Macworld ClarisWorks 3.0 Co

by Steven A. Schwart

Quick Reference C

Working with Tools

Basic Tool Panel

Expanded Tool Panel (when working in a paint document or frame)

- Environment tools
- Drawing tools
- Painting tools
- Pop-up Fill palettes
- Pop-up Pen palettes

- Object selection tool
- Text tool
- Spreadsheet tool
- Paint tool
- Draw a straight line
- Draw a rectangle
- Draw a rectangle with rounded corners
- Draw an oval
- Draw a curved line
- Draw an irregular shape composed of straight lines
- Draw a freehand shape
- Draw an irregular shape with control points
- Draw a regular shape with equal sides
- Pick up the pen and fill attributes of an object
- Select a rectangular area
- Select an irregular area
- Select adjacent pixels of same color
- Paint
- Paint fine lines
- Fill an area with a color, pattern, or gradient
- Paint with an airbrush
- Erase an area
- Current fill color, pattern, or gradient
- Set a fill color, pattern, or gradient
- Current pen color, pattern, and line width
- Set a pen color or pattern
- Set line thickness and whether a line will have arrowheads

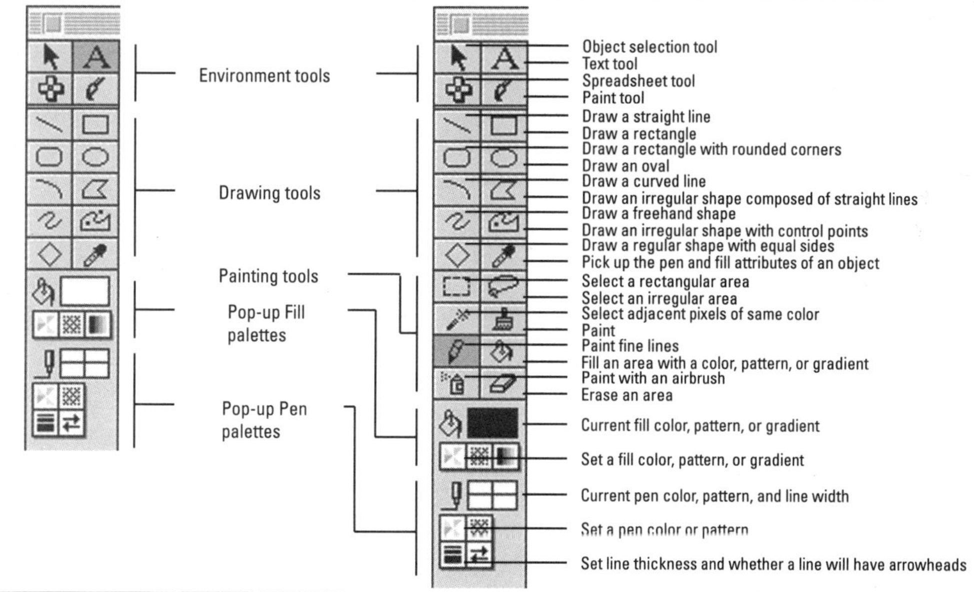

Working with Text and Windows

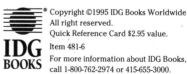

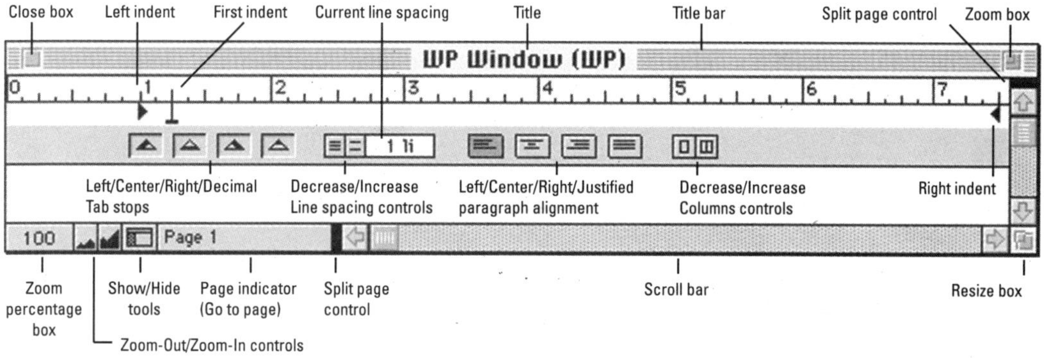

Close box · Left indent · First indent · Current line spacing · Title · Title bar · Split page control · Zoom box

WP Window (WP)

Left/Center/Right/Decimal Tab stops · Decrease/Increase Line spacing controls · Left/Center/Right/Justified paragraph alignment · Decrease/Increase Columns controls · Right indent

Zoom percentage box · Show/Hide tools · Page indicator (Go to page) · Split page control · Scroll bar · Resize box

Zoom-Out/Zoom-In controls

Macworld ClarisWorks 3.0 Companion, 3rd Edition

by Steven A. Schwartz Ph.D.

Quick Reference Card

Working with the Shortcuts Palettes

No Open Documents

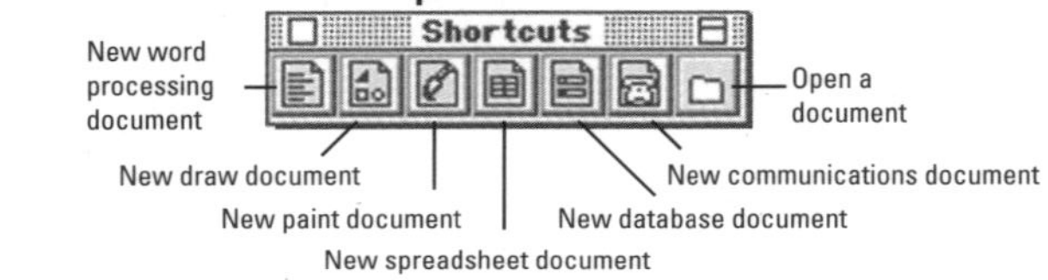

Word Processing Shortcuts

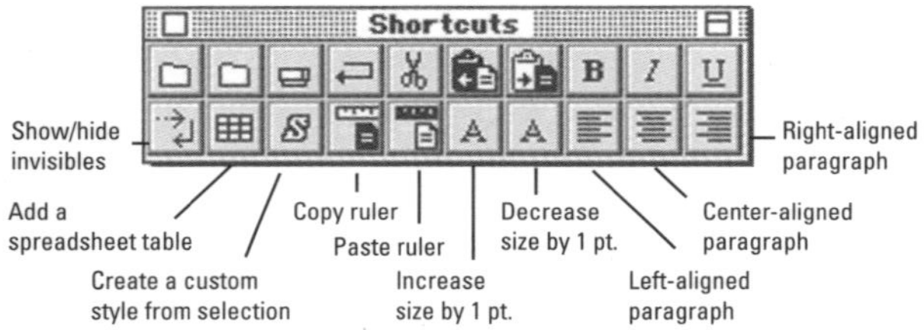

Database Shortcuts

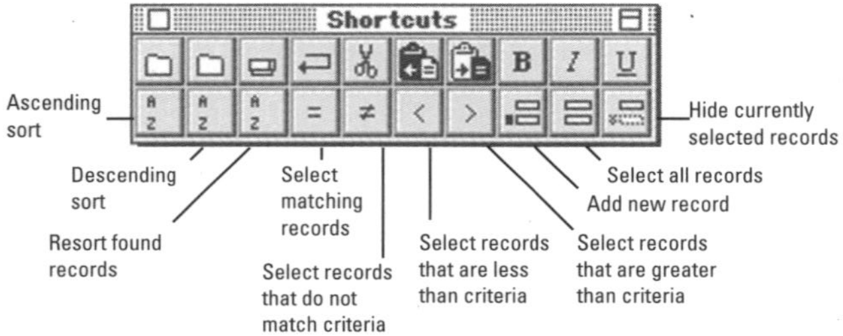

Communications Shortcuts

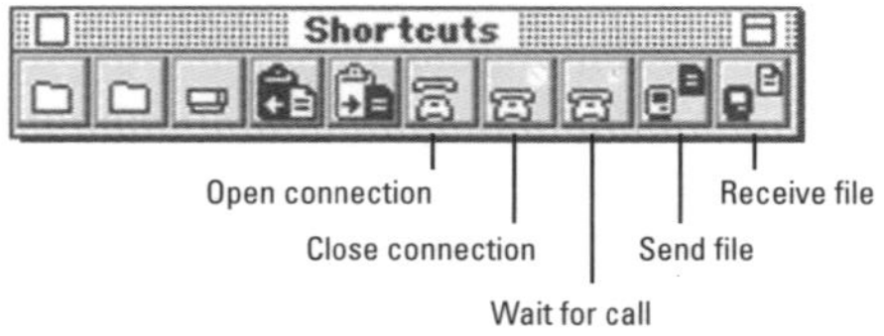

General Shortcuts
(available in most environments)

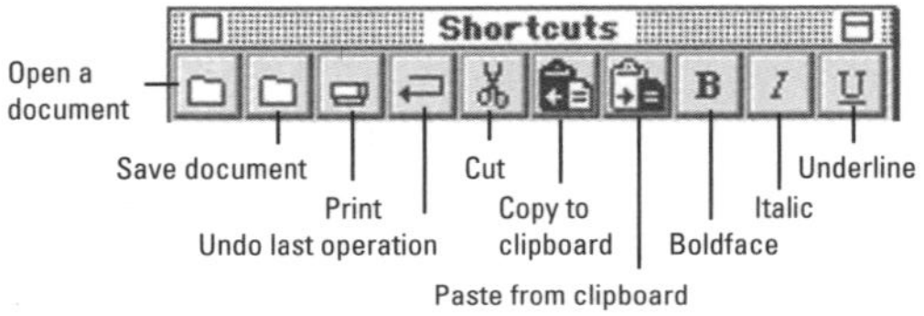

Spreadsheet Shortcuts

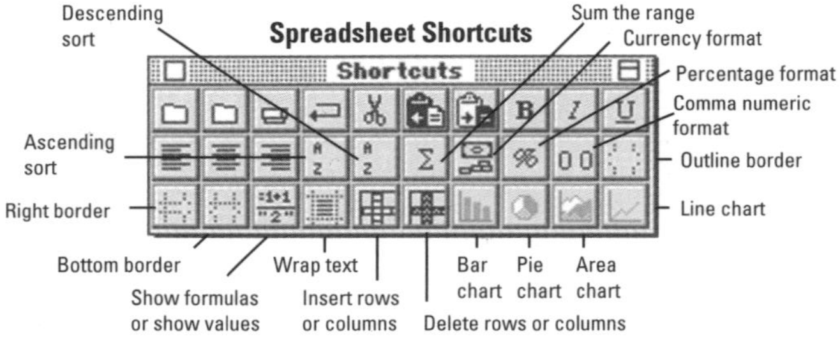

Draw Shortcuts

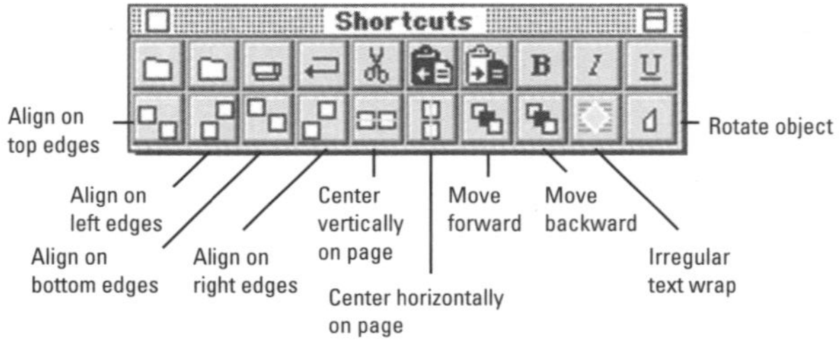

Paint Shortcuts

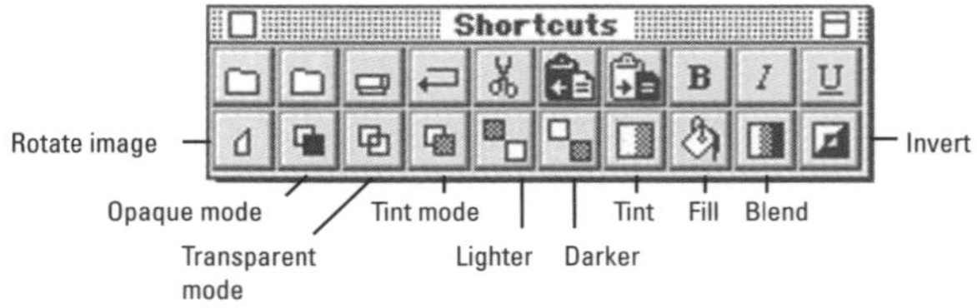

About *Macworld Companion* Books

Macworld ClarisWorks 3.0 Companion, 3rd Edition, is part of the *Macworld Companion* series of books, brought to you by IDG Books, the leading publisher of computer information worldwide. This is a new kind of book designed to meet your growing need to quickly find what you want to do and learn how to do it.

These books work the way you do: They focus on accomplishing specific tasks — not learning random functions. *Macworld Companion* books are not long-winded tomes, manuals, or even quick reference guides, but are the result of drawing from the best elements of these three types of publications. These books have the easy-to-follow step-by-steps sections of a manual, the comprehensive coverage you'd expect to find in a long tome, and the brevity you need from a quick reference guide — it's all here.

The designers of the *Macworld Companion* series use the following visual elements to make it easy to find the information you need:

Step-by-Steps sections provide easy-to-follow instructions that demonstrate the concepts introduced in the Overview sections. If you're a beginner, these Step-by-Steps sections will go a long way toward getting you up to speed on unfamiliar topics.

Version 2.1 icons mark sections that bring you up to date on what's new in ClarisWorks 2.1. These icons are especially useful if you already use ClarisWorks 2.0.

New Feature 3.0 icons point out features that appear only in ClarisWorks 3.0.

Quick Tips sections include tips and insights on the material in the Topic; Quick Tips enable you to get the most out of your application or operating system no matter what level user you are.

The authors of the *Macworld Companion* books are leading *Macworld* columnists, technology champions, and Mac gurus, who are uniquely qualified to provide you with expert advice and insightful tips and techniques not found anywhere else. We're sure you'll agree that the *Macworld Companion* approach is the best.

— David Solomon
Executive Vice-President,
Strategic Product Planning and Research

MACWORLD®

ClarisWorks® 3.0 Companion,

3rd Edition

MACWORLD AUTHORIZED EDITION™

MACWORLD® ClarisWorks® 3.0 Companion, 3rd Edition

by Steven A. Schwartz, Ph.D.

FIFTH ANNIVERSARY IDG BOOKS WORLDWIDE

IDG Books Worldwide, Inc.
An International Data Group Company

Foster City, CA ✦ Chicago, IL ✦ Indianapolis, IN ✦ Braintree, MA ✦ Dallas, TX

Macworld® ClarisWorks® 3.0 Companion, 3rd Edition

Published by
IDG Books Worldwide, Inc.
An International Data Group Company
919 E. Hillsdale Blvd.
Suite 400
Foster City, CA 94404

Library of Congress Catalog Card No.: 95-75379

ISBN: 1-56884-481-6

Printed in the United States of America

10 9 8 7 6 5 4 3 2

3B/SU/QY/ZV

Distributed in the United States by IDG Books Worldwide, Inc.

Distributed by Macmillan Canada for Canada; by Computer and Technical Books for the Caribbean Basin; by Contemporantea de Ediciones for Venezuela; by Distribuidora Cuspide for Argentina; by CITFC for Brazil; by Ediciones ZETA S.C.R. Ltda. for Peru; by Editorial Limusa SA for Mexico; by Transworld Publishers Limited in the United Kingdom and Europe; by Al-Maiman Publishers & Distributors for Saudi Arabia; by Simron Pty. Ltd. for South Africa; by IDG Communications (HK) Ltd. for Hong Kong; by Toppan Company Ltd. for Japan; by Addison Wesley Publishing Company for Korea; by Longman Singapore Publisher Ltd. for Singapore, Malaysia, Thailand and Indonesia; by Unalis Corporation for Taiwan; by WS Computer Publishing Company, Inc. for the Philippines; by WoodsLane Enterprises Ltd. for New Zealand.

For general information on IDG Books Worldwide's books in the U.S., please call our Consumer Customer Service department at 800-762-2974. For reseller information, including discounts and premium sales, please call our Reseller Customer Service department at 800-434-3422.

For information on where to purchase IDG Books Worldwide's books outside the U.S., contact IDG Books Worldwide at 415-655-3021 or fax 415-655-3295.

For information on translations, contact Marc Jeffrey Mikulich, Director, Foreign & Subsidiary Rights, at IDG Books Worldwide, 415-655-3018 or fax 415-655-3295.

For sales inquiries and special prices for bulk quantities, write to the address above or call IDG Books Worldwide at 415-655-3200.

For information on using IDG Books Worldwide's books in the classroom, or ordering examination copies, contact Jim Kelly at 800-434-2086.

For authorization to photocopy items for corporate, personal, or educational use, please contact Copyright Clearance Center, 222 Rosewood Drive, Danvers, MA 01923, or fax 508-750-4470.

About the Author

In 1978, Dr. Steven Schwartz bought his first microcomputer, a new Apple II+. Determined to find a way to make money with it, he began writing software reviews, BASIC programs, and user tips for *Nibble* magazine. Shortly thereafter, he was made a Contributing Editor.

Over the past 15 years, Steven has written hundreds of articles for more than a dozen computer magazines. He currently writes for *Multimedia World.* He was also a founding editor of *Software Digest*, as well as Business Editor for *MACazine,* and a regular contributor to *Macworld.*

Steven is the author of more than 20 books, and he was the Director of Technical Support for Funk Software from 1985 to 1990. Steven has a Ph.D. in psychology and presently lives in the Arizona desert, where the wildlife — particularly the lizards — keeps him perpetually amused.

ABOUT IDG BOOKS WORLDWIDE

Welcome to the world of IDG Books Worldwide.

IDG Books Worldwide, Inc., is a subsidiary of International Data Group, the world's largest publisher of computer-related information and the leading global provider of information services on information technology. IDG was founded more than 25 years ago and now employs more than 7,500 people worldwide. IDG publishes more than 235 computer publications in 67 countries (see listing below). More than 60 million people read one or more IDG publications each month.

Launched in 1990, IDG Books Worldwide is today the #1 publisher of best-selling computer books in the United States. We are proud to have received 8 awards from the Computer Press Association in recognition of editorial excellence, and our best-selling *...For Dummies*™ series has more than 17 million copies in print with translations in 25 languages. IDG Books Worldwide, through a recent joint venture with IDG's Hi-Tech Beijing, became the first U.S. publisher to publish a computer book in the People's Republic of China. In record time, IDG Books Worldwide has become the first choice for millions of readers around the world who want to learn how to better manage their businesses.

Our mission is simple: Every one of our books is designed to bring extra value and skill-building instructions to the reader. Our books are written by experts who understand and care about our readers. The knowledge base of our editorial staff comes from years of experience in publishing, education, and journalism — experience which we use to produce books for the '90s. In short, we care about books, so we attract the best people. We devote special attention to details such as audience, interior design, use of icons, and illustrations. And because we use an efficient process of authoring, editing, and desktop publishing our books electronically, we can spend more time ensuring superior content and spend less time on the technicalities of making books.

You can count on our commitment to deliver high-quality books at competitive prices on topics consumers want to read about. At IDG Books Worldwide, we value quality, and we have been delivering quality for more than 25 years. You'll find no better book on a subject than an IDG book.

John Kilcullen
President and CEO
IDG Books Worldwide, Inc.

VIII
WINNER
Eighth Annual Computer Press Awards 1992

IX
WINNER
Ninth Annual Computer Press Awards 1993

IDG BOOKS WORLDWIDE

IDG Books Worldwide, Inc., is a subsidiary of International Data Group, the world's largest publisher of computer-related information and the leading global provider of information services on information technology. International Data Group publishes over 235 computer publications in 67 countries. More than sixty million people read one or more International Data Group publications each month. The officers are Patrick J. McGovern, Founder and Board Chairman; Kelly Conlin, President; Jim Casella, Chief Operating Officer. International Data Group's publications include: **ARGENTINA'S** Computerworld Argentina, Infoworld Argentina; **AUSTRALIA'S** Computerworld Australia, Computer Living, Australian PC World, Australian Macworld, Network World, Mobile Business Australia, Publish!, Reseller, IDG Sources; **AUSTRIA'S** Computerwelt Oesterreich, PC Test; **BELGIUM'S** Data News (CW); **BOLIVIA'S** Computerworld; **BRAZIL'S** Computerworld, Connections, Game Power, Mundo Unix, PC World, Publish, Super Game; **BULGARIA'S** Computerworld Bulgaria, PC & Mac World Bulgaria, Network World Bulgaria; **CANADA'S** CIO Canada, Computerworld Canada, InfoCanada, Network World Canada, Reseller; **CHILE'S** Computerworld Chile, Informatica; **COLOMBIA'S** Computerworld Colombia, PC World; **COSTA RICA'S** PC World; **CZECH REPUBLIC'S** Computerworld, Elektronika, PC World; **DENMARK'S** Communications World, Computerworld Danmark, Computerworld Focus, Macintosh Produktkatalog, Macworld Danmark, PC World Danmark, PC Produktguide, Tech World, Windows World; **ECUADOR'S** PC World Ecuador; **EGYPT'S** Computerworld (CW) Middle East, PC World Middle East; **FINLAND'S** MikroPC, Tietoviikko, Tietoverkko; **FRANCE'S** Distributique, GOLDEN MAC, InfoPC, Le Guide du Monde Informatique, Le Monde Informatique, Telecoms & Reseaux; **GERMANY'S** Computerwoche, Computerwoche Focus, Computerwoche Extra, Electronic Entertainment, Gamepro, Information Management, Macwelt, Netzwelt, PC Welt, Publish, Publish; **GREECE'S** Publish & Macworld; **HONG KONG'S** Computerworld Hong Kong, PC World Hong Kong; **HUNGARY'S** Computerworld SZT, PC World; **INDIA'S** Computers & Communications; **INDONESIA'S** Info Komputer; **IRELAND'S** ComputerScope; **ISRAEL'S** Beyond Windows, Computerworld Israel, Multimedia, PC World Israel; **ITALY'S** Computerworld Italia, Lotus Magazine, Macworld Italia, Networking Italia, PC Shopping Italy, PC World Italia; **JAPAN'S** Computerworld Today, Information Systems World, Macworld Japan, Nikkei Personal Computing, SunWorld Japan, Windows World; **KENYA'S** East African Computer News; **KOREA'S** Computerworld Korea, Macworld Korea, PC World Korea; **LATIN AMERICA'S** GamePro; **MALAYSIA'S** Computerworld Malaysia, PC World Malaysia; **MEXICO'S** Compu Edicion, Compu Manufactura, Computacion/Punto de Venta, Computerworld Mexico, MacWorld, Mundo Unix, PC World, Windows; **THE NETHERLANDS'** Computer! Totaal, Computable (CW), LAN Magazine, Lotus Magazine, MacWorld; **NEW ZEALAND'S** Computer Buyer, Computerworld New Zealand, Network World, New Zealand PC World; **NIGERIA'S** PC World Africa; **NORWAY'S** Computerworld Norge, Lotusworld Norge, Macworld Norge, Maxi Data, Networld, PC World Ekspress, PC World Nettverk, PC World Norge, PC World's Produktguide, Publish& Multimedia World, Student Data, Unix World, Windowsworld; **PAKISTAN'S** PC World Pakistan; **PANAMA'S** PC World Panama; **PERU'S** Computerworld Peru, PC World; **PEOPLE'S REPUBLIC OF CHINA'S** China Computerworld, China Infoworld, China PC Info Magazine, Computer Fan, PC World China, Electronics International, Electronics Today/Multimedia World, Electronic Product World, China Network World, Software World Magazine, Telecom Product World; **PHILIPPINES'** Computerworld Philippines, PC Digest (PCW); **POLAND'S** Computerworld Poland, Computerworld Special Report, Networld, PC World/Komputer, Sunworld; **PORTUGAL'S** Cerebro/PC World, Correio Informatico/Computerworld, MacIn; **ROMANIA'S** Computerworld, PC World, Telecom Romania; **RUSSIA'S** Computerworld-Moscow, Mir - PK (PCW), Sety (Networks); **SINGAPORE'S** Computerworld Southeast Asia, PC World Singapore; **SLOVENIA'S** Monitor Magazine; **SOUTH AFRICA'S** Computer Mail (CIO),Computing S.A.,Network World S.A., Software World; **SPAIN'S** Advanced Systems, Amiga World, Computerworld Espana, Communicaciones World, Macworld Espana, NeXTWORLD, Super Juegos Magazine (GamePro), PC World Espana, Publish; **SWEDEN'S** Attack, ComputerSweden, Corporate Computing, Macworld, Mikrodatorn, Natverk & Kommunikation, PC World, CAP & Design, Datalngenjoren, Maxi Data,Windows World; **SWITZERLAND'S** Computerworld Schweiz, Macworld Schweiz, PC Tip; **TAIWAN'S** Computerworld Taiwan, PC World Taiwan; **THAILAND'S** Thai Computerworld; **TURKEY'S** Computerworld Monitor, Macworld Turkiye, PC World Turkiye; **UKRAINE'S** Computerworld, Computers+Software Magazine; **UNITED KINGDOM'S** Computing /Computerworld, Connexion/Network World, Lotus Magazine, Macworld, Open Computing/Sunworld; **UNITED STATES'** Advanced Systems, AmigaWorld, Cable in the Classroom, CD Review, CIO, Computerworld, Computerworld Client/Server Journal, Digital Video, DOS World, Electronic Entertainment Magazine (E2), Federal Computer Week, Game Hits, GamePro, IDG Books Worldwide, Infoworld, Laser Event, Macworld, Maximize, Multimedia World, Network World, PC Letter, PC World, Publish, SWATPro, Video Event; **URUGUAY'S** PC World Uruguay; **VENEZUELA'S** Computerworld Venezuela, PC World; **VIETNAM'S** PC World Vietnam.
05/17/95

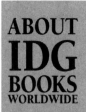

Acknowledgments

I am grateful to the many people who offered their encouragement and support for this updated edition of the book, including Jay Lee (Claris Corporation); Andy Cummings, Greg Croy, Megg Bonar, Bill Barton, Valery Bourke, Drew Moore, Mark Owens, and CEO John Kilcullen (IDG Books Worldwide); Matt Wagner (Waterside Productions); and last — but definitely not least, Pat Seiler, the best editor in the business.

(The publisher and the author would like to give special thanks to Patrick J. McGovern, without whom this book would not have been possible.)

Dedication

To Sheldon and Barbara Schwartz, the best parents anyone could wish for.

Credits

Publisher
Brenda McLaughlin

Acquisitions Manager
Gregory Croy

Acquisitions Editor
Nancy E. Dunn

Brand Manager
Pradeepa Siva

Editorial Director
Andy Cummings

Editorial Executive Assistant
Jodi Lynn Semling

Editorial Assistant
Nate Holdread

Production Director
Beth Jenkins

Supervisor of Project Coordination
Cindy L. Phipps

Supervisor of Page Layout
Kathie S. Schnorr

Pre-Press Coordinator
Steve Peake

Associate Pre-Press Coordinator
Tony Augsburger

Media/Archive Coordinator
Paul Belcastro

Project Editors
Pat Seiler
Jeremy Judson
Laurie Ann Smith

Editors
Kezia Endsley
H. Leigh Davis
Shawn MacLaren
William A. Barton

Technical Reviewers
Jay Lee
Dennis Cohen

Project Coordinator
Valery Bourke

Production Staff
Gina Scott
Carla C. Radzikinas
Patricia R. Reynolds
Melissa D. Buddendeck
Dwight Ramsey
Robert Springer
Theresa Sánchez-Baker
Elizabeth Cárdenas-Nelson
Drew R. Moore
Mark C. Owens
Laura Puranen

Proofreader
Jennifer Kaufeld

Indexer
Sharon Hilgenberg

Book Design
Drew R. Moore
and University Graphics

Cover Illustration
Don Baker

Cover Design
Kavish + Kavish

Contents at a Glance

Table of Contents

Topic 6: The Database Environment 203

Introduction

About This Book

The *Macworld ClarisWorks 3.0 Companion,* 3rd Edition, is a different kind of computer book. First, it's not a manual. Many people don't like computer manuals — perhaps because they feel obligated to read them from cover to cover to avoid missing something important or because manuals are designed to explain how features work rather than how to put a program to work for you. The *Macworld ClarisWorks 3.0 Companion,* 3rd Edition, is not a book you *have* to read. It's a book that you'll *want* to read — because it provides easy-to-find, easy-to-understand explanations of many of the common tasks for which you bought ClarisWorks in the first place. When you want to know how to use a particular program feature, you can use the Table of Contents, the Task Index, or the Index to quickly identify the section of the book that you need to read.

Second, unlike many computer books, this one is *task oriented.* The reason most people buy computer books is not because they want to become an expert with a particular piece of software. Instead, they have a task that they want to accomplish. In addition to the step by step explanations of normal ClarisWorks procedures, the book also provides many worked-through task examples. Rather than spend your time reinventing the wheel, you can just follow the numbered steps to accomplish many common business and home computing tasks.

Finally, the philosophy of this book — as well as the other books in the Macworld *Companion* series — is that you don't want or need a handful of books on a computer program; one should suffice. The *Macworld ClarisWorks 3.0 Companion,* 3rd Edition, is an all-in-one book that covers ClarisWorks 2.0, 2.1, and 3.0. Rarely will you be referred back to your manual. You can find almost anything you want to know about ClarisWorks 2.0 and higher in this book.

What Is ClarisWorks?

ClarisWorks belongs to a class of programs known as *integrated software.* The idea behind integrated software is that — within a single box — you acquire a core set of programs that fulfill all your basic computing needs. The typical program components or modules are word processing, spreadsheet, database, graphics, and telecommunications. And the modules function together as a cohesive unit — more or less. I say "more or less" because the early integrated software packages (as well as many of the current ones) were often only a collection of programs. They frequently had little in common with each other beyond being in the same box. There may have been no way to share data between the modules or significant differences in the command structure in the different modules. Learning how to use one module may have taught you nothing about using the other modules.

As a class of software, integrated software was often viewed with disdain by computing purists. In order to squeeze the entire package into a reasonable amount of memory, the modules were often stripped down to bare-bones programs. "Big time" features — such as a spelling checker, thesaurus, character and paragraph styles, and advanced searching and sorting — were routinely missing. Thus, many users felt (rightfully so) that the integrated modules couldn't hold a candle to full-featured stand-alone programs.

Microsoft Works was the first major integrated package for the Mac. The Mac's native support for cut-and-paste made it relatively easy to merge data from different types of documents, enabling you to paste a graphic into a word processing file, for example. Although integration was considerably better than in the early programs, each Works module was essentially a stand-alone tool. To create a new spreadsheet that you wanted to incorporate into an annual report, you had to work in both the spreadsheet and word processing modules and then cut and paste the spreadsheet into the final document.

Why Choose ClarisWorks?

ClarisWorks, on the other hand, has carried the integration concept forward to the next logical step. It, too, has separate components, but you can use features of the different components no matter what type of document you're currently working on. For example, although a word processing document is primarily composed of words, you can add a spreadsheet section to the document simply by selecting the spreadsheet tool and then drawing a frame (see Figure INT-1). While you are working in the spreadsheet frame, the menu bar and menu commands change to ones relevant to spreadsheets — hiding the irrelevant word processing commands. If you click in any part of the word processing text, the menus change back to ones appropriate for word processing. This tight integration between components makes ClarisWorks significantly easier and more convenient to use than its competitors. In fact, Claris prefers that the ClarisWorks components be referred to as *environments* rather than modules — to emphasize the high level of integration between the different parts of the program.

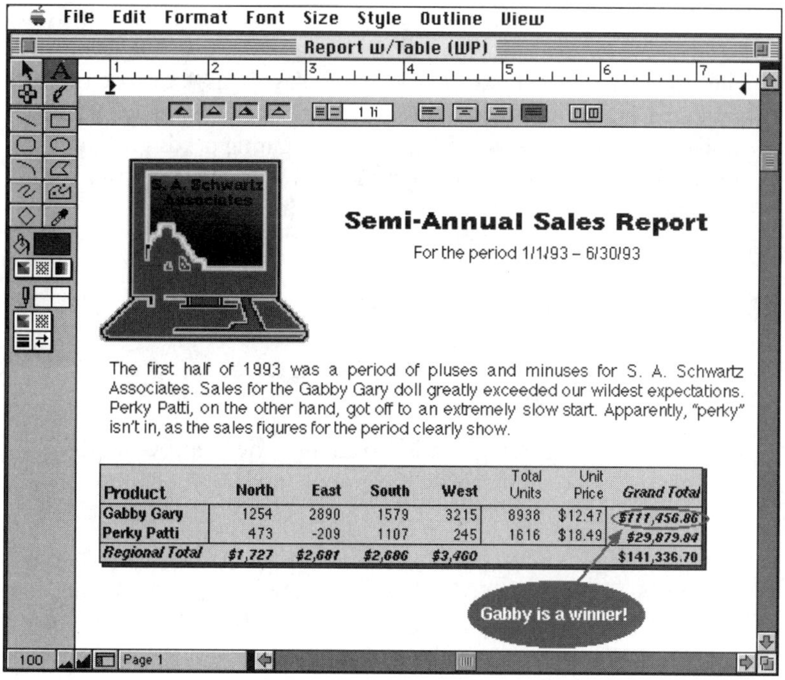

Figure INT-1: A spreadsheet frame within a word processing document.

ClarisWorks has also made great strides toward including the "power features" that have traditionally been absent from integrated programs. The word processor includes a spelling checker, thesaurus, and outliner, as well as support for custom text styles. The paint environment offers gradients, and the draw environment has advanced drawing tools. The spreadsheet includes charts, text wrap within cells, and variable row heights and column widths, and it allows multiple fonts per worksheet. The communications environment provides standard file transfer protocols and support for the Communications Toolbox. The database offers pop-up list fields and enables you to create multiple custom layouts for each database file. The built-in macro recorder enables you to automate common or repetitive tasks with ease.

ClarisWorks provides solid integration with *other* programs, too. Numerous import and export filters that are included with ClarisWorks enable it to exchange data with many popular business programs, such as Microsoft Office. And with the System 7 feature called Publish & Subscribe, you can easily embed ClarisWorks documents (or portions of documents, such as a spreadsheet chart) in documents created in other programs. You may want to publish a ClarisWorks spreadsheet chart for inclusion in a desktop publishing layout, for example. When the underlying ClarisWorks documents change, you can set the desktop publishing program (in this case, the *subscriber*) to automatically replace the old chart with the new one. Publish & Subscribe works in the opposite direction, too. You can use it to embed non-ClarisWorks documents into ClarisWorks files and have them automatically update whenever changes are made to the external documents.

Finally, ClarisWorks offers a clear upgrade path. Many of its environments are based on more powerful, stand-alone Claris programs. The database is based on FileMaker Pro, and the word processor is based on MacWrite Pro. Although the draw environment was based on the now defunct MacDraw Pro it has many similarities to ClarisDraw. When your computing needs grow, you can easily transfer the skills you've learned in these environments to a more powerful Claris program.

Whom This Book Is for

The *Macworld ClarisWorks 3.0 Companion* is for anyone who uses Version 2.0, 2.1, or 3.0 of ClarisWorks:

- If you're a beginning ClarisWorks user, the Step-by-Steps sections help you get up to speed quickly with common (and not-so-common) ClarisWorks features and procedures.
- If you're an intermediate or advanced ClarisWorks user — someone who wants only the ClarisWorks essentials but doesn't need much hand holding — the tips and insights in each Topic will help you get the most from ClarisWorks. You'll find Quick Tips sections, sidebars, icons indicating new ClarisWorks features, and the Quick Reference tear-out card handy tools for your ClarisWorks toolbox.

How This Book Is Organized

Rather than chapters, this book has Topics — tasks you're likely to perform in ClarisWorks. Each Topic covers a specific task, such as working with the word processor, setting preferences, recording macros, and so on. When you need to perform a particular ClarisWorks task, scan the table of contents to locate the Topic that addresses your needs. You can also flip through the pages of the book to quickly find the Topic you need — every Topic's name appears at the edge of each right-hand page. Topics contain the following sections:

- **Overview** provides an introduction to the Topic.
- **Step-by-Steps** sections appear throughout each Topic. Each Step-by-Steps section spells out the specific instructions — in order — needed to accomplish a particular task.
- **Quick Tips** give useful tips about additional tasks that you can perform in the ClarisWorks environment or about the subject being discussed. You also can turn to this section for ideas on how to better use the features or the environment.
- **Moving On Up** provides you with information on upgrading from a ClarisWorks environment to a more advanced program.

- **Summary** is a list of the main points covered in the Topic. You can turn to the Summary section of any Topic to see whether it contains the information you need at the moment.

Other icons that are used to help streamline your learning experience include the following:

The Version 2.1 icon marks discussions of features that are available only in ClarisWorks 2.1 or higher.

The New Feature 3.0 icon marks discussions of features that are found only in ClarisWorks 3.0.

The Tip icon offers an insight into the feature or task being discussed, in many cases suggesting better or easier ways of accomplishing it.

The Note icon provides additional information relevant to a particular feature or task.

The Caution icon warns you about potentially dangerous situations — particularly those in which data may be lost.

The *Macworld ClarisWorks 3.0 Companion,* 3rd Edition, is divided into five parts:

- **Part I, "The Basics,"** is a gentle introduction to using the Macintosh and performing basic ClarisWorks procedures, such as opening and saving documents, printing, and managing windows. It also lists the major features and enhancements that were introduced in ClarisWorks 2.1 and 3.0.
- **Part II, "Using the ClarisWorks Environments,"** explains the workings of each of the six major ClarisWorks components (word processing, spreadsheet, database, draw, paint, and communications).
- **Part III, "Integrating the ClarisWorks Environments,"** offers suggestions and examples for using elements of two or more environments in the same document (generating a mail merge and using spreadsheet frames to create word processing tables).

- **Part IV, "Advanced Topics,"** covers material that helps you make more productive use of ClarisWorks. It isn't essential to learn about these features immediately, but you will want to tackle them after you're comfortable with the ClarisWorks basics.
- **Part V, "Appendixes,"** includes four appendixes to aid you in your work:
- **Appendix A, "Installing ClarisWorks 2 or 3,"** provides information on how to install ClarisWorks. If you will be installing on any disk other than your start-up hard disk, reading this appendix is especially important.
- **Appendix B, "Installing the ClarisWorks 2.1 Updater,"** explains how to update ClarisWorks 2 to Version 2.1.
- **Appendix C, "Keyboard Shortcuts,"** lists the many keyboard shortcuts in ClarisWorks. If you're new to using a mouse or don't want to take your hands off the keyboard, you'll want to check out this appendix.
- **Appendix D, "Task Index,"** is an index that lists the page on which each Step-by-Steps procedure is explained.

How to Use This Book

Far be it from me to tell you how to read this book. Reading and learning styles are all very personal. When I get a new computer program, I frequently read the manual from cover to cover before even installing the software. Of course, I'll be flattered if you read the *Macworld ClarisWorks 3.0 Companion,* 3rd Edition, the same way, but I'll be *surprised* if you do, too.

This book is written as a reference to "all things ClarisWorks." When you want to learn about the database environment, there's a specific Topic to which you can turn. If you just need to know how to use the spelling checker, you can flip to the Table of Contents or the Index and find the pages where the spelling checker is discussed. Most procedures are explained in step-by-step fashion, so you can quickly accomplish even the most complex tasks. So, you can read this book as you would a Stephen King novel (but with fewer surprises, and less snappy dialog and bloodletting), read just the Topics that interest you, or use it as a quick reference for when you need to learn about a particular feature or procedure.

For those who prefer a little more direction than "whatever works for you," I've listed the following general guidelines — arranged according to your level of Mac expertise and previous ClarisWorks experience.

NOTE

I do have one general suggestion: *If at all possible, read this book with ClarisWorks 2.0, 2.1, or 3.0 on-screen.* Sure, you can read about editing a user dictionary for the spelling checker while relaxing in the tub, but — unless you have exceptional recall — what you read will be more meaningful if you're sitting in front of the computer.

For the beginner

Although this book discusses many of the basic concepts and procedures necessary for the beginning user to start working productively on the Macintosh (Topic 1, "Macintosh Essentials"), it is *not* a substitute for the documentation that came with your Mac. As you work on the desktop and begin experimenting with ClarisWorks, you're bound to encounter additional Mac issues that are only touched on — or ignored altogether — in Topic 1. When that happens — *and it will* — it's time to drag out the manuals for your Macintosh, peripherals (printers, modems, and so on), and system software, and see what you've missed. After you fill in the gaps in your Mac education, you'll feel more confident and comfortable tackling ClarisWorks and any other programs you eventually purchase.

If you're relatively new to the Mac, start by reading all of Part I. You'll become acquainted with the fundamentals of using the Mac, as well as with the ClarisWorks basics. From that point on, you should pick a ClarisWorks environment — the word processor is a good place to start — and, with book in hand, work through the appropriate Topic in Part II. Each Topic in Part II explains the fundamentals for a single ClarisWorks environment. The really advanced stuff is in Part III, "Integrating the ClarisWorks Environments," and Part IV, "Advanced Topics." Although you'll eventually want to check out the material in those Parts, too, you'll note that I've purposely separated the advanced matters from the basics in order to keep new users from being overwhelmed.

For the more experienced Mac user

You can safely skip Topic 1, "Macintosh Essentials." The material in this Topic is very basic and is probably second nature to you.

Topic 2, "ClarisWorks Essentials," is must reading for every ClarisWorks user. Many ClarisWorks tasks, such as arranging windows and printing, are not specific to any one environment. Rather than discuss them again in each of the environment Topics, I have included these procedures and features only in Topic 2.

The remainder of the book can be treated as reference material and read as needed.

For those who have upgraded from ClarisWorks 1.0 or 2.0

If you're an experienced ClarisWorks 1.0 or 2.0 user, the best place for you to start is in Topic 3, "New Features in ClarisWorks 2.1 and 3.0." Essentially, this Topic is a quick guide to the additional features that you need to learn about in these versions of ClarisWorks. Topic 3 briefly explains each of the new features, and cross-references tell you where to turn in the book for more detailed discussions.

Before you jump ahead, however, be sure to at least skim through Topic 2, "ClarisWorks Essentials." Although the basics of using the program haven't changed drastically, you need to be familiar with some new procedures and options.

Part I
The Basics

Topic 1 Macintosh Essentials

Overview

ClarisWorks is often one of the first programs that new Macintosh owners purchase. If you're new to the Mac, you will find that using ClarisWorks is much easier after you have a firm grasp of the Macintosh basics — understanding the Macintosh desktop and using the mouse, for example. Topic 1 is written especially for you. Although it covers much of the same material that is in the Macintosh user's guide, it stresses information that is essential for operating the Mac and running ClarisWorks. (After reviewing this short Topic, you may have the impetus needed to work through the Macintosh user's guide, too.)

Even if you have a solid understanding of Mac basics, giving this Topic a fast read may still be worthwhile. For example, the instructions on starting up and shutting down the Mac — if you follow them exactly — can save you enormous grief by preventing damage to data on the hard disk. And the section on printing explains the meaning of those odd Page Setup options.

An Ounce of Prevention

In this Topic, I begin with two important subjects that are often poorly understood or ignored by Macintosh users: the correct way to start up and shut down the Mac and the importance of backing up data. If you learn and practice the procedures described in this Topic, you can avoid the majority of pitfalls and disasters that befall poorly prepared Mac owners.

Starting up and shutting down

Unlike a clock radio, the Mac has a right way and a wrong way for you to start it up and shut it down. Correctly starting up ensures that any external drives are ready to go. Shutting down correctly ensures that all data that is floating around in the Mac's memory is properly written to the hard disk before you shut the Mac off.

To start up:

1. **Turn on all external SCSI (Small Computer System Interface) devices that are connected to the Mac.** These devices normally include external hard disks, CD-ROM drives, tape drives, and scanners.

   A *SCSI ("scuzzy") device* is any mechanism that is connected — either directly or in a chain — to the SCSI port on the back of the Mac. Figure 1-1 shows the icon that identifies the SCSI port.

   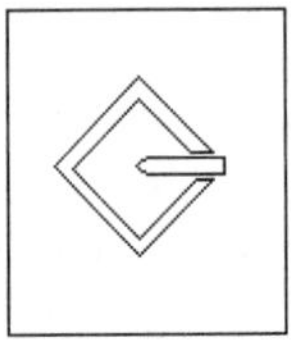

   Figure 1-1: The SCSI port icon.

   If you don't have any external SCSI devices (you may have only an internal hard disk, for example), move directly to Step 3.

2. **Wait for the external SCSI devices to warm up.**

   Most SCSI drives go through an audible power-up sequence. After they stop grinding, clanking, and making other interesting noises (usually within 20 to 45 seconds), they are ready to go.

3. **Flip the power switch on the back of the Mac or press the power key on the keyboard.** (For Macs so equipped, the *power key* is the one with a left-facing open triangle symbol.) The Mac goes through its normal start-up procedure.

NOTE

You can normally turn other external devices (those that are *not* connected to the SCSI port) on and off whenever you like. To be sure, however, refer to the manuals for printers, modems, and so on.

To shut down:

1. **When you're through with the Mac for the day, quit all programs that are currently running.** (Normally, you choose Quit from the File menu and, optionally, save any open files.)

2. **At the desktop, choose Shut Down from the Special menu, as shown in Figure 1-2.**

   Depending on the model, the Macintosh either shuts down automatically at this point or displays a message that tells you that you can safely turn off the Mac.

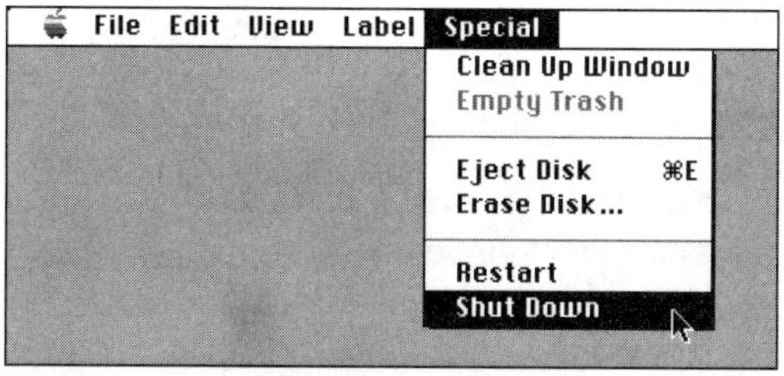

Figure 1-2: The Shut Down menu command.

3. **If the Mac doesn't shut off automatically in Step 2, turn its power off by flipping the power switch to the Off position.**

4. **Turn off all external SCSI devices.**

   After you have used this procedure to shut down the Mac gracefully, you can safely turn off all external hard disks and other SCSI devices.

If you shut down the Mac in any way other than by choosing Shut Down from the Special menu — just turning off the power or pressing the reset switch, for example — unfortunate consequences such as the following may result:

- Any documents or data files that you did not save will be gone.
- If the Mac was in the process of writing information to the hard disk, that particular file may be unreadable or may contain erroneous, garbage data.
- The next time you turn on the Mac, the start-up process will take considerably longer. The system software will have to figure out which windows were open and where the various files and folders were located when you so abruptly shut down the system.

The importance of making backups

Backing up (or *making a backup*) is the process of making an extra copy of important files. Although some people find it comforting to think that their Mac is immune to disaster, this approach is foolhardy. Here are just a few of the ways that you can lose crucial data files:

- You throw a folder that you no longer need into the Trash — only to discover that it was the wrong folder.
- While cleaning your desk, someone bumps your Mac (or your external hard disk). The bump results in a *head crash* — a catastrophic event that renders the disk inoperable.
- The hard disk's power supply dies. Although the data is still intact, you have no way of getting at it until the hard disk is repaired. How long can your business survive without access to that information?

- You borrow a program disk from a friend, not realizing that it is infected with a computer virus. The first time that you run the program, it erases every file on the hard disk while pretending to do something useful.
- A *real* disaster occurs (a fire or theft leaves you with a smoking or missing Mac), and your data goes along for the ride.

To be safe, you should always have one or more duplicate copies of every important data file on your system. Even if you can't afford a special backup device, such as a tape drive or removable cartridge system, you can always back up onto floppy disks. Whenever you make significant changes to an important file, first save it to the hard disk and then copy it onto a floppy.

TIP

If you think that you need to keep multiple generations of a file that you're working on — perhaps a budget proposal or a spreadsheet that you're developing over a period of time — name each new draft something slightly different. You may want to use a numbering scheme (Budget 1, Budget 2, and so on) or add the date to the end of the filename (Budget 6/4/93, Budget 6/9/93). Because you are giving a unique name to each generation of the file, the backup copies will have unique names too — preventing you from inadvertently saving over any of the earlier drafts.

If you want to make the backup process more manageable, you can use one of the many good commercial backup programs that are available. My favorites are the following programs from Dantz Development Corporation (510-849-0293):

- DiskFit Direct (floppy and removable cartridge backups)
- DiskFit Pro (floppy and removable cartridge backups, plus server and scheduled backup support)
- Retrospect (floppy, tape, and removable cartridge backups, server support, scheduled backups, compression, and data encryption)

In addition to providing extra features, backup programs make backing up the entire hard disk just as easy as backing up only important data files. Having a full backup of the hard disk makes restoring the entire disk a snap if the need arises (following its total destruction, for example).

The Macintosh Desktop

When you first turn on the Mac, you see the *desktop* — sort of a Command Central for Mac operations. The desktop is where you perform many disk-related and file-related activities, such as making copies of disks and files, erasing disks and files, formatting disks (preparing them so that they're ready to receive Mac data), creating folders in which to organize files, and choosing programs to run. Figure 1-3 points out some of the key features of the desktop.

A note on crashes

Sometimes you have no choice but to cut the power to the Mac or press the reset switch. Such is the case when the Mac crashes. (A *crash* is when the cursor freezes, the current program no longer responds to keyboard or mouse clicks, or a system crash dialog box with a bomb icon appears. For whatever reason, the current program or the Macintosh system software is so messed up that the Mac is unable to continue.) The only fix for a crash is to restart the Mac.

Before giving up entirely after a crash, try pressing ⌘-Option-Esc. This emergency quit command sometimes enables you to quit from the program that crashed. A dialog box appears asking if you want to *Force [program] to quit? Unsaved changes will be lost.* Click the Quit button. Although any unsaved changes to open documents will indeed be lost, you may be able to save changes made to documents in *other* programs that are currently running.

If this procedure works, immediately save any files that are open in other programs, quit from those programs, and then choose the Restart or Shut Down command from the Finder's Special menu.

One of the most common causes of crashes is known as an *INIT conflict*. INITs (called *extensions* in System 7) are programs that load from your System Folder at start-up and run in the background on the Mac. Examples of INITs include macro utilities, fax modem drivers, and appointment reminder utilities. Some control panel documents also have an INIT attached to them. Problems can arise when two INITs perform similar functions, when an old INIT is used with a new version of system software, or when an INIT is incompatible with a particular program you're running. (***Note:*** Apple-supplied INITs and Control Panel documents — ones that are part of the system software — are seldom the culprits.)

To determine if you have an INIT problem, try removing all INITs and restarting the Mac. If the problem does not recur during the session, it is likely that it was caused by an INIT conflict.

Under System 7, turning off all INITs is easily accomplished by holding down the Shift key as you turn on or restart the Mac. You'll see a message in the Welcome to Macintosh box that says `Extensions off`.

If you're running System 6, however, the process is more complex. You must drag all extensions and Control Panel documents out of the System Folder and then restart. As an alternative, you can start up the Mac with the System Tools disk that comes with the different versions of the System 6 system software.

After you determine that an INIT is the likely cause of the crashes, the next step is to determine which particular INIT is the problem. The only way to do this is by trial and error — slowly returning them to the System Folder until the problem returns.

If you have many INITs, an easier approach to managing them is to pick up a software utility called an *extension manager.* An extension manager is a special INIT/Control Panel document that enables you to selectively turn INITs on or off during the start-up process. Some utility programs (such as NOW Utilities) include an extension manager as part of the package. You also can find freeware and shareware extension managers on most of the major on-line information services.

If you need more help diagnosing and correcting common Mac problems, pick up a copy of my book *Help! The Mac Answer Book,* a troubleshooting guide for Macintosh novices.

Because a crash can occasionally wreak havoc with hard disks, you may want to use a utility program (such as Disk First Aid, which is free with the Apple system software; Norton Utilities; Public Utilities; or MacTools) to examine the hard disk(s) following a crash. If the crash caused any damage, these utilities can often correct it.

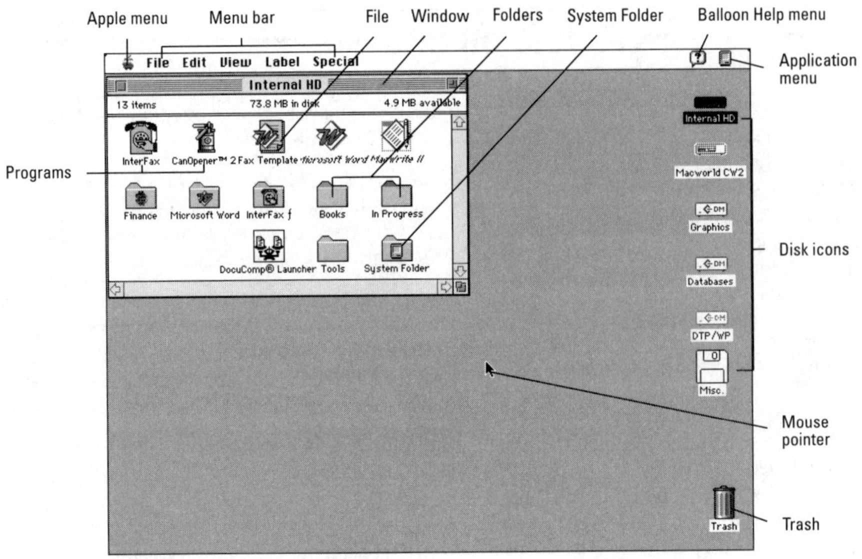

Figure 1-3: The Macintosh desktop.

Items on the desktop

The desktop contains the following items:

- *Menu bar.* Whether you're at the desktop or working within a program, you always see a set of menus across the top of the screen. Click any of these menus to pull down the menu so that you can view and choose from the menu commands.

- *Apple menu.* The apple icon tops a special menu. Click it to examine and use desk accessories (miniprograms) that you've installed.

In System 7, you also can put programs, important data files, and folders in the Apple menu by simply dropping their icons (or *aliases* of their icons) into the Apple Menu Items folder inside the System Folder. (For information on creating aliases, see the Quick Tips at the end of this Topic.)

- *Window.* Any open disk or folder is represented by a rectangular window, such as the window named Internal HD in Figure 1-3 that represents the hard disk. When you are running a program, each document that you open is also enclosed in a window.

- *Programs.* A program is a set of instructions that performs a computer task. A word processor is an example of a program.

- *File.* A file contains information of some sort. Documents that you create within ClarisWorks are examples of files, as are preference data, help information, and other documents that come with or are created for you by different programs.

- *Folders.* You use folders to organize files and programs. You can place them inside other folders, nesting them as deeply as you need to in order to achieve the level of organization that you want. (On a PC, folders are called *directories* and *subdirectories.*)

- *System Folder.* The System Folder is a special folder that contains the Macintosh system software (the System, Finder, fonts, and other important files). When you, Apple, or your dealer install the system software on your Mac, a System Folder is automatically created for you. The presence of a System Folder makes a disk *bootable* (that is, you can use it to start up the Mac).

  Whether the disk is a hard disk or a floppy disk, you can have only one System Folder per disk. Only disks that are capable of starting up the Mac need to have a System Folder, however. (Disks that you use only to store data, for example, do not require a System Folder.)

- *Balloon Help menu.* If you are running System 7, you see a balloon icon. Click it to pull down a special menu that enables you to turn the Balloon Help feature on or off. When Balloon Help is on and the mouse pointer moves over an object that has help information attached to it, a pop-up cartoon-style balloon with helpful information appears (see Figure 1-4).

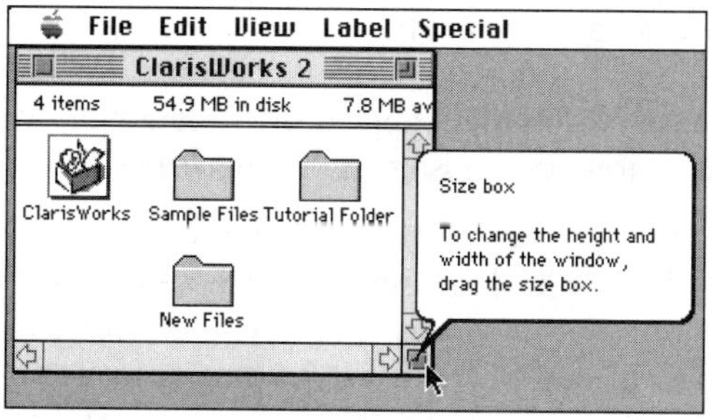

Figure 1-4: An example of Balloon Help.

- *Application menu.* If you're running System 6 with the MultiFinder turned on or you're using System 7, you see a tiny icon in the upper-right corner of the screen — whether you're at the desktop or running a program. This icon is the Application menu icon, and you use it to switch between programs that are running. The icon shows the program that is currently active.

  Under System 7, click the icon to view a menu of the programs and desk accessories that are open (see Figure 1-5). To switch to any of these programs or desk accessories, choose it with the mouse.

  If you see a tiny Macintosh icon at the far right side of the menu bar, it means that you're at the Finder desktop and can perform normal Finder activities, such as copying files. To return from the Finder to any of your open programs, choose the program from the Application menu or click in any of the program's open windows.

Figure 1-5: The System 7 Application menu.

Under System 6, you switch between open programs by clicking the Application menu icon. Each time you click, the Mac cycles to the next open program. As in System 7, you can click in any open window to switch back to that program.

- *Disk icons.* Every disk drive that is connected to the Mac — whether internal or external — is represented by an icon that appears on the right edge of the desktop. Any disk that appears on the desktop is referred to as *mounted.* Disk drives that use removable media (floppy drives, removable hard disk drives, and CD-ROM drives, for example) appear on the desktop only after a disk has been inserted into them. Some types of drives never appear on the desktop. Tape drives, for example, usually do not appear on the desktop because they are not designed to be directly accessible from the desktop. You need to run a special tape backup program to access the information that's stored on the tape. Notice that floppy disks (for example, Misc. in Figure 1-3) have icons that clearly distinguish them from hard disks.
- *Trash.* The Trash serves two purposes. First, if you want to *delete* a file (erase it), you drag its icon to the Trash and then choose Empty Trash from the Special menu. Second, to remove a disk from the desktop (usually a floppy, a CD-ROM, or a removable hard disk), you drag its icon to the Trash. Unlike dragging a file's icon, this action does not erase the disk. It merely removes the disk's icon from the desktop and then automatically ejects the disk from the floppy drive or the CD-ROM drive (or it may enable you to manually remove other types of disks, such as removable hard disks).
- *Mouse pointer.* The mouse pointer (shaped like an arrow or arrowhead) tracks movements that you make with the mouse. You use it to select objects and perform other desktop activities, such as dragging files to the Trash and choosing commands from menus.

Icons and more icons

Almost everything on the desktop is represented by an *icon* (a pictorial symbol). In Figure 1-3, you can see icons for the different programs, folders, hard disks, floppy disks, and the Trash. Programs and data documents have their distinctive icons assigned to them by the programmers who created the programs. Whenever you save a new document with a program, a special icon is automatically created for it. Different programs create different icons. Notice the icon in Figure 1-3 for Fax Template, a Microsoft Word document.

Actions performed on these icons affect the data files, programs, folders, and disks that they represent. On a PC running DOS, to copy a file from one drive to a directory on another drive, you may type the following:

```
C> COPY MEMO.DOC D:\WP\DOCS
```

To perform the same copy on a Mac, all that you need to do is use the mouse to select the MEMO file and then drag the icon to where you want the copy to go. One simple action. You have nothing to type and no commands to remember. This visual, icon-oriented work environment is what makes the Macintosh so easy to use.

Using the Mouse

The mouse is key to most operations on the Mac. On the desktop, you'll notice a tiny arrowhead-shaped pointer. This pointer is the *cursor*, and it moves as you move the mouse. As you use the Mac, you'll notice that the cursor frequently changes shape. When you are typing a word processing document, the cursor may be a straight vertical line. Move it outside the document window, and it changes into a pointer. If the program is performing a lengthy process — sorting a large database, for example — it may change into a watch or spinning beach ball icon. You get the idea: The cursor changes shape when the program is performing a new operation. It changes to reflect the operation.

Clicking and dragging

The two basic operations that you perform with the mouse are *clicking* and *dragging*. All operations involve one or both of these actions.

To *click* means to press the mouse button once and then release it. To *drag*, you press and hold the mouse button while you move the mouse pointer to a different on-screen location. A description of a few of the most common mouse maneuvers follows.

Selecting items on the desktop

Launching programs, copying files, opening folders, and almost everything else that you do on the desktop involve selecting items. The directions for selecting different items and objects follow.

To select an item on the desktop (and objects in most programs):

1. **Move the mouse so that the pointer is over the item you want to select.**
2. **Click the mouse button once.** The item is highlighted to indicate that it has been selected.

To select multiple items on the desktop:

1. **Hold down the Shift key and click once on each item that you want to select.**

— or —

1. **Click once outside the area where the items are located and, while continuing to hold down the mouse button, drag a rectangle around or through the items that you want to select, as shown in Figure 1-6.** (The rectangle, which is composed of tiny dots, is called a *selection rectangle.*)

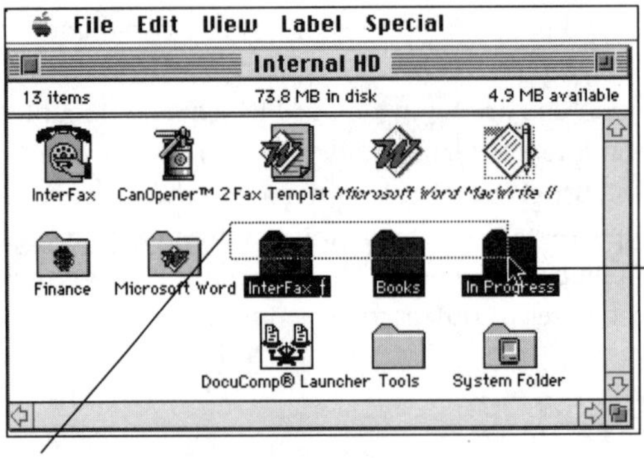

Drag mouse cursor over last item to be selected to complete the selection rectangle.

Click here to begin the selection rectangle.

Figure 1-6: Dragging to select three folders.

The latter technique is an example of *dragging.* Again, to drag, you move the mouse while holding down the mouse button. On the desktop, the selection rectangle merely needs to touch each item that you want to include. In some programs, however, you need to completely surround the items with the selection rectangle.

Choosing menu commands

Another common example of dragging is choosing menu commands — both on the desktop (in the Finder) and in programs.

Step-by-Steps

To choose a command from a menu:

1. **Move the mouse so that the pointer is over the menu that you want to open.**
2. **Click the menu name (File or Edit, for example) and continue to hold down the mouse button.** The menu name is highlighted, and the menu appears, exposing the commands that it contains.
3. **While continuing to hold down the mouse button, drag the pointer down until the command that you want to choose is highlighted, as shown in Figure 1-7.**

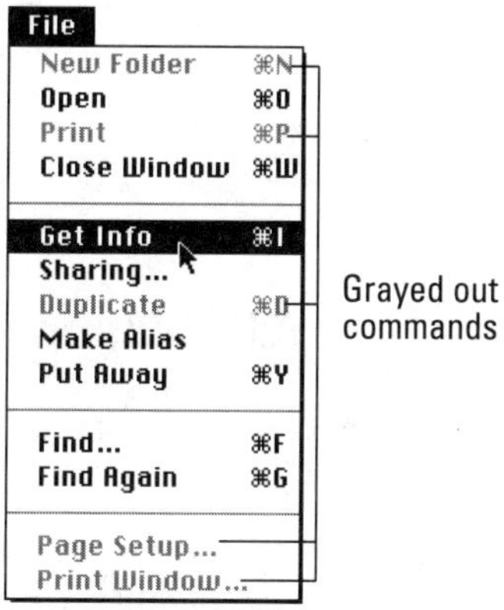

Figure 1-7: Choosing a menu command.

4. **Without moving the mouse, release the mouse button.** The chosen command executes.

   If you decide not to choose a command, continue to hold down the mouse button while you drag the pointer away from the menu area. As long as a command is not highlighted when you release the mouse button, no command will execute.

Sometimes menu commands are *grayed out* (appear in gray type) to indicate that, currently, you cannot choose them. The pointer merely slides over them without ever highlighting them. Usually, grayed-out commands are not available in the current condition of the program or the desktop. For example, the Empty Trash command in the Special menu is grayed out if the Trash is already empty. A program's Save command may be grayed out if you don't have a file on-screen or if you've just finished saving the current file.

Some programs also have *hierarchical* or *pop-up menus*. The ClarisWorks Outline Format command in the Outline menu is an example of this type of menu (see Figure 1-8). Pop-up menus are often indicated by a triangle symbol that appears after an option in a menu. After you select the command with the mouse, another menu appears with a set of commands for you to choose from.

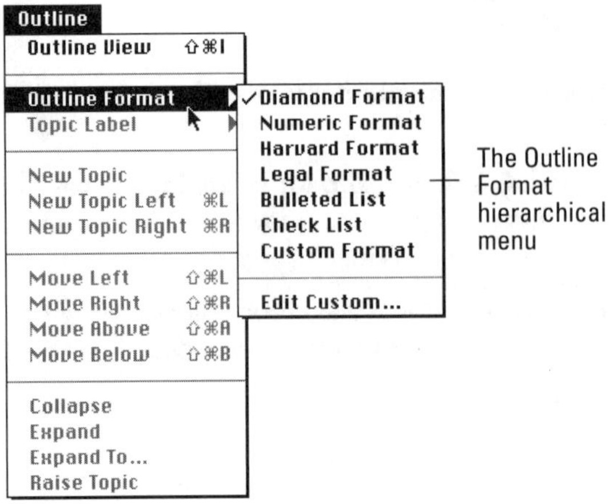

Figure 1-8: An example of a hierarchical menu in the ClarisWorks word processor.

To choose a command from a hierarchical (pop-up) menu:

1. **Move the mouse so that the pointer is over the menu that you want to open.**
2. **Click the menu name (File or Edit, for example) and continue to hold down the mouse button.** The menu name is highlighted, and the menu appears, exposing the commands that it contains.
3. **While continuing to hold down the mouse button, drag the pointer down until the command that you want to select is highlighted.** The list of choices (pop-up menu) for the command appears — usually to one side or the other of the menu.
4. **Drag the mouse pointer into the pop-up menu and highlight the command that you want.**
5. **Without moving the mouse, release the mouse button.** The command that you chose executes.

NOTE

Dialog boxes (discussed in "Dealing with Dialog Boxes," later in this Topic) may also incorporate pop-up menus.

Both on the desktop and within programs, some menu commands list a cloverleaf symbol (⌘) that is followed by a letter, number, or character. This symbol is the *Command* symbol, which is shown on most keyboards as ⌘ and . Instead of choosing these menu commands with the mouse, you can use the Command-key combinations that are listed in the menu to issue the commands directly from the keyboard. For example, on the desktop, you can close the active window by holding down ⌘ and pressing W. You can request information about a file by selecting it and pressing ⌘-I. Some programs — particularly the more powerful or complex ones — also use the Shift key in combination with the Command key to expand the number of keyboard shortcuts that the program offers. In the ClarisWorks 2 word processor, for example, ⌘-I changes selected text to italic, and Shift-⌘-I toggles between the program's outline and normal display modes.

Double-clicking

In addition to single mouse clicks, some operations require a double-click. Double-clicking a program icon on the desktop launches the program. Double-clicking a document icon normally launches its creating program and loads the file. Double-clicking a word in a word processor selects the entire word for further editing, such as changing the font or text style. In many programs, double-clicking an object may display a dialog box that is appropriate for that object. In a charting program, for example, double-clicking a graph element may bring up a color and pattern dialog box.

Step-by-Steps

To double-click:

1. **Position the cursor over the icon, object, or text item.**
2. **Press the mouse button twice in rapid succession.**

Some programs support other mouse commands, such as clicking and dragging while holding down a modifier key (⌘, Shift, or Option). In some word processors, triple-clicking selects an entire sentence or paragraph. Check program manuals for details.

TIP

If you find that the Mac isn't responding correctly to double-clicks, you're probably taking too much time between clicks, making the Mac think that you have executed two single clicks rather than one double-click. You can adjust the double-click speed in the Mouse control panel.

Step-by-Steps

To change the double-click speed:

1. **Choose Control Panels from the Apple menu.**
2. **Under System 6, click the scroll bar until you see the Mouse icon and then click the icon.**

— or —

2. **Under System 7, double-click the Mouse control panel icon.**
3. **The Mouse control panel supports three double-click speeds, as shown in Figure 1-9.** If you tend to click slowly, choose the option on the left by clicking its radio button (see "Common dialog elements" for more details on radio buttons). The middle option is normal, and the one on the right is the fastest.

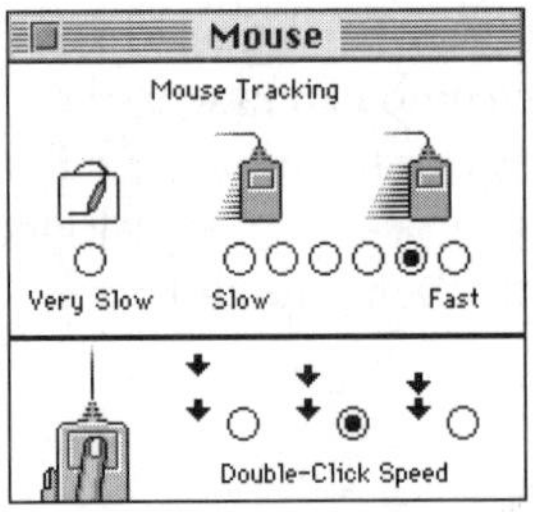

Figure 1-9: The Mouse control panel.

4. **Close the control panel by clicking its close box (the tiny square in the upper-left corner of the window).** Any changes take effect immediately.

Dealing with Dialog Boxes

Whether you're selecting menu commands from the desktop or working in a program such as ClarisWorks, dialog boxes frequently confront you. A *dialog box* is a special window in which you select options, answer questions, and communicate choices to the Mac's system software and to programs. At its simplest, a dialog box may present a single question for you to answer with Yes, No, and Cancel buttons, as shown in Figure 1-10, or with OK and Cancel buttons. To respond to such a dialog box, you just click the button that corresponds to your choice.

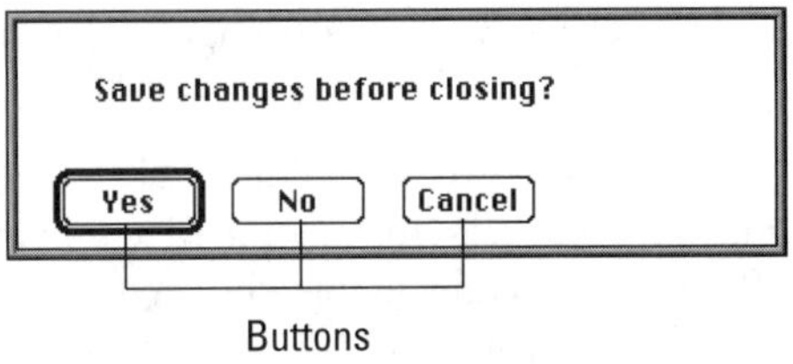

Figure 1-10: A simple dialog box that appears when you attempt to close a document window without saving the document.

TIP

In most dialog boxes, you can use two keyboard shortcuts instead of clicking buttons. To choose the Cancel option, press ⌘-. (the Command key and the period). To select the *default option* (the button surrounded by the thick border), press Return or Enter.

Common dialog box elements

For an example of a complex dialog box, from the desktop File menu, choose Page Setup. If you have a LaserWriter, you see a dialog box like the one in Figure 1-11.

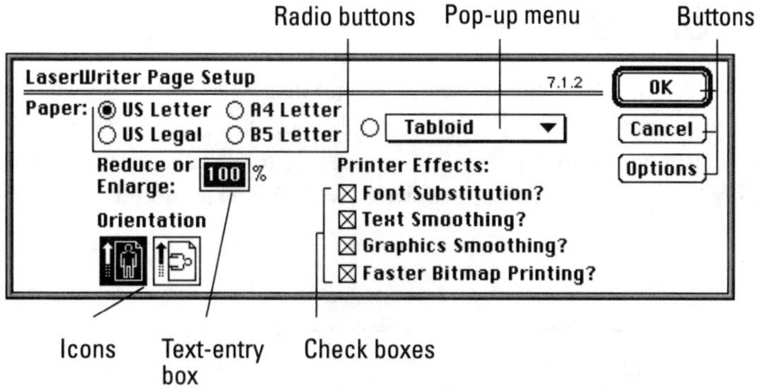

Figure 1-11: The LaserWriter Page Setup dialog box.

The LaserWriter Page Setup dialog box incorporates many of the elements that you generally see in dialog boxes — including radio buttons, text-entry boxes, check boxes, buttons, icons, and pop-up menus. Here's how each element works:

- *Radio buttons.* Radio buttons present a group of mutually exclusive choices. In the Page Setup dialog box, you use radio buttons to choose paper size. To select an option, click once in the circle beside your choice. A black dot appears in the radio button to denote that you have chosen the item. After you choose a radio-button item, the previously selected item's button changes to an empty circle (indicating that it is no longer selected).
- *Text-entry boxes.* A text-entry box is one in which you type an entry. The Reduce or Enlarge box is an example of a text-entry box.
- *Check boxes.* Like radio buttons, check boxes are presented as a group. However, the items are not mutually exclusive; you can choose as many as you like. Clicking in a check box toggles the current condition of the box. If it was checked, it becomes unchecked. If it was unchecked, it becomes checked.
- *Buttons.* Instead of setting options, buttons in dialog boxes cause an action to occur. You click a button to change the dialog box (presenting more choices, as in the case of the Options button) or to select a final action (OK or Cancel, for example). After you click a button, you exit the dialog box.
- *Icons.* Dialog boxes occasionally use icons as options. In this example, the portrait and landscape paper orientations are portrayed by two icons that show normal and sideways printing. This pair of icons is mutually exclusive. To select one, you merely click the appropriate icon, and it is highlighted to show that you have chosen it.
- *Pop-up menus.* The radio button next to the box that contains the word *Tabloid* incorporates a pop-up menu. After you click the box surrounding the arrow and the word *Tabloid,* you see a new set of options, including, for example, Envelope — Center Fed. While holding down the mouse button, choose one of the items in the pop-up menu and then release the mouse button. The radio button will be selected, and the option that you chose will replace the word *Tabloid* in the box.

File dialog boxes

One type of dialog box that warrants special discussion is the standard file dialog box that appears whenever you open a file from within a program or choose the Save As command from the File menu (see Figure 1-12). Because you see these dialog boxes almost every time you work with the Mac, understanding them is important.

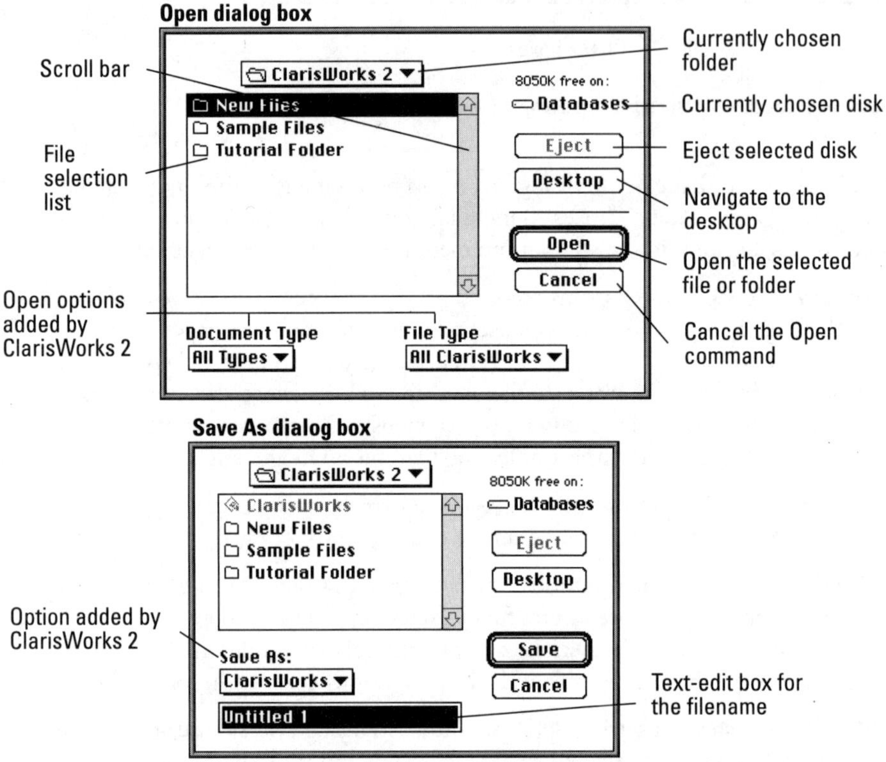

Figure 1-12: The ClarisWorks 2 Open and Save As file dialog boxes (System 7).

The examples shown in Figure 1-12 contain all the elements of the standard Open and Save As file dialog boxes as they appear in System 7. (If you're running System 6, you see a Disk button, rather than the Desktop button, but in other respects, the dialog options work the same way.) Some programs add elements to the file dialog box. The dialog boxes in Figure 1-12 show the Document Type, File Type, and Save As pop-up menus that ClarisWorks has added. Refer to the program manuals for information regarding these extras.

Using either of these dialog boxes is a two-step process. First, you navigate to the desired disk and folder. Then, you open or save the file. (See Topic 2 for information about these dialog boxes in ClarisWorks 3.0.)

Navigation

When you choose Open or Save As from the File menu, the program presents one of the dialog boxes that is shown in Figure 1-12. The disk and folder that are displayed when the dialog box appears are the ones most recently used by the program in this session. When you save a file that was opened during the session, its original disk and folder are automatically selected. In some instances, however, you want to change to a different disk or folder.

To switch to a different disk (System 7):

1. **Click the Desktop button.** The file selection list now contains a list of all mounted disks, as well as any files that are stored on the desktop.
2. **Select the disk that you want to open by double-clicking the disk's name or by highlighting it and clicking the Open button (if one is available).**

NOTE: Under System 6, you change disks by clicking the Disk button. Each time you click the button, you cycle to the next disk in the list of all currently mounted disks.

To switch to a different floppy disk:

1. **Use the preceding set of steps to select the currently inserted floppy disk.**
2. **Click Eject.** The floppy pops out.
3. **Insert the floppy that you intend to use.**
4. **If the new floppy is not automatically selected for you, double-click the floppy's name in the file selection list or highlight it and click the Open button (if one is available).**

NOTE: If you want to use a particular floppy disk and no floppy is currently inserted in the drive, you can skip Steps 1 and 2.

After ensuring that the correct disk is selected, you frequently need to change to a different folder.

To navigate to a lower (more deeply nested) folder on the current disk:

1. **Choose a folder in the file selection list.** You can click the scroll bars to move quickly through a list that is larger than the window.
2. **Double-click the folder name or highlight it and click the Open button (if one is available).**

To navigate to a higher (less deeply nested) folder on the current disk:

1. **Click the current folder pop-up menu above the file selection list.** A list of folders that are higher in the hierarchy drops down.
2. **While continuing to hold down the mouse button, drag to select the folder that you want to open.**

TIP

If you are running System 7, you can use a shortcut to move up through the folder hierarchy. Click the name of the current disk (in this case, Databases). Each time you click it, you automatically move up one level in the folder hierarchy.

Opening a file

After you select the disk and folder, you open the desired file by selecting it in the file list and taking one of the following actions:

- Double-clicking its filename
- Clicking the Open button (or pressing Return or Enter)

The file is then loaded into the program.

Saving a file

After navigating to the destination disk and folder, you save a file in a similar fashion.

To save a file:

1. **Type a name into the text-edit box.**
2. **Click the Save button (or press Return or Enter).**

If you enter the name of a file that already exists on that disk and in that folder, you see a new dialog box that asks the question *Replace existing "[filename]"?*. Click Replace to overwrite the old file. Click Cancel if you decide to save the new file with a different name, to a different disk, or in a different folder.

Basic Text Editing

Whether you are typing a word processing, spreadsheet, or database document; entering text in dialog boxes; or simply renaming an icon, the Mac has its own distinctive conventions for text editing. The following step-by-steps cover the essentials.

To enter text:

1. **Move the cursor to where you want to start typing.**
2. **Click once.** The cursor positions itself where you clicked.
3. **Begin typing.**

Selecting text

To manipulate text — to cut it, change the font or style, and so on — you first have to select the text. After you position the cursor at either the start or the end of the intended selection, you can choose from one of the following methods to select the text:

- Drag to complete the selection.
- Press Shift and then click at the other end of the selection.

The selected text — like a selected menu command — is highlighted, as shown in Figure 1-13. You can extend a text selection by pressing Shift again and clicking in an area past the position of the previous second click.

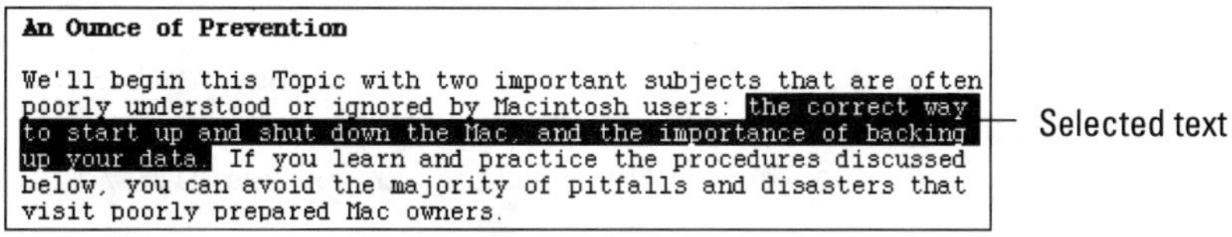

An Ounce of Prevention

We'll begin this Topic with two important subjects that are often poorly understood or ignored by Macintosh users: the correct way to start up and shut down the Mac, and the importance of backing up your data. If you learn and practice the procedures discussed below, you can avoid the majority of pitfalls and disasters that visit poorly prepared Mac owners.

Figure 1-13: The highlighted text is selected.

Many programs also support text-selection shortcuts. One shortcut that you can use in almost all editing — including editing that you do on the desktop and in dialog boxes — is double-clicking to select a word.

To select a word:

1. **Position the cursor anywhere on the word.**
2. **Click once.** The cursor positions itself within the word. (***Note:*** Where the cursor positions itself within the word doesn't matter.)
3. **Double-click, and the entire word is selected.**

Deleting text

You can delete individual characters by positioning the cursor and then pressing the Delete or Backspace key. Each time you press the key, the character to the immediate left of the cursor position is removed.

To delete a larger group of text (a phrase, sentence, or paragraph, for example), use one of the text-selection methods described in the preceding section and then issue the appropriate command or perform the appropriate procedure:

Menu Command	*Key*	*Action*
None	Delete or Backspace	Deletes the text without placing a copy of it on the Clipboard (see "Pasting text or objects")
Clear	None	Deletes the text without placing a copy of it on the Clipboard
Cut	⌘-X	Deletes the text and places a copy of it on the Clipboard
None	Type the replacement text	Whatever is typed instantly replaces the selected text without placing a copy of it on the Clipboard

If you don't intend to reuse the text, the deletion method you use doesn't matter. If you want to paste the text into another spot in the document, into a different document, or into another program, use the Cut command (⌘-X).

Pasting text or objects

Text or objects that have been cut or copied are placed on the *Clipboard,* a temporary storage area in the Mac's memory. Whatever has been cut remains in the Clipboard and is available for pasting until you cut or copy something else or shut down the Mac.

Step-by-Steps

To paste text or objects:

1. **Move the cursor over the area where you want to paste the text or object and click once to position the cursor.**
2. **Choose Paste from the Edit menu (or press ⌘-V).**

Printing 101

Printing is one of the most basic computer operations. Although it is usually straightforward (you choose Print from the File menu and then click the Print button), things can quickly become muddled when you have several printers to choose from, are printing over a network, or are trying to decipher the meaning of the Page Setup options.

Preparation for printing requires three steps:

1. Selecting a printer in the Chooser desk accessory
2. Setting Page Setup dialog box options
3. Setting Print dialog box options

Using the Chooser

You use the Chooser desk accessory (shown in Figure 1-14) to select the printer or other device to which you want to send the next print job. Subsequent print jobs continue to go to that device until you select a different device in the Chooser.

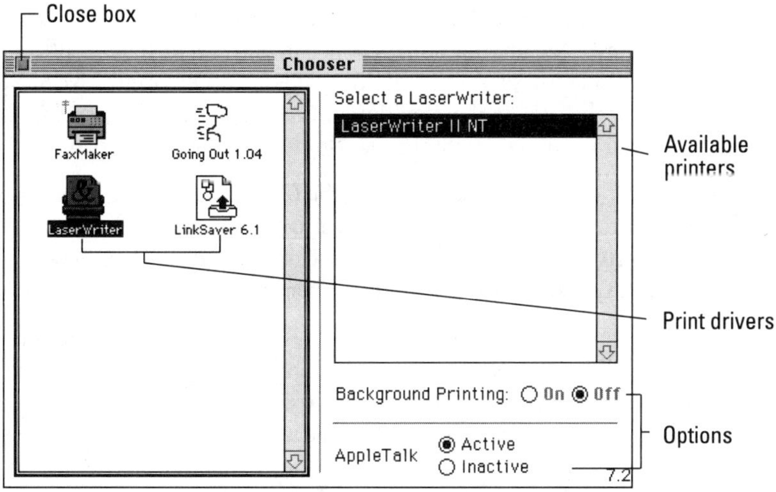

Figure 1-14: The Chooser desk accessory.

To use the Chooser to select a printer:

1. Select Chooser from the Apple menu.

The left side of the Chooser window displays all print drivers that are installed in the System Folder. (Under System 6, they're stored loose in the System Folder. Under System 7, they're stored in the Extensions folder inside the System Folder.) Although most Chooser drivers are for printers, other programs and utilities may also supply drivers that redirect printing. In Figure 1-14, for example, FaxMaker is a driver for a fax modem. When selected, FaxMaker intercepts all Print commands and converts the current document to fax format for transmission to a fax machine.

2. **In the left side of the window, click once to select the appropriate driver for the printer you want to use.**

3. **In the right window is a list of printers that can use the selected driver; click to select the printer to which you want to send the next print job.** If you are on a network, you may be able to choose from multiple printers, including printers that are not directly connected to the Mac. (***Note:*** The printer has to be turned on in order for it to appear in the list.)

4. **Set options for the printer.**

   The options that are listed vary according to the type of printer that you select. See the printer manual for a list of the printer's capabilities and the meaning of the options.

5. **To record changes, click the close box in the upper-left corner of the Chooser window.**

NOTE

You also may see drivers for printers that you do not own or that are not connected to your Mac or your network. When you install system software on the Mac, the installation procedure often installs all Apple print drivers. You may want to throw out the drivers that you don't need. Be sure, however, that you are throwing out print drivers rather than something else.

If you've just changed printer types in the Chooser, the Mac reminds you to check the Page Setup options to make sure that they're correct for the new printer. To check the settings and change them if necessary, choose Page Setup from the File menu on the desktop or from within any program.

TIP

If you have only one printer that you always use, you can select it once in the Chooser and then never have to use the Chooser again until you want to change options. The only exception to this rule is when you install or reinstall the system software. Doing so usually leaves the Mac without a selected printer.

The Print and Page Setup dialog box options

Whether you're printing from the desktop or from within ClarisWorks or another program, you need to understand the Print and Page Setup dialog box options. The Page Setup options deal with paper and image issues: size, rotation, scaling, and similar options. The Print options govern the print quality, the number of copies, the page range, and the paper source.

Page Setup options

Normally, you need to adjust Page Setup options only when you want to do one of the following tasks:

- ◆ Select a new printer in the Chooser
- ◆ Print on a different paper type or size, such as an envelope or legal-sized paper
- ◆ Change the orientation of a printout (from portrait to landscape or vice versa)

Figure 1-15 shows the Page Setup dialog boxes for three of the most common Apple printers: the LaserWriter, the ImageWriter, and the StyleWriter. (If you have a non-Apple printer that came with its own Chooser print driver, the Page Setup options may differ somewhat from the options in these boxes. Refer to your printer manual for an explanation of the options.)

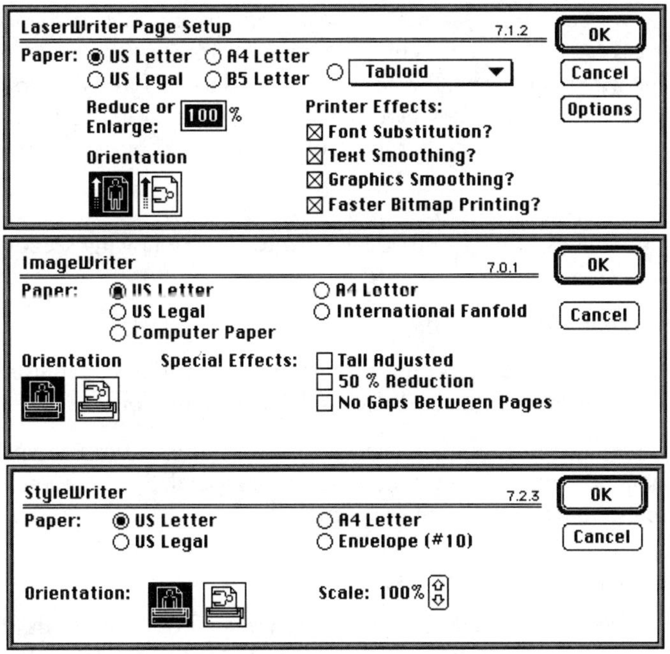

Figure 1-15: The Page Setup dialog boxes for three printers.

The three dialog boxes have the following options in common:

- ◆ *Paper sizes.* At the top of the dialog box is a set of radio buttons for several paper sizes. Select the one that's correct for the paper you intend to use.

Although most printing is done on standard 8.5 x 11-inch paper (the US Letter option), some of the other options you may encounter are A4 Letter (8.5 x 11.67-inch paper), a popular European paper size for letters; B5 letter (7 x 10-inch paper), another European paper size for correspondence; Computer Paper (standard 15 x 11-inch fan-fold computer paper), a popular choice for ImageWriter printers; and Tabloid (an 11 x 17-inch paper that, because of its large size, is normally supported only by special laser printers).

If you have a LaserWriter (or a printer that uses the LaserWriter driver), be sure to examine the Tabloid pop-up menu. It contains support for envelope printing, as well as for other special paper types and sizes.

- *Orientation icons.* All Macintosh printers can print documents in two orientations: *portrait* (right side up) and *landscape* (sideways). You print most documents in portrait mode (click the first Orientation icon). If a document is too wide to fit within the eight or so printable inches of a standard 8.5 x 11-inch page, click the landscape icon.
- *Reduction and scaling options.* Occasionally, you may want to change the size of what you're printing — either to make it fit on one page or to make it take up more room on the page. This option is available for many printers, but it may come with restrictions. PostScript printers, such as LaserWriters, generally enable you to specify any percentage for reducing or enlarging an image. ImageWriters, on the other hand, offer only two choices: full size or 50% reduction.

Some options are specific to a particular printer. The following sections discuss these unique options.

Unique ImageWriter options

- *Tall Adjusted.* Select this option when printing graphics. It adjusts for the difference between ImageWriter and screen resolution.
- *No Gaps between Pages.* When printing to continuous-form computer paper, making a continuous printout is sometimes useful. Spreadsheets and program listings, for example, often are printed this way.

Unique LaserWriter options

- *Font Substitution.* When this option is checked, PostScript fonts (Times, Helvetica, and Courier) are automatically substituted for their lower-resolution counterparts (New York, Geneva, and Monaco) if the latter fonts are in the current document. Unless you routinely format documents with ImageWriter fonts, you usually don't need to check this option. (On the other hand, it doesn't hurt to have it checked.)
- *Text Smoothing.* This option minimizes jagged edges when you are printing non-PostScript fonts.

- *Graphics Smoothing.* This option minimizes jagged edges on graphics images.
- *Faster Bitmap Printing.* When you check this option, bitmapped images are preprocessed for faster printing. However, this option was apparently intended to be used only with the original LaserWriter and LaserWriter Plus printers. Checking this option for more recent printers can slow the printing or prevent some images from printing at all.

If you click the Options button in the LaserWriter Page Setup dialog box, another group of settings appears, as shown in Figure 1-16. The Apple *dogcow* image to the left changes to show the effects of options selected on this screen.

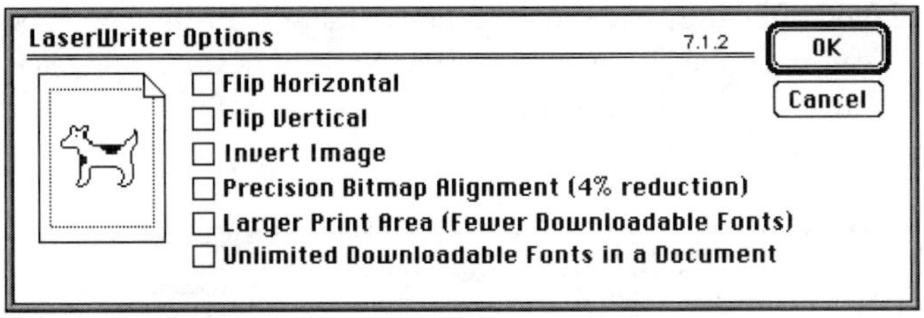

Figure 1-16: Additional LaserWriter setup options.

The additional options are as follows:

- *Flip Horizontal.* Reverse the page from left to right.
- *Flip Vertical.* Reverse the page from top to bottom (so the image is upside down).
- *Invert Image.* Reverse blacks and whites in the image.
- *Precision Bitmap Alignment (4% reduction).* Choose this option if you need the printout to precisely match that of the original bitmapped image. The printout is printed at 288 dots per inch — precisely four times the Mac's screen resolution of 72 dots per inch. Usually this option is necessary only for printing things such as blueprints and schematic diagrams — where the dimensions must be exact.
- *Larger Print Area (Fewer Downloadable Fonts).* Enlarge the printable area slightly (at the expense of having fewer downloadable fonts in the document).

NOTE

There are three ways that a laser printer can generate fonts for a printout. First, most laser printers have a number of fonts that are built into their memory. These are called *resident* fonts and are always available to the printer. Second, fonts can be sent by the Mac to the printer. This process is called *downloading.* If you format part of a document by using a font that is not resident in the printer, the system software searches the System Folder for a special font outline file that can be used to describe the font to the printer. If the file is found, its information is downloaded to the printer.

Third, if the font outline file is not found, the printer can attempt to create the font based on the *screen font* that is used to display the font on-screen. Unfortunately, screen fonts can result in poor printed output — particularly if the fonts have to be scaled to a new size.

- *Unlimited Downloadable Fonts in a Document.* This option enables you to print a document that contains a large number of fonts that must be *downloaded* (ones that are not built into the printer). Printing time may increase substantially.

Print options

The final (and often only) step in printing is to set the Print dialog box options. (Choose Print from the File menu, choose the Print options, and click the Print button.) The screen shown in Figure 1-17 shows the standard Print dialog box for the three printers discussed previously.

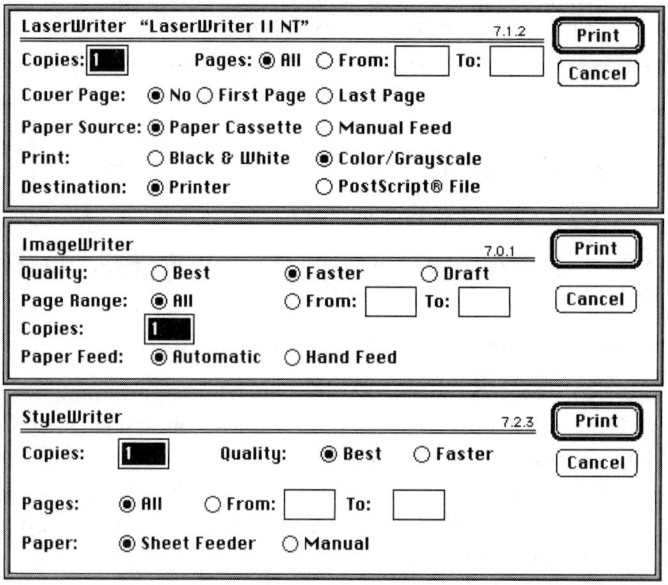

Figure 1-17: Print dialog boxes for the Apple LaserWriter, ImageWriter, and StyleWriter.

You use the various options to do the following:

- *Copies.* Specify the number of copies to print.
- *Page Range (Pages).* Determine whether the entire document (leave the boxes blank) or only a subset of the pages (type a page range) will be printed.
- *Quality (Print).* Different printers offer different Quality settings. Normally, the lower the quality, the faster the job prints. On an ImageWriter, choose Draft printouts to use the printer's built-in font and ignore fonts that have

been set in the document. On LaserWriters, choose Black & White to produce a two-tone printout or Color/Grayscale to use a halftone process that produces shades of gray.

- *Paper Source (Paper Feed, Paper).* This option determines where the paper will be drawn from when printing. Select Hand Feed when inserting cut-sheet paper into an ImageWriter or Automatic when using continuous-form computer paper. The meanings of the other options are self-explanatory.

The only unique Print option is the LaserWriter's support for a Cover Page. Set a Cover Page when you want the first or last page to provide identifying information about the print job: the user's name, the application, the document name, the date, the time, and the printer. This feature is most useful for distinguishing the owner of different print jobs on a shared printer.

Quick Tips

The following tips tell you how to access programs and documents quickly by using aliases, drag-and-drop, and keyboard shortcuts.

Making aliases

If you're running System 7 and have favorite programs or documents that you use frequently, *aliases* (file, folder, or disk stand-ins) offer speedy access to the files without the usual folder sifting. An alias is a tiny 1–2K file that represents another single file, folder, or disk. After you double-click an alias, the program it represents launches, or in the case of a disk or folder alias, a window with the contents of that disk or folder appears on the desktop.

You can place aliases anywhere you like; the desktop is one popular spot. When you pop them in the Apple Menu Items folder (inside the System Folder), you can launch programs and open current project documents by selecting the alias file from the Apple menu.

Step-by-Steps

To create an alias:

1. **On the desktop, use the mouse to select the program, document, folder, or disk for which you want to make an alias.** If you want quick access to ClarisWorks, for example, select its icon.
2. **Choose Make Alias from the File Menu.** The alias icon appears. (Note that alias names are italic.) As with other files, you can rename an alias if you want to. (I usually eliminate the *alias* part of the name because it makes the name unnecessarily long. After all, the name is already in italic, making it readily identifiable as an alias.)

3. **Place the alias wherever you want it.** No matter where you put it, it maintains its link with the original program, document, folder, or disk that it represents. If, for example, you want to add an alias to the Apple menu, open the System Folder and then drag the alias icon into the Apple Menu Items folder. The alias is immediately added to the Apple menu.

Translating files with drag-and-drop

System 7 adds a cool new feature called *drag-and-drop* that enables you to simultaneously launch a program (ClarisWorks, for example) and convert a foreign file so it can be used in that program. Follow this simple procedure:

Step-by-Steps

To use drag-and-drop:

1. **At the desktop, drag the icon of the foreign document onto the program icon.** If the program recognizes that type of document, the program icon turns dark.
2. **Release the mouse button.** The program launches, interprets the foreign file, and displays the contents of the file in a new document window.

ClarisWorks has a large number of translator files. For a further discussion of working with foreign files in ClarisWorks, see "Opening non-ClarisWorks documents" in Topic 2.

Fast file selection

Many times, the file selection list in Open dialog boxes can be quite lengthy. Although you can use the scroll bars and boxes to move through the list and make your choice, the Mac also provides some useful keyboard shortcuts:

- *Press the up- or down-arrow key.* You can quickly scroll to the filename without using the mouse. To open a selected folder or file, press Return or Enter.
- *Press the Page Up, Page Down, Home, or End keys (if you have an Apple Extended keyboard).* Although these keys do not select files or folders, they do move through the list. Page Up and Page Down are the equivalent of a single click in the scroll bar. Home and End display the beginning and end of the file list, respectively.
- *Type the first letter of the filename.* The list automatically scrolls to the first matching entry. For example, to open a file named Memo, press M. The list displays the first filename that begins with *M.* If no name starts with *M,* the next filename that follows alphabetically is selected. If you type fast enough, you can string several letters together as a search string. If you have many files that begin with *M,* for example, typing **ME** locates the Memo file more precisely.

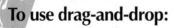

Summary

- The Mac has a right way and a wrong way for you to start it up and shut it down.
- You should make regular copies (backups) of important data files. In many cases, the value of the information stored in the Mac is many times the value of the hardware and programs you own.
- When not working in a program, you spend much of your time on the Mac desktop — manipulating files and disks and organizing documents within folders.
- All mouse operations involve clicking, dragging, or a combination of these two actions.
- You can double-click to launch programs, select documents to open, or select a word in most documents. If the Mac doesn't respond consistently to your double-clicks, you can adjust the double-click speed in the Mouse control panel.
- Dialog boxes enable you to communicate important information and option choices to programs and to the Mac system software.
- File dialog boxes enable you to open and save documents. Some programs (ClarisWorks, for example) change the file dialog boxes by adding other options, such as file filtering and export format lists.
- The Mac has special procedures for editing and selecting text. After you learn them, you can apply them at the desktop and within almost every Mac program.
- Readying a document for printing consists of three steps: selecting a printing device in the Chooser desk accessory, specifying Page Setup options, and setting Print options.

Topic 2

ClarisWorks Essentials

Overview

Before you leap into ClarisWorks, you need to get some basics under your belt. If you're new to the Mac, this Topic is particularly helpful. Many of the procedures that it describes — such as starting the program, opening and saving documents, and printing — are applicable to almost any Mac program. Even if you consider yourself an experienced Mac user, you can benefit from at least skimming through this Topic. You may pick up a time-saving tip or two that improves your productivity with ClarisWorks.

In Topic 2, you learn how to start the program; create new documents; open existing documents (including *foreign* files, which are documents created in other programs); save documents; use the Tool panel and Shortcuts palette; add frames to documents; change the display (by hiding/showing tools, altering the magnification level, arranging and resizing document windows, creating split screens, and generating new views); print documents; use the Help System; and quit the program.

Starting ClarisWorks

As with most Macintosh programs, you can start ClarisWorks in several ways. From the desktop, which is shown in Figure 2-1, you have two methods to choose from:

- Double-click the ClarisWorks program icon.
- Click the ClarisWorks program icon to select it and then choose Open from the File menu (or press ⌘-O).

The desktop shows icons for all mounted disks (both hard disks and floppy disks), the Trash, windows for open drives and folders, and icons for programs and data files. Topic 1 describes the desktop in detail.

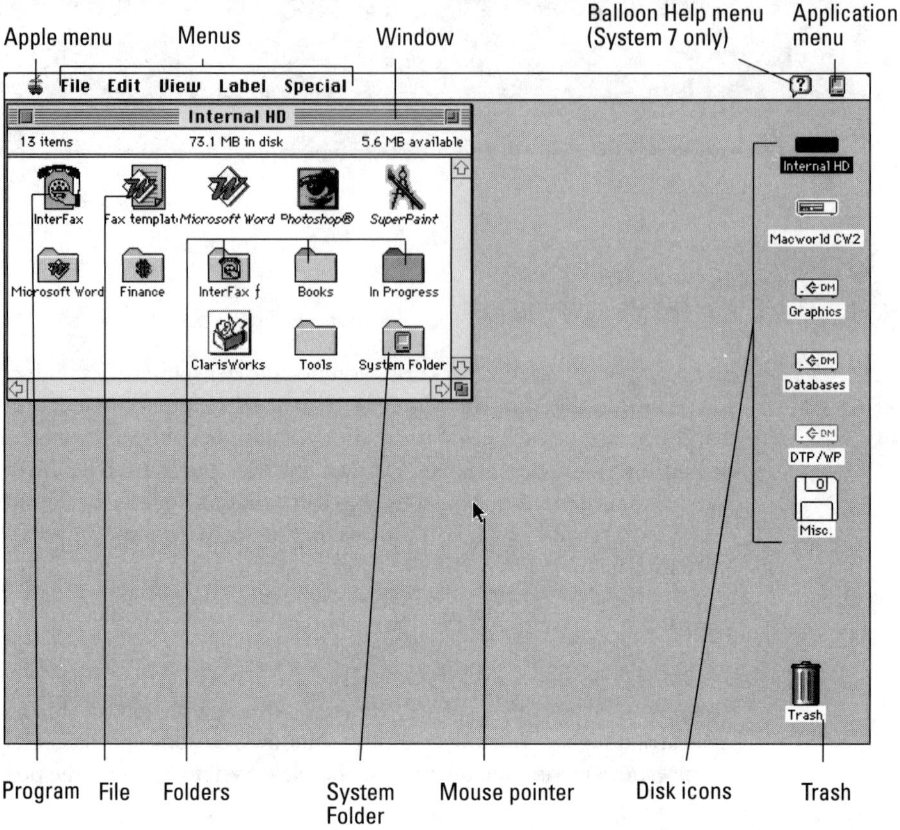

Figure 2-1: The Macintosh desktop.

If you want to load a document (or perhaps several) as you launch the program, you can use one of the following methods:

- ◆ Double-click a ClarisWorks document icon.
- ◆ Select several ClarisWorks document icons (by Shift-clicking the icons or by drawing a selection rectangle around them) and then choose Open from the File menu (or press ⌘-O).

Whether you open documents from the desktop or load them from within ClarisWorks, you can open as many documents as memory allows.

Creating a New Document

Each time you start ClarisWorks, the program loads, and the New Document dialog box (ClarisWorks 2.0 or 2.1) or the Welcome dialog box (ClarisWorks 3.0) automatically opens so that you can create a new document. (Other options presented in the ClarisWorks 3.0 Welcome dialog box are discussed later in this Topic.)

To create a new document at start-up in ClarisWorks 2.0 or 2.1:

1. **Load ClarisWorks.** The New Document dialog box, which is shown in Figure 2-2, automatically opens.

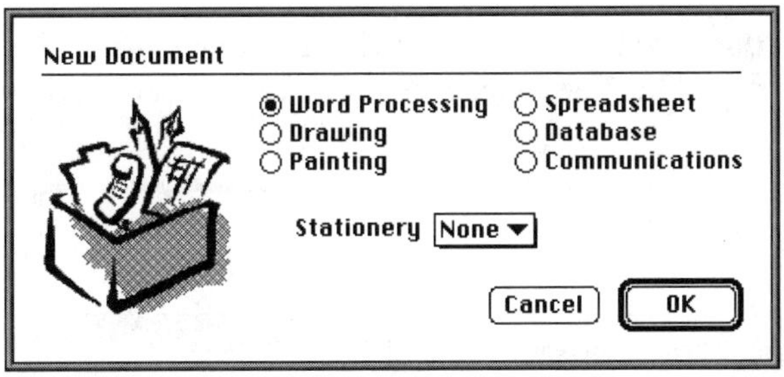

Figure 2-2: The New Document dialog box.

2. **Click a radio button to choose the type of document (called an *environment*) that you want to create.**
3. **Click OK.**

If you want to load an existing document instead of creating a new one, click Cancel. Then choose Open from the File menu to select a document to load (following the steps described in "Opening Existing Documents," later in this Topic).

To create a new document at start-up in ClarisWorks 3.0:

1. **Load ClarisWorks.** The Welcome dialog box, which is shown in Figure 2-3, automatically opens. (Note that if you have changed the general preference setting for On startup, show, as described in Topic 12, you may see the New Document or Open dialog box instead.)

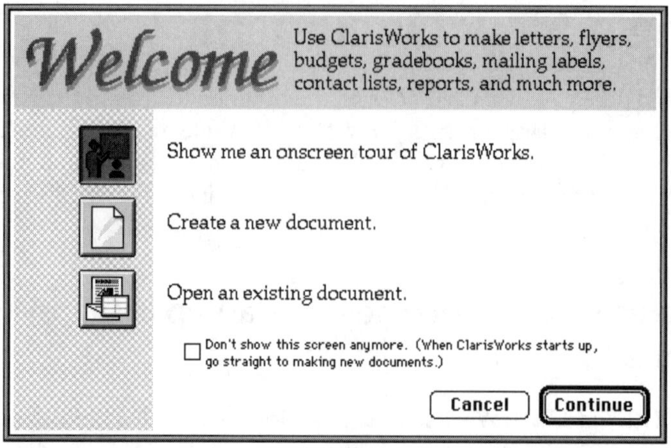

Figure 2-3: ClarisWorks 3.0's Welcome dialog box.

2. **Click the middle icon, labeled Create a new document, and then click Continue.** The New Document dialog box appears, as shown in Figure 2-4.

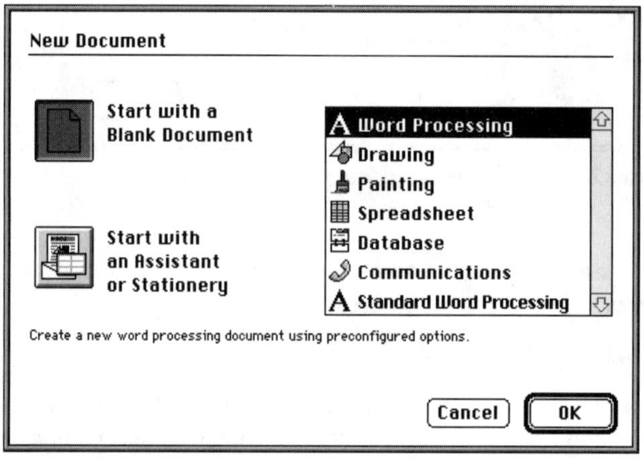

Figure 2-4: The New Document dialog box.

3. **To start with a blank document from any of the six ClarisWorks environments, click the first icon, select a document type from the scrolling list, and click OK.**

— or —

3. **To start with a ClarisWorks Assistant or a stationery document (that is, a document template), click the second icon, select a document or Assistant type from the Category pop-up menu, choose a specific document from the scrolling list, and click OK.** For more information on working with stationery documents and Assistants, see Topic 11.

If you have created an *options stationery document* for an environment (see "Using Stationery to Set New Environment Defaults" inTopic 11), you see two different stationery documents listed for that environment (as shown for word processing in Figure 2-4, for example). The options stationery document is simply shown as Word Processing. The ClarisWorks *default* document for that environment, on the other hand, is listed as Standard Word Processing.

If you want to open an existing document instead of creating a new one, click the icon labeled Open an existing document (see Figure 2-3) and click Continue. In the standard file dialog box that appears, select the file and click Open to load it into ClarisWorks.

If you want to create a new document after the program has been running for a while, you can either choose New from the File menu or press ⌘-N. The New Document dialog box appears. Select a document type and then click OK.

You can create new documents or open existing documents at any time during a ClarisWorks session. The only limitation on the number of documents you can have open at the same time is the amount of memory available to ClarisWorks. See the Quick Tips at the end of this Topic for help with changing the memory allocation for ClarisWorks.

New documents are assigned a temporary name that consists of the word *Untitled*, a number that represents the number of documents created and opened so far in the session, and a pair of letters in parentheses that represents the document type. Thus, *Untitled 4 (PT)* indicates that the document is a new Paint document that is the fourth document created during the session.

Remember that new documents are not automatically saved to disk. If you neglect to save one (see "Saving Documents," later in this Topic), it disappears forever after you click its close box or quit the program. If a document is important to you, be sure to save early and save often. Note that if you attempt to close a document without saving, ClarisWorks presents an alert box that offers an option to save the document.

Opening Existing Documents

As mentioned in "Starting ClarisWorks," earlier in this Topic, you can open existing ClarisWorks documents from the desktop by double-clicking them. Doing so simultaneously launches ClarisWorks and opens the selected document. After the program is running, you can open other ClarisWorks documents, as well as documents created in many other programs.

Opening ClarisWorks documents from within the program

The following instructions describe how to open ClarisWorks documents when the program is running.

To open ClarisWorks documents from within ClarisWorks:

1. **Choose the Open command from the File menu (or press ⌘-O).** You see a file dialog box like one of those in Figure 2-5 or Figure 2-6.

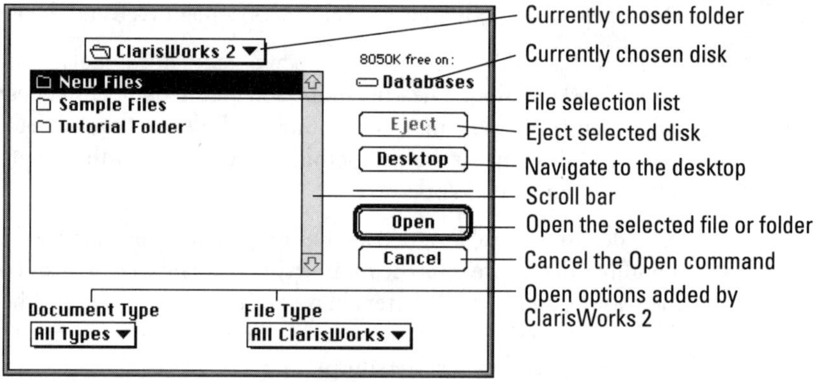

Figure 2-5: The Open dialog box for ClarisWorks 2.0/2.1.

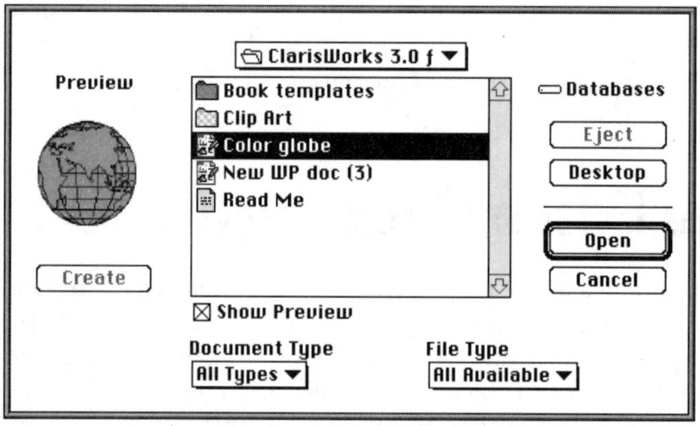

Figure 2-6: The Open dialog box for ClarisWorks 3.0.

2. **Using the mouse or arrow keys, select the particular file that you want to open and either click Open or double-click the filename.**

The ClarisWorks Open dialog box has a special pair of pop-up menus at the bottom. You use the Document Type pop-up menu on the left to restrict the documents that appear in the file list to a particular type, such as database files. If you have a large number of files in a particular folder, using the Document Type pop-up menu can make it simpler to find the file you want. If you don't feel like opening the menu, you can press Command-key equivalents to restrict the list to a single document type. Table 2-1 shows the Command-key equivalents.

Table 2-1
Document Type Command-Key Equivalents

Document Type	***Command-Key Equivalent***
All types	⌘-0
Word processing	⌘-1
Drawing	⌘-2
Painting	⌘-3
Spreadsheet	⌘-4
Database	⌘-5
Communications	⌘-6

To enter a Command-key equivalent, press the Command key (⌘) and, while holding it down, press the number, letter, or character that is to accompany the Command key.

You use the File Type pop-up menu on the right side of the Open dialog box to specify whether you want to see regular ClarisWorks documents (ClarisWorks), stationery documents (Stationery), or both stationery and document files (All ClarisWorks). See Topic 11 for additional information on stationery documents.

The ClarisWorks 3.0 Open dialog box (as shown in Figure 2-6) adds a Preview option that enables you to see a thumbnail representation of any graphic document selected in the file list. (Note that the Preview option is presented only if Apple's QuickTime system software extension is currently loaded. Otherwise, the dialog box is identical to the one used in ClarisWorks 2.0/2.1.)

By clicking the Show Preview check box, you instruct ClarisWorks to show a preview image for any graphic or movie file that has had a preview saved for it. If no preview is shown for a particular file, you can tell ClarisWorks to construct one by clicking the Create button. (Note that previews are available for some text files, too.)

Finally, if a preview is no longer correct for a file, the Create button changes to Update. Click it to create an updated preview for the file.

Opening non-ClarisWorks documents

Claris programs include a file translation system called the *XTND system.* Depending on which Claris translator files are in the Claris folder within the System Folder, the XTND system also can interpret documents that were created by many other programs, such as Microsoft Word, WriteNow, and MacPaint. This capability is particularly useful if you have recently switched from a non-Claris word processor, spreadsheet, or graphics program or if a friend has given you a document for which you don't have the creating program.

To open a non-ClarisWorks document from within ClarisWorks:

1. **Choose Open from the File menu (or press ⌘-O).**
2. **In the Open dialog box, click the Document Type pop-up menu and choose the type of file that you want to open (Word Processing, Drawing, Painting, Spreadsheet, Database, or Communications).**
3. **Navigate to the disk and folder where the document files are stored and select the file that you want to open.** If the file that you want does not appear in the file list, you do not have the translator that is needed to open the file.
4. **Click Open or double-click the filename to load the file and convert it to the ClarisWorks format.**

After you select the file, the Converting dialog box shown in Figure 2-7 appears. A progress thermometer shows how much of the conversion has been completed. You can click Cancel at any time during the conversion if you change your mind about loading the file. Otherwise, after the conversion is finished, ClarisWorks opens the document for you. The file is given a temporary name that consists of its original filename followed by - *Converted* and a pair of letters in parentheses that indicate the document type (such as *DB* for a database document).

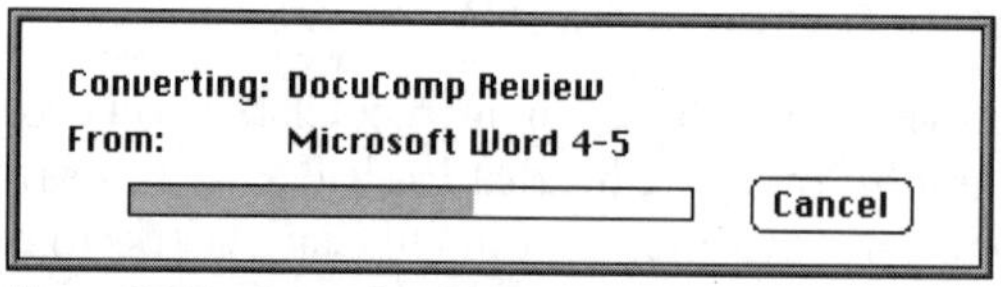

Figure 2-7: The Converting dialog box.

VERSION 2.1

ClarisWorks 2.1 includes a new *XTND* filter for Microsoft Excel 4.0.

NEW FEATURE 3.0

ClarisWorks 3.0 adds a MacWrite Pro filter.

One other type of conversion that many users are curious about is the manner in which ClarisWorks 2 and 3 handle documents created by earlier versions of ClarisWorks. You don't need to worry. When you open a Version 1 file with any later version of ClarisWorks, a dialog box appears that states: *This is a ClarisWorks 1.0 document. A copy will be opened in 2.0 (or 3.0) format and "[v2.0]"(or "[v3.0]") will be added to the filename.* Note that this message says that a *copy* will be opened. As with XTND translations of foreign files, the original document is merely read into memory — not replaced on disk. If you want to make a permanent copy of the document in the current version's format, you need to use the Save or Save As command to save a new copy of the file.

ClarisWorks 2.1 added a new *XTND* filter that enables you to both open *and save* text documents in ClarisWorks 1.0 format. (***Note:*** This works *only* with word processing documents; you cannot save documents created in any other environment in 1.0 formats.)

ClarisWorks 3 files are compatible with those of ClarisWorks 2.0 and 2.1, as well as with those of ClarisWorks 3 for Windows.

The conversion process does nothing to the original file; ClarisWorks simply reads the file and makes a converted copy of it. Note that the file ClarisWorks creates is not automatically stored on your disk. If you neglect to save the converted file, it disappears at the end of the current session.

When you save a converted file, you have two options:

- Save it with a different name from that of the original file.

  This option leaves the original file intact and creates a second file that is in the ClarisWorks format.

- Save it with the same name as that of the original file.

  This option deletes the original file and replaces it with the new ClarisWorks-formatted file. Use this option only if you have no further use for the original document.

If you're running System 7, you also can use the *drag-and-drop* procedure to make ClarisWorks simultaneously launch and open a non-ClarisWorks document. (To find out which version of system software is installed on your Mac, click an item on the desktop — such as a disk or file icon — and then choose About the Finder or About This Macintosh from the Apple menu.)

To use the drag-and-drop technique to open a foreign file:

1. **On the desktop, click once to select the icon for the non-ClarisWorks document that you want to open.**
2. **Drag the icon onto the ClarisWorks program icon.**

If ClarisWorks is able to interpret the document type that you've selected, the ClarisWorks icon turns dark, and the program launches and attempts to convert the document — just as it does when you open a foreign document from within ClarisWorks. If the document is not one of the types that ClarisWorks can read, the ClarisWorks icon doesn't become dark, and the program doesn't launch.

Inserting documents

ClarisWorks provides one additional way for you to make use of foreign documents. The Insert command on the File menu enables you to place the entire contents of a non-ClarisWorks document into whatever document you're currently working on. (***Note:*** If you need to use only *part* of a file — a paragraph of text or a single graphic, for example — it may be faster to simply open the second file and copy and paste the portion that you need.)

Step-by-Steps

To insert a document:

1. **If you're working in a word processing document or frame, position the cursor where you want to place the insert; in other types of frames and documents, click where you want to place the insert.**
2. **Choose Insert from the File menu.** A standard file dialog box appears.
3. **If you want to restrict your choices to a particular file type, choose the type from the Show pop-up menu.**
4. **Navigate to the drive and folder that contain the file.**
5. **Select the file that you want to insert by clicking it and clicking Insert or by double-clicking the name of the file.**

NOTE

Only file types that are supported for the frame or document environment will appear in the Show pop-up menu. As always, the Show list is created from the Claris XTND translator files that are installed in the System Folder.

NEW FEATURE 3.0

In addition to opening files directly as Draw documents, you can insert any of the files in the new Clip Art folder into existing documents by using the Insert command. Be sure to browse through these first-class images. You're certain to find some that you can use to dress up your memos, newsletters, spreadsheet charts, or correspondence.

TIP

You cannot use the Insert command to place a ClarisWorks 2 or 3 document within another ClarisWorks 2 or 3 document. Normally, the Insert command is reserved for *foreign* files, or files created in other programs. Because ClarisWorks 2.1 and 3.0 include an XTND filter for ClarisWorks 1.0 files, however, you *can* insert ClarisWorks 1.0 word processing files into ClarisWorks 2.1 or 3.0 word processing documents or text frames. And, as a result, you can insert a ClarisWorks 2 or 3 word processing document into another ClarisWorks 2 or 3 document if you know the following trick.

To insert a ClarisWorks word processing document into another ClarisWorks 2 document:

1. **Open the ClarisWorks 2 or 3 word processing document that you want to insert.**
2. **Choose the Save As command from the File menu.**
3. **Select the ClarisWorks 1.0 Text filter in the Save As pop-up menu, as shown in Figure 2-8.**

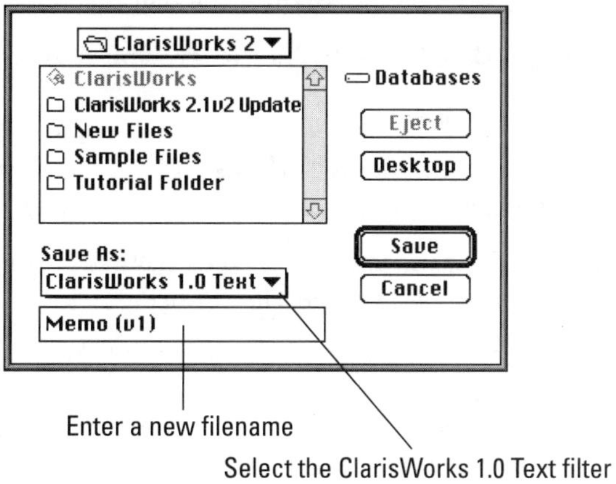

Figure 2-8: Saving a ClarisWorks 2 or 3 word processing document as a ClarisWorks 1.0 text file.

4. **Enter a new name for the converted file in the text-edit box and click the Save button.** The document is saved as a ClarisWorks 1.0 text file.
5. **Position the cursor in the ClarisWorks 2.1 or 3.0 document where you want to insert the text, select Insert from the File menu, and choose the newly converted ClarisWorks 1.0 text file.**

Saving Documents

To save a ClarisWorks document to disk, you use either the Save or the Save As command from the File menu. For new Mac owners, determining which of these commands is the correct one to use is often a major source of confusion. This section clears up the confusion once and for all.

Saving existing files

You use the Save command (⌘-S) to save existing files. If the file is already on disk, the Save command merely replaces the old copy of the file with the new copy. No dialog box appears.

Because the Save command automatically deletes the previous copy of the file, at times you may prefer to use the Save As command to save an existing file. The Save As command enables you to assign a new name to the file, as well as to specify a different location on disk in which to store it. You can use the Save As command when you want to keep multiple versions of a file instead of just replacing the old version. You also can use Save As when you want to save a document in a different format.

Step-by-Steps

To use the Save As command to save an existing file:

1. **Choose Save As from the File menu**. The standard file dialog box appears.
2. **Navigate to the disk drive and folder where you want to save the file.**
3. **Type a name for the file.**
4. **Use the Save As pop-up menu to choose a file type (if you want to save it as something other than a standard ClarisWorks file).**
5. **Click the Save button (or press Return or Enter).** If you change your mind and decide not to save the file, click Cancel.

If you are saving a file that already exists on disk and don't change the name from the one suggested, the program asks whether you want to *Replace existing "Memo"?* — or whatever the file is named (see Figure 2-9). Click Replace if you want to replace the old file on disk with the new one. Click Cancel if you don't want to replace the old file. You can then specify a new name or location (a different disk or folder), or you can cancel the Save altogether.

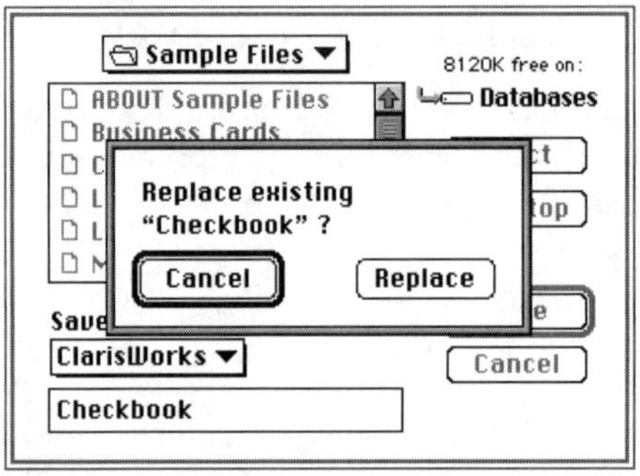

Figure 2-9: The Replace dialog box.

The Replace dialog box, shown in Figure 2-9, appears whenever you choose the Save As command and try to save a file under its original name (or under any other filename that's already in use).

Saving new files

You can save new files by using either the Save or Save As command. After you select either command from the File menu, a standard file dialog box appears and gives you the opportunity to name the new file and specify a location on disk in which to store it. To avoid overwriting any files that are already on the disk, be sure to enter a name that is different from that of your other files.

NOTE

If the file you want to save has never been saved before (that is, it's a new file) *and it's empty,* ClarisWorks *grays out* the Save command (makes it unselectable). Until at least one character has been typed into the document, the only save option presented is Save As.

NEW FEATURE 3.0

ClarisWorks 3.0 enables you to save identifying information with any file. By providing Document Summary Info (by choosing the File menu command with that name), you can do the following:

- ◆ Provide a more elaborate title for a document
- ◆ Identify the author
- ◆ Specify a version number (to distinguish multiple revisions of a file, for example)
- ◆ Assign keywords that can be used to help locate the file with the Find ClarisWorks Documents Assistant
- ◆ Specify a category and some descriptive text (to classify and explain the purpose of a stationery document when it appears in the New Document dialog box)

An example of a Document Summary is shown in Figure 2-10. Because this information is primarily for your benefit, you can enter as much or as little information as you like. If you later want to change some of the entries, just choose the Document Summary Info command again, make the changes, and then save the document again. Document Summary Info also is discussed in Topic 11.

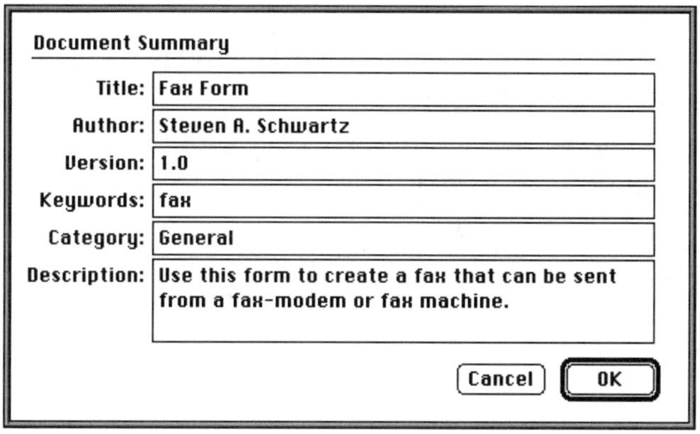

Figure 2-10: The Document Summary dialog box.

Save As options

When you use the Save As command to save a file, you can select from several file format options by clicking the Save As pop-up menu, as shown in Figure 2-11. In most cases, you leave the pop-up menu alone. The default setting is ClarisWorks, which means that the file will be saved as a standard ClarisWorks file.

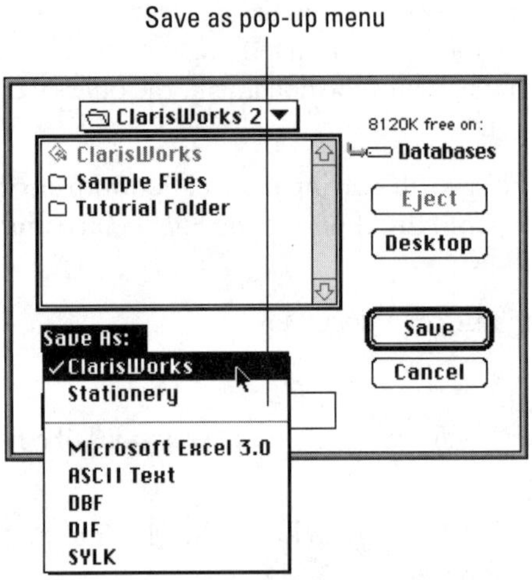

Figure 2-11: The Save As dialog box in ClarisWorks 2.0/2.1.

A second option is to save the document as a *stationery* file — a template for frequently-used documents, such as fax forms and memos. See Topic 11 for additional information on working with stationery files.

Depending on the Claris XTND translators that have been installed, you may have options for saving the document as a non-ClarisWorks document. You may want to save a spreadsheet in Microsoft Excel format, for example, if you plan to give it to a friend who uses Excel rather than ClarisWorks. You can save Draw graphic files in PICT format so they can be opened by any draw program. The file format options that are presented vary, depending on the ClarisWorks environment that you're in when you choose Save As. For example, if you're saving a spreadsheet, the Save As pop-up menu lists only spreadsheet formats.

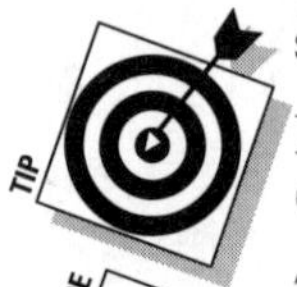

If you intend to use the file in ClarisWorks again, saving a copy of the file in ClarisWorks format is a smart idea.

The Save As dialog box is slightly different in ClarisWorks 3.0. You still use the Save As pop-up menu to select a file format: a ClarisWorks file, a foreign file (such as Microsoft Word), or a generic file type (such as PICT). But you now choose a normal or stationery file by clicking a radio button rather than by choosing an option from the Save As pop-up menu (see Figure 2-12). Note that these options work together. You must select a file format from the Save As pop-up menu *and* choose a file type by clicking the Document or Stationery radio button.

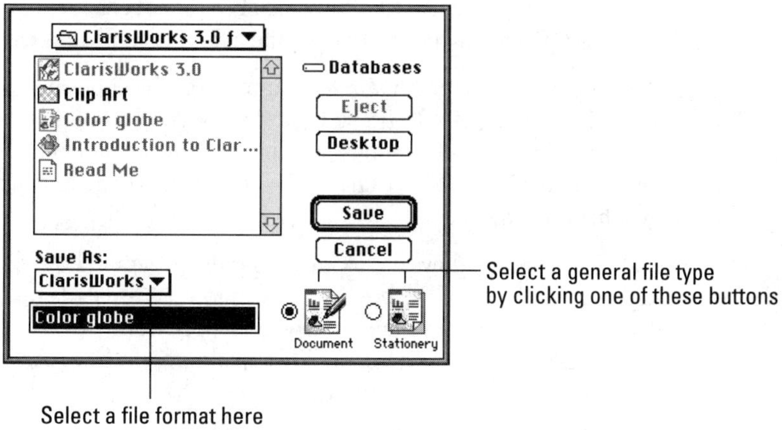

Figure 2-12: The new ClarisWorks 3.0 Save As dialog box.

If you click the Stationery radio button, ClarisWorks automatically navigates to the ClarisWorks Stationery folder. You can then open any stationery document saved in this folder by clicking the Start with an Assistant or Stationery icon in the New Document dialog box. (Choose New from the File menu or press ⌘-N.)

Closing Document Windows

Saving a document copies its contents to a file on disk. It does not close the document window. After you finish using a document, you can close its window by using one of the following methods:

- Clicking once in its close box (in the upper-left corner of the window, as shown in Figure 2-13)

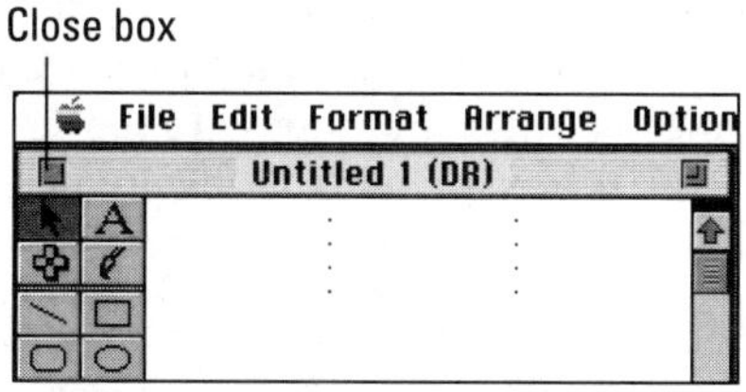

Figure 2-13: Use the document window close box to close a window.

- Choosing Close from the File menu
- Pressing ⌘-W

If the file has been saved, the window immediately closes. If changes have been made to the file, you are given a chance to save the file before ClarisWorks closes it.

You can close all of the document windows at one time by choosing Quit from the File menu (or by pressing ⌘-Q). If you have already saved all of the documents, ClarisWorks simply closes all windows and quits. If any documents have not been saved — new files or files you have changed — ClarisWorks gives you an opportunity to save them one by one.

To close all document windows without quitting the program, hold down the Option key and click in the close box for any window. As usual, if you haven't saved some documents, the program gives you an opportunity to save them or to cancel before their windows are closed. (This tip also works from the desktop and is a fast way to eliminate window clutter.)

Selecting and Using Tools

Along the left side of most document windows is the Tool panel. (If the tools aren't visible, choose Show Tools from the View menu. Other ways to show and hide the Tool panel are discussed later in this Topic in "Hiding and showing tools.") The tools enable you to create new frames (such as adding paint graphics or a spreadsheet to a word processing document); select drawing and painting tools; and set fill and pen colors, patterns, gradients, and line styles.

You can divide the objects in the Tool panel into the following categories, according to their functions: environment tools, drawing tools, painting tools, fill palettes, and pen palettes. The Tool panel has two different states (as shown in Figure 2-14), which you can call *basic* and *expanded.* The *expanded Tool panel* adds painting tools to the basic panel, and it appears only when you are working on a paint document or have selected the Paintbrush tool to create a paint frame in a document of another type.

To create a new frame in the current document, click an environment tool: Click *A* for a word processing frame, the plus symbol for a spreadsheet frame, or the paintbrush for a paint frame. To add a draw object to the document, click any of the draw icons. To work with colors, patterns, gradients, or line styles, click any of these tool icons at the bottom of the panel and select the option you prefer.

The color, pattern, gradient, and line style tools are *tear-off* palettes. If you use any of them frequently, you can keep them open and on-screen.

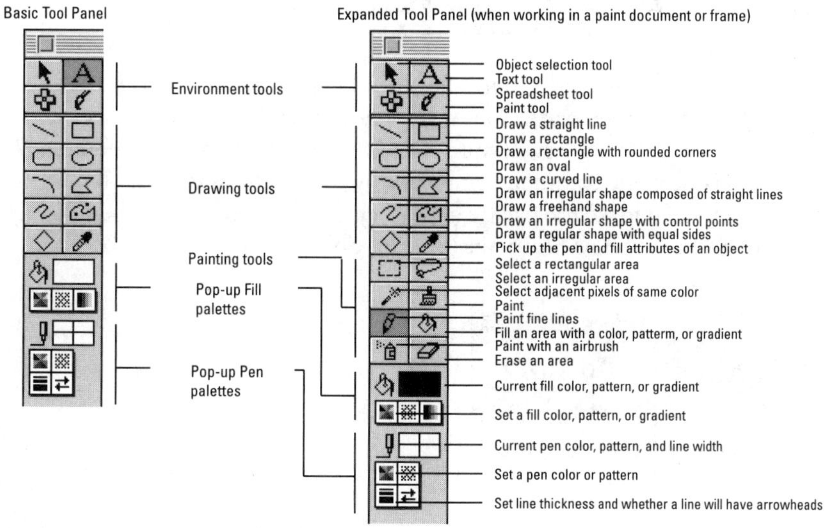

Figure 2-14: The basic and expanded Tool panels.

To tear off a palette:

1. **Click on the palette icon of interest.** The panel drops down.
2. **While holding down the mouse button, drag the palette away from the Tool panel.**
3. **Release the mouse button.**

After you release the mouse button, the palette is in its own tiny window, where it's easily accessible (see Figure 2-15). To close a floating palette of this type, click its close box (in the upper-left corner). To temporarily shrink the palette, click the box in the palette's upper-right corner. To move the palette, click in its title bar and drag it to the desired position.

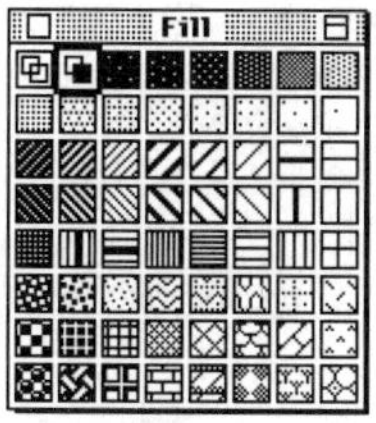

Figure 2-15: A tear-off palette.

Using the Shortcuts Palette

To save you the effort of needlessly pulling down menus to choose commands or of having to memorize Command-key equivalents, ClarisWorks 2 and later versions provide a new feature called the Shortcuts palette (see Figure 2-16). You can issue many common commands by simply clicking a button on the Shortcuts palette. To make the palette appear, choose Shortcuts from the File menu and then choose Show Shortcuts (or press Shift-⌘-X).

Figure 2-16: The Shortcuts palette.

The contents of the palette change to match the environment or frame in which you are working. After you draw a spreadsheet frame, for example, the buttons change to become relevant to spreadsheet operations.

Like the graphic palettes, the Shortcuts palette floats above the current document. You can move, reduce, or close the palette by following the procedures that are discussed in the preceding section, "Selecting and Using Tools." You can even customize the Shortcuts palette by adding and removing buttons or assigning *macros* (user-created ClarisWorks scripts) to buttons. Topic 13 discusses customizing the Shortcuts palette.

Creating and Using Frames

To integrate information from the various ClarisWorks environments, you use *frames.* A frame is a rectangular area within a document that is — in most cases — a different environment than that of the underlying document. For example, Figure 2-17 shows a spreadsheet frame within a word processing document. The three types of frames correspond to the three environment tools in the Tool panel: text, paint, and spreadsheet.

NOTE

ClarisWorks does not have a separate frame type for draw objects. You can add a draw object to most documents by selecting a draw tool from the Tool panel and then drawing.

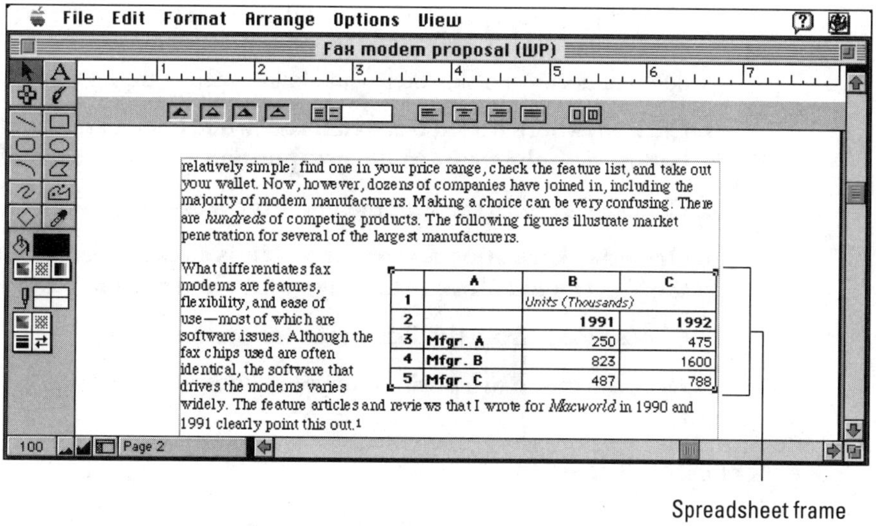

Figure 2-17: A spreadsheet frame in a word processing document.

To create a frame:

1. **Select one of the three environment tools (text, spreadsheet, or paint) from the Tool panel.**
2. **Click the mouse button over the spot where you want to position one of the frame's corners.**
3. **Drag until the frame is the size and shape that you desire.**
4. **Release the mouse button.**

NOTE

You can place additional word processing frames into a word processing document or spreadsheet frames into a spreadsheet document by pressing Option as you draw the frame.

After you create a frame, you can immediately begin working in it: entering data in spreadsheet frames, typing in text frames, and creating graphics in paint frames.

You may discover, however, that a particular frame is incorrectly positioned, is the wrong size, or is no longer needed. The following instructions describe how to remedy these situations.

To move a frame:

1. **Select the pointer from the Tool panel.**
2. **Click the frame to select it.** A set of black dots (called *handles*) appears around the frame to show that it is selected.

If you want to move the frame to a different position in the current document, follow Step 3 and you're done. If you want to move the frame to a different document, skip Step 3 and follow Steps 4 through 7.

3. **Click anywhere within the frame and, while holding down the mouse button, drag the frame to the new position.**
4. **Choose Cut from the Edit menu (or press ⌘-X).**
5. **Open the destination document or, if it is already open, choose it from the View menu. Move to the page where you want to paste the frame.**
6. **Choose Paste from the Edit menu (or press ⌘-V).**
7. **Drag the frame to a position of your choosing.**

Step-by-Steps

To resize a frame:

1. **Select the pointer from the Tool panel.**
2. **Click the frame to select it.** A set of black dots (called *handles*) appears around the frame to show that it is selected.
3. **Using the pointer tool, select one of the frame handles, and then drag it to change the size of the frame.**

Step-by-Steps

To delete a frame:

1. **Select the pointer from the Tool panel.**
2. **Click on the frame to select it.** A set of black dots (called *handles*) appears around the frame to show that it is selected.
3. **Press the Delete or Backspace key.**

See Topic 15 for additional information about frames.

Changing the Display

In ClarisWorks, you can control what you see on-screen in several ways:

- ◆ Show or hide the Tool panel to see more of a partially hidden or wide document.
- ◆ Switch magnification levels to focus in on important areas or get a bird's-eye view of the document.
- ◆ Stack or tile windows to make working with several documents at the same time more convenient.

- ◆ Zoom document windows to switch between two window sizes with a single mouse click.
- ◆ Split the screen to see two or four parts of a document at the same time.
- ◆ Create new views of a document to work with two or more copies of the same document.

Hiding and showing tools

Although you usually want to keep the Tool panel handy, sometimes you may want to make it disappear. If you have a small screen or are working on a very wide document, for example, hiding the Tool panel enables you to see more of the document. You can hide or show the tools in one of two ways:

- ◆ Choose Show Tools or Hide Tools from the View menu. (The wording for this command changes, depending on whether the Tool panel is presently visible or hidden.) You also can issue this command by pressing ⌘-Shift-T.
- ◆ Click the Show/Hide Tools control at the bottom of the document (see Figure 2-18).

Figure 2-18: Use the Show/Hide Tools control to view or hide the Tool panel.

Each time you issue the Show/Hide Tools command or click the control, the state of the Tool panel switches. If the Tool panel is currently hidden, it appears. If the panel is visible, it is removed.

Setting the magnification level

Occasionally, you may want to change a document's magnification level. Although this feature is extremely helpful in the paint environment (because it enables you to zoom in to touch up tiny areas), it is also available in the other environments. You can zoom out to get a thumbnail view of the layout for a word processing document without being distracted by the text, for example. You change the magnification with the Zoom Percentage box, the Zoom-Out control, or the Zoom-In control, which are located in the bottom left corner of every document window (see Figure 2-19).

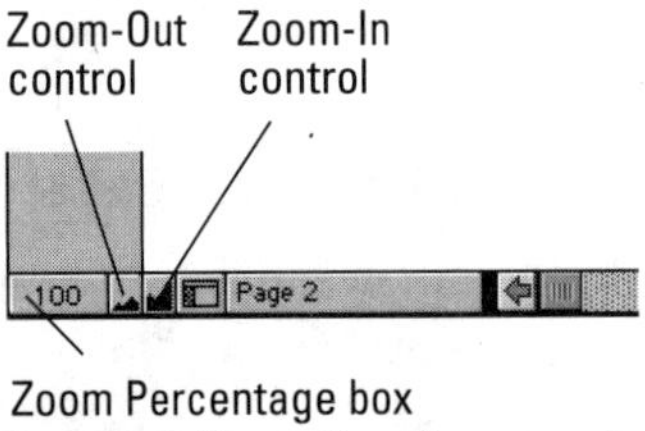

Figure 2-19: Use the Zoom Percentage box, the Zoom-Out control, and the Zoom-In control to change a document's magnification.

You can change the magnification in two ways:

- Click the Zoom Percentage box and drag to select a new percentage. (If you select Other, a dialog box appears, where you can type a specific percentage, including percentages that are not listed in the menu.)
- Click the Zoom-Out or Zoom-In control. Each click reduces or increases the magnification by one step.

Resizing windows

Resizable windows, such as ClarisWorks document windows, contain two special boxes: the size box and the zoom box, which are shown in Figure 2-20. To change the size of a window, click in the size box and drag until the window is the desired size. Each time you click a window's zoom box, it switches between a full-screen window and the size and position that you last set for the window. Zooming isn't just a ClarisWorks feature. It works with any Macintosh window that contains a zoom box.

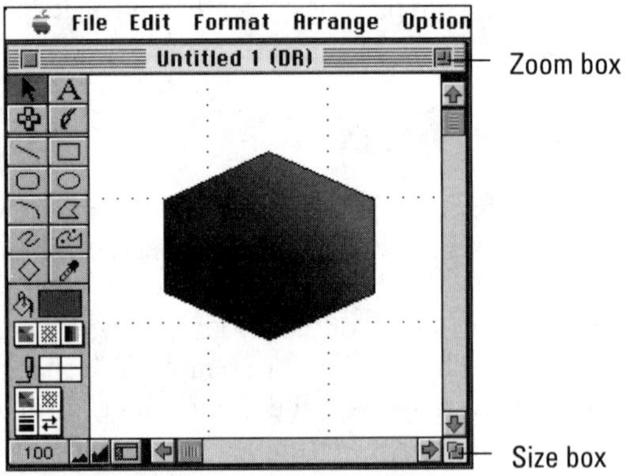

Figure 2-20: Use the zoom and size boxes to change the size of a window.

Arranging windows

ClarisWorks enables you to open and work with as many documents at one time as the computer's memory permits. Two commands in the View menu — Tile Windows and Stack Windows — make juggling several open files easy.

The Tile Windows command arranges document windows in a vertical stack, one above the other. Documents are full width, but their height is reduced, as shown in Figure 2-21. You can make any document active by simply clicking it.

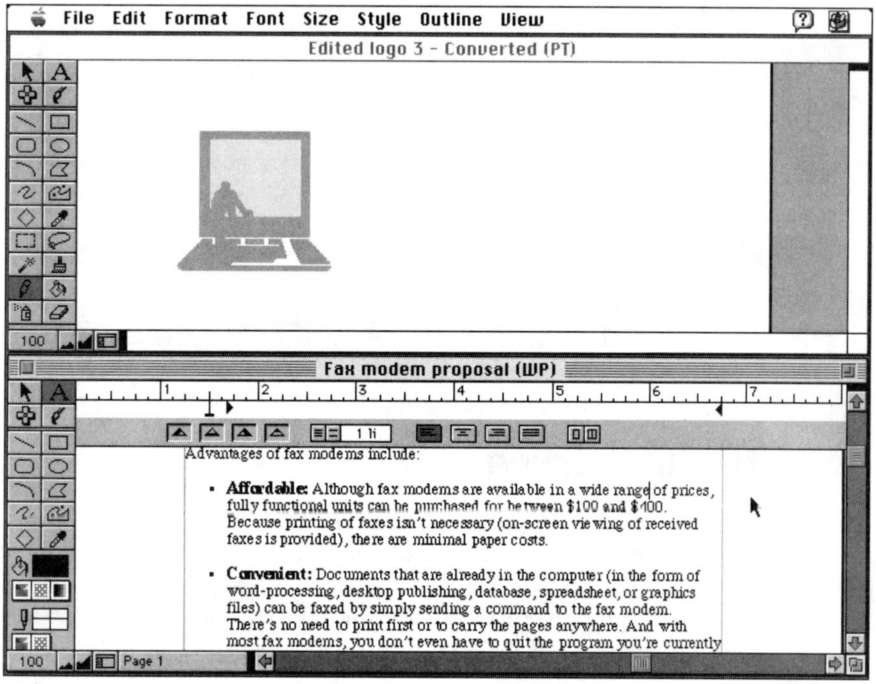

Figure 2-21: Tiled windows.

TIP

If you don't need to refer constantly to any of the other open documents, you can expand the current document so that it takes over the entire screen by clicking its zoom box (in the right corner of the document's title bar). When you're ready to switch to a different document window, click the current window's zoom box again to make it shrink to its original, tiled position.

The Stack Windows command arranges documents so that they cascade from the upper-left corner of the screen to the bottom right, as shown in Figure 2-22. Because a tiny portion of each document always shows, you can easily switch between documents by clicking the edge of the one you want to bring to the front.

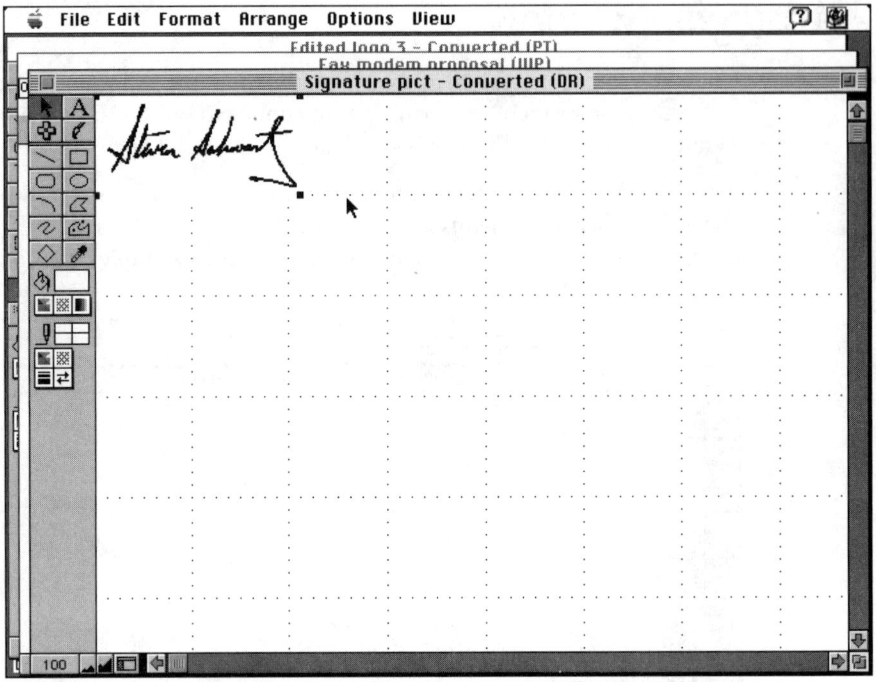

Figure 2-22: Stacked windows.

Splitting the screen

ClarisWorks enables you to split any document horizontally and/or vertically into two or four panes (see Figure 2-23). In each pane, you can examine or edit a different part of the document. Each pane scrolls independently of the other pane(s) so that working on one part of the document while viewing another part of it is easy to do. Changes that you make in any pane are simultaneously recorded in all panes.

Step-by-Steps

To split the screen:

1. **Click the vertical or horizontal pane control and drag it to the spot where you want to divide the document.**
2. **Release the mouse button.** A pair of dividing lines marks the edge of each pane.

To remove a split pane, click on the dividing line and drag it to the edge of the document window.

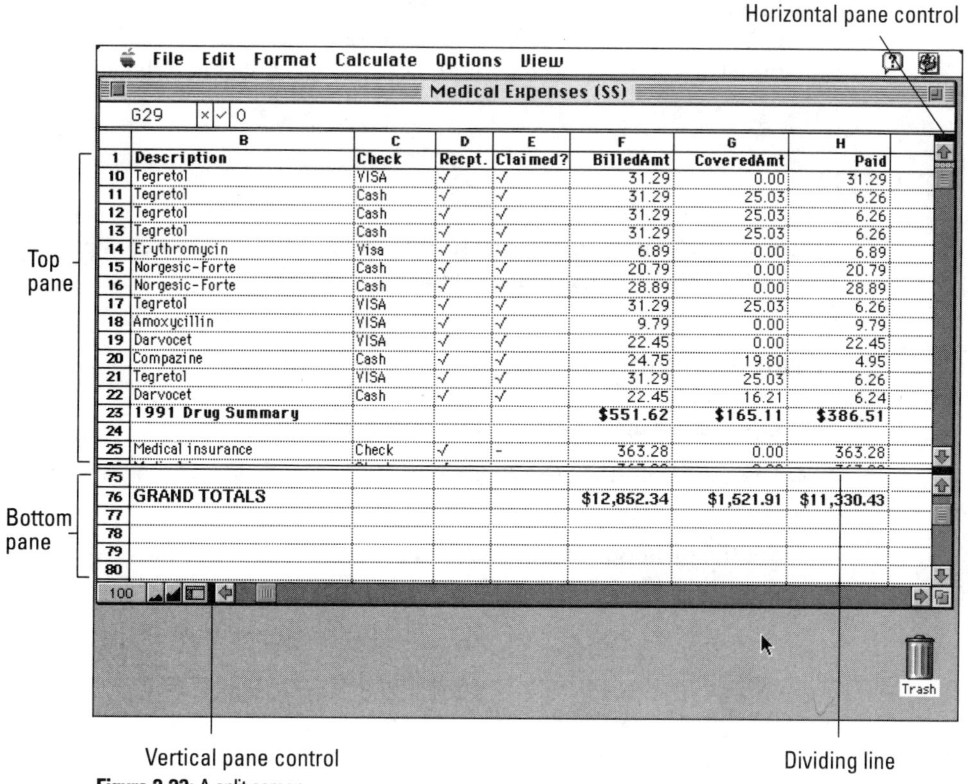

Horizontal pane control
File Edit Format Calculate Options View
Medical Expenses (SS)
G29 0
B C D E F G H
1 Description Check Recpt. Claimed? BilledAmt CoveredAmt Paid
10 Tegretol VISA √ √ 31.29 0.00 31.29
11 Tegretol Cash √ √ 31.29 25.03 6.26
12 Tegretol Cash √ √ 31.29 25.03 6.26
13 Tegretol Cash √ √ 31.29 25.03 6.26
14 Erythromycin Visa √ √ 6.89 0.00 6.89
15 Norgesic-Forte Cash √ √ 20.79 0.00 20.79
16 Norgesic-Forte Cash √ √ 28.89 0.00 28.89
17 Tegretol VISA √ √ 31.29 25.03 6.26
18 Amoxycillin VISA √ √ 9.79 0.00 9.79
19 Darvocet VISA √ √ 22.45 0.00 22.45
20 Compazine Cash √ √ 24.75 19.80 4.95
21 Tegretol VISA √ √ 31.29 25.03 6.26
22 Darvocet Cash √ √ 22.45 16.21 6.24
23 1991 Drug Summary $551.62 $165.11 $386.51
24
25 Medical insurance Check √ - 363.28 0.00 363.28
75
76 GRAND TOTALS $12,852.34 $1,521.91 $11,330.43
77
78
79
80
100
Trash
Top pane
Bottom pane
Vertical pane control
Dividing line

Figure 2-23: A split screen.

Creating a new view of a document

If you want to open two copies of the same document, choose New View from the View menu. Any changes that you make in one copy are instantly reflected in the other copy. To distinguish the copies, ClarisWorks appends a number at the end of each name in the title bar. If the original document is called Memo (WP), you end up with two documents on-screen: Memo:1 (WP) and Memo:2 (WP).

What's the point of having multiple copies of the same document on-screen? Creating multiple views of a document has the following advantages:

- ◆ It enables you to see a zoomed out view (the entire document) and a 100% view (the normal view) at the same time. Editing changes are reflected in both views so that you can see their effects.
- ◆ If you have a spreadsheet frame in a word processing or database document, the only way to increase the number of rows and columns in the frame is by creating a new view of the frame (by using the Open Frame command).

◆ In the database environment, you can use two views to look at the document in both browse and layout modes at the same time. As you make changes to the layout, you can instantly see how it will affect the formatting of the data.

Printing

The final step for most documents is creating a *printout* — a printed copy of the spreadsheet, memo, graphic image, or database report.

To print a document:

1. **Open or create a ClarisWorks document.**
2. **Choose Print from the File menu.** The Print dialog box appears on-screen.
3. **Set the print options as you like.**
4. **Click Print to send the print job to the printer.**

The Print dialog box that you see depends on the printer that you select in the Chooser and the version of system software that is installed on the Mac. Figure 2-24 shows three print dialog boxes.

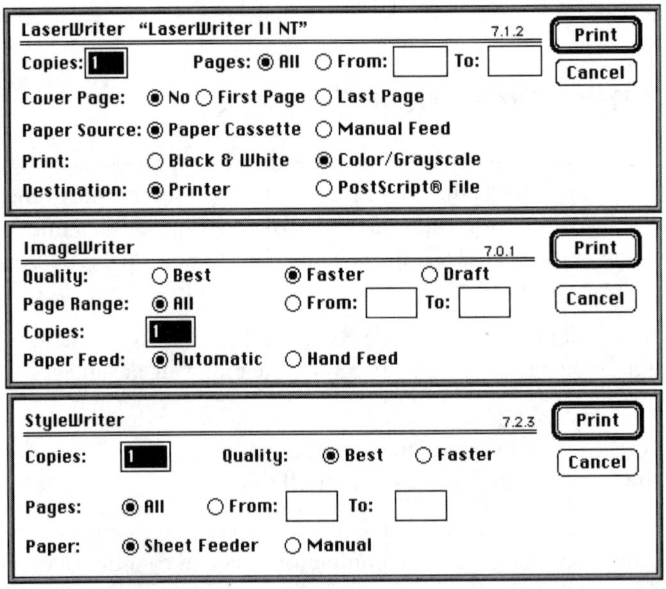

Figure 2-24: Print dialog boxes for LaserWriter, ImageWriter, and StyleWriter printers.

NOTE: Be sure that you have selected a printer in the Chooser desk accessory, particularly if you have more than one printing device. The printer that is currently selected receives the print job. Whenever you change the printer selection in the Chooser, you also should use the Page Setup command to make sure that the options are correct for the newly selected printer.

To select a printer, open the Chooser desk accessory (see Figure 2-25), click the appropriate Chooser icon in the left side of the window, and select the printer and other options in the right side of the window.

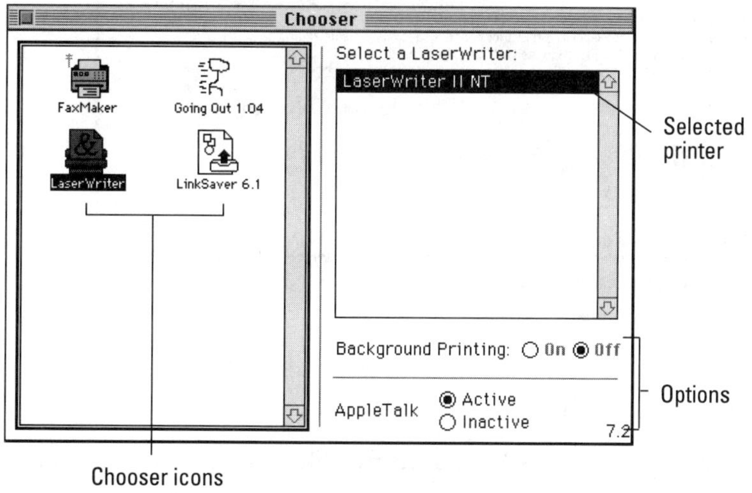

Figure 2-25: Use the Chooser desk accessory to select the printer and set other options.

For information about Print and Page Setup options, refer to Topic 1.

Using the ClarisWorks Help Features

Depending on which version of ClarisWorks you have (2.0/2.1 versus 3.0), the manner in which the ClarisWorks Help System operates, its contents, and how you invoke it differ considerably.

Using the ClarisWorks Help System (ClarisWorks 2.0/2.1)

Instead of having to reach for a manual, you often can find the information that's necessary to accomplish a task by referring to the ClarisWorks Help System. The Help System is organized as a deck of cards, much like a HyperCard stack. The system is *context sensitive;* that is, when you invoke ClarisWorks Help, it normally opens to a card that is relevant to what you are currently doing. For example, if you select some text in a word processing document and then invoke Help, you see the Help screen that is shown in Figure 2-26.

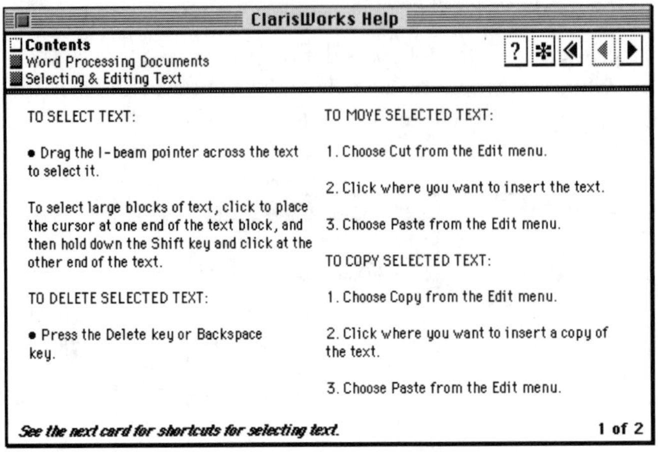

Figure 2-26: A ClarisWorks 2 help screen.

You can use several methods to invoke the help system:

- ◆ Choosing Help from the Apple menu
- ◆ Choosing ClarisWorks Help from the Balloon Help menu (System 7 only)
- ◆ Pressing ⌘-?
- ◆ Pressing the Help key (if you have an Apple Extended keyboard)

Click in the following locations to navigate among the help cards:

- ◆ The icons in the upper-right corner of the window
- ◆ Any of the unshaded boxes in the upper-left corner of the window
- ◆ The hand icon that appears at the bottom of some cards
- ◆ Subject matter text that appears on the Contents and Index cards

For a complete explanation of Help navigation, click the icon with the question mark on it (?) on any Help card. The first card of the Using Help topic appears. Read it and the eight cards that follow by clicking the right triangle icon.

When you're ready to continue working with the document, you can leave the Help window open so that you can refer to the Help information as you're accomplishing the task. When you're done with Help, click the close box in the upper-left corner of its window.

TIP

The reason that the ClarisWorks Help System for Version 2.0/2.1 looks so much like a HyperCard stack is that it *is* a HyperCard stack! As a result, in addition to being able to access Help information from within ClarisWorks, you also can read the Help text from within HyperCard (assuming that you have the program); and you can use HyperCard techniques to search the stack for key terms.

To search for key terms, launch HyperCard and use the Open command to load the ClarisWorks help file (it is named ClarisWorks 2.0 Help and is in the Claris folder within the System Folder). After the stack has loaded, press ⌘-M to display the HyperCard message box, press ⌘-F to request a Find, and then — between the pair of quotation marks — type the name of the ClarisWorks term for which you want to search. When you press Return to execute the search, HyperCard displays the first located instance of the term (special thanks for this tip to Nicholas dePaul of Claris Technical Support).

For System 7 users, a second form of help, known as *Balloon Help*, is available. Whenever the pointer passes over an object on-screen that has a Balloon Help message attached to it, a cartoon-style thought balloon pops up, providing some general information about the object. Resizing controls, icons in the Tool panel, and parts of the document window are some of the items within ClarisWorks that have Help balloons. ClarisWorks 2.1 also includes Balloon Help for buttons in the Shortcuts palette. Figure 2-27 shows an example of a Help balloon.

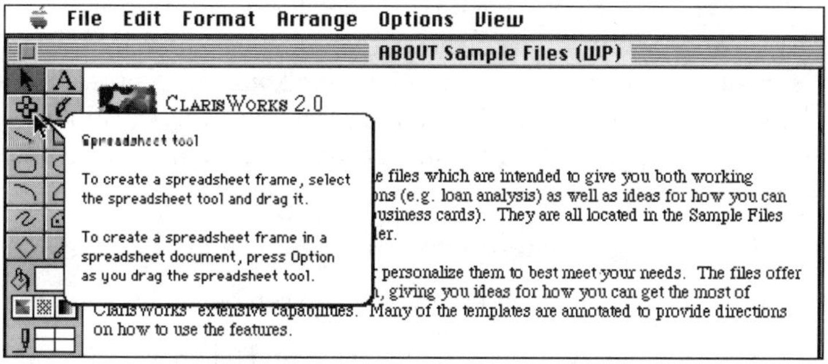

Figure 2-27: A Balloon Help example.

Step-by-Steps

To turn on Balloon Help:

1. **Click the balloon icon in the upper-right corner of the screen.** The Balloon Help menu appears, as shown in Figure 2-28.

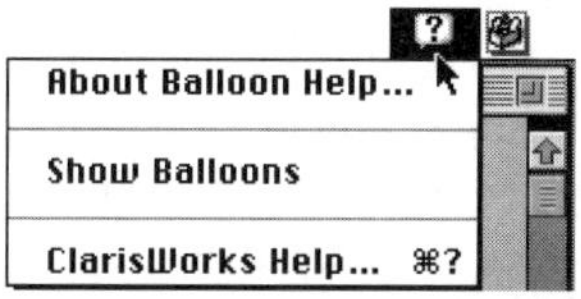

Figure 2-28: The Balloon Help menu.

If you don't see the icon, you are running a version of the system software that is earlier than System 7, and Balloon Help is not available to you.

2. **While holding down the mouse button, choose Show Balloons.**

3. **Release the mouse button.**

Now, whenever you point to a Balloon Help object, a balloon will appear. Because most people find the balloons distracting when they are attempting to work, you'll probably want to turn Balloon Help off after you find out what you need to know.

To turn off Balloon Help:

1. **Click the balloon icon in the upper-right corner of the screen.** The Balloon Help menu appears.

2. **While holding down the mouse button, choose Hide Balloons.**

3. **Release the mouse button.**

Using the ClarisWorks Help System (ClarisWorks 3.0)

The ClarisWorks Help System was completely revised for ClarisWorks 3.0. In earlier versions of ClarisWorks, most program information is in the manual. Help serves mainly as a reminder of how things work, instead of providing detailed explanations. In ClarisWorks 3.0, on the other hand, this situation has been reversed. The manual has been trimmed considerably, and much of the program information is now available *only* in the Help System.

You can invoke Help in several ways:

- Choose a Help command from the Help submenu of the Apple menu
- Choose a Help command from the Balloon Help menu (System 7 only)
- Press ⌘-?
- Press the Help key (if you have an Apple Extended keyboard)

As in ClarisWorks 2.0/2.1, Balloon Help also is available (for System 7 users only). By turning on Balloon Help with the Show Balloons command (as described previously), you can get helpful information about icons in the Tool panel and in the ruler.

In addition to the general Balloon Help commands that are always available (Show Balloons/Hide Balloons), the Balloon Help menu also displays the same set of ClarisWorks help commands as in the Help submenu of the Apple menu. There's no advantage to invoking help from one menu or the other; use whichever one happens to be most convenient for you. Remember that you must be running System 7 for Balloon Help to be available.

Help is no longer context-sensitive in ClarisWorks 3.0. However, the type of help information, as well as the particular Help screen shown, can be controlled by making an appropriate selection from the Help submenu of the Apple menu or from the Balloon Help menu (see Figure 2-29).

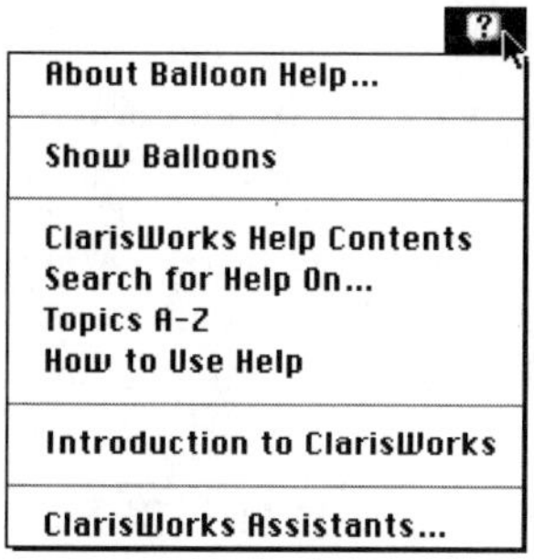

Figure 2-29: These commands are available in both the Balloon Help menu and in the Help submenu of the Apple menu.

- To reach the opening screen of the ClarisWorks Help System (see Figure 2-30), choose ClarisWorks Help Contents from the Balloon Help menu or Help submenu of the Apple menu, press ⌘-?, or press the Help key (Apple Extended keyboards only).

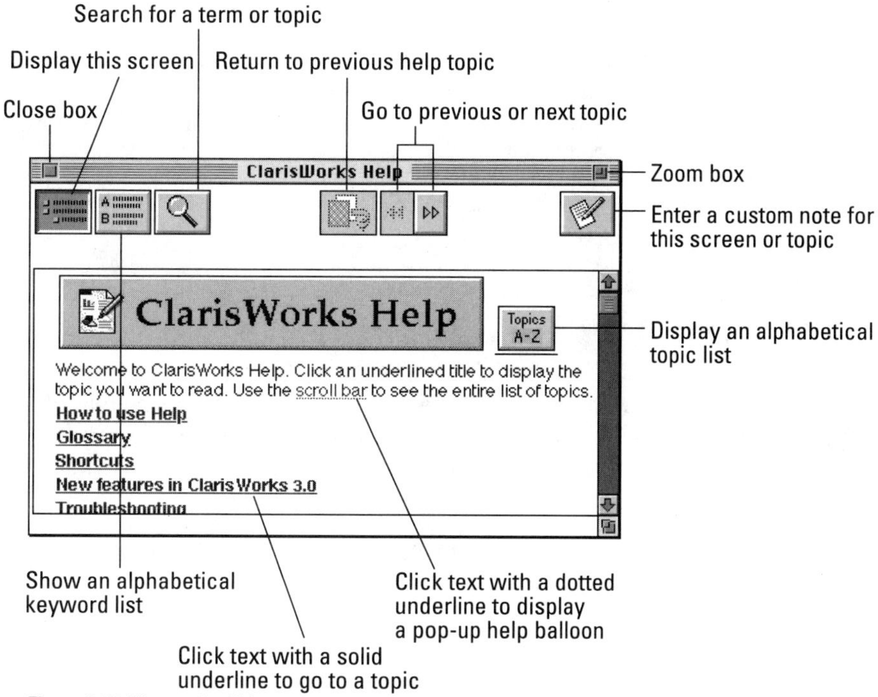

Figure 2-30: The opening Help screen.

- To display an alphabetical list of help topics, choose Topics A–Z from the Balloon Help menu or Help submenu of the Apple menu or — after you have invoked Help — click the Topics A–Z button (see Figure 2-30).
- For an alphabetical list of keywords, invoke Help and then click the button indicated in Figure 2-30.
- To search for help on a particular topic or a keyword, choose Search for Help On from the Balloon Help menu or Help submenu of the Apple menu or click the icon indicated in Figure 30.
- To view a guided tour of ClarisWorks 3.0, choose Introduction to ClarisWorks from the Balloon Help menu or Help submenu of the Apple menu or click the top icon on the Welcome screen (immediately after ClarisWorks has been launched).
- For general information on using the ClarisWorks Help System, select How to Use Help from the Balloon Help menu or Help submenu of the Apple menu or choose this topic from the opening Help screen.

TIP

Often, the fastest way to find help on a particular subject is to display the alphabetical list of keywords (as described previously). In the alphabetical *topic* list, the keyword is frequently embedded somewhere within the topic name (such as *Set preferences*). The *keyword* list, on the other hand, arranges entries alphabetically according to the most important term (such as *Preferences* and *Preferences command*). You can further speed up the process by typing the first letter of the keyword for which you're searching. The keyword list automatically scrolls to the first keyword that begins with the letter you press.

Finally, you should note that Help can remain on-screen while you continue to work on ClarisWorks documents. When you are through with Help, you can dismiss it by clicking its close box (found in the upper-left corner of the ClarisWorks Help window).

For information on ClarisWorks Assistants (the final Help/Balloon Help menu command), refer to Topic 11.

Viewing the On-Screen Tour

NEW FEATURE 3.0

A new feature in ClarisWorks 3.0 is an on-screen guided tour of the program. New ClarisWorks users can run the tour to get a quick overview of ClarisWorks 3.0's features and capabilities. More experienced users may want to refer to the tour the first time they explore an environment.

You can start the tour from within ClarisWorks 3.0 or run it from the desktop by using one of the following methods:

- *From the desktop.* Double-click the Introduction to ClarisWorks icon in your ClarisWorks 3.0 folder.
- *When launching ClarisWorks.* Click the Show me an on-screen tour of ClarisWorks button in the Welcome dialog box.
- *When ClarisWorks is already running.* Choose Introduction to ClarisWorks from the Help or Balloon Help menu.

To move from screen to screen within the tour, click the arrow buttons or choose a new topic from the Menu screen. When you want to leave the tour, click the Exit button.

NOTE

If you launch the tour from the desktop, you are returned to the desktop after you finish the tour. If you start the tour from within ClarisWorks by choosing the command from the Help menu, after you are done with the tour, you are returned to whatever you were last doing in ClarisWorks. Finally, if you launch the tour from the Welcome screen, you also return to ClarisWorks, but no documents are open. To continue the ClarisWorks session, choose New or Open from the File menu.

Quitting the Program

After you finish using ClarisWorks, choose Quit from the File menu (or press ⌘-Q). If you have open documents that haven't been saved, ClarisWorks gives you an opportunity to save each file before quitting (see Figure 2-31). If a file has never been saved (that is, it's a new file that you created in the current session) and you click Yes to save the file, ClarisWorks presents the standard Save file dialog box (as described previously in this Topic in "Saving Documents"). If, on the other hand, the file has been saved before, clicking the Yes button simply saves the new version of the file over the older one.

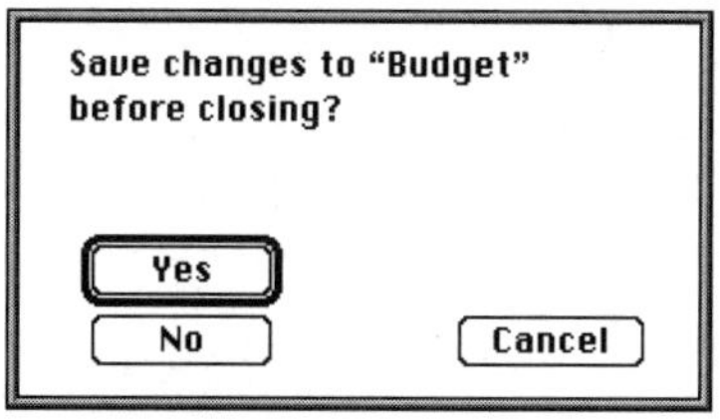

Figure 2-31: Last chance to save!

The Yes, No, Cancel dialog box repeats for every unsaved document. If you change your mind about quitting, click the Cancel button. The ClarisWorks session immediately picks up where you left off.

CAUTION!

Clicking No tells ClarisWorks to close the document without saving it. After you close a document in this manner, all your changes are lost. Be sure that you don't click No by mistake.

Quick Tips

The following tips help ensure that you have enough memory for your ClarisWorks sessions, tell you how to skip the New Document dialog box when you launch ClarisWorks, explain how to shrink and expand windows, describe a special procedure for printing from the desktop, tell you what to do when you don't have a translator for a file that you want to open or insert, and help you find misplaced ClarisWorks documents quickly.

Changing the memory allocation for ClarisWorks

While running ClarisWorks, you may occasionally receive a message that there is insufficient memory to open a document or that a paint document will be opened in a reduced size. You can increase the memory available to ClarisWorks and your documents by using the following steps.

Step-by-Steps

To change the memory allocation:

1. **Quit ClarisWorks by choosing Quit from the File menu (or pressing ⌘-Q).** If any open documents are new or have been changed, you are given an opportunity to save them.

   Quitting returns you to the desktop.

2. **Select the ClarisWorks icon by clicking it and then choose Get Info from the File menu (or press ⌘-I).** You see an Info window similar to the one shown in Figure 2-32. (Refer to the ClarisWorks Installation Guide if you are using an earlier version of the system software.)

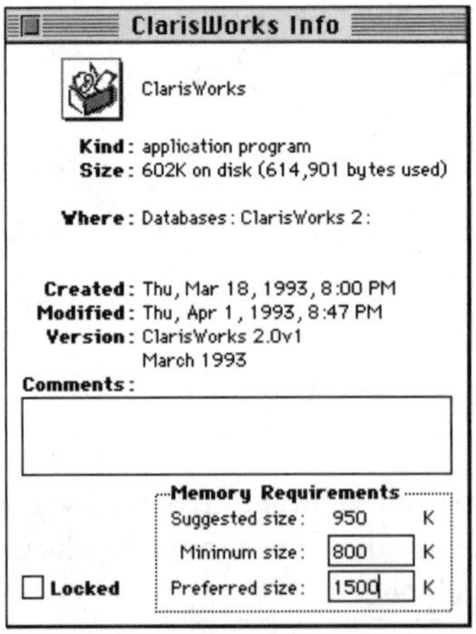

Figure 2-32: A ClarisWorks Info window in System 7.1.

3. **Type a larger number into the Preferred size box. Increase the Suggested size by 25 to 50 percent to start.** (Later, as you determine the amount of memory that you require for a typical ClarisWorks session, you can fine-tune the memory allocation.)

4. **Click the close box in the upper-left corner of the Info window to save the changes.** The next time you run ClarisWorks, the additional memory will be available for your documents.

You use the Info window to set the total memory available for loading a program and document files. The window looks slightly different if you are running System 6 rather than System 7. (Figure 2-32 shows the System 7 window.)

Skipping the New Document dialog box at start-up

If you want to skip the New Document dialog box that normally accompanies the program start-up, hold down the Command key as you launch ClarisWorks 2.0 or 2.1. After the program loads, it immediately presents the Open dialog box, rather than the New Document dialog box. (This procedure does *not* work in ClarisWorks 3.0.)

An alternative to tiled and stacked windows

If tiled or stacked windows don't appeal to you, you can take more control over your document window arrangement by shrinking and expanding them.

Step-by-Steps

To shrink and expand document windows:

1. **Using the size box, shrink each document window to the smallest possible size.**

2. **Manually arrange the document windows so that the title bar of each one is exposed.**

3. **To make one of the documents active (so you can work with it), click once in its window.** (When several windows are on-screen, the active window is the one with a series of horizontal lines in its title bar. The title bars for the other windows are blank.)

4. **Click the zoom box to expand the document to its full size.**

When you're ready to switch to a different document, click the active document's zoom box again; it shrinks back to its reduced size and position. Then repeat Steps 3 and 4 for the next document that you want to use.

Printing ClarisWorks files from the desktop

If you aren't currently in ClarisWorks and just want to print an existing document without making changes to it, you can do so by using a special procedure.

To print from the desktop:

1. **Go to the desktop and select the file or files that you want to print.**
2. **Choose Print from the File menu.** (If you are running System 7, you also can press ⌘-P to execute the Print command.)

   Instead of starting ClarisWorks in the usual way, choosing Print from the desktop loads the selected document(s) into ClarisWorks and then immediately presents the Print dialog box.
3. **Select print options and then click Print.**

   After the document has been printed, ClarisWorks automatically quits and you are returned to the desktop.

You can use this Print procedure with most other programs. The only drawback is that if you change your mind about printing the document or decide that you need to make some changes before printing it, you need to restart the program and reload the documents.

File conversion tips

Although ClarisWorks can understand dozens of foreign file formats, plenty of formats exist that ClarisWorks can't read. What do you do if ClarisWorks doesn't have a translator for the foreign file that you want to use with the Open or Insert commands? The solution is to use the originating program to save or export the file into a format that ClarisWorks does support.

Suppose, for example, that you have a spreadsheet that was created in Microsoft Excel 4.0. Although Version 4.0 isn't supported by ClarisWorks 2.0, ClarisWorks does have a translator for Excel 3.0. All that you have to do is load the file into Excel 4.0 and then use the Options command from the Save As menu to save a new copy of the file in the Excel 3.0 format. Alternatively, if you don't have Excel 4.0, see whether you have another spreadsheet program that understands Excel 4.0 files. Then load the file into that particular program and save or export it to a format that ClarisWorks supports, such as SYLK, Text, or DIF.

VERSION 2.1

Note: ClarisWorks 2.1 and 3.0 *do* have a translator for Excel 4.0.

In general, when you create a file for export, you should shoot for one of the more specific translators that ClarisWorks supports — that of a particular program, such as Excel, Word, MacWrite, or another popular program of the correct type. When ClarisWorks translates such files, it attempts to retain the proper formatting, margins, styles, formulas, and so on. The next best solution is translating the file to a general format, such as ASCII text or SYLK (spreadsheet). Although much of the original formatting will disappear, at least you can work with the basic text of the document and save some retyping time.

TIP

In the case of a word processing document, if you can't find a popular word processing format that's supported, see whether the program can create an *RTF* file (a Microsoft document format that has wide support in the computer industry). Unlike straight ASCII text, you'll find that much of the original formatting is retained.

Locating misplaced ClarisWorks documents

NEW FEATURE 3.0

You're probably already familiar with the Find File desk accessory (System 6) or the Find menu command (System 7) that are built into Apple's system software. Simply put, this utility and command enable you to search for files on the hard disk. All you have to know is part of the filename. To make it easy to locate files *without leaving ClarisWorks 3.0*, an Assistant called Find ClarisWorks Documents is provided.

Step-by-Steps

To use the Find ClarisWorks Documents Assistant:

1. **Choose ClarisWorks Assistants from the Help submenu of the Apple menu or from the Balloon Help menu (System 7 only).** The Select Assistant dialog box appears (see Figure 2-33).

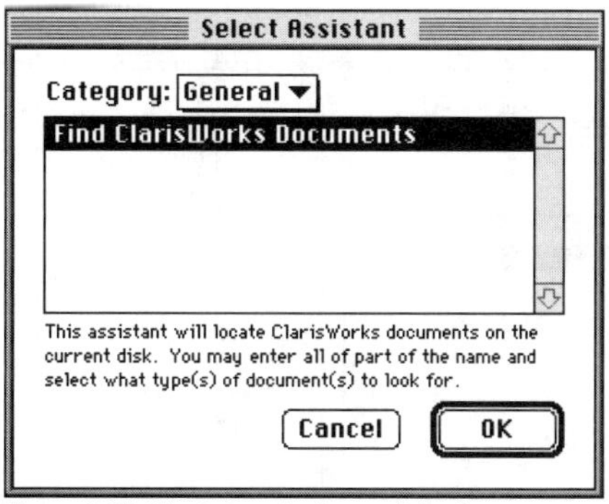

Figure 2-33: The Select Assistant dialog box.

2. **From the General category pop-up menu, choose Find ClarisWorks Documents and click OK.** The Find Document Assistant dialog box appears (see Figure 2-34).

3. **Enter search instructions consisting of any combination of the file's name (or a part of its name), the file date or period that you want to consider, and the document type.**

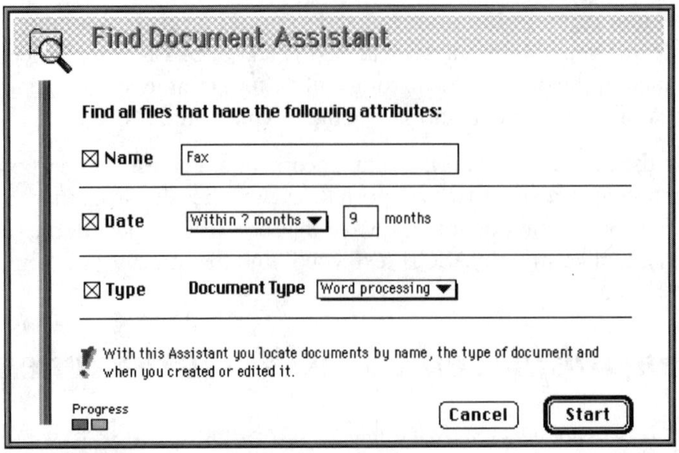

Figure 2-34: The Find Document Assistant dialog box.

4. Click Start to execute the search.

5. The search progress is displayed in a new dialog box (see Figure 2-35). In the Documents Found box, highlight the file you want to load and click the Open button. If the desired file is not found, click Cancel.

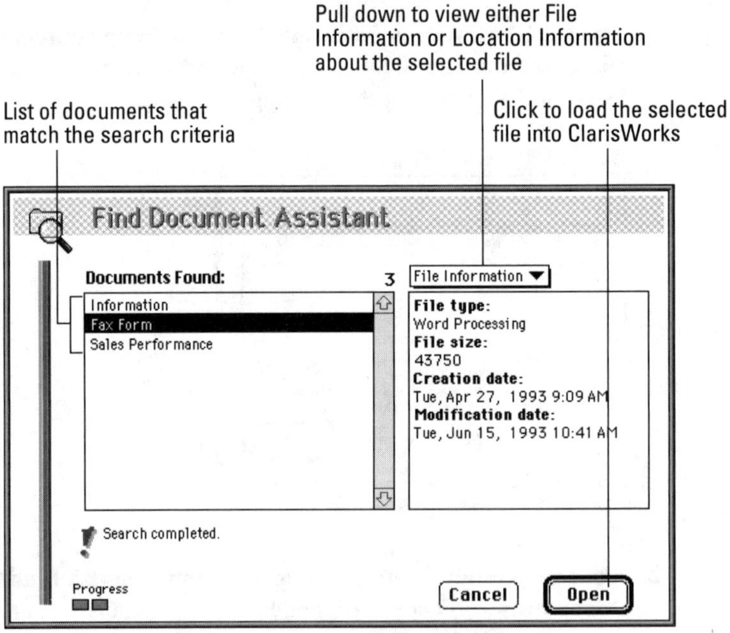

Figure 2-35: Choose a document to open from the Documents Found list.

Note that the Find Document Assistant searches only the *active* hard disk — the one from which ClarisWorks is launched. If you have more than one hard disk or the hard disk is partitioned into multiple volumes, the usefulness of this Assistant may be somewhat limited.

TIP

If you want to see *every* ClarisWorks document on the active drive, leave all the search criteria blank and unchecked.

Summary

- You can launch ClarisWorks in several ways. It can open with a particular document on-screen (or several documents), to the New Document dialog box, or to the Open dialog box — depending on your needs for the session.
- To make finding a particular document easier, the ClarisWorks Open dialog boxes contain a Document Type pop-up menu that can restrict document choices to an environment of your choosing.
- Using the provided Claris Translator filters, ClarisWorks (and other Claris programs) can open or insert many types of non-ClarisWorks files.
- You use the Save command to quickly resave documents that are already stored on disk. You use the Save As command to save new files and multiple generations of existing files.
- When you're through with a particular document, you can close its window by clicking its close box or by choosing Close from the File menu. You can simultaneously close all document windows by holding down the Option key while clicking any close box.
- You use objects in the Tool panel to add different environment frames to a document, to select drawing tools, and to specify colors, gradients, and patterns for objects. You can hide the Tool panel so that you can see larger areas of the document.
- The Shortcuts palette enables you to execute common commands quickly. Its contents change to match the current environment.
- You can integrate two or more environments in a single document by using frames.
- You can change the display for any document by hiding or showing tools, resizing the document window, and splitting the screen. If you're working with multiple documents, you can arrange them optimally with the Tile Windows or Stack Windows commands in the View menu.
- You can print documents from within ClarisWorks or from the desktop.
- ClarisWorks offers two forms of program help: the ClarisWorks Help system — a HyperCard-like deck of information and procedures — and Balloon Help (which is available only to System 7 users).

Topic 3

New Features in ClarisWorks 2.1 and 3.0

Overview

If you previously used ClarisWorks 2.0 and have just upgraded to ClarisWorks 2.1 or 3.0, or if you are thinking about upgrading, this Topic acquaints you with the new features and enhancements of ClarisWorks 2.1 and 3.0. The description of each new feature is followed by a reference to the Topic in which it is fully discussed. Thus, this Topic leads you directly to the feature that you want to learn about next.

NOTE

If you're still using the original ClarisWorks or any version prior to 3.0, you can contact Claris Corp. at 800-544-8554 or 408-727-8227 for upgrade information.

New in ClarisWorks 2.1 and 3.0

Although ClarisWorks 3.0 is currently the latest version of the program, most of the major ClarisWorks features were introduced in version 2.0. Small improvements were added in versions 2.1 and 3.0, but the basic program, the six environments, and the way things work have changed very little. As such, this book is based on ClarisWorks 2.0. When a feature is discussed in this book and a specific version number isn't mentioned, you can assume that the feature exists in ClarisWorks: 2.0, 2.1, and 3.0. When a *newer* feature is discussed, you see an icon in the margin that indicates the minimum ClarisWorks version that you need to have to use that particular feature.

The following sections briefly discuss the changes that were introduced in ClarisWorks 2.1 and 3.0. These features are dealt with in greater depth in the Topics to which they are related.

New in ClarisWorks 2.1

In February 1994, Claris released ClarisWorks 2.1, which included not only a handful of changes that made ClarisWorks easier to use, but also two important new features:

- *Hyphenation.* A custom hyphenation dictionary enables you to set automatic hyphenation for any word processing document, database, or text frame. You also can enter *discretionary hyphens* (which appear only when a word is split across two lines), keep certain words from being hyphenated, and edit the hyphenation dictionary. Hyphenation is covered in Topic 4.
- *PowerTalk electronic mail support.* As long as you have System 7.5, System 7 Pro, or a later version of the system software, you can add a mailer (an address header) to a ClarisWorks document, making the document a letter that you can send to other PowerTalk users. Documents sent via PowerTalk can include enclosures, such as other ClarisWorks 2.1 documents. Topic 21 discusses PowerTalk messaging.

NOTE

In general, there are few differences between Versions 2 and 2.1. And files created in one version can be read by the other version, making it easy to exchange ClarisWorks documents with other users. Note, however, that discretionary hyphens included in ClarisWorks 2.1 documents appear as box characters when the document is opened in ClarisWorks 2.0.

New in ClarisWorks 3.0

Although the main purpose of ClarisWorks 3.0 was to bring the Windows version of the program up to par with the Macintosh version, a few significant features and enhancements were added to the Mac program:

- *Introduction to ClarisWorks.* New users of ClarisWorks will appreciate this guided tour of the program. You can run the tour as often as you like by selecting the option for it from the Welcome screen or from the Help menu.
- *Welcome screen.* Rather than assume that you always want to create a new document, the new Welcome screen enables you to either create a new document, load an existing document, invoke a ClarisWorks Assistant, or view an on-screen tour of ClarisWorks. See Topic 2 for help with using the Welcome screen.
- *Assistants.* Assistants are built-in "experts" that make it simple to perform tasks such as formatting footnotes, printing mailing labels and envelopes, and designing newsletters and presentations. Assistants are discussed in Topic 11.
- *Revised Help System.* Help was changed dramatically for Version 3.0 and is discussed in Topic 2.

- *Document Summary Info.* You can save identifying information with any file to show a more descriptive title, the name of the person who created the file, a version number, keywords, a category, and a description. An explanation of the Document Summary Info dialog box is in Topic 2.
- *Word Count.* You can now get an accurate count of the number of characters, words, lines, paragraphs, and pages in the current document. See Topic 4 for more information.
- *Improved Save As and Open dialog boxes.* The new Save As dialog box now makes it extremely simple to save any document as a stationery template. If you have Apple's QuickTime extension loaded, the Open dialog box can show you a thumbnail preview of any graphic image or QuickTime movie *before* you open the file. The Save As and Open dialog boxes are discussed in Topic 2.
- *Automatic macros.* Tucked away in the ClarisWorks Help System is a description of a neat feature that enables certain macros to automatically play whenever you launch ClarisWorks, create a new document in a particular environment, or open a document in a particular environment. See Topic 14 for a description of this new kind of macro.
- *Fonts and clip art.* To help you create more interesting, attractive documents, ClarisWorks 3.0 includes half a dozen free fonts and 75 clip art images.
- *MacWrite Pro file filter.* ClarisWorks 3.0 can now translate files that were created with MacWrite Pro.

NOTE

The files created in the Mac and Windows versions of ClarisWorks 3.0 are compatible with each other, as are files created in all Mac versions between 2.0 and 3.0. As in ClarisWorks 2.0 and 2.1, ClarisWorks 3.0 can interpret and translate files created in Version 1.0. However, when you transfer Mac files to the Windows version of ClarisWorks, you need to follow DOS filenaming conventions. The main part of the filename can be no more than eight characters long and must be followed by .CWK, which is a DOS extension.

Deducing Your ClarisWorks Version Number

Because ClarisWorks 2.1 and 3.0 incorporate some features that do not exist in Version 2.0, knowing which version of ClarisWorks you have is important. To determine which version you are using, do the following:

- *If ClarisWorks is running,* choose About ClarisWorks from the Apple menu. A dialog box appears (see Figure 3-1), listing the version number. Click OK to close the dialog box.

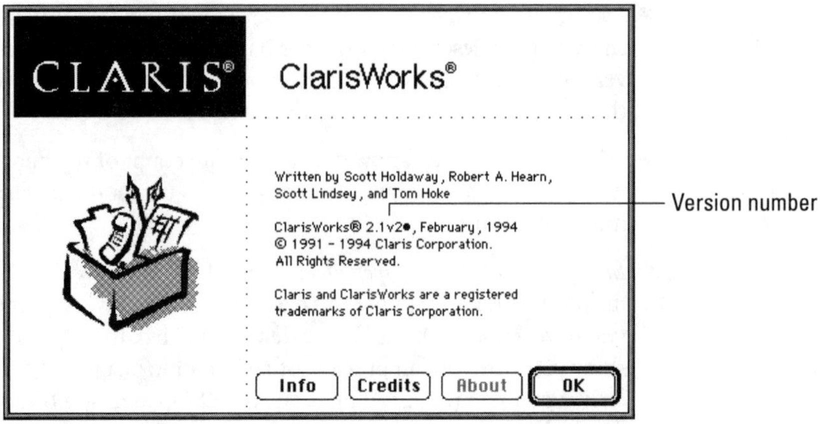

Figure 3-1: The About ClarisWorks dialog box.

- *If ClarisWorks is not running,* from the desktop, click the ClarisWorks program icon. Then choose Get Info from the File menu or press ⌘-I. An Info window appears (see Figure 3-2), listing the version number. Click the Info window's close box.

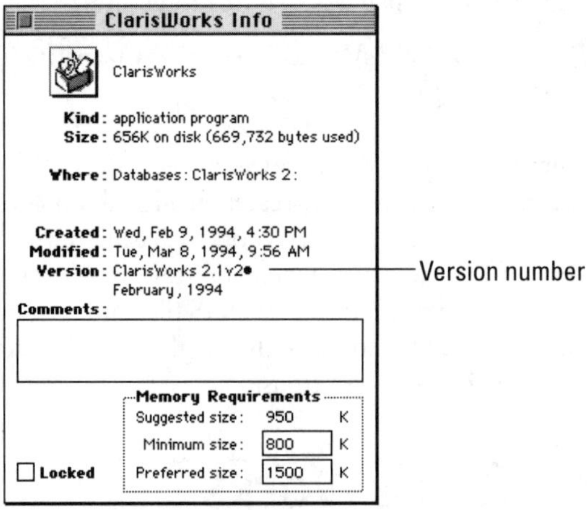

Figure 3-2: The ClarisWorks Info window.

Updating Your Copy of ClarisWorks

To update to ClarisWorks 2.1, you need to run a program called ClarisWorks 2.1v2 Updater, which converts a copy of ClarisWorks 2 to version 2.1. For more information on how to obtain and install the Updater, see Appendix B.

For information on updating to ClarisWorks 3.0, contact Claris Customer Relations (800-544-8554 or 408-727-8227).

Part II
Using the ClarisWorks Environments

Topic 4

The Word Processing Environment

Overview

Everyone writes. And whether you're working on a letter, memo, fax, report, or the Great American Novel, the computer is the ideal writing tool.

Before you bought a Mac, you probably wrote with a combination of pen, pencil, and typewriter. All three of these tools have drawbacks, however. Although a handwritten note is considered more personal than a typed one, you may not be able to say exactly what you want to say without a lot of rewrites and wasted stationery. Typewritten documents are cleaner and more uniform, but they can require an amazing amount of retyping — *and white-out* — to eliminate typographical errors and spelling errors. And when you want to move, insert, or delete a paragraph, you often have to retype every page of text that follows.

What Is a Word Processor?

A word processing program makes it easy for you to edit, reorganize, and polish your writing. Spelling checkers, thesauruses, and grammar checkers help you choose the best (and correct) words. Because you create documents on the Mac's screen, you can avoid paper waste by not printing until the document is exactly as you want it. Instead of making copies of documents for your files, you can simply save them on disk. If you ever need to refer to the original document again or want another printed copy, you just open the document in the word processor. Finally, you can store frequently used paragraphs on disk and reuse them whenever you like. You can copy and paste them into the document or save them as reusable stationery documents (as described in Topic 11).

As you read this Topic, keep in mind that everything in it applies to word processing *frames* as well as to documents. In addition, some of the features that you traditionally associate with word processing, such as the spelling checker and rulers, are also available in other ClarisWorks environments. This Topic includes a discussion of these features (because this is where you'd normally expect to read about them), and other Topics refer you back to this Topic as necessary.

Word Processing Essentials

The first step in using the word processor is to create a new word processing document.

To create a new word processing document:

1. **Choose New from theFile menu (or press ⌘-N).**
2. **Click the Word Processing radio button.**
3. **Click OK or press Return.** A blank document opens (see Figure 4-1) with the cursor positioned at the top of the page, ready for you to start entering text.

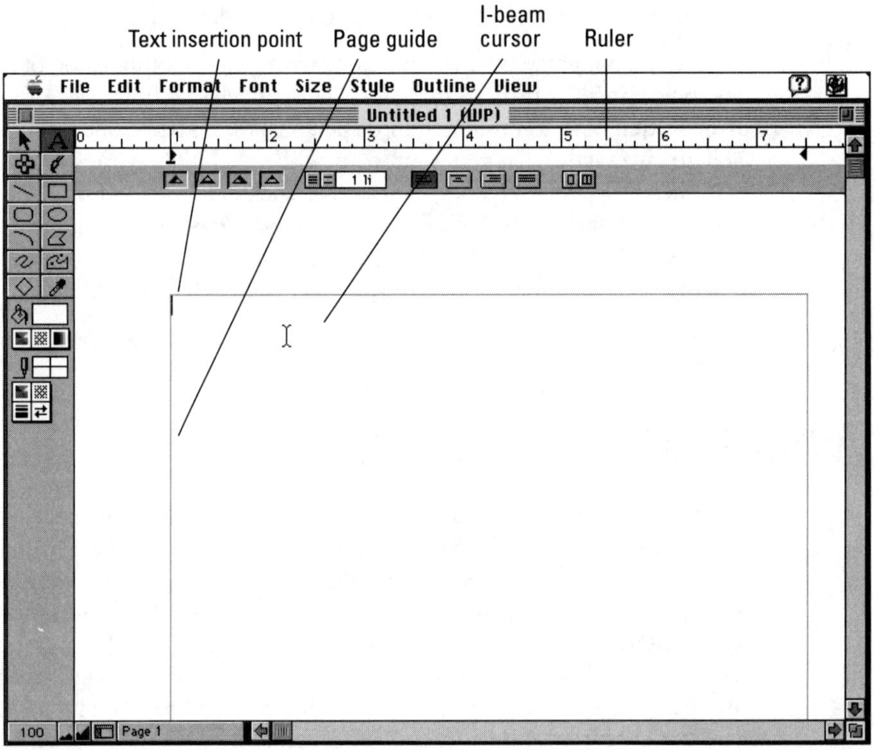

Figure 4-1: A new word processing document.

Text that you type or paste always appears at the location of the cursor (which is also called the *text insertion point*). The insertion point is marked by a tiny vertical line. You can change the insertion point by moving the mouse and then clicking in a new location. To help you accurately position the text insertion point, ClarisWorks displays an *I-beam cursor* (shown in Figure 4-1) as you move the mouse over the page.

As you type, ClarisWorks automatically handles line ends by wrapping extra text to the next line. As you approach the end of a line, the word processor checks whether the word you are typing, plus the other words in the line, exceed the printable page width. If so, the last word is automatically moved or *wrapped* to the next line. Unlike with a typewriter, you don't have to press Return to start a new line in a word processing document. You just keep typing. In fact, the only times that you should press Return are to end a paragraph or to insert an extra blank line between paragraphs.

In addition to reformatting lines for you, the word processor features *automatic repagination.* As you insert, delete, or move text in the document, the program automatically adjusts the composition of the pages. Suppose, for example, that you add a couple of paragraphs to the middle of a report. If you are using a typewriter, you have to retype all the pages that follow the insertion. In the ClarisWorks word processor, however, any text following the two new paragraphs automatically shifts down, and the program forms new pages as required. Large deletions work the same way. When you delete, the word processor automatically closes up the space and repaginates the document.

Like all current word processing programs, the ClarisWorks word processor is *paragraph oriented.* Tabs, indents, and text alignment options that you apply always affect an entire paragraph — not just the line where the text insertion point happens to be. When you press Return, a new paragraph is started, which — by default — contains the same settings as the previous paragraph. Because each paragraph is treated as a separate entity, you can change settings on a paragraph-by-paragraph basis.

You also can apply text-formatting options such as fonts, sizes, and styles to entire paragraphs or to selected text strings within a paragraph. With a typewriter, you have to change type balls or wheels to change the formatting. In the word processor, you simply select some text and then choose the appropriate text formatting commands from the Font, Size, and Style menus.

Navigation

ClarisWorks provides several ways to navigate through a document without changing the insertion point. If you're just reading a document on-screen or checking what was written on page 7, for example, you can use the techniques in Table 4-1 to move through the document. Again, when you are using these techniques, the text insertion point does not change.

Table 4-1
Navigational Techniques

Navigation	***Key or Action***
Move up or down one line of text	Click the up- or down-arrow symbol on the scroll bar
Move up or down one screenful of text	Press the Page Up or Page Down key (Extended keyboard only) or click in the gray area of the vertical scroll bar
Move up or down to an approximate location	Drag the box in the vertical scroll bar to a new position
Move to the beginning or end of the document	Press the Home or End key (Extended keyboard only) or drag the box in the scroll bar to the top or bottom
Go to a specific page	Double-click in the page number area at bottom of the document and type a page number in the dialog box that appears

Elementary Text Editing

Few of us are blessed with the ability to write precisely what we want the very first time. In fact, depending on the type and complexity of the document, we may actually spend more time editing than doing the initial writing. This section describes some essential techniques for text editing in the word processing environment.

Inserting text in a word processing document or frame

Whether you type text, paste it, or insert it with the Insert command, it is always entered at the text insertion point (described previously). You can enter new text into a word processing document or into a frame.

Step-by-Steps

To insert text:

1. **Position the cursor over the spot where you want to insert the text and click the mouse button once.** The cursor — a small vertical line — is positioned for you, ready for text entry.

— or —

1. **Use the arrow keys to move the cursor as described in Table 4-2.**
2. **Type the text, paste it, or enter it with the Insert command from the File menu.**

Table 4-2
Insertion Point Navigational Shortcuts

Cursor Movement	***Keystroke***
One character left or right	Left- or right-arrow key
One line up or down	Up- or down-arrow key
To the start or end of a line	⌘-left-arrow key or ⌘-right-arrow key
One word to the left or right	Option-left-arrow key or Option-right-arrow key
To the beginning or end of a paragraph	Option-up-arrow key or Option-down-arrow key
To the beginning or end of the document	⌘-up-arrow key or ⌘-down-arrow key
Continuous scrolling	Hold down the up- or down-arrow key

NOTE

When you position the cursor, you need to place it immediately before, after, or within the current text of the document. In a new, blank document, for example, no matter where you click, the insertion point will be set at the start of the first page. Similarly, even if you click several inches below the last paragraph in a partially written document, the insertion point will be placed immediately following the last character of the document. If you want to start typing well below the current end of the document, you can press Return several times to add the necessary white space so that you can position the insertion point where you want it.

Deleting text from a word processing document or frame

Nobody's perfect. Part of the writing process is deleting text. The following instructions describe how to delete a character or a selection of text.

Step-by-Steps

To delete a character:

1. **Position the cursor to the right of the character that you want to delete.**
2. **Press Delete or Backspace. Each keypress deletes one character to the left of the cursor.**

— or —

1. **Position the cursor to the left of the character that you want to delete.**
2. **Press the Delete key on the Extended keyboard.** Each press of the Delete key deletes one character to the right of the cursor.

To delete a text selection:

1. **Select the text to be deleted.**
2. **Press Delete or Backspace, or choose Clear from the Edit menu.** Each of these operations deletes the text selection without copying it to the Macintosh Clipboard.

— or —

2. **Choose Cut from the Edit menu (or press ⌘-X).** This method simultaneously deletes the text selection and copies it to the Macintosh Clipboard. Use this approach when you want to paste the text elsewhere — either in the current document or in another one.

Copying and reusing text

The Copy command is useful when you have text strings or phrases that you want to use in several places in a document or copy to a different document.

To copy text:

1. **Select the text to be copied.**
2. **Choose Copy from the Edit menu (or press ⌘-C).** A copy of the selected text is transferred to the Clipboard, and the text is immediately available for pasting.

As long you don't copy or cut (⌘-X) anything else to the Clipboard, you can paste the copied text repeatedly (⌘-V) in the current document as well as in other documents.

Text-selection techniques

In addition to the text-selection techniques that are described in the discussion of selecting text in Topic 1, ClarisWorks offers a couple of special tricks of its own:

- To select a single *word,* double-click anywhere within the word.
- To select the *current line,* triple-click anywhere within the line.
- To select the *current paragraph,* quadruple-click anywhere within the paragraph.
- To select the *entire document,* choose Select All from the Edit menu (or press ⌘-A).

After you select text, you can act on the selection as a whole. For example, you can change its font, copy or cut it, or move it to a new location.

Using the Macintosh Clipboard

Throughout this book, and in many other Macintosh books, magazines, and manuals, you see frequent references to the *Clipboard.* What is the Clipboard, and how does it work?

The Clipboard is a temporary storage area in Macintosh RAM (memory). The last object or text selection that you copied with the Copy command (⌘-C) or deleted with the Cut command (⌘-X) is stored in the Clipboard. Each time you copy or cut a new object or text selection, the new object or text replaces the current contents of the Clipboard.

The beauty of the Clipboard is that whatever it currently contains is available for pasting with the Paste command (⌘-V). And not only can you paste the object or text into the current document, you also can paste it into other documents, even into documents in other programs. You can, for example, copy a name and address from a word processing document and paste it into an address book desk accessory (or vice versa).

Note that the Clipboard works the same way whether you are running System 6 with the Finder, System 6 with MultiFinder, or System 7. The only things that clear the contents of the Clipboard are cutting or copying a new object or text selection and turning off the Mac. Otherwise, you can quit one program and start another, confident that the Clipboard's contents are still intact.

Moving text in a word processing document or frame

In ClarisWorks, moving text is a two-step process: cut and then paste. You cut selected text from the document and then paste it in another position in the document.

Step-by-Steps

To move text by cutting and pasting:

1. **Select the text to be moved.**
2. **Choose the Cut command from the Edit menu (or press ⌘-X). Cutting the text deletes it and moves it to the Clipboard.**
3. **Move the text insertion point to the position where you want to move the text.**
4. **Choose the Paste command from the Edit menu (or press ⌘-V).** The Paste command makes a copy of the text that is in the Clipboard and pastes it at the text insertion point.

TIP

ClarisWorks also provides a shortcut for directly moving a text selection to a new location without using the normal cut-and-paste routine.

Step-by-Steps

To directly move text:

1. **Select the text to be moved.**
2. **Hold down the Command and Option keys while you use the mouse button to click the destination location in the document.** The text is transferred from its original location to the destination.

Undoing your actions

While typing or editing a document, you'll probably make errors. You may find that you've typed a phrase in the wrong spot — perhaps in the middle of a word — or that you've chosen the wrong formatting command. You may be able to correct the damage by using the Undo command.

ClarisWorks keeps track of the last thing that you did to change the current document, such as cutting text, typing new text, or saving changes to a file. If the program can undo the last action, choosing the Undo command from the Edit menu (or pressing ⌘-Z) puts the document back to the condition it was in immediately before you performed the action. The wording of the Undo command changes to reflect the last action. If, for example, the last change that you made was a cut, the command reads *Undo Cut.*

After choosing Undo, you can still change your mind. The Undo menu command now reads *Redo command* (in this case, *Redo Cut*). Choose the Redo command, and the Undo is undone.

CAUTION!

Undo tracks only the last change that you made to the document. If you delete some text and then type new text, you cannot undo the deletion. For the Undo command to work, you have to catch the error immediately — before you make any other change to the document. Also, you cannot undo some actions. Saving a new version of a file over an existing file is one example. In those instances, the Undo command reads *Can't Undo.* Think carefully before you make major changes (and be sure to keep current backups).

If you've been experimenting with a document and want to undo *all* the changes you've made, choose the Revert command from the File menu. Revert replaces the document on-screen with a copy of the most recently saved version of the file. It's as though you closed the current document without saving it and then reloaded the original document from disk. Be careful when you are using Revert, however. You cannot undo it by using the Undo command. (Also note that you can use Revert with *any* type of ClarisWorks document, not just with word processing files.)

Formatting: Word Processing with Style

Formatting is what distinguishes an ordinary document from one with style. Sure, you can just pick a standard font (such as Times or Helvetica) and type the entire document, pausing only to press Return now and then to begin a new paragraph. But the word processor enables you to do much more. You can choose different fonts for headers and body text, apply italic to selected phrases to add emphasis, set left and right indents differently for different paragraphs, create hanging indents to format bulleted lists, and use tabs to align items in a list or columns of numbers. You learn to master these formatting commands, and others, in this section.

Within the word processing program, the three classes of formatting are text formatting, paragraph formatting, and document formatting.

- Text formatting is concerned with applying fonts, sizes, and styles to characters, words, phrases, sentences, and paragraphs.
- Paragraph formatting enables you to set tabs, indents, line spacing, and between-paragraph spacing for paragraphs.
- Document formatting governs the look of the entire document. It includes setting margins, inserting headers and footers, forcing page breaks, creating multicolumn documents, and specifying an optional title page.

Formatting words

Formatting words, as discussed here, is concerned only with applying different fonts, sizes, and styles. Although you can apply these formats to individual characters within a document, you'll usually stick to formatting words and phrases.

Changing fonts and styles

Most correspondence and reports consist of a single font in a single size. When you want to make some text stand out (for example, by applying italic to emphasize a phrase or by changing the font to differentiate a header from body text), ClarisWorks enables you to apply different fonts, sizes, and styles.

To assign fonts, sizes, and styles:

1. **Select the text with the font, size, or style you want to change.**

— or —

1. **Position the text insertion point where you want the new font, size, or style to begin.**
2. **Choose a new font, size, or style from the Font, Size, or Style menus.** The selected text changes to reflect the options you've chosen. If no text was selected, new text that you type will reflect the chosen options.

Although each character can have only one font and size combination (Helvetica 12 point, for example), you can assign multiple styles to any text string. To apply additional styles, select some text and then choose the Style commands that you want to apply to the text (see the Style menu in Figure 4-2). Styles that you can combine include the following:

- **Bold** (⌘-B)
- *Italic* (⌘-I)
- Underline (⌘-U)
- ~~Strike Thru~~
- Outline
- Shadow

In addition, you can apply a color to selected text by choosing a color from the Text Color pop-up menu in the Style menu, move letters in a text string closer together (Condense) or farther apart (Extend), and format characters so that they appear higher (Superscript, Shift-⌘-+) or lower (Subscript, Shift–⌘-–) than the surrounding text. The Condense and Extend styles are mutually exclusive, as are Superscript and Subscript.

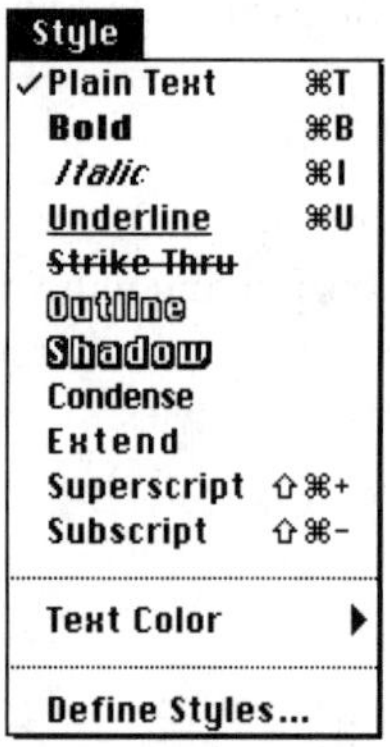

Figure 4-2: The Style menu.

Removing styles

Each Style command works as a toggle. To remove a single style from a text string, select the text and choose the Style command that you want to remove. This method of removing styles is particularly useful when a text string has several styles and you want to remove one or some of them but leave the other styles intact.

You can instantly remove all styles from text by selecting the text and then choosing Plain Text (⌘-T) from the Style menu. The one exception is that any color that is applied to the text will remain.

Choosing and using fonts

Regardless of the type of document that you're working on, you'll do well to restrict your use of fonts to a small number — perhaps two. (Too many fonts can make a document look like a ransom note.) Within a selected font (Helvetica or Times, for example), you can freely apply other typefaces and styles, such as italic, bold, and so on.

Fonts can be divided into two general types that are referred to as *serif* and *sans serif.* A serif font, such as Times, has angular points and lines (which are called serifs) at the base and top of each character. Serif fonts are designed to be easy on the eyes and are regularly used to format body text. Sans serif fonts, such as Helvetica, are essentially smooth (they have no serifs) and are often used as headings (*sans* means *no* or *without).*

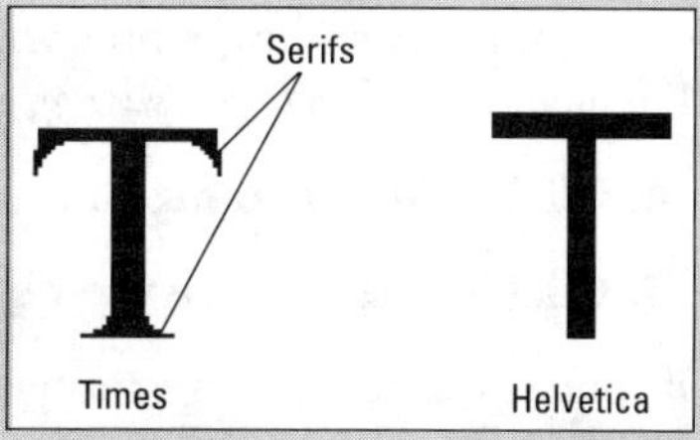

If you're new at selecting and using fonts (as most of us are), try these suggestions as a starting point:

- For body text, choose a serif font (such as Times, Palatino, or Adobe Garamond).
- For heads, use a sans serif font (such as Helvetica Bold or Franklin Gothic).

Custom text styles

As you work with the word processor, you may find that you use some special text styles frequently. You can use the Define Styles command in the Style menu to create custom text styles for those styles.

To define a custom style by example:

1. **In a word processing document, format some text with the desired combination of font, size, and styles.**
2. **Choose Define Styles from the Style menu.** The Define Custom Styles dialog box appears, as shown in Figure 4-3.

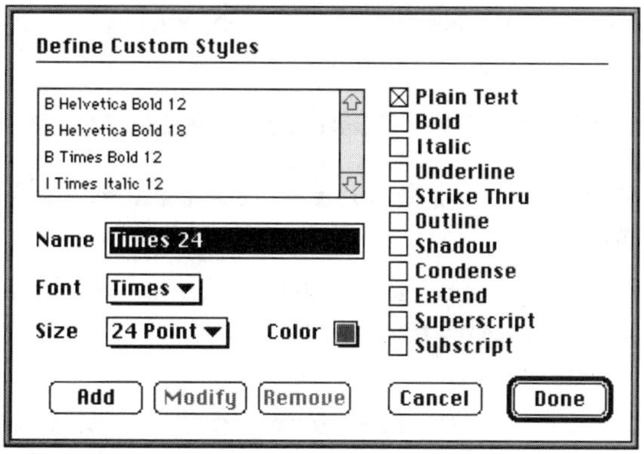

Figure 4-3: The Define Custom Styles dialog box.

3. **Type a name for the style in the Name box or accept the default name that is presented.** (The default name consists only of the font name and point size. You may want to name it something a bit more descriptive, such as a name that indicates how you intend to use the style. Examples might include *Title, Main Heading*, and *Body Text*.)
4. **Click Add to add the new custom style to the Style menu.**
5. **Click Done to close the dialog box and return to your work.**

Of course, you also can create styles from scratch by choosing options from the Define Custom Styles dialog box.

Step-by-Steps

To create a custom style from scratch:

1. **Choose Define Styles from the Style menu.** The Define Custom Styles dialog box appears.
2. **Choose a font, a size, a color, and style options for the custom style.**
3. **Type a name for the style in the Name box or accept the default name that is presented.** (The default consists only of the font name and point size. You may want to name it something a bit more descriptive.)
4. **Click Add to add the new custom style to the bottom of the Style menu.**
5. **Repeat Steps 2 through 4 for additional custom styles that you want to define.**
6. **Click Done to close the dialog box and continue your work.**

TIP

Custom styles exist only in the document in which they are defined. Open a new document, and you'll see that no custom styles are in the Style menu. A problem immediately presents itself: Who wants to create the same custom styles over and over again? You may find that you'd like to use a key set of custom styles in almost every new document. Instead of redefining the styles each time, you can create one or more stationery documents that contain the custom styles you need.

Step-by-Steps

To save custom styles in a stationery document:

1. **Choose New from the File menu to create a new, blank word processing document.**
2. **Choose Define Styles from the Style menu, create the custom styles, and assign a descriptive name to each custom style (following the steps outlined previously).**
3. **Choose Save As from the File menu and choose Stationery from the Save As pop-up menu.**
4. **Enter an appropriate name for the file (Memo Template or Report Template, for example) and click Save to save it to disk.**

Whenever you need to create a new memo or report, you can simply open the stationery document. The custom styles will be ready for you to use. (If you want to be able to select a stationery template from the New Document dialog box, see the instructions for creating stationery documents in Topic 11.)

Applying a custom style to text

As each new style is defined, ClarisWorks adds it to the bottom of the Style menu. To apply a custom style, select some text and then choose a custom style from the bottom of the Style menu (see Figure 4-4).

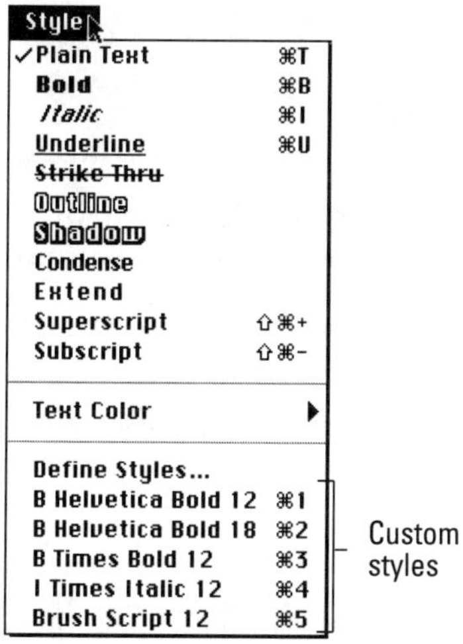

Figure 4-4. The Style menu with custom styles added.

Because the first eight custom styles also have an associated Command-key combination (from ⌘-1 through ⌘-8), you can apply the styles by either selecting from the custom style list or pressing the appropriate Command-key combination. For example, after you select some text, you can apply the first custom style to the text by pressing ⌘-1. Because pressing Command-key combinations is easier (and faster) than choosing menu commands, assigning the styles that you use the most as the first eight custom styles is beneficial.

Modifying a custom text style

If you later discover that a custom style isn't precisely what you need (perhaps you want a different font or point size), you can modify the style's definition.

Step-by-Steps

To redefine a custom style:

1. **Choose Define Styles from the Style menu.** The Define Custom Styles dialog box appears, as shown in Figure 4-3.
2. **In the list box of the custom styles that you've previously defined, select the style that you want to change.**
3. **Make the required modifications by changing the font, size, color, or styles.**
4. **If the style name no longer accurately reflects the style definition, you can change it, too.**
5. **Click Modify to record the changes.**
6. **Click Done to close the dialog box and return to your work.**

Modifying a style has no impact on text that has been formatted with that style. If you want to apply the modified style to that text, you have to choose the menu command again.

Removing a custom text style

If you find that you no longer need a custom style, you can delete it.

Step-by-Steps

To delete custom styles:

1. **Choose Define Styles from the Style menu.** The Define Custom Styles dialog box appears, as shown in Figure 4-3.
2. **In the list box of the custom styles that you've previously defined, choose the one that you want to delete.**
3. **Click Remove.**
4. **Click Done to close the dialog box and return to your work.**

NOTE

You can remove several styles at the same time by clicking each one while pressing Shift (for contiguous selections) or ⌘ (for noncontiguous selections).

As in modifying a style, removing a custom style has no effect on text that has already been formatted with that style.

NOTE

If you have used a desktop publishing program or other word processing programs (such as Microsoft Word or MacWrite Pro), be sure that you don't confuse the ClarisWorks styles with the more powerful style feature, paragraph styles. You use the ClarisWorks custom styles only for formatting selected text with font, style, and size options. Paragraph styles, such as the ones found in high-end word processing and desktop publishing programs, also deal with character font, size, and style. In addition, however, they contain paragraph formatting information, such as margin settings, tab stops, and line spacing. And when you redefine a paragraph style, all paragraphs that you have formatted with that style automatically update to reflect the new style.

Formatting paragraphs

The ClarisWorks word processor treats every paragraph as a distinct entity. If you want to, you can give every paragraph different settings for tabs, indents, alignment, and the spacing between lines and between paragraphs. You can set these paragraph formatting options with the ruler or choose the Paragraph command from the Format menu.

NOTE When you type new paragraphs, each time you press Return to end one paragraph and begin another, ClarisWorks automatically applies the format of the previous paragraph to the new paragraph. These formatting options remain in effect for additional paragraphs until you specifically change them.

Using the ruler

The word processing ruler serves a greater function than simply showing the page width. By clicking and dragging, you can use the ruler to set most paragraph formatting options (see Figure 4-5). The options that you can set with the ruler include:

- Indents (left, right, and first)
- Tab stops (left, center, right, or decimal)
- Line spacing
- Paragraph alignment (left, center, right, or justified)
- Number of columns (described in "Working with columns" later in this Topic)

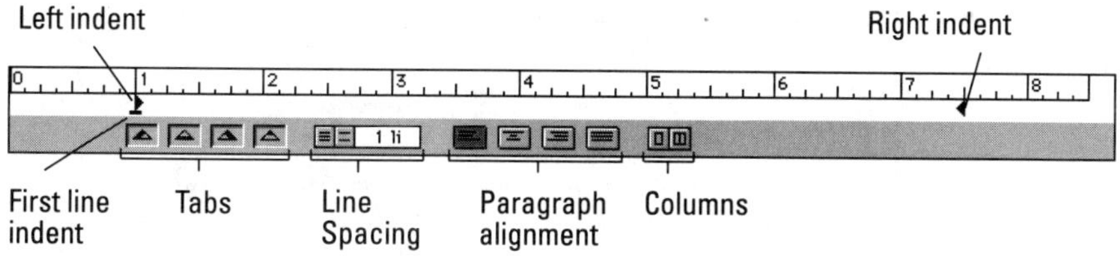

Figure 4-5: The ruler and its components.

When you want to make minor changes to paragraph formatting, this visually-guided approach is easy to use. Just change ruler settings until the paragraph looks right.

If the ruler isn't visible, choose Show Rulers from the View menu (or press Shift-⌘-U). To hide the ruler(s), choose Hide Rulers from the View menu (or press Shift-⌘-U).

Although most people prefer a ruler that measures in inches, you can change the measurement units, as well as specify the number of ruler divisions (up to 14). Examples of the different measurement units are shown in Figure 4-6.

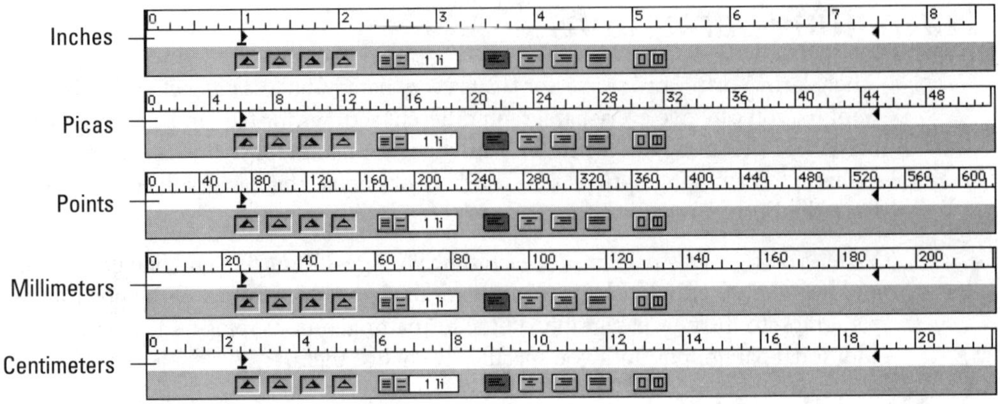

Figure 4-6: Text ruler measurement units.

To set ruler measurement units and divisions:

1. **Open an existing word processing document or create a new document.**
2. **Choose Rulers from the Format menu.** The Rulers dialog box appears, as shown in Figure 4-7.

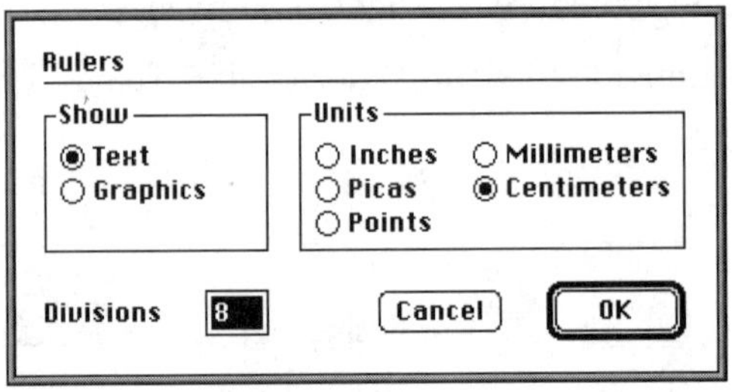

Figure 4-7: The Rulers dialog box.

3. **Select either the Text ruler or the Graphics ruler by clicking the appropriate radio button in the Show box.**

   The Text ruler is a standard horizontal ruler that appears at the top of the page. Selecting the Graphics ruler creates a pair of rulers: a horizontal ruler across the top of the page and a vertical ruler down the left side of the page. Graphics rulers, however, are only aids for positioning; they do not contain the same controls that Text rulers have. Thus, Graphics rulers are not recommended for use with word processing documents.

4. **Select a unit of measurement by clicking the appropriate radio button in the Units box.**

5. **Type a number in the Divisions text-edit box to indicate the number of minor divisions that you want in each segment of the ruler.** You can specify a maximum of 14 divisions.

6. **Click OK.** A ruler appears with the units and divisions you specified.

ClarisWorks saves the ruler with the document. Note that every document can have a different type of ruler with different divisions.

TIP

If you find, for example, that you prefer a ruler with points as the units of measurement, rather than inches, you may want to create a blank stationery document with that style of ruler. You also can make that style of ruler the default for all new word processing documents by including the ruler in an options stationery document. Topic 11 includes instructions for creating both types of stationery files.

Indents

Indents are paragraph-specific settings that indicate how far in from the left or right margins the text should be positioned. In ClarisWorks, as in other word processors, you can set a first line indent so that the first line is treated differently from other lines in the paragraph. First line indents can be used to create *hanging indents.* Indents are useful for formatting bulleted lists, numbered lists, and quotations (see Figure 4-8).

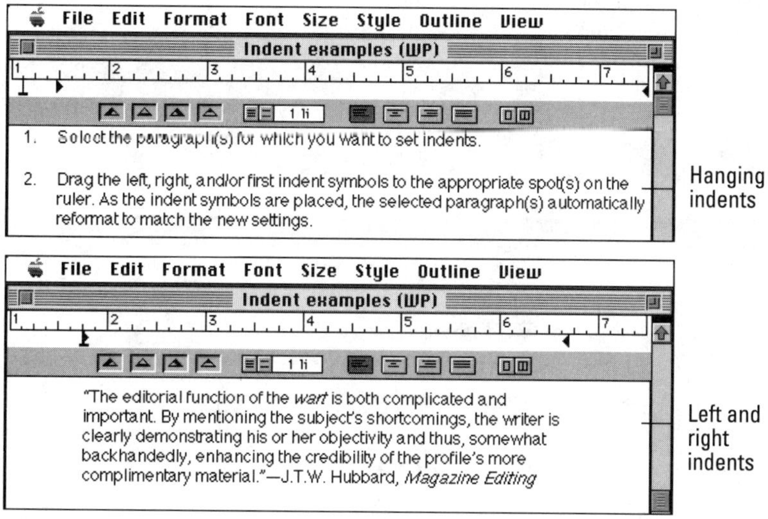

Figure 4-8: Examples of different indents.

To set indents with the ruler:

1. **Select the paragraph(s) for which you want to set indents.**
2. **Drag the left, right, and/or first indent symbols to the appropriate spot(s) on the ruler.** As the indent symbols are placed, the selected paragraphs automatically reformat to match the new settings.

Hanging indents

Hanging indents are frequently used in documents, particularly for formatting numbered lists and bulleted lists. (In a *hanging indent,* the first line begins farther to the left than the remaining lines.) The following figure shows hanging indents with bullets and numbered points.

To create a hanging indent:

1. **On the ruler, drag the left indent marker (the solid right-pointing triangle) to the right.** Its location marks the spot where the text will begin.
2. **Drag the first line marker to the desired position.** Its location marks the spot where the numbers or bullets will appear. (If you want the numbers or bullets to be flush with the left margin, you don't need to change the position of the first line marker.)

To form the hanging indent, start by typing the number or bullet symbol. Then press Tab and type the text of the step or point. If the text is longer than one line, the remaining text automatically wraps to the position of the left indent marker.

Normally, when you attempt to drag the left indent marker, the first line marker also comes along for the ride. To move the left indent marker by itself (so you can easily create a hanging indent), hold down Option while you click and drag the left indent marker.

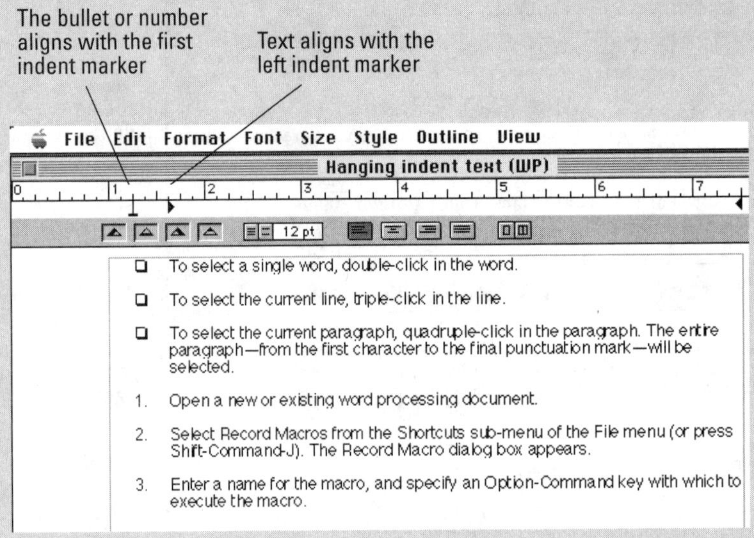

Tab stops

If you're familiar with a typewriter (I haven't touched one in 15 years), you already know about tabs. Tabs are used to align text in columns, to create tables, and to precisely position important text strings (enabling you to right-align a page number in a footer, for example). ClarisWorks offers four tab stop options: left, center, right, and decimal. Figure 4-9 shows examples of the four types of tab stops.

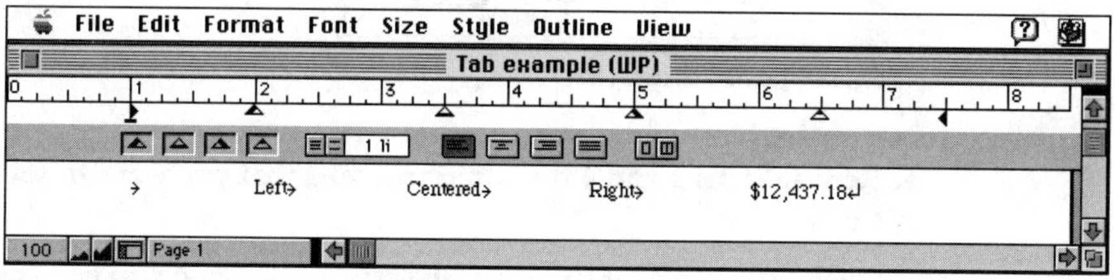

Figure 4-9: Left, center, right, and decimal tabs.

To set tab stops with the ruler:

1. **Select the paragraph(s) for which you want to set tab stops.**
2. **Click a tab icon and drag it into position on the ruler.**
3. **Repeat Step 2 until you have set all the tabs that are required for the paragraph.**

After you set a tab, you can reposition it by simply dragging it to a new location on the ruler. You can remove a tab by dragging it off the ruler.

You can also use the Tab command to specify a *leader character* (a character, such as a period, that fills the blank space leading up to the tab). Leader characters are particularly useful in formatting entries in a table of contents and separating invoice items from prices (for example, Jello .... $0.49).

To set tab stops with the Tab command:

1. **Select the paragraphs for which you want to set tab stops.**
2. **Choose the Tab command from the Format menu.** The Tab dialog box appears, as shown in Figure 4-10.
3. **Choose the settings for the first tab stop that you want to set.** Click the radio button for the Alignment desired, type a number in the Position text-edit box, and (optional) click a radio button to select a Fill pattern (which is also called a *leader*).
4. **Click Apply to insert the new tab.**

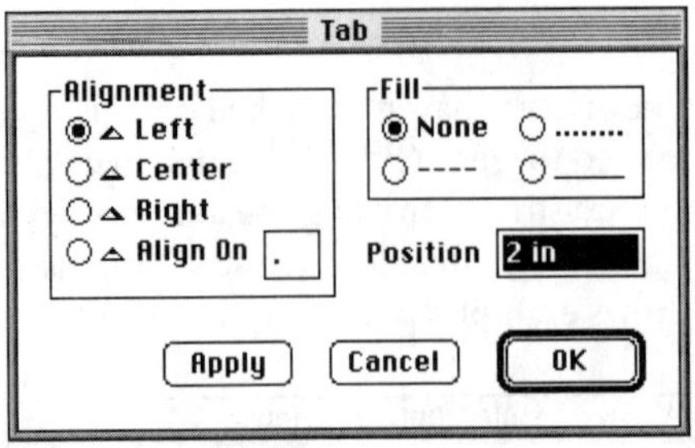

Figure 4-10: The Tab dialog box.

5. **Repeat Steps 3 and 4 for additional tabs that you want to set at this time.**
6. **Click OK to accept the new tab settings or Cancel to revert to the original tab settings.**

NOTE

The decimal tab (the Align On option) is followed by a text-edit box. Although you normally set this tab to align on a decimal point (.), you can specify any character you like. You may, for example, want a column of numbers to align on the percent sign (%).

TIP

If the Tab dialog box covers any of the paragraphs that will be affected by the command, you can drag the dialog box to a different position.

Also note that the Tab dialog box does not provide a method for removing tab stops. Regardless of how you set tabs, you have to remove them manually by dragging them off the ruler.

When you are creating a document, such as a résumé, that uses many different indentations, use tabs instead of a space. Though it may look good on the screen, the printout may look quite different. Tabs are also much easier to adjust than spaces.

Line spacing

Most documents are printed single spaced (with no blank lines between lines of text). Occasionally, however, you need to alter the between-line spacing. High school and college homework, for example, often must be double-spaced (with one blank line between every pair of text lines). Manuscripts submitted to magazines and book publishers sometimes must be double-spaced as well — to make it easier for an editor to edit and write comments on the printed copy.

TIP

Like other ruler settings, line spacing can be different for every paragraph in a ClarisWorks word processing document. If you want to set line spacing for the entire document, choose Select All from the Edit menu (or press ⌘-A) and then select a line spacing option.

Step-by-Steps

To set line spacing with the ruler:

1. **Select the paragraphs for which you want to set between-line spacing.**
2. **In the ruler bar, click the line spacing icon on the left to decrease the between-line spacing or click the line spacing icon on the right to increase the between-line spacing.**

   Line spacing always increases or decreases in half-line increments. Figure 4-11 shows examples of several of the most common settings for line spacing.

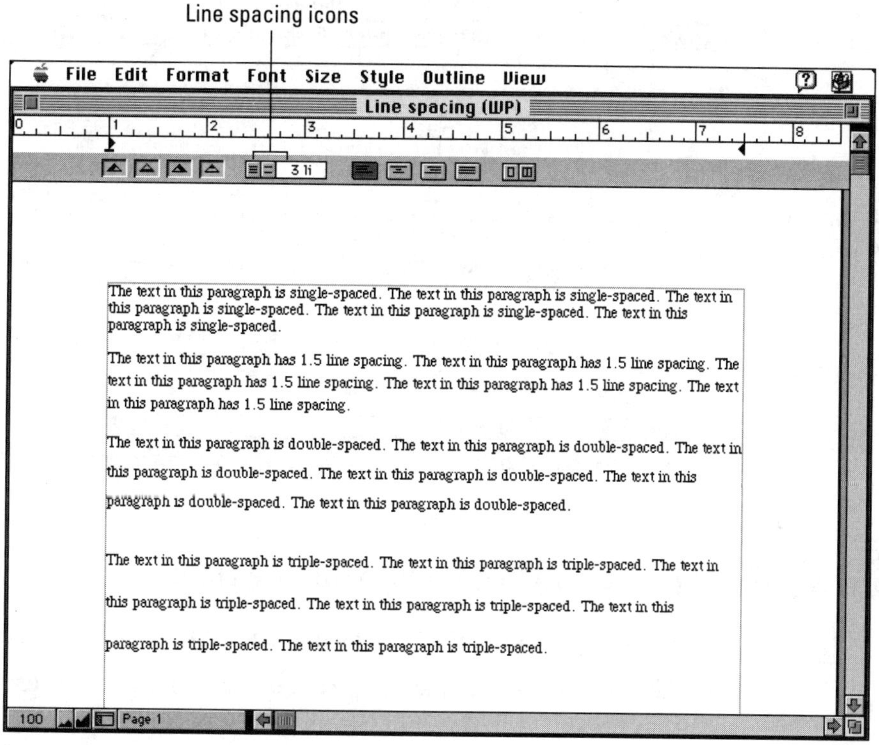

Figure 4-11: Some line spacing examples.

Paragraph alignment

Most documents are *left-aligned* (flush with the left margin and with a ragged right margin). For those times when you need it, however, ClarisWorks also provides options for center-aligned, right-aligned, and justified paragraphs. (See Figure 4-12 for examples of the four types of paragraph alignment.) Making a document title *center-aligned* centers it instantly on the page; you don't need to mess with tabs or the spacebar. You can use the *right-align* setting to position the current date in a letter.

Justified paragraphs are flush with both the left and right margins. ClarisWorks automatically adds extra space between words to make each line edge square with the margins. Magazine articles often have justified paragraphs.

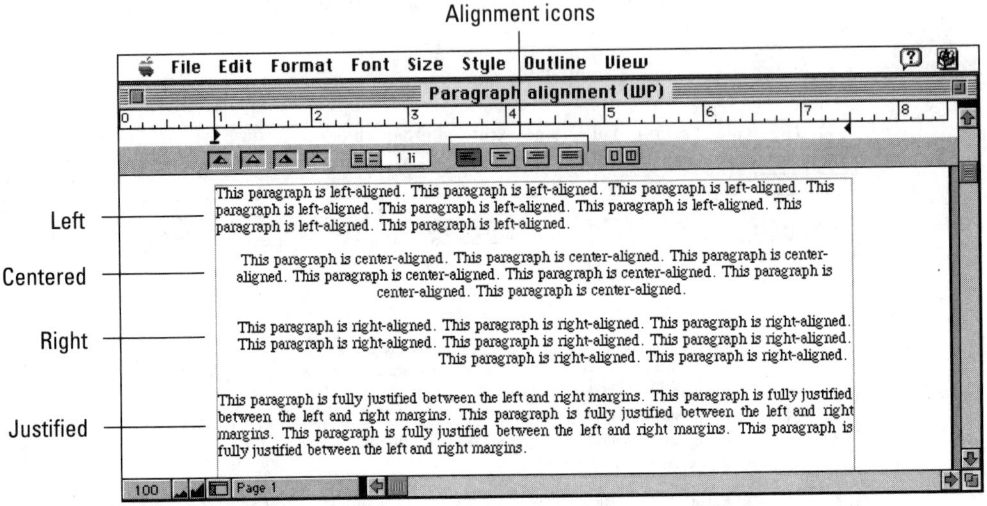

Figure 4-12: The four paragraph alignment icons on the ruler and examples of aligned paragraphs.

To set paragraph alignment with the ruler:

1. **Select the paragraph(s) for which you want to set an alignment.**
2. **Click one of the four paragraph alignment icons in the ruler bar.** The chosen alignment is applied to the selected paragraphs.

Using the Copy Ruler and Apply Ruler commands

After you set formatting options for a paragraph, you may want to repeat these settings in other paragraphs in the document. For example, when writing a report, you may create a paragraph format for bulleted lists and another for long quotations. Manually recreating these formats each time you have a new quote or bulleted list is time-consuming and prone to error. To make transferring paragraph formats to new paragraphs easy, ClarisWorks provides the Copy Ruler and Apply Ruler commands.

To apply ruler settings to a new paragraph:

1. **Move the cursor into the paragraph whose ruler settings you want to copy.**
2. **Choose Copy Ruler from the Format menu (or press Shift-⌘-C).**
3. **Move the cursor into the target paragraph.** (Alternatively, you can use normal text selection techniques to select several contiguous paragraphs to which you want to apply the ruler settings.)
4. **Choose Apply Ruler from the Format menu (or press Shift-⌘-V).** The ruler settings from the copied ruler are applied to the selected paragraph(s).

Note that the Apply Ruler command remains active (not gray) even after you paste the settings. You can continue to paste these settings into additional paragraphs until you quit ClarisWorks or issue a new Copy Ruler command.

TIP

You also can use the Copy Ruler and Apply Ruler commands to transfer ruler settings between documents.

Using the Paragraph command

Although the ruler is handy, you also can use the Paragraph command from the Format menu to set paragraph indents and line spacing directly. The advantages of using the Paragraph command over using the ruler include:

- The Paragraph command gives you improved precision in establishing settings.
- You can set several options in a single dialog box (as opposed to setting them one by one with the ruler).
- You can use any measurement system that you like — not just the one shown on the current ruler — for line and paragraph spacing.
- The only way to set spacing above and below a paragraph is with the Paragraph command.

To choose paragraph settings with the Paragraph command:

1. **Select the paragraph(s) for which you want to alter paragraph format settings.** The Paragraph dialog box appears, as shown in Figure 4-13.
2. **Type numbers in the text-edit boxes for the settings that you want to change.**

   The Left indent, First line, and Right indent settings are preceded by their corresponding ruler symbols. The only settings that do not appear on the ruler are Space before and Space after. Fill in their boxes in the Paragraph dialog box to set the amount of blank space that you want to appear before or after the selected paragraph(s).

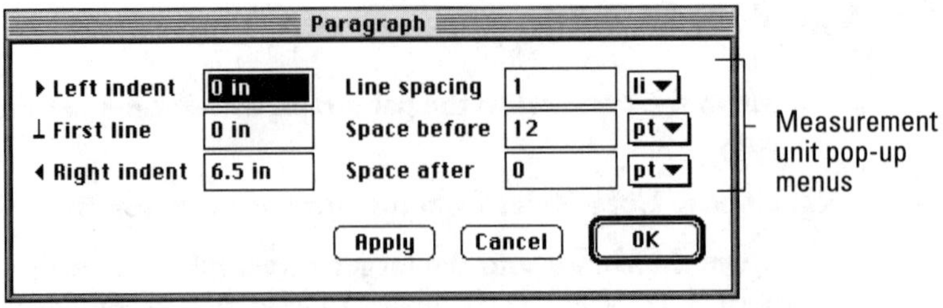

Figure 4-13: The Paragraph dialog box.

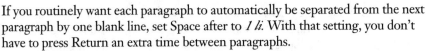

You can change the measurement system for Line spacing, Space before, or Space after by selecting an option from their respective pop-up menus. As Figure 4-13 shows, you can mix and match measurement systems as needed.

3. **Click Apply to apply the new settings to the selected paragraph(s).** (Apply is a tentative option. You can remove changes made with Apply by clicking Cancel; the formatting instantly reverts to the original settings.)

4. **Click OK to accept the paragraph formatting changes or Cancel to revert to the original settings.**

TIP

If you routinely want each paragraph to automatically be separated from the next paragraph by one blank line, set Space after to *1 li*. With that setting, you don't have to press Return an extra time between paragraphs.

Formatting documents

Document formatting controls the overall appearance of each page — both on-screen and when printed. Document options include:

- Margins (top, bottom, left, and right)
- On-screen page display (single page, two pages side by side, or multiple pages)
- Margin and page guides (shown or invisible)
- Title page (treat the first page of a word processing document differently from other pages)
- Starting page number

You set document formatting options by choosing Document from the Format menu. The Document dialog box appears, as shown in Figure 4-14. Set options and click OK to put your choices into effect (or click Cancel if you change your mind).

Note that several of the options (Margins, Title page, and Starting page #) affect the way the document will be printed. The remaining options (Display, Show margins, and Show page guides) affect only the document's on-screen appearance.

All settings in the Document dialog box affect only the active document. When you create a new document, you have to reset the Document options again. Although you can't save these options as preferences, you can avoid the boring, repetitious task of resetting the options. Create a new blank document, set the document preferences, and then save the file as an options stationery document, as described in Topic 11. New word processing files then use your preferred Document settings automatically. (You can use this same tactic for any ClarisWorks environment.)

```
┌──────────────────────────────────────────────┐
│ Document                                       │
│ ┌─Margins──────┐  ┌─Display─────────────────┐ │
│ │ Top    [1 in]│  │ ◉▤  ○▤▤  ○[3]           │ │
│ │ Bottom  1 in │  │ ⊠ Show margins           │ │
│ │ Left    1 in │  │ ⊠ Show page guides       │ │
│ │ Right   1 in │  │ ☐ Title page             │ │
│ └──────────────┘  └─────────────────────────┘ │
│                                                │
│ Starting page # [1]    ( Cancel )  ( OK )      │
└──────────────────────────────────────────────┘
```

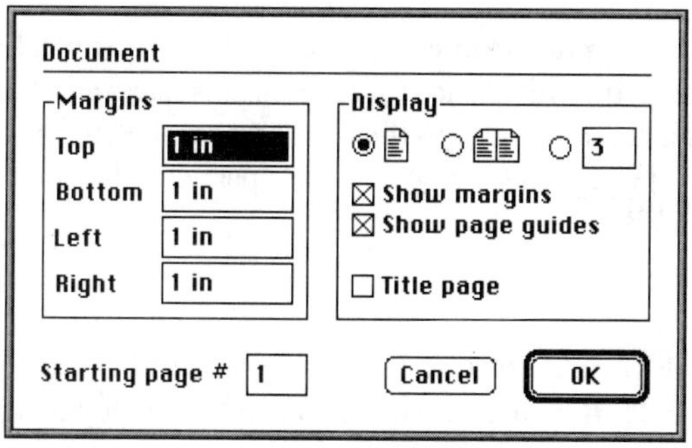

Figure 4-14: The Document dialog box.

Setting margins

To change a margin setting (in the Document dialog box), simply type a number in the appropriate margin text-edit box. If you do not specify a measurement unit, ClarisWorks uses the unit that was originally in the box. You can specify a different unit of measurement by following the number with one of these abbreviations:

Abbreviation	Unit of Measurement
in	inches
p	picas
pt	points
mm	millimeters
cm	centimeters

If you find yourself constantly typing a new unit of measurement in the Document dialog box, you can change it to the one you use most often by choosing Rulers from the Format menu and changing the unit of measurement in the Rulers dialog box.

Number of pages displayed

By default, ClarisWorks is set to display every document one page at a time. If you would rather see pages side by side, click the middle Display icon (showing a pair of pages) in the Document dialog box. This type of display is particularly useful if you have a monitor that has room to show two complete pages at the same time. You can display several pages side by side (three or more) by clicking the third radio button and then entering a number in the text-edit box.

Show margins and Show page guides

The setting for Show margins determines whether the body text will be separated from the edges of the page by white space (Show margins checked). Checking Show page guides causes the work area of the document to be outlined by a faint gray border. Having the page guides visible is useful particularly when you are working with headers and footers.

Title page

When you click the Title page check box, ClarisWorks treats the first page of the document as a title page. It eliminates the headers and footers for that page only. Normally, you do not want to display page numbers and date stamps (common items for a header or footer) on the first page. If the document doesn't have a header or footer, this setting is irrelevant.

Starting page

This option works in conjunction with the automatic page-numbering feature (Insert Page # on the Edit menu). You can specify a starting page number by entering a number in the text-edit box. Although you usually want page numbering to begin with 1 (the default), this feature can be useful. For example, if you are writing a book and you know that Chapter 1 ended on page 27, you can specify a starting page number of 28 for Chapter 2.

Working with columns

One last document formatting option that you should be familiar with is working with multiple columns. Newsletters and church bulletins are often formatted with two or more columns. Although this option affects the entire document, ClarisWorks does not provide access to column-related settings in the Document command. Instead, the Format menu contains the Columns command. And although this option has nothing to do with paragraph formatting, you can use a pair of icons in the ruler bar to quickly change the number of columns for a word processing document (see Figure 4-15).

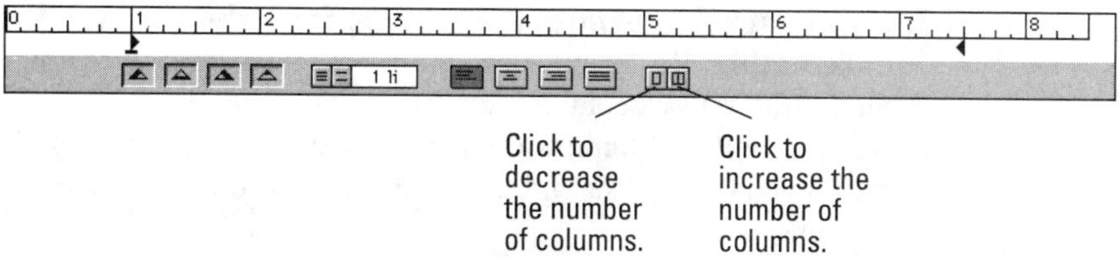

Click to decrease the number of columns.
Click to increase the number of columns.

Figure 4-15: Setting the number of columns by using the ruler.

To set the number of columns by using the ruler:

1. Click the left icon to decrease the number of columns by one.

— or —

1. Click the right icon to increase the number of columns by one.

If you want greater control over the way columns are set up (setting the space between for equal-width columns or setting specific column widths for variable-width columns), you can use the Columns command to set columns up the way you want them.

To set multiple columns with the Columns command:

1. **Choose Columns from the Format menu.** The Columns dialog box appears, as shown in Figure 4-16.

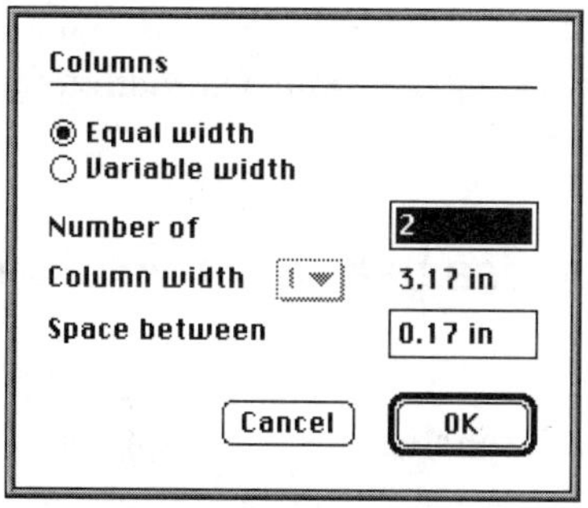

Figure 4-16: The Columns dialog box.

2. **Type a number in the Number of text-edit box.**
3. **If you want all columns to be the same width, click the Equal width radio button.** The default Column width and Space between for that number of columns are shown on the right side of the dialog box. You can change the column widths by increasing or decreasing the number shown for Space between.

— or —

3. **If you want the columns to be different widths, click the Variable width radio button.** By default, all columns are set to the same width. To change the widths, select a column number (the columns are numbered from left to right) from the Column width pop-up menu and enter the column's width in the text-edit box to the right. Repeat this procedure for the remaining columns.

4. **Click OK to use the new column settings or Cancel to revert to the settings that were in effect before you chose the Columns command.** If you click OK, ClarisWorks automatically reformats the text to flow into the columns that you created.

NOTE

If you enter an individual column width that is wider than the allowable maximum, the program displays an error message, and you have to enter a new width number. Similarly, if the combined width of all columns and *gutters* (the space between columns) exceeds the page width, you are asked to enter new numbers.

In addition to using the Columns command, you can manually adjust column widths and the space between columns.

Step-by-Steps

To manually adjust the widths of two adjacent columns:

1. **Move the pointer into the space between a pair of columns and press Option.** The pointer changes to a pair of arrows surrounding a hollow box.

2. **Press the mouse button and move the pointer to the left or right.** As you move the pointer, the widths of the two columns change.

3. **Release the mouse button to set the new column widths.**

   Throughout this procedure, the space between the columns does not change. You are merely allocating the combined widths of the two columns in a new way.

Step-by-Steps

To manually change the space between two adjacent columns:

1. **Move the pointer so that it touches the inside edge of a column and press Option.** The pointer changes to a pair of arrows surrounding two vertical lines.

2. **Press the mouse button and move the pointer to the left or right.** As you move the pointer, the width of the column that the pointer is touching and the space between the columns change.

3. **Release the mouse button to set the new column width and between-column spacing.**

Page and column breaks

One feature that ClarisWorks lacks is the capability to handle widows and orphans in text. A *widow* is a lone line of text that ends a page or column (the first or only line of a paragraph or a heading). An *orphan* is a lone line of text that starts a page or column (usually the final line of a paragraph). Widows and orphans make a document look unprofessional. To eliminate them, manually insert breaks as needed as the final editing step before you print the document.

Step-by-Steps

To insert a break:

1. **Position the text insertion point at the beginning of the line that you want to be the first line in the new page or column.**
2. **Choose Insert Break from the Format menu (or press Enter).** The break appears, and the line of text is moved to the next page or column.

If Show Invisibles is on (that is, you have checked it in Preferences in the Edit menu, have clicked its button on the Shortcuts palette, or have pressed ⌘-; [semicolon]), a break is indicated by a tiny downward-pointing arrow. You can remove a break by selecting the arrow and pressing Delete or Backspace. If the arrow is invisible, move the text insertion point to the start of the text line that begins the break and then press Delete or Backspace.

VERSION 2.1

ClarisWorks 2.1 and 3.0 support auto-hyphenation, a formatting feature that can greatly enhance the appearance of your word processing documents, databases, and text frames. You now can ask ClarisWorks to hyphenate a word at the end of a line; in previous versions, ClarisWorks forced the whole word to wrap to the next line, leaving some really ragged right margins. This feature is fully described in the section "Using Hyphenation," later in this Topic.

Advanced Editing Tools and Techniques

The features and editing techniques that are discussed in this section are nonessentials. Although you can initially do without them, you'll eventually find many of the following tools and techniques helpful in creating clean, attractive, readable documents:

- Finding and replacing text
- Headers and footers
- Footnotes
- Inserting automatic date, time, and page numbers
- Using the spelling checker and thesaurus
- Using the hyphenation feature (ClarisWorks 2.1 and 3.0)
- Working with outlines

Finding and replacing text

Like other word processing programs, the ClarisWorks word processing environment includes a set of Find/Change commands. Use Find to locate a particular section of a document quickly (where you talked about social security, for example). Use the Change option to replace one text string with another. Find/Change enables you to do the following:

- ◆ Find the next occurrence of a particular text string
- ◆ Find subsequent occurrences of the same text string
- ◆ Replace a found text string with another text string (or simultaneously replace all instances of one text string with another text string)
- ◆ Find a text string that matches the currently selected text in the document

To find a text string:

1. **Choose Find/Change from the Find/Change submenu of the Edit menu (see Figure 4-17) or press ⌘-F.** The Find/Change dialog box that is shown in Figure 4-18 appears.

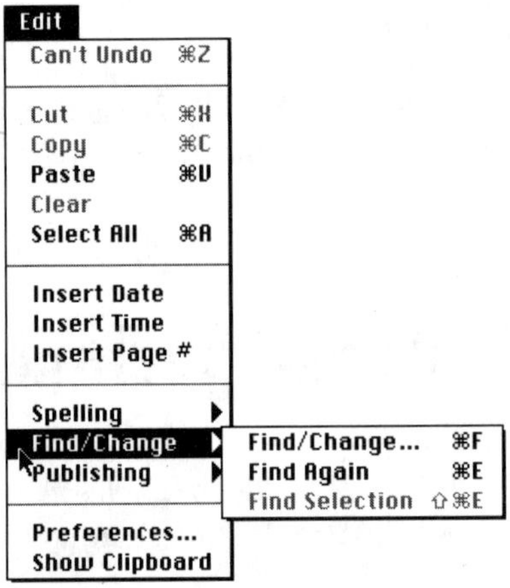

Figure 4-17: The Find/Change menu commands.

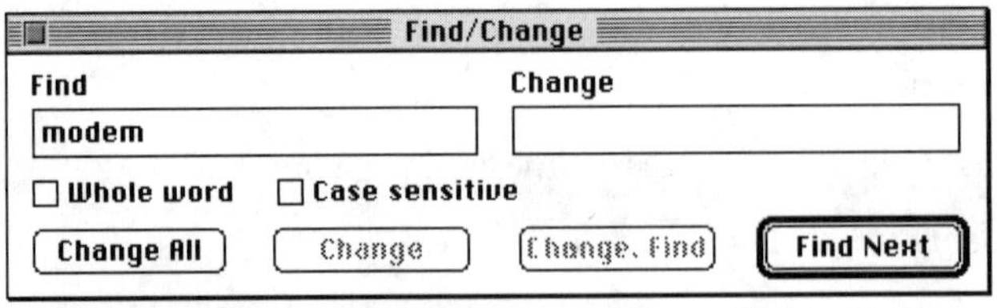

Figure 4-18: The Find/Change dialog box.

2. **In the Find box, type the text string for which you want to search. Leave the Change box empty.**

   - *Whole word.* If you want to search only for complete words, click the Whole word check box. With Whole word checked, searching for *and* will find only *and*— not *sand* or *bandage.*
   - *Case sensitive.* Click the Case sensitive check box if you want the case of each character in the Find string to be considered during the search. If you check this box, a search for *Young* would not match *young* or *YOUNG.* If you're unsure of the capitalization, you probably don't want to check Case sensitive.

3. **Click the Find Next button (or press Return or Enter).** The search commences downward from the current cursor position. Eventually, the search wraps around so that the whole document is searched — including text that is above the initial cursor position.

   If the document contains a match, ClarisWorks highlights the first instance of the text string. If no match is found, a message to that effect appears.

4. **If the found text is not the instance for which you are searching, click Find Next again.** Each click restarts the search from the point of the last found text.

5. **When you are finished, click the close box of the Find/Change dialog box.**

You can repeat a search by choosing Find Again (⌘-E) from the Find/Change pop-up menu of the Edit menu.

TIP

Sometimes the Find/Change dialog box obscures the found text. If necessary, you can move the dialog box to a different location by clicking its title bar, holding down the mouse button, and dragging.

You probably noticed that the Find/Change dialog box also contains a Change text-edit box. Text that you type into this box can replace instances of found text — either one match at a time (with your approval) or globally (automatically replacing all instances without one-by-one approval).

Step-by-Steps

To find and change text:

1. **Choose Find/Change from the Find/Change pop-up menu of the Edit menu (or press ⌘-F).** The Find/Change dialog box shown in Figure 4-19 appears.

2. **In the Find text-edit box, enter the text string to be located, and in the Change text-edit box, enter a replacement text string.**

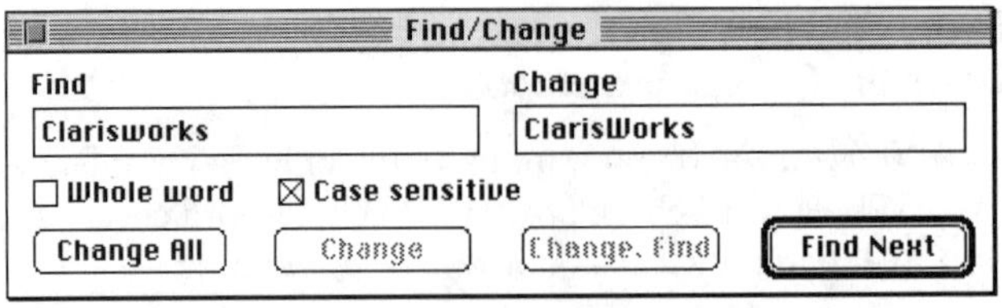

Figure 4-19: You can use the Find/Change dialog box to change text.

3. Set the Whole word and Case sensitive settings as desired.

- If you check Whole word, ClarisWorks will find only whole words that match the Find string.
- If you check Case sensitive, the program will locate only strings that have capitalization that is identical to the Find string's capitalization.

4. To change all instances of the Find string to the Change string without prompting from the program, click Change All. A dialog box appears stating: *The Change All feature is not undoable.* Click OK to continue or click Cancel.

— or —

4. To examine each Find result before you change the text, click Find Next. As text is found, click Change, Find or click Change.

- Click Change, Find to change the current instance and then find the next one.
- Click Change to change only the current instance. Normally, you choose this option when you are ready to end the search (after you have found the single or final instance of text that you want to change). If you decide that you want to continue the search after you click Change, click Find Next.

5. When you are finished, click the close box of the Find/Change dialog box.

NOTE

On subsequent finds, the Find/Change dialog box will contain the last set of Find/Change text strings and settings that you used.

Finding special characters

Occasionally, you may want to locate — and optionally replace — some special ClarisWorks characters, such as tabs, paragraph returns (end-of-paragraph markers), or automatic dates. To search for these characters or use them as replacements, you have to enter the symbols that are shown in Table 4-3 in the Find or Change text-edit boxes of the Find/Change dialog box.

Table 4-3
Find/Change Symbols for Special Characters

Search Character	***Characters to Type***
Space	Spacebar
Nonbreaking space	Option-spacebar
Tab	\t or ⌘-Tab
Paragraph return	\p or ⌘-Return
Line break (soft return)	\n
Column or page break	\c or ⌘-Enter
Automatic date	\d
Automatic time	\h
Automatic page number	\#
Backslash	\\

VERSION 2.1

ClarisWorks 2.1 and 3.0 enable you to search for two additional special characters: discretionary hyphens (⌘-Hyphen) and line breaks (⌘-Shift-Return).

NOTE

Because the backslash character (\) is used to define many of the special characters in the table, you have to type a pair of backslashes (\\) to find a backslash that appears in the text.

Because the need to search for such characters or use them as replacements may not be readily apparent, consider the following examples:

- *Removing double spaces.* Modern typesetting conventions frown on double spaces between sentences. (I know that you were taught to use double spaces when you learned to type, but double spaces are not necessary when you are using a computer, a word processing program, and a high-quality printer.) Use the Find/Change command to substitute a single space for every instance of a double space. In addition to eliminating double spaces between sentences, you'll also get rid of extra spaces between words.

- *Substituting spaces for tabs in communications text.* Some information services and bulletin boards aren't prepared to handle tabs in text files. Search for the tab character (\t) and replace each instance with a fixed number of spaces (5 or 8, for example).

- *Eliminating extra space at the end of paragraphs.* Some of my publishers are sticklers for this one. Search for Space Return (\p) and replace with Return (\p).

- *Replacing automatic date and time with a fixed date or time.* Automatic dates or times (which you enter by choosing Insert Date or Insert Time from the Edit menu) change every time you open the document. These features are useful if you want to show a new date or time whenever you print the document. If you want to show when a document was written, on the other hand, you can replace the automatic date and time with a fixed date and time.

If you can't remember what to type when you want to execute a search for a particular character, or if Table 4-3 isn't handy, you can copy and paste the special characters.

To copy and paste special characters:

1. **Find an example of the character in your document.**

   To more easily find characters that are normally hidden, click the Show/Hide Invisibles button in the Shortcuts palette (Figure 4-20), choose Preferences from the Edit menu and check the Show Invisibles check box in the Text options, or press ⌘-; (semicolon).

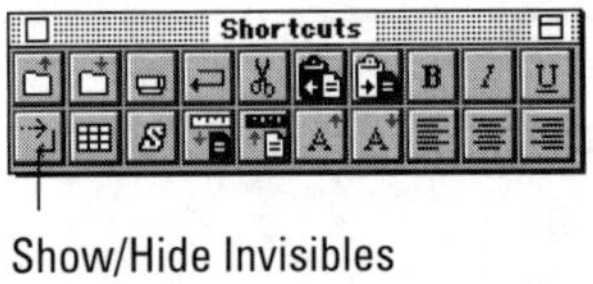

Figure 4-20: The Show/Hide Invisibles button in the word processing Shortcuts palette.

2. **Select the character and choose the Copy command from the Edit menu (or press ⌘-C).**
3. **Choose Find/Change from the Find/Change pop-up menu of the Edit menu (or press ⌘-F).** The Find/Change dialog box appears.
4. **Press ⌘-V to paste the character into the Find or the Change text-edit box, as appropriate.** When pasting into a Find/Change text-edit box, ClarisWorks automatically substitutes the correct symbols for the special character.

Headers and footers

Headers and footers can contain any text or graphics that you want to separate from the body of the document. Because they are printed on the top or bottom of every page, headers and footers are very useful for displaying document-identification text, such as the date, your name, a document filename, and the report title. You also can place logos and other graphics in headers and footers to save yourself the trouble of repeatedly pasting images onto every page of the document. Figure 4-21 shows a header and a footer for a typical letterhead.

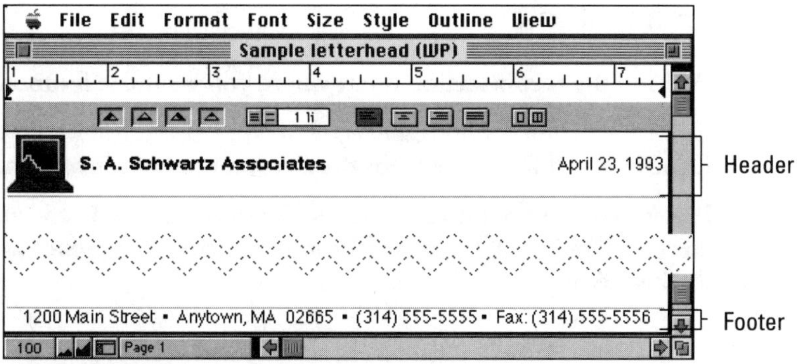

Figure 4-21: Examples of a header and a footer.

Page numbers also are routinely placed in the header or footer. For page numbers that automatically change to reflect pagination changes in the text, see "Inserting automatic date, time, and page numbers," later in this Topic.

To create a header or footer:

1. **Choose Insert Header or Insert Footer from the Format menu.** A header or footer appears in the document, and the cursor moves to the header or footer area.
2. **Type the header or footer text.**

As with other text, you can format header and footer text with different fonts, styles, sizes, and paragraph/ruler bar settings.

NOTE

Unless you check the Show page guides check box in the Document dialog box (choose the Document command in the Format menu), you may have a difficult time distinguishing the header and footer text from the body text. After you check Show page guides, faint gray outlines surround the header and footer.

If you later decide that you do not need a header or a footer, you can eliminate them by choosing Remove Header or Remove Footer from the Format menu. Doing so instantly deletes all text and graphics in the header or footer.

Footnotes

If you're working on a school report or a professional paper, you'll appreciate the ClarisWorks features for managing footnotes.

To insert a footnote:

1. **Position the text insertion point where you want the footnote to appear.**
2. **Choose Insert Footnote from the Format menu (or press Shift-⌘-F).**
3. **If you have checked Auto Number Footnotes in the Preferences dialog box (see Topic 12), the next footnote number in sequence appears at the insertion point.**

— or —

3. **If you have not checked Auto Number Footnotes, the Mark with dialog box appears, as shown in Figure 4-22. Type the character that you want to use to mark the footnote and click Enter.** The character appears at the insertion point.

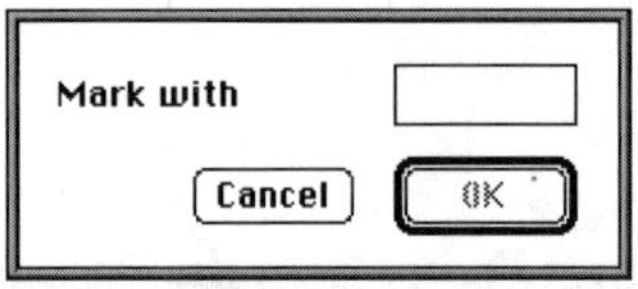

Figure 4-22: Use the Mark with dialog box to specify a special footnote character.

After the program inserts the footnote mark, the cursor automatically moves into the footnote area at the bottom of the current page.

4. **Type the footnote and then click in the body text area to continue working with the document (see Figure 4-23).**

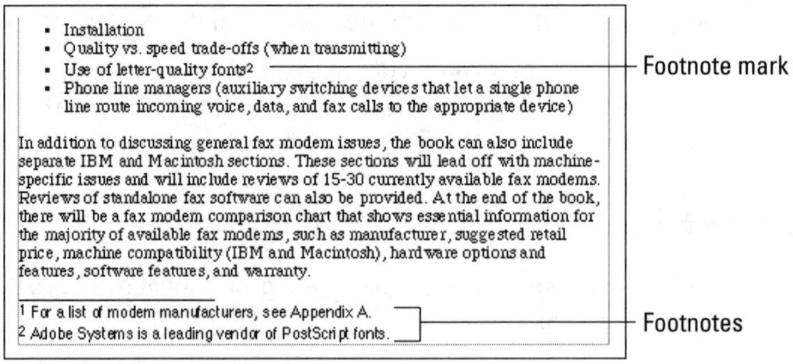

Figure 4-23: Footnote examples.

If you decide to create your own footnote symbols instead of using a simple numbered sequence, you may want to consider the characters that appear in the following table. The symbols may not appear correctly in the Mark with dialog box. (Some symbols appear as an empty square.)

Character	***Keystroke***
*	Shift-8
†	Option-T
‡	Shift-Option-7

To remove a footnote, select the footnote number or symbol where it appears in the body text and then press Delete or Backspace. The program automatically removes the footnote reference at the bottom of the page and renumbers the remaining footnotes if necessary.

NEW FEATURE 3.0

For more information about creating footnotes, see "Using the Word Processing Assistants," later in this topic.

Inserting automatic date, time, and page numbers

Whether for record keeping purposes or for use in headers and footers, you may want to date stamp or time stamp certain documents to show when you printed or last updated them.

Step-by-Steps

To insert today's date or the current time in a document:

1. **Position the insertion point.**
2. **Choose Insert Date or Insert Time from the Edit menu.** The program inserts the current date or time for you.

NOTE

The program takes the date and time from the Mac's clock. If the wrong date or time appears, you can correct it by entering the proper information in the General control panel. (In System 7.1 or higher, you also can set this information in the Date & Time control panel.)

Dates or times that you insert in this manner automatically change to reflect the new date and time whenever you reopen the document. To permanently affix today's date or time in the document (so that it will not update), press Option as you choose Insert Date or Insert Time.

You use a similar command, Insert Page #, to add page numbers to documents. If you add them inside a header or footer, page numbering automatically carries through to every page in the document.

To add page numbers to a document:

1. **If the document doesn't already contain a header or footer, choose Insert Header or Insert Footer from the Format menu.**

— or —

1. **If the document already contains a header or footer, skip to Step 2.**
2. **Position the text insertion point in the header or footer.**
3. **Choose Insert Page # from the Edit menu.** The program inserts the current page number and numbers all pages in the document, beginning with the number *1.*

Page numbers inserted in this manner automatically change as the document changes (that is, as you add, delete, or move pages). If you want the page numbers to be fixed, press Option when you choose Insert Page #.

If you want to set a different starting page number for the document, use the Document command in the Format menu. See "Formatting Documents" earlier in this Topic for details.

TIP

Depending on the type of document that you're working on, plain numbers may look odd. You may prefer to precede each number with the word *Page,* for example. To accomplish this task, simply type **Page**, followed by a space, in front of where you have inserted or are about to insert the automatic page number. Remember that you can add formatting to header and footer text, just as you can to body text. For example, you can right- or center-justify page numbers by clicking the appropriate alignment icon below the ruler or by using tabs. (If the ruler isn't visible, choose Show Ruler from the View menu.) You also can apply different fonts or styles. After you apply formatting to an element of a header or footer, the program automatically repeats the formatting on every page.

Using the spelling checker

The inclusion of a built-in spelling checker was one of the first great advancements in word processing. A spelling checker examines every word in a document and compares it to words found in its massive dictionary. The program then flags unknown words for you and gives you an opportunity to replace them — either by typing the replacement word or by selecting a word from a list of the most likely replacements. Now with only a modicum of effort, every man, woman, and child can produce correctly spelled letters, memos, and reports.

Checking spelling

ClarisWorks provides two spell-checking options: Check the entire document or check only the currently selected text. Spell checking is available for all ClarisWorks documents that contain text except communications documents. To spell check a communications document, select the text, copy it to the Clipboard (⌘-C), paste it into a word processing document (⌘-V), and then invoke the spell checker.

You initiate spell checking by choosing the Spelling pop-up menu from the Edit menu and choosing either Check Document (⌘-=) or Check Selection (Shift-⌘-Y).

Note: The Spelling submenu is named Writing Tools in ClarisWorks 2.1 and higher.

- ◆ *Check Document.* Select this option if you want to spell check the entire document. Note that when you choose the command, the position of the cursor doesn't matter. Spell checking automatically starts at the beginning of the document.
- ◆ *Check Selection.* Select this option if you want to spell check only the currently selected text. Check Selection is particularly useful for checking a single word or just a paragraph or two that you've recently edited.

Regardless of which command you use to start the spelling checker, ClarisWorks displays the spelling checker's progress in the Spelling dialog box, which is shown in Figure 4-24.

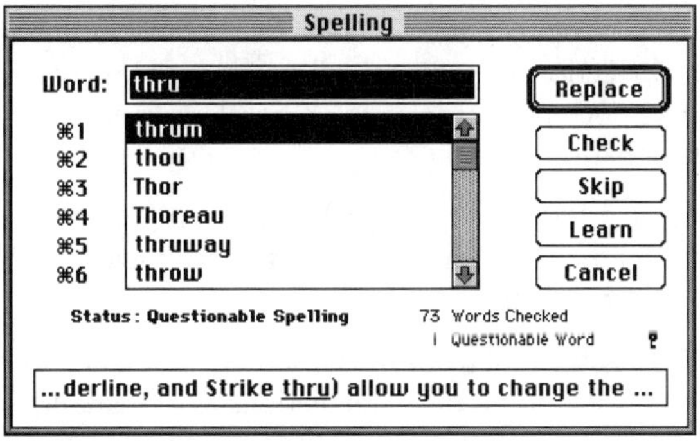

Figure 4-24: The Spelling dialog box.

As the spelling checker examines the document or selection, it stops at each word that it doesn't find in its dictionary or in the user dictionary that you created. For each word, you can do the following:

- ◆ Correct the spelling by typing the proper word in the Word text-edit box. (After making a manual correction in this fashion, you can click the Check button to make sure that the replacement you've typed is spelled correctly.)
- ◆ Select a replacement by double-clicking any of the words in the list box, by typing its Command-key equivalent (⌘-1, ⌘-2, and so on), or by highlighting the replacement and clicking the Replace button.
- ◆ Accept the spelling as correct by clicking Skip.
- ◆ Accept the spelling as correct and add it to the current user dictionary by clicking Learn.
- ◆ End the spell check by clicking Cancel.

You can click the tiny flag icon in the bottom-right corner of the dialog box to toggle between showing the potentially misspelled word in context and showing only the word itself.

As the spell check continues, ClarisWorks reports the number of words checked, as well as the number of questionable words found. After you deal with each questionable word, the spell checker progresses through the document (or selection) until it finds the next questionable word or the spell check is completed. When all words have been checked, you end the spell check by clicking Done.

TIP: As good as spell checking is, it is not a substitute for proofreading. The ClarisWorks spelling checker does not flag duplicate words (*and and*), grammatical errors, or mistakes in punctuation. Nor will it find words that are spelled correctly but happen to be the wrong words (She *one* the game *to* many times.) If you need help in these areas, consider one of the many Macintosh grammar-checking programs, such as RightWriter (Que Software), Grammatik Mac (Reference Software International), or Sensible Grammar (Sensible Software).

Working with dictionaries

At any given moment, you can have two dictionaries available for use with the spelling checker: a main dictionary and a user dictionary (one that you've created). When you spell check a document or selection, ClarisWorks automatically uses the words in both dictionaries.

ClarisWorks comes with a 100,000-word dictionary that it normally uses as the main dictionary, although replacement dictionaries (most notably for foreign languages) are available from Claris.

The *user dictionary* contains a list of words that you want ClarisWorks to accept as correct, even though they are not in the main dictionary. Whenever you click Learn in the Spelling dialog box, the spell checker adds the current word that it is questioning to the active user dictionary. You also can add words manually by using the User Dictionary command from the Spelling (or Writing Tools) pop-up menu of the Edit menu. Examples of words that you may want to add to a user dictionary include proper nouns (such as product names and company names), technical terms, and current slang.

If you like, you can create several user dictionaries, each for a particular type of writing. If you write about computers, for example, you may want to create a separate user dictionary for computer terminology. If you write many interoffice memos, you may want a second user dictionary that includes the spelling of every employee's name.

TIP: When you create multiple user dictionaries, keep in mind that only one of them can be active during a spell check. If the writing in any document covers several dictionary content areas, you have to check the document in multiple passes — one for each different user dictionary that you need. If this situation occurs frequently, you may be better off creating a single, composite user dictionary.

Creating and opening dictionaries

The following instructions tell you how to open a different main, user, or thesaurus dictionary; create a new user dictionary; or not use any dictionary at all.

To install a dictionary:

1. **Choose Install Dictionaries from the Spelling pop-up menu of the Edit menu.** The Select Dictionary dialog box appears, as shown in Figure 4-25.

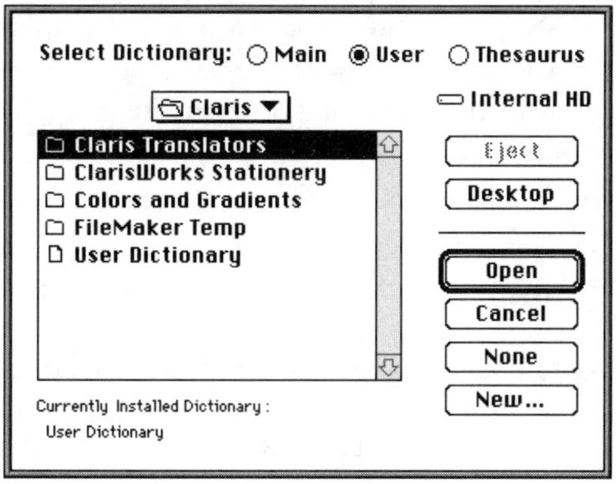

Figure 4-25: The Select Dictionary dialog box.

Note: The Spelling submenu is named Writing Tools in ClarisWorks 2.1 and higher.

2. **Click one of the three radio buttons at the top of the dialog box (Main, User, or Thesaurus) to indicate the type of dictionary that you want to install.** The name of the currently installed dictionary of the selected type appears at the bottom of the dialog box.
3. **Select the new dictionary file and click Open.** The program now uses the new dictionary.

To create a new user dictionary:

1. **Choose Install Dictionaries from the Spelling (or Writing Tools) pop-up menu of the Edit menu.** The Select Dictionary dialog box appears, as shown in Figure 4-25.
2. **Click the User radio button at the top of the dialog box.** The name of the currently installed user dictionary appears at the bottom of the dialog box.
3. **Click New.** A Save dialog box appears.
4. **Type a filename for the new user dictionary.**
5. **Click Save to create the new dictionary file or Cancel if you change your mind.**

After you create a new user dictionary in this fashion, ClarisWorks automatically puts it into use.

NOTE

If you decide that you don't want to use a main dictionary, user dictionary, or thesaurus, select the appropriate radio button in the Select Dictionary dialog box and then click None.

Dictionary editing

As mentioned earlier, you can add words to the active user dictionary during a spell check by clicking the Learn button. Periodically, however, you may want to examine the complete contents of the user dictionary to see whether it contains incorrect entries or words that you no longer need. While editing the dictionary, you also can add words. If you have a list of terms that you've already added to a user dictionary in another word processing program, for example, you can add them to the ClarisWorks dictionary without waiting for them to be flagged as questionable during a spelling check.

Step-by-Steps

To edit a user dictionary:

1. **If the appropriate user dictionary is not already open, choose the Install Dictionaries command from the Spelling (or Writing Tools) pop-up menu of the Edit menu. Select the user dictionary and click Open.**

2. **Choose User Dictionary from the Spelling (or Writing Tools) pop-up menu of the Edit menu.** The User Dictionary dialog box shown in Figure 4-26 appears. The name of the current user dictionary is at the top of the dialog box.

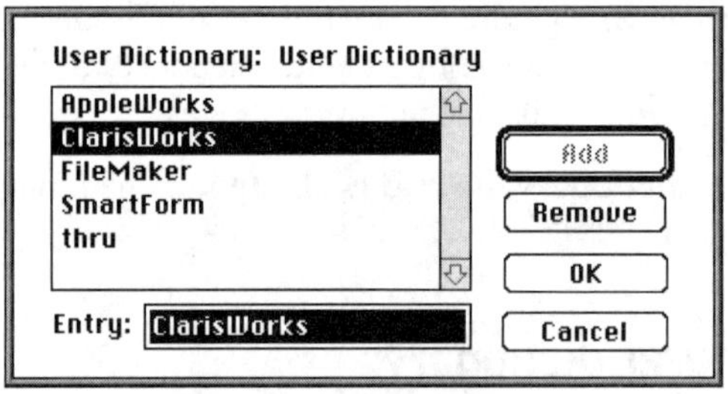

Figure 4-26: The User Dictionary dialog box.

3. **Add or remove words from the dictionary.** To remove a word, select the word and click Remove. To add a new word, type the word in the Entry text-edit box and click Add.

4. **After you finish editing the dictionary, click OK to save the changes and return to the document (or click Cancel to ignore the changes).**

Using the thesaurus

When you're stuck for a word or find yourself using the same pet phrase over and over again, you can turn to the Word Finder thesaurus for assistance. Because it contains more than 220,000 *synonyms* (words with the same or similar meanings), chances are excellent that you can find a new word or phrase that will add a little variety and style to your writing.

To find a synonym:

1. **Invoke the thesaurus by choosing Thesaurus from the Spelling pop-up menu of the Edit menu (or by pressing Shift-⌘-Z).** (***Note:*** The Spelling submenu is named Writing Tools in ClarisWorks 2.1 and higher.)

   If you invoke the thesaurus while a word in the document is selected, the program displays synonyms for that word in the Word Finder Thesaurus dialog box (see Figure 4-27).

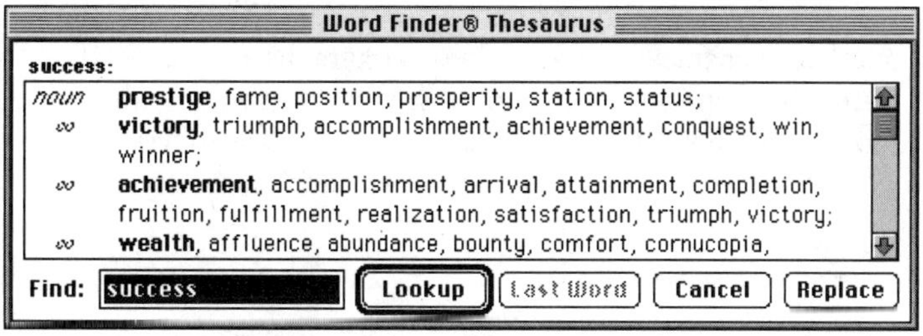

Figure 4-27: The World Finder Thesaurus dialog box.

   If no word is selected, the dialog box is initially blank. In the Find box, type the word for which you want to display synonyms.

2. **Scroll through the list of synonyms. If you find a word that you want to use, select it and click Replace (or double-click the word).** The dialog box closes, and the word is inserted at the current cursor position in the document. (If a word was highlighted in the document, that word is replaced by the synonym.)

   To exit from the thesaurus without replacing a word, click Cancel.

— or —

2. **If you don't see a synonym that you like, but you do see a word with a similar meaning, select it with the cursor.** To see synonyms for that word, click Lookup. When you find a word that you like, click Replace.

   To exit from the thesaurus without replacing a word, click Cancel.

If you want to re-examine other words that you've looked at during this thesaurus session, click Last Word. The Last Words dialog box appears, as shown in Figure 4-28. To recheck one of these words, select it and click Lookup. To return to the thesaurus as you left it, click Cancel.

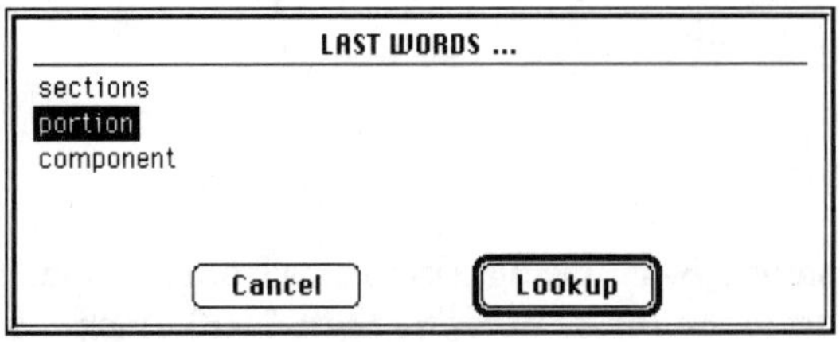

Figure 4-28: The Last Words dialog box.

Performing a Word Count

By selecting Word Count from the Writing Tools submenu of the Edit menu, you can get statistical information about the text in a document, including the number of characters, words, lines, paragraphs, and pages. The Word Count feature is an enormous help to those who must write within a specific length limit (no more than 400 words, for example), as well as to writers who are paid by the word. Figure 4-29 shows a typical word count summary.

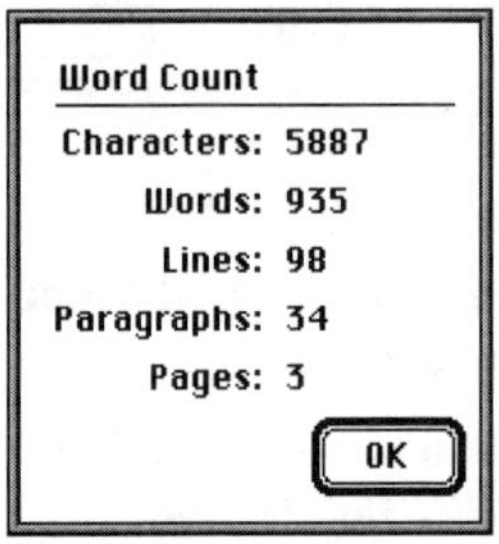

Figure 4-29: The Word Count dialog box.

Note that the Word Count feature is somewhat limited in that it can only summarize an *entire* document. However, with a little effort, you can create a ClarisWorks macro that can perform a *selective* word count (that is, count the words on a single page or in selected paragraphs).

To create a macro that performs a selective word count:

1. **Open any existing ClarisWorks word processing document and highlight the text that you want to count.**
2. **Choose Record Macro from the Shortcuts submenu of the File menu (or press Shift-⌘-J).**

3. **In the Record Macro dialog box (see Figure 4-30), enter a name for the macro and choose the Option-Command-Key combination or Function key that you will use to execute the macro.** Because the macro must play only in the word processing environment or frames, be sure that Play In Word Processing is checked.

```
┌──────────────────────────────────────────────────────────┐
│ Record Macro                                             │
│                                                          │
│                               ┌─Play In──────────────┐   │
│  Name  │Selective Word Count│  │ ☐ All Environments   │   │
│                               │ ☒ Word Processing    │   │
│  ○ Function Key      ┌───┐    │ ☐ Drawing            │   │
│  ● Option + ⌘ + Key  │ w │    │ ☐ Painting           │   │
│                      └───┘    │ ☐ Database           │   │
│  ┌─Options─────────────┐      │ ☐ Spreadsheet        │   │
│  │ ☐ Play Pauses       │      │ ☐ Communications     │   │
│  │ ☐ Document Specific │      └──────────────────────┘   │
│  │ ☐ Has Shortcut      │  ┌──┐                           │
│  │ ☐ In Shortcuts Palette│ │  │  ┌────────┐ ┌────────┐   │
│  └─────────────────────┘  └──┘  │ Cancel │ │ Record │   │
│                                 └────────┘ └────────┘   │
└──────────────────────────────────────────────────────────┘
```

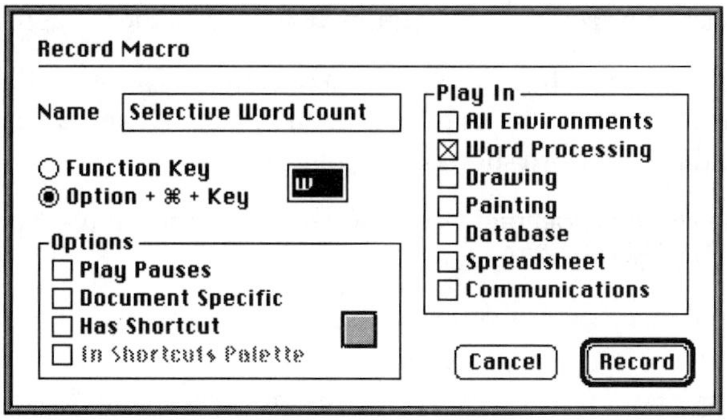

Figure 4-30: The Record Macro dialog box.

4. **Click Record to begin recording the macro. Then perform the following macro steps:**

 ◆ Press ⌘-C (or choose Copy from the Edit menu) to copy the selected text to the Macintosh Clipboard.

 ◆ Press ⌘-N (or choose New from the File menu).

 ◆ In the New Document dialog box that appears, indicate that you want to create a new word processing document.

 ◆ Press ⌘-V (or choose Paste from the Edit menu) to paste the copied text into the blank document.

 ◆ Choose Word Count from the Writing Tools submenu of the Edit menu. The word count for the document appears.

5. **Press Shift-⌘-J to stop recording.** (You cannot choose this command from the ClarisWorks menus, as you would normally do, because all menus are disabled when a dialog box is on-screen.) ◖◗

Whenever you want to run this macro to do a selective word count, all you have to do is select the text that you want to count and then press the Option-Command-Key combination or Function key to run the macro. After viewing the word count, you can close the temporary word processing document without saving it.

Topic 4

Using Hyphenation

A lack of hyphenation features formerly separated the ClarisWorks word processing environment from the "big-time" stand-alone word processing programs such as Microsoft Word, MacWrite Pro, WriteNow, Nisus, and WordPerfect. From the release of Version 2.1, however, ClarisWorks no longer has had this shortcoming. As a result, you can easily improve your documents' appearance.

After you turn on auto-hyphenation for a document, ClarisWorks automatically examines line ends, consults its hyphenation dictionary, and then determines whether (and how) a word should be hyphenated.

Auto-hyphenation is document-specific; that is, turning auto-hyphenation on affects only the current document.

If you want to make auto-hyphenation the default for all *new* word processing documents, you can do so by creating an options stationery document, as I explain in the "Using Stationery to Set New Environment Defaults" section in Topic 11.

To turn on auto-hyphenation for a document:

1. **Select Auto Hyphenate from the Writing Tools submenu of the Edit menu.**

   When auto-hyphenation is on, a check mark appears in front of the command. Selecting the command again turns auto-hyphenation off and removes the check mark.

— or —

1. **Click the Auto Hyphenate button in the Shortcuts palette, as shown in Figure 4-31.**

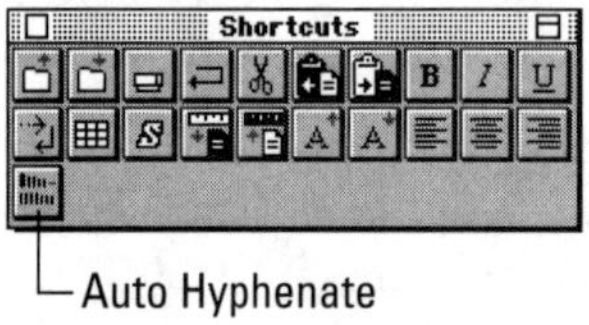

Figure 4-31: The Auto Hyphenate button.

Updating to ClarisWorks 2.1 does not change the contents of the original ClarisWorks 2 Shortcuts palettes. You must add the Auto Hyphenate button manually, as I explain in the "Adding buttons" section in Topic 13.

Hyphenating a word your way

Auto-hyphenation is an "all-or-nothing" affair — that is, it affects the entire document or text frame.

If you decide that you don't want a particular word hyphenated, or if ClarisWorks fails to hyphenate a word because the word isn't in the hyphenation dictionary, you can edit the hyphenation dictionary.

NOTE

Only words of five or more letters can be added to the hyphenation dictionary.

Step-by-Steps

To edit a hyphenation dictionary:

1. **Select Install Dictionaries from the Writing Tools submenu of the Edit menu.** The Select Dictionary dialog box appears, as shown in Figure 4-32.

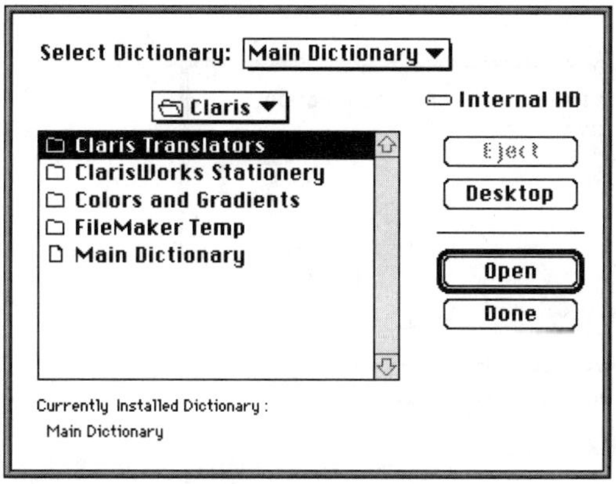

Figure 4-32: The Select Dictionary dialog box.

By default, the dialog box opens to the Claris folder, where the various Claris dictionaries are stored. Notice that the dialog box also defaults to the spelling checker dictionary (Main Dictionary).

2. **Click the Select Dictionary pop-up menu and choose Hyphenation Dictionary (see Figure 4-33).**
3. **If you're using the standard dictionary supplied with ClarisWorks 2.1 or 3.0, choose US English – Hyphenation.** If you want to use another hyphenation dictionary, select it instead.
4. **Click Edit.** The Hyphenation File dialog box appears (see Figure 4-34).

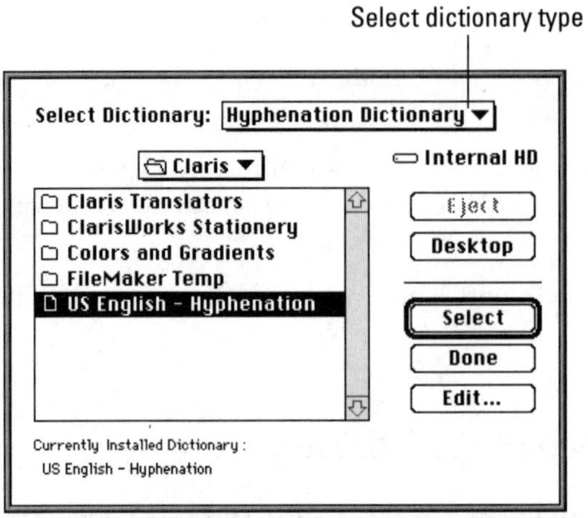

Figure 4-33: After you choose the Hyphenation Dictionary option from the Select Dictionary pop-menu, all hyphenation dictionaries appear in the file list.

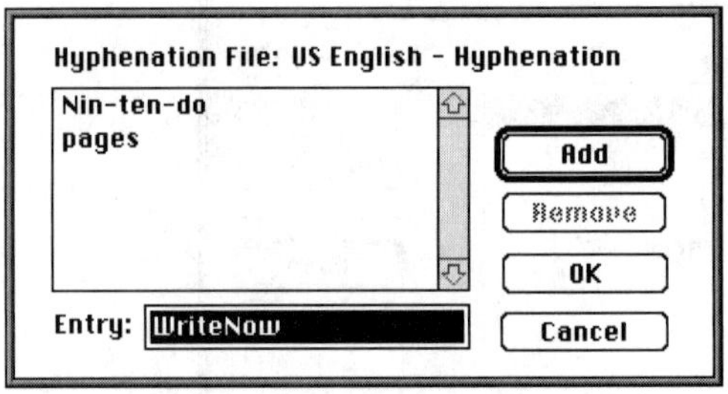

Figure 4-34: The Hyphenation File dialog box.

5. Edit the hyphenation dictionary as desired.

- To specify a word's hyphenation, type the word in the Entry text-edit box, inserting the appropriate hyphens. Then click Add.
- To prevent ClarisWorks from hyphenating a particular word, type the word in the Entry text-edit box without hyphens. Then click Add.
- To change the hyphenation for a word previously added to the hyphenation file, select the word and make the appropriate changes in the Entry text-edit box. Then click Replace.
- To remove a word previously added to the hyphenation file, select it and then click Remove.

6. Click OK to accept the changes to the hyphenation file and return to your document; otherwise, click Cancel.

Even when auto-hyphenation is on, you can adjust a word's hyphenation by manually inserting regular and discretionary hyphens:

- To insert a regular hyphen, set the text insertion point where you want the hyphen to appear and then press the hyphen key (-).

  A hyphen inserted in this manner will always show up at that spot in the word — regardless of where the word appears in the line. As a result, if the text is later edited or reformatted, regular hyphens can show up in the middle of a line. (If you ever see a word like *Mac-intosh* in the middle of a line, someone probably inserted a regular hyphen, edited the surrounding text, and then forgot to proofread the text.) You should insert a regular hyphen only if a word is always hyphenated, as in *data-entry screen.*

- To insert a *discretionary hyphen*, set the text insertion point where you want the hyphen to appear and then press ⌘-hyphen. Unlike regular hyphens, discretionary hyphens appear only when the word must be split between two lines; otherwise, they're invisible.

Installing a different hyphenation dictionary

ClarisWorks 2.1 and 3.0 are shipped with a U.S. English hyphenation dictionary. If you work in other languages, you can purchase other language-specific hyphenation dictionaries from Claris.

To install a hyphenation dictionary:

1. **Select Install Dictionaries from the Writing Tools submenu of the Edit menu.** The Select Dictionary dialog box appears, as shown in Figure 4-32.

   By default, the dialog box opens to the Claris folder, where the various Claris dictionaries are stored. Notice that the dialog box also defaults to the spelling checker dictionary (Main Dictionary).

2. **Click the Select Dictionary pop-up menu and choose Hyphenation Dictionary (see Figure 4-33).**

3. **Select the hyphenation dictionary you want to use and click Select.**

   ClarisWorks installs the new hyphenation dictionary, which will be used for all documents until you choose a different dictionary.

Although most users associate hyphenation with word processing, don't forget that you can use it with database fields and text frames that are inserted into other types of documents, such as spreadsheets.

Adding Graphics to Word Processing Documents

The selective use of graphics can go a long way toward enhancing a report or memo. For example, you can add a company logo to letterhead or presentation pages and embed spreadsheet charts in reports. ClarisWorks enables you to add graphics to a word processing document in two ways: as free-floating *objects* or as *in-line graphics* (part of the text).

Because objects are not part of the text, you can move them wherever you like. And because they are objects, you can add a new background color, gradient, or bounding lines to them. Finally, you also can specify a text wrap for each object (none, regular, or irregular).

Figure 4-35 shows examples of both types of graphics.

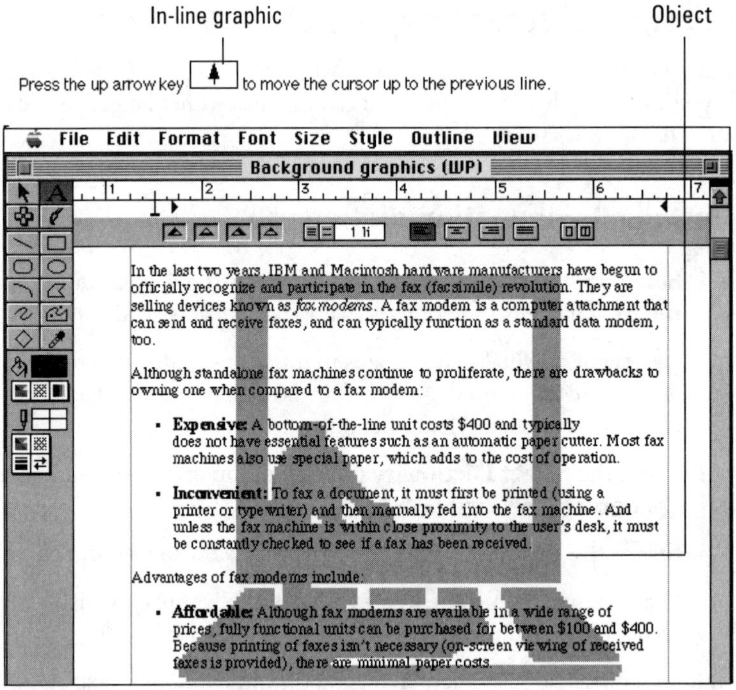

Figure 4-35: An in-line graphic that is embedded in a paragraph and an object that is moved to the back so that the text shows through.

In-line graphics

An in-line graphic in a word processing document is treated exactly the same as text. For all practical purposes, you can think of it as just another character. As a result, if the graphic is in a paragraph by itself, you can use paragraph formatting commands to align the graphic to a tab stop or to center it.

TIP

In most cases, the best place for an in-line graphic is in a paragraph by itself — without any surrounding text. An in-line graphic that is in the same line with text can cause serious problems with spacing between lines because line height is defined by the largest font or image in the line.

Step-by-Steps

To add an in-line graphic:

1. **Set the text insertion point where you want to insert the graphic.**
2. **To insert a graphic from a file, choose Insert from the File menu and choose a graphic file to insert.** The entire contents of the file appear at the text insertion point.

— or —

2. **To insert a graphic from the Clipboard, select and copy the graphic (⌘-C) from a ClarisWorks paint or draw document, from within another graphics program, or from the Scrapbook.** Within the ClarisWorks document, choose Paste from the Edit menu (or press ⌘-V). The graphic appears at the text insertion point.
3. ***Optional:* Resize the graphic as needed by dragging its handle to a new position.** You can maintain the original proportions by pressing Shift as you drag.

Graphic objects

You can paste graphic objects into a document, insert them with the Insert command, create them from scratch with the drawing tools, or embed them in a Paint frame.

Step-by-Steps

To paste a picture from the Clipboard as a free-floating graphic:

1. **In the graphics program, select the picture.**
2. **Choose Copy from the Edit menu (or press ⌘-C).** A copy of the image is temporarily stored in the Clipboard.

3. **Select the Pointer tool from the ClarisWorks Tool panel.** (If the Tool panel isn't visible, click the Show/Hide Tools control at the bottom of the document window.) Selecting the Pointer tool takes you out of word processing mode and instructs ClarisWorks to treat the graphic to be pasted as a free-floating object rather than as an in-line graphic.

4. **Choose Paste from the Edit menu (or press ⌘-V).** The picture is pasted as an object that you can resize or move.

   After the picture is pasted, it should be surrounded by handles. If the handles are not visible, the picture has probably been pasted as an in-line graphic (part of the text), rather than as an object. Press Delete once to remove the picture and go back to Step 3.

Step-by-Steps

To paste a picture from the Scrapbook as a free-floating graphic:

1. **Choose the Scrapbook desk accessory from the Apple menu.** The Scrapbook opens.

2. **Select the desired picture from the Scrapbook by clicking the right or left arrows until it appears.**

3. **To copy the picture to the Clipboard, choose Copy from the Edit menu (or press ⌘-C).**

4. **Close the Scrapbook by clicking its close box (in the upper-left corner of the Scrapbook window).**

5. **Select the Pointer tool from the ClarisWorks Tool panel.** (If the Tool panel isn't visible, click the Show/Hide Tools control at the bottom of the document window.) Selecting the Pointer tool takes you out of word processing mode and instructs ClarisWorks to treat the graphic to be pasted as a free-floating object rather than as an in-line graphic.

6. **Choose Paste from the Edit menu (or press ⌘-V).** The picture is pasted as an object that you can resize or move.

   After the picture is pasted, it should be surrounded by handles. If the handles are not visible, the picture has probably been pasted as an in-line graphic (part of the text), rather than as an object. Press Delete once to remove the picture and go back to Step 5.)

To insert a picture from a file as a free-floating graphic:

1. **Select the Pointer tool from the ClarisWorks Tool panel.** (If the Tool panel isn't visible, click the Show/Hide Tools control at the bottom of the document window.) Selecting the Pointer tool takes you out of word processing mode and instructs ClarisWorks to treat the graphic to be pasted as a free-floating object rather than as an in-line graphic.
2. **Choose Insert from the File menu.** A standard file dialog box appears.
3. **Navigate to the proper drive and folder and choose the graphics file that you want to insert in the document.** As an example, you can insert the file Pegasus Logo found in the Tutorial Folder.
4. **Click Insert.** The program inserts the file in the document as an object that you can resize or move about.

   After the picture is pasted, it should be surrounded by handles. If the handles are not visible, the picture has probably been pasted as an in-line graphic (part of the text), rather than as an object. Press Delete once to remove the picture and go back to Step 1.)

Topic 7 discusses the details of creating a picture from scratch. In general, you select drawing tools from the Tool panel and drag to create different shapes.

Wrapping text around graphic objects

If you are going to surround the graphic object with text, you can specify how (or whether) the text should wrap around the object (see Figure 4-36). You can choose from the following text wrap options:

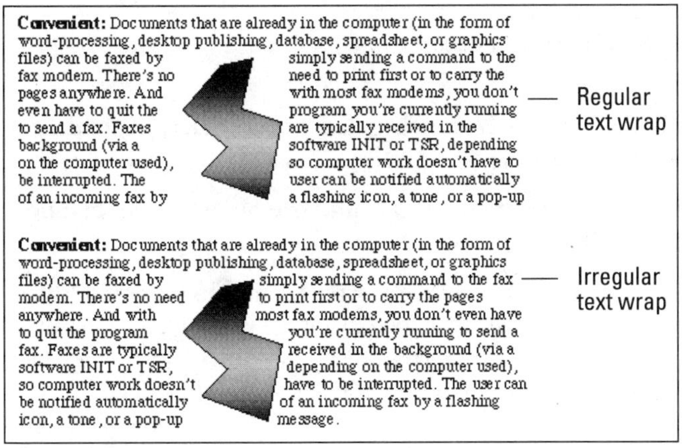

Convenient: Documents that are already in the computer (in the form of word-processing, desktop publishing, database, spreadsheet, or graphics files) can be faxed by simply sending a command to the fax modem. There's no need to print first or to carry the pages anywhere. And with most fax modems, you don't even have to quit the program you're currently running to send a fax. Faxes are typically received in the background (via a software INIT or TSR, depending on the computer used), so computer work doesn't have to be interrupted. The user can be notified automatically of an incoming fax by a flashing icon, a tone, or a pop-up
Regular text wrap
Convenient: Documents that are already in the computer (in the form of word-processing, desktop publishing, database, spreadsheet, or graphics files) can be faxed by simply sending a command to the fax modem. There's no need to print first or to carry the pages anywhere. And with most fax modems, you don't even have to quit the program you're currently running to send a fax. Faxes are typically received in the background (via a software INIT or TSR, depending on the computer used), so computer work doesn't have to be interrupted. The user can be notified automatically of an incoming fax by a flashing icon, a tone, or a pop-up message.
Irregular text wrap

Figure 4-36: Text wraps.

- *None.* The object obscures any text that it is covering. If you move the object to the back, the text appears over the object.
- *Regular.* An invisible rectangle is drawn around the object, and text wraps to the edges of the rectangle.
- *Irregular.* Text wraps as closely as possible to the original edges of the object.

NOTE: You also can specify a text wrap for other objects, such as spreadsheet frames.

To set text wrap around an object:

1. **Add a picture to the document by using one of the methods described previously.**
2. **Select the picture.** (After you select it, handles appear around the object.)
3. **Choose Text Wrap in the Options menu.** The Text Wrap dialog box appears, as shown in Figure 4-37.

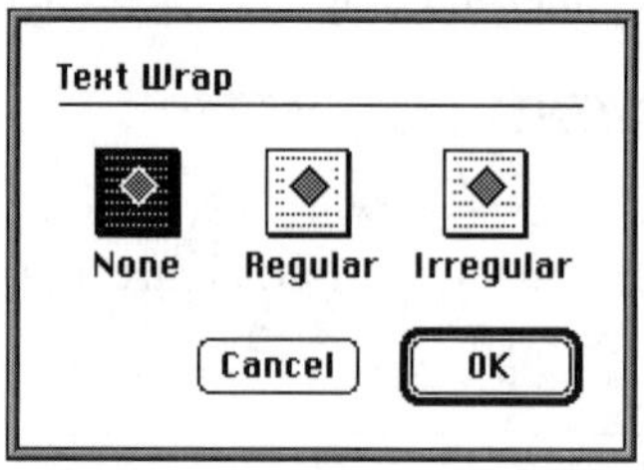

Figure 4-37: The Text Wrap dialog box.

4. **Click the icon for None, Regular, or Irregular, depending on the type of wrap you want.**
5. **Click OK. The text wraps around the object in the manner that you specified.**

TIP: When you try to do an irregular text wrap around an imported PICT image, the object often appears to be embedded in a large rectangle — regardless of the actual shape of the image. To get the wrap that you want, ungroup the object in ClarisWorks and then group it again. The text should wrap correctly. (Note, however, that if the object really is surrounded by a rectangular box — as in the case of most scans, for example — this procedure may change nothing.)

Layering pictures and text

Of course, text does not have to be wrapped around graphic objects. With Text Wrap set to None, you can make a graphic float on top of the document, hiding the text beneath it. By using the Move to Back command, you can make text print over a graphic. This technique is useful for creating a letterhead watermark or a rubber stamp effect (as shown earlier in Figure 4-35).

Step-by-Steps

To place a picture behind or in front of text:

1. **Select the picture.**
2. **If a text wrap has been set for the object, choose Text Wrap in the Options menu. Click the None icon and then click OK.**
3. **From the Arrange menu, choose Move Forward, Move to Front, Move Backward, or Move to Back.**

TIP

Objects that have been moved to the back of a word processing document usually work best if they are light colored. Dark objects, or ones with dark areas, may make reading the overlaying text difficult or impossible.

Using the Word Processing Assistants

NEW FEATURE 3.0

When you're working in a word processing document or frame, you can select ClarisWorks Assistants from the Help submenu of the Apple menu or from the Balloon Help menu (System 7 only) to get help with three common tasks: addressing envelopes, inserting and formatting footnotes, and creating tables. After you select ClarisWorks Assistants, the Select Assistant dialog box appears (as shown in Figure 4-38). The following instructions explain how to use these three Assistants.

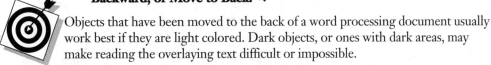

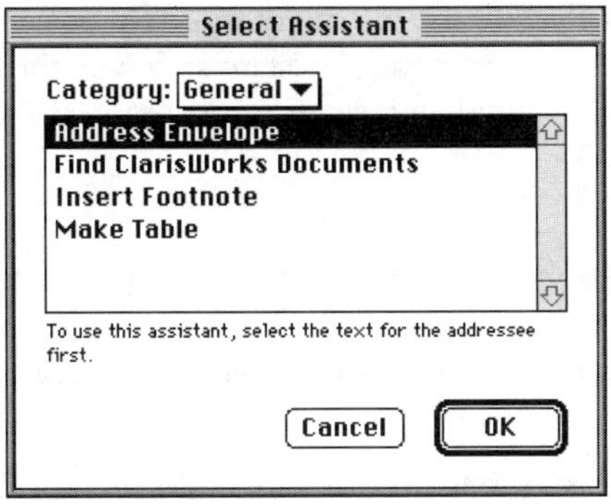

Figure 4-38: ClarisWorks 3.0 Assistants that are available from word processing documents.

Using the Address Envelope Assistant

The Address Envelope Assistant makes it easy to address and print envelopes from within ClarisWorks. Just follow these simple steps.

Step-by-Steps

To address an envelope:

1. **In the document, select (highlight) the address of the individual or company to whom you want to send the letter.** Note that you do not need to Copy (⌘-C) or Cut (⌘-X) the address to the Clipboard.
2. **Choose ClarisWorks Assistants from the Help submenu of the Apple menu or from the Balloon Help menu (System 7 only).**
3. **In the Select Assistant dialog box, choose Address Envelope and click OK.** The Assistant incorporates the highlighted address into a new word processing document that is formatted as a business envelope. If your envelopes do not include a preprinted return address, you can add one to the document now.

When you are ready to print, choose Page Setup from the File menu and make sure that the options are correct (on most laser printers, envelopes are printed in landscape mode, for example), insert an envelope into the printer or its tray, and choose Print from the File menu (or press ⌘-P). If you have any problems, refer to the printer manual for the special options and procedures necessary when printing envelopes.

Using the Insert Footnote Assistant

Whether you are writing a college term paper, a professional article, or any other work in which you include footnotes, the Insert Footnote Assistant is an enormous help in ensuring that each footnote contains the necessary information. Unlike footnotes that you create manually with the Insert Footnote command in the Format menu (Shift-⌘-F), the Insert Footnote Assistant steps you through the process of composing the footnote and then formats it according to the footnote style you've chosen.

Step-by-Steps

To add a footnote with the Insert Footnote Assistant:

1. **In a word processing document, position the cursor where you want to insert the footnote.**
2. **Choose ClarisWorks Assistants from the Help submenu of the Apple menu or from the Balloon Help menu (System 7 only).**
3. **In the Select Assistant dialog box, choose Insert Footnote and click OK.**

4. In the dialog box that appears (see Figure 4-39), click the radio button for the type of source you want to cite and then click Next.

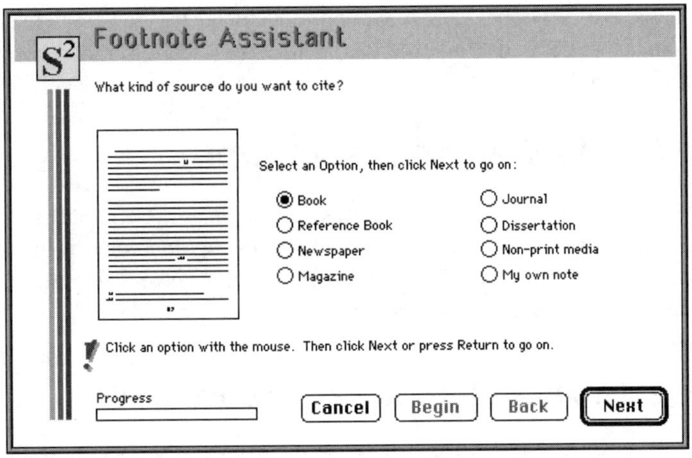

Figure 4-39: Indicate the type of source that you are citing.

5. Another dialog box appears (such as the one in Figure 4-40), where you fill in the appropriate information for your source. The information requested varies with different types of sources. Any field that you leave blank is marked with a placeholder in the footnote, and you can fill it in later.

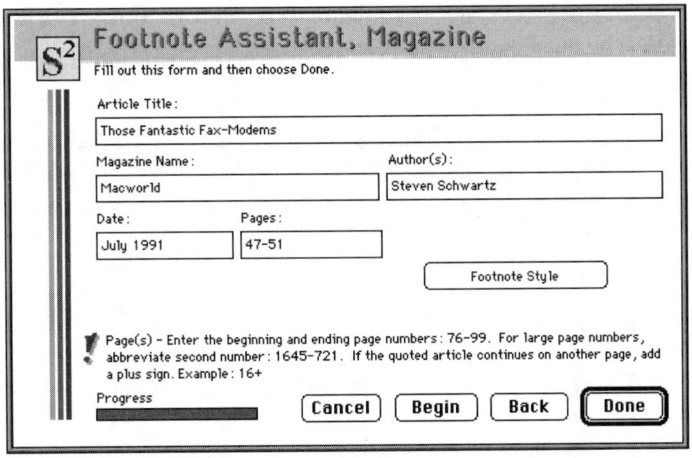

Figure 4-40: Fill in the blanks with your source information.

6. *Optional:* Some source forms include a Footnote Style button that you click to select one of two footnote styles: Modern Language Association or *Chicago Manual of Style*. Click OK to continue. If you do not make a style selection, the Modern Language Association style is used.

7. Click Done. The new footnote number is inserted at the cursor position, and the footnote is added to the bottom of the current page.

NOTE: Although the Insert Footnote Assistant is listed in the Select Assistant dialog box when you invoke this dialog box from a word processing *frame*, you can use this Assistant only in a word processing *document*. Also, this Assistant creates footnotes at the bottom of pages. If what you really need are *endnotes* (a list of references that appears at the end of a paper or article, as in a bibliography), copy and paste the individual footnotes.

Using the Make Table Assistant

As shown in the “Down to Business” example at the end of this Topic, one of the easiest ways to add a table to a word processing document is by inserting a spreadsheet frame. By taking advantage of the Make Table Assistant, you can reduce much of the work required in designing a table.

Step-by-Steps

To add a spreadsheet table to a document:

1. **Decide whether you want the table to be a free-floating graphic or an in-line graphic (as described in “Adding Graphics to Word Processing Documents,” earlier in this Topic). To create a floating table, click the pointer tool in the Tool panel. For an in-line graphic, position the text insertion point at the spot in the document where you want the table.**
2. **Choose ClarisWorks Assistants from the Help submenu of the Apple menu or from the Balloon Help menu (System 7 only).**
3. **In the Select Assistant dialog box, choose Make Table and click OK.** The opening dialog box appears (see Figure 4-41).

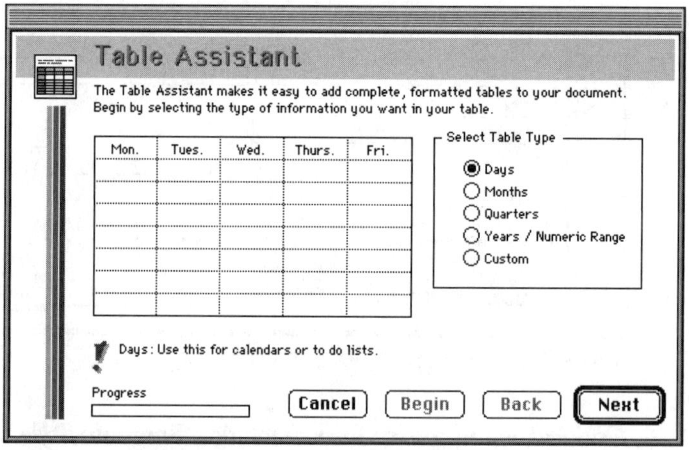

Figure 4-41: Set column headings in this dialog box.

4. **Click a radio button to indicate the type of column headings that the table will have and then click Next.** If none of the numeric options is appropriate, click Custom.

5. **Set additional headings and options by choosing from the pull-down menus in the dialog box that appears next (see Figure 4-42) and then click Next to continue.** The options and their wording vary depending on the table headings chosen in the preceding dialog box. Check the Show Extra Category check box to add a blank column at the start of the table. (If you want to enter row headings manually as well, the extra blank column creates the necessary space for you to do so.)

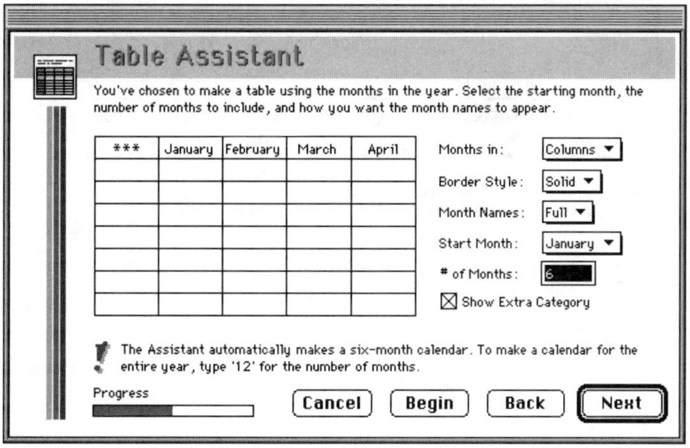

Figure 4-42: Set additional table options.

6. **In the final dialog box, set data-formatting options. Click Create to generate the table.** The table appears in the current document.

If the table is too large to fit within the margins of the document, you may have to adjust either the size or number of rows or columns.

NOTE

In addition to helping you create tables in the word processing environment, the Make Table Assistant also can be invoked from a draw document or from Layout mode in a database.

Down to Business: An Improved Fax Form Template

Although ClarisWorks includes a fax form template (called Fax Cover Sheet), I think you can do better. First, I believe in conservation. Attaching a cover sheet to a fax automatically adds an extra page to the transmission. This extra page wastes the recipient's fax paper and adds unnecessarily to the transmission time (which increases your phone bill). Second, although Fax Cover Sheet does provide an area for a message, the space is too tiny for most faxes.

My approach to faxing is to combine the cover page information with the body of the fax. As you can see in the finished fax form that is shown in Figure 4-43, the essential To:/From: information takes up less than a third of the page, leaving plenty of room for the fax message. If you use this form, rather than a cover page, you can probably reduce most transmissions to a single page.

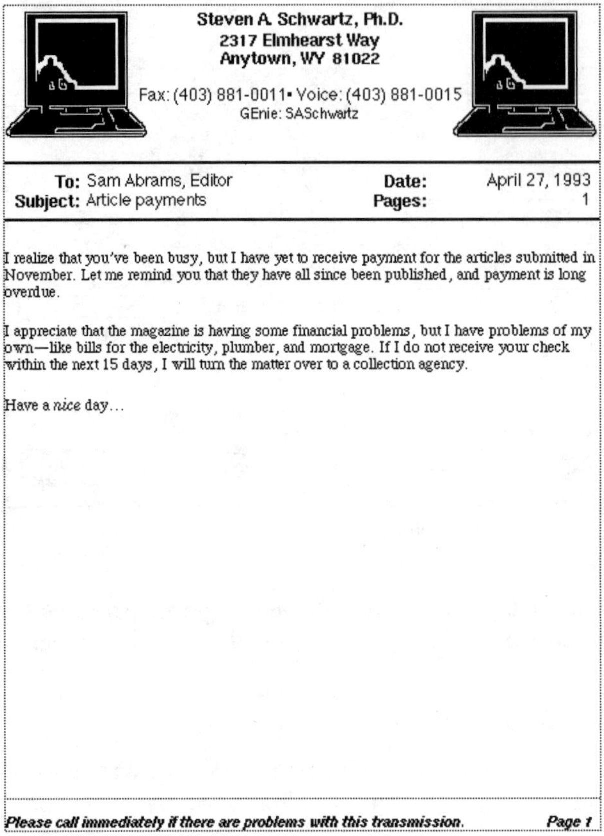

Steven A. Schwartz, Ph.D.
2317 Elmhearst Way
Anytown, WY 81022

Fax: (403) 881-0011• Voice: (403) 881-0015
GEnie: SASchwartz

To:	Sam Abrams, Editor	**Date:**	April 27, 1993
Subject:	Article payments	**Pages:**	1

I realize that you've been busy, but I have yet to receive payment for the articles submitted in November. Let me remind you that they have all since been published, and payment is long overdue.

I appreciate that the magazine is having some financial problems, but I have problems of my own—like bills for the electricity, plumber, and mortgage. If I do not receive your check within the next 15 days, I will turn the matter over to a collection agency.

Have a *nice* day...

Please call immediately if there are problems with this transmission. ***Page 1***

Figure 4-43: A filled-in Fax Form Template

This exercise illustrates the following ClarisWorks features:

Graphics

- ◆ Placing and drawing graphics in a word processing document
- ◆ Locking graphic elements (so they cannot be moved or altered inadvertently)

Text

- ◆ Using multiple fonts, styles, and sizes
- ◆ Paragraph formatting

- ◆ Creating a footer
- ◆ Automatic page numbering

Spreadsheet

- ◆ Using a spreadsheet frame as a table
- ◆ Changing spreadsheet column widths
- ◆ Pasting formulas
- ◆ Protecting spreadsheet cells
- ◆ Automatic date entry

Designing the template

To create the template, begin by creating a new word processing document (choose the New command from the File menu or press ⌘-N). Then choose the Document command from the Format menu. In the Document dialog box that appears, set the Left and Right Margins to *1 in*. This setting ensures that you will not lose text from the sides of the document when you send it as a fax.

The key elements of the fax form are numbered in Figure 4-44. The discussion that follows refers to each element by number.

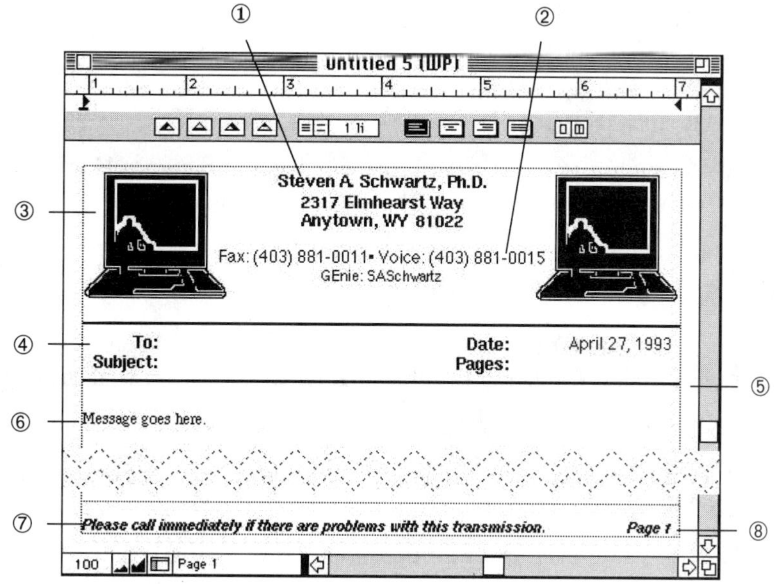

Figure 4-44: The elements of the fax form.

1: Name/company name/return address

Center your name, company name, and return address on the page. (Click the center alignment icon in the ruler bar to center text between the margins.) Use 12 point Helvetica Bold for the font.

2: Fax and voice phone numbers

You center these lines as you centered the address information. The phone numbers are 12 point Helvetica, and the electronic mail account information (GEnie) is 10 point Helvetica.

You can replace the GEnie account information with your electronic mail address (if you have one) or with other pertinent information, or you can simply delete it.

Finally, separate the last line of the phone number or electronic mail information from the body text below it. Although you can accomplish this task by pressing Return several times to insert blank lines, inserting them by setting Space after for the final line is preferable.

Step-by-Steps

To separate the return address text from the body text:

1. **Position the text insertion point anywhere in the electronic mail text line.**
2. **Choose the Paragraph command from the Format menu.** The Paragraph dialog box appears.
3. **Set Space after to 6 li and then click OK.**

3: Logo or graphic

I like to use graphics or logos in my faxes. The logos in Figure 4-44 are pasted onto the document as objects rather than as in-line graphics.

Step-by-Steps

To add a graphic to a template:

1. **In the Scrapbook or a graphics program (the ClarisWorks Draw environment, for example), select the image that you want to copy.**
2. **Choose Copy from the Edit menu (or press ⌘-C).**
3. **Return to the fax form in ClarisWorks and select the Pointer from the Tool panel.**
4. **Choose Paste from the Edit menu (or press ⌘-V).** The graphic appears on-screen, surrounded by handles to show that it is selected. (If the handles are not visible, the graphic has been pasted as in-line text rather than as an object. Press Delete to remove the image and return to Step 3.)

5. **With the image still selected, drag it to the upper-left corner of the fax form.** If the image is too large or too small, click its bottom right handle and, while pressing Shift, drag to resize the image. (Using Shift while resizing a graphic helps to maintain the same proportions.)

6. ***Optional:* To make an exact copy of the graphic for use in the upper-right corner of the fax form, select the graphic and choose Copy from the Edit menu (or press ⌘-C).**

7. ***Optional:* Choose Paste from the Edit menu (or press ⌘-V). A copy of the graphic is pasted directly on top of the original graphic.**

8. ***Optional:* Select the new graphic and, while pressing Shift, drag it horizontally to the right edge of the fax form.** (Pressing Shift while dragging an image assures that all movements are exactly horizontal or vertical and keeps the two graphics perfectly aligned.)

4: The spreadsheet table (addressee information)

The addressee information is a spreadsheet frame. Figure 4-45 shows what the spreadsheet frame looks like as you work with it.

	A	B	C	D
1	To:		Date:	April 27, 1993
2	Subject:		Pages:	

Figure 4-45: The spreadsheet frame.

To create the addressee table:

1. **Click the Spreadsheet tool in the Tool panel and draw the frame.**

2. **In cells A1, A2, C1, and C2, enter the following text strings:**

Cell	*Text*
A1	To:
A2	Subject:
C1	Date:
C2	Pages:

Format these four cells with 12 point Helvetica Bold and make them right-aligned. To set the font (Helvetica), style (Bold), and point size (12), select the cells and then choose the appropriate options from the Font, Style, and Size submenus of the Format menu. To set the alignment, choose Right from the Alignment pop-up menu in the Format menu.

3. **Use 12 point Helvetica and the General alignment (the default setting) for the remaining cells (B1, B2, D1, and D2).** Set the font and point size for these cells by using the procedure described in Step 2.

4. **Add a formula to cell D1 that automatically inserts the current date: select the cell and then choose Paste Function from the Edit menu.** The Paste Function dialog box appears, as shown in Figure 4-46.

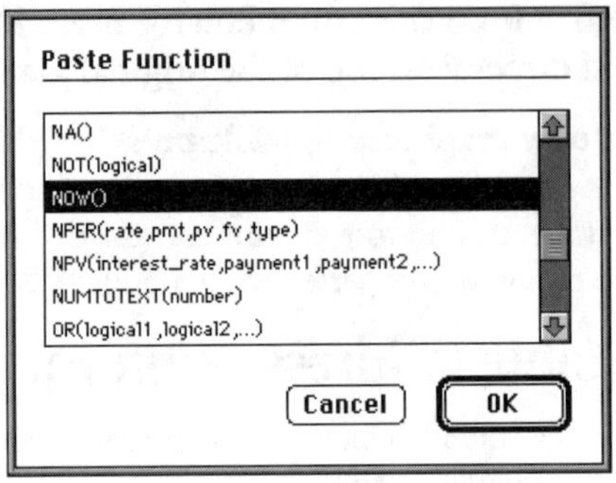

Figure 4-46: The Paste Function dialog box.

5. **Select NOW() and click OK.** The function appears in the entry bar at the top of the spreadsheet.

6. **Press Enter to enter the formula in the cell.**

7. **To display cell D1 as a date, rather than as a numeric string, choose Number from the Format menu.** The Numeric dialog box appears, as shown in Figure 4-47.

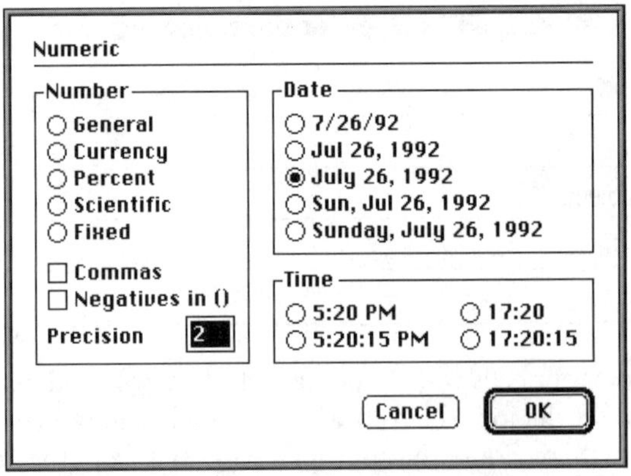

Figure 4-47: The Numeric dialog box enables you to set numeric, date, and time formats for selected cells.

8. **Click a radio button for a date format and then click OK.** Cell D1 is now formatted as a date.

9. **When you first created the spreadsheet frame, the column widths were all uniform. To change them to their final sizes, select a column, choose Column Width from the Format menu, and enter the width. Set the widths as follows:**

Column Name	*Width*
A	56
B	212
C	46
D	120

10. **To get rid of the ugly grid lines and row/column labels, select any cell in the spreadsheet (which cell you select doesn't matter) and then choose Display from the Options menu.** The Display dialog box appears, as shown in Figure 4-48.

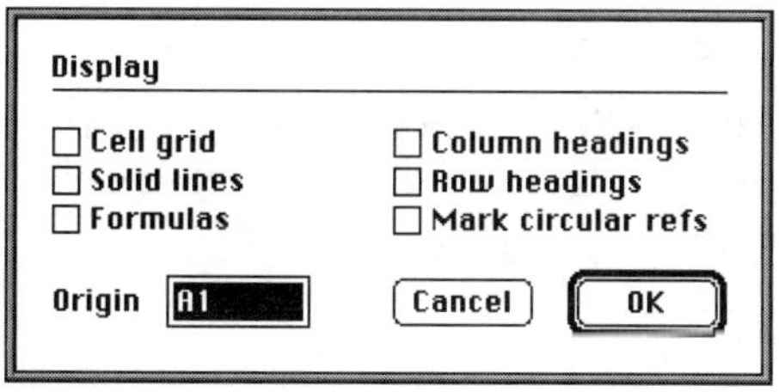

Figure 4-48: The Display dialog box.

11. **Remove all check marks from the check boxes and then click OK.**

12. **To prevent the formatting or formula from being changed inadvertently, select cells A1 and A2 and then choose Protect Cells from the Options menu (or press ⌘-H).** Repeat this procedure for cells C1, C2, and D1.

13. **Drag the spreadsheet frame to its proper position on the fax form.** When it is in position, choose Lock from the Arrange menu (or press ⌘-H). This procedure locks the frame into position and displays a gray handle on each corner of the table. (If you later need to change the position of the table, choose Unlock from the Arrange menu.)

5: The horizontal lines

A pair of thick horizontal lines separates the addressee information from the rest of the fax form.

To create the lines:

1. **Select the Line tool from the Tool panel.**
2. **Starting at the left margin, hold down Shift and drag until you reach the right margin.** Then release the mouse button.
3. **With the newly drawn line still selected, choose *2 pt.* from the line width palette in the Tool panel.**
4. **To make a copy of the line, choose Copy from the Edit menu (or press ⌘-C). Then choose Paste from the Edit menu (or press ⌘-V).** A new copy of the line is pasted directly on top of the original copy. (You also can use the Duplicate command to make a copy of the line, but it will be pasted away from the original rather than on top of it.)
5. **Select the copy of the line and, while pressing Shift, drag the line down to the bottom of the spreadsheet table.**
6. **Finally, to keep the two lines from ever shifting by mistake, select them both (click one and then Shift-click the other) and choose Lock from the Arrange menu.**

6: The body text

To enter the dummy line of body text (*Message goes here.*) so that you can set the paragraph format and choose a font for the fax text, move the text insertion point to the end of the electronic mail line in the return address information, press Return, and type the dummy text.

Every paragraph of the body text uses the same font and paragraph format settings. To set the paragraph format, choose Paragraph from the Format menu. The Paragraph dialog box appears. Match the settings that appear on the screen to those shown in Figure 4-49. Click OK to accept the new settings.

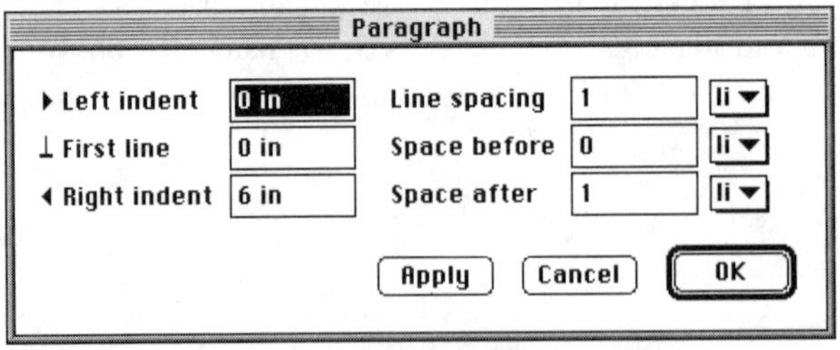

Figure 4-49: Paragraph settings for the body text.

As a last step, choose a font for the body text from the Font menu and use it to format the dummy text line. Make sure that the font you choose is very legible so that the recipient's copy will be clear. Times is a good choice for the font.

7 and 8: The footer

The footer repeats on every page of the fax, displaying a standard message and the page number for each page.

Step-by-Steps

To create the footer:

1. **Choose Insert Footer from the Format menu.** A blank area at the bottom of the page is now reserved for the footer.
2. **Press Return once to add a blank line at the top of the footer (to separate it from the body text).**
3. **Set the font, style, and size as Helvetica, Bold and Italic, and 10 point, respectively.**
4. **Type the following message:** Please call immediately if there are problems with this transmission.
5. **Press Tab once and then type** Page, **followed by a space.**
6. **Drag a right tab — the third tab icon — to the 7-inch mark on the ruler (as shown in Figure 4-44).** Doing so causes the page number information to align with the right margin.

To complete the footer, insert the automatic page number (see Figure 4-44). With the text insertion point at the end of the footer text, choose Insert Page # from the Edit menu.

Because you want to have ready access to the template and ensure that you do not change it by mistake, save it as a stationery document.

Step-by-Steps

To save the template as a ClarisWorks stationery document:

1. **Choose Save As from the File menu.** The standard Save file dialog box appears.
2. **Choose Stationery from the Save As pop-up menu.**
3. **Enter a name for the document, such as Fax Form Template.**
4. **Save the stationery document to the desired folder.**

If you want to be able to choose the stationery document from the Stationery pop-up menu in the New Document dialog box, save it in the ClarisWorks Stationery folder located in the Claris folder in the System Folder. Any ClarisWorks stationery file that you save or move into this folder is automatically added to the Stationery pop-up menu, and you can choose it when you issue the New command.

To open a stationery document in ClarisWorks 3.0, choose New Document from the File menu (or press ⌘-N), click the Start with an Assistant or Stationery button, navigate to the correct file list by choosing from the Category pop-up menu, choose a stationery file, and click OK. Note that you also can open a stationery document at the *start* of a ClarisWorks session by clicking the Create a new document button on the Welcome screen.

Using the template

Now that you have created the fax form template, you need to know how to use it.

To create a fax:

1. **Choose New from the file menu.** The New Document dialog box appears.
2. **Choose Fax Form Template (WP) from the Stationery pop-up menu.**
3. **Click OK.** An untitled copy of the Fax Form Template appears.
4. **Fill in the address information.** Begin by clicking to the right of the *To:* cell. Enter the name of the fax recipient and press Return. The cursor moves to the cell below, where you can now enter the subject of the fax.
5. **Select the line of text that reads *Message goes here*, and type the body of the fax.** You'll notice that each time you press Return to start a new paragraph, the program automatically inserts a blank line for you.
6. **When you've completed the body text, select the spreadsheet cell to the right of *Pages:* and enter the total number of pages for the fax.**
7. **If you are going to transmit the fax on a standard fax machine, turn on the printer and choose Print from the File menu.** The Print dialog box appears. Change settings as necessary (you can usually accept the default settings) and click OK. The fax prints.

— or —

7. **If you are going to transmit the fax on a fax modem, select the Chooser desk accessory from the Apple menu.** The Chooser dialog box appears. (***Note:*** The specific procedure for sending a document with a fax modem may differ, depending on the fax software installed on the Mac. See the software manual for exact instructions.)
8. **Select the fax modem driver from the left side of the Chooser dialog box and click the close box to make that driver the current driver.**

9. **In ClarisWorks, choose Page Setup from the File menu and change settings as needed.** Click OK to return to the document.
10. **Choose Print from the File menu, change settings as necessary, specify a recipient for the fax, and click OK.** The document is now translated into fax format and transmitted to the recipient.

From looking at the completed fax form in Figure 4-44, you may have been surprised that it took so many steps to create what — from first glance — appears to be a relatively simple form.

Quick Tips

The following Quick Tips describe how to use the Outliner to reorganize word processing text and how to create glossary terms. They also suggest ways to improve the quality of your documents by using special papers and tell you about more powerful word processing programs.

Using the Outliner as an editing tool

The word processor's Outliner, which is discussed in detail in Topic 16, has a special feature that makes reorganizing text easy. Unlike the normal text move procedure (using the Cut and Paste commands or pressing Option-⌘ as you click a new location), moving text in the Outline view is direct and easy to accomplish.

To move text in the Outliner:

1. **Choose Outline View from the View menu (or press Shift-⌘-I).** The current word processing document is reformatted as an outline.
2. **Select the paragraph that you want to move by clicking to the left of its topic label.** (In default mode, the label is a diamond.) When selected, the entire paragraph is highlighted, as shown in Figure 4-50.

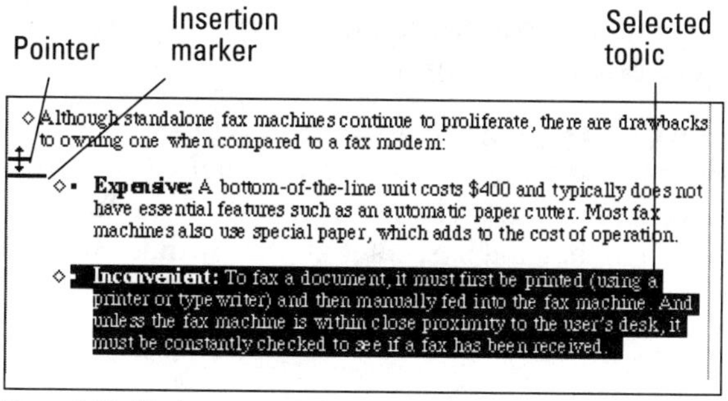

Figure 4-50: Moving a paragraph to a new location.

3. **While continuing to hold down the mouse button, move the pointer.** It immediately changes to a horizontal bar with arrows at the top and bottom (as shown in Figure 4-50).

4. **Continue to move the pointer until the insertion marker (a long horizontal line) is where you want to move the selected topic/paragraph.**

5. **Release the mouse button.** The paragraph moves to the new location.

6. **Choose Outline View again from the View menu (or press Shift-⌘-I).** The document is displayed in its normal form.

The only disadvantage to moving text in the Outliner is that you can move only one paragraph at a time. (Each paragraph is treated as a separate point in the outline.)

A do-it-yourself glossary

You may have noticed that the ClarisWorks word processor lacks a glossary feature. (A *glossary* enables you to insert frequently used terms and phrases into documents easily by simply selecting them from lists or by pressing hot keys.) However, with minimal effort, you can create glossary terms. Two approaches work fairly well: using the Find/Change command and using macros.

To use the Find/Change method, you define one or more abbreviations to represent a longer word or phrase, use them in the text, and then issue the Find/Change command to replace each abbreviation with the expanded phrase.

Step-by-Steps

To create a glossary term with the Find/Change command:

1. **Decide on a term or phrase for which you want to define an abbreviation.** The phrase can contain up to 255 characters, including spaces.

2. **Pick an abbreviation for the phrase.** Ideally, the abbreviation should not be a real word or a portion of a word. For example, you can use three asterisks (***) or a nonsense syllable (cpt).

3. **When typing the document, use the abbreviation, rather than the full word or phrase that it represents.**

4. **After you finish typing the document, replace all abbreviations with the full word or phrase.** Do so by choosing Find/Change from the Find/Change submenu of the Edit menu (or by pressing ⌘-F), entering the abbreviation in the Find box, entering the expanded word or phrase in the Change box, and clicking Change All.

To create a glossary term macro:

1. **Open a new or existing word processing document.**

2. **Choose Record Macros from the Shortcuts submenu of the File menu (or press Shift-⌘-J).** The Record Macro dialog box appears, as shown in Figure 4-51.

```
Record Macro

Name  [Untitled 1]              ┌─Play In──────────────
                                □ All Environments
○ Function Key          [    ]  ⊠ Word Processing
● Option + ⌘ + Key              □ Drawing
                                □ Painting
┌─Options─────────────          □ Database
□ Play Pauses                   □ Spreadsheet
□ Document Specific             □ Communications
□ Has Shortcut          [  ]
□ In Shortcuts Palette          [ Cancel ] ( Record )
```

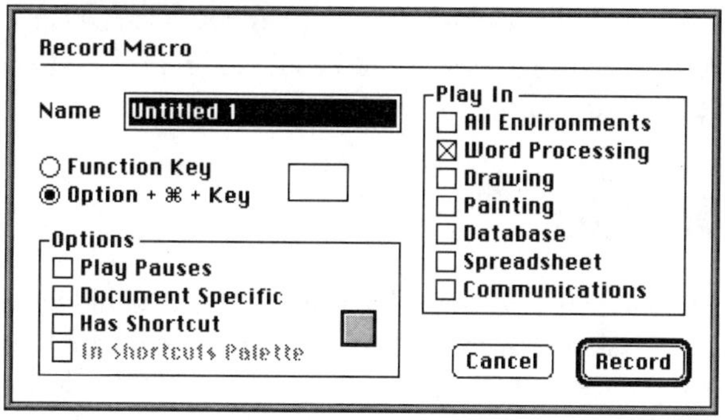

Figure 4-51: The Record Macro dialog box.

3. **Enter a name for the macro and specify an Option-⌘ key with which to execute the macro.**

4. **Choose from the following options:**

 ◆ If you don't intend to use the glossary term anywhere other than in the present document, click Document Specific. If you want the macro to be available in other documents, leave that check box blank.

 ◆ If you want to add the macro to the Shortcuts palette, click Has Shortcut and In Shortcuts Palette and then create an icon for the macro (as described in Topic 14).

 ◆ By default, the Play In check box for the current environment is checked. Click any additional environments in which the glossary term may also be needed.

5. **Click Record.** You are returned to the document, and the macro recorder starts.

6. **Type the term or phrase that you want to record.** In most cases, you will probably want to end the macro term or phrase with a space (that is, you will type "ClarisWorks" rather than "ClarisWorks"). If you include a space at the end of the macro, you don't have to press the spacebar before you type the next word when you execute the macro.

7. **Choose Stop Recording from the Shortcuts submenu on the File menu (or press Shift-⌘-J).** 👣

Whenever you want to insert the new glossary term in a document, simply press the Option-⌘ key that you assigned to the macro or click its button on the Shortcuts palette.

Paper, paper . . . who's got the paper?

Letterhead and fan-fold computer paper do not meet every word processing need. Whether you just want to make a document look its best or you have something different in mind (such as a brochure, an imprinted postcard, or an award certificate), a special paper may be exactly what you need.

Unless you happen to have a heavy-duty stationery shop nearby, one of the best sources of specialty papers is Paper Direct (800-272-7377). Call and ask for a copy of the catalog. If you own a laser printer, you'll be amazed at the printing capabilities you have but didn't know about.

Moving On Up

At some point, you may find yourself wishing that you could handle a particular word processing task more easily. That's the time to start thinking about a more powerful word processor. Currently, Microsoft Word is the leading Macintosh word processing program. In addition to the features in the ClarisWorks word processor, Word 5.1 offers the following:

- Custom paragraph styles (to assure consistency within and between documents)
- A built-in grammar checker (which checks for correct syntax, passive constructions, run-on sentences, and so on)
- User-defined glossaries
- An integrated charting program
- A table feature
- Voice and *sticky note* document annotations
- Table of Contents and Index generation
- Drop caps
- A change case feature (to change a text string to uppercase, lowercase, title case, and so on)
- In-text numeric calculations
- A hyphenation command (which searches for words at line ends that can be hyphenated to improve the appearance of the text)
- Envelope printing

On the other hand, if you're concerned about making the smoothest transition possible, you should take a close look at MacWrite Pro, which is another Claris product that has many of the above-mentioned features. Other popular, powerful, stand-alone word processing programs to consider include WordPerfect (WordPerfect Corporation), WriteNow (WordStar International), and Nisus (Paragon Concepts).

Summary

- Word processing text can contain any combination of fonts, sizes, and styles. You can apply multiple styles to the same text string. If you use certain text styles often, you can add their definitions to the Style menu by defining them as custom styles.
- Paragraph formatting controls the look of a particular paragraph. It includes settings for tabs, indents, line spacing, and text alignment. You can set most paragraph options directly on the ruler or choose the Paragraph command from the Format menu.
- ClarisWorks offers four kinds of tab stops: left, centered, right, and character. Character tab stops are frequently used to align a column of numbers on the decimal point. You can also specify a fill or leader character for tab stops.
- The four alignment options enable you to create left-, right-, center-, or full-justified paragraphs.
- Document commands enable you to see multiple pages of text on-screen at the same time, set margins, and create a title page.
- If you want to lay out a newsletter or a magazine article, you can easily change to a multicolumn layout. You can use the Insert Break command to manually adjust page and column breaks and to avoid widows and orphans.
- The Find/Change commands enable you to search for words and, optionally, to replace them with other words.
- Headers and footers are sections that can appear on every page of a document. They are useful for displaying page numbers, a company logo, and so on.
- ClarisWorks can automatically number and manage footnotes, or you can mark them with special characters that you have selected.
- You can insert automatic dates, times, or page numbers into any document. Dates and times automatically update each time you open the document. Page numbers automatically adjust as the pagination for the document changes.
- The spelling checker enables you to check the entire document or just the text that is currently selected. You can create user dictionaries that contain the spellings of words that are not in the main dictionary. The Word Finder thesaurus helps you find synonyms when you're stuck for the right word.
- ClarisWorks 2.1 and 3.0 have an auto-hyphenation feature that can dramatically improve the appearance of documents.
- You can add pictures to word processing documents as in-line graphics or as objects. ClarisWorks treats the former as text. The latter are free-floating, and you can position them next to, behind, or in front of text. You also can wrap text around graphics.

Topic 5

The Spreadsheet Environment

Overview

A spreadsheet program is like an electronic version of a bookkeeper's ledger page. A spreadsheet document (or *worksheet*) is a grid composed of numbered rows and lettered columns. You enter data into worksheet *cells* — the intersections of the rows and columns. The default size for a ClarisWorks worksheet is 500 rows by 40 columns. Figure 5-1 shows the components of a worksheet.

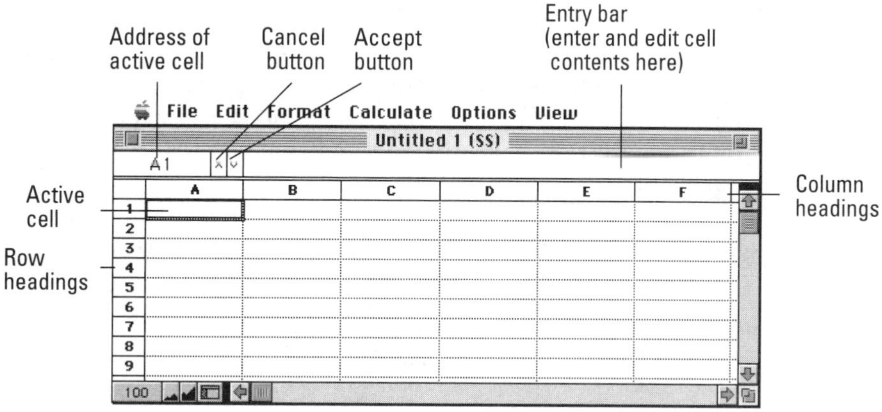

Figure 5-1: The parts of a worksheet.

The power of the spreadsheet lies in its calculation capabilities. You can mathematically combine the contents of cells by creating *formulas* that add, subtract, divide, or multiply cells by each other or by constants. The ClarisWorks spreadsheet environment also offers a large number of mathematical, statistical, time, text, financial, and logical *functions* that enable you to perform complex calculations, such as determining the average of a group of numbers or computing a modified internal rate of return.

The spreadsheet is the ideal environment for data that requires calculations. As such, it is frequently used for accounting, bookkeeping, and record keeping. You can use the charting capabilities to summarize any portion of your data pictorially. And although the ClarisWorks spreadsheet does not contain the database commands that other spreadsheet programs offer, you can still keep simple lists in a worksheet and sort them as needed. You also can use worksheet frames as tables in other ClarisWorks environments.

NOTE

A *spreadsheet* is a type of program, or, in ClarisWorks, an environment. A *worksheet* is a spreadsheet document. These terms are sometimes used interchangeably when referring to the document.

Understanding Spreadsheet Basics

Worksheet cells are identified by the letter and number combination of the intersection of the cell's column and row. For example, the cell in the upper-left corner of every worksheet is A1 (column A, row 1). The current cell has a double border and is called the *active cell.* To make a different cell active, you can click it with the mouse, move to it by using the cursor keys, or choose the Go To Cell command (⌘-G) from the Options menu.

The letter and number combination for a cell is called its *cell address.* A cell address uniquely identifies every cell in the worksheet. You can use cell addresses in formulas. For example, to add the contents of cells A1 and B1 and display the result in cell C1, you enter this formula in C1: **=A1+B1.**

NOTE

The equal sign (=) informs ClarisWorks that you are entering a formula.

You can use a combination of cell addresses and constants in formulas, as shown in the following formulas: =B3*15 and =(A17/5)+2.37.

You also can work with a rectangular group of cells that is known as a *range* (see Figure 5-2). You can include ranges in some types of formulas, such as SUM(A1..A4), where A1..A4 is a range that represents the four cells from A1 to A4 (that is, A1, A2, A3, and A4). This formula adds the contents of the four cells. When you want to quickly apply a format (a font, style, size, or numeric format, for example) to a large number of cells by using a single command, you can select a range prior to issuing a formatting command.

To specify a range in a formula, you separate the upper-left and lower-right cells in the range (called the *anchor cells*) with a pair of periods, as in =SUM(A1..A5).

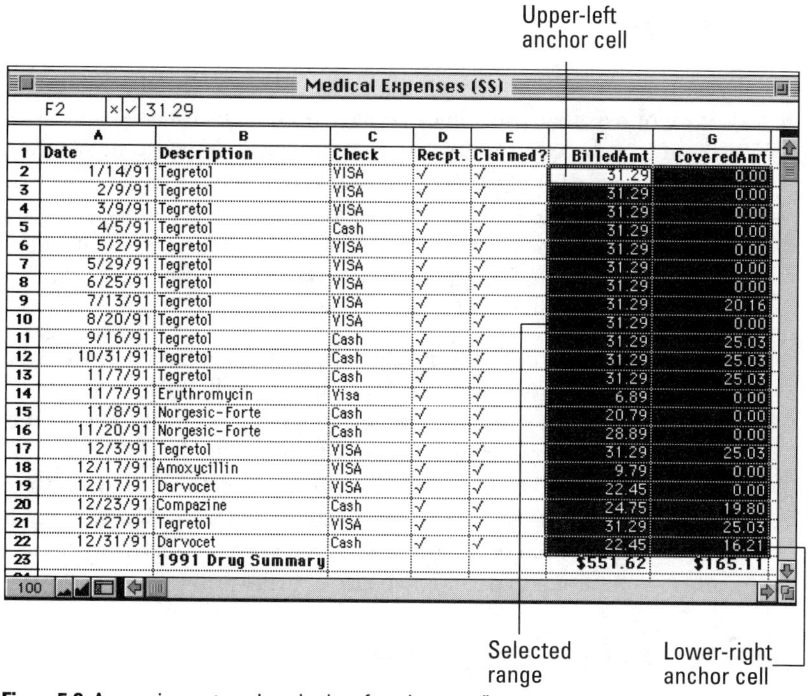

	A	B	C	D	E	F	G
1	Date	Description	Check	Recpt.	Claimed?	BilledAmt	CoveredAmt
2	1/14/91	Tegretol	VISA	√	√	31.29	0.00
3	2/9/91	Tegretol	VISA	√	√	31.29	0.00
4	3/9/91	Tegretol	VISA	√	√	31.29	0.00
5	4/5/91	Tegretol	Cash	√	√	31.29	0.00
6	5/2/91	Tegretol	VISA	√	√	31.29	0.00
7	5/29/91	Tegretol	VISA	√	√	31.29	0.00
8	6/25/91	Tegretol	VISA	√	√	31.29	0.00
9	7/13/91	Tegretol	VISA	√	√	31.29	20.16
10	8/20/91	Tegretol	VISA	√	√	31.29	0.00
11	9/16/91	Tegretol	Cash	√	√	31.29	25.03
12	10/31/91	Tegretol	Cash	√	√	31.29	25.03
13	11/7/91	Tegretol	Cash	√	√	31.29	25.03
14	11/7/91	Erythromycin	Visa	√	√	6.89	0.00
15	11/8/91	Norgesic-Forte	Cash	√	√	20.79	0.00
16	11/20/91	Norgesic-Forte	Cash	√	√	28.89	0.00
17	12/3/91	Tegretol	VISA	√	√	31.29	25.03
18	12/17/91	Amoxycillin	VISA	√	√	9.79	0.00
19	12/17/91	Darvocet	VISA	√	√	22.45	0.00
20	12/23/91	Compazine	Cash	√	√	24.75	19.80
21	12/27/91	Tegretol	VISA	√	√	31.29	25.03
22	12/31/91	Darvocet	Cash	√	√	22.45	16.21
23		1991 Drug Summary				$551.62	$165.11

Figure 5-2: A range is a rectangular selection of contiguous cells.

Selecting cells

Many actions in a spreadsheet program require that you preselect one or more cells and then choose the action that you want to perform on those cells. After you choose cells, you can apply formats to them, fill them to the right or down, clear them, create a chart based on the selected values, sort them, and so on.

- *To select a single cell,* click it. The cell is surrounded by a double border and becomes the active cell.
- *To select a cell range,* click to select the first cell and then drag the mouse or Shift-click to choose the remaining cells. (***Note:*** The upper-left and lower-right cells in the range are called *anchors* or *anchor cells.*)
- *To select an entire row or column,* click the heading for that row or column or drag through the row or column.
- *To select the entire worksheet,* click the blank box above the *1* heading for row 1 or choose Select All from the Edit menu.
- *To select the active area of the worksheet* (those cells that contain entries), press Option as you click the blank box above the *1* heading for row 1.

Cell contents

Every cell can contain a text string, a number, or a formula. Numbers can be positive or negative, and you can type them directly (as in 43 and –123.654). You also can type directly any entry that begins with a letter (as in Sam Jones and Social Security #123-45-6789). As soon as you enter a space or other text character, that cell is treated as text. On the other hand, you always have to precede formulas with an equal sign (as in = A5+B4). If you want to treat a number as text, enter it as if it were a formula; that is, precede the number with an equal sign and enclose it in quotation marks (as in ="1993").

NOTE

ClarisWorks treats cell data and the formatting that has been applied to the data as separate entities. If you delete the contents of a cell, the formatting remains. Understanding this concept is particularly important when you want to print a worksheet. The print range defaults to printing all cells that have data in them — which is interpreted by ClarisWorks to mean all cells that have data or formatting. For example, if you used the Select All command to apply a different font or size to all cells when you created the worksheet, every cell in the worksheet will be printed — resulting in pages and pages of blank printout.

Entering and editing data

The following steps describe how to enter data into a cell.

Step-by-Steps

To enter data:

1. **Select a cell.** The cell is surrounded by a double border, showing that it is the active cell.
2. **Type the text, number, or formula that you want to enter into the cell.** Whatever you type appears in the entry bar at the top of the document window.
3. **To accept the entry, press Return, Enter, Tab, or an arrow key, or click the Accept button in the entry bar.** To cancel the entry, click the Cancel button in the entry bar or press Esc.

VERSION 2.1

The arrow keys work differently in ClarisWorks 2.1. To accept an entry and move to an adjacent cell, you need to press Option-arrow key. Pressing an arrow key by itself moves the insertion point within the cell text.

NEW FEATURE 3.0

In ClarisWorks 3.0, the way that the arrow and Option-arrow keys work is determined by the setting chosen in spreadsheet preferences. See Topic 12 for details.

If you press any key other than Enter or Esc to conclude a cell entry, the cursor moves to an adjacent cell and makes that cell the active cell.

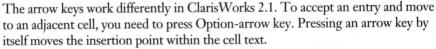

The direction in which the cursor moves depends on the key you press:

Key/Button	*Cursor Moves to*
Esc, Cancel button	Stays in the current cell and cancels the entry
Enter, Accept button	Stays in the current cell and accepts the entry
Return, down arrow (Option-down arrow in 2.1)	Cell below
Right-arrow (Option-right arrow in 2.1), Tab	Cell to the right
Left-arrow (Option-left arrow in 2.1), Shift-Tab	Cell to the left
Up-arrow (Option-up arrow in 2.1), Shift-Return	Cell above

You can also edit or clear the cell contents.

Step-by-Steps

To edit the contents of a cell:

1. **Click the cell that you want to edit.** The contents of the active cell appear in the entry bar.
2. **In the entry bar, click to position the text insertion point. Use normal editing procedures to add or delete characters and to insert new cell references.** (Note that you are always in insertion mode when you are editing or entering text.) To move the cursor within an entry, press the left- or right-arrow key in ClarisWorks 2.0; press Option-left arrow key or Option-right arrow key in ClarisWorks 2.1. In ClarisWorks 3.0, press either an arrow key or an Option-arrow key, depending on the setting you've chosen for spreadsheet preferences (see Topic 12).
3. **To complete the entry, press Return, Enter, Tab, or an arrow key, or click the Accept button.**

Step-by-Steps

To clear the contents of a cell or range of cells:

1. **Select the cell or cell range that you want to clear.**
2. **Choose Clear from the Edit menu or press the Clear key (if your keyboard has one).** The cell contents, as well as any formats that were applied to the cell(s), are cleared.

— or —

2. **Choose Cut from the Edit menu (or press ⌘-X).** The program copies the cell contents to the Clipboard and then clears the cells, as well as any formats that were applied to the cell(s).

— or —

2. **Press Delete.** ClarisWorks clears the cell contents, but formats applied to the cell(s) remain intact.

Entering cell names and ranges by pointing

To prevent inaccuracies when you enter or edit formulas, you can use the cursor to *point* to cell addresses and ranges instead of typing them. Suppose, for example, that you want to add the contents of cells A2 and A3. After selecting the destination cell (A4, for example), you would normally type the formula = **A2 + A3.**

Using the pointing method, you can accomplish the same task as follows:

1. **Select cell A4 and press the equal sign (=).**
2. **Using the pointer, click cell A2, press + (the plus sign), and click cell A3.** Clicking a cell has exactly the same effect as typing its cell address.

In fact, you can even skip entering the plus sign, if you want to. If no symbol separates two selected cell addresses or ranges, ClarisWorks assumes that you want to add them, and it inserts the plus sign for you.

Pointing is particularly useful for selecting a range. To compute the sum of a particular range (A1 through A6, for example), you can type this formula: **=SUM(A1..A6)**.

Using the pointing method, you can accomplish the same thing by doing the following:

1. **Select the destination cell and press = (the equal sign).**
2. **Choose Paste Function from the Edit menu, choose SUM, and click OK.** The SUM function appears in the entry bar.
3. **Highlight the arguments in the SUM function and then use the pointer to highlight the desired range (A1 through A6).**
4. **Click the Accept button (or press Return, Enter, Tab, or an arrow key) to complete the entry.**

Worksheet navigation

The ClarisWorks spreadsheet environment offers a number of ways for you to move about the worksheet:

- ◆ Use the horizontal or vertical scroll bars.
- ◆ Press the Page Up or Page Down keys to move up or down one screen.
- ◆ Press Home or End to move to the top or bottom of the worksheet.
- ◆ Press Enter to make the worksheet scroll to display the active cell.

None of these commands changes the active cell. They are pure navigation commands. If you want to change your view of the worksheet and also change the active cell, do one of the following:

- ◆ Choose Go To Cell (⌘-G) from the Options menu to go to a specific cell and make it active.
- ◆ Press an arrow key, Tab, Return, Shift-Tab, or Shift-Return to move one cell in the appropriate direction (as described previously).

Formulas

Formulas are the raison d'être for spreadsheets. A formula can be as simple as adding the contents of two cells (for example, =A1+A2) or so complex that it contains several nested spreadsheet functions. As mentioned earlier in this Topic, you need to begin every formula with an equal sign (=).

You can use the following numeric operators in formulas:

Symbol	***Meaning***	***Examples***
+	Addition	= A5+3
–	Subtraction or negative number	= B7–6; –15
*	Multiplication	= A2*A3
/	Division	= A7/3
^	Exponentiation (raise to the power of)	=A1 ^ 2

The ampersand (&) is the only text operator. You use it to *concatenate* (combine) pairs of text strings. If A1 contains the word *Steve* and B1 contains *Schwartz,* you can place a formula in C1 that creates a full name, as in =A1 & " " & B1 (that is, *Steve,* a space, and *Schwartz*). Note that you need to surround text constants in formulas, such as the space in the preceding example, with quotation marks.

Precedence in formulas

TIP

When a formula contains multiple operators, the precedence of the operators determines the order in which the program performs calculations. Higher-precedence operations are performed before lower-precedence operations. If all operators have the same precedence level, the program evaluates the formula from left to right.

You can use parentheses to change the precedence level. When you use parentheses, the program first performs calculations on the innermost set of parentheses.

The precedence levels for different operators are as follows:

Operator	***Precedence Level***
% (divide by 100)	7
^ (exponentiation)	6
+, – (sign)	5
*, / (multiplication, division)	4
+, – (addition, subtraction)	3
& (text concatenation)	2
=, >, >=, <, <=, <> (logical comparison)	1

The following examples explain how ClarisWorks evaluates different formulas:

- = *7+2–5* The result is 4. Because addition and subtraction have the same precedence, the program evaluates the formula from left to right.
- =*5+4*3* The result is 17. Because multiplication has a higher precedence than addition, the program evaluates *4*3* first and then adds *5* to produce the result.
- = *(5+4)*3* The result is 27. The parentheses change the calculation order, forcing the program to evaluate *5+4* first and then multiply that result by *3*.
- = *3+(2*(4+5))–5* The result is 16. The program evaluates the contents of the innermost parentheses first, giving a result of 9. Then it evaluates the next set of parentheses, producing 18. Finally, because the formula contains no more parentheses and the remaining operators are the same precedence level, it evaluates the rest of the formula from left to right, giving a result of 16.

Using functions in formulas

ClarisWorks provides 100 built-in functions that you can use in formulas. Function categories include business and financial, numeric, statistical, text, trigonometric, logical, date/time, and information. For additional information on using the ClarisWorks database and spreadsheet functions, refer to the *ClarisWorks User's Guide.* (If you have ClarisWorks 3.0, refer to ClarisWorks Help instead.)

Step-by-Steps

To enter a formula that contains a function:

1. **Select the cell in which you want to enter the formula.**
2. **Type an equal sign (=).**
3. **Choose Paste Function from the Edit menu.** The Paste Function dialog box appears, as shown in Figure 5-3.

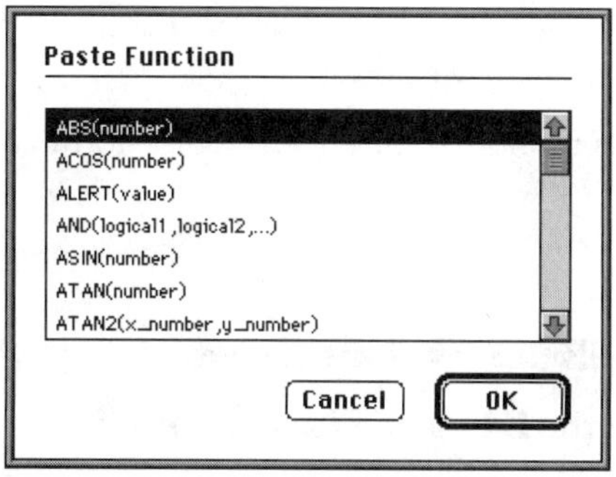

Figure 5-3: The Paste Function dialog box.

You can move quickly to any function in the list by pressing the letter key for the first letter in the function name.

4. **Choose a function from the scrolling list.** (To choose a function, click OK or double-click the function name.) The function and its arguments appear at the text insertion point in the entry bar.

5. **Replace the arguments in the function with real numbers and/or cell references.**

6. **To add more functions to the formula, click in the entry bar to set the text insertion point and repeat Steps 3 through 5.**

7. **Click the Accept button (or press Return, Enter, Tab, or an arrow key) to complete the entry.**

You also can enter functions into formulas manually. Simply type the function and its arguments at the appropriate spot in the formula. You can nest functions (have one function act on another one). An example is =DAYOFYEAR(NOW( )). The NOW( ) function returns a number from the system clock that represents this moment in time. The DAYOFYEAR function converts the number to the day of the current year. On June 22, 1993, the result was 173. Note that the inner function — NOW( ) — is surrounded by parentheses to set it apart from the outer function, DAYOFYEAR.

Copying and pasting cells

One way to duplicate or move cells is to copy or cut the cells and then paste them into a new location. To copy and paste, you select the cells of interest, choose Copy from the Edit menu, select a destination, and then choose Paste from the Edit menu. When you copy a formula, the program reflects the new location by updating the cell references that the formula contains.

You cannot paste the copied contents of a single cell into more than one cell at a time. During a paste, the program automatically replicates the shape of the copied cell grouping. Thus, if you copy a single cell and select multiple cells for the paste, the data or formula is copied only to the first cell in the destination range. If you select a string of three cells when copying (A1 through A3, for example), regardless of the area selected for pasting, ClarisWorks fills the first cell of the destination range and the two cells immediately below it.

You also can paste formula results (or *values*), leaving the formulas behind.

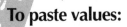

To paste values:

1. **Select the cell or cells that you want to copy.**

2. **Choose Copy from the Edit menu (or press ⌘-C).**

3. **Select a destination.**

4. **Choose Paste Special from the Edit menu.** The Paste Special dialog box appears.

5. **Click the Values only radio button and click OK.** ◖

Absolute and relative cell references

When a formula in a cell refers to another cell or range of cells, it is called a *cell reference.* For example, you may have a formula in cell B1 that multiplies the contents of cell A1 by 0.15, as in =A1*0.15. If you copy cell B1 and then paste it into cell B2, the formula updates to read = A2*0.15. The cell that the formula refers to is no longer the original cell. The reason for the change is that the initial cell reference is a *relative reference;* that is, the reference is relative to the position of the active cell. ClarisWorks interprets the formula in B1 to mean: "Take the contents of the cell to my immediate left and multiply it by 0.15." No matter which cell you copy this formula to, ClarisWorks interprets it in the same manner.

Normally, a relative cell reference is what you want. When you copy a cell that contains a formula or apply Fill Down or Fill Right to a group of cells that begins with a cell containing a formula, you want the new cells to contain the same formula — but with the appropriate cell references. Occasionally, however, you may want the row or column reference to remain unchanged — pointing to the original row and/or column of the cell. Any reference that does not change when you copy the cell elsewhere is called an *absolute reference*.

Perhaps cell A1 contains an estimate of inflation (.15, for example), and the range from A2 to A7 contains various expense figures. In cells B2 through B7, you want to calculate new expense figures after taking inflation into account. The formula in B2 may read =A2+(A1*A2).

To keep the reference to cell A1 from changing when you copy or fill the formula to the remaining cells (B3

through B7), however, you need to make it into an absolute reference, as in =A2+(A1*A2). The $ in front of the A makes the column reference absolute. The $ in front of the 1 makes the row reference absolute. When you copy the new formula to cells B3 through B7, every instance refers directly to cell A1. The references to A2, on the other hand, are still relative and are updated to point to the correct relative cell.

	Inflation calc (SS)		
B5	×✓ =A5+(A1*A5)		
	A	**B**	**C**
1	0.15		
2	12	13.8	
3	134	154.1	
4	34	39.1	
5	24	27.6	
6	123	141.45	
7	27	31.05	

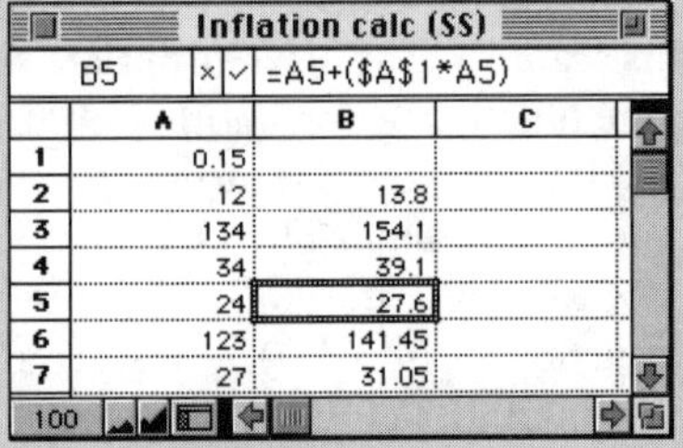

When you enter a formula, you can automatically make a reference absolute by holding down Option and ⌘ when clicking the cell.

You also can create *mixed references,* in which the row reference is absolute and the column reference is relative (or vice versa), as in =B$1+7.

Circular references, on the other hand, are errors, and you should avoid them. They occur when two or more cells depend on the contents of each other. The following formulas contain circular references: A1=B3+7 and B3=A1/5. Because cells A1 and B3 are mutually dependent, the program cannot calculate the results. Cells that contain circular references are indicated by bullets that surround the cell contents, as in •8.75•.

Filling Cells

ClarisWorks provides two commands for copying a formula into a series of cells quickly: Fill Down and Fill Right. (You also can use these commands to copy a single number or text string into a series of cells.)

Step-by-Steps

To fill cells down or to the right:

1. **Select the source cell whose formula you want to copy.**
2. **Drag the pointer or press Shift to select the additional cells to the right or below that will serve as the destination for the copied formula.**
3. **Choose Fill Right (⌘-R) or Fill Down (⌘-D) from the Calculate menu, as appropriate.** The program copies the formula into every selected cell to the right or below the source cell.

TIP

In other spreadsheet programs, you can use Fill Right or Fill Down to conveniently number a series of cells, increasing each one by an increment of your choice. In ClarisWorks, you can achieve the same effect by using a formula. As an example, suppose that you want to enter a number for each row or record in cells A1 through A50. To perform this task, type **1** in cell A1. In cell A2, enter the formula **=A1+1.** Then select cells A2 through A50 and choose Fill Down (⌘-D) from the Calculate menu. You can use this technique to number any string of cells, modifying the starting number cell or using a different increment in the formula as required. To change to an increment of 5, for example, you just alter the formula to =A1+5.

Rearranging the Worksheet

Creating a useful worksheet is an evolving process. The basic structure changes frequently. New rows and columns are inserted, ranges are moved, and columns are sorted as you determine the best way to display the data. ClarisWorks provides all the commands that are necessary to ensure that rearranging the worksheet is as easy and trouble free as possible.

Inserting and deleting cells, columns, and rows

Clearing the contents of a cell or range of cells has no other effect on the worksheet (unless formulas in other cells refer to the cleared cells). Sometimes, however, you may want to add one or more new cells, a new row, or a new column to a worksheet; or you may want to delete cells, rows, or columns.

When you add cells, you need to shift other cells below or to the right to make room for the new cells. (The shift is automatic if you insert entire rows or columns.) When you delete cells, you need to close up the hole that is left by the departing cells. (The shift is automatic if you delete entire rows or columns.)

Using the Insert Cells or Delete Cells command is much faster than the alternative: cutting, pasting, and otherwise manually rearranging the worksheet. You may find, for example, that you haven't left sufficient space at the top of a worksheet for a general label ("Budget Worksheet for Fall 1995") or other identifying information. You can use the Insert Cells command to easily insert a row or two.

To insert new cells:

1. **Select the cell or range where you want to add the new cells.**
2. **Choose Insert Cells from the Calculate menu (or press Shift-⌘-I).** The Insert Cells dialog box appears, as shown in Figure 5-4.

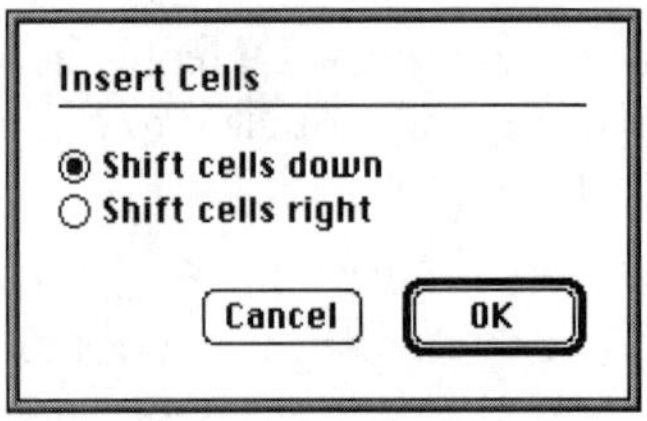

Figure 5-4: The Insert Cells dialog box.

3. **Choose Shift cells down if you want the selected cells and all cells directly below the selection to move down.**

— or —

3. **Choose Shift cells right if you want the selected cells and all cells directly to the right of the selection to move to the right.**
4. **Click OK.** The program inserts the new cell or cells and rearranges the worksheet as requested.

To insert new columns or rows:

1. **Select the headings for the columns or rows where you want to insert the new columns or rows.**
2. **Choose Insert Cells from the Calculate menu (or press Shift-⌘-I).** New blank columns or rows are inserted in place of the selected columns or rows, and the originally selected columns or rows automatically shift to the right or down to make room.

To delete cells:

1. **Select the cell or range that you want to delete.**
2. **Choose Delete Cells from the Calculate menu (or press Shift-⌘-K).** The Delete Cells dialog box appears, as shown in Figure 5-5.

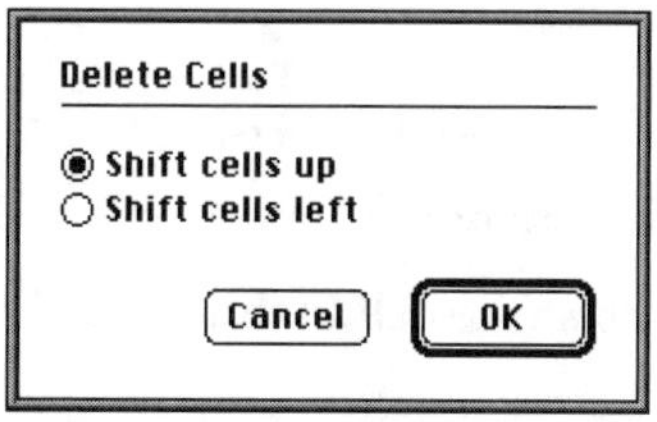

Figure 5-5: The Delete Cells dialog box.

3. **Choose Shift cells up if you want the cells below the selection to move up to fill the hole left by the deletion.**

— or —

3. **Choose Shift cells left if you want the cells to the right of the selection to move left to fill the hole left by the deletion.**
4. **Click OK.** The program deletes the cell or cells and rearranges the worksheet as requested.

To delete entire columns or rows:

1. **Select one or more columns or rows to be deleted by clicking the column or row headings.**
2. **Choose Delete Cells from the Calculate menu (or press Shift-⌘-K).** The program removes the selected columns or rows, and the columns to the right or rows below automatically move to close the gap.

Moving cells

When you use the cut-and-paste method to move cells from one worksheet location to another, the program updates the relative cell references that are contained within the moved cells so that they refer to the new locations. If you want the cell references to remain unchanged, use the Move command instead.

Suppose, for example, that cell A1 contains *10* and cell B1 contains the formula *=A1+5* (which evaluates as 15). If you use the Move command to move cell B1 to D10, the formula remains unchanged (=A1+5). On the other hand, if you cut cell B1 and paste it into D10, the formula reads *=C10+5* and evaluates incorrectly — assuming that you still wanted the cell to reflect the contents of cell A1 plus 5.

If you want to move both cells A1 and B1, you can use either the Cut and Paste commands or Move. The result is the same. If a move contains all cells that are referred to by other cells in the move, the program updates the references, just as it does when you cut and paste.

To move cell contents:

1. **Select the cell or range that you want to move.**
2. **Choose Move from the Calculate menu.** The Move to dialog box appears.
3. **Enter a destination cell address (the cell in the upper-left corner of the range) for the move.**
4. **Click OK.** The program moves the cell or range to the new location.

CAUTION! When executing a move or a paste, be sure that there is room at the destination for the moved or pasted cells. Existing data in the destination cells will be overwritten by the moved or pasted data. If you make this mistake, choose Undo from the Edit menu immediately.

TIP You can accomplish a move quickly by pointing. Select the cell or range that you want to move. Then hold down the Command and Option keys while you click the destination cell.

Sorting

ClarisWorks has flexible sorting options that enable you to perform one- to three-way ascending or descending sorts on columns (vertical) or rows (horizontal). At the simplest level, a sort can affect a single string of cells in a row or column. To perform this type of sort, you select the cells, issue the Sort command, select an *order key* (a cell within the string), choose ascending or descending order, and specify whether the sort is horizontal or vertical.

More common, however, is sorting a range of cells that consists of several columns and rows, based on the values in one or more of the columns or rows.

To perform a sort:

1. **Select the area of the worksheet that you want to sort.**
2. **Choose Sort from the Calculate menu (or press ⌘-J).** The Sort dialog box appears, as shown in Figure 5-6.
3. **If a range has not been preselected, enter the range in the Range text-edit box.** (Separate the two anchor cells with a pair of periods, as in A1..D7.)
4. **Click the Vertical radio button to sort columns or the Horizontal radio button to sort rows.**

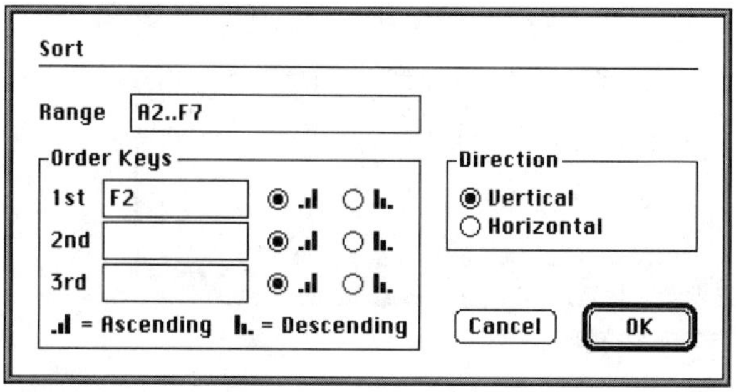

Figure 5-6: The Sort dialog box.

5. **In the 1st Order Keys text-edit box, enter a cell address from the first column that you want to base the sort on (for a vertical sort) or from the first row that you want to base the sort on (for a horizontal sort).**
6. **If you want to perform additional sorts, enter a cell address for a second and third column or row on which you want to base the sort.**
7. **For each order key, click a radio button to indicate whether you want to sort in *ascending order* (from A to Z and lowest to highest number) or *descending order* (from Z to A and highest to lowest number).**
8. **Click OK.** The program performs the requested sort or sorts.

When sorting on a single order key, the program sorts the selected range on the basis of the contents of the key's column (vertical sort) or row (horizontal sort).

When performing a multikey sort, the program sorts the selected range on the basis of the contents of the first key's column (vertical sort) or row (horizontal sort). It then re-sorts on the basis of the second key, where all *ties* (duplicate values) in the first key sort are reordered according to the second key. If you selected a third key, records that are still tied after the program sorts on the second key are reordered according to the third key.

As an example, Figure 5-7 shows a simple address worksheet with fields in columns A through F. To sort the data, start by specifying the data range — **A2..F7**, in this case. (Don't include the labels in row 1 as part of the sort, because you don't want them to change positions.) To perform a sort that reorganizes the records into ascending ZIP code order, specify a Vertical sort and enter a key (cell address) from the ZIP code field (**F2**, for example). The Sort settings that you use to order the records according to their ZIP codes are shown in Figure 5-6.

The result of the sort is shown in Figure 5-8. Because you are simultaneously sorting columns A through E as well, each entire *record* changes position — not just the ZIP code. If you set the range as **F2..F7**, on the other hand, the program reorders only the ZIP codes — not the accompanying data in columns A through E.

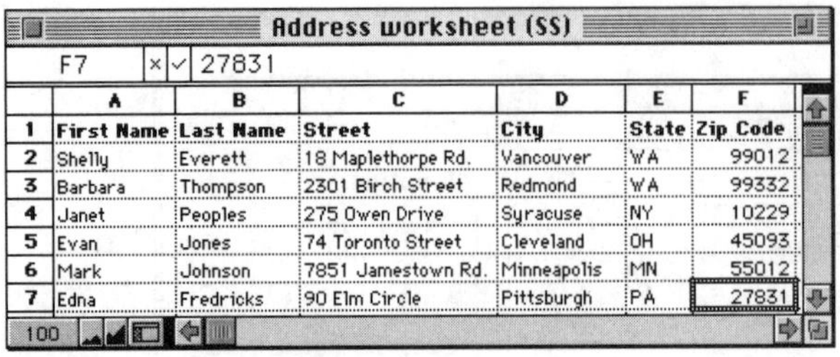

Address worksheet (SS)
F7 27831
First Name | Last Name | Street | City | State | Zip Code
Shelly | Everett | 18 Maplethorpe Rd. | Vancouver | WA | 99012
Barbara | Thompson | 2301 Birch Street | Redmond | WA | 99332
Janet | Peoples | 275 Owen Drive | Syracuse | NY | 10229
Evan | Jones | 74 Toronto Street | Cleveland | OH | 45093
Mark | Johnson | 7851 Jamestown Rd. | Minneapolis | MN | 55012
Edna | Fredricks | 90 Elm Circle | Pittsburgh | PA | 27831

Figure 5-7: The original address database.

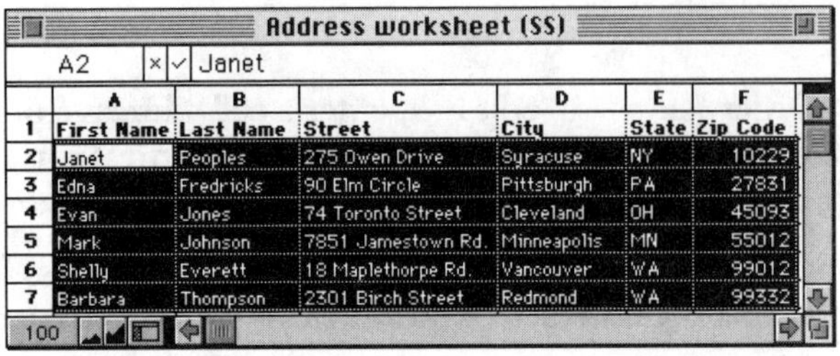

Address worksheet (SS)
A2 Janet
First Name | Last Name | Street | City | State | Zip Code
Janet | Peoples | 275 Owen Drive | Syracuse | NY | 10229
Edna | Fredricks | 90 Elm Circle | Pittsburgh | PA | 27831
Evan | Jones | 74 Toronto Street | Cleveland | OH | 45093
Mark | Johnson | 7851 Jamestown Rd. | Minneapolis | MN | 55012
Shelly | Everett | 18 Maplethorpe Rd. | Vancouver | WA | 99012
Barbara | Thompson | 2301 Birch Street | Redmond | WA | 99332

Figure 5-8: The database reordered by ZIP code.

Figure 5-9 shows the settings for and the results of a two-way sort of the same database. The first sort is on State (column E), and the second sort is on Last Name (column B). When the program executes the sort instructions, it sorts the entire database (A2..F7) alphabetically based on State. It then re-sorts any duplicate entries (*WA,* in this case) alphabetically according to the person's Last Name. (***Note:*** When performing a multiway sort, list the sort keys in the order of decreasing importance.)

TIP

If you make a mistake during a sort (specify the wrong range, sort in the wrong order, or sort rows instead of columns, for example), you can restore the data to its original condition by immediately choosing the Undo command from the Edit menu (⌘-Z), which should read *Undo Sort.*

Transposing a range

Another way to rearrange information is to *transpose* it. Transposing a range swaps columns for rows and vice versa. Figure 5-10 shows a range before and after it has been transposed.

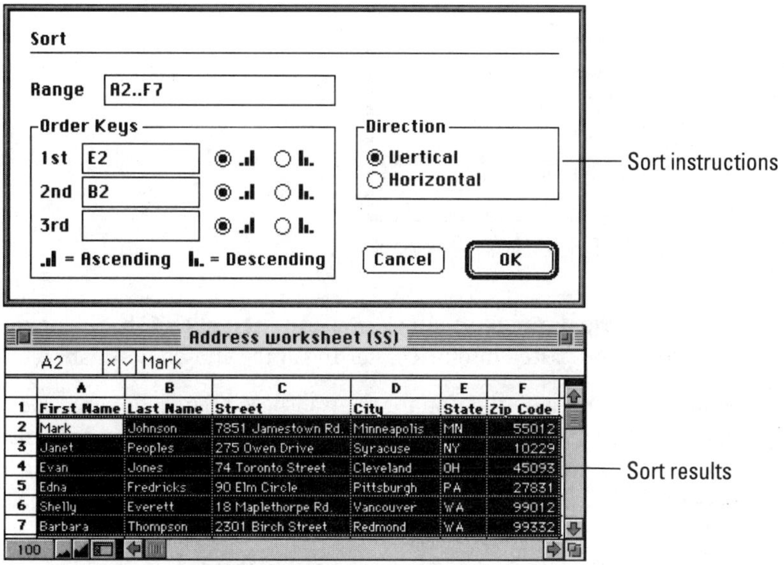

Figure 5-9: A two-way sort on the same data.

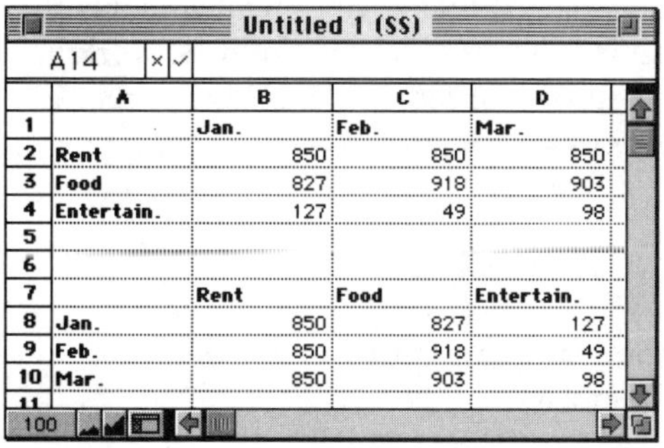

Figure 5-10: Range A7..D10 contains transposed information from range A1..D4.

To transpose information:

1. **Select the area that you want to transpose.**
2. **Choose Copy (⌘-C) or Cut (⌘-X) from the Edit menu to place a copy of the range on the Clipboard.**
3. **Select a destination cell for the range.**
4. **Choose Paste Special from the Edit menu.** The Paste Special dialog box appears, as shown in Figure 5-11.

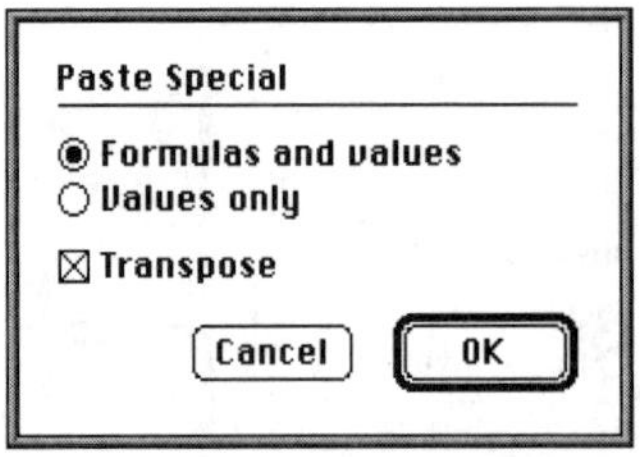

Figure 5-11: The Paste Special dialog box.

5. **Click the Transpose check box and then click OK.** The range is transposed and pasted into place, starting at the chosen destination cell.

CAUTION!

When you select a destination for the transposed range, be sure to leave yourself enough room in the cells to the right and below. The transposed range overwrites data that is in the cells that it covers. If you overwrite important data, immediately choose Undo from the Edit menu (⌘-Z) and select a different destination.

Changing the size of the worksheet

When you create a worksheet, it contains 40 columns and 500 rows. (A new spreadsheet frame in another ClarisWorks environment contains 10 columns and 50 rows.) Although these dimensions are adequate for most worksheets, you may occasionally find that you've run out of room. ClarisWorks enables you to increase or decrease the numbers of worksheet rows and/or columns as your needs change.

Step-by-Steps

To change the size of a worksheet:

1. **Select Document from the Format menu.** The Document dialog box appears, as shown in Figure 5-12.

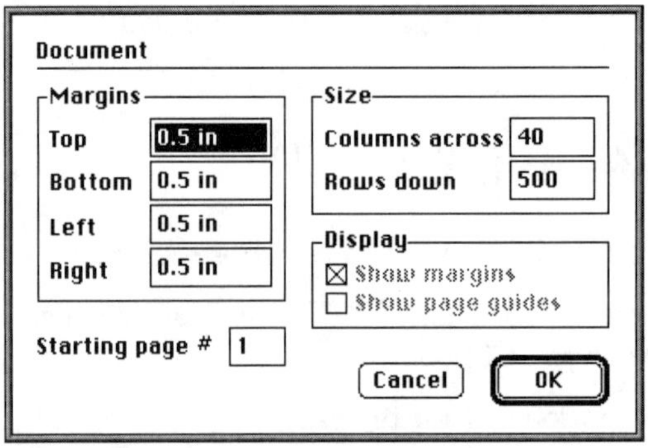

Figure 5-12: The Document dialog box.

2. **To alter the size of the current worksheet, enter numbers in the Size section of the Document dialog box (Columns across and Rows down).**

To double the width of the worksheet, for example, you type 80 in the Columns across text-edit box. Remember, too, that you can also use this dialog box to *reduce* the size of a worksheet.

3. **Click OK to close the dialog box.** The worksheet is resized according to your specifications.

To reach the Document dialog box from a spreadsheet *frame*, however, you first have to open the frame to full size by choosing Open Frame from the View menu. Then choose the Document command from the Format menu.

Formatting Cells

As recently as a few years ago, worksheets were pretty drab. They were usually restricted to a single font in a single point size. Modern spreadsheet programs, such as the ClarisWorks spreadsheet environment, encourage you to be creative when you format worksheets. You can use multiple fonts, sizes, and styles; add color to text; surround cells with border lines; hide the cell gridlines or row and column headings; and change the width and height of individual columns and rows.

Setting cell formats

ClarisWorks provides a host of methods for dressing up the contents of any cell:

- Assigning a font, size, and style
- Applying a color
- Setting an alignment (general, left, right, or center)
- Making text wrap in the cell if it is too wide to fit
- Assigning a number format for displaying numbers, dates, or times

Step-by-Steps

To assign format attributes to a cell:

1. **Select a cell or range of cells.**
2. **Choose options from any of the following submenus of the Format menu: Font, Size, Style, Text Color, or Alignment.** The program applies the new settings to the entire contents of the selected cells.

NOTE

- The General Alignment option (the default) automatically left-aligns cells that contain text and right-aligns cells that contain numeric data.
- If you set a large point size for a cell, you should note that ClarisWorks does not automatically adjust row height to accommodate the largest font in the row. If you do not change the row height, some of the text may be clipped at the top. (Instructions for changing row heights are provided in "Making cell contents fit" later in this Topic.)

To add or remove cell borders:

1. **Select a cell or range of cells.**
2. **Choose Borders from the Format menu.** The Borders dialog box appears, as shown in Figure 5-13.

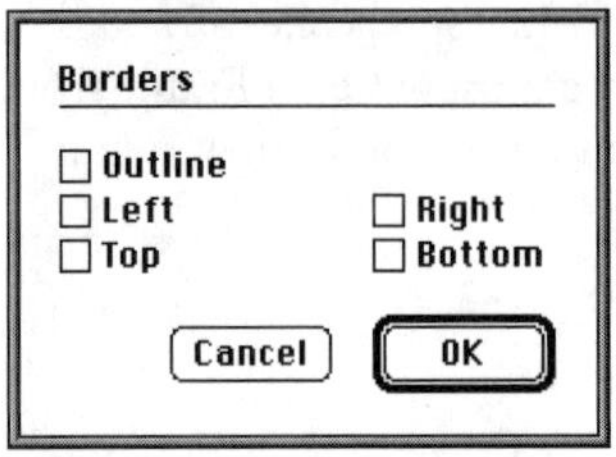

Figure 5-13: The Borders dialog box.

3. **Each check box works as a toggle.** Place check marks to indicate the sides on which the program should apply border lines.

   A dash in a check box means that some, but not all, of the selected cells have that particular border option set.

   Removing a check mark clears the border on that side of the selected cell or cells.
4. **Click OK.** The program applies the selected border options individually to every selected cell. However, if you check Outline, an outline border appears around the *group* of cells that you selected — not around every individual cell.

To set a numeric format:

1. **Select a cell or range of cells.**
2. **Choose Number from the Format menu (or press Shift-⌘-N).** The Numeric dialog box appears, as shown in Figure 5-14.

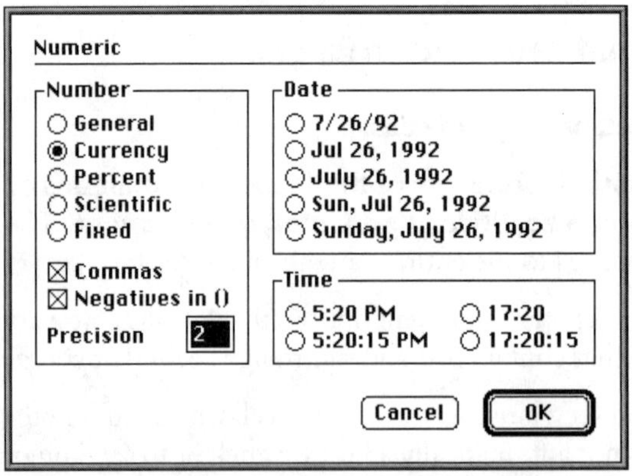

Figure 5-14: Use the Numeric dialog box to assign a number, date, or time format to any cell or range of cells.

3. **Set options and click OK to apply the options to the selected cell or cells.**

TIP

You can directly summon the Numeric dialog box by double-clicking any cell.

Reusing cell formats

When you are formatting cells, ClarisWorks also provides a pair of commands that enable you to copy an existing cell format and apply it to other cells.

Step-by-Steps

To copy and paste cell formats:

1. **Select a cell that contains the format options that you want to duplicate.**
2. **Choose Copy Format from the Edit menu (or press Shift-⌘-C).**
3. **Select the cell or range to which you want to apply the format options.**
4. **Choose Paste Format from the Edit menu (or press Shift-⌘-V).** The program applies the formats to the target cell(s).

Making cell contents fit

When you make an entry into a cell, sometimes it doesn't fit. If the cell contains text, it overflows into blank cells on the right, left, or both the right and the left (depending on the Alignment option that you choose for the original cell). If the cell next to the current cell is not empty, only as much of the text string as will fit in the current cell is displayed. (***Note:*** If a *number* doesn't fit in its cell, the program converts it to scientific notation or displays it as a string of # symbols.)

You can make text fit within a cell by applying the Wrap option from the Alignment submenu of the Format menu. Wrap works like the word wrap feature in a word processing program. (You may have to change the row height to see all of the wrapped text, however.)

In many cases, you may prefer to simply change the width of the column that contains the cell. ClarisWorks enables you to widen or narrow columns selectively. You also can change the height of rows.

Step-by-Steps

To set row heights or column widths:

1. **Select a cell or group of cells from the rows or columns whose height or width you want to change.**
2. **Choose Row Height or Column Width from the Format menu.** The Row Height or Column Width dialog box appears, as shown in Figure 5-15.

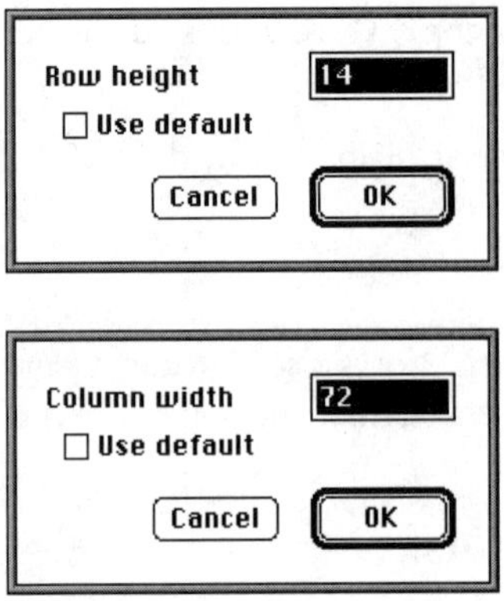

Figure 5-15: The Row Height and Column Width dialog boxes.

3. Type the number of points for the desired height or width. (One inch equals 72 points.) As an alternative, if you click the Use default check box, ClarisWorks enters the default height (14 points) or width (72 points).

4. Click OK. The program applies the new height or width to the selected rows or columns. ◆

You also can set the row height or column width manually. Move the pointer into the heading area at the top or left side of the worksheet. Whenever the pointer is over the dividing line between a pair of rows or a pair of columns, it changes into a special cursor, as shown in Figure 5-16. Click and drag to change the width or height of a column or row.

This pointer appears when you manually change a column width

	Checkbook

	A	B	C	D
C4	× ✓	Ace Hardware		
1				
2	Date	Check #	Payee	Description
3	6/19/93			Starting balance
4	6/20/93	127	Ace Hardware	Repair materials
5	6/20/93	128	Citizen's Electric	May electric bill
6	6/22/93		Deposit	Paycheck
7	6/28/93		Withdrawal	ATM
8				
9				

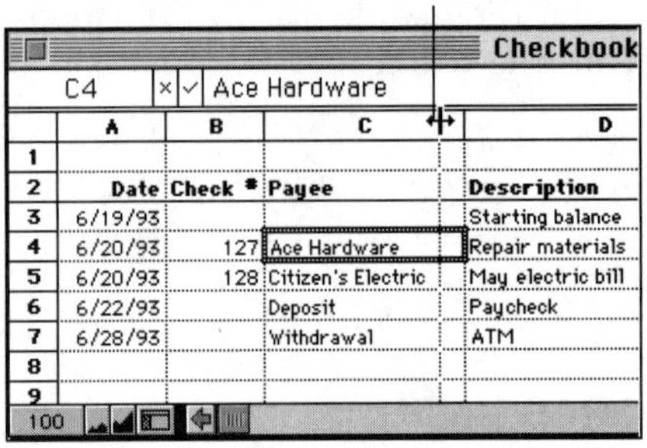

Figure 5-16: Manually changing a column width.

Making Charts

Question of the Day: If a picture is worth a thousand words, how much data is a chart worth? Charts and graphs provide a pictorial representation of data, making it easy to see significant trends, for example.

ClarisWorks has the capability to produce bar, area, line, scatter, pie, pictogram, stacked bar, stacked area, X-Y line, X-Y scatter, hi-low, stacked pictogram, and combination charts.

NOTE

As long as a chart is attached to a worksheet, changes that you make to the data are instantly reflected in the chart. If you copy a chart to another ClarisWorks document, however, the chart loses its link with the data. If the data changes, the chart remains the same. If you are running System 7, however, the link between the ClarisWorks document and the chart can be maintained by using Publish & Subscribe (as explained in Topic 20).

Step-by-Steps

To create a chart:

1. **Select the data range that you want to express as a chart.**

   If you also select the labels above and to the left of the data, they will appear in the chart and be used in the legend. Any text in the upper-left corner of the range becomes the chart title.

2. **Choose Make Chart from the Options menu (or press ⌘-M).** The Chart Options dialog box appears, as shown in Figure 5-17.

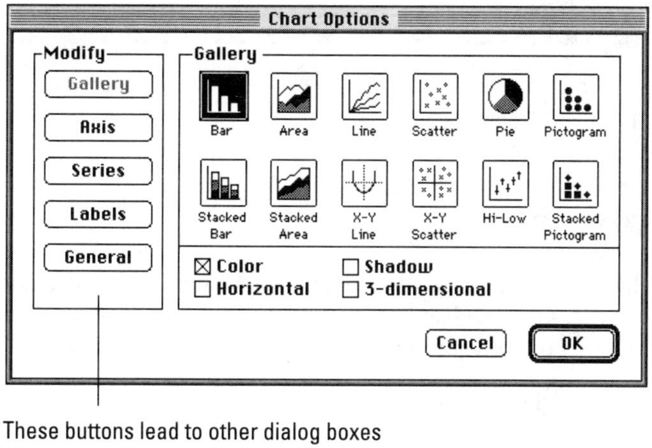

Figure 5-17: The Chart Options dialog box.

3. **Select a chart type from the Gallery section of the dialog box.**

4. ***Optional:* Choose chart enhancements at the bottom of the dialog box by clicking in check boxes.** The enhancements that are listed vary according to the type of chart that you select.
5. ***Optional:* Set other chart options by clicking the Axis, Series, Labels, or General buttons (these options are discussed in the next section).** A different dialog box appears for each button.
6. **Click OK.** A chart appears with the characteristics that you chose. Figure 5-18 explains the parts of a chart.

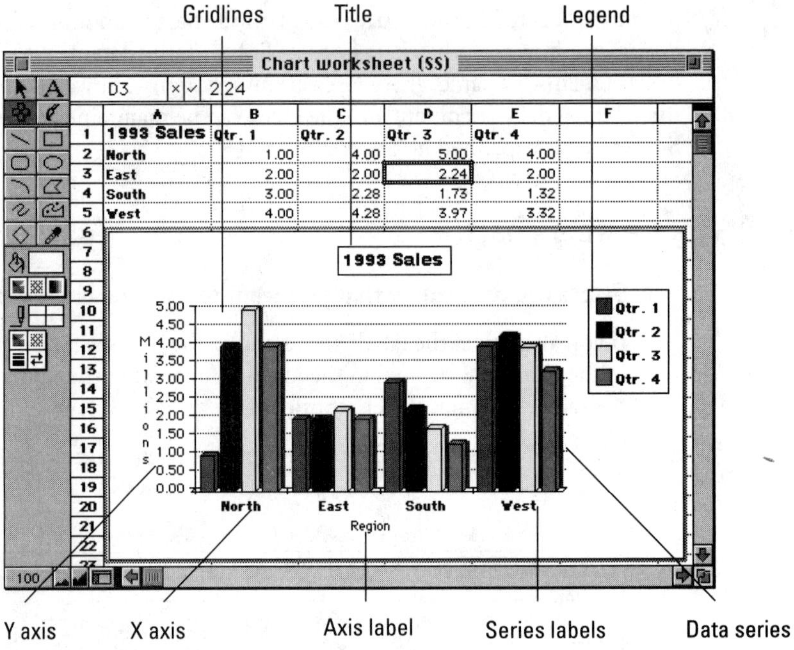

Figure 5-18: Essential chart components.

Chart options

If a chart doesn't look exactly the way you want it to look, ClarisWorks provides plenty of options for changing it without starting over. The following sections discuss chart options according to the Chart Options dialog box that is displayed.

Gallery options

ClarisWorks presents Gallery options (see Figure 5-17) whenever you issue the Make Chart or Modify Chart command. You use this dialog box to select a chart type initially, to change an existing chart to another chart type, or to set basic display options for the chart (such as color vs. black & white, horizontal vs. vertical, 2-dimensional vs. 3-dimensional, and whether shadows appear behind each plotted data series). The options that are presented at the bottom of the dialog box vary according to the chart type chosen.

Axis options

Axis options (shown in Figure 5-19) enable you to do the following:

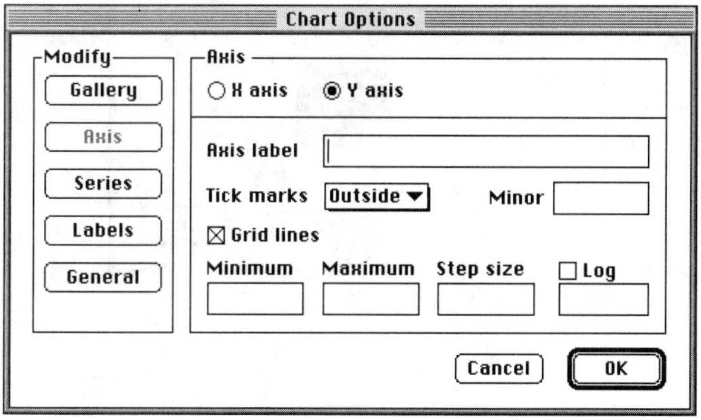

Figure 5-19: The Chart Options (Axis) dialog box.

- Add labels to the X (horizontal) and Y (vertical) axes
- Specify whether grid lines are displayed
- Set minimum, maximum, and/or step values for axis divisions
- Use a log scale
- Specify whether tick marks are shown and, if so, how they appear

You have to change the elements of each axis individually. Select an axis by clicking the X axis or Y axis radio button at the top of the Chart Options (Axis) dialog box. All other settings that you choose affect that axis only.

To change the color, pattern, or line width for an axis and its gridlines, select the axis on the chart and then choose these options from the Tool panel. To alter the font attributes for the axis text, select the axis on the chart and then choose options from the Format menu.

Series options

You use the Series options (shown in Figure 5-20) to specify settings for one or all of the data series included in the current chart. You can label data points with their values and change the type of display for individual data series. The latter option enables you to create combination charts. For example, you can show one data series with bars and the second data series as a line.

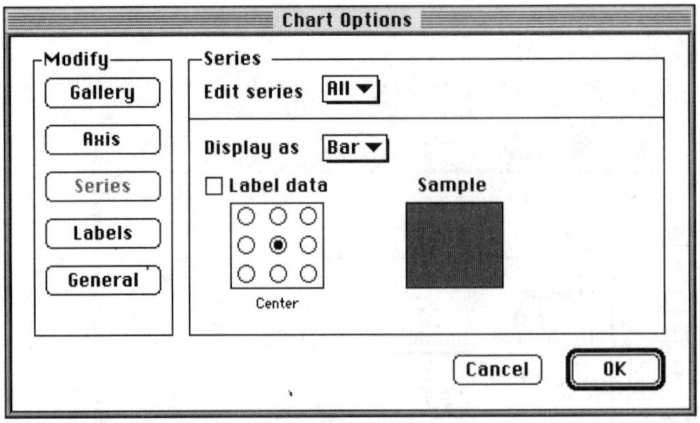

Figure 5-20: The Chart Options (Series) dialog box.

To specify a series option:

1. **In the Edit series pop-up menu, choose All or the specific series that you want to change.**
2. ***Optional:* For the chosen series, choose a graph type from the Display as pop-up menu.**

   Some graph types also enable you to pick a symbol to use for data points, as shown in Figure 5-21. To select a symbol for the data points for a particular series, choose a series from the Edit pop-up menu and then click a new symbol. To change a symbol's color, click the box to the right of the Symbol check box and select a color from the pop-up palette. To change the size of a symbol, enter a new number (in points) in the Size text-edit box. (One inch equals 72 points.)

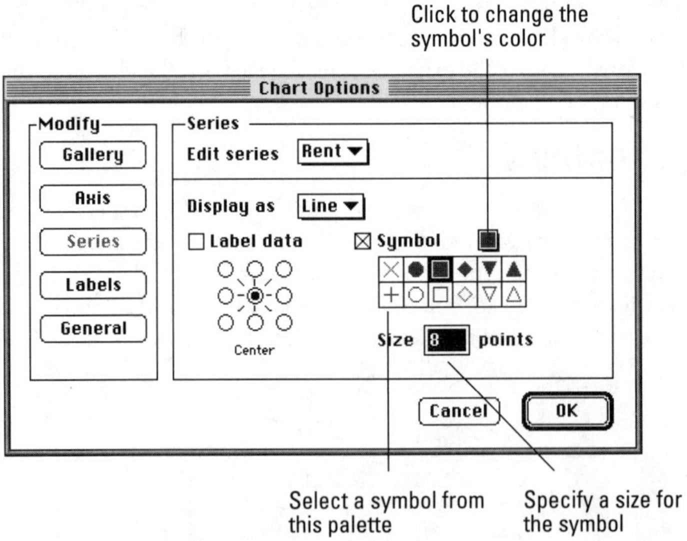

Figure 5-21: You use this dialog box to choose the shape, size, and color of the symbol for data points.

Other graph types, such as pie charts, offer different options, such as the ability to *explode* a slice.

3. ***Optional:* To label data points with their values, click the Label data check box. Click any of the nine radio buttons below the check box to indicate where the data label will appear in relation to each data point.** For some graph types, such as bar and pictogram, an example of a data label is shown in a Sample box.

4. **Click OK to put the new options into effect.**

To change the color or pattern of any series, select its box in the chart legend and then select another color, pattern, or gradient from the Tool panel.

Labels options

Use Labels options (see Figure 5-22) to specify settings for the chart title and legend.

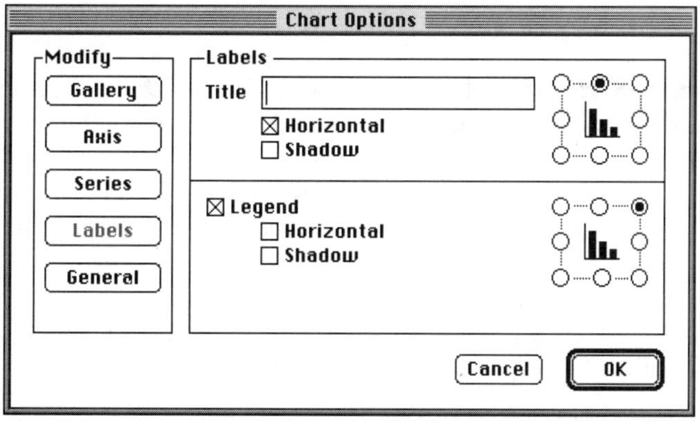

Figure 5-22: The Chart Options (Labels) dialog box.

To add or modify the chart title:

1. **If a title was in the upper-left corner of the chart range, it appears in the Title text-edit box.** You can change it there or create a new title in the box if none exists.

2. **To display the title horizontally, check the Horizontal check box.** To display the title vertically, remove the check mark.

3. **To add a drop shadow behind the chart title, check the Shadow check box.**

4. **To specify a different location for the chart title, click one of the eight title placement radio buttons that are to the right of the Title text-edit box.**

Font, size, and other text characteristics for the title come directly from the formatting that you apply to the title's cell in the worksheet. To change the formatting, change it in the cell. To change the title text, change it in the cell or in the Labels section of the Chart Options dialog box. To eliminate the title, delete it from the cell.

If a title did not come from the worksheet (that is, you created it in the Chart Options [Labels] dialog box), you can change the title's attributes by selecting it in the chart and then choosing options from the Format menu.

Regardless of where the title was created, you can alter its bounding box by selecting the title in the chart and then choosing a pattern, gradient, background color, line width, or pen color from the Tool panel.

Labels in the legend are determined by the series labels at the left and top of the worksheet range that you specify when you create the chart. To change any of the labels, change the contents of the appropriate cells.

To modify the legend:

1. **To change from the labels of one series to the labels of another series, click the General button in the Chart Options dialog box (see Figure 5-23).** The names in the Series names list box will be used in the legend. Click the radio button for Series in Rows or Series in Columns to change the series used for the legend. (***Note:*** This action also changes the chart layout.)

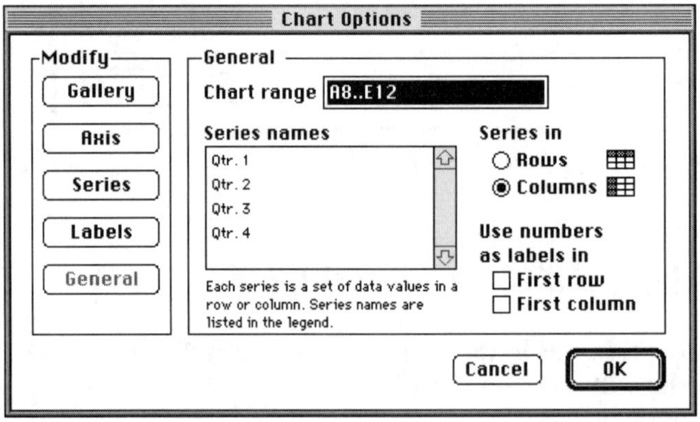

Figure 5-23: The Chart Options (General) dialog box.

2. **To change the position of the legend relative to the chart, click one of the eight position radio buttons in the Chart Options (Labels) dialog box (see Figure 5-22).**

3. **Use the Horizontal check box in the Chart Options (Labels) dialog box to designate whether the legend elements are to be displayed in a vertical or horizontal list.**

4. To place a shadow behind the legend box, click the Shadow check box.

5. To hide the legend, remove the check mark from the Legend check box.

You also can alter the legend's bounding box by selecting the legend in the chart and then choosing a pattern, gradient, background color, line width, or pen color from the Tool panel.

General options

Use the General options (see Figure 5-23) to change the data range for the chart, use numbers as axis labels, and indicate whether the data series in the selected range is in rows or in columns.

To specify a new chart range, type it into the Chart range text-edit box. Remember to separate the anchor points in the range with a pair of periods, as in A1..D7.

In most cases, you will use text from the worksheet as axis labels. If the first row or first column of the selected chart range contains numbers that you want to use as labels, click the (Use numbers as labels in) First Row or First Column check box, as appropriate.

To indicate whether the data series in the selected range is arranged in rows or in columns, click the (Series in) Rows or Columns check box, as appropriate. The labels that appear in the Series names list box are the data that will be plotted.

Pictograms

Pictograms use pictures, rather than bars, lines, and so on, to represent data. Pictogram images can be a single image or a series of repeating images, one above the other. To use pictogram images in a chart, you do one of the following:

- Select Pictogram or Stacked Pictogram as the chart type.
- Set one or more of the series to display as pictograms in the Chart Options (Series) dialog box.

The default pictogram symbol is a large arrow, but you can provide your own symbols (as shown in Figure 5-24).

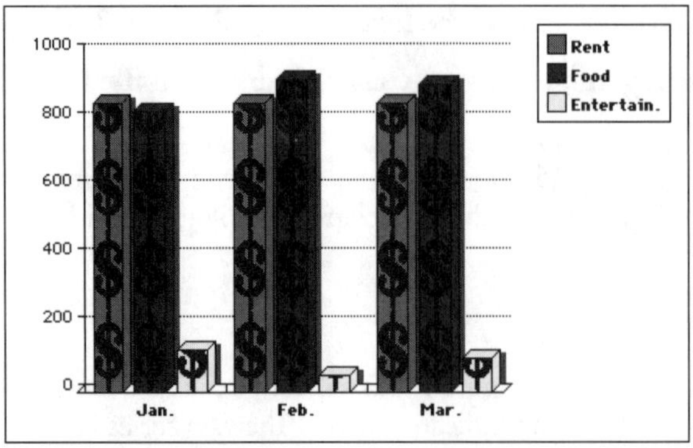

Figure 5-24: A pictogram with a repeating custom symbol.

Chart-editing shortcuts

So that you can avoid wading through dialog boxes and buttons, ClarisWorks provides several shortcuts that take you directly to the appropriate Chart Options dialog box:

- ◆ Double-click an open area of a chart to make the Chart Options (Gallery) dialog box appear. This action is equivalent to choosing Modify Chart (Shift-⌘-I) from the Options menu. The Chart Options (Gallery) dialog box enables you to change the chart type or to set basic display options.
- ◆ Double-click the X or Y axis of a chart to make the Chart Options (Axis) dialog box appear.
- ◆ Double-click a chart symbol in the legend to make the Chart Options (Series) dialog box appear.
- ◆ Double-click the chart title (if the chart has a title) or a label in the legend to make the Chart Options (Labels) dialog box appear.

Step-by-Steps

To change a pictogram symbol:

1. **In the Scrapbook or a graphics program, select the image that you want to use as a pictogram.** Choose Copy from the Edit menu to place a copy of the image on the Mac's Clipboard. (Claris recommends using a draw image rather than a paint picture.) For a financial chart, you could use a large dollar sign ($) as a pictogram image, for example.
2. **In the Chart Options (Series) dialog box (see Figure 5-25), choose All or a specific data series from the Edit series pop-up menu.** (You can use the same image for all series or a different image for each series.) The current pictogram image appears in the Sample box.
3. **Click the Sample box.** A dark border surrounds the box.
4. **Choose Paste from the Edit menu (or press ⌘-V).** The image on the Clipboard replaces the one in the Sample box and is used for the selected series or all series, depending on the choice that you made in the Edit series pop-up menu.

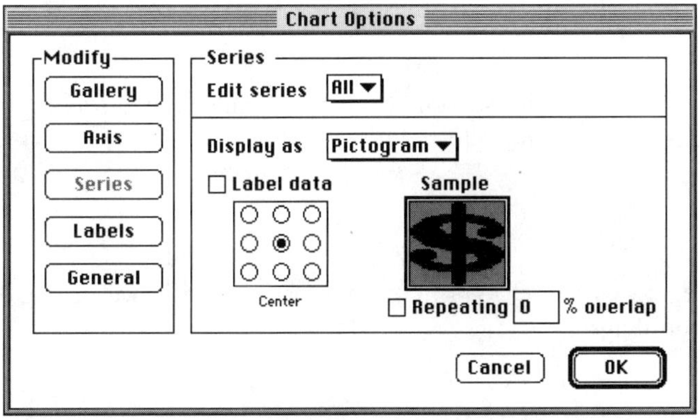

Figure 5-25: Use this box to change pictogram images.

5. **Click the Repeating check box to make a constant-sized symbol repeat in each bar.** If you want repeating symbols to overlap each other, enter a number in the % overlap text-edit box. Leave the Repeating check box blank if you want the symbol to be sized to match the height of the bar.

6. **If you want to use additional images for other data series, repeat Steps 2 through 5 as required.**

TIP

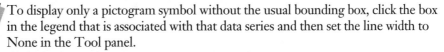

To display only a pictogram symbol without the usual bounding box, click the box in the legend that is associated with that data series and then set the line width to None in the Tool panel.

Other chart changes and embellishments

In addition to using the options in the Chart Options dialog boxes, you can use other methods to modify and embellish charts. After you create a chart, it acts like any other ClarisWorks object. When you first click a chart, handles appear at its corners. You can drag it to a new location or resize it by dragging a handle. You also can change the size precisely by choosing Scale Selection from the Options menu.

You can embellish the chart by adding text (for callouts, for example) and graphics. As an example, you can draw attention to an important element in the chart, such as an outstanding quarterly sales figure, by using the drawing tools to add an arrow pointing to the bar or data point. Finish off the effect by selecting the text tool to create a comment ("Best quarter since the company's inception!"), and then surround the comment with a colored box or oval.

You also can add a background color for the chart, color the legend box, and change the line width or color of the box that encloses the chart by choosing options from the palettes in the Tool panel. Because a chart is just another object, to achieve an uncluttered look, you can use the chart to hide the data used to create it. When you copy a chart into a word processing document, you can specify a text wrap for a more professional appearance.

Printing

ClarisWorks contains several features that apply only to printing worksheets. It enables you to do the following:

- Add manual page breaks
- Specify a print range
- Decide whether to print or omit the cell grid, as well as the column and row headings

Adding page breaks

Although ClarisWorks automatically determines where page breaks occur based on full pages, you may want to force a page break at a strategic spot in the worksheet — usually to keep important information from being split across pages.

To insert a page break, select the cell that you want to print as the last item on a page and choose Add Page Break from the Options menu. Any cells to the right or below the selected cell will print on other pages.

You can remove a manual page break by selecting the same cell and choosing Remove Page Break from the Options menu. To remove all manual page breaks simultaneously, choose Remove All Breaks from the Options menu.

TIP

If you want to see how the worksheet will print (and where the page breaks will occur), choose Page View (Shift-⌘-P) from the View menu.

Specifying a print range

When the time comes to print the worksheet, ClarisWorks intelligently defaults to printing the entire active portion of the worksheet; that is, it prints all areas of the worksheet (beginning with cell A1) that contain data. If you want to specify a different print range, choose Print Range from the Options menu. A Print Range dialog box appears, as shown in Figure 5-26. Click the Cell range radio button and type the specific range that you want to print. (Remember that a range consists of the upper-left cell coordinate and the lower-right cell coordinate, separated by a pair of periods.) Click OK to set the new range.

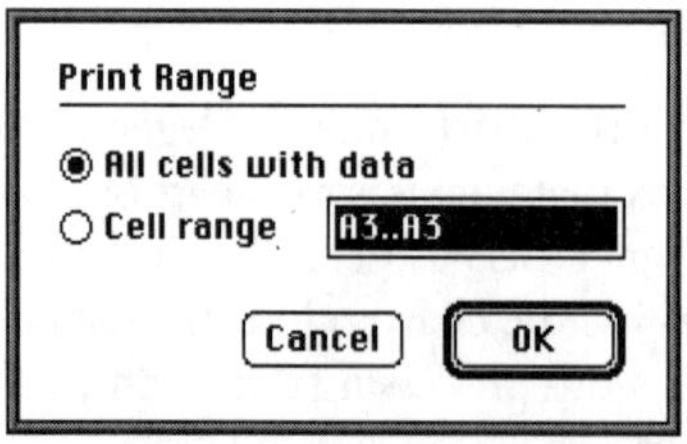

Figure 5-26: You use this dialog box to set a specific print range.

TIP

If you preselect a range by dragging and then go directly to the Print command, you do not have to use the Print Range command. The program automatically sets the Print Range to match the highlighted range.

Working with a modified Print dialog box

When you choose Print from the File menu (or press ⌘-P), you'll notice that the Print dialog box (see Figure 5-27) has been modified slightly. At the bottom of the dialog box is a series of check boxes that appear only when you are printing a worksheet. Depending on the boxes that are checked, you can print or omit column headings, row headings, and the cell grid. Initially, these settings match the options that you have chosen in the Display dialog box (which is discussed in "Changing display options" later in this Topic).

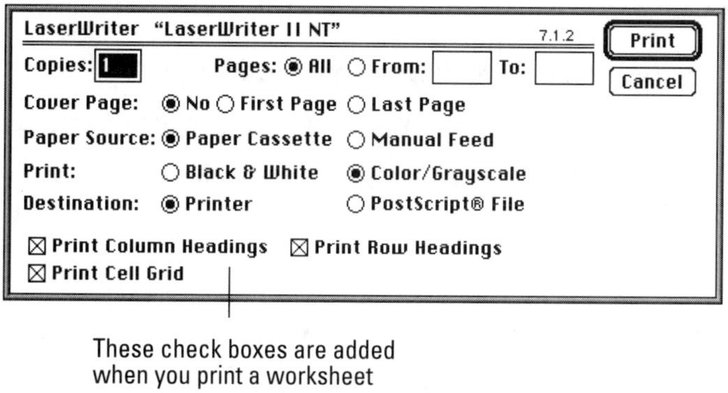

Figure 5-27: When you print a worksheet, a modified Print dialog box appears.

Looking at Other Procedures and Options

This section explains the remaining commands, procedures, and options that are available to you in the spreadsheet environment. (In short, other stuff. . . .) Although you don't have to use any of these features (some you may *never* use), knowing that they're around is nice.

Automatic and manual recalculation

Normally, ClarisWorks recalculates the worksheet whenever it is necessary. If a cell contains a formula that refers to another cell (B17, for example) and you change the contents of B17, the program automatically recalculates the formula. In very large worksheets or on slow Macs, recalculation can be time-consuming. If you like, you can turn off the automatic recalculation by choosing Auto Calc from the Calculate menu and removing its check mark.

When Auto Calc is turned off, ClarisWorks recalculates the worksheet only when you choose Calculate Now from the Calculate menu (or press Shift-⌘-=). (***Note:*** If you check Auto Calc, you *never* have to choose Calculate Now.)

Protecting cells

Like any other computer document, a worksheet can be a fragile thing. If you make a wrong entry in a critical cell, many of the worksheet's underlying assumptions may become incorrect and lead you to wrong conclusions about the data or its summary figures. If you edit a formula and make a mistake, similar consequences can result. To prevent inadvertent changes of this sort, ClarisWorks enables you to protect selected cells.

Step-by-Steps

To protect a cell or range:

1. Select the cell or range that you want to protect.

2. Choose Protect Cells from the Options menu (or press ⌘-H).

If you attempt to edit, delete, or move a protected cell, ClarisWorks displays an alert box with the message *Some cells are protected.* If a protected cell contains a formula, on the other hand, the calculation will still be recomputed as necessary.

To remove protection from a cell or range, select the cell or range and then choose Unprotect Cells from the Options menu (or press Shift-⌘-H).

NOTE

If you protect an entire column of data (by clicking the column heading and then choosing the Protect Cells command), you can still enter data into blank cells in the column. Any cells in the column that already contain data will be protected.

Locking titles

Depending on the nature of the worksheet, locking row or column titles in place is sometimes useful. As you scroll the worksheet, the titles remain in view. Figure 5-28 shows a worksheet with column A and rows 1 and 2 locked in place.

- *To lock a set of row and column titles in place,* select the cell that intersects the row and column titles (cell A2 in Figure 5-28) and choose Lock Title Position from the Options menu.
- *To lock a set of column titles in place,* select the entire bottom row of the titles (by clicking the row number heading) and choose Lock Title Position from the Options menu.
- *To lock a set of row titles in place,* select the entire right-most column of the titles (by clicking the column number heading) and choose Lock Title Position from the Options menu.

To unlock the titles (to choose a different set of locking titles, to edit a cell in the title region, or to remove the locking titles), choose Lock Title Position again.

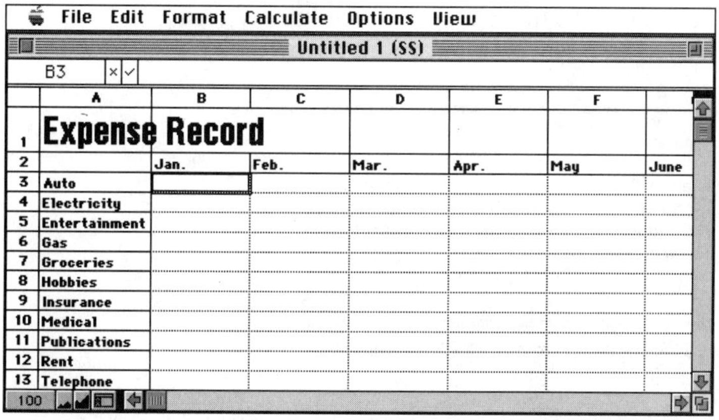

Figure 5-28: Solid lines, rather than the usual dotted gridlines, surround the cells in the locked rows (1 and 2) and column (A).

Setting a default font

Normally, the default font for worksheets is 9 point Geneva. Unless you manually select another font for a cell, the program uses the default font for all formatting.

To set a different default font for the current worksheet, choose Default Font from the Options menu. The Default Font dialog box appears, as shown in Figure 5-29. Select a new font from the list box (all fonts installed in the system are displayed in the list), type a point size in the Size text-edit box, and click OK. All cells that have not had a different font or size manually applied to them change to the new default font and size. Cells that you have manually set to a specific font or size retain that font or size.

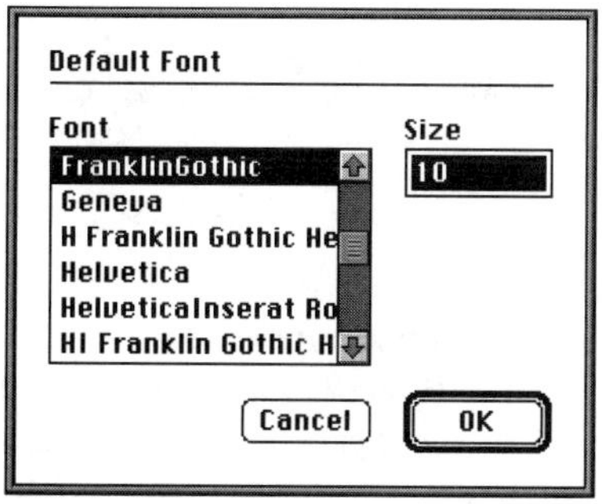

Figure 5-29: The Default Font dialog box.

Changing display options

The Display command in the Options menu enables you to exert some control over the way ClarisWorks displays the current worksheet. You may want to alter the display before printing a worksheet or using it as part of a presentation or slide show, for example. In the Display dialog box (see Figure 5-30), checking or clearing a particular check box has the following effects:

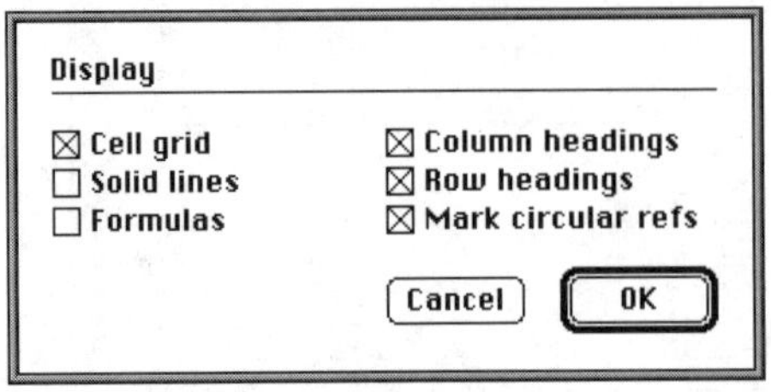

Figure 5-30: The default settings in the Display dialog box.

- *Cell grid.* When this box is unchecked, ClarisWorks displays the worksheet without a cell grid.
- *Solid lines.* When this box is checked, the program displays the cell grid as solid lines. When it is unchecked (default), a dotted cell grid is displayed.
- *Formulas.* When this box is checked, ClarisWorks displays formulas in cells, instead of displaying the results of the formulas. This option is useful for checking the accuracy of a worksheet.
- *Column headings.* When this box is unchecked, the program does not display column headings (letters).
- *Row headings.* When this box is unchecked, the program does not display row headings (numbers).
- *Mark circular refs.* When this box is checked, data in a cell that contains a circular reference is surrounded by bullet characters (•).

Down to Business: Creating a Check Register Worksheet

As an illustration of some of the ClarisWorks spreadsheet capabilities, you can create a worksheet that fulfills the reason that many new users say they bought their computer: to balance their checkbook. (Of course, when you think about it, paying several thousand dollars for slightly more capability than a hand calculator doesn't make a great deal of sense, does it?)

This worksheet is useful if you don't like to balance your checking account manually or if you want a clean printed copy of your checking activity. But because the worksheet duplicates the check register, you have to enter your checks and deposits twice — once in the check register and once in the worksheet.

In addition to duplicating a standard check register, the worksheet tosses in a few extra features:

- Separate Payee and Description columns, so that you can record whom each check was made out to as well as what it was for
- Automatic calculation of the balance
- Automatic calculation of the total of uncleared checks, withdrawals, and deposits (the uncleared total)

Creating the worksheet

Figure 5-31 shows the worksheet with a half dozen sample entries. Use the following steps to create a working copy of the worksheet.

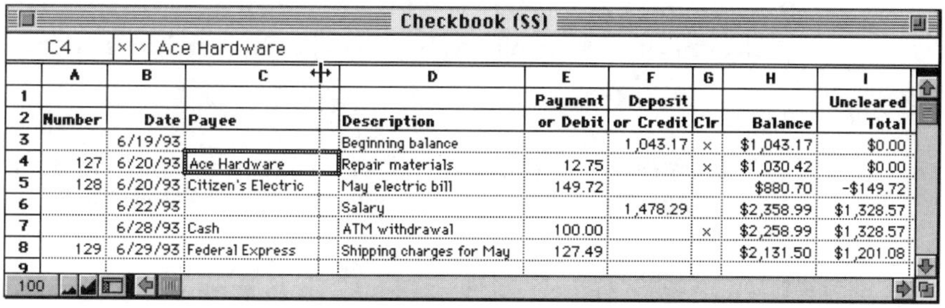

Checkbook (SS)

C4 | Ace Hardware

	A	B	C	D	E	F	G	H	I
1					Payment	Deposit			Uncleared
2	Number	Date	Payee	Description	or Debit	or Credit	Clr	Balance	Total
3		6/19/93		Beginning balance		1,043.17	×	$1,043.17	$0.00
4	127	6/20/93	Ace Hardware	Repair materials	12.75		×	$1,030.42	$0.00
5	128	6/20/93	Citizen's Electric	May electric bill	149.72			$880.70	-$149.72
6		6/22/93		Salary		1,478.29		$2,358.99	$1,328.57
7		6/28/93	Cash	ATM withdrawal	100.00		×	$2,258.99	$1,328.57
8	129	6/29/93	Federal Express	Shipping charges for May	127.49			$2,131.50	$1,201.08
9									

Figure 5-31: The check register worksheet.

To lay out the worksheet:

1. **Create the column labels in rows 1 and 2.**

   All label text is 9 point Geneva bold. (All other text is 9 point Geneva.)

2. **Set the alignment for each column.**

   To set the alignment for a column, click a column heading to select the entire column and then choose an option from the Alignment submenu of the Format menu. Columns A, B, E, F, H, and I are right-aligned (⌘-]); columns C and D are left-aligned (⌘-[); and column G is center-aligned (⌘-\).

3. **Set column widths by using the Column Width command in the Format menu as follows: A (44), B (52), C (104), D (124), E and F (56), G (20), and H and I (64).**

4. **Add a bottom border to cells A2 through I2 by using the Borders command in the Format menu.**

5. **To set number formats for data in the worksheet, select column A by clicking its column heading, choose Number from the Format menu (or press Shift-⌘-N), choose Fixed with a Precision of 0 (zero), and click OK.**

Repeat this procedure for the other columns, setting options as follows: B (choose the first Date option), E and F (Fixed, Commas, Precision 2), and H and I (Currency, Commas, Precision 2).

6. **The record in row 3 is reserved for the beginning balance; for now, enter today's date in B3,** Beginning balance **in D3,** 1000 **in F3,** =F3 **in H3, and** 0 **in I3.** (Later, you can change this information to match your real beginning balance.)

7. **Enter this formula in cell H4 to calculate the running balance (Balance):**

```
=IF(B4<>"",H3-E4+F4,"")
```

After entering the formula, copy it to the remaining cells in column H by selecting cells H4 through H500 and choosing Fill Down (⌘-D) from the Calculate menu.

8. **Enter this formula into cell I4 to calculate the running total of uncleared checks, withdrawals, and deposits (Uncleared Total):**

```
=IF(B4="","",IF(G4<>"x",I3-E4+F4,I3))
```

After entering the formula, copy it to the remaining cells in column I by selecting cells I4 through I500 and choosing Fill Down (⌘-D) from the Calculate menu.

9. **To keep the labels in rows 1 and 2 from scrolling off-screen as additional transactions are entered, make them into titles: Select row 2 by clicking the row heading (the number 2) and choose Lock Title Position from the Options menu.** After you lock the rows, you cannot edit any of the cells in rows 1 or 2. Later, if you need to make changes in either row, choose Lock Title Position again.

10. ***Optional:* Select columns H and I by clicking their headings and choose Protect Cells from the Options menu (or press ⌘-H) to keep the entries in these columns from being altered accidentally.** (The entries in columns H and I are all calculated automatically, based on your transactions.)

Understanding the formulas

The formulas are fairly complex, so they require further examination. The formula in H4 is

```
=IF(B4<>"",H3-E4+F4,"")
```

First, the formula checks cell B4 — the date for the current record — to see whether it is empty. If B4 contains something (a date, presumably), the first action is performed. That is, the formula takes the previous balance (H3), subtracts any payment entered for this record (E4), and adds any deposit entered for this record

(F4). If, on the other hand, the date field is blank for the record, the second action is taken: The Balance entry is left blank. (You test for the existence of a date because every legitimate record should contain one. If no date is found, you assume that the record does not yet exist.)

NOTE

This formula could have been written as =H3–E4+F4. When filled down to the remaining records, however, transactions that didn't exist yet would all display the current balance. Using this more complex approach to test whether a transaction exists produces a more attractive worksheet.

The formula in I4 is even more complex. It contains an IF function nested within another IF function.

```
=IF(B4="","",IF(G4<>"x",I3-E4+F4,I3))
```

The formula performs two actions. First, if the Date field is blank IF(B4="", it assumes that the record does not yet exist and leaves the Uncleared Total entry blank — just as the previous formula left the Balance entry blank. Because the first test has been met, the remainder of the formula is not evaluated.

Next, if the Date field is not blank, the formula checks the Clr entry (G4) for the current record to see whether it contains an *x*. (You use an *x* to indicate that — according to the bank statement — a check, withdrawal, or deposit has cleared.) If an *x* is not found, the formula takes the previous Uncleared Total (I3), subtracts the current Payment from it (E4), and adds the current Deposit (F4). Thus, if an entry has not cleared, its payment or deposit is reflected in the Uncleared Total. If an *x* is found, on the other hand, the previous Uncleared Total in I3 is simply copied to the cell.

Using the worksheet

The best time to begin using this worksheet is when you open a new account or immediately after you've received a bank statement and balanced your checkbook.

Begin by editing the first record (row 3). Replace the temporary date (B3) and balance (F3) with today's date and your balance. Placing the balance in F3 automatically copies it to the Balance column (H3). Because the beginning balance won't be part of a later reconciliation, type a lowercase *x* in the Clr column (G3) for the entry.

Now go back through your check register and, beginning in row 4, make an entry for every outstanding check, withdrawal, and deposit. (If you don't want gaps in the register, you can go back to the oldest outstanding check, withdrawal, or deposit, and enter *every* transaction up to the current date. If you do so, be sure to add an *x* in the Clr field for every item that has cleared.)

When a bank statement arrives, the Checkbook worksheet can help with the reconciliation. Going down G (the Clr column), add an *x* for every item that has cleared. When you are through, the last figure in the Uncleared Total column will represent the total of the outstanding deposits minus the outstanding checks.

Quick Tips

The following quick tip tells you how preselecting a range of data can speed data entry.

Speeding data entry by preselecting a range

Although you can tab and click to move from cell to cell when you enter data, you can use a faster method to enter data into a specific section of the worksheet. Start by preselecting the range into which you will be entering data. In the checkbook worksheet, the range might look like the one in Figure 5-32.

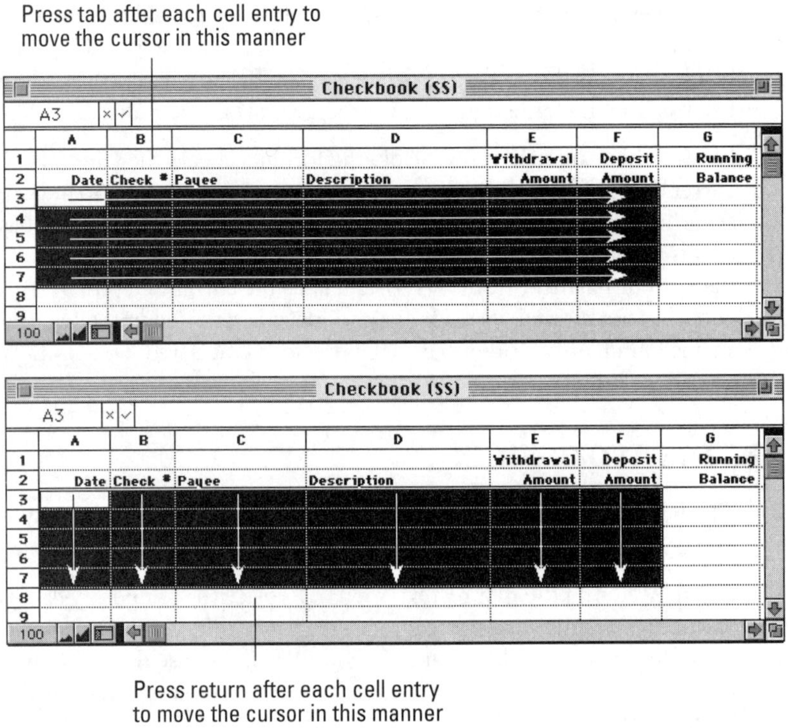

Figure 5-32: A preselected range.

In a preselected range, the active cell is white, while all other cells are dark. After entering information in the first cell, press Tab. The cell to the right becomes active. If you continue to press Tab after each cell entry, the active cell shifts across each row, one cell at a time. When a row is completed, the cursor drops down to the first cell in the next row. If you press Return (rather than Tab) after each cell entry, the cursor moves down one cell at a time through each selected column.

Moving On Up

Although the ClarisWorks spreadsheet environment suffices for many users, as your needs become more complex, you may want to check out a more full-featured spreadsheet program. Features such as a macro language, the ability to define your own functions, additional chart types and functions, and linked and three-dimensional worksheets are all commonplace in commercial spreadsheets. Currently, the leading Mac spreadsheet program is Microsoft Excel (Microsoft Corporation).

TIP

The export capabilities of ClarisWorks make upgrading to other spreadsheets easy to do. If you save a ClarisWorks worksheet in Microsoft Excel or SYLK format, most other spreadsheet programs can interpret it correctly. Similarly, if you use a different spreadsheet program at the office and want to continue working on it at home, you can probably import the spreadsheet into ClarisWorks by using the Open command. Note, however, that macros that have been attached to the worksheet (in Excel or 1-2-3, for example) will not function in ClarisWorks.

If you're looking for additional charting capabilities, check out DeltaGraph Professional (DeltaPoint) for business charts. KaleidaGraph (Synergy Software) and CA-Cricket Graph (Computer Associates) are excellent for scientific and statistical graphing.

Summary

- A worksheet is a grid that is composed of numbered rows and lettered columns. A cell is the intersection of a row and a column. You enter text strings, numbers, and formulas into cells. Formulas can refer to other cells, contain constants, and use any of the 100 built-in ClarisWorks functions.
- The cell in which the cursor is positioned is known as the active cell. The location of any cell is given by its cell address.
- A group of cells is known as a range. A range is identified by its anchor points — the upper-left and lower-right cells in the range.
- Formulas are normally evaluated from left to right. The precedence levels of the operations performed within the formula can change the calculation order, however, as can the use of parentheses to enclose operations.
- You can type functions directly into formulas, or you can paste them there (along with dummy arguments) by using the Paste Function command.
- You can copy and paste formulas to other cells. You also can paste just the values contained in cells, ignoring the formulas. The Fill Down and Fill Right commands expedite copying a formula to a large range.
- ClarisWorks provides many commands that make reorganizing a worksheet simple. It includes commands that insert and delete cells, columns, and rows; move ranges of cells to new locations; sort data; and transpose a range (swapping the positions of rows and columns).
- To make worksheets more attractive, you can selectively apply font, size, style, color, and alignment options to cell contents. To make the contents of the cell fit inside the cell borders, you can widen column widths, change row heights, or apply a Wrap format. You can control the way the program displays numbers, dates, and times by choosing options in the Numeric dialog box.
- The Copy and Paste Format commands enable you to easily apply existing cell formats to other cells.
- ClarisWorks provides a dozen different styles of charts that you can use to embellish a worksheet. Because every chart is also an object, you can copy and paste charts into other documents.
- When printing a worksheet, ClarisWorks defaults to selecting the entire active area of the worksheet. You can specify a particular print range, add manual page breaks, and turn off the printing of some worksheet elements, such as the cell grid and row or column headings.
- You can protect important cells to prevent them from being changed inadvertently. You can lock important information (titles, for example) at the top and left sides of the worksheet in place so that it doesn't disappear when you scroll the worksheet.

Topic 6

The Database Environment

Overview

A *database* is an organized set of information — usually on one particular topic. One common example of a database is a card file that contains the names, addresses, and phone numbers of business associates, customers, or friends. Other everyday examples of databases that you can find around the office or home include employee records, inventory records, a recipe file, and a list of videotapes.

Every database is composed of *records*. In the previous examples, each record contains all the pertinent information about one friend, one employee, one inventory part, one recipe, or one videotape.

Each record is composed of *fields*. A field contains one piece of information about the employee (a social security number, for example), videotape (the name of the star), recipe (cooking time), or friend (date of birth). In an address database, you may have separate fields for each person's first name, last name, street address, city, state, and ZIP code.

Unlike a word processing document (which is free-form), a computer database has an order that comes from its use of fields. Every field holds one particular type of information (an employee identification number, for example). As you skim through the records of the database, you see that the same type of information is in that field in every record. Figure 6-1 shows the relationship between a database, records, and fields.

If you're still having trouble understanding what a database is, I'll put it in simpler terms. Think about file folders — the kind that are found in office filing cabinets. Each folder contains a different type of information, such as receipts, invoices, or employee information. A folder is the equivalent of a *database* and contains all the information that you've collected on a particular topic.

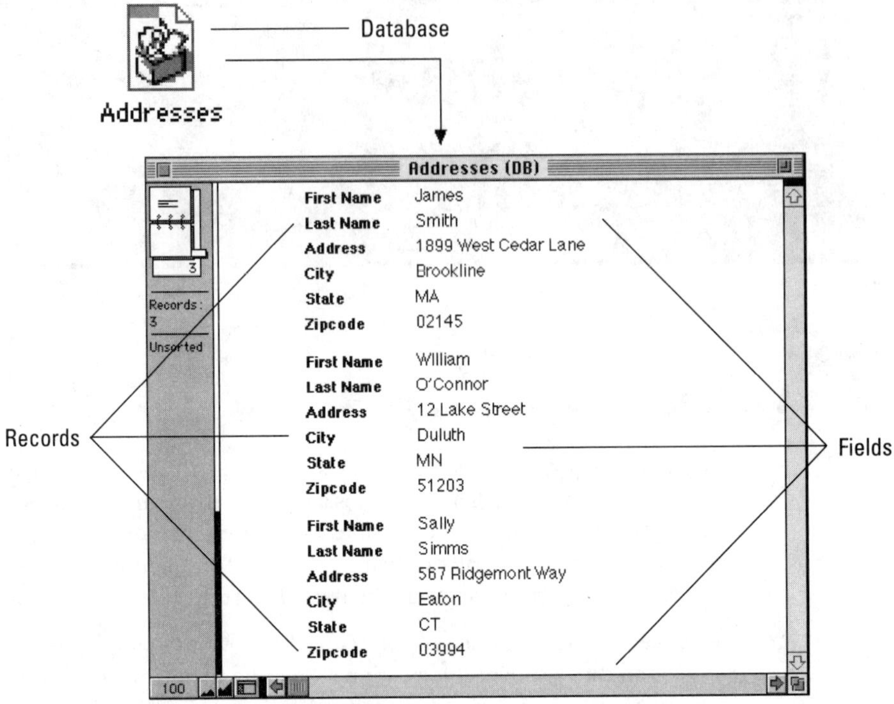

Figure 6-1: A computer database contains a series of records; each record is composed of a set of fields.

Inside each folder is a bunch of forms. The forms are the database *records*. Each record contains specific information about one person, place, or thing.

The lines that have been filled in on the forms are called *fields*. Examples of fields in an employee form may include first and last names, address, phone number, and social security number.

Thus, a database is a hierarchy of information: the database file, records, and fields.

Although you can keep database information in a word processing document, you lose the data manipulation advantages that a database provides, such as the capability to select subsets of records (for example, only employees who make between $20,000 and $30,000 per year), sort records by one or more fields (for example, by ZIP code, last name, years of employment, or cost of ingredients), create fields that perform calculations and computations (for example, totaling all items ordered or combining two text fields), and generate custom reports.

Another great thing about a computerized database, as compared to a paper version, is the ease with which you can modify and reorganize its contents. Early database programs required you to define every field before you started to enter data. If you later decided to add a field, delete a field, or change the type of a particular field (from text to numeric, for example), you had to execute a complex procedure to reorganize the database.

Current database programs, such as the ClarisWorks database environment, make reorganizing a database remarkably easy. If you need a new field, for example, you simply define it and add it to the appropriate layouts.

When Should I Use a Database?

If you are new to computing or have never used a database program before, you may not readily understand why or when to create a database instead of using another ClarisWorks environment. Databases excel at organizing information — both text and numeric. Think in terms of the card file analogy again. Every database has a unifying topic. In the case of a card file, the central topic or theme is information about colleagues or friends. Each card in the file is the equivalent of a database record. The card contains all the pertinent information about a person, such as the person's name, address, phone number, birth date, and miscellaneous notes.

In a database, you create a separate field for each of these pieces of information. Because you are using a database, rather than scraps of paper or a word processing document, you can view and use the data in ways that would otherwise be impossible. Using a database, you can do the following:

- Quickly identify records that match simple criteria (Name = Sam Jones) or very complex criteria (Salary <= $40,000 and Age > 45)
- Sort the records by the contents of one or more fields (by Last Name within City)
- Create multiple layouts for any database (create data entry, phone directory, and label layouts for the same database)
- Set data validation criteria for some fields (the field must be unique, or its data must be within a particular range)
- Specify a data type for each field (text, number, date, time, calculation, or summary)
- Automatically enter certain data (today's date or an invoice number)
- Perform calculations (totals or averages for each record, a subset of records, or the entire database)

Working with the ClarisWorks Database

You use a ClarisWorks database in three modes: Layout, Browse, and Find. In *Layout* mode, you arrange fields and other database objects on a screen page so that the program will display and print them the way you want it to. You use *Browse* mode to view, edit, add, delete, and sort records. You do all data entry in Browse mode. *Find* mode enables you to search for records that meet one or more criteria (Last Name = Smith, for example).

Defining Fields

Every database is composed of fields into which you enter information. In fact, you cannot begin to enter data until you have defined at least one field by specifying its name and the type of data that it will contain.

Although the database environment is packed with fancy features, sometimes simplest is best. You can just define the necessary fields, accept the default layout, and start entering data. The following example shows the steps for designing a basic address book database. As you progress in this Topic, you'll learn how to customize the layout and work with special data types and options.

Step-by-Steps

To create a simple database:

1. **Choose New from the File menu (or press ⌘-N).** The New Document dialog box appears.

2. **Click the Database radio button, followed by the OK button.** A new database is created, and the Define Fields dialog box appears (see Figure 6-2).

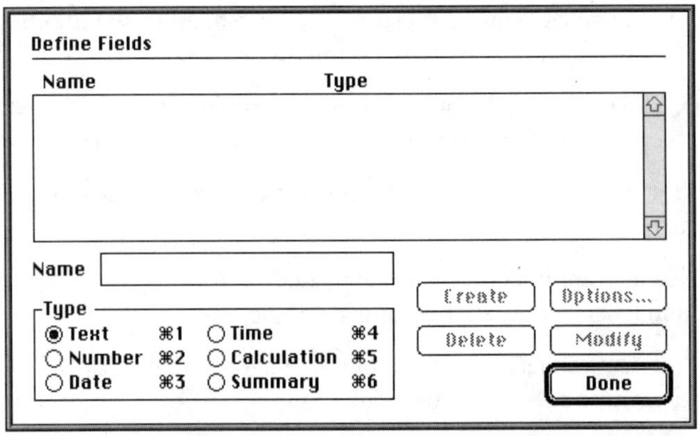

Figure 6-2: You can use the Define Fields dialog box to specify name, field type, and options for every field in the database. You also can use it to modify a field definition or delete a field.

3. **Define the fields you want to use in the database.** For the address book database, you'll define the following fields (in order): First Name, Last Name, Address, City, State, ZIP, and Birthdate. Birthdate is a Date field; all others are Text fields.

   For each field, type its name in the Name text-edit box, click the appropriate Type radio button (or press its Command-key equivalent), and then click Create. The field is added to the list box.

Note that the name of the field just defined is still in the text-edit box. When you begin typing a name for the *next* field, the text-edit box automatically clears.

4. **After you have defined all fields, click Done.** A database with the default layout (field sizes, placements, fonts, and so on) appears (as shown in Figure 6-3), ready for you to enter the first record.

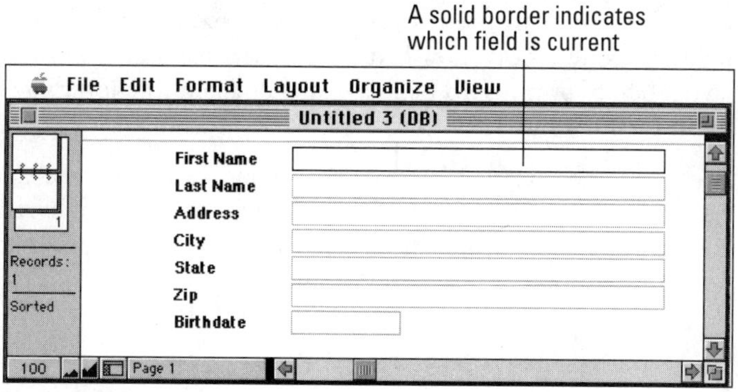

Figure 6-3: After you define the fields, ClarisWorks displays the first record.

Field types

As the Define Fields dialog box in Figure 6-2 shows, ClarisWorks offers six types of fields, each for a different type of data: text, number, date, time, calculation, and summary. By assigning the correct data type to each field, you enable ClarisWorks to do some simple validation (for example, making sure that only dates are entered in date fields and only numbers are entered in numeric fields).

Although you can define every field as text, you'll miss out on the validation features that ClarisWorks offers, as well as some of the real power of the program, if you don't take advantage of the other field types. The following sections describe how each field type works.

Text fields

Although it's called a *text* field, you can enter any type of character into a text field. Letters, numbers, punctuation marks, spaces, and so on are all legal characters. Data that you enter into a text field will word wrap, just as it does in a word processing document. This feature makes text fields ideal for notes, as well as for any type of information that contains a mixture of letters and numbers (street addresses, for example).

As with other fields in a ClarisWorks database, you can apply selective formatting to any portion of the field's contents. For example, if you create a Comments field that you define as a text field, you can selectively change the font for some words or add a style such as italic to others.

The size of the bounding box for a text field does not restrict the amount of text that you can enter in the field. As you type, the bounding box expands vertically as needed to accommodate additional text. When you exit the field (by pressing the Tab key or by clicking in a different field), the bounding box returns to its normal size, obscuring any overflow text. (***Note:*** To print the contents of a text field that contains overflow text, you must expand the size of the field on the layout before printing.) The field expands again whenever you move the text insertion point into it.

NOTE

A ClarisWorks text field can hold a maximum of about 500 characters. If you exceed this limit, a message to that effect appears. You will have to edit the contents of the field manually by removing some of the text or style formatting before ClarisWorks will accept the entry.

Number fields

Number fields are for numeric data only, such as prices, quantities, and so on. Legitimate numeric characters include the digits 0 through 9, parentheses or a minus sign (for negative numbers), the plus sign (+), a percent sign (%), and an *e* (for scientific notation). ClarisWorks automatically flags other characters and requests that you reenter the number. It ignores commas or dollar signs during data entry.

If you enter a number that exceeds the width of the field, the program automatically converts the number to scientific notation (1.234571+e19, for example). As with overly long text entries, you have to move the text insertion point into the number field to see a number that exceeds the field width.

You can assign a display format, such as Currency or a particular number of decimal places, to any number field. See "Field formatting" later in this Topic, for more information.

TIP

You should define some fields as text fields even though they are composed entirely of numbers. ZIP codes are a perfect example. Because number fields cannot display leading zeros, a ZIP code of 01535 would display as *1535* in a number field. Similarly, numbers that contain parentheses or dashes are not allowed. Thus, social security numbers and phone numbers are best defined as text fields, too.

Date fields

You use date fields, of course, to record calendar dates, such as 7/19/93. Examples include birth dates, the date a product was ordered, the date an employee was hired, or the date a school project is due. You can enter dates in a number of different ways. All of the following setups are acceptable:

- 7/19/93
- 7-19-93
- July 19, 1993
- Jul 19, 93
- 7/19
- Jul 19

As you can see, the methods for entering information into a date field are extremely flexible. As long as you enter enough information to identify each portion of the date (the first three letters of the month's name, for example), ClarisWorks will do its best to interpret what you type. If you omit the year, as in the last two examples, ClarisWorks assumes that you are referring to the current year and inserts it for you.

You also can display dates within their fields in several ways. For a discussion of formatting options, see "Field formatting" later in this Topic.

Time fields

Time fields enable you to record times in hours, minutes, and seconds. The various time formats (discussed in "Field formatting," later in this Topic) enable you to record times with AM and PM suffixes, as well as in 12- or 24-hour formats.

Calculation fields

As shown in the preceding date calculation examples, the availability of calculation fields sets a ClarisWorks database apart from a paper-based database or one created in a word processor.

A calculation field is based on a formula that you specify. You can use calculation fields to perform simple math, such as the computation of state sales tax ('Price'*.07), a product mark-up ('Cost'*1.5), or the sum of several fields ('Qty1'+'Qty2'+'Qty3'). Calculation fields also can incorporate any of the ClarisWorks database functions that are described in the *ClarisWorks User's Guide.*

Step-by-Steps

To define a calculation field:

1. **Choose Define Fields from the Layout menu (or press Shift-⌘-D).** The Define Fields dialog box appears, as shown in Figure 6-4.

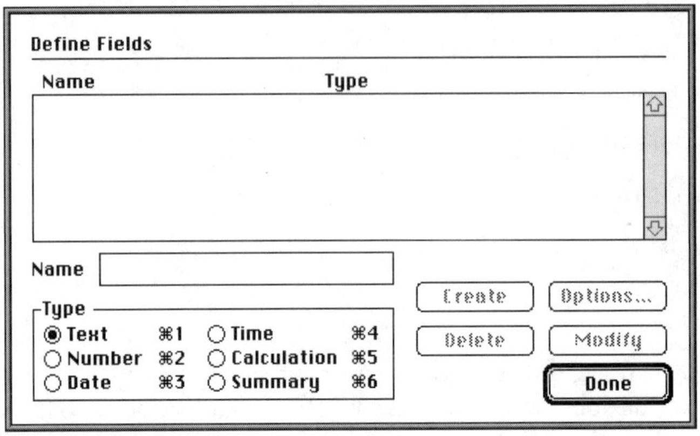

Figure 6-4: The Define Fields dialog box.

2. **Enter a name for the calculation field in the Name text-edit box and click the Calculation radio button in the Type section of the dialog box (or press ⌘-5).**

3. **Click Create.** The Enter Formula dialog box appears, as shown in Figure 6-5.

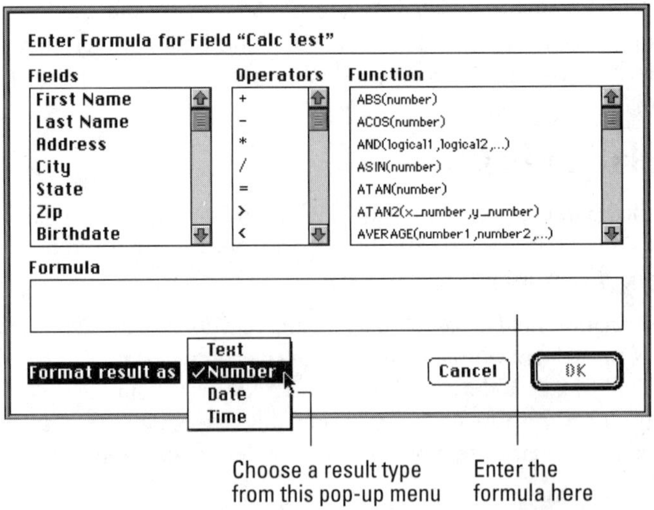

Figure 6-5: The Enter Formula dialog box.

4. **Enter the formula in the Formula text-edit box.** You can create formulas by typing directly into the box; by selecting fields, operators, and functions from the three scrolling list boxes (click an option to insert it into the formula at the text insertion point); or by combining the two approaches.
5. **Choose a result type from the Format result as pop-up menu.** The choices are Text, Number, Date, and Time.
6. **Click OK to accept the formula.** ClarisWorks notifies you if there is an error in the formula. Otherwise, you return to the Define Fields dialog box where you can define, modify, or delete additional fields.

NOTE

You cannot enter data into a calculation field. The program fills it in automatically, based on the results of the formula for the field. Consequently, during data entry or editing, you cannot move into the field by tabbing or by selecting it with the mouse. To show which fields in a database are user modifiable and which ones are calculation fields, ClarisWorks surrounds normal fields with a light gray bounding box when you're in Browse mode (for data entry and editing). Calculation fields have no bounding box.

Summary fields

Summary fields play an important role in ClarisWorks databases. They can change a database from a static collection of data to something that really works for you — providing information that cannot be gleaned from a simple scan of the records.

A calculation field makes a computation within each record (adding the total of three invoice fields, for example). Summary fields, on the other hand, make calculations *across a group of records* — either a subset of records (for a sub-summary) or all records in the database (for a grand summary).

Every summary field is based on a formula. The built-in database functions in ClarisWorks make it easy to calculate totals, averages, and counts to summarize groups of records or the entire database. Where a summary field is placed in the layout determines whether it summarizes each group of records (the field is in a sub-summary part) or the whole database (the field is in a leading or trailing grand summary part).

When you place a summary field in a sub-summary layout part, you have to specify a sort field for the summary field. The sort field serves to *group* the records. Suppose, for example, that you run a business and want to track total sales in different cities. You can create a summary field called Sales Total, define its formula as =SUM('Sales'), and set the City field as the "sort by" field for the summary field. Then after you sort the database by City, the records for each city would form a separate group (all customers from Chicago would be listed together, for example).

At the end of every city group, the total sales for only that particular city would be shown — above or below all the individual records for that city (the location of the summary figure depends on where you place it in the layout). You should note that you also can *nest* summary fields. For example, you might use two summary fields to look at total sales within each city within each state.

When you place a summary field in a grand summary layout part, the summary field summarizes all the records in the database. There are two types of grand summaries: leading and trailing. A *leading grand summary* appears above the data that it summarizes. A *trailing grand summary* appears below the data.

The Credit Card Charges database described later in this Topic provides additional examples of summary fields — in both sub-summary and grand summary layout parts.

As with calculation fields, you cannot enter information into a summary field. Instead, ClarisWorks automatically calculates results for the field, based on the criteria you set. To see the results for a summary field, you need to either be in Page View or print the database. To have summary fields in a sub-summary part contain the correct information, you need to sort the database by the sort field (the one specified in the Insert Part dialog box when the sub-summary part was created). To be safe, you should always sort the database just before printing a report.

Creating a summary field requires several steps: creating a new field to hold the summary information (similar to the way you create a calculation field), adding a Summary part to the layout, placing the summary field in the Summary part, and — if the field has been added to a Sub-summary part — sorting the records.

The fine points of formula creation

You need to keep the following points in mind when creating formulas:

- Only calculation or summary fields can contain formulas. The program computes the results of a calculation field individually for each record in the database. Summary field formulas, on the other hand, summarize information across all or a subset of records. In a product catalog database, for example, you can use a summary field to calculate the total price of every product in the database.
- You need to surround field names with single quotes ('Sales') and text strings with double quotes ("Smithers").
- You can add extra space around operators that you manually enter (+, – , and so on) to improve readability when you are creating the formula, but ClarisWorks removes extra spaces when it checks the formula.
- When evaluating a formula, ClarisWorks examines the elements from left to right. Different mathematical and logical operators (+, *, >, and so on) have different precedence, however. When you include more than one operator in a formula, the precedence of the operators determines the order in which ClarisWorks performs the calculations.

You can add parentheses to a formula to improve readability or to change the precedence for performing a calculation. If, for example, A=2 and B=3 in a given record, the formula A+B*2 gives a result of 8. Because multiplication has a higher precedence than addition, ClarisWorks evaluates the formula in this order: (B*2) equals 6, to which A is added, giving an answer of 8. By adding parentheses to the formula, as in (A+B)*2, you can change the precedence. Now the program adds A to B first (because elements that are enclosed in parentheses have a higher precedence than elements that are not enclosed in parentheses), giving a result of 5. Next, the program multiplies 5 by 2, giving an answer of 10.

Note: A common error is to have unbalanced parentheses in a formula. The number of left and right parentheses must always be equal.

Precedence levels in database formulas — from highest to lowest — are as follows:

Operator	*Meaning*
%	percentage (divide by 100)
^	exponentiation (raise to a power, such as 'Length'^2)
+, –	change sign (for example, –'Cost')
*,/	multiplication, division
+, –	addition, subtraction
&	concatenate text strings ("Jim" & " " & "Uris" equals Jim Uris)
=,>,>=,<, <=,<>	comparison operators (equal, greater than, greater than or equal to, less than, less than or equal to, not equal)

- Selecting a function from the Function list inserts the function (as well as any appropriate arguments to the function) at the text insertion point. An example of a function is AVERAGE(number1,number2,...), where number1, number2, and ... are the arguments to the function. The *number1,number2, ...* means that the fields that you replace the arguments with must be number fields and that you can have as many of them as you like.

Arguments are placeholders. You often replace them with field names. The fastest way to replace an argument with a field name is to double-click the argument to select it and then click a field in the Fields list.

An ellipsis (. . .) in an argument list means that the number of elements of the number data type that you use is up to you. In the Average example, a completed formula may read AVERAGE('Qtr1','Qtr2','Qtr3','Qtr4'), where each of the Qtr fields contains a sales figure or a numeric grade for the quarter.

Note: You also can replace any or all number arguments with real numbers by typing them directly into the formula, as in AVERAGE('Sales',25000).

- Although most of the functions are available for use in both spreadsheet and database environments, database functions cannot refer to a range of fields. You must include every individual field name in a database formula, and separate the field names with commas. You can use this formula in a database:

```
SUM('QTY1','QTY2','QTY3')
```

But you cannot use this formula:

```
SUM('QTY1'..'QTY3')
```

- A formula can consist entirely of a single function. You also can embed functions within a larger formula, as well as use one function to modify the result of another function. An example of the latter use is 'Due Date'–TRUNC(NOW()). This formula computes the number of days from the current date until the due date. The decimal portion of today's date and time (NOW()) is eliminated by the TRUNC function, and the result is subtracted from Due Date.

For additional information on using the ClarisWorks database and spreadsheet functions, refer to the *ClarisWorks User's Guide*. (If you have ClarisWorks 3.0, refer to ClarisWorks Help instead.)

To create a summary field:

1. **Choose Define Fields from the Layout menu (or press Shift-⌘-D).** The Define Fields dialog box appears.

2. **Type a name for the summary field, click the Summary radio button (or press ⌘-6), and click Create.** The Enter Formula dialog box appears (the same dialog box that appears when you create a calculation field).

3. **Enter the formula for the summary field in the Formula text-edit box.** You can create formulas by typing them directly into the box; by selecting fields, operators, and functions from the three scrolling list boxes (click an option to insert it into the formula at the text insertion point); or by combining the two approaches.

4. **Choose a result type from the Format result as pop-up menu.** The choices are Text, Number, Date, and Time.

5. **Click OK to accept the formula (ClarisWorks notifies you if the formula contains an error) and click Done to exit the dialog box.**

6. **At the bottom of the Layout menu, choose the layout to which you want to add the summary field.**

7. **Choose Layout from the Layout menu (or press Shift-⌘-L).**

8. **Choose Insert Part from the Layout menu.** The Insert Part dialog box shown in Figure 6-6 appears.

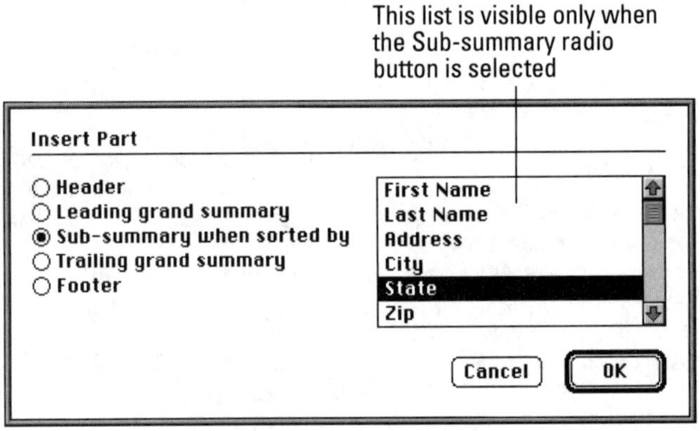

Figure 6-6: The Insert Part dialog box.

9. **Choose "Leading grand summary," "Sub-summary when sorted by," or "Trailing grand summary."** (You cannot use the Header or Footer parts for summary items.)

   You use the Leading and Trailing grand summary options to provide a summary for the entire database. In a sales database, for example, you can use either of these choices to total or average all sales for the database.

   If you choose the Sub-summary option, you have to choose a sort field from the list on the right side of the dialog box. When you sort the database by the contents of that field, the program groups records by the sort field and calculates a subtotal of the found set for each group. If you want to examine sales on a state-by-state basis, for example, you can create a sales sub-summary that is sorted by state.

10. **Click OK to leave the dialog box.** (If you selected the Sub-summary option, the program asks whether you want the sub-summary part to appear above or below each record group. Choose Above, Below, or Cancel.) The program adds the sub-summary part to the appropriate location in the current layout.

11. **Add the summary field to the layout by selecting Insert Field from the Layout menu.** The Insert Field dialog box appears, as shown in Figure 6-7.

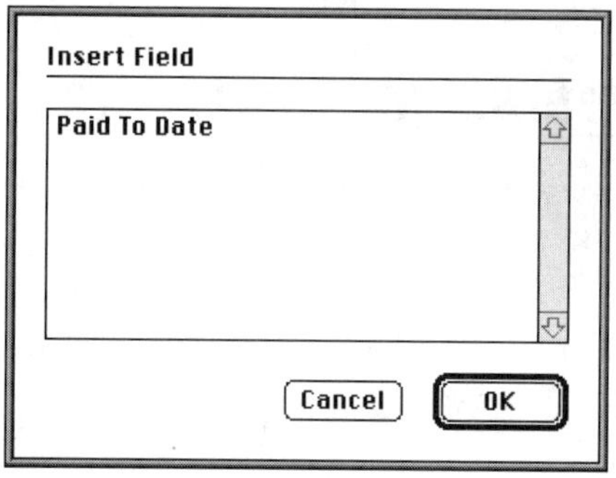

Figure 6-7: The Insert Field dialog box.

12. **Select the summary field in the list box and click OK.** (You also can double-click the summary field). In either case, the field and its label appear in the current layout. Drag the summary field and its label into the summary part.

13. **Switch to Browse mode by selecting Browse from the Layout menu (or press Shift-⌘-B).**

14. **If the database is not in Page View, you don't see summary fields. If necessary, choose Page View from the View menu (or press Shift-⌘-P).**

15. **If the field is a sub-summary field (rather than a grand summary), you need to sort the database by the field specified in the Insert Part dialog box. Choose Sort Records from the Organize menu (or press ⌘-J).** The Sort Records dialog box appears, as shown in Figure 6-8.

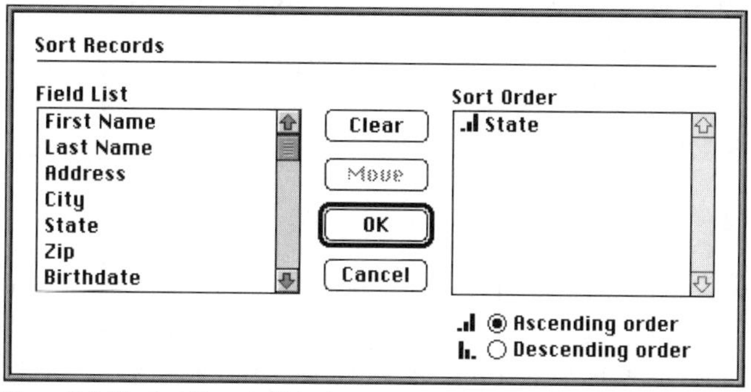

Figure 6-8: The Sort Records dialog box.

Use the Move and Clear buttons, as appropriate, to select the sort field. You can sort each field in ascending or descending order, depending on which radio button you click. Click OK to conduct the sort. The sub-summary information is displayed, grouped according to the contents of the sort field.

TIP

If you want to see all of the summary data at one time or want to move it into another environment (such as the spreadsheet or word processor), change to Page View (Shift-⌘-P) and choose Copy Summaries from the Edit menu. ClarisWorks transfers the contents of summary fields to the Clipboard, where it is available for pasting into other documents and applications.

Setting data entry options for fields

ClarisWorks 2 includes several automatic data entry and data validation options that you can set for any text, number, date, or time field. They include the following:

- Entering the same value in every new record (as a default)
- Date- or time-stamping a field to show when it was created or when it was last modified
- Inserting a serial number that increases with each new record
- Creating a list of values that will appear in a pop-up menu
- Specifying that a particular field must not be empty
- Specifying that every entry in a field must be unique
- Setting a range of acceptable values for a field

Setting field options is a two-step process. First, you define the field. Second, you reselect the field from the field list in the Define Fields dialog box and click Options. The Entry Options dialog box shown in Figure 6-9 appears. The following sections discuss the purpose of each option.

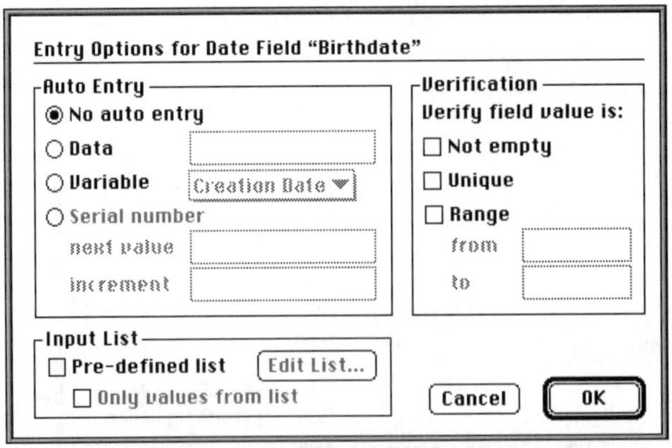

Figure 6-9: The Entry Options dialog box. The name of the field for which you are setting options appears at the top of the dialog box.

NOTE

Setting Entry options for a field affects only new records. Previously entered records have to be adjusted manually.

No auto entry

No auto entry is the default option and is automatically selected the first time you open the Entry Options dialog box for a given field.

Data

The Data option inserts a fixed value into every record of the database. The purpose of this option is to set a default for the field and save you some data-entry work. If a majority of entries for a field are usually the same (all of your friends are from California, for example), you can specify CA as the default data for the State field.

To specify a default value, click the Data radio button and type the value in the Data text-edit box. Note that the value that you enter has to be the same data type as the data type that you defined for the field. As an example, you cannot enter text in a number or time field.

Variable

You use the Variable option to automatically enter a record creation date, creation time, or creator's name or a record modification date, modification time, or modifier's name. As with the other auto-entry options, the purpose of the Variable option is to save you some unnecessary typing and to ensure consistency in the way that data is entered.

Step-by-Steps

To set a Variable option:

1. **Choose Define Fields from the Layout menu (or press Shift-⌘-D).** The Define Fields dialog box appears.
2. **Select the text, date, or time field to which you want to assign a Variable option. Click Options (or double-click the field name).** The Entry Options screen appears, as shown in Figure 6-10.
3. **Click the Variable radio button and choose an option from the pop-up menu.**

   The type of the current field determines which menu choices are available for the Variable options. A text field, for example, shows only Creator Name and Modifier Name in the Variable pop-up menu.
4. **Click OK to accept the new settings and return to the Define Fields dialog box or click Cancel to ignore the new settings.**
5. **Click Done to leave the Define Fields dialog box.**

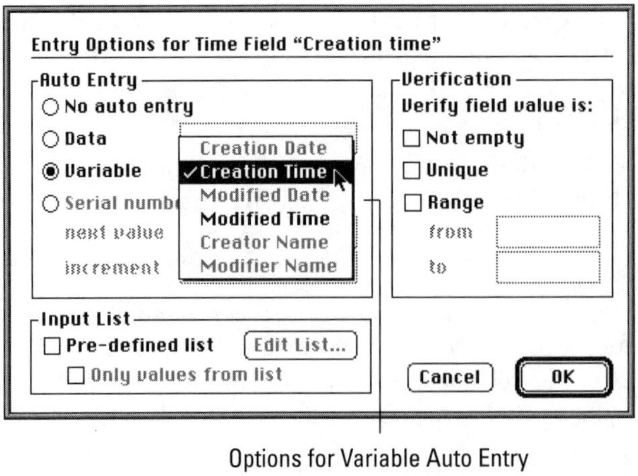

Figure 6-10: You can choose an auto-entry option from the Variable pop-up menu in the Entry Options screen.

If you choose any of the three *Creator* options for a field, ClarisWorks automatically fills in the creator field when you create a new record.

If you choose a *Modifier* option for a field, the program checks each record only when you save the database (using the Save or Save As commands in the File menu). If you have modified the record in any way — that is, added, deleted, or changed data in at least one field — ClarisWorks fills in the modifier field for that record.

To fill in Creator or Modifier Name, ClarisWorks takes information from the Chooser desk accessory (if you are running System 6) or the Sharing Setup control panel (if you are running System 7). If the Creator or Modifier Name information is blank in the database records or if the information is erroneous, open the Chooser desk accessory (System 6) or the Sharing Setup control panel (System 7) and enter the information as you want it to appear.

TIP

If you construct a name and address database, you can use the Creation and Modification Date options to show when you entered each address and when you last updated it. This feature ends the guesswork concerning whether a particular address or phone number in the database is current.

Serial number

With the Serial number option, you can assign an auto-incrementing number to a field. Typical examples include invoice numbers or numbers for the records themselves.

To set a Serial number option:

1. **Choose Define Fields from the Layout menu (or press Shift-⌘-D).** The Define Fields dialog box appears.
2. **Select a number field to which you want to assign the serial number option.** Click Options (or double-click the field name); the Entry Options screen appears.
3. **Click the Serial number radio button.**
4. **Type numbers into the next value and increment text-edit boxes.** *Next value* indicates the number that the program will assign to the next new record that you create. *Increment* indicates how much succeeding values will increase over the current value. The default next value and increment are both 1.
5. **Click OK to accept the new settings and return to the Define Fields dialog box or click Cancel to ignore the new settings.**
6. **Click Done to leave the Define Fields dialog box.**

Because the serial number option affects only *new* records, existing records remain unchanged. Thus, if you have already manually entered records for invoice numbers 1000 through 1047, you can easily pick up where you left off by setting the next value to 1048.

Pre-defined list

Choose the Pre-defined list option to add a pop-up menu of choices to any text, date, or time field. In Browse mode, whenever the cursor moves into a field that contains a pre-defined list, the pop-up menu appears.

To create a pre-defined list for a field:

1. **Choose Define Fields from the Layout menu (or press Shift-⌘-D).** The Define Fields dialog box appears.
2. **Select the text, date, or time field for which you want to create a pre-defined list. Click Options (or double-click the field name).** The Entry Options dialog box appears.
3. **In the Input List section of the Entry Options dialog box, click the Pre-defined list check box.**
4. **Click the Edit List button.** A new dialog box appears in which you can create the value list (see Figure 6-11). The values that you add to the list box will appear in the same order when you attempt to enter data into the field.

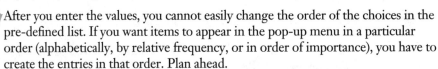

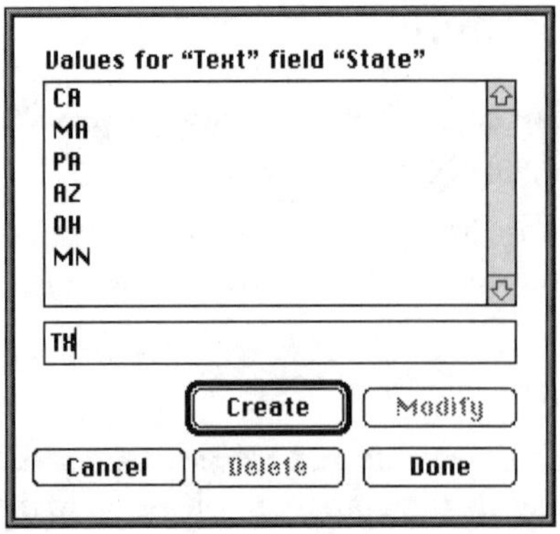

Figure 6-11: Enter the values for the pre-defined list in this dialog box.

5. **Type a value that you want to add to the pop-up menu for the field and click Create to add the value to the list.** The program adds the value to the bottom of the list.
6. **Repeat Step 5 for additional values that you want to add at this time.**
7. **To save the changes to the value list, click Done to return to the Entry Options dialog box, OK to return to the Define Fields dialog box, and then Done to return to the database.**
8. ***Optional:* To restrict entries to those that appear in the pre-defined list, click the Only values from list check box in the Entry Options dialog box.**

Note that the value list creation dialog box also includes buttons for modifying and deleting values. You can use these buttons to change the wording or spelling for any value (Modify) or to remove a value from the list (Delete).

TIP

After you enter the values, you cannot easily change the order of the choices in the pre-defined list. If you want items to appear in the pop-up menu in a particular order (alphabetically, by relative frequency, or in order of importance), you have to create the entries in that order. Plan ahead.

While you are using the database, the pop-up menu that you created appears automatically whenever you move into a field that contains a pre-defined list. You can then select items from the list to enter into the field.

Step-by-Steps

To select an item from a pre-defined list:

1. **Tab into the field or click it with the mouse.** The choice list pops up.
2. **Highlight the item that you want and press Return or Enter to accept it.** (You also can double-click your choice.)

— or —

2. **If you want to enter a response that isn't in the pop-up menu, ignore the pop-up menu and click once in the field.** You can now type your entry — unless you have checked the Only values from the list check box.

TIP

You can use a couple of tricks to speed up choice selection in pop-up menus without using the mouse. First, you can use the up-arrow and down-arrow keys to scroll through the list and highlight a choice. Second, you can type the first letter of a choice. The program automatically searches through the list and highlights the first choice that begins with that letter. After you make a selection, just press Return or Enter to copy it into the field.

The database environment also includes three verification options that you can use to make sure that data meets your criteria: Verify that the field is not empty, verify that the field value is unique, and verify that the field value is within a range of values. You can use these three options in combination with each other.

NOTE

If you violate a verification option and attempt to either save the file, move to a different record, or create a new record, ClarisWorks displays a warning message like the one in Figure 6-12. As you can see, you can override the verification setting for the field by simply clicking the appropriate button in the dialog box.

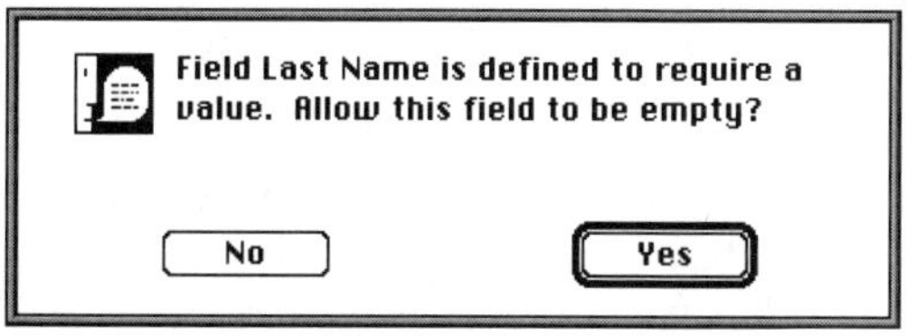

Figure 6-12: A verification violation warning message.

Verify field value is not empty

Check this verification option to insist that a particular field always contain a value. Some database programs call this a *required field.*

Verify field value is unique

Check this option to specify that no two records in the database can contain the same value for the field (no duplicates are allowed). You may want to set this option for an invoice number field or for a part number in a catalog database.

Verify field value is within a specific range

Check this option to specify that the contents of a number, date, or time field must be within a specific range of values.

To set a verification range:

1. **Choose Define Fields from the Layout menu (or press Shift-⌘-D).** The Define Fields dialog box appears.
2. **Select a numeric, date, or time field for which you want to set a range and click Options (or double-click the field name).** The Entry Options dialog box appears.
3. **In the Verification section of the Entry Options dialog box, click the Range check box.**
4. **Type the minimum value to be allowed in the from text-edit box and the maximum value in the to text-edit box.**
5. **Click OK to return to the Define Fields dialog box and then Done to return to the database.**

Modifying field definitions

After you define a field, you can change its definition or even delete the field. You also can change the field type or change the formula for a calculation or summary field.

TIP

Changing a field definition from one data type to another sometimes has unfortunate effects, and you cannot use the Undo command to undo changes to field definitions. Saving the database before you alter a field definition is a smart idea. If the transformations don't work as you intended, you can simply close the database without saving the changes.

To change field types:

1. **Choose Define Fields from the Layout menu (or press Shift-⌘-D).** The Define Fields dialog box appears.
2. **Select the field for which you want to set a new type.** The field's name appears in the Name text-edit box.
3. **Click the radio button that corresponds to the new type that you want to assign to the field and then click Modify.**

   The following warning message appears:

   ```
   When modifying the field type, any data that cannot be con-
   verted will be lost.
   ```

4. **Click OK to continue or Cancel to leave the original field type unchanged.**
5. **Click Done to return to the database.**

Deleting fields

Some fields outlive their usefulness, and you can easily delete them. However, deleting a field also deletes all information contained in that field *from every record in the database.*

To delete a field:

1. **Choose Define Fields from the Layout menu (or press Shift-⌘-D).** The Define Fields dialog box appears.
2. **Highlight the field that you want to delete.**
3. **Click the Delete button.** A dialog box appears with the following question:

   ```
   Permanently delete this field and all of its contents?
   ```

4. **Click OK to delete the field or Cancel if you change your mind.**
5. **Repeat Steps 2 and 3 for any additional fields that you want to delete.**
6. **Click Done to exit the Define Fields dialog box.**

Adding new fields

You can add new fields to the database at any time.

To create a new field:

1. **Choose Define Fields from the Layout menu (or press Shift-⌘-D).** The Define Fields dialog box appears.
2. **Type the name of the new field in the Name text-edit box, click one of the Type radio buttons (or press its Command-key equivalent), and then click Create.** The program adds the field to the list box.
3. **Create additional fields or click Done.** ClarisWorks adds the new fields and their labels to the database and to the currently selected layout.
4. **Edit the layout to accommodate or omit the new fields, as you prefer (as described in the next section, "Organizing Information with Layouts").**

Organizing Information with Layouts

In most database programs, every database has a single screen on which you do data entry, and you create reports in a separate part of the program. ClarisWorks doesn't force you to make a distinction between data-entry forms and reports. Instead, it introduces the concept of layouts.

A *layout* is a particular arrangement of the fields that you've defined for a database. In each layout, you can use as many or as few of the defined fields as you like. There are no fields that you *must* use. And you can have as many layouts for each database as you need. Using an address database as an example, you can create the layouts shown in Figure 6-13.

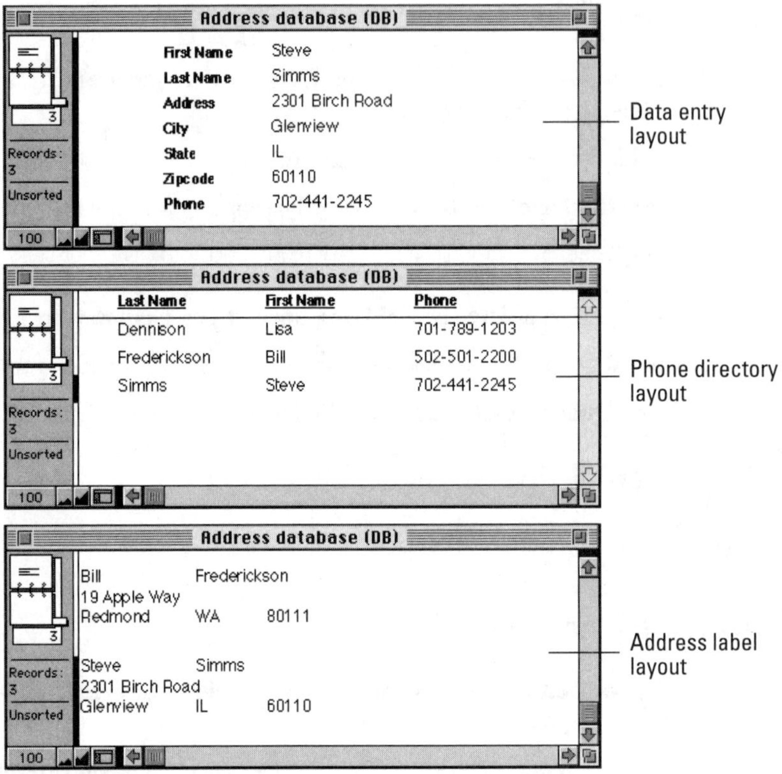

Figure 6-13: Different layouts provide different views of the same data.

To create a new layout for a database:

1. **Choose New Layout from the Layout menu.** The New Layout dialog box appears (Figure 6-14).
2. **Type a name for the new layout or accept the default name that ClarisWorks presents (Layout [number]); click a radio button to choose one of the five layout formats (Standard, Duplicate, Blank, Columnar report, or Labels); and click the OK button.**
3. **After you choose the layout type, choose fields and settings, if required.** ClarisWorks creates the new layout.

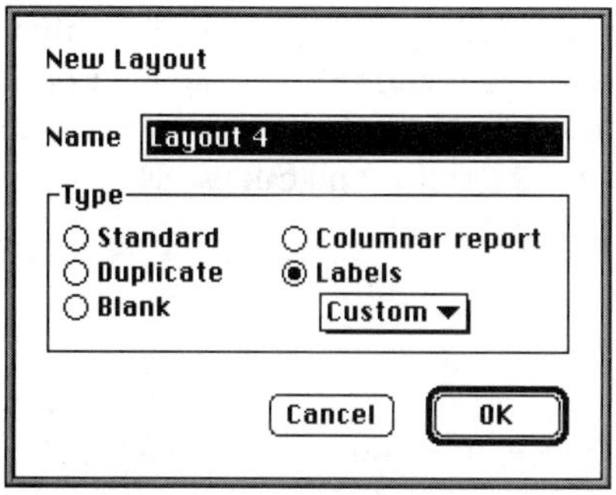

Figure 6-14: The New Layout dialog box.

The five layout formats provide the following results:

- If you choose a *Labels* layout, you can pick from any of the predefined label layouts or create your own layout by selecting the Custom choice. See "Working with mailing labels," later in this Topic, for a complete discussion of label options.
- If you choose *Standard,* ClarisWorks creates a default database layout that contains every field that you defined for the database. The fields appear one above the other in a vertical list.
- If you choose *Duplicate,* ClarisWorks creates an exact copy of the currently selected layout. This option is useful if you want to make a variation of the current layout — perhaps adding a few fields or rearranging the fields. You also can create a duplicate when you want to experiment with the layout. If the experiment doesn't work out, you can simply delete the layout.
- If you choose *Blank,* ClarisWorks creates a blank layout. You add all fields by choosing the Insert Field command from the Layout menu. (This option is useful when you want to start from scratch in designing a layout.)
- If you choose *Columnar report* or *Labels* (see the phone directory and label layouts in Figure 6-13 for examples), the Set Field Order dialog box appears, as shown in Figure 6-15.

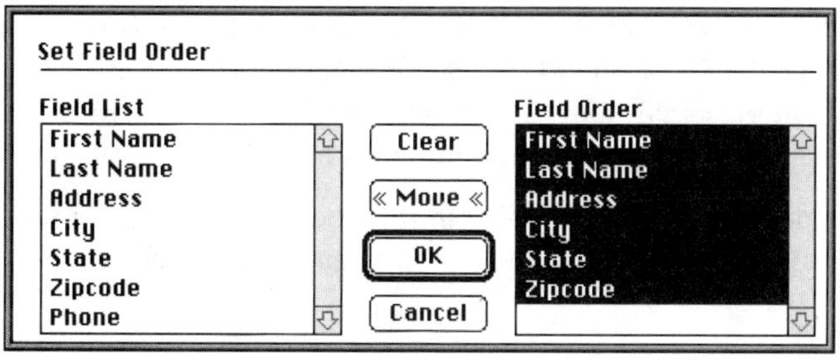

Figure 6-15: The Set Field Order dialog box.

The purpose of the Set Field Order dialog box is to specify the fields that you want to include in the new layout and to designate their order. Choose a field from the Field List (on the left side of the dialog box) and click Move to add it to the Field Order list on the right. You can use as many or as few fields in the layout as you like.

Layout parts

As shown in Figure 6-16, every layout is composed of labeled *parts*. The *Body* is the main part of any layout. The Body holds the bulk of the data fields, mainly those into which you enter data. All other parts of a layout are optional. The optional parts include the *Header* and *Footer* (which hold information that repeats on every page of the layout), leading or trailing *Grand Summaries* (which display summary data at the beginning or end of a report), and one or more *Sub-summaries* (which display summary information for groups of records — all records with the same ZIP code, for example).

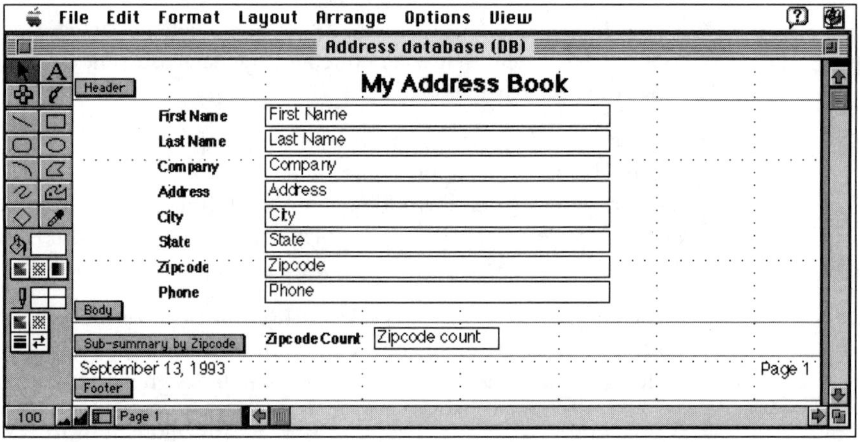

Figure 6-16: The parts of a database layout.

You can change the size of any part by simply clicking on the dividing line for the part and dragging to make the part smaller or larger. As long as a part doesn't contain any fields or other objects, you can remove the part by dragging it up into the part immediately above it. (If the part does contain fields or other objects, you must delete them or move them into other parts before you can remove the part.)

Although you can place any field in the Body, Header, or Footer, you can place only summary fields in a grand summary or sub-summary part.

Arranging fields on the layout

Initially, ClarisWorks arranges fields on the layout according to the layout type that you selected when you created the layout (Standard, Duplicate, Blank, Columnar report, or Labels). Everything that you place on a layout — fields, field labels, text, and graphics — is considered a draw object. As such, you can do anything with items on the layout that you can do with an object. Click on any object, and you see its handles. You can drag a handle to resize a field (making it larger or smaller); drag fields to different positions; change or delete field labels; align fields with each other or the grid (using the Align commands in the Arrange menu); change the font, size, or style of text in the field or the label; place graphics on the layout; and so on. See Topic 7 for additional information on working with objects.

Field formatting

The default layouts create serviceable databases, but they aren't particularly attractive. The following instructions describe how to improve a layout by changing the text attributes for field contents and labels; by setting numeric, date, and time formats for fields; and by adding a border around a field.

Step-by-Steps

To set text attributes:

1. **At the bottom of the Layout menu, choose the layout in which you want to work.**
2. **Choose Layout from the Layout menu (or press Shift-⌘-L).**
3. **Click or Shift-click to select the fields and field labels for which you want to set new text attributes.**
4. **Choose options from the Font, Size, Style, Text Color, and Alignment submenus of the Format menu.** The selected fields and labels change to match the new settings.

You can change the display format for number, date, and time fields, as well as for calculation and summary fields that produce a number, date, or time result.

Step-by-Steps

To set number, date, and time formats:

1. **At the bottom of the Layout menu, choose the layout in which you want to work.**
2. **Choose Layout from the Layout menu (or press Shift-⌘-L).**
3. **Click to choose a number, date, time, calculation, or summary field.**

4. Choose Field Format from the Options menu (or press Shift-⌘-I).
Depending on the field type, one of the three dialog boxes in Figure 6-17 appears.

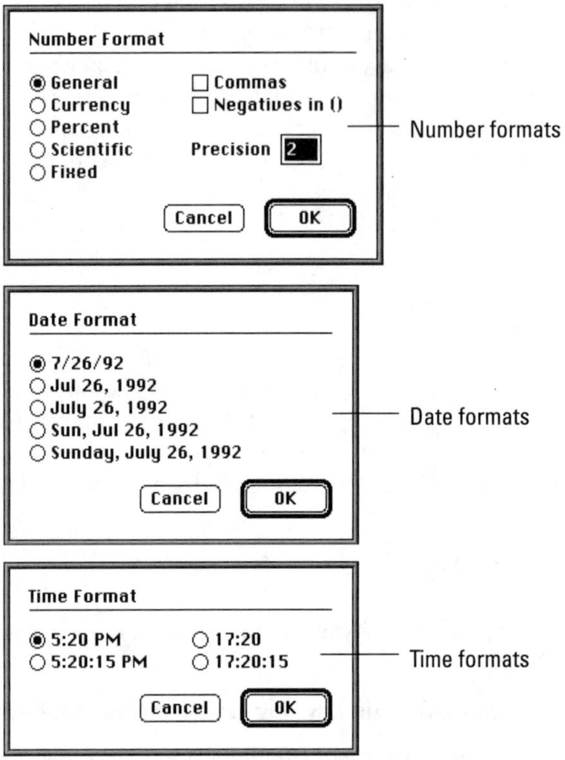

Figure 6-17: Use these dialog boxes to set the display format for number, date, and time fields.

5. Choose options in the Format dialog box and then click OK.
ClarisWorks formats the field according to your selections.

Date format options include slashes, abbreviations, and day names. Time format options include AM/PM, the display of seconds, and normal versus military (24-hour) time. The various number format options produce the following results:

- *General.* Displays numbers without commas and shows the number of decimal places entered (or required by a calculation).
- *Currency.* Displays a dollar sign and two decimal places, as in $19.81. (You can change the display of commas, negative amounts, and number of decimal places with the Commas, Negatives, and Precision options.)

- *Percent.* Adds a percent sign as a suffix and multiplies the field's contents by 100 (for example, 0.1235 x 100 is 12.35%). The Precision setting determines the number of decimal places.
- *Scientific.* Uses exponential notation, as in 1.245e+3 (for 1,245), which is useful for handling extremely large or very small numbers.
- *Fixed.* Rounds the results to the number of decimal places that are shown in the Precision text-edit box, as in 21.433 (for a precision setting of 3).
- *Commas.* Inserts commas every three digits, as in 18,221.
- *Negatives in ().* Surrounds numbers less than zero with parentheses, as in *(24)*, instead of using a minus sign.
- *Precision.* Sets the number of decimal places to be shown.

Step-by-Steps

To create field borders:

1. **At the bottom of the Layout menu, choose the layout in which you want to work.**
2. **Choose Layout from the Layout menu (or press Shift-⌘-L).**
3. **Using the Pointer tool, select the fields to which you want to add a border.**
4. **In the Tool palette, set the pen pattern to opaque.** You also can select a different pen color and a line width. After you change to Browse mode (Shift-⌘ B), the fields appear with a border.

Adding and deleting fields from a layout

As mentioned earlier, you can have as many or as few fields in each layout as you like. You can add fields to any layout that doesn't currently display every defined field, and you can remove unnecessary fields.

Step-by-Steps

To add a field to a layout:

1. **At the bottom of the Layout menu, choose the layout to which you want to add a field.**
2. **Choose Layout from the Layout menu (or press Shift-⌘-L).**
3. **Choose Insert Field from the Layout menu.** The Insert Field dialog box appears, as shown in Figure 6-18. Its list box contains only the defined fields that are not in use in the current layout.

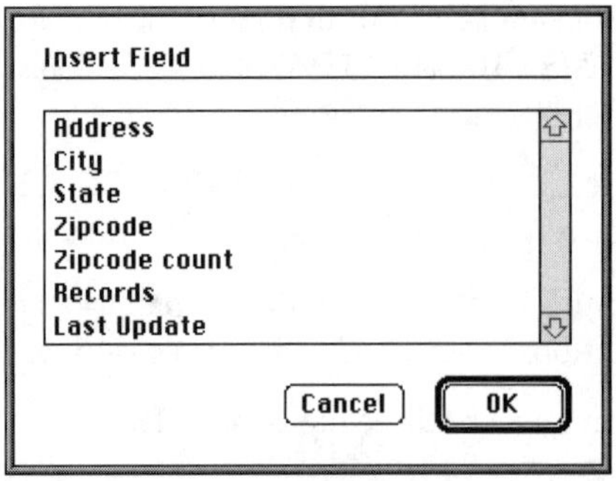

Figure 6-18: The Insert Field dialog box.

4. **Select a field and click OK.** ClarisWorks inserts the field and its label into the layout.
5. **If necessary, move and resize the field and its label.**

To remove a field from a layout:

1. **At the bottom of the Layout menu, choose the layout from which you want to remove a field.**
2. **Choose Layout from the Layout menu (or press Shift-⌘-L).**
3. **Use the Pointer tool to select the fields that you want to remove from the layout.**
4. **Press Delete or Backspace or choose Clear or Cut (⌘-X) from the Edit menu.** ClarisWorks removes the field or fields from the layout.

NOTE

Removing a field from a layout is not the same as *deleting* the field. Removing a field from a layout does nothing to the data in the field. The field can still appear in other layouts with its data securely intact. And if you insert the field back into the layout from which you removed it, its data reappears. On the other hand, after you delete a field in the Define Fields dialog box (Shift-⌘-D), ClarisWorks removes the field from all layouts and permanently deletes the field's data from the entire database.

Deleting a layout

To delete any layout that you no longer want to use, choose the layout by name from the list at the bottom of the Layout menu and then choose Delete Layout from the Layout menu. A dialog box appears and asks whether you want to *Permanently delete this layout?* Click OK to delete the layout or click Cancel to leave it intact.

Deleting a layout does not delete the fields that you defined for the database or any of the data that appeared in the layout. It merely eliminates one possible view or arrangement of the data. To delete a field, select the field in the Define Fields dialog box (Shift-⌘-D) and then click the Delete button. To delete data, remove it from the record or delete the record.

Special layout options

The Layout menu contains two other commands: Layout Info and Tab Order. Layout Info enables you to assign a name to the current layout, specify the number of columns that will appear in Page View, and close up the space between fields when printing (which is particularly useful for labels).

You can use the Tab key to move from field to field when you are entering data. The Tab Order command enables you to set a new order for navigating between fields when you press Tab.

To use the Layout Info command:

1. At the bottom of the Layout menu, select the layout for which you want to change settings.

2. Choose Layout Info from the Layout menu. The Layout Info dialog box appears, as shown in Figure 6-19.

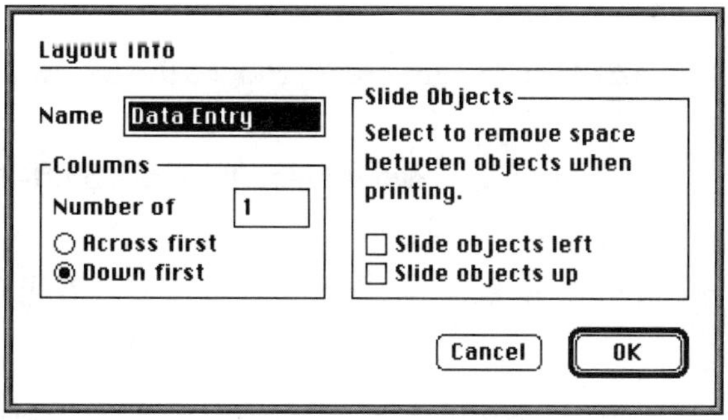

Figure 6-19: Use the Layout Info dialog box to choose optional settings for the current layout.

3. *Optional:* Enter a name for the layout by typing it in the Name text-edit box.

4. *Optional:* In the Columns section of the dialog box, set the number of columns to be displayed in reports and on-screen (in Page View only) by typing a number in the Number of text-edit box. Then click a radio button (Across first or Down first) to indicate the order in which records will be displayed in the columns.

5. ***Optional:* Use the Slide Objects section to close up space between fields when printing.** This option is often useful for labels. The Slide objects left check box closes up space between objects on the same line. For example, the address line

```
Bemidji    , MN  56601
```

would print as

```
Bemidji, MN 56601
```

The Slide objects up check box eliminates blank lines in records. When you print an address label layout that contains fields arranged in five lines (1 – name; 2 – company name; 3 – first address line; 4 – second address line; and 5 – city, state, and ZIP code), labels that contain only one address line or no company name print without blank lines in those spots.

6. **Click OK to accept the layout options and return to the database.**

When you are entering data, tabbing from field to field is much faster than selecting each field with the mouse. By default, ClarisWorks sets the tab order for a database to match the order in which you created the fields. If you have altered the default layout by rearranging fields on-screen, the tab order may cause the cursor to jump willy-nilly all over the screen. You can change the tab order so that the cursor moves more efficiently.

To set a new tab order:

1. **At the bottom of the Layout menu, choose the layout for which you want to specify a new tab order.**
2. **Choose Layout from the Layout menu (or press Shift-⌘-L).**
3. **Choose Tab Order from the Layout menu.** The Tab Order dialog box shown in Figure 6-20 appears. The current (or default) tab order is shown in the Tab Order list box on the right side of the dialog box.

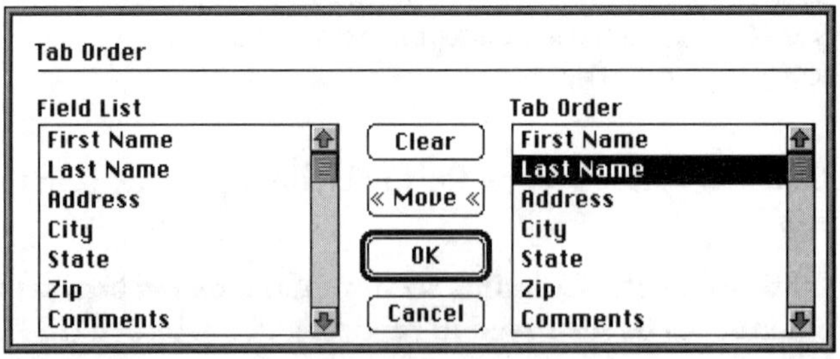

Figure 6-20: The Tab Order dialog box.

4. **To create a tab order from scratch, click Clear.** ClarisWorks clears the Tab Order list box.

5. **To specify the new order, choose a field name from the Field List and click Move (or double-click the field name).** The program adds the field to the bottom of the Tab Order list. Continue selecting fields, in the order you prefer, until you have copied all of the fields into the Tab Order list.

You also can Shift-Click to choose several contiguous field names simultaneously or ⌘-Click to choose several noncontiguous field names.

If you don't want users to be able to tab into some fields, leave those fields out of the list. When a user is in Browse mode, a press of the Tab key skips right over the fields. Note, however, that users can still enter data in those fields by clicking in them.

Browse Mode: Viewing, Entering, and Editing Data

After you have designed a database and created layouts, you will spend most of your time in Browse mode — entering, editing, and viewing the data.

If you've created more than one layout for a database, you can enter and edit records in *any* layout. To select a layout in which to work, choose its name from the bottom of the Layout menu. (Normally, however, you will want to do data entry in a layout that contains all of the essential fields.)

Adding and deleting records

To create a new record for the current database, choose New Record from the Edit menu (or press ⌘-R). The new record appears with the text insertion point in the first field.

The following instructions describe how to delete a record.

To delete a record:

1. **Select the record by clicking any place in the record *other than inside a field*.** To show that the record is selected, ClarisWorks highlights the entire record.

2. **Choose Cut (⌘-X) or Clear from the Edit menu.** ClarisWorks removes the record from the database.

Entering and editing data

When a new record appears on-screen, the cursor automatically appears in the first field (or in the field which you set as first with the Tab Order command). Complete the field and then press the Tab key to move to the next field. You also can move directly to any field by clicking it with the mouse. Note, however, that you cannot click in or tab to a field that does not allow user input — namely, calculation and summary fields.

You edit data in exactly the same manner as in any other text-oriented environment. After entering Browse mode (Shift-⌘-B) and tabbing or clicking into a field, you use normal editing techniques to add to, delete, or alter the information in any field.

TIP

If a record is substantially similar to an existing record, you can save typing time by creating a duplicate of the existing record and then making the necessary editing changes to the duplicate. To create a duplicate record, select the record and then choose Duplicate Record from the Edit menu (or press ⌘-D).

Navigating among records

You can move among the database records in a number of ways. The following options are available:

- *To move to the next or preceding record,* click the bottom or top page of the book icon (see Figure 6-21). In normal view, this action selects the next or previous record. In Page View, it merely scrolls the records in the appropriate direction.

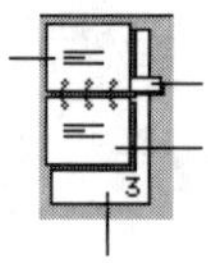

Click to move to the previous record
Drag to any record number
Click to move to the next record
3
Click and type the record number to which you want to move

Figure 6-21: The book icon.

- To move to the next or previous record while leaving the cursor in the same field, press ⌘-Return or Shift-⌘-Return, respectively.
- To move to a specific record (by number), drag the tab on the right side of the book icon until you see the record number; choose Go To Record from the Organize menu (or press ⌘-G); or click once to select the record number at the bottom of the book icon, type a record number, and press Return.
- To move up or down through the records, use the scroll bar at the right side of the database window or press Page Up or Page Down (if your keyboard has these keys).
- To move to a specific page of the database, double-click the page number indicator at the bottom of the database window (you have to be in Page View). The Go To dialog box appears. Type a page number and click OK.

◆ To move to the beginning or end of the database, press the Home or End keys.

Finding and Selecting Records

Flipping through a database one record at a time is the hard way to find specific information. ClarisWorks has two different commands that you can use to find and select records, based on criteria that you supply. You use the Find command to restrict displayed records to a particular subset (the program temporarily hides all other records). For example, you may want to look only at records in which State equals Ohio. The Match Records command leaves all records visible and simply selects (highlights) those records that match the criteria.

Using the Find command

To use the Find command, you type search criteria on a blank copy of a record that appears when you issue the Find command. To find an exact or partial match, you simply type the text or number that you want to search for in the appropriate field. To find all address records for people whose last name contains the string *Sch,* for example, you type **Sch** in the Last Name field. In this type of search, the program considers a record a match if it contains the string *anywhere within the field,* not just at the beginning of the field.

You also can use logical operators to specify search criteria, as described in Table 6-1.

Table 6-1
Logical Search Operators

Operator	***Meaning***	***Examples***
=	Find records that exactly match the contents of this field.	(=435; =18 Apple Street)
<	Find records that are numerically or alphabetically less than this value.	(<100; <S)
>	Find records that are numerically or alphabetically greater than this value.	(>180; >Bob)
≤ (Option-<)	Find records that are numerically alphabetically less than or equal to or this value.	(≤2000; ≤D; ≤10:00AM)
≥ (Option->)	Find records that are numerically or alphabetically greater than or equal to this value.	(≥4/19/93; ≥3000)
<>	Find records that are not equal to this value.	(<>10; <>CA; <>11:15)

VERSION 2.1

You can search for blank database fields in ClarisWorks 2.1 or 3.0 by entering only an equal sign (=) in a field.

To find records:

1. **At the bottom of the Layout menu, choose the layout that you want to use as a search template.** (Be sure that the fields that you intend to use as criteria appear in the layout.)
2. **Choose the Find command from the Layout menu (or press Shift-⌘-F).** A screen with a blank record appears, as shown in Figure 6-22.

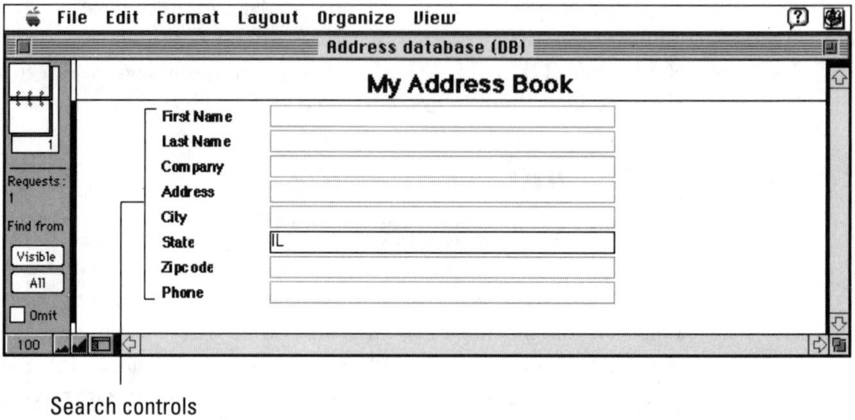

Figure 6-22: You type the search criteria into fields on this blank record.

3. **Type the search criteria into the appropriate fields.**
4. ***Optional:* If you want to find all records that do *not* match the search criteria, click the Omit check box.**
5. **Click All to search the entire database or click Visible to search only records that are visible; that is, the ones that are not currently hidden.** (***Note:*** Pressing Return or Enter automatically selects the All button.) Claris-Works conducts the search. It displays matching records and hides all others.

   After you're through examining the records that match the criteria, you can make the entire database visible again by choosing Show All Records (Shift-⌘-A) from the Organize menu.

When you specify multiple criteria in a single Find request, you are conducting an *AND* search. In an AND search, ClarisWorks finds only records that satisfy all the criteria. For example, entering **Santa Clara** for the city and **CA** for the state identifies only the address records for people who come from Santa Clara, California. It does not find records for people from other California cities or from cities named Santa Clara in other states.

Sometimes, you may want to conduct an OR search — in which the program finds a record if the record matches any one of several criteria. To conduct this type of search, you have to issue multiple Find requests.

Step-by-Steps

To conduct an OR search:

1. **At the bottom of the Layout menu, choose the layout that you want to use as a search template.** (Be sure that the fields that you intend to use as criteria appear in the layout.)
2. **Choose the Find command from the Layout menu (or press Shift-⌘-F).** A screen with a blank record appears.
3. **Enter a set of search criteria in the record.**
4. **Before clicking the All or Visible buttons, choose New Request from the Edit menu (or press ⌘-R).** Another blank record appears, as shown in Figure 6-23.

First search request

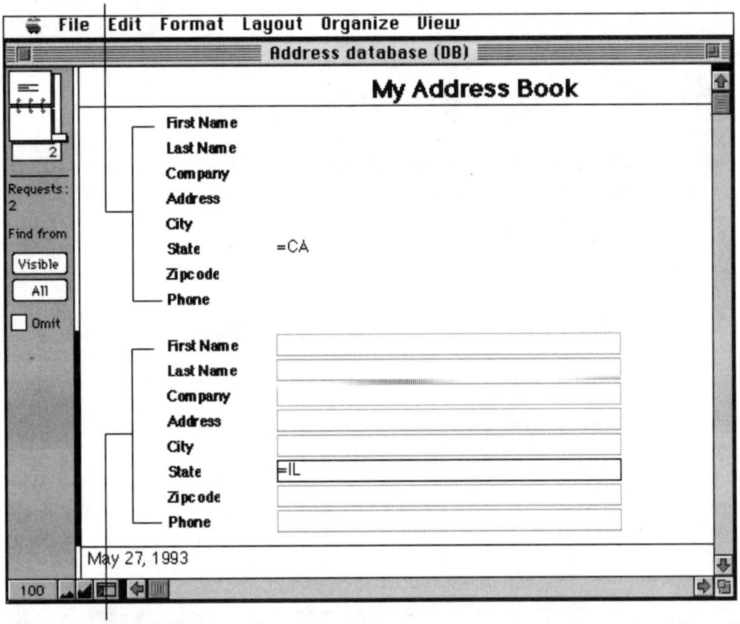

Second search request

Figure 6-23: This pair of search requests identifies all records in which State equals CA (California) or State equals IL (Illinois).

5. **Enter the next set of search criteria in the new record.**
6. **Repeat Steps 4 and 5 for each additional set of criteria that you want to impose.**
7. **Click All to search the entire database or click Visible to search only the records that are visible; that is, the ones that are not currently hidden.** The search is conducted. Records that satisfy any of the search requests are displayed and all others are hidden.

You can issue a Find command from any layout, as long as the fields on which you want to base the search are present. Some layouts, however, are easier to search from than others. A layout that is designed to print mailing labels, for example, makes the task more difficult because the fields are not labeled. Change to a better layout by selecting a layout from the bottom of the Layout menu before initiating the search. After the program finds the records, you can change back to the original layout to view or print the records.

Using the Match Records command

The Find command is intended for simple searches. If you want to perform a more complex search, you may prefer to use the Match Records feature. A Match Records search selects (highlights) all records that meet the criteria, but it leaves the other records on-screen. Because the records are selected (highlighted), using Match Records is an ideal way to identify and delete records that you no longer need.

To select matching records:

1. **Choose Match Records from the Organize menu (or press ⌘-M).** The Enter Match Records Condition dialog box appears, as shown in Figure 6-24. It is identical to the dialog box that you use to define a formula for a calculation field or a summary field.

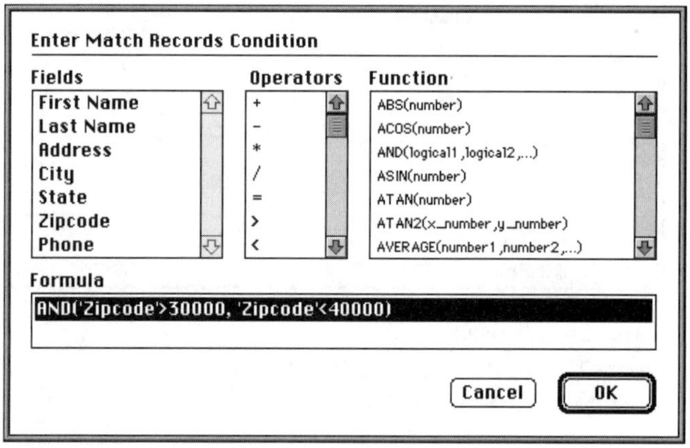

Figure 6-24: Use this dialog box to specify the search conditions formula.

2. **Enter the match formula in the Formula text-edit box.** You can create formulas by typing them into the box; by selecting fields, operators, and functions from the three scrolling list boxes (click an option to insert it into the formula at the text insertion point); or by combining the two approaches. Field names must be enclosed in single quotes (') and text strings in double quotes (").

3. **Click OK.** ClarisWorks evaluates the formula. If it finds an error, it displays the message *Bad formula.* Otherwise, it displays the database, showing the records that match the formula as selected (highlighted).

After using the Match Records command to select a set of records, you can use two additional commands from the Organize menu to help you focus your attention on the new record subset: Hide Selected (⌘-left parenthesis) and Hide Unselected (⌘-right parenthesis). Hide Unselected has the same effect as the normal Find command. It hides all records that do not match the Match Records formula. Hide Selected has the same effect as a Find command with the Omit check box checked.

You also can use the Hide Selected and Hide Unselected commands after you manually select records. To select a single record, click anywhere in the record except in a field. To select multiple contiguous records, hold down the Shift key as you select the records. To select noncontiguous records, hold down the Command key as you select the records.

Changing the display order of records

You can change the order in which records are displayed by sorting them by the contents of one or several fields. You can do an ascending (A to Z) or descending (Z to A) sort for each sort field. When you select multiple sort fields, ClarisWorks sorts the database once for each field, using the order in which you selected the sort fields. Sorting changes the order of records in the database for all layouts, not just for the one that is currently displayed.

Step-by-Steps

To sort records:

1. **Choose Sort Records from the Organize menu (or press ⌘-J).** The Sort Records dialog box appears, as shown in Figure 6-25. (If you have sorted the database previously, the program displays the last sort instructions.)
2. **Choose the first sort field from the list on the left. Click the Ascending order or Descending order radio button to set the direction of the sort for that field and then click the Move button.** ClarisWorks adds the field to the Sort Order list on the right.
3. **Choose additional sort fields, as required.**
4. **Click OK to execute the sort instructions.** The program displays the records in the new order.

NOTE

If the layout has sub-summary fields, you have to sort the database by the designated sort field if you want the summary information to be displayed. For example, if you have created a sub-summary when sorted by Last Name, you must sort by Last Name. See "Summary fields," earlier in this Topic, for more information.

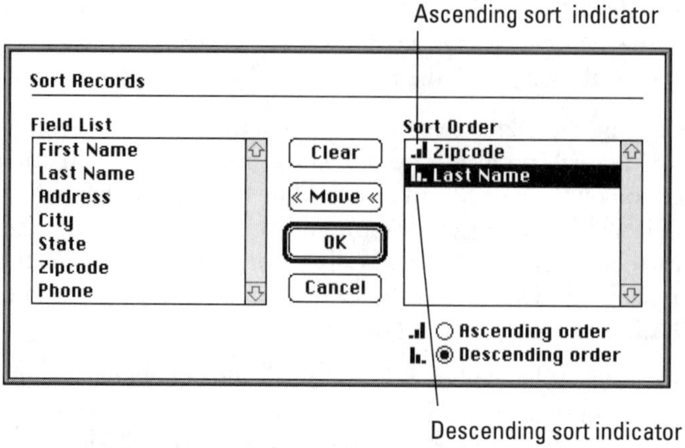

Figure 6-25: The Sort Records dialog box.

Creating Reports

One of the main reasons for building a database is the ease with which you can create custom reports and mailing labels. Although you can print any layout, creating special layouts for reports often makes more sense, especially if you create layouts that show the particular fields and summary information that you require, organized in a manner that makes sense for a report.

Adding headers and footers

You can add a header and a footer to a database layout. A header or footer appears in every report page and can be used to include a title — explaining what a report is about — or page numbers, for example.

Step-by-Steps

To create a header or a footer:

1. **At the bottom of the Layout menu, choose the layout to which you want to add a header or footer.**
2. **Choose Layout from the Layout menu (or press Shift-⌘-L).**
3. **Choose Insert Part from the Layout menu.** The Insert Part dialog box appears.
4. **Click the Header or Footer radio button and then click OK.** A header or footer area is inserted at the top (header) or bottom (footer) of the current layout.
5. **Add graphics or text in the header or footer area.** Whatever you insert will appear in that position at the top or bottom of every page. To see how the header or footer will look when printed, change to Browse mode (Shift-⌘-B) and choose Page View (Shift-⌘-P) from the View menu.

TIP

Headers and footers frequently include a report date and page numbers. To add automatic page numbering (so that page numbers increment by one for each new page) and date-stamping, select the Text tool, click the spot in the header or footer where you want to place the element, and then choose Insert Page # or Insert Date from the Edit menu. You should note, however, that every time you open the database, the date changes to match the current date. If you want to insert today's date and make sure that it does not change, press the Option key when you choose Insert Date.

Calculating summary and sub-summary information

By creating summary fields and adding them to a layout, you can calculate statistics that span the entire database or that summarize data based on record groupings (generating subtotals for each type of household expense, for example). Summary information can come at the beginning or end of a report or be displayed at the break between each group of records. And you aren't restricted to just totals. You can use any formula that you like, as well as take advantage of the dozens of database functions that ClarisWorks offers. For instructions for adding summary and sub-summary fields to a database, see "Summary fields," earlier in this Topic.

Working with mailing labels

Although you can design your own layouts for printing labels, ClarisWorks comes with more than 50 predefined layouts for popular Avery label formats. And if you don't find a layout to match the size of labels that you use, you can easily create a custom layout.

Step-by-Steps

To use a predefined label layout:

1. **Choose New Layout from the Layout menu.** The New Layout dialog box appears, as shown in Figure 6-26.

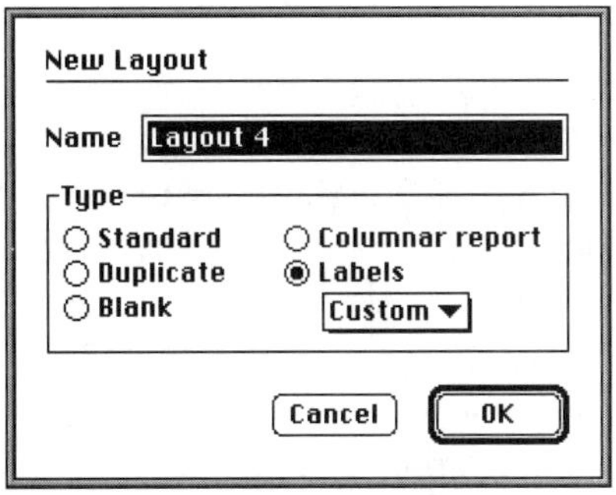

Figure 6-26: The New Layout dialog box.

2. **Click the Labels radio button and then click the Custom pop-up menu.** A list of the supported label formats pops up. (If you aren't using an Avery label, measure your label and match it to the equivalent Avery label format or create a custom label layout by following the next set of instructions.)

3. **Choose a label format and click OK.** The Set Field Order dialog box appears, as shown in Figure 6-27.

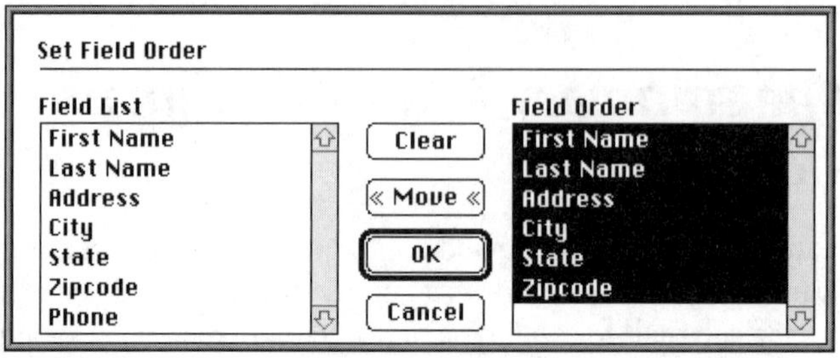

Figure 6-27: The Set Field Order dialog box.

4. **Select the fields that you want for the labels in the order in which they will appear and click the Move button to transfer each field to the Field Order list box.**

5. **Click OK.** The label layout appears.

6. **Resize and move the fields to correspond with the way they should appear on the labels.** Figure 6-28 shows a typical layout after editing.

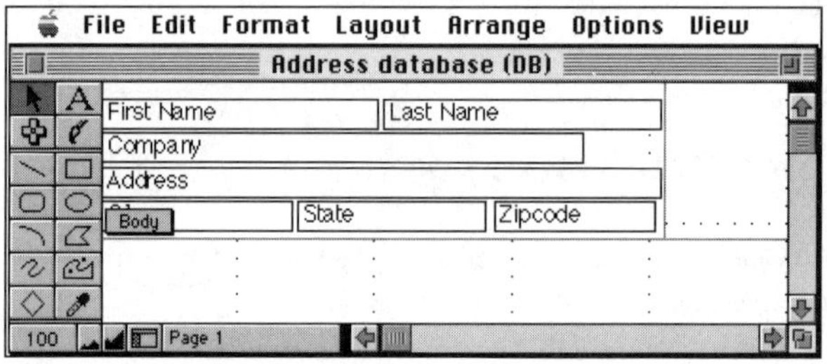

Figure 6-28: A sample label layout.

7. **If you want an idea of how the labels will look, choose Browse from the Layout menu (or press Shift-⌘-B).** Make sure that Page View (Shift-⌘-P) is also in effect. (Note that the space between fields, as well as blank lines, will be closed up when you print the labels but not when you view them on-screen.)

NOTE

ClarisWorks has unusual requirements that you need to adhere to when you are attempting to close up space during printing. These requirements apply not only to labels but also to any other type of database layout:

- *Objects do not slide toward other objects that are smaller than they are.* In order for a field to slide left, therefore, the field to the left must be exactly the same size or larger than the sliding field. Also, the top edges must be aligned if the fields are on the same line. The left edges must be aligned if fields are stacked one above the other (on different lines).

  To check the dimensions of each field, choose Object Size from the Options menu and then click each field. The Size palette lists each field's distance from the margins, as well as its height and width. See Topic 7 for information on using the Size palette to set the dimensions of an object.

- Fields will not slide at all if their edges are touching on the layout.

Also, if you are using a laser printer, you should note that the printer cannot print on the entire page. Most laser printers require a minimum margin of 0.2 to 0.25 inches all around the page. To ensure that you can print as close to the edges as possible, choose Page Setup from the File menu, click Options, and then click the check box for Larger Print area (fewer downloadable fonts).

TIP

Finally, because of the difficulty of getting text to align perfectly on labels, you're well advised to print a test page on standard paper and then place the test printout over a page of labels to see how they align. Continue to adjust the fields and make test printouts until the alignment is correct.

If you don't see a predefined label format that matches the labels you want to use, you can create a custom label layout.

Step-by-Steps

To create a custom label layout:

1. **Choose New Layout from the Layout menu.** The New Layout dialog box appears.
2. **Click the Labels radio button and be sure that the Custom option is selected.**
3. **Enter a descriptive name for the label layout in the Name text-edit box and click OK.** The Label Layout dialog box appears, as shown in Figure 6-29.

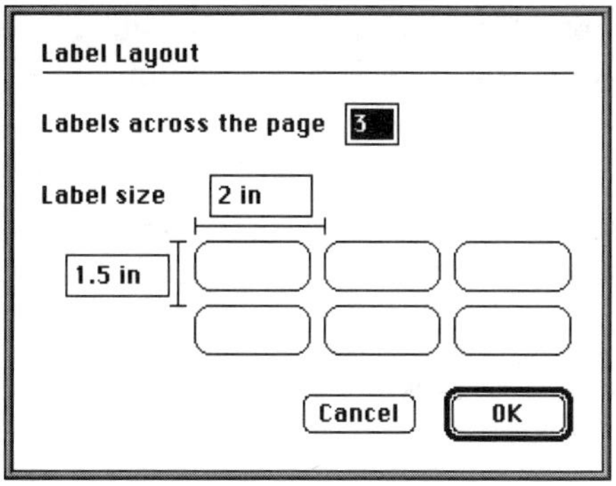

Figure 6-29: The Label Layout dialog box.

4. **Enter the number of labels across (enter 3 for a page with three labels across it, for example) and the dimensions for a single label, and then click OK.** The Set Field Order dialog box appears.

5. **Select the fields that you want to appear on the labels, click the Move button to transfer them to the Field Order list, and click OK.** The new layout appears.

6. **Resize and move the fields to correspond with the way they should appear on the labels.** The initial placement of the Body dividing line is correct for the size of label that is specified. Do not move it and be sure that all fields stay within its boundaries.

7. **If you want an idea of how the labels will look, choose Browse from the Layout menu (or press Shift-⌘-B).** Make sure that Page View (Shift-⌘-P) is also in effect. (Note that the space between fields, as well as blank lines, will be closed up when you print the labels but not when you view them on-screen.)

NOTE

You measure the width of a label from the left edge of the first label to the left edge of the next label. Similarly, you measure label height from the top of one label to the top of the label below it. That is, the gaps that follow each label to the right and below are considered part of the label's size.

Database printing

To generate a database report or other printout from a database, you can just select an appropriate layout and choose Print. However, you also can choose other options to make reports and printouts more meaningful and attractive. (***Note:*** Every printout can consist of all visible [nonhidden] records or only the currently selected record.)

Step-by-Steps

To print from a database:

1. **At the bottom of the Layout menu, choose the layout that you want to use to generate the printout.**

2. **Use the Find command (see "Finding and Selecting Records," earlier in this Topic) to select the records that you want to include.** If you want to use all of the records, choose Show All Records from the Organize menu (or press Shift-⌘-A).

3. **If you want the records to display in a particular order, sort the records (as described in "Changing the display order of records," earlier in this Topic).**

4. **Choose Print from the File menu (or press ⌘-P).** The Print dialog box appears, as shown in Figure 6-30.

Creating and saving custom label definitions

All permanent label layout definitions are stored in a text file named ClarisWorks Labels. By editing this file, you can add your own custom label definitions, as well as change the names of existing layouts (Diskette Label — 3-up, rather than Avery 5096, 5196, 5896, for example). After you make the changes to the file, you can choose your own label definitions from the Labels pop-up menu in the New Layout dialog box.

To create a new label definition:

1. **Locate the ClarisWorks Labels file.** It is inside the Claris folder, which is inside the System Folder on the start-up hard disk.
2. **Select the ClarisWorks Labels icon and choose Duplicate from the Finder's File menu (or press ⌘-D).** The file is copied and named Copy of ClarisWorks Labels or ClarisWorks Labels Copy, depending on whether you are running System 6 or System 7. Making a duplicate helps protect the original file.
3. **To protect the original ClarisWorks Labels file, change its name (to ClarisWorks Labels.bak, for example).** Keep it as a backup copy in case you have problems with the editing.
4. **Double-click the duplicate copy of the ClarisWorks Labels file.** ClarisWorks launches, and the file is converted from plain text to ClarisWorks format. The figure shows the contents of the ClarisWorks Labels file when you open it in the word processor.

As you can see in the figure, every label definition consists of eight lines: the label name enclosed in brackets, the number of columns, the horizontal pitch (label width), the vertical pitch (label height), the top margin, the bottom margin, the left margin, and the right margin. (Ignore any information that is preceded by a pair of slashes [//]; it is a comment.)

5. **Use one of the existing label definitions as a template for designing a new label.** Select any 8-line segment, starting with a label name and ending with its right margin data. Choose Copy from the Edit menu (or press ⌘-C).
6. **Select the spot in the label list where you want to insert the new label definition.** You may want to keep your own definitions together — at the end of the list, for example.
7. **Place the text insertion marker at the spot where you want to insert the definition and choose Paste from the Edit menu (or press ⌘-V).** Be sure that you do not break up an existing definition when you paste the template.
8. **Edit the pasted text by entering your own label name within the brackets and replacing the other lines with the number of columns, width, height, top margin, bottom margin, left margin, and right margin for your label.**
9. **Save the file by choosing the Save As command from the File menu (or pressing Shift-⌘-S). Choose Text in the Save As pop-up menu and type ClarisWorks Labels as the new filename.**
10. **Quit ClarisWorks.** The next time you launch ClarisWorks, the new label layouts will be available.

Changing the name for any of the label layouts is even easier. Simply follow the preceding steps; but, instead of adding an entirely new layout, just change the text string between any pair of brackets to something more meaningful, such as [Audio Cassette — 2-up] rather than [Avery 5198]. After you change the name for a label layout and save the file, the new name appears in the Labels pop-up menu.

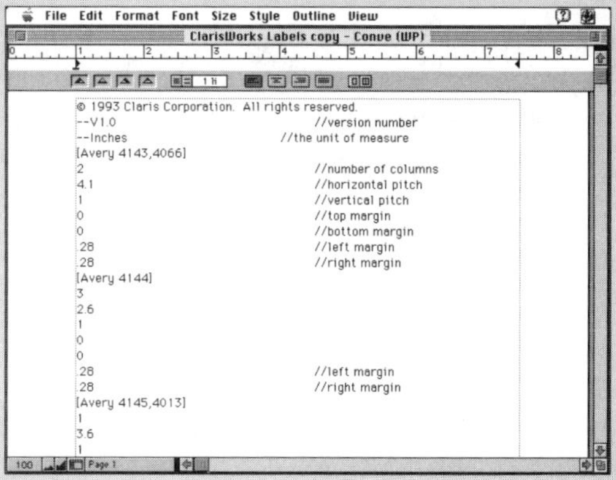

```
┌─────────────────────────────────────────────────────────────────────┐
│ LaserWriter  "LaserWriter II NT"              7.1.2    ┌─────────┐   │
│                                                        │  Print  │   │
│ Copies: █         Pages: ⦿ All  ○ From: [    ] To: [    ] └───────┘   │
│                                                        ┌─────────┐   │
│ Cover Page:   ⦿ No ○ First Page  ○ Last Page          │ Cancel  │   │
│                                                        └─────────┘   │
│ Paper Source: ⦿ Paper Cassette   ○ Manual Feed                       │
│ Print:        ○ Black & White    ⦿ Color/Grayscale                   │
│ Destination:  ⦿ Printer          ○ PostScript® File                  │
│ ─────────────────────────────────────────────────────────────────── │
│ Print:        ○ Current Record   ⦿ Visible Records                   │
└─────────────────────────────────────────────────────────────────────┘
```

Click one of these buttons to
determine what will be printed

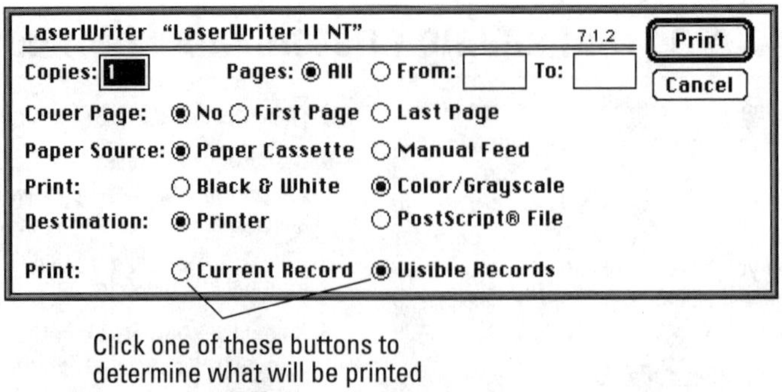

Figure 6-30: The Print dialog box, as it appears when you are printing a ClarisWorks database. (This Print dialog box is for a LaserWriter; dialog boxes for other printers are different.)

5. **Click the Current Record or Visible Records radio button at the bottom of the dialog box, depending on what you want to print.**

6. **Click Print to send the report to the printer.** (Topic 1 explains other Print and Page Setup options.) ◊

Saving Changes

If you've used FileMaker Pro or any of its earlier incarnations, you've undoubtedly noticed the many features that it shares with the ClarisWorks database environment. One of the major differences, however, is the way that the two programs handle data and layout storage.

FileMaker and FileMaker Pro automatically save any database changes, whether they are layout modifications or data additions, deletions, or alterations. In fact, FileMaker Pro doesn't even have a Save command. The plus side of this feature is that users never have to worry about whether their changes have been saved. The minus side is that the program saves *all* changes — both deliberate changes and unintentional or ill-advised changes. Unless you have a backup of your important FileMaker files, experimentation can be dangerous.

ClarisWorks, on the other hand, does not have an automatic save feature. You can experiment to your heart's content, secure in the knowledge that you can close the file at any time without saving changes. When you do want to save, on the other hand, choose the Save or Save As command from the File menu.

Importing and Exporting Data

Unless you just bought your Mac, you may already have several databases that you designed in other programs. They may be FileMaker Pro or HyperCard databases, or they may be databases that you created in an address book program, a word processor, a spreadsheet, or a desk accessory. You can easily import databases into ClarisWorks.

You use the Insert command in the File menu to add information from other databases into a ClarisWorks database. Instead of reorganizing the source database so that its fields match those of the target ClarisWorks database, you use the Import Field Order dialog box to match fields between the two databases — regardless of their order and whether the databases have the same number of fields. Thus, importing data is easier than ever.

To import information into a ClarisWorks database:

1. **In the source program, save or export the data file as a tab-delimited text file.** Some programs, such as spreadsheets, may simply call this file a Text file, ASCII Text file, or Text-Only file. See the program's manual for instructions. (In a tab-delimited text file, each record is a separate paragraph. Every field in a record is separated from the next field by a tab character.)
2. **Open or create a ClarisWorks database to receive the imported data.**
3. **In ClarisWorks, choose the Insert command from the File menu, choose the tab-delimited text file created in Step 1, and click Insert.** The Import Field Order dialog box appears, as shown in Figure 6-31. The fields in the left side of the dialog box are from the file that you're importing (the source file). The fields on the right are in the ClarisWorks database (the destination file).

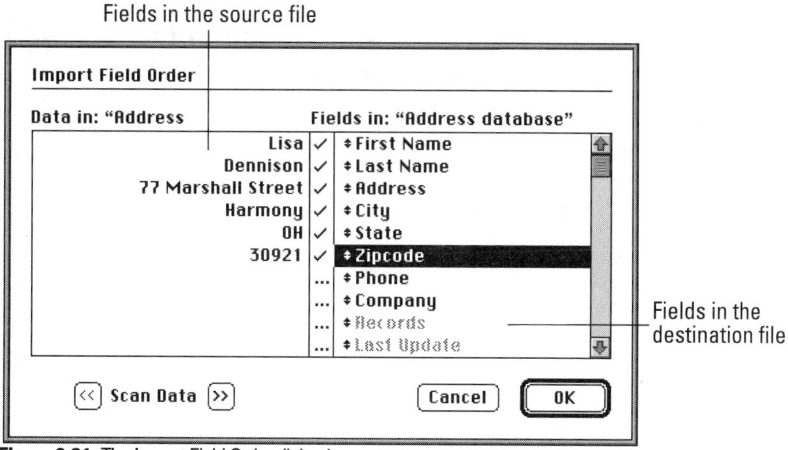

Figure 6-31: The Import Field Order dialog box.

4. **Rearrange the fields in the right side of the dialog box so that they match the appropriate fields on the left side.** Fields with a counterpart that you want to import should have a check mark in front of them. Fields with no counterpart are indicated by ellipses (...) and are not imported.

   NOTE

   Not every field needs to have a counterpart. You may well have more fields in one database than in the other. No restrictions govern how many or how few fields you can import. If you find, however, that the target ClarisWorks database lacks a key field that the source file possesses, you may want to cancel the import, add the new field to the ClarisWorks database, and then proceed with the import.

5. **Using the Scan Data buttons, check several records of the source file to see whether the fields match correctly. If you're satisfied with the matchup, click OK to import the data.** The new records are imported into the database.

As with importing data, when you export data from a ClarisWorks database to use in another program, tab-delimited ASCII text is often the best format to use. Virtually every type of Macintosh program (including word processors) can correctly handle such a file. (A tab-delimited text file contains one record per line, and each field in the record is separated from the next field by a tab character.)

Step-by-Steps

To export a ClarisWorks database file:

1. **Open the ClarisWorks database by choosing Open from the File menu (or press ⌘-O).**
2. **Choose Save As from the File menu (or press Shift-⌘-S).**
3. **Choose ASCII Text from the Save As pop-up menu and enter a new filename for the export file.** (If the receiving program can read them, you also can choose a DBF, DIF, or SYLK format for the exported data.)
4. **Click Save to save the file.**
5. **Open or import the file into the destination program.** (See the program's manual for instructions on opening or importing foreign files.)

Using a spreadsheet to clean up import data

Although you can use the Import Field Order dialog box to match fields as well as possible when you import data into a database, the matchup between fields isn't always as clean as it could be. When you import address data, for example, two problems are common:

- The address, phone number, or name fields in the import file are split into two fields (address line 1 and address line 2, area code and phone number, and first name and last name), but they are in one field in the ClarisWorks database — or vice versa.
- ZIP codes shorter than five digits are missing the leading zero (1276 rather than 01276).

Instead of importing the data as is and cleaning it up in the database afterward, you can use the ClarisWorks spreadsheet to make the necessary transformations to the data and do it more efficiently. Using the spreadsheet changes the steps in the ClarisWorks database import process.

To use a spreadsheet to import data into a ClarisWorks database:

1. **Export the data from the database, spreadsheet, or address book program as a tab-delimited ASCII text file.**
2. **Open the ASCII text file as a ClarisWorks spreadsheet; make the transformations to the data, creating new fields as necessary; and save the revised file as an ASCII text file again.**
3. **Open the ClarisWorks database and use the Insert command to import the ASCII text file into the database.**

The simplest way to make the transformations in the spreadsheet is to create additional columns at the right end of the spreadsheet. Each column will contain a formula that combines or converts one or more columns of the original data. After you create the appropriate formula, use the Fill Down command (⌘-D) to copy it into the remaining cells in the column. The figures illustrate three typical conversions.

In the first figure, Column A contains first names, and column B contains last names. The combination formula in the entry bar, *=A2&" "&B2,* takes the first name in cell A2 (*Jody*), adds a space to it (" "), and then adds the last name from cell B2 (*Privette*) to the end of the text string. The combined fields appear in column C as one name.2

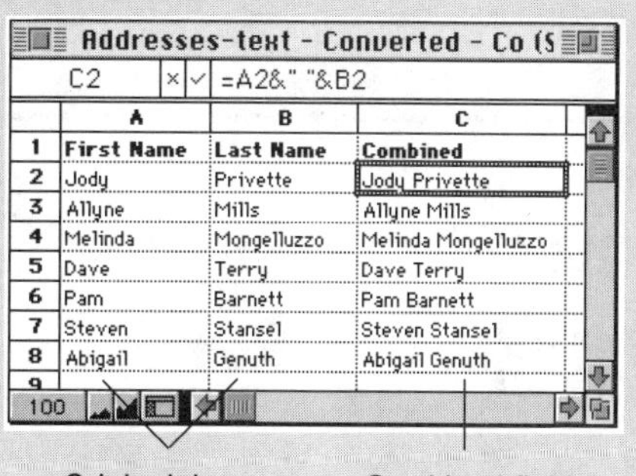

	A	B	C
1	First Name	Last Name	Combined
2	Jody	Privette	Jody Privette
3	Allyne	Mills	Allyne Mills
4	Melinda	Mongelluzzo	Melinda Mongelluzzo
5	Dave	Terry	Dave Terry
6	Pam	Barnett	Pam Barnett
7	Steven	Stansel	Steven Stansel
8	Abigail	Genuth	Abigail Genuth

The second figure is an example of combining two address fields into a single address field. Unlike the names in the preceding example, some addresses contain only one part. The equation *=IF(B2<>"",A2&", "&B2,A2)* checks to see whether the address has a second part (*B2<>""*). If the second portion is not

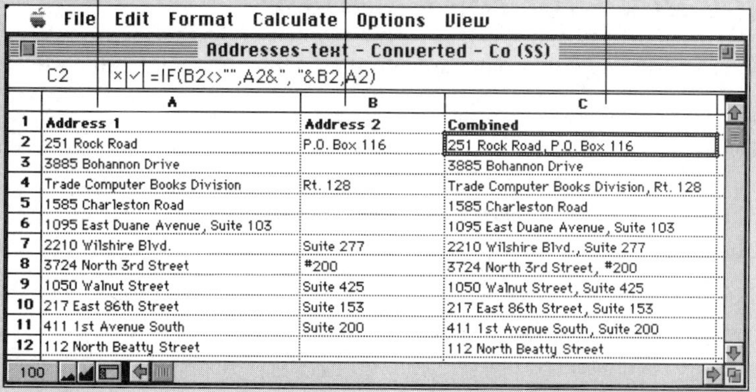

	A	B	C
1	Address 1	Address 2	Combined
2	251 Rock Road	P.O. Box 116	251 Rock Road, P.O. Box 116
3	3885 Bohannon Drive		3885 Bohannon Drive
4	Trade Computer Books Division	Rt. 128	Trade Computer Books Division, Rt. 128
5	1585 Charleston Road		1585 Charleston Road
6	1095 East Duane Avenue, Suite 103		1095 East Duane Avenue, Suite 103
7	2210 Wilshire Blvd.	Suite 277	2210 Wilshire Blvd., Suite 277
8	3724 North 3rd Street	#200	3724 North 3rd Street, #200
9	1050 Walnut Street	Suite 425	1050 Walnut Street, Suite 425
10	217 East 86th Street	Suite 153	217 East 86th Street, Suite 153
11	411 1st Avenue South	Suite 200	411 1st Avenue South, Suite 200
12	112 North Beatty Street		112 North Beatty Street

(continued)

(continued)

blank, the formula combines the two portions, separating them with a comma followed by a blank, as in *251 Rock Road, P.O. Box 116.* If the address does not have a second part, the formula simply copies the first address part (*A2*) into the cell.

In the example in the third figure, a zero is added to four-digit ZIP codes. Because ZIP codes are often treated as numbers, the leading zero may disappear, resulting in an improper four-digit code. The lengthy formula *=IF(LEN(A2)=4,"0"&A2, NUMTOTEXT(A2))* checks to see whether the length of the ZIP code is four digits (*LEN(A2)=4*). If so, a leading zero is appended to the ZIP code (*"0"&A2*), and the ZIP code is converted to text. If the ZIP code does not contain four digits, it is converted to text and passed through unaltered (*NUMTOTEXT(A2)*). Converting ZIP codes to text is necessary to display leading zeroes and to handle blank ZIP codes. If the formula simply ended with *A2,* rather than with *NUMTOTEXT(A2),* a blank ZIP code would translate as 0 (zero).

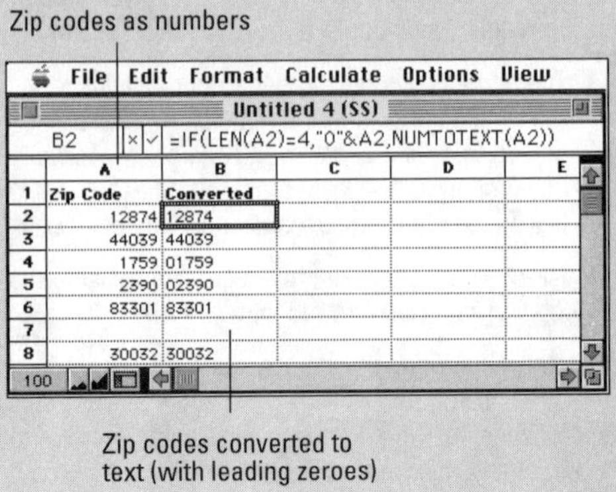

Down to Business: Creating a Credit Card Charge Tracker

If all you want to do is keep track of how you're doing on your credit cards, you don't need a dedicated home finance program. You can use a simple ClarisWorks database to record charges and payments, as well as to show how you're doing overall. Figure 6-32 shows what such a database looks like.

The database enables you to record the following information for every charge: the date of the transaction, the store or business where the charge was made, a description of what was charged, the amount of the charge, and the particular credit card that was used.

Defining fields for the database

Start by creating a new database and then define the fields listed in Table 6-2.

The first four fields (Date, Store, Item Description, and Amount) are self-explanatory. To save typing time and ensure accurate, consistent spelling, Charge Card is declared as a Text field based on a value list — in this case, a list of the names of all charge cards you intend to track. When you select it in the database (by clicking the field or tabbing into it), the Charge Card field displays a pop-up list of your credit cards.

The Paid field is also a pop-up list, but it contains only a single item: a check mark symbol (Option-V). Because it's difficult to remember what to type to create the check mark character, placing it in a value list relieves you of the need to type the character manually — you can just choose it from the pop-up list.

Charge Total is a summary field that calculates an individual charge total for each credit card when the database is sorted by Charge Card.

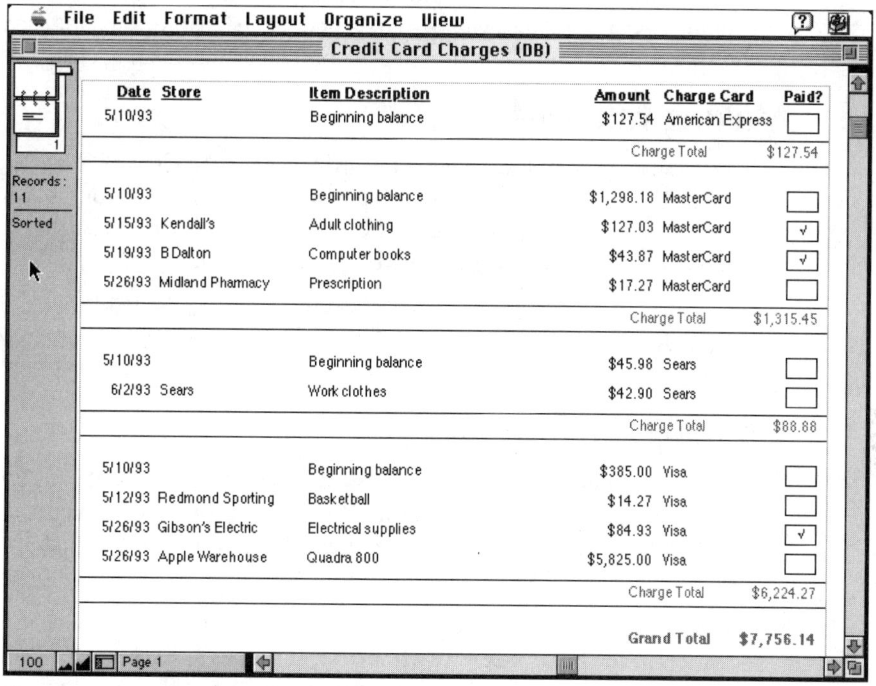

Figure 6-32: The Credit Card Charges database.

Table 6-2
Fields for the Credit Card Charges Database

Field Name	***Type***	***Formula***
Date	Text	
Store	Text	
Item Description	Text	
Amount	Number	
Charge Card	Text	Value list: American Express, MasterCard, Visa, and so on
Paid?	Text	Value list: √ (Option-V)
Outstanding amount	Calculation	=IF('Paid?'="√",0,'Amount')
Charge Total	Summary	(Sub-summary by Charge Card) =SUM('Outstanding amount')
Grand Total	Summary	(Trailing grand summary) =SUM('Outstanding amount')

Outstanding Amount is a calculation field that is used to determine whether each charge has already been reconciled (paid). If paid, Outstanding Amount is set to 0 (zero). Otherwise, it is set to whatever number is currently in the Amount field for the record. Unlike the other database fields, Outstanding Amount is not displayed on the layout. It is, however, used to generate the Charge Total for each credit card, as well as the Grand Total (the total amount of all outstanding charges for all cards).

Making value lists

To create a pop-up menu of credit card types for the Charge Card field, choose the field name in the Define Fields dialog box and click Options. Click the Predefined list check box and then click Edit list. Create a value list that consists of the names of all the credit cards that you intend to track.

Use the same technique to create a pop-up menu for the Paid? field. The only value that should be used for this field is a check mark. Press Option-V to create the check mark character (√).

Creating the formulas

You use two summary formulas in the database. Charge Total adds up the outstanding charges for each credit card, and the total is displayed as a sub-summary when the database is sorted by Charge Card. Grand Total adds up the outstanding charges for all credit cards.

Outstanding amount is a simple calculation field. It determines whether a check mark is in the Paid? box for each record. If it finds a check mark, it notes that the outstanding amount for the item is now 0 (zero). If it does not find a check mark, it assumes that the amount for the record is outstanding. Outstanding amount is used only for calculations; it does not appear on the layout.

To create the Charge Total and Grand Total fields, enter each name in the Define Fields dialog box, click the Summary radio button, and then click Create. A new dialog box appears in which you can enter the formula shown in Table 6-2. To create the Outstanding amount field, follow the same steps but click the Calculation radio button rather than the Summary radio button.

Making the layout

This database requires only one layout. Not only will it serve for data entry, but you also can use it to display on-screen and printed reports.

After you define the fields, the program automatically creates a standard layout. Because you don't need this layout, choose Delete Layout from the Layout menu to remove it. Now, create the *real* layout.

To design the layout:

1. **Choose New Layout from the Layout menu.**
2. **In the dialog box that appears, name the layout Data Entry, click the Columnar Report radio button, and then click OK.**
3. **In the Set Field Order dialog box that appears (see Figure 6-33), select every field except Outstanding amount and click Move. Make sure that the order matches that of the figure, and click OK to create the columnar layout.**

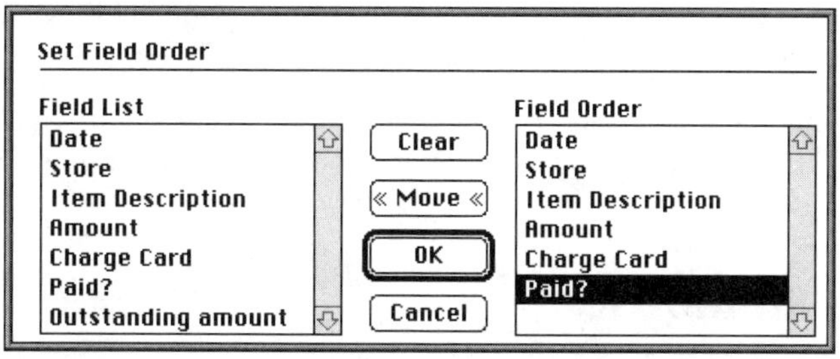

Figure 6-33: The Set Field Order dialog box for the Credit Card Charge Tracker.

4. **Arrange the fields (in the body) and labels (in the header) so they look like the layout in Figure 6-34.**

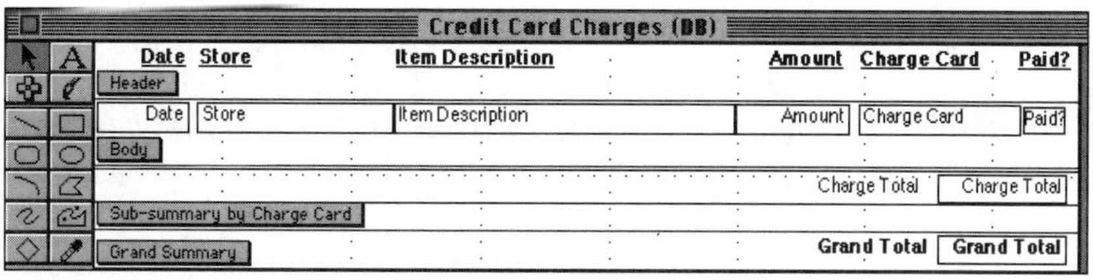

Figure 6-34: The final layout.

5. **To create the Charge Total sub-summary, choose Insert Part from the Layout menu. Then choose Sub-summary when sorted by Charge Card and click OK. Click Below in the dialog box that follows.** The sub-summary part is added to the layout.
6. **To create the Grand Total summary, choose Insert Part from the Layout menu. Then choose Trailing grand summary and click OK.** The Grand Summary part is added to the bottom of the layout.
7. **To insert the two summary fields into the layout, choose Insert Field from the Layout menu and then double-click Charge Total and Grand Total. After the fields are placed on the layout, drag them to the locations that are shown in Figure 6-34.**

You can add several finishing touches to pretty up the database layout:

- Above and below the Charge Total field, add solid lines that extend the full width of the page.
- Apply the Currency format to all monetary fields (Amount, Charge Total, Grand Total).
- Set right justification as the text alignment for the Date, Amount, Charge Total, and Grand Total fields; set center justification for the Paid? field.
- Create a box around the Paid? field by setting the pen pattern for the field to opaque and its color to black (using the Pen tools in the tool panel).
- Add boldface to the Grand Total by selecting the field and choosing Bold from the Style submenu of the Format menu.
- Drag the Header and Body dividers up to reduce the space that they take up on the layout. (Figure 6-34 shows them with extra space so that you can see all the field names.)

Using the database

Using the database is fairly simple. The basic procedures include starting up, entering new records, establishing a sort order in which to display the records, reconciling the individual charges with payments made to the credit card companies, and deleting records.

Starting up

The first time that you use the database, you are likely to have outstanding balances on some of your credit cards. If so, create a Beginning balance record for each charge card, as shown in Figure 6-32. As you pay off (or pay down) the balance, you will reduce it by your payment amounts (as described in "Reconciling the charge statement," later in this Topic).

Entering new charges

Whenever you have a new charge to enter, choose New Record from the Edit menu (or press ⌘-R). A new record appears, and you can enter the charge details. Leave the Paid? field blank (unchecked).

Establishing a sort order

Although you can leave the records in the order in which you entered them, that order complicates reconciliation and makes finding specific records difficult. Furthermore, the Charge Total summaries won't be available to you. You can solve all of these problems by specifying a sort order for the database.

Choose Sort Records from the Organize menu (or press ⌘-J), set ascending sorts for the Charge Card and Date fields (in that order), and then click OK. ClarisWorks sorts the database by charge card and, within each charge card, by date of purchase. If the Charge Totals are still not visible, make sure that you have selected Page View from the View menu.

NOTE

Each time you finish entering new records, be sure to sort the database again.

Reconciling the charge statement

When a charge statement arrives in the mail, you can reconcile it in one of two ways, depending on whether you pay off the entire balance or pay less than the balance due.

Step-by-Steps

To reconcile a statement when you pay off the entire balance:

1. **Check each record against the statement to make sure that it contains no mistakes.**
2. **Using the pop-up menu in the Paid? field, select the check mark character for each record that is on the statement (marking them paid).** The Charge Total for that credit card should now show as *0* (zero).

Step-by-Steps

To reconcile a statement when you pay off less than the entire balance:

1. **Check each record against the statement to make sure that it contains no mistakes.**
2. **Subtract the amount that you intend to pay on this statement from any of the outstanding charges for that credit card.**

   For example, suppose that you have $500 worth of Visa charges in your database ($300 of it as the beginning balance and two other charges of $100 each). If you are paying $75 today, you can edit any of the original Amount fields for that card by subtracting the $75 payment. Thus, you may reduce the $300 beginning balance to $225.

   If you are paying $100, you can simply mark one of the $100 charges as paid (which would instantly remove that amount from the Charge Total for the credit card).

   Remember, the object is to show the correct outstanding amount for each card (the Charge Total). What the individual charges show is irrelevant — at least after you've verified that the credit card company has recorded them correctly.

Deleting records

After you've paid off some charges, you can, at your option, delete their records to prevent them from cluttering up the database. (However, you may want to make a printout of the database for your permanent records first.) The simplest way to remove all of the paid records is to use the Match Records command.

Step-by-Steps

To select and delete the paid records:

1. **Choose Match Records from the Organize menu (or press ⌘-M).** The Match Records dialog box appears.
2. **Enter the formula shown in Figure 6-35 (press Option-V to type the check mark symbol) and then click OK.** The records that have been paid are selected.

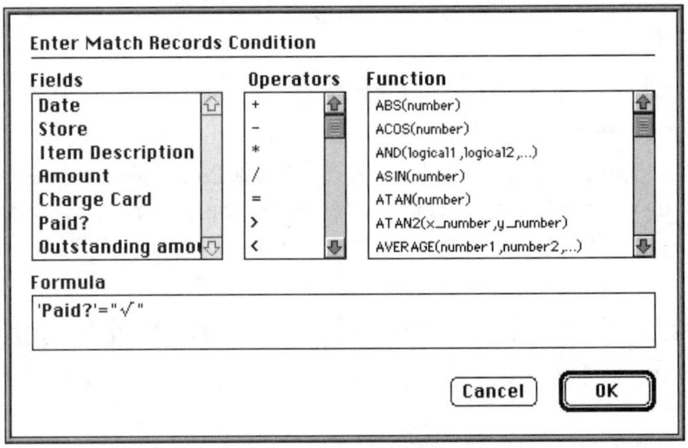

Figure 6-35: Enter the formula shown in the text-edit box to highlight all records that you've marked as paid.

NOTE

Instead of trying to remember this formula, you can create a ClarisWorks macro to type it for you. See Topic 14 for instructions.

3. **Choose Clear from the Edit menu.** The paid records are removed from the database.

Quick Tips

The following Quick Tips describe how to empty a database field for an entire database, explain how to perform date calculations, suggest ways to use the spelling checker and thesaurus, and list several database programs to consider when you're ready for a more powerful database.

Emptying a database field for an entire database

Suppose that you want to erase the contents of a single field within every record in the database. The database environment does not provide an easy way to perform this task, but you can do it if you enlist the spreadsheet to help you.

To empty a database field:

1. **Open the database in ClarisWorks and choose the Save As command from the File menu (or press Shift-⌘-S).**
2. **Save the file in ASCII text format (choose this option from the Save As Pop-up menu) and use a new filename.**
3. **Choose Open from the File menu (or press ⌘-O), and choose Spreadsheet from the Document Type pop-up menu.** The ASCII Text file appears in the file list.
4. **Choose the ASCII Text file and click Open.** The text file is converted to a spreadsheet that has one database field in each column.
5. **Select the column of data that corresponds to the database field that you want to empty — Phone in this example.** (Click the letter at the top of a column to select the column.)
6. **Choose Clear from the Edit menu.** The cells are cleared.
7. **Save the file as text again by choosing Save As from the File menu, choosing ASCII text in the Save As pop-up menu, and changing the filename back to the one you used in Step 2.** This step replaces the original ASCII text file with the modified version that you just created in the spreadsheet.
8. **Switch to the database screen; choose Show All Records from the Organize menu (Shift-⌘-A), followed by Select All from the Edit menu (⌘-A).** All records in the database are highlighted/selected.
9. **Choose Clear from the Edit menu to remove all records simultaneously.**
10. **Choose Insert from the File menu and choose the ASCII Text version of the spreadsheet that you saved in Step 7; click Insert.** The Import Field Order dialog box appears, as shown in Figure 6-36. This box shows you, one record at a time, how the imported data will be entered into the database fields. The match should be perfect. (Of course, the field you just emptied — Phone, in this example — should be blank.)

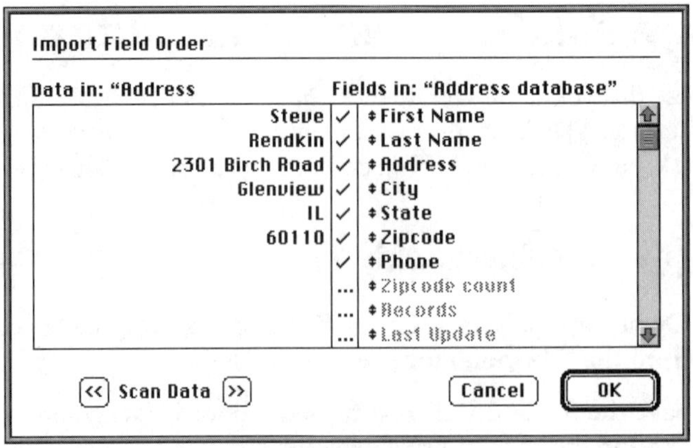

Figure 6-36: The Import Field Order dialog box.

11. After using the Scan Data buttons to check several records, click OK.
The procedure is now complete. Figure 6-37 shows the results of clearing the Phone field for all records.

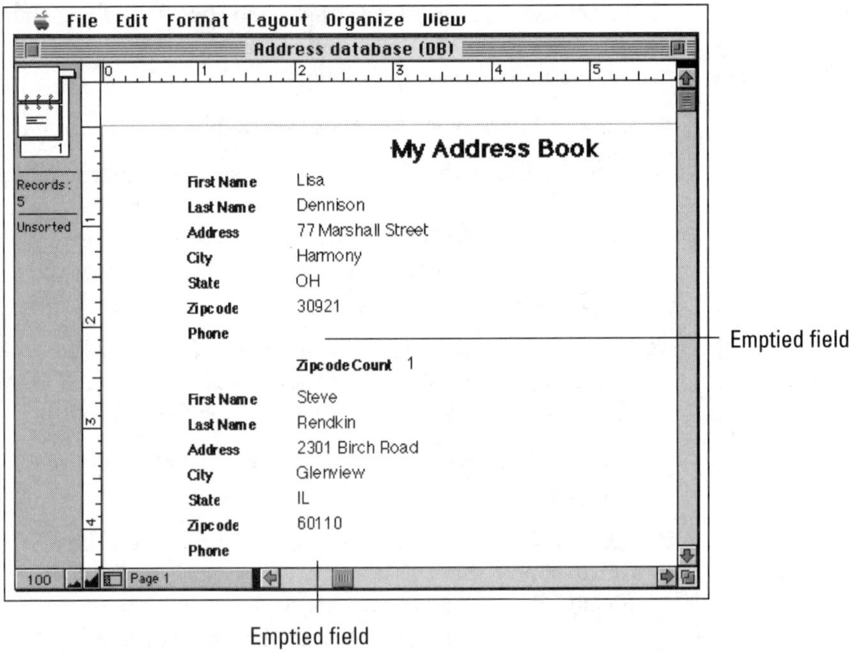

Figure 6-37: The revised database records.

Date calculations

Because the ClarisWorks database environment also enables you to create calculation fields, you may sometimes want to record two dates and then determine the number of days between them. You can calculate the number of days that completing a project required or the number of days until a special event will occur (days until your mother's birthday or payday, for example). The following steps show how to accomplish this task in your own databases.

Step-by-Steps

To calculate the number of days between two dates:

1. **Choose Define Fields from the Layout menu (or press Shift-⌘-D).** The Define Fields dialog box appears.
2. **Create a pair of date fields (Start Date and End Date, for example).**
3. **Create a calculation field to compute the difference between the dates (Total Days, for example).** The formula for the field is 'End Date'–'Start Date'. Set Number as the result type by using the Format result as pop-up menu.

Step-by-Steps

To calculate the number of days until an upcoming event:

1. **Choose Define Fields from the Layout menu (or press Shift-⌘-D).** The Define Fields dialog box appears.
2. **Create a date field (such as Due Date) in which to record the target date.**
3. **Create a calculation field to compute the number of days between today and the target date.** The formula for the field would be 'Due Date'–TRUNC(NOW( )). Set Number as the result type by using the Format result as pop-up menu.

   The NOW( ) function takes the current date and time from the Mac's internal clock. When you truncate the date and time by adding the TRUNC function, the program discards the fractional portion of the day. Because you want to know only how many full days remain until the event, this formula produces a whole number as the result: 7 days, rather than 7.1852 days, for example.

NOTE

If the Due Date has already occurred, the result of this formula is a negative number. A result of –5 indicates that the event occurred five days ago.

Don't forget the spelling checker and thesaurus!

The name of this section says it all. Although you normally think of the spelling checker and thesaurus in connection with word processing documents, you also can use them in other ClarisWorks environments, such as the database. You may even want to create special user dictionaries for some databases. A dictionary that contains the spellings for company and customer names would be useful for a contacts or client database, for example, and would help to ensure the accuracy of the data that you enter.

If your database includes large text fields, such as ones for notes or comments, you may want to turn on the auto-hyphenation feature (in ClarisWorks 2.1 and higher versions). To do so, select Auto Hyphenate from the Writing Tools submenu of the Edit menu.

Moving On Up

If you're lusting for more database power, you'll find the transition to Claris's FileMaker Pro an easy one. The features in the ClarisWorks database environment are a subset of the features in FileMaker Pro. FileMaker Pro enables you to create powerful database scripts with a simple-to-use scripting system, add script buttons to layouts, and exercise greater control over the way that layouts display on-screen.

If you need programming and relational database capabilities, check out 4th Dimension (ACI US Inc.), FoxBase (Microsoft), and Double Helix (Helix Technologies).

Summary

- A database is an organized set of information on one particular topic. Every database is composed of records, and the records are made up of fields.
- The ClarisWorks database has three essential modes: Layout, Browse, and Find.
- ClarisWorks offers six types of database fields: text, number, date, time, calculation, and summary. You use different field types to allow only certain types of data to be entered into the fields.
- Entries in calculation and summary fields are always the result of a formula that you have specified. You cannot manually enter data into a calculation or summary field.
- The ClarisWorks database environment includes several data validation and auto-entry options that you can set for fields. These options can help ensure the accuracy of the data that you enter and speed up the data-entry process.
- For each database, you can create as many layouts (arrangements of data fields and other objects) as you need. Each layout can offer a different view of the data and use different subsets of fields.
- In addition to the Body part of each layout (where most of the fields are), you can create Header and Footer parts (for placing information that you want to appear on every page of the database), as well as Summary and Sub-summary parts (where you can calculate statistics or formulas for the entire database or selected record groupings).
- By sorting the database on the contents of one or more fields, you can change the order in which the records are displayed and the way in which they are grouped.
- You can search for records by using two commands: Find and Match Records. The Find command displays the subset of records that match the search criteria and hides all other records. Match Records merely selects the subset without hiding the other records.
- Entering multiple criteria in a single Find request results in an AND search (find records that match this criterion *and* that criterion). You also can issue multiple Find requests to execute an OR search (find records that match this criterion *or* that criterion).
- ClarisWorks provides more than 50 layouts for Avery labels. You also can create custom label layouts.
- As with the other environments, the database can import and export records in a number of different formats. Importing enables you to merge records from other data files with an existing ClarisWorks database. Exporting data is useful when you want to examine or use the database data in another program (a spreadsheet or desktop publishing program, for example).

Topic 7

Graphics: The Draw and Paint Environments

Overview

ClarisWorks has two graphics environments: Draw and Paint. Using the draw tools, you create *objects* — graphics that you can move, resize, and place in layers over each other. Because the graphics are objects, they maintain a separate identity from everything else on the page. You can select any draw object separately from other images. Editing, however, affects the entire object. You cannot, for example, remove a few dots from an object or cut a section away. But changing the color, pattern, or line width for an object is simple.

In paint documents or frames, on the other hand, images are composed entirely of dots, and you can edit them at the dot level. This capability makes the paint environment excellent for creating detailed images, such as illustrations.

Here are the major differences between the two environments:

- Draw tools are always available (except in the communications environment). The paint tools remain hidden until you select the Paintbrush tool (to work in or create a paint frame) or open a paint document.
- Draw objects are solid; you can edit them only as a whole. Paint images are composed of dots; you can edit them at the dot level.
- Selecting and manipulating draw objects is easy. Working with portions of paint images can be more difficult because they do not maintain a separate identity. (A paint image is just a mass of dots.)
- You can place draw objects in layers, with some objects obscuring portions of other objects. The objects retain their independence, enabling you to change their attributes and their position in the layers. In the paint environment, after you cover part of an image with another image, the obscured portion is gone forever (unless you immediately choose the Undo command).
- There is no such thing as a draw frame. You can place draw objects directly onto the pages of most ClarisWorks documents. Paint images, however, must be in a paint document or in a paint frame. If you copy and paste a portion of a paint image into another document, the program automatically embeds it in a rectangular paint frame.

- ◆ You can align draw objects to each other or to the grid.
- ◆ You can rotate either type of image, and you can flip them horizontally or vertically and scale them to a different size.
- ◆ The paint environment enables you to apply a variety of special effects to selections. Some of the effects are invert, blend, tint, shear, distort, and perspective.
- ◆ You can alter the resolution and depth of paint documents.

Because the two environments share similar purposes and capabilities, this Topic discusses both of them.

The Draw Environment

The draw environment enables you to create graphics objects that you can easily move, resize, and combine. You can place these objects on any document page, copy them to other applications, and store them in the Scrapbook desk accessory.

The draw tools are available in every environment other than communications. Because everything on a draw page is treated as an object (including frames from other environments), the draw environment is excellent for laying out newsletters and ad copy.

Creating objects with the draw tools

To create any draw object, you select a drawing tool from the Tool panel (see Figure 7-1) and then click and drag in the current document. When you release the mouse button, the object is surrounded by tiny dark squares that are called *handles* (see Figure 7-2). By dragging the handles, you can change the object's size.

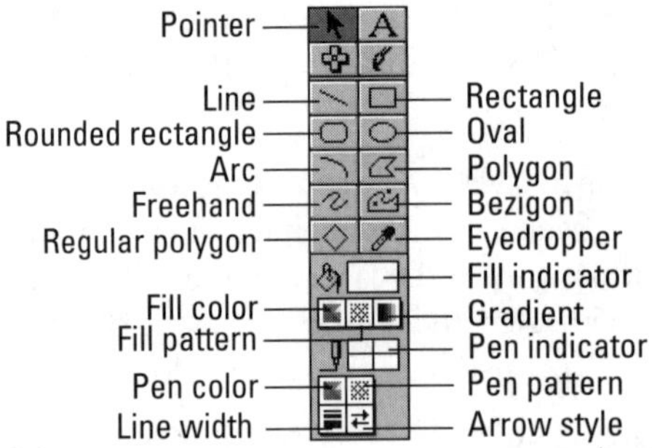

Figure 7-1: The draw tools.

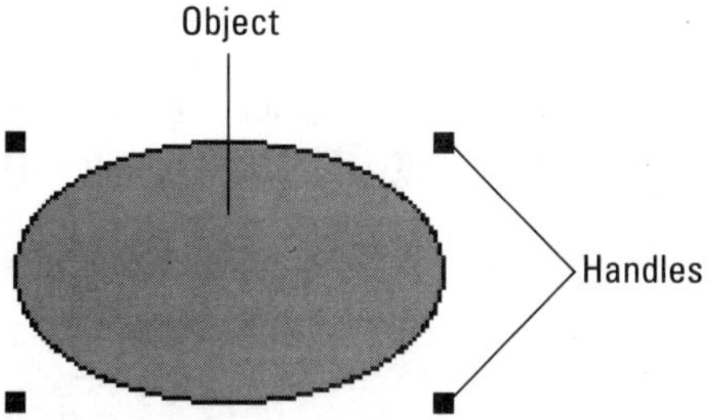

Figure 7-2: A simple draw object.

TIP

After you create an object, ClarisWorks normally selects the Pointer tool from the Tool panel. To keep the original drawing tool selected, double-click it when you select it, instead of single-clicking it. When you select a tool by double-clicking it, the tool's symbol becomes black, instead of merely darkening in the Tool panel, and you can draw multiple objects of the same type without having to select the tool each time.

NOTE

Pressing Shift as you create an object constrains the effects of the following drawing tools:

- *Rectangle or Rounded Rectangle tool.* A square or rounded square is drawn.
- *Oval tool.* A circle is drawn.
- *Arc tool.* A quarter circle is drawn.
- *Line tool.* Only lines that are a multiple of the Shift constraint angle (as set in the Graphics section of the Preferences dialog box) can be drawn. To find out how to change the Shift constraint, refer to Topic 12.

Lines

A line has two endpoints. You can draw lines at any angle or restrict them to multiples of the Shift constraint angle (as set in Preferences). You can apply only pen attributes (pen color, pen pattern, line width, and arrows) to a line.

Step-by-Steps

To draw a line:

1. **Select the Line tool in the Tool Panel.**
2. **Click the document page once to select the starting point and then drag to create the line.** When you release the mouse button, the line is completed.

If you press Shift as you draw the line, the line's angle is restricted to multiples of the Shift constraint that is set for the mouse in the Graphics Preferences. By default, the Shift constraint angle is set to 45 degrees. To draw a perfectly straight line, press Shift as you draw.

Rectangles

A rectangle is an object with four sides, and every corner angle is 90 degrees. In addition to normal rectangles and squares, ClarisWorks also supports *rounded rectangles* (rectangles with rounded corners).

To draw a rectangle:

1. **Select the Rectangle tool in the Tool Panel.**
2. **Click the document page once to select the starting point and then drag to create the rectangle.** When you release the mouse button, the rectangle is completed.

If you press Shift as you draw the rectangle, the resulting object will be a square.

To draw a rounded rectangle:

1. **Select the Rounded Rectangle tool in the Tool Panel.**
2. **Click once on the document page to select the starting point and then drag to create the rounded rectangle.** When you release the mouse button, the rounded rectangle is completed.

If you press Shift as you draw the rounded rectangle, the resulting object will be a rounded square.

You also can adjust the roundness of the corners or add round corners to a standard rectangle.

To create or adjust rounded corners:

1. **Select a rectangle or a rounded rectangle.**
2. **Choose the Round Corners command from the Options menu, press Shift-⌘-I, or double-click the rectangle.** The Round Corners dialog box appears, as shown in Figure 7-3.

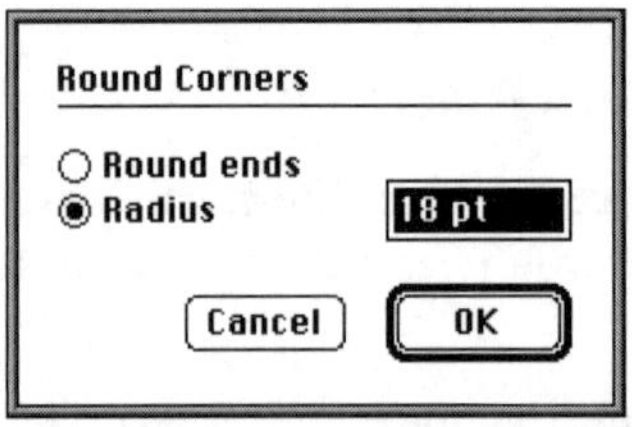

Figure 7-3: The Round Corners dialog box.

3. To create a rectangle with semicircles at the corners, click the Round ends radio button and then click OK.

— or —

3. Click the Radius radio button, enter a new radius (in the text-edit box) for the circle that forms the curve, and click OK.

NOTE

If you change the Round ends setting when an object is not selected, the setting is automatically used for all new rounded rectangles that you create.

Ovals

An oval is a closed object that is shaped as an ellipse or a circle.

Step-by-Steps

To draw an oval:

1. **Select the Oval tool in the Tool Panel.**
2. **Click the document page once to select the starting point and then drag to create the oval.** When you release the mouse button, the oval is completed.

If you press Shift as you draw the oval, the resulting object will be a circle.

Arcs

An arc is a curved line. Although arcs are typically drawn as open objects, you can assign fill colors, patterns, or gradients to them.

Step-by-Steps

To draw an arc:

1. **Select the Arc tool in the Tool Panel.**
2. **Click the document page once to select the starting point and then drag to create the arc.** The direction in which you drag determines the arc's curve. When you release the mouse button, the arc is completed.

If you press Shift as you draw the arc, the resulting object will be a quarter circle.

Normal drawing will result in a quarter ellipse. To increase or decrease the arc angle, you must modify it. You can reshape an arc in three different ways:

- Select a handle and drag — changes the size (diameter) of the arc.
- Use the Reshape command — allows manual resizing of the arc angle.
- Use the Modify Arc command — allows precise angle adjustment and framed edges.

To reshape an arc:

1. **Select the arc with the Pointer tool.**
2. **Choose Reshape from the Edit menu (or press ⌘-R).** A special *reshape cursor* appears.
3. **Click one of the arc's handles and drag to reshape the arc.** The cursor is constrained to the arc's diameter.
4. **To complete the editing, select another tool or choose the Reshape command again.**

To modify an arc:

1. **Select the arc with the Pointer tool.**
2. **Choose Modify Arc from the Options menu (or press Shift-⌘-I).** The Modify Arc dialog box appears, as shown in Figure 7-4.

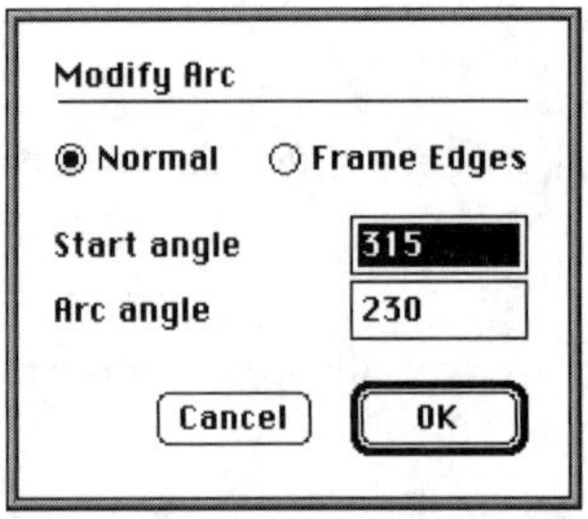

Figure 7-4: The Modify Arc dialog box.

3. **Choose Normal for a normal arc or choose Frame Edges to create a *pie wedge* (closing the arc).**
4. **Enter numbers for the Start angle and the Arc angle.**
5. **Click OK to execute the instructions and close the dialog box.**

Polygons

A polygon is any figure with three or more sides. Polygons can be closed or open, contain uneven sides, or have sides of equal length (regular polygons).

To draw a polygon:

1. **Select the Polygon tool in the Tool Panel.**
2. **Click the document page once to select the starting point and then move the mouse to create the first line of the polygon.** (If you press Shift as you move the mouse, the angle of the line will be restricted to an increment of the Shift constraint that is set in the Graphics Preferences.)
3. **Click once to set the endpoint for the line.**
4. **Move the mouse again and click to complete the next line. Repeat this step as many times as necessary to complete the polygon.**
5. **To finish the polygon, click the starting point (to create a closed polygon), double-click, or press Enter.**

To make polygons close automatically (the equivalent of clicking the starting point), choose the Graphics Preferences option for Automatic Polygon Closing. For information on setting preferences, see Topic 12.

To draw a polygon that has equal sides, use the Regular Polygon tool. A regular polygon has three or more sides, and all sides are equal in length. The default setting is for a six-sided polygon (a hexagon).

To draw a regular polygon:

1. **Select the Regular Polygon tool in the Tool Panel.**
2. **To set the number of sides for the polygon, choose Polygon Sides from the Options menu (or press Shift-⌘-I).** The Number of sides dialog box appears. Enter the number of sides desired and click OK.
3. **Click the document page once to select the starting point and then drag to create the polygon.** You can rotate the polygon as you drag. When you release the mouse button, the polygon is completed.

If you press Shift as you draw the regular polygon, its angle is restricted to the Shift constraint that is set for the mouse in the Graphics section of the Preferences dialog box. By default, the angle is set to 45-degree increments.

NOTE: The Polygon Sides command is available only when the Regular Polygon tool is selected. The keyboard shortcut (Shift-⌘-I) has other meanings when other drawing tools are selected.

You can use the Reshape command to change the angles between polygon sides, add anchor points, or change a straight line into a curve.

To reshape a polygon:

1. **Select the polygon with the Pointer tool.**
2. **Choose Reshape from the Edit menu (or press ⌘-R).** The reshape pointer appears.
3. **Drag an anchor point to reshape the polygon.**

— or —

3. **Click an anchor point and, while pressing the Option key, drag to create a curve.**

— or —

3. **Click between any pair of anchor points to add a new anchor point.**
4. **To complete the editing, select another tool or choose the Reshape command again.**

Other shapes

You can also use the Freehand tool to create free-form objects and the Bezigon tool to create objects that contain a combination of curved and straight lines. Unlike other objects, which are set to have a white fill, freehand objects have a transparent fill.

To draw a freehand shape:

1. **Select the Freehand tool in the Tool Panel.**
2. **Click the document page once to select the starting point and then drag to create the shape.** When you release the mouse button, the shape is completed.

By default, ClarisWorks automatically smooths freehand shapes (removes some of the irregularities in the lines and curves). To avoid smoothing, uncheck the Automatically Smooth Freehand check box in the Graphics Preferences options. For information on setting preferences, see Topic 12.

The Bezigon tool enables you to draw complex shapes composed of curves and straight lines.

To draw with the Bezigon tool:

1. **Select the Bezigon tool in the Tool Panel.**
2. **Click to select the starting point and then move to select the endpoint for the first line or curve.**

3. Click to set the endpoint.

To create an angular point, press Option as you click. To create a more dramatic curve, click and drag.

4. Repeat Steps 2 and 3 as required.

5. Double-click to close the shape.

To reshape any of the curves in a Bezigon shape, choose Reshape from the Edit menu (or press ⌘-R) and click the object. Select any of the hollow handles that appear and drag to reshape. To add a new anchor point, click anywhere on a line. To delete an anchor point, select it and press the Delete or Backspace key. When you've finished reshaping the object, choose the Reshape command again or select another tool.

Note that there are two types of hollow handles: circles for curved points and squares for sharp points. Pressing Option while clicking a square handle enables you to change to a curve, click on the handle, and then drag right and/or left. Option-clicking a *Bezier handle* (one of the tiny dots that appears when creating or modifying a curve) resets the curve to a sharp point.

Editing objects

Drawing an object is often only the first step. You can use the different commands, procedures, and palettes to change an object's size, shape, color, pattern, and so on.

Selecting and deselecting objects

In order to do anything with an object (change its size, position, or attributes, for example), you must first select it. To select an object, choose the Pointer tool from the Tool panel and click the object. Handles appear around the object's border to show that it is selected. (Normally, four handles appear, but you can increase the number of handles by changing the Graphics Preferences. See Topic 12 for details.)

You also can select multiple objects. This capability is useful when you want to apply the same command to a number of objects. To select more than one object, do one of the following:

- ◆ Select the Pointer tool and press Shift as you click objects.
- ◆ Select the Pointer tool and drag a selection rectangle around the objects.
- ◆ Select the Pointer tool and press the Command key as you drag *through* the objects.
- ◆ Choose Select All from the Edit menu (or press ⌘-A) to select all objects on the current document page.
- ◆ Click an object type in the Tool panel and then choose Select All from the Edit menu to select all objects of that type.

NOTE: The last technique works differently with bezigons, polygons, regular polygons, and freehand shapes. If you select one of these objects from the Tool panel and issue the Select All command, objects of all of these types are selected.

To deselect an object, click anywhere outside the object. To deselect individual objects when several have been selected, Shift-click them.

Changing the size of an object

You can change the size of a selected object in three ways:

- ◆ Dragging one of its handles
- ◆ Using the Scale Selection command
- ◆ Using the Object Size command

When dragging one of an object's handles to change the size of the object, you can constrain the angle of movement by pressing Shift as you drag. You can change this angle, which is referred to as the *Shift constraint,* in the Graphics Preferences. By default, the angle is set to increments of 45 degrees.

To change an object's size by using the Scale Selection command:

1. **Select the object or objects whose size you want to change.**
2. **Choose Scale Selection from the Options menu.** The Scale Selection dialog box appears (see Figure 7-5).

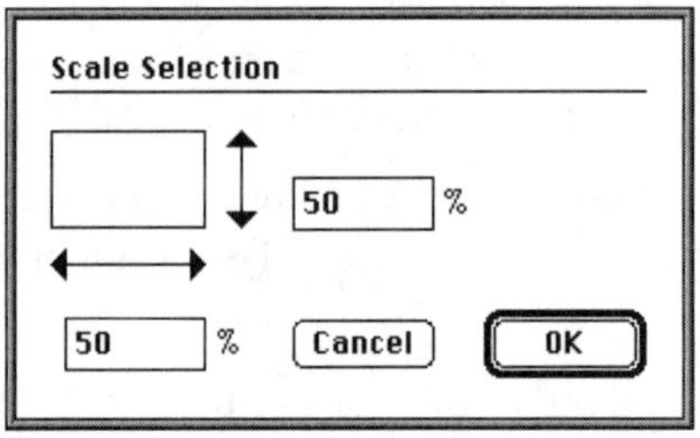

Figure 7-5: The Scale Selection dialog box.

3. **Enter new figures for the vertical or horizontal dimensions of the selected object.** (To change the dimensions proportionately, enter the same percentage for both dimensions.)
4. **Click OK.**

To change an object's size by using the Object Size command:

1. **Select the object whose size you want to change.**
2. **Choose Object Size from the Options menu.** The Size *floating windoid* appears (see Figure 7-6).

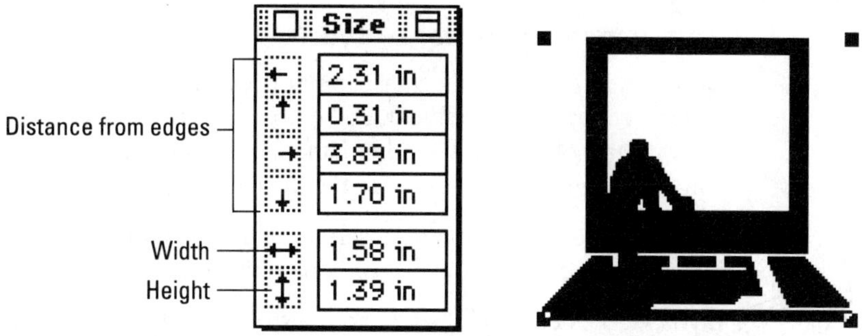

Figure 7-6: The numbers in the Size floating windoid refer to the currently selected object.

3. **To change the horizontal or vertical dimensions (width or height) of the selected object, type new figures in the two text-edit boxes at the bottom of the windoid.**

Smoothing and unsmoothing objects

You can *smooth* or *unsmooth* polygons, regular polygons, bezigons, and freehand shapes. Smoothing an object converts all angles into curves. Unsmoothing an object changes curves into angles. To smooth an object, select it and choose Smooth from the Edit menu or press ⌘-(. To unsmooth an object, choose Unsmooth from the Edit menu or press ⌘-).

NOTE

When you are working with a bezigon, smoothing and unsmoothing are not necessarily opposites of each other. You may prefer to use the Undo command in the Edit menu to return to the original shape after you use either the Smooth or Unsmooth command for a bezigon.

Setting object attributes

You can set attributes (fill color, fill pattern, gradient, pen color, pen pattern, line width, and arrowheads for lines) before or after you create an object. To set attributes beforehand, select them from the Tool panel pop-up palettes (see Figure 7-7) and then draw the object. The object will automatically use the current attributes. To assign or change attributes for an existing object, select the Pointer tool, select the object, and then select the new attributes from the various fill and pen palettes in the Tool panel.

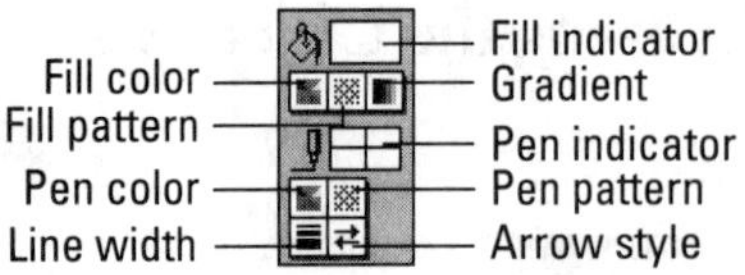

Figure 7-7: Tool panel pop-up palettes.

Although lines are normally solid, you can apply a pen pattern to a line to achieve interesting effects. For example, try different dot pen patterns to create dotted lines.

Transparent and opaque objects

Every object can be either transparent or opaque. An *opaque* object has a fill pattern, color, and/or gradient, and it obscures anything on the page that it covers. A *transparent* object, on the other hand, has no fill color, pattern, or gradient, and you can see anything on the page that it covers.

To make an object transparent, select the first fill pattern in the palette (the two linked blank squares). Any fill color, pattern, or gradient is temporarily removed.

If you set the default fill pattern to transparent — by selecting the transparent icon (the pair of linked blank boxes) when no object is currently selected — the transparent icon is displayed as a reminder in the pattern indicator in the tool panel (see Figure 7-8).

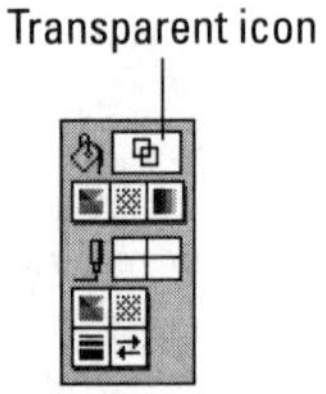

Figure 7-8: The default fill pattern is transparent.

To make an object opaque (the default for all objects other than freehand shapes), select the second fill pattern in the palette (the two linked blank and black squares). Any fill color, pattern, or gradient that was previously applied to the object is restored.

You can tear off any attribute palette and drag it onto the page as a floating windoid. After you expose the palette in this manner, you can quickly set a particular attribute for many objects without having to pop-up the attribute palette again. To move a floating palette, drag it by its title bar. To close the palette, click its close box (in the upper-left corner). To shrink or expand the palette, click the box in the palette's upper-right corner.

Copying object attributes with the Eyedropper tool

After setting attributes for an object, you can copy those attributes to other objects by using the Eyedropper tool.

Step-by-Steps

To use the Eyedropper tool to copy attributes to other objects:

1. **Select the Eyedropper tool from the Tool panel.**
2. **Click the object whose attributes you want to copy.** The current attributes change to match those of the copied object.
3. **Select the Eyedropper tool again and Command-click the objects to which you want to apply the attributes.**

NOTE

If a destination object has a transparent fill, you need to Command-click its border with the Eyedropper to apply the attributes.

You can also change the default attributes by clicking on an object that already has what you want. Note the change in the palettes. All new objects that are drawn now take on these attributes.

Arranging objects

The Arrange menu contains commands for moving, aligning, and reorienting objects. You also can move objects manually by dragging them.

Moving objects

To reposition an object manually, select it with the Pointer tool and drag the object to a new location. When you move a line, arc, rectangle, or oval, an outline of the object is visible as you drag. When you move other objects, only the bounding box is displayed as you drag. To see the outline of the object itself (to facilitate placement of the object), press ⌘ as you drag a polygon, bezigon, or freehand shape. To restrict movements to the current Shift constraint angle (set in the Graphics Preferences), hold Shift as you drag. This technique is particularly useful when you want to keep objects aligned with each other.

You also can move a selected object by pressing any of the arrow keys. When Autogrid is turned off, the object moves one pixel in the direction of the arrow key. When Autogrid is turned on, the distance that the object moves is determined by the ruler type that is currently set. To turn Autogrid on or off, press ⌘-Y or choose the appropriate command from the Options menu (Autogrid On or Autogrid Off).

One other way to move an object is to use the Size palette (see Figure 7-9), which is displayed when you choose Object Size from the Options menu. To change the position of a selected object, simply type new numbers in the Size palette to set the object's distance from the left edge, right edge, top, or bottom of the page.

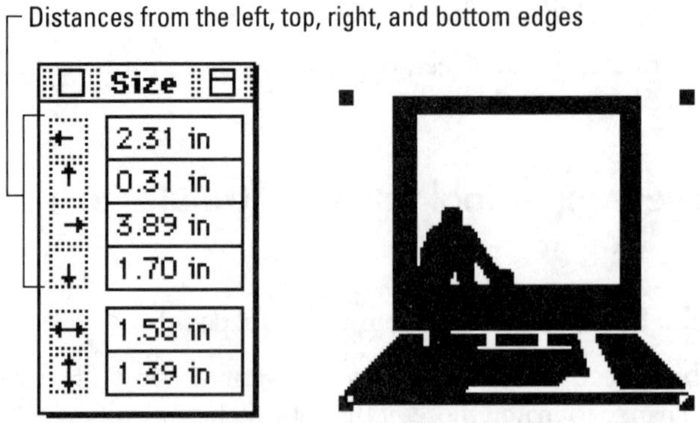

Figure 7-9: You can precisely position an object on the page by typing new figures in the Size palette.

About the graphics grid and Autogrid

The dotted lines that you see on a new draw document are called the *graphics grid.* The ruler type that is in effect and the number of divisions specified for that ruler govern the spacing of the dots. (By default, the unit of measurement is inches, and each inch has eight divisions.) When you use the Rulers command on the Format menu to change the ruler or the number of divisions, you change the grid.

The grid can be shown or hidden. To hide the grid, choose Hide Graphics Grid from the Options menu. To make it visible again, choose Show Graphics Grid from the Options menu.

Only a portion of the grid is visible. You may want to think of the visible portion as being grid border markers. As Figure 7-10 illustrates, many additional grid points are inside each rectangular grid section.

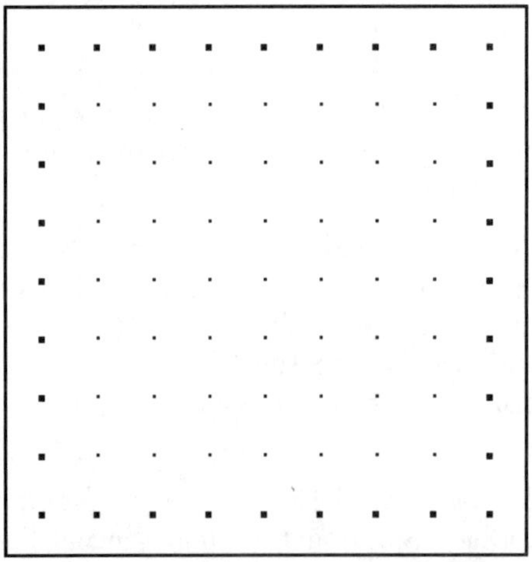

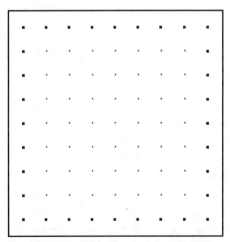

Figure 7-10: This single grid section is magnified 200 percent. The small dots inside the grid represent the grid points that you can't see.

Aligning objects

The Autogrid feature causes objects to align with the nearest point on the gridline. When Autogrid is off, you can place objects without being constrained to a grid point. Choose Turn Autogrid On or Turn Autogrid Off from the Options menu (or press ⌘-Y) to change the state of the grid.

When Autogrid is off, you can still make objects align with the grid by using the Align to Grid command.

To align objects to the grid:

1. **Select the object that you want to align to the grid.**
2. **Choose Align to Grid from the Arrange menu (or press ⌘-K).** The object aligns with the nearest gridpoint.

In many cases, having a set of objects align perfectly with each other is more important than having them align with the grid.

To align objects to each other:

1. **Select the objects that you want to align to each other.** (Drag or Shift-click to select multiple objects.)
2. **Choose Align Objects from the Arrange menu (or press Shift-⌘-K).** The Align Objects dialog box appears, as shown in Figure 7-11.

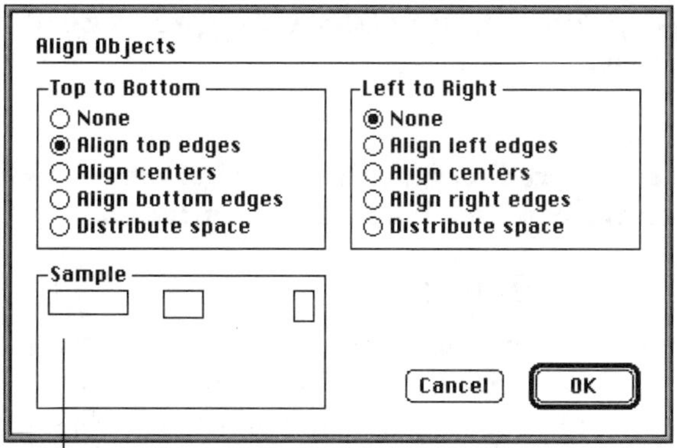

A sample that shows how objects will be aligned

Figure 7-11: The Align Objects dialog box.

3. **Click the radio buttons for the desired alignment options.** The Sample box shows how the objects will align.
4. **Click OK to perform the alignment.**

NOTE

If the result is not what you intended, immediately choose Undo from the Edit menu and perform the steps again.

Object layers

You can place objects over each other, creating *layers*. Using the appropriate menu command, you can move an object to the top or bottom layer of a drawing or one step up or down in the layer hierarchy. Figure 7-12 shows two different stacking orders for the same set of objects.

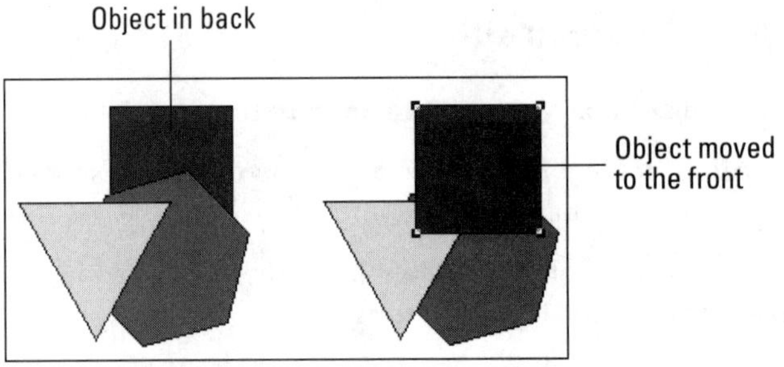

Figure 7-12: Bring the box in back to the top or front layer by choosing the Move to Front command.

Step-by-Steps

To change an object's layer:

1. **Select an object.** Handles appear around its border.
2. **To move one layer toward the front or back, choose Move Forward (Shift-⌘-+) or Move Backward (Shift-⌘-– [minus sign]) from the Arrange menu.**

— or —

2. **To move the object directly to the top or bottom layer, choose Move to Front or Move to Back from the Arrange menu.**

Flipping and rotating objects

The Arrange menu has three commands that you can use to change the orientation of objects: Flip Horizontal, Flip Vertical, and Rotate (Shift-⌘-R). Figure 7-13 shows the result of applying each of these commands to an object.

- ◆ *Flip Horizontal* creates a mirror image of an object, reversing the left and right sides.
- ◆ *Flip Vertical* creates a reflection of the object (as though it were sitting on the edge of a lake), reversing the top and bottom.
- ◆ *Rotate* rotates the image 90 degrees clockwise. Each time you issue the Rotate command, the object is rotated an additional 90 degrees.

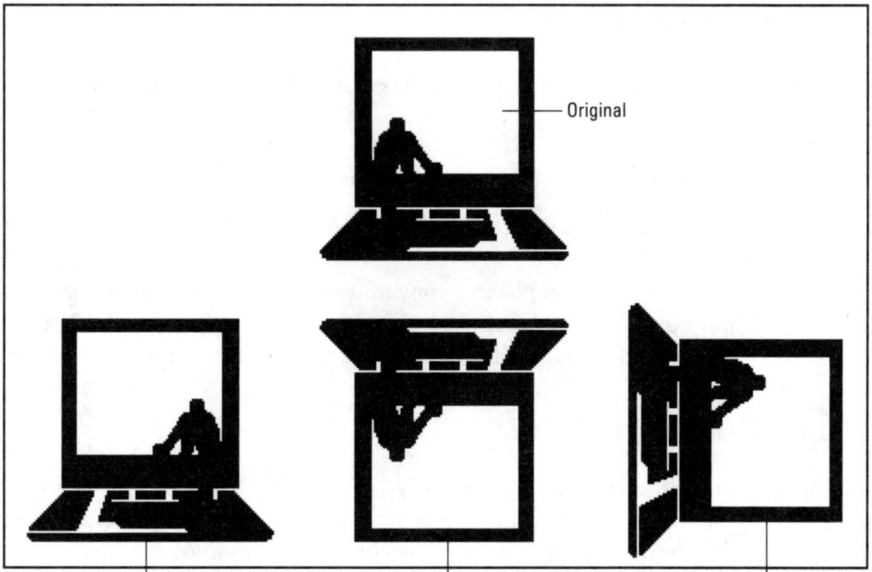

Figure 7-13: The original object and the object after the Flip Horizontal, Flip Vertical, and Rotate commands are applied to it.

NOTE

When text is rotated, it is treated as an object. You will lose some resolution as a result (text goes to 72 dpi). Rotate back to the original position and text will again have its original attributes.

Step-by-Steps

To change an object's orientation:

1. **Select the object.** Handles appear at the corners.
2. **Choose Flip Horizontal, Flip Vertical, or Rotate (Shift-⌘-R) from the Arrange menu.** The object is reoriented.

TIP

When you reorient an object, working with a copy of the object is safer than working with the original, particularly if you are experimenting. Remember, too, that you can use the Undo command to undo the last change.

Duplicating objects

In addition to the normal Copy and Paste routine, you can use the Duplicate command to make a copy of an object and paste it simultaneously. To duplicate an object, select it and choose Duplicate from the Edit menu (or press ⌘-D). A copy of the object appears. If you immediately move the duplicate to its new position and then choose the Duplicate command again, the new duplicate will be offset the same distance and direction as the preceding one. Duplicate is extremely useful for quickly creating a series of parallel, equidistant lines or other objects, for example.

Deleting objects

To delete an object, select it and use one of the following methods:

- ◆ Press Delete, Backspace, or Clear.
- ◆ Choose Clear from the Edit menu.
- ◆ Choose Cut from the Edit menu (or press ⌘-X).

The Cut command places a copy of the object on the Clipboard. The other options delete the object without copying it to the Clipboard. (***Note:*** You also can use any of these procedures to delete multiple objects at the same time.)

Combining objects

Sometimes, combining objects is useful. ClarisWorks provides two methods of combining objects: grouping (which enables you to treat several objects as a single object) and reshaping (which links objects end-to-end).

Combining objects with the Group command

After you painstakingly create a complex series of interrelated objects, dealing with the objects as a whole is often easier and safer than dealing with the individual objects. After you select all of the components of the image, you can create a single object with a single set of handles by choosing the Group command from the Arrange menu (or pressing ⌘-G). You can then, for example, move all of the objects at the same time without fear of leaving a piece or two behind. You also can apply other Arrange commands to the new object to flip or rotate it, or you can choose a new color, gradient, or pattern for the object.

If you ever need to work with the component parts, simply select the object and choose Ungroup from the Arrange menu (or press Shift-⌘-G).
The components reappear, and you can work with them individually.

Combining objects with the Reshape command

The Group command enables you to treat several distinct objects as a united group. The Reshape command, on the other hand, enables you to physically link two or more freehand shapes, polygons, or bezigons end-to-end. This technique can be useful when you are designing repeating patterns, such as those often used in picture borders.

To link freehand shapes, polygons, or bezigons:

1. **Choose Reshape from the Edit menu (or press ⌘-R).** The reshape cursor appears.
2. **Select the freehand shape, polygon, or bezigon that you want to attach to another object.** Hollow handles appear around the selected object.
3. **Choose Copy from the Edit menu (or press ⌘-C).** A copy of the object is placed on the Clipboard.
4. **Select the second object (the one to which you want to attach the first object).**
5. **If you want to attach the object to the second object's starting point, select the starting point.** Otherwise, the object will be attached to the endpoint.
6. **Choose Paste from the Edit menu (or press ⌘-V).** A copy of the first object is connected to the second object.
7. **If required, repeat Step 6 to attach additional copies end-to-end.**
8. **Choose Reshape from the Edit menu or select another drawing tool to complete the process.**

If you press Option while choosing the Paste command in Step 6, the last point (rather than the first point) of the copied object will be attached to the second object.

Locking and unlocking objects

If the position of certain objects is critical to a document, you can lock them in place and keep them from being altered by selecting the objects and choosing Lock from the Arrange menu (or pressing ⌘-H). If you later want to modify, delete, or move the objects, choose Unlock from the Arrange menu (or press Shift-⌘-H).

Creating custom colors, patterns, and gradients

If you want to use special colors, patterns, or *gradients* (fills that blend from one color to another) that are not already in the palettes, you can create your own by replacing existing colors, patterns, or gradients with new ones.

Custom colors, patterns, and gradients are saved with the document in which they are created. To make custom patterns and gradients reusable, you can create them in a blank document and then save it as a stationery document. To create a reusable color palette, you have to use the Editable 256 Color Palette in the Palettes section of the Preferences dialog box and then save the palette as a color palette document.

NOTE: You can also edit colors, patterns, and gradients in the paint environment.

To create a custom color:

1. **Use the Editable 256 Color Palette: Choose Preferences from the Edit menu, click the Palettes icon in the left side of the Preferences dialog box, click the Editable 256 Color Palette radio button, and click OK.**
2. **Click the Fill color or Pen color palette and tear off the palette by dragging it onto the screen.**
3. **Double-click the color that you want to replace.** A color wheel dialog box appears, as shown in Figure 7-14.

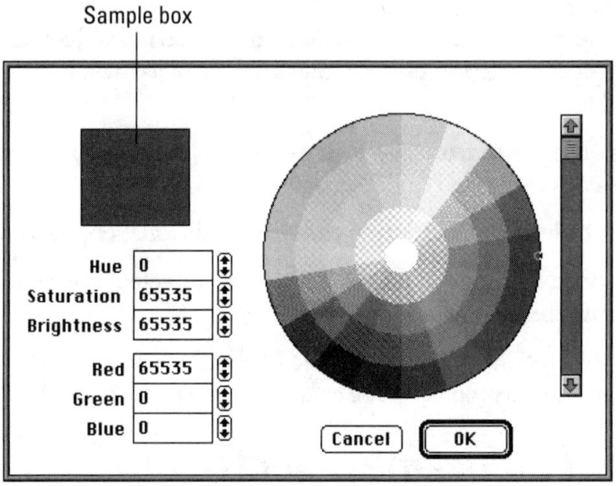

Figure 7-14: Select a new color from this color wheel.

4. **To select a replacement color, you can do any of the following (or use a combination of these approaches):**
   - ◆ Click a different color on the wheel.
   - ◆ Drag the scroll bar on the right side of the dialog box to change the brightness of the colors.
   - ◆ Enter new numbers for Hue, Saturation, Brightness, Red, Green, or Blue.
5. **Click OK to save the change.** The new color replaces the original one in both the fill and pen color palettes. (To revert to the original color, click Cancel or the lower half of the sample color square in the upper-left corner of the dialog box.)

If you want to be able to reuse the revised color palette in other documents, you can save it. Choose Preferences from the Edit menu, click the Palettes icon in the left side of the Preferences dialog box, and click Save Palette. A standard file dialog box appears. Enter a name for the palette and click Save. When the Preferences dialog box reappears, click OK.

To create a custom pattern for the current document:

1. **Choose Patterns from the Options menu.** The Fill pattern palette and the Pattern Editor appear (see Figure 7-15). Select the pattern to be edited by clicking it in the Fill pattern palette.

— or —

1. **Tear off the Fill pattern or Pen pattern palette and double-click the pattern that you want to replace.** The Pattern Editor appears, set for the chosen pattern.

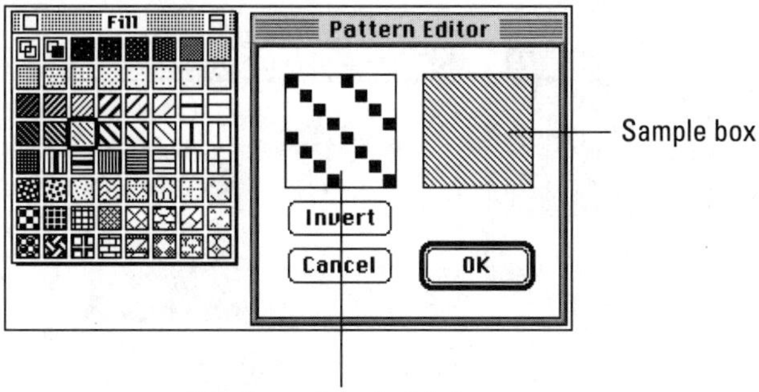

Figure 7-15: The Pattern Editor.

2. **In the box on the left side of the Pattern Editor, click or drag to change the pattern.** White spots that are clicked turn black; black spots turn white. To reverse the pattern (swapping whites for blacks and vice versa), click Invert.

3. **Click OK to accept the new pattern or Cancel to revert to the previous pattern.**

Every gradient is a sweep from one color to another and can contain two to four colors. ClarisWorks supports three types of sweeps: directional, circular, and shape burst. Every sweep has a *focus* (shown as a hollow circle in the Focus section of the Gradient Editor). In a directional sweep, the focus is the spot at which the final color appears. In a circular sweep, the focus is the point around which the gradient sweeps. A shape burst sweep is based on a rectangle, around which the gradient sweeps. The focus is the bottom-right corner of the rectangle.

When working in the Gradient Editor, you can immediately see the effects of your changes by watching the Sample box.

Step-by-Steps

To create a custom gradient for the current document:

1. **Choose Gradients from the Options menu. The Gradient palette and the Gradient Editor appear (see Figure 7-16). Select the gradient to be edited by clicking it in the Gradient palette.**

— or —

1. **Tear off the Gradient palette and double-click the gradient that you want to replace.** The Gradient Editor appears, set for the chosen gradient.

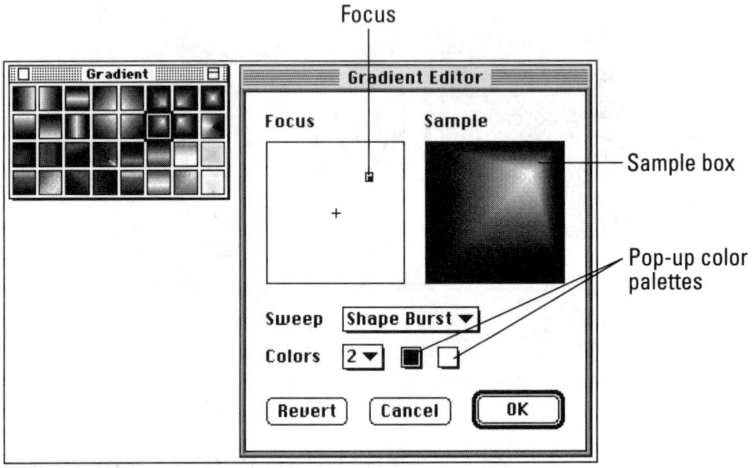

Figure 7-16: The Gradient palette and the Gradient Editor.

2. **Choose a sweep type from the Sweep pop-up menu.**
3. **Make the changes that you want.**

   ◆ *Directional sweep.* You can set the number of colors (by choosing a number from the Colors pop-up menu); select the specific colors (the starting color is shown in the left pop-up color palette, and the ending color is shown in the right pop-up color palette); change the focus (by dragging the hollow circle in the Angle section of the Gradient Editor); and set a new angle for the sweep (by dragging the line or typing an angle in the text-edit box).

   ◆ *Circular sweep.* You can set the number of colors (by choosing a number from the Colors pop-up menu); select the specific colors (the starting color is shown in the left pop-up color palette, and the ending color is shown in the right pop-up color palette); change the focus (by dragging the connected pair of circles in the Angle section of the Gradient Editor); and set a new angle for the sweep (by dragging the filled circle or typing an angle in the text-edit box).

- *Shape burst sweep.* You can set the number of colors (by choosing a number from the Colors pop-up menu); select the individual colors (the starting color is shown in the left pop-up color palette, and the ending color is shown in the right pop-up color palette); change the size of the shape burst focus (by dragging the black handle of the focus box in the Focus section of the Gradient Editor); and change the location of the focus (by dragging the focus box to a new spot).

4. **Click OK to save the new gradient, Cancel to ignore the changes, or Revert to change the gradient back to its ClarisWorks default.**

Adding pages to a draw document

By default, a graphics document contains only a single page. Adding more pages can be useful (for example, when you are creating a slide show).

Step-by-Steps

To add pages:

1. **Choose Document from the Format menu.** The Document dialog box appears.
2. **Increase the number of Pages across and/or Pages Down in the Size section of the dialog box.**
3. **Click OK.** The pages you specified are added to the document.

Down to business: Creating border designs

Whether you're getting ready for a presentation or just want to add some pizzazz to your graphics, enclosing your images in a border frame is often a nice touch. For example, adding a border to a master page can lend consistency to slide show presentations. This task shows you how to quickly create a simple but attractive border that is composed of overlapping diamonds.

Step-by-Steps

To create a simple border:

1. **Launch ClarisWorks and create a new draw document.**
2. **Make sure that Autogrid is on.** (The command in the Options menu should read Turn Autogrid Off.) Having Autogrid turned on makes aligning the shapes easy.
3. **Select the Regular Polygon tool from the Tool panel. It's shaped like a diamond.**
4. **Choose Polygon Sides from the Options menu, type** 4 **in the dialog box that appears, and click OK.**

5. **Select a fill color from the Fill pop-up palette in the Tool panel.**
6. **Drag to create a small diamond shape and place the shape in the upper-left corner of the page.**
7. **With the shape still selected, choose Duplicate from the Edit menu (or press ⌘-D).**
8. **Press the up-arrow key once.** The second diamond overlaps the first one and is slightly offset to the right.
9. **Press ⌘-D repeatedly to create additional diamonds for the top border.** Each one should overlap the previous diamond in exactly the same way as the first duplicate did. Stop when the top border is the desired width.
10. **Using the pointer, drag a selection rectangle around the row of diamonds.**
11. **Choose Group from the Arrange menu (or press ⌘-G).** The row of diamonds is now treated as a single object.
12. **With the row selected, choose Copy from the Edit menu (or press ⌘-C).**
13. **Choose Paste from the Edit menu (or press ⌘-V).** A copy of the row is pasted over the original row.
14. **Choose Rotate from the Arrange menu (or press Shift-⌘-R).** A vertical column of diamonds appears.
15. **Drag the column to the left side of the page and place it so that it overlaps with the left end of the original row of diamonds.**
16. **With the column still selected, choose Copy and then Paste from the Edit menu.** A copy of the column is pasted over the original column.
17. **Drag the column to the right side of the page and place it so that it overlaps with the right end of the original row of diamonds.** If you press Shift as you drag, the column moves in a perfectly straight line.
18. **Click to select the top row of diamonds and choose Copy and then Paste from the Edit menu.** A copy of the row is pasted over the original row.
19. **Drag the copy down until it overlaps with the bottom ends of the two columns.** The resulting border should look like the one shown in Figure 7-17.

After the border is satisfactory, you can lock the rows and columns in place. Shift-click to select the four elements (or choose Select All from the Edit menu) and then choose Lock from the Arrange menu (or press ⌘-H).

If you plan to use this border frequently, you can save it as a ClarisWorks stationery document rather than as a normal document. For instructions on working with stationery documents, see Topic 11.

Figure 7-17: The finished diamond border.

The Paint Environment

The Paint environment enables you to create and edit *bit-mapped images*, which are graphics composed entirely of dots. Unlike when you work with draw objects, you can edit paint images at the dot level. The precise control that this capability provides is what makes the paint environment so useful in creating complex illustrations.

Creating a new paint document or frame

Although you can create draw objects in almost any document type, you have to either design paint images in a paint document or place them in a paint frame in another ClarisWorks environment. To create a new paint document, choose New from the File menu (or press ⌘-N). When the New Document dialog box appears, click the Painting radio button and then click OK.

NOTE

If insufficient memory is available, you may be notified that the document size will be reduced. For instructions on increasing the available memory (and, in turn, the size of your paint documents), see the Quick Tips at the end of this Topic.

To create a paint frame in another ClarisWorks environment, click the Paintbrush tool in the Tool panel and drag to draw the paint frame.

Paint frames and paint documents can contain only bit-mapped graphics. Although you can place draw objects and frames from other environments into a paint frame or document, the object or frame from the other environment loses its environmental identity the instant you stop working in the frame. At that moment, the frame is converted to a paint image, which you can edit only by using the paint tools. The same is also true for text that you type or paste into a paint document or frame.

TIP

Like other frames, a paint frame is surrounded by a rectangular border. To make the border invisible (so the paint image will blend with the rest of the document), set the pen color to white or set the pen pattern to transparent.

While you are working in a paint frame or in a paint document, the normally hidden paint tools are displayed and available for use (see Figure 7-18).

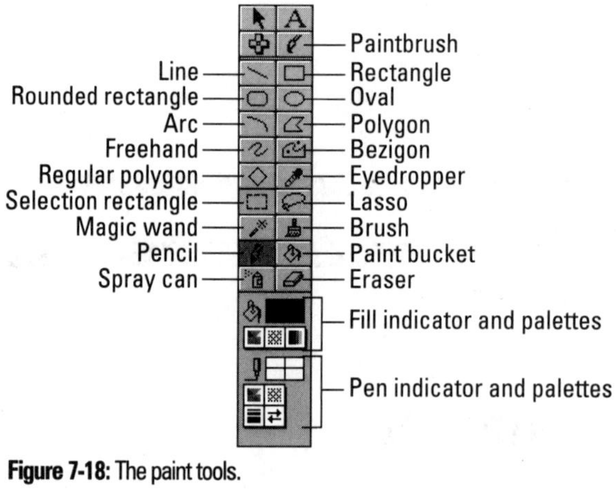

Figure 7-18: The paint tools.

NOTE

You should note that the top ten tools, which, in ordinary circumstances, produce draw objects, are now paint tools. When you use them in a paint frame or a paint document, these tools create bit-mapped graphics — not objects. For instructions on using these tools in a paint frame or paint document, see "Creating objects with the draw tools," earlier in this Topic. The information in that section concerning Shift constraint also applies.

Many of the object modification commands are no longer available as menu commands when you are working in the paint environment. However, you can make the following dialog boxes appear:

- *Round Corners.* Double-click the Rounded Rectangle tool in the Tool panel.
- *Modify Arc.* Double-click the Arc tool in the Tool panel.
- *Number of sides.* Double-click the Regular Polygon tool in the Tool panel.

Paint modes

ClarisWorks supports three paint modes: opaque, transparent pattern, and tint.

- In *opaque mode,* any color, pattern, or gradient placed on another image completely covers the image beneath.
- In *transparent pattern mode,* any pattern that contains white areas or dots allows the image beneath to show through. A gradient or solid color placed over another image, however, is still treated as opaque (completely covering the image beneath).
- In *tint mode,* a color, pattern, or gradient placed on another image will result in a blending of the colors. Depending on the colors chosen, the overlap may not show change. For best results, use colors with greater contrast.

Figure 7-19 shows examples of the three paint modes.

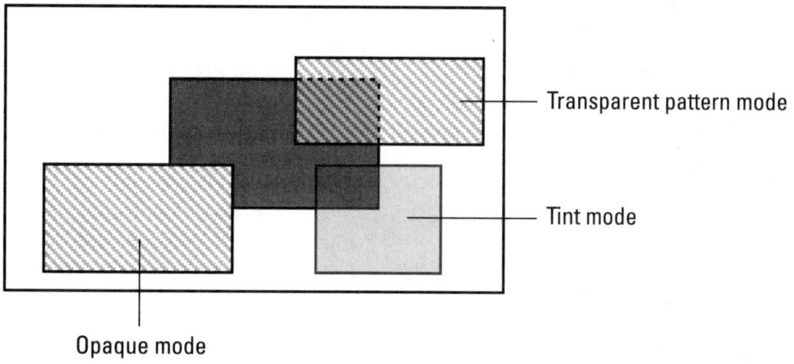

Figure 7-19: The three paint modes.

To set the paint mode, choose Paint Mode from the Options menu, click the radio button for Opaque, Transparent pattern, or Tint in the Painting Mode dialog box, and click OK.

Using the paint tools

When you create draw objects, you can set attributes before or after you create the object. When you work in the paint environment, on the other hand, you should generally select fill and pen attributes *before* you use each tool. Except for filling closed images, assigning attributes after you create an image can be very difficult.

When you select a paint tool from the Tool panel, it automatically remains selected until you choose a different tool. You do not have to double-click the tool to keep it selected, as you do in the draw environment.

Using the Pencil

You use the Pencil tool to create and edit single dots, make freehand drawings (much as you do with the Freehand tool), and draw thin lines. When you first open a paint document or paint frame, the Pencil is automatically selected.

Only the pen color setting affects the pencil. Fill settings, as well as pen pattern, line width, and arrows, have no effect.

You can click to create single dots or click and drag to create lines. If you press Shift as you draw with the Pencil, you can make straight vertical or horizontal lines.

When you click a blank pixel on the screen with the Pencil, a dot of the current pen color is produced. If you click a black or colored pixel, on the other hand, the pixel changes to white.

Double-clicking the Pencil tool zooms the document window to 800 percent, making it easy to do fine editing. To return to the 100 percent view, click the Zoom Percentage box in the lower-left corner of the document window and select 100%.

Using the Brush

Use the Brush to paint in the current fill color and pattern. (You cannot use a gradient fill with the Brush.) To change to a different brush shape, double-click the Brush icon in the Tool panel. The Brush Shape dialog box appears, as shown in Figure 7-20.

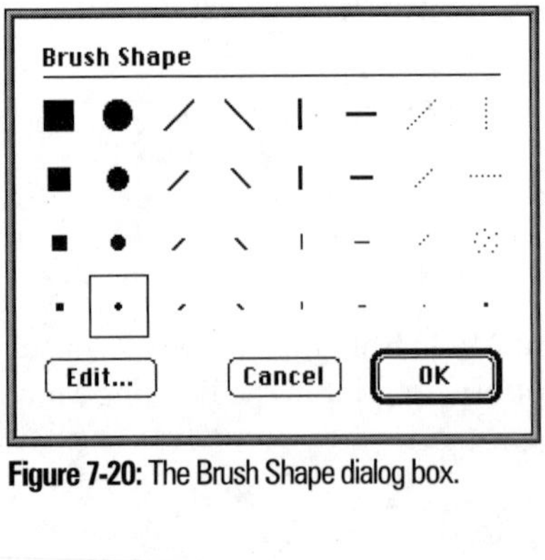

Figure 7-20: The Brush Shape dialog box.

To choose a different brush, select it and click OK. To create a new brush (by editing one of the existing brush shapes), select a brush shape and click Edit. The Brush Editor appears, as shown in Figure 7-21.

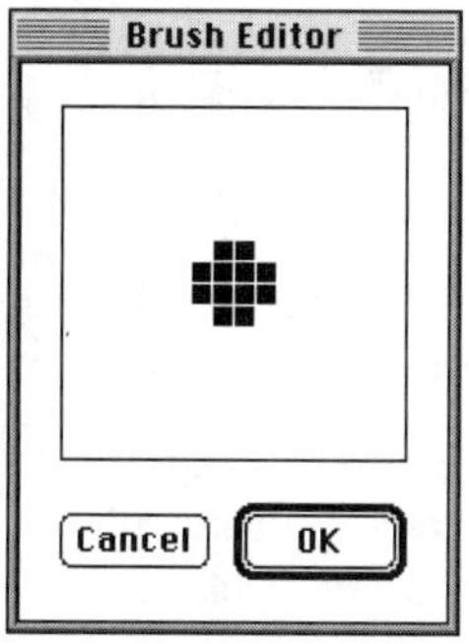

Figure 7-21: The Brush Editor.

Alter the brush shape by clicking and dragging in the box. When you click a white spot, it becomes black. When you click a black spot, it becomes white. Click OK to accept the new brush shape (for this document only) and then click OK again to close the Brush Shape dialog box.

TIP

You can cut patterns out of images by setting the fill color to white or the fill pattern to transparent before you use the brush.

Using the Paint Bucket

The Paint Bucket's sole function is to fill a closed area with a color, pattern, or gradient. The tip of the bucket (the tiny stream of paint that is pouring over its side) is the active area of the Paint Bucket cursor (see Figure 7-22). It shows where the paint will be applied.

Figure 7-22: The Paint Bucket is poised to fill the pimento in this olive.

If the Paint Bucket is applied to an area that is currently filled with a pattern or gradient, a solid color fill will not be successful. The procedure for refilling an area that contains a pattern or gradient is to select it and then choose Fill from the Transform menu. (If the area is filled with a solid color, on the other hand, you can use the Paint Bucket to successfully fill the area with a color, pattern, or gradient.)

TIP: If the area that you're attempting to fill is not completely closed, the fill color, pattern, or gradient may be applied to many unintended areas in the document or frame. Choose Undo immediately to remove the fill. Before filling again, zoom the screen to locate and fill in the pixels needed to close the area. If you deliberately apply the Paint bucket to a blank area in the background, you can quickly add a color, pattern, or gradient to the entire background for a picture or paint frame.

Using the Spray Can

The Spray Can works like an artist's airbrush. (Set free the graffiti artist in you!) You can change both the dot size and the flow rate to achieve different effects.

To use the Spray Can, select a fill color, select the Spray Can in the Tool panel, and either click the mouse to spray or press the mouse button and drag. To spray in a straight vertical or horizontal line, press Shift as you click and drag.

To change the Spray Can settings:

1. **Double-click the Spray Can icon in the Tool panel or choose Spray Can from the Options menu.** The Edit Spray Can dialog box shown in Figure 7-23 appears.

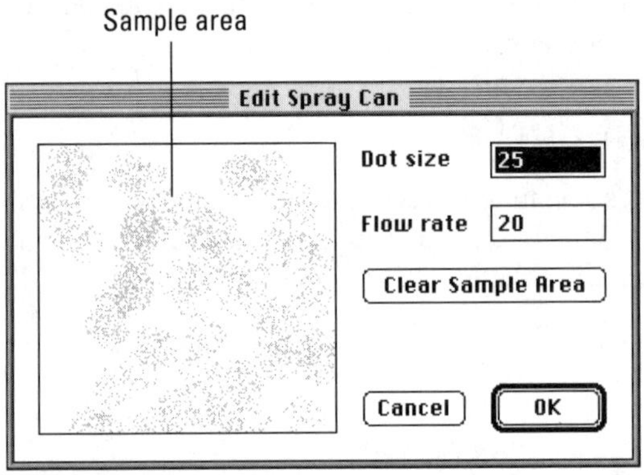

Figure 7-23: The Edit Spray Can dialog box.

2. **Enter new figures for Dot Size (1 to 72) and Flow Rate (1 to 100).**
3. **To test different combinations of Dot Size and Flow Rate with the current fill color, click and drag in the sample area of the dialog box**. (If you want to test different combinations in a clean sample area, you can click Clear Sample Area at any time.)
4. **Click OK when the settings are to your liking.**

Dot Size is in pixels, and there are 72 pixels in an inch.

Dot Size doesn't really vary the size of the dots; it changes the size or spread of the dot pattern.

Flow Rate governs how fast the paint flows. At the highest setting, you get splotches of color everywhere the spray pattern touches.

Editing paint images

As in most other graphics programs, you usually spend as much time editing an image as you do creating it. Editing tools include the Eraser, the Selection Rectangle, the Lasso, and the Magic Wand.

Using the Eraser

You use the Eraser to erase portions of a paint image. Click to erase the part of the image that is covered by the Eraser. You can click and drag to erase larger portions of the image. If you press Shift as you erase, you can drag the Eraser in a straight horizontal or vertical line. (The first move that you make as you drag determines the direction.)

You cannot resize the Eraser. If it's too big to erase a small section of a painting, zoom the screen to a greater magnification.

If you double-click the Eraser icon in the Tool panel, you erase the entire paint document or frame.

Selecting images and portions of images

When you want to work with a portion of a picture — whether to cut, copy, move, change the fill, or add a special effect to it — you first have to select the specific portion of the picture that you want to edit. With draw objects, this task is simple. You just click the particular object that you're interested in. In a paint document or frame, on the other hand, everything is just dots. Three tools are available for selecting a portion of a picture: the Selection Rectangle, the Lasso, and the Magic Wand.

The Selection Rectangle

The Selection Rectangle tool enables you to make rectangular selections.

To use the Selection Rectangle:

1. **Choose the Selection Rectangle tool in the Tool panel.**
2. **Click to position one corner of the selection rectangle and then drag.** When you release the mouse button, the selection is defined by the area that is enclosed in the flashing rectangle.

To deselect an image, click outside of the selection, click any tool icon, and choose Undo Select from the Edit menu, or press ⌘-Z.

You also can use a selection rectangle in the following ways:

- ◆ Press ⌘ while you drag a selection rectangle around an image to make the selection snap around the image, just as the Lasso tool does.
- ◆ Double-click the Selection Rectangle icon in the Tool panel to select the entire paint document or frame.
- ◆ Press ⌘ while you double-click the Selection Rectangle icon to select only the images within the paint document or frame (ignoring blank space).
- ◆ Press Option while you drag a selection to make a copy of it. (For example, you can use this feature to take a picture of one car and change it into a traffic jam.)

The Lasso

The Lasso enables you to make irregular selections in a paint document or frame.

Step-by-Steps

To use the Lasso:

1. **Choose the Lasso tool in the Tool panel.**
2. **Click and then drag around the area that you want to select.** When you release the mouse button, the Lasso snaps around the images that you have selected, ignoring blank background areas.

You can double-click the Lasso icon in the Tool panel to select only the images within the paint document or frame. You also can press Option while you drag a selection to make a copy of it.

To deselect an image, click outside of the selection, click any tool icon, or choose Undo Select from the Edit menu (or press ⌘-Z).

The Magic Wand

Use the Magic Wand to make selections that are based on color. When you position the head of the Magic Wand over the desired color or pattern and click the mouse button, all adjacent pixels that are the same color or pattern are selected.

Step-by-Steps

To use the Magic Wand:

1. **Choose the Magic Wand tool in the Tool panel.**
2. **Position the head of the Magic Wand over the color of pixel or the pattern that you want to select and click the mouse button.**

To make a copy of a selection, press Option while you drag the selection.

To deselect an image, click outside of the selection, click any tool icon, and choose Undo Select from the Edit menu, or press ⌘-Z.

TIP

When you are attempting to select a pattern, dragging the Magic Wand through a small area of the pattern may be easier than just clicking. As you drag, a Freehand-style line is displayed. When you release the mouse button, the selection is made.

Moving, cutting, copying, or duplicating a selection

When you move the cursor over a selection that you have made, the cursor changes to a pointer. If you click while the pointer is visible, you can drag the selection to a new location. If you press Shift as you drag, you drag straight horizontally or straight vertically.

You also can use the arrow keys to move the selection one pixel at a time. (If Autogrid is on, the selection moves one gridpoint at a time.)

Commands in the Edit menu become available after you select an image or a portion of an image. You can Cut (press ⌘-X) or Copy (press ⌘-C) the image to the Clipboard, Clear the image, or Duplicate it (press ⌘-D).

Applying special effects to a selection

Special effects in the Transform menu also become available after you make a selection. These effects include Shear, Distort, and Perspective. *Shear* adds vertical or horizontal slant to an image. *Distort* enables you to stretch an image in any direction. *Perspective* makes the image appear as if you are viewing it from an angle.

Step-by-Steps

To shear, distort, or add perspective to a selection:

1. **Select a portion of the image by using one of the selection tools (Selection Rectangle, Lasso, or Magic Wand).**
2. **Select Shear, Distort, or Perspective from the Transform menu.** Blank handles appear around the selection.
3. **Drag a handle to achieve the desired effect.**
4. **Click away from the selection to remove the handles.** Figure 7-24 shows the effects of applying Shear, Distort, and Perspective to an image.

NOTE

You lose resolution when you modify an object by using these commands. Because you're in a 72 dpi mode and are in a bitmapped document, the pixels are modified during the transformation. Some pixels become larger, some smaller. This change is normal. If there are too many jagged edges for you, clean up by zooming in and using the tools to smooth out the image. Another trick is to use the Blend option. This option makes the edges less noticeable.

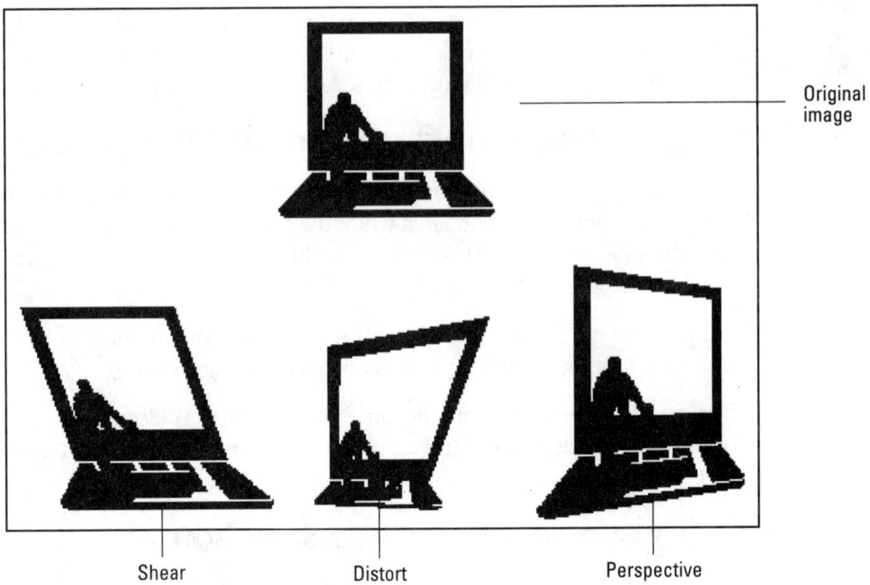

Figure 7-24: Special effects.

Changing the size of a selection

Two commands in the Transform menu enable you to change the size of a selection: Resize and Scale Selection. To change the size manually, use the Resize command. To change the size by specifying scaling proportions, use Scale Selection.

Step-by-Steps

To use the Resize command:

1. **Select a portion of the image by using one of the selection tools (the Selection Rectangle, Lasso, or Magic Wand).**
2. **Choose Resize from the Transform menu.** Blank handles appear around the selection, as shown in Figure 7-25.

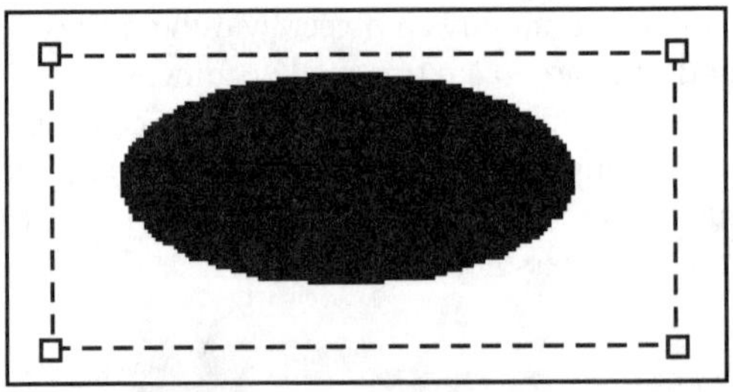

Figure 7-25: The Resize command adds handles to the selection.

3. **Drag a handle to change the size of the selection.** When you release the mouse button, the selection is redrawn to the specified size.
4. **Click away from the image to eliminate the Resize handles.**

If you press Shift as you drag a handle, the original proportions of the selection rectangle are maintained.

To use the Scale Selection command:

1. **Select a portion of the image by using one of the selection tools (the Selection Rectangle, Lasso, or Magic Wand).**
2. **Choose Scale Selection from the Transform menu.** The Scale Selection dialog box appears, as shown in Figure 7-26.

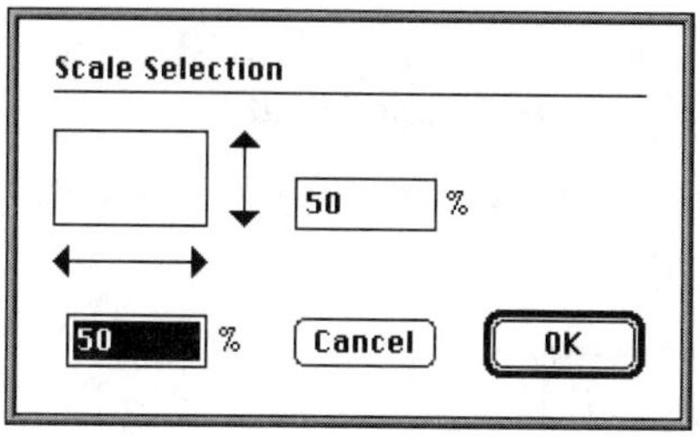

Figure 7-26: The Scale Selection dialog box.

3. **Type percentages for enlargement (greater than 100%) or reduction (smaller than 100%).** If you want to maintain proportions, enter the same percentage for both the horizontal and vertical dimensions.
4. **Click OK.** The selection is resized.

Orientation transformations

The same commands that are available in the draw environment for changing an object's orientation are also available in the paint environment. To change the orientation of a selection, select a portion of the image and choose Flip Horizontal, Flip Vertical, or Rotate. Flip Horizontal and Flip Vertical work exactly the same as the commands in the draw environment. For additional information, see the description of these commands in the "Flipping and rotating objects" section, earlier in this Topic.

The Rotate commands in the Paint environment, on the other hand, are considerably more powerful than those for draw objects. Rotate and Free Rotate enable you to set the rotation of a selection to *any* angle — not just to 90-degree increments as you're restricted to in the draw environment.

Step-by-Steps

To use the Free Rotate command:

1. **Select a portion of the image by using one of the selection tools (the Selection Rectangle, Lasso, or Magic Wand).**
2. **Choose Free Rotate from the Transform menu.** Blank handles appear at the corners of the selection.
3. **Drag one of the handles to rotate the selection.**
4. **Click away from the selection to complete the command.**

Step-by-Steps

To use the Rotate command:

1. **Select a portion of the image by using one of the selection tools (the Selection Rectangle, Lasso, or Magic Wand).**
2. **Choose Rotate from the Transform menu.** The Rotate dialog box that is shown in Figure 7-27 appears.

Figure 7-27: The Rotate dialog box.

3. **Enter a number (in degrees) for the clockwise rotation that you desire.**
4. **Click OK.** The selection is rotated.

Color transformations

At the bottom of the Transform menu are a number of useful color-related transformation commands. Here is what they do:

- *Fill.* This command duplicates the function of the Paint Bucket tool, enabling you to fill any selection with a color, pattern, or gradient. The difference is that the fill is applied only to the selected area, so it does not matter whether an image is closed or open; nor does it matter whether the selected area contains a solid color, a gradient, or a pattern.
- *Pick Up.* This command enables you to transfer the design and attributes of one image to another image. To use the command, select an image, drag it over another image, and choose Pick Up from the Transform menu.

  TIP

  One interesting application of Pick Up is for creating patterned text. Type the text, select it by pressing ⌘ as you drag the Selection Rectangle tool around it, move it over an interesting pattern, and choose the Pick Up command. Figure 7-28 shows some text with a gradient pattern that was created in this manner.

Figure 7-28: Gradient text created with the Pick Up command.

- *Invert.* Use this command to make a negative image of a selection. Colors in the image are reversed, but perhaps not as you might expect them to be. An inverted gray scale gradient, for example, may show shades of yellow, green, and blue.
- *Blend.* Use Blend to provide a smooth transformation between colors by adding intermediate shades.
- *Tint.* Choose Tint to tint a selection with the current fill color.
- *Lighter and Darker.* Use these commands to add white or black to a selection, making it lighter or darker.

TIP

When you use any of the color transformation commands, make sure that you select only the outline of an object and not part of the background, too. Each command applies to *everything* within the selection. To select only an object without the surrounding background, use the Lasso or press ⌘ while you drag the Selection Rectangle.

Creating custom colors, patterns, and gradients

As in the draw environment, you can replace colors, patterns, and gradients in the palettes with ones of your own choosing. Follow the instructions presented earlier in this Topic (under the same heading for the draw environment).

Other paint settings

Other menu commands that appear in the paint environment enable you to change the document size, the depth and resolution of the image, and the grid size (in conjunction with the Autogrid feature).

Step-by-Steps

To change the document size:

1. **Choose Document from the Format menu.** The Document dialog box appears, as shown in Figure 7-29.

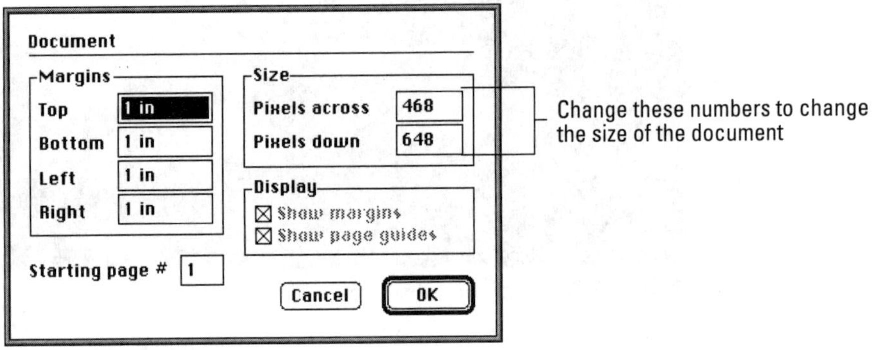

Figure 7-29: The Document dialog box.

2. **In the Size section of the dialog box, enter new numbers for Pixels across and Pixels down.** As with points, there are 72 pixels per inch. The maximum for either dimension is 2,000 pixels; the minimum is 36 pixels.
3. **Click OK.** The document is resized as specified. Any new paint documents created during the remainder of this ClarisWorks session also will be the new size.

The *resolution* of a paint document is initially set to match the resolution of a typical Macintosh screen — 72 dots per inch (dpi). If you are printing on a high-resolution printer, such as an Apple LaserWriter (most of which print at 300 dpi), you can change the resolution to match that of the printer.

As you increase the resolution, however, the document and its contents shrink accordingly. At 300 dpi, for example, a standard paint document reduces to about 1.5 x 2.25 inches. If you have enough free memory, you can increase the size of the document by following the steps listed in the preceding instructions. You should note, however, that the higher the resolution and the larger the document size, the more memory is required. For this reason, many users will prefer to use the default 72 dpi setting for resolution.

Depth refers to the number of colors that are available for displaying the document. Depth is initially set to match the setting in the Monitors control panel.

To change the depth and resolution of a paint document or frame:

1. **Choose Resolution & Depth from the Format menu.** The Resolution and Depth dialog box appears, as shown in Figure 7-30.

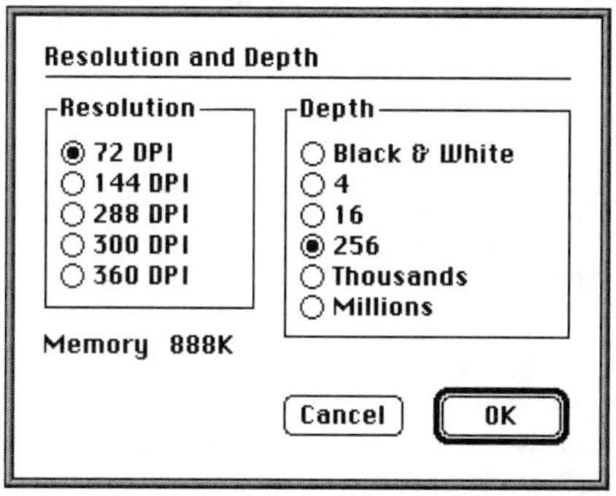

Figure 7-30: The Resolution and Depth dialog box.

2. **Choose a resolution by clicking its radio button.**
   - Use 72 dpi for a document that you intend to display only on-screen or print on an ImageWriter printer. You also can use higher multiples of 72 (144 and 288) to maintain proportions when you print to an ImageWriter or equivalent printer.
   - Use 300 dpi to match the resolution of most laser printers.
   - Use 360 dpi to match the resolution of most ink-jet printers.
3. **Choose a depth by clicking its radio button.** The amount of memory that the new depth setting requires is shown at the bottom of the dialog box.

NOTE

If you are working in a paint frame, rather than in a paint document, select the frame and then choose Modify Frame from the Options menu. A similar dialog box appears that enables you to set the resolution, depth, and the *origin* (starting point) for displaying the contents of the frame. Enter values (in pixels) for the horizontal and vertical coordinates. See Topic 15 for additional information.

When importing a PICT file into a paint frame or document, ClarisWorks 2.1 or 3.0 automatically matches the resolution of the image and uses the document's original color table.

When the Autogrid option is on (set in the Options menu), the grid size determines where you can place objects and how far they will move at each step when you drag or nudge them with an arrow key. The larger the setting for grid size, the farther apart the grid locations are.

You can set the grid size to 2 pixels for fine control over image placement.

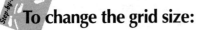

To change the grid size:

1. **Choose Grid Size from the Options menu.** The Painting Grid Size dialog box appears, as shown in Figure 7-31.

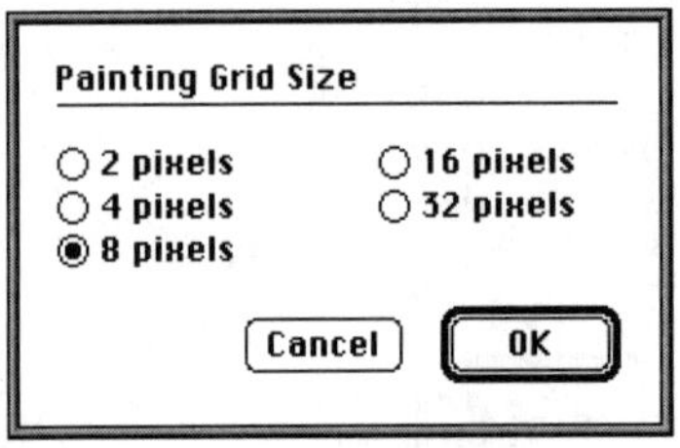

Figure 7-31: The Painting Grid Size dialog box.

2. **Click the radio button for the desired grid size and click OK.**

Down to business: Editing a screen capture

If you're new to the Mac or haven't read your system software manual, you may not be aware that the Mac has a built-in screen capture utility. By pressing Shift-⌘-3, you instruct the Mac to capture (make a copy of) the current screen image. Commercial screen capture utilities add other functions, such as the ability to capture a selected portion of the screen, capture pull-down menus, hide or display the cursor in the capture, and so on.

After you capture the screen, you'll often want to edit the capture. In this task, you learn to capture a screen that displays one of the Paint dialog boxes, edit the capture so that only the dialog box remains, and then change the image into a draw object so that you can place and resize it in any type of document.

This task demonstrates the following paint activities:

- Editing a full-screen capture at a high-zoom magnification
- Using the eraser

◆ Using the selection rectangle

◆ Using the Scrapbook to change a paint image into a resizable PICT object

Step-by-Steps

To clean up a screen capture:

1. **In ClarisWorks, create a new paint document and add some shapes to it.**
2. **Choose Spray Can from the Options menu.** The Edit Spray Can dialog box appears.
3. **Test the current spray pattern by clicking and dragging in the sample box.**
4. **If you do not have a separate capture utility, press Shift-⌘-3.** A copy of the screen is saved on disk as a new file, with the name Picture [x] or Screen [x] (depending on whether you are using System 7 or System 6).

— or —

4. **If you have a separate screen capture utility, you may be able to capture a specific portion of the screen, determine whether the cursor will be included in the screen shot, and choose many other useful options.** Issue the utility's capture command to capture the full screen or a selection that includes the dialog box.
5. **Close the paint document by clicking its close box.** Do not save the document.
6. **Choose Open from the File menu (or press ⌘-O).** A file dialog box appears.
7. **Choose Painting from the Document Type pop-up menu at the bottom of the dialog box.** Choosing Painting restricts the file list to documents that you can open in the paint environment.
8. **Navigate to the drive and folder where the screen capture is stored, select the file, and click Open.** The screen capture opens as a paint document. Figure 7-32 shows what the screen may look like.

   NOTE

   If you have performed a full-screen capture, the program may inform you that the document will be opened at a reduced size. If the entire dialog box is not visible in the document window, quit ClarisWorks and increase the memory that is available to the program. (See the Quick Tips at the end of this Topic for instructions.) Then restart ClarisWorks and go to Step 6.
9. **Choose the Selection Rectangle from the Tool panel.** Drag to select the dialog box.
10. **Choose Cut from the Edit menu (or press ⌘-X).** A copy of the dialog box is transferred to the Clipboard.

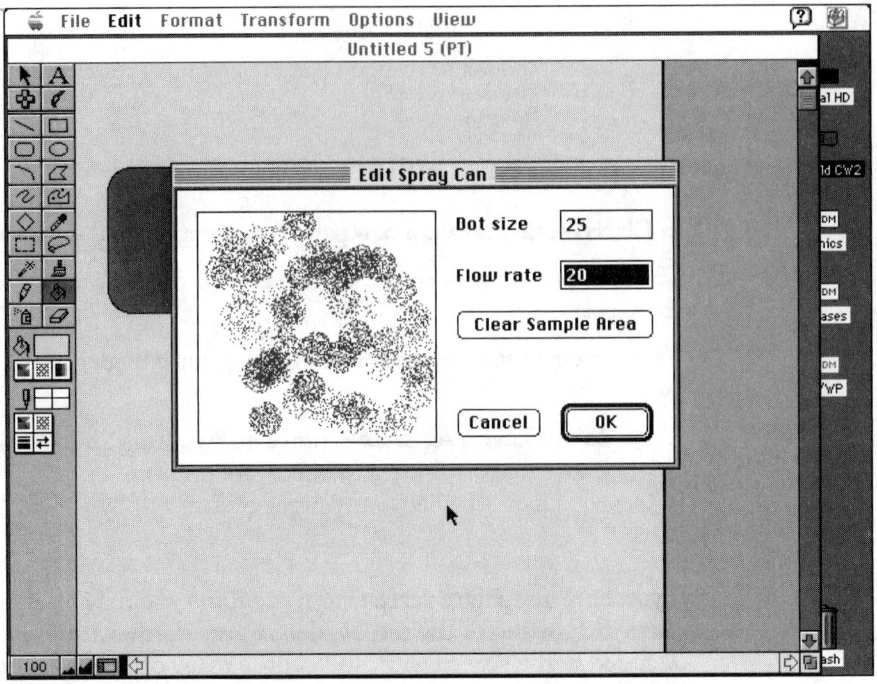

Figure 7-32: The screen capture opened as a ClarisWorks paint file.

11. **Double-click the Eraser tool.** The entire painting is erased.
12. **Choose Paste from the Edit menu (or press ⌘-V).** A copy of the dialog box is pasted onto the blank document page.
13. **Click the Zoom Percentage box in the lower-left corner of the document window and select 200%.** This setting makes editing the image easier. (With practice and a steady hand, you also can do this kind of editing at 100%.)
14. **If the Eraser isn't still selected, choose it now. To remove the stray patterns and colors from around the border of the dialog box, position the eraser so that its edge is touching — but not covering — one of the sides of the dialog box. Press Shift, click the mouse button, and drag to erase the stray material along that side of the dialog box. Repeat for the other three sides.**
15. **Click the Zoom Percentage box in the lower-left corner of the document window and select 100%.** The image returns to its normal size, as shown in Figure 7-33.
16. **Save the edited picture of the dialog box.** (In case anything goes wrong in the remaining steps, you can reopen the edited file and proceed from this step.)

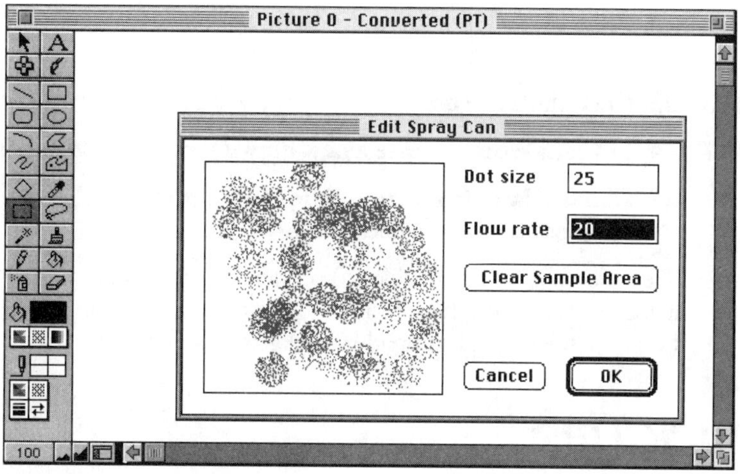

Figure 7-33: The edited screen capture.

17. **Choose the Selection Rectangle tool from the Tool panel. While pressing the Command key, drag a selection rectangle around the dialog box.** When you release the mouse button, the selection rectangle snaps around the dialog box.

18. **Choose Copy from the Edit menu (or press ⌘-C).** A copy of the edited dialog box is transferred to the Clipboard.

19. **Close the paint document.** If you are asked whether you want to save the document, click No.

20. **Open the Scrapbook desk accessory by selecting it from the Apple menu.** (***Note:*** Using the Scrapbook to change images from painting to PICT format is also discussed in the Quick Tips at the end of this Topic.)

21. **Press ⌘-V.** A copy of the dialog box picture is added to the Scrapbook, as shown in Figure 7-34.

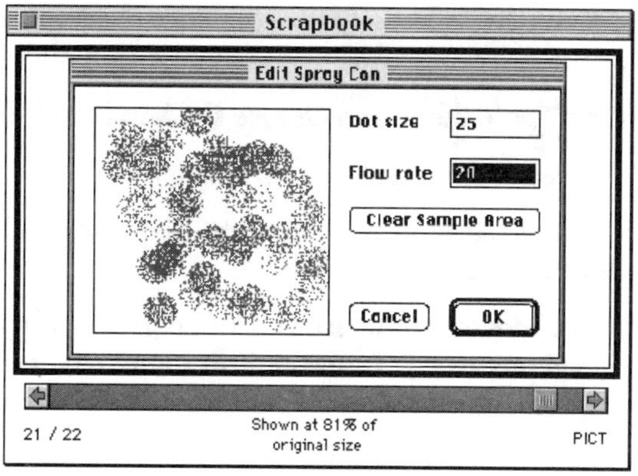

Figure 7-34: The dialog box pasted into the Scrapbook.

22. **Press ⌘-X.** The copy of the dialog box picture is removed from the Scrapbook and changed into a PICT image (an object).
23. **Click the close box on the Scrapbook to put it away.**
24. **In ClarisWorks, create a new drawing or word processing document.**
25. **Choose Paste from the Edit menu (or press ⌘-V).** A copy of the dialog box is pasted into the document.

The dialog box is now an object. You can now perform any manipulations to the dialog box that you can perform on other objects. You can, for example, change the size of the dialog box or add a background color to it.

Quick Tips

The following Quick Tips describe how to edit draw objects in the paint environment, change an edited paint image into a draw object, increase the memory that is available to ClarisWorks, create and work with a second copy of a paint document, and preview images before opening them.

Editing draw objects in the paint environment

Occasionally, being able to edit draw objects at the dot level is useful. To perform this task, you simply copy the object, paste it into a paint document, edit, copy again, and then paste it back into the original document.

Although this procedure works, it has an unfortunate side effect. When you paste the image back into the original document, it is a paint frame — a bitmap. It is enclosed by a border, and you can no longer resize it the way you can resize an object. Here's a better method.

Step-by-Steps

To change a paint image into a draw object:

1. **After you finish editing in the paint document, select and copy the image.**
2. **Pull down the Apple menu and choose the Scrapbook desk accessory.**
3. **Press ⌘-V.** The image is pasted into the Scrapbook.
4. **Press ⌘-X.** The image is removed from the Scrapbook and copied to the Clipboard as an object.
5. **Open the target document (a draw or word processing document, for example) and choose Paste from the Edit menu (or press ⌘-V).** The image is pasted into the document as a normal object.

Paint memory requirements

If you plan on working in the paint environment regularly — particularly with full-screen images — increasing the memory that is available to ClarisWorks is a good idea. Otherwise, you'll frequently see the following message:

```
The document size has been reduced to fit available memory.
```

To increase the memory that is available to ClarisWorks:

1. **Quit ClarisWorks (if it is running), go to the desktop, and select the ClarisWorks program icon.**
2. **Choose Get Info from the File menu (or press ⌘-I).** The Info window for ClarisWorks appears, as shown in Figure 7-35. The Info window enables you to change the program's *memory allocation* (the amount of memory that the system will give you to run ClarisWorks and work with ClarisWorks documents).

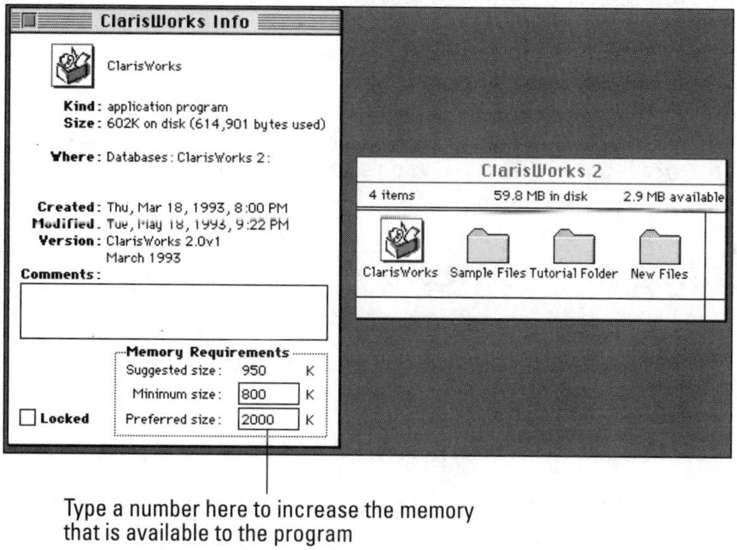

Figure 7-35: The ClarisWorks Info window for System 7 (shown here) looks slightly different from the window for System 6.

3. **Type a larger number in the Preferred size text-edit box.** (In this example, I increased it to 2000K, or 2MB.) In earlier versions of the system software, the text-edit box may be labeled Current size or Application memory size.
4. **Click the Info window's close box.**

You can change the memory allocation as often as necessary. To track how much memory you're using in ClarisWorks, go to the desktop and select About This Macintosh (under System 7) or About the Finder (under System 6) from the Apple menu. A window appears, showing how much memory the System and any open programs (ClarisWorks, for example) are currently using (see Figure 7-36). You also can see the amount of memory that is still free for use by other programs, desk accessories, and so on.

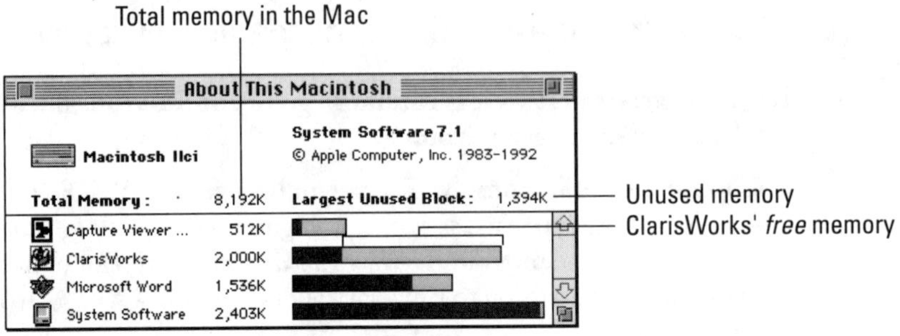

Figure 7-36: The About This Macintosh window in System 7 shows how much memory the System and any open programs are currently using and how much memory is still free.

A bar for each program shows the total memory that is allocated to that program. The dark area of each bar represents memory that is currently in use. The light area is memory that you can use to open additional documents or expand the size of current documents.

Painting in two views

When you edit a paint image at a high magnification, seeing a normal view of the image at the same time is sometimes helpful.

To create and work with a second copy of a paint document:

1. **Choose New View from the View menu.** A second copy of the document appears.
2. **Choose Tile Windows from the View menu.** The two copies are displayed together, one above the other.
3. **Set the magnification for one of the copies to a higher level (between 200% and 800%, for example) by clicking the Zoom Percentage box in the lower-left corner of the document.**

Changes made in one copy of the document are simultaneously reflected in the other copy. However, scrolling is not synchronized between the two documents. You have to scroll the copies manually to make sure that the same portions of the document are displayed in both copies.

Previewing Documents

If you load Apples's QuickTime extension at the start of your computing session, you can preview graphics files before you open them in ClarisWorks 3.0. In the Open dialog box, ClarisWorks can present a thumbnail image of every graphics file. If you have a large number of files, using the Preview feature can help you avoid opening the wrong document. For information on creating previews, see Topic 2.

Moving On Up

When — or if — your image creation and editing needs expand, you can choose from dozens of commercial graphics programs. They can be classified roughly according to their capabilities:

- *High-end paint programs.* These programs extend paint capabilities by enabling you to create or edit 8-, 16-, 24-, or 32-bit color or gray scale images. Studio 8 and Studio 32 (Electronic Arts) are examples of such programs.
- *Draw programs.* If objects are your thing, you may prefer a capable draw program, such as MacDraw Pro (Claris).
- *PostScript drawing programs.* These programs are capable of creating extremely complex and detailed PostScript images — the natural choice of illustrators and designers. The most popular of these programs are Illustrator and FreeHand. PostScript drawing programs tend to have a very steep learning curve, however. They're not for casual artists or users with simple graphics needs.
- *Image editors.* If you need to edit scanned images or captures of still video, a program such as Adobe PhotoShop is a godsend.
- *QuickTime editors.* If you want to make your own QuickTime movies, you need software tools that make it possible. Adobe Premiere is a popular choice.
- *Special-purpose graphics programs.* A wide variety of graphics niche programs is also available. Some specialize in 3-D images (RayDream Designer, addDepth, and Adobe Dimensions), enable you to switch freely between paint and PICT modes or combine them in the same document (SuperPaint), or imitate an artist's brush strokes (Fractal Design Painter).

Depending on your graphics needs, you may find that you require several programs — each for a different purpose. (You may also need more memory.)

Summary

- ClarisWorks includes a pair of graphics environments. You use the draw environment to create objects and the paint environment for bitmapped images.
- Draw objects are solid; you can edit them only as a whole. Paint images are composed of dots; you can edit them at the dot level.
- The first step in editing a draw object is to select it. After you have made a selection, you can move the object, apply different fill and pen attributes to it, or choose editing commands. You also can select several objects at the same time.
- When you want to edit a paint image, three tools enable you to select a portion of a picture: the Selection Rectangle, the Lasso, and the Magic Wand. After you make a selection, you can move it, resize it, or alter its attributes.
- Unlike draw objects (which you can place in almost any environment), you can use paint images only in paint documents and paint frames.
- Although you can easily add to or change the attributes of a draw object at any time, setting paint attributes is easier before you create each portion of an image than it is afterward.
- Paint documents are memory hogs. You may have to increase the memory that is available to ClarisWorks if you regularly work with large paint documents.

Topic 8

The Communications Environment

Overview

Communications (also called *telecommunications*) is the process of exchanging information between computers. This Topic discusses communications by means of a direct connect cable or a device called a modem. Another way that computers can exchange information is on a network (not discussed here).

A modem is a hardware device that is connected to a computer, either internally in an available slot or externally to the computer's serial port. The job of the modem is to translate outgoing data from its original digital form (ones and zeros) to an analog form (sounds) that telephone lines can carry. The modem attached to the receiving computer translates these sounds back into a digital form that the computer can understand. The name *modem* comes from the description of what the device does. It *mod*ulates and *dem*odulates computer data. Because modems exchange data over phone lines, you can use a modem to communicate with a computer down the street or across the country.

Modems can do the following:

- Connect your computer to *information services,* such as CompuServe, Prodigy, and America Online
- Connect your computer to bulletin board systems (BBSs)
- Communicate directly with computers used by your colleagues and friends
- Connect to networks and larger computers (mainframes)

Information services charge you according to the amount of time that you spend *on-line* (connected) each month. Some services have a flat monthly fee that provides unlimited use of basic services, and they charge separately for other parts of the system (for downloading programs and other files from their computer to your Mac, for accessing financial services, and so on). If you live in a metropolitan area, you can frequently connect to the service without incurring long-distance phone charges. The larger information services provide local phone numbers (*access nodes*) that you dial to connect with their systems. When you buy a modem, sign-up information for several information services is often included in the box.

NOTE

A BBS is like a miniature information service and is often run by just one person. Users can typically download files and send messages to other subscribers. A BBS can be as small as a single modem and phone line, or it can contain a bank of phone lines to handle multiple subscribers simultaneously — much the same as the information services do. Fees for becoming a subscriber, if any, are usually quite reasonable.

One-to-one communications is also very popular. You can exchange documents and programs with any other person who has a modem — even if you are using different types of machines (a Mac and a PC, for example). Overnight delivery services take a full day to deliver a document, but a pair of high-speed modems can deliver an important document in a few minutes, and often at a fraction of the cost of using a delivery service.

Unlike most of the other Topics in this book, this Topic is primarily oriented to teaching by example. It contains several "Down to Business" sections that show you, step by step, how to use the ClarisWorks communications environment to perform the following tasks:

- Connecting with an information service or BBS by using a modem
- Connecting with another Mac by using a modem
- Transferring files between a pair of Macs by using a direct connect cable
- Transferring files between a Mac and a PC by using a direct connect cable

Communications Terminology

Like most areas of computing, communications has its own language. The following list explains some communications terms that you need to understand:

- *Access number, access node.* A phone number that you can dial to reach an information service or BBS. Larger services frequently provide local access numbers for major cities. When you dial an access number, it automatically connects you with the system, and you avoid long-distance charges.
- *Baud, bps (bits per second).* The operating speed of a modem. Although the terms have different meanings, they're often used interchangeably. Whether the advertising says that a modem is 2400 baud or 2400 bps, it simply means that the modem's top speed (without compression) is 2400 bits per second.
- *Download, downloading.* Retrieving a file or program for your own use from an information service, BBS, or another user's computer.
- *E-mail (electronic mail).* Private messages that you leave for another user or another user leaves for you.

- *Log on, logging on.* Connecting with an information service or BBS. Often you have to provide a user ID and password to complete the connection and gain access to the service or BBS.
- *Log off, logging off.* Ending a session with an information service or BBS. Most systems have a command (such as Bye, Off, Logoff, End, or Quit) that you must type to end the session.
- *Protocol, protocol transfer.* The computer algorithm that you've selected for assuring error-free data transfers between your computer and the other system when you are uploading or downloading files. Each protocol has its own method of making sure that each block of data is received correctly. In most cases, when an error occurs, the protocol instructs the system to resend the block. Examples of protocols include XMODEM, 1K XMODEM, Kermit, YMODEM, ZMODEM, and CompuServe B. Different information services, BBSs, and communications programs support different protocols.
- *Session.* The period during which you are connected to another computer, information service, or BBS.
- *SIG (Special Interest Group).* Information services are often divided into sections that are each devoted to a particular topic, such as legal issues, writing, Macintosh users, game playing, hang-gliding, and so on. Within each SIG, you may be able to participate in interactive discussions, read and post messages, and download files that interest you.
- *Upload, uploading.* Transmitting a file or program from your Mac to an information service, BBS, or another user's computer.

Communication Essentials

Whether you are connecting by modem to an information service, a BBS, or another computer, or transferring files between two computers by using a direct connect cable, the two communications programs need to have matching parameters. Both modems have to transmit data at the same speed, use the same file transfer protocols, and so on. If any of the essential communication parameters do not match, you may see garbage characters on-screen, have difficulty transferring data, lose the connection inadvertently, or not be able to connect at all. Having mismatched parameters is like trying to converse with someone when each of you is speaking a different language.

After you create a standard communications document for a modem, you can use it as the starting point for any new communications session that you undertake. Figure 8-1 shows the components of a communications document window.

Choosing a modem or fax modem

If your Mac didn't come with an internal or external modem (most don't), several factors can help you decide which modem is best for you.

Speed

Different modems support different maximum data transmission speeds. Speed is stated in terms of *baud* or *bps.* When a modem is advertised as a 2400 bps unit, for example, the ad is stating the modem's top transmission speed. Most modems also can perform at lower speeds for compatibility with older or less capable modems.

In general, the faster the modem, the more expensive it is. For communicating with information services (such as CompuServe, GEnie, America Online, and Prodigy), a 2400 bps modem is usually sufficient. Although you can purchase a faster modem (9600 or 14400 bps, for example), not all of the information services support the higher speeds. Those that do may charge a premium for connecting at any speed above 2400 bps.

If much of your communicating will be with friends or colleagues, on the other hand, the faster the modems, the better. And if this two-way communication has to occur at long-distance phone rates, the faster the transmissions occur, the lower the charges will be.

You can increase *throughput* (the data transfer rate) in a file transfer if both modems have data compression routines in their *ROMs* (read-only memory). Data compression squeezes information into a smaller package, reducing the time required to transmit files. Because it is handled entirely by the modems rather than in software, the compression occurs very quickly. One standard that is called MNP5 (Microcom Networking Protocol) offers compression of approximately two to one. Another standard, V.42 bis, which was developed by CCITT (the Consultative Committee for International Telephone and Telegraph), offers four-to-one compression. The amount of compression varies, depending on the type of data that you are transferring. Graphics and text tend to compress very well. Computer programs compress very little. To use compression at all during a communications session, however, both modems must support the same compression features.

Note: If two modems cannot perform compression, you can use one of the many Mac compression programs to compress files prior to going on-line. Examples of some of the more popular compression programs include StuffIt Deluxe (Aladdin Systems), DiskDoubler (Symantec), and CompactPro (a shareware program from Cyclos). If the files are precompressed in this manner, however, make sure that you are not also using modem-provided compression. This causes the files to be compressed a second time, which — in most cases — will not improve the compression and will result in the files taking *longer* to transmit.

Data modems versus fax modems

As its name implies, you use a *data modem* strictly to exchange computer data — documents, graphics, programs, and so on. A *fax modem* is a data modem that also can send and receive faxes. Many fax modems now offer the same feature set as advanced data modems, as well as providing the ability to fax documents that reside in a Mac and to read incoming faxes on the Mac's screen.

Essentially, a fax modem is a paperless fax machine. Using a special print driver that comes with the fax software, you can issue the Print command from within almost any program. The current document is then translated into fax format and sent through the modem to the destination fax machine or fax modem. Documents that you send or receive with a fax modem are indistinguishable from documents that you send or receive with a standard fax machine. If anything, documents that you send with a fax modem tend to be a little clearer because the original document isn't scanned. It is simply converted into fax format by software.

The one drawback of fax modems is that you cannot fax an external document, such as a lease or a photograph, unless you also have a scanner. All documents have to be in the Mac in order for you to fax them.

Special features

The many useful and esoteric features that you can add to a modem are like the add-ons that a dealer offers when you buy a new car. The following features are among the options that are available:

- Advanced error correction and data compression protocols, which, because they are coded into the modem's ROM, work much faster than the same features in a communications program
- Voice capabilities, for modems that also work as answering machines
- Voice/fax switching, for modems that can sense what type of information is conveyed in an incoming call and automatically switch it to the appropriate device — either ringing the phone or sending a fax answer tone

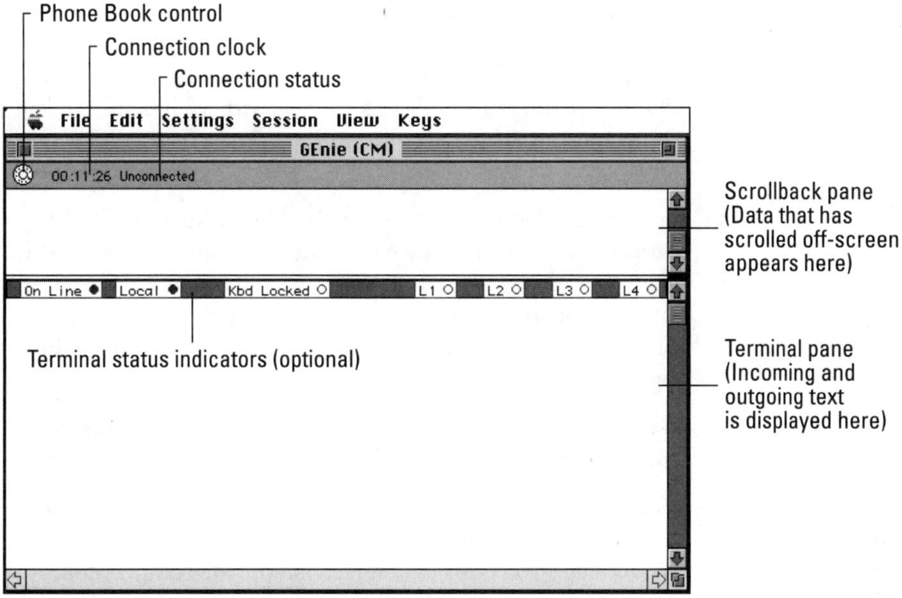

Figure 8-1: A communications document window.

To create a general communications document for use with a modem:

1. **Choose Connection from the Settings menu.** The Connection Settings dialog box appears, as shown in Figure 8-2. Use this dialog box to set up the current communications document for use with a modem (Apple Modem Tool) or for a direct connection (Serial Tool).

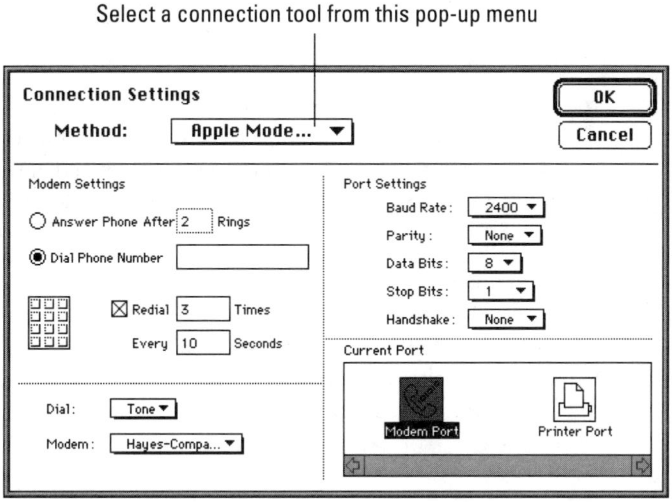

Figure 8-2: The Connection Settings dialog box.

2. **Choose Apple Modem Tool from the Method pop-up menu.** The default settings in the Port Settings section of the dialog box are 2400 bps (bits per second), no parity, 8 data bits, 1 stop bit, and no handshake. Generally, these settings are correct for a Mac with a 2400 bps modem that will be communicating with an on-line information service, a BBS, or a friend with a similar modem.

   If you have a 9600 bps or faster modem, however, you need a special cable that is wired for a *hardware handshake.* The computer uses one line of the cable to tell the modem that data is being sent to the Mac faster than the Mac can handle it and that the modem needs to pause until the Mac catches up. If you have such a cable, choose the appropriate setting from the Handshake pop-up menu.

3. **In the Modem Settings section of the dialog box, choose your modem from the Modem pop-up menu.**

   If your specific brand or model isn't listed, the Hayes-Compatible Modem choice will work for most modems. If your modem offers MNP (Microcom Networking Protocol) error correction or data compression, you can select Generic MNP Modem. Similarly, if the modem supports the V.32 CCITT standard, you can select Generic V.32 Modem. Check your modem user's guide for more details about your modem.

4. **Click the Disconnect when NO CARRIER detected check box if you want the modem to hang up the phone line automatically when you fail to make a connection with the other computer or when the connection is broken.**

5. **In the Current Port section of the dialog box, click the icon of the port (the modem port or the printer port) to which the modem cable is connected.**

6. **In the Phone Settings section, set the following options:**

   - *If you want the computer to be able to receive a call,* set the number of rings that the modem must detect before it answers.

   - *If you want the computer to be able to initiate a call,* enter the telephone number of the other computer system, BBS, or information service; the number of times that you want the modem to redial the number if it detects a busy signal; the number of seconds between redials; and the type of phone line that you are using (touch-tone, pulse, or mixed).

     When you type the phone number, include all digits that must be dialed. For example, if the call is long-distance, the number is usually preceded by 1. If the phone system requires you to dial 9 to get an outside line, the first digit of the number should be 9. You can include hyphens in the number to improve readability.

You also can add pauses by inserting one or more commas between numbers. Each comma normally represents a two-second pause. If you need to reach an outside line before you dial the phone number, for example, the entry may look similar to the following:

```
9,,555-8812
```

In this example, the modem dials 9, waits four seconds, and then dials the rest of the number.

7. **Click OK to retain the new connection settings.**
8. **Choose Terminal from the Settings menu.** The Terminal Settings dialog box appears. Set the following options:
   - *Terminal mode.* When a Mac is connected with another computer by modem or by cable, the ClarisWorks software enables the Mac to *emulate* (pretend to be) a number of different computer terminals. Different emulation choices provide varying degrees of control over how text and graphics are displayed on the Mac's screen. The default choice — ANSI/VT102 — is fine for most connections. (When you are connecting with an information service, check its manual for information about the features that are offered with different terminal emulations.)

     This section discusses only the terminal settings that you are most likely to use. For an explanation of the other settings, refer to the *ClarisWorks User's Guide.*

     Terminal choices include VT102, VT52 (two varieties of terminals from Digital Equipment Corporation), and TTY (Teletype). If the information service or BBS does not respond properly to the ANSI/ VT102 setting (or if you don't need the features and special keys that are defined for the VT102), try the TTY Tool setting.

     NOTE: The sample file called VT320 Keys modifies the Shortcuts palette to include function keys that are equivalent to those found on a VT220 or VT320 terminal.

ANSI/VT102 General options

- *On Line.* When this box is checked, you can connect and communicate with the other computer system. Leaving it unchecked means that you want to work off-line. Normally, you should check the On Line box.
- *Local Echo.* When this box is checked, everything that you type is automatically displayed in the terminal window. When this box is unchecked, you are relying on the other computer to echo back to your screen whatever you just typed. After you connect with the other computer, check this box if nothing that you type appears on your screen. Remove the check mark if you see double characters for everything you type (*HHeelllloo,* for example).

- *Show Status Bar* and *Show Tab Ruler*. Checking Show Status Bar adds some informative display lights to the top of the communications window. Checking Show Tab Ruler adds a ruler bar to the top of the window. Neither option is critical, and neither affects communications.
- *Answerback Message*. If you want to, you can enter a brief text string ("Connected with Steve's Mac," for example) that will automatically be transmitted when another computer connects with yours.

ANSI/VT102 Screen options

As you select Screen options, the effects of your choices are shown in the tiny text box on the right side of the dialog box.

- *Text width* and *Character Text size*. Column width options are 80 or 132 characters per line. Characters can be displayed in 9 or 12 point type (size).
- *Auto Wrap to Next Line*. If a line contains more characters than the number specified for the terminal width, it will automatically wrap to the next line.
- *Insert Characters*. When checked, this option enables you to insert characters in the middle of a text string that you are typing. When unchecked, characters will replace existing text.
- *Scroll Text*. This option (Jump or Smooth) determines how incoming text will be displayed on your screen.
- *Inverse Video*. Checking this option displays white text on a black background, rather than black text on a white background.

ANSI/VT102 Keyboard options

- *Keyclick Sound*. When this box is checked, you hear a click whenever a key is pressed.
- *New Line on a Return*. Click this check box if the cursor does not automatically move to a new line when you press the Return key to end a paragraph.

TTY Tool options

If you choose the TTY Tool, rather than the VT102 Tool, a single screen appears. The screen contains options that are a subset of the options that are available for the VT102.

9. **Click OK to record the Terminal settings.**
10. **Choose File Transfer from the Settings menu to choose a default method for conducting file transfers.** The File Transfer Settings dialog box appears. If you prefer, you can wait until you're on-line to make a selection. (File transfer options are discussed later in this Topic. Refer to the "Down to Business" sections for suggested protocols.)

11. **Save the communications document.** If you want to use the document as the basis for most communication documents, refer to the section in Topic 11 on using stationery to set new defaults for an environment.

NOTE: When you save a communications document, text in the terminal and scrollback panes also is saved. If you want to use the document as a communications template, you may want to clear both panes by choosing the Clear Screen and Clear Saved Lines commands from the Session menu.

Making the connection

When you are ready to connect with another computer, turn on the modem, open the communications document, and check the Connection, Terminal, and File Transfer settings. Then, if you want to initiate the call, choose Open Connection from the Session menu (or press Shift-⌘-O). The program dials the number that you entered in the Dial Phone Number text-edit box in the Connection Settings dialog box. If the text-edit box is blank (that is, you haven't entered a number), ClarisWorks prompts for the number to dial.

NOTE: As an alternative, if you have created a Phone Book entry for the service, BBS, or computer (as discussed later in this Topic under "Using the Phone Book feature"), you also can initiate the connection by choosing Phone Book from the Settings menu (or pressing ⌘-B), choosing the name of the system with which you want to connect, and clicking Connect (see Figure 8-3). If you can't find the name of the system that you want to call or if you change your mind, click Done.

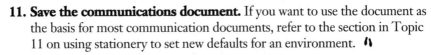

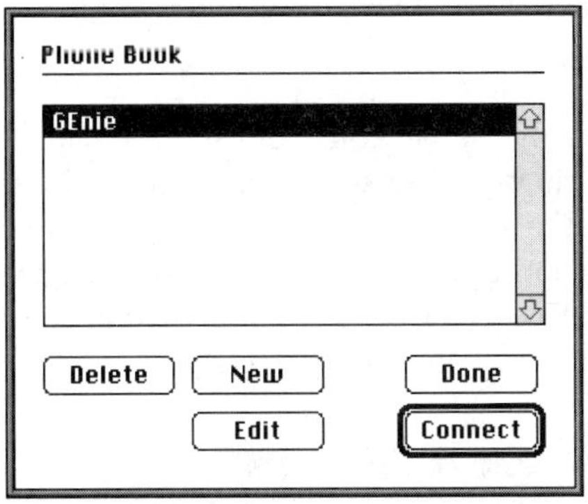

Figure 8-3: You can dial the number for the system that you want to connect with by choosing its name from the Phone Book.

NOTE: Normally, you can turn on a modem just before you initiate a connection. You don't have to leave the modem on when you don't need it. However, you need to turn on some modems, particularly some fax modems, prior to starting up the Mac. Otherwise, the software that controls the modem may not be in effect for that computing session. Check your manual to see whether your modem has any special on/off requirements.

On the other hand, if the other person or system will be calling you, choose Wait for Connection from the Session menu (or press Shift-⌘-W). A Modem Status window appears, as shown in Figure 8-4, and the modem is instructed to wait for and automatically answer the call. You can click Cancel at any time to reset the modem so that it will not continue to wait for an incoming call.

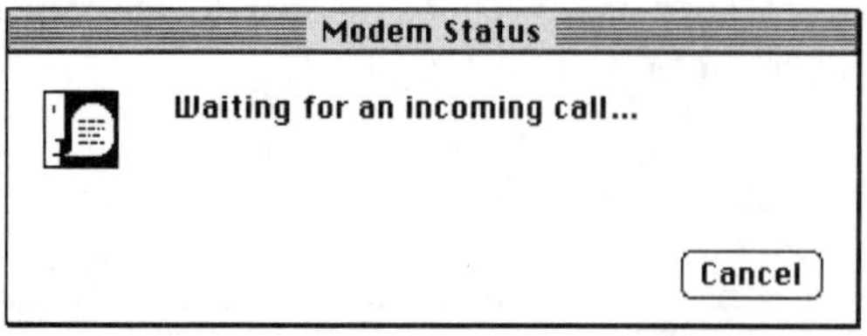

Figure 8-4: The Modem Status window when the modem is waiting for a call.

TIP

The first time that you attempt to connect with another person's computer, an information service, or a BBS, you should agree on the communication parameters beforehand. At a minimum, you need to agree on the following parameters:

- Baud rate
- Parity
- Data bits
- Stop bits
- A protocol for file transfers (if you intend to exchange files during the session)

During the initial few seconds of the connection, many modems can negotiate some of the more important settings, such as speed and protocols for error correction and compression; but many other modems can't negotiate these settings. If one of the users attempts to correct a mismatch by changing the settings while on-line, the connection may be lost. You can avoid potential aggravation by agreeing on settings before you try to connect.

Setting communication preferences

The Preferences command in the Edit menu enables you to set defaults for how the scrollback pane operates; choose the method for capturing incoming data; determine what to do when a communications document is opened; select a folder in which downloads will automatically be stored; and choose tools for the connection, terminal emulation, and the file transfer protocol. You can establish different preference settings for each communications document. You also can set global defaults to be used with every new communications document. See Topic 12 for details.

Controlling the scrollback

Most communications programs automatically track all data that is sent or received during a session. As you type new text and information is transmitted to you, the session data scrolls off the screen. As in working with a word processing document, if you want to see what someone said to you earlier in the session or find the ID number of a file that you want to download which has scrolled off-screen, you just drag the scroll bar back until the information reappears.

To accommodate Macs that have little memory to spare, ClarisWorks takes another approach to recording session data. First, instead of being automatic, recording the data is an optional part of a communications session. Second, you can use the Preferences dialog box to specify how the program should handle scrollback data. Third, ClarisWorks displays the information in a separate pane at the top of the communications window.

There are two ways of looking at the ClarisWorks scrollback options:

- The ClarisWorks scrollback options offer extensive control over how much old data is retained in memory and whether it is saved to disk when an information service or BBS sends a command to clear your screen.
- The ClarisWorks scrollback options introduce an unnecessary set of procedures for handling something that is normally transparent to communications users.

Anyway, you're stuck with the scrollback options. The following sections describe how they work.

Viewing the scrollback

As the terminal window fills with data, old information scrolls off the top of the window. As long as the Save Lines Off Top command (⌘-T) in the Session menu is preceded by a check mark, the old data is recorded rather than discarded. Whether the scrollback pane is displayed or hidden, the data is still being recorded.

When you first open a communications document, the scrollback pane is hidden. To view the scrollback, you can use either of the following methods:

- Choose Show Scrollback from the Settings menu (or press ⌘-L).
- Drag down the scrollback pane divider (as shown in Figure 8-5).

As soon as the system has received a screenful of data, the data begins to appear in the scrollback pane.

To hide the scrollback pane, press ⌘-L again, choose Hide Scrollback from the Settings menu, or drag the scrollback pane divider upwards until it disappears.

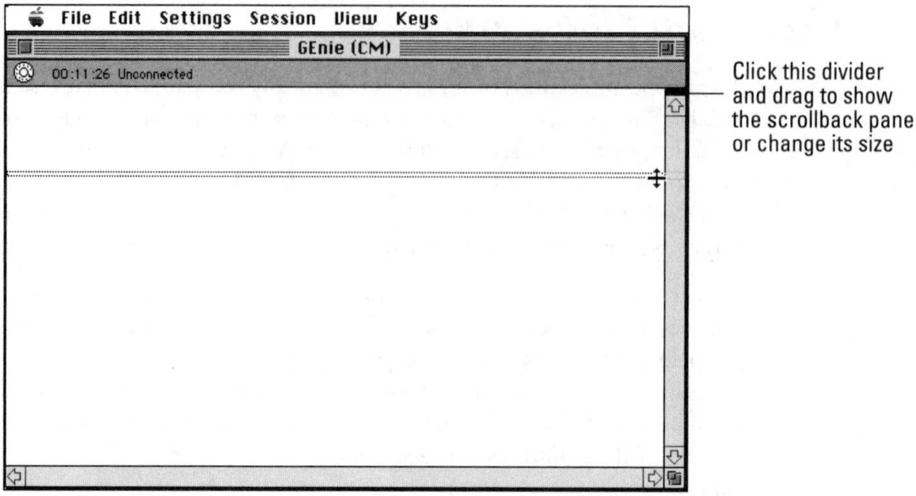

Figure 8-5: You can manually open or resize the scrollback pane by dragging the divider.

Setting scrollback preferences

You set scrollback defaults in the Preferences dialog box. Choose Preferences from the Edit menu and click the Communication icon in the Preferences dialog box that appears (see Figure 8-6).

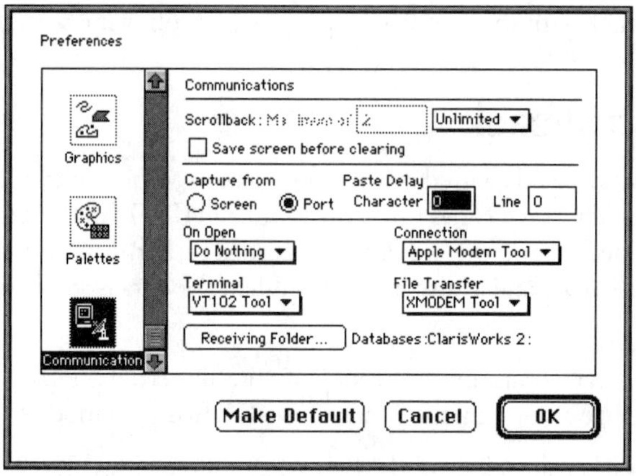

Figure 8-6: You set communications defaults in the Preferences dialog box.

The top section of the dialog box contains the scrollback settings; Unlimited scrollback is the default setting. You can limit scrollback to a specific number of data lines, screens, or Kilobytes (groups of 1,024 characters) by using the pop-up menu and text-edit box.

Some information services and BBSs send information one screen at a time and send a command to clear the current screen before transmitting the next one. To avoid losing the previous screen, click the Save screen before clearing check box. For more information about setting communications preferences, see Topic 12.

Working with the scrollback pane

When the scrollback pane is open, you can do several things:

- Scroll forward and backward to see data from earlier in the session by using the scroll bar.
- Copy the current screen in the terminal window into the scrollback pane by choosing Save Current Screen from the Session menu.
- Eliminate all data in the scrollback pane by choosing Clear Saved Lines from the Session menu.
- Copy selected data from the scrollback pane and paste it into the terminal window. The system sends information that you paste into the terminal window to the other computer or information service, just as if you typed it manually.

TIP

Copying information from the scrollback and then pasting it into the terminal window can be handy. For example, you can use this method to identify files when you want to download them from CompuServe or GEnie. In order to download a file, you have to identify it by its ID number. You can request a directory of new files and then, after you receive the directory, go back into the scrollback. Next, select and Copy (⌘-C) the ID number for the first file that you want to download. When the program prompts you for the file to download, use the Paste command (⌘-V) to type the ID number.

Capturing text

In most cases, using one of the more advanced file transfer protocols, such as XMODEM or Kermit, to transfer files from one computer to another is preferable. Regardless of whether the file is a formatted word processing document, a Macintosh program, or a simple ASCII text file, you can still use a file transfer protocol.

Occasionally, however, you may want to make a record of incoming text, such as a lengthy help message from an information service or an author's description of a program that he or she has uploaded. Because such information is normally just displayed on the screen (it doesn't have to be downloaded), a different procedure is used to capture the text. (No file transfer protocol is needed.)

To capture a text stream:

1. **Just before the information that you want to capture appears on-screen, choose Capture to File from the Session menu.** A standard file dialog box appears.
2. **Type the filename under which the text will be saved and click Save.** All incoming data is saved to the file.

   When you want to stop capturing incoming text, choose Stop Capture from the Session menu.

You can capture data in two different formats: Port or Screen. You select the format in the Preferences dialog box that appears when you choose Preferences from the Edit menu (see Topic 12 for instructions).

Port format captures data exactly as it is sent, along with any tabs, line-feeds, or form-feeds that have been embedded in the text. *Screen* format, on the other hand, is straight ASCII text.

Working with tables

You can convert some tables that you get from information services into a table format that is suitable for manipulating in a spreadsheet. Stock information is a common example.

To copy data in tabular format:

1. **Select the table in the terminal window.**
2. **Choose Copy Table from the Edit menu.**

   If the table is in the middle of the terminal window, you can copy just the contents of the table and ignore information in the left and right margins by pressing the Command key as you drag to highlight the table.
3. **Paste the table into a spreadsheet by clicking a destination cell and choosing Paste from the Edit menu (or pressing ⌘-V).**

Using the Phone Book feature

The Phone Book is an optional directory that you can use to record and dial the phone numbers of information services, BBSs, and other computers with which you want to connect. Every communications document can have its own Phone Book. If you use the same communication parameters for several information services or BBSs, you can create a generic communications document and add all of the appropriate phone numbers to the document's Phone Book.

To create a Phone Book:

1. **Open the communications document to which you want to attach a Phone Book.**
2. **Choose Phone Book from the Settings menu (or press ⌘-B).** The Edit Phone Book Entry dialog box appears, ready for you to create a new listing (see Figure 8-7).

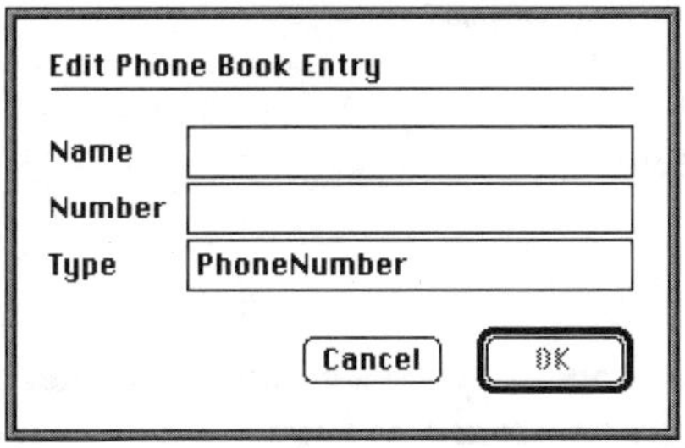

Figure 8-7: A blank page for a new Phone Book entry.

3. **In the appropriate text-edit boxes, enter a name for the service or computer and a complete phone number (including any required prefixes).**
4. **For a modem connection, leave *PhoneNumber* in the Type text-edit box.**
5. **Click OK to accept the new entry.**

To dial with the Phone Book:

1. **Turn on the modem.**
2. **Open the communications document to which the Phone Book is attached.**
3. **Choose Phone Book from the Settings menu (or press ⌘-B).** The Phone Book for the current document appears (see Figure 8-8), listing all of the entries that you have created.
4. **Select the entry that you want to dial and click Connect.** The number is dialed, and a connection is attempted, using the current communication parameters for the document.

— or —

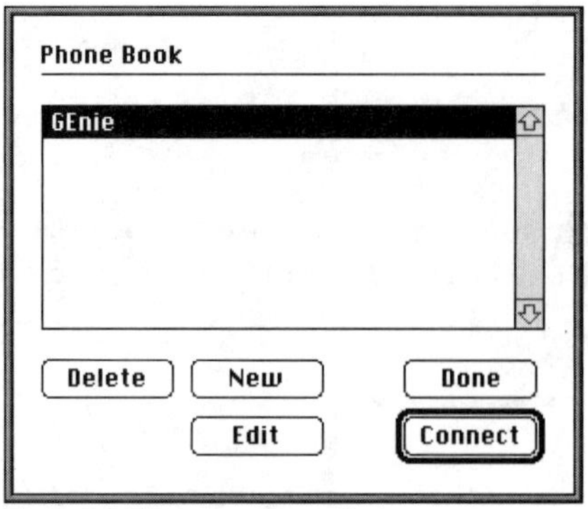

Figure 8-8: The current Phone Book.

1. **Turn on the modem.**
2. **Click the Phone Book control (the telephone dial icon at the top right of the communications document window).** A pop-up menu that lists all services, BBSs, and other computers in the current document's Phone Book appears below the control. Drag down until the correct service is selected and release the mouse button. The number for the service is dialed, and a connection is attempted, using the current communication parameters for the document.

You can edit Phone Books to add new numbers, delete unwanted numbers, and edit existing numbers. To edit the Phone Book, choose Phone Book from the Settings menu, press ⌘-B, or click the Phone Book control and choose Edit Phone Book. You can make any of the following changes:

- Click New to create a new entry.
- Select an entry and click Delete to remove it from the Phone Book.
- Select an entry and click Edit to change the name or number for an entry.

Click Done when you finish making changes.

Connecting via Modems

The most common use of communications is connecting with an information service, a BBS, or another user's computer by using a modem. This section explains how to use a modem with the ClarisWorks communications environment. After you have established the correct numbers and settings, save the document as a stationery document for future sessions to eliminate the setup time.

Down to business: Connecting with an on-line information service

Many of the larger information services, such as America Online, Prodigy, and eWorld, have their own communications software that you need to use in order to connect with their service. These services either include the cost of the software in their sign-up fee or provide it at no cost.

You can access other information services, such as CompuServe, GEnie, and most BBSs, with any standard communications program, including the ClarisWorks communications environment.

Step-by-Steps

To access an on-line information service or BBS by using ClarisWorks:

1. **Obtain an access number and a list of connection parameters from the service.**

   Information service access numbers are often restricted to particular modem speeds. Be sure to select one that corresponds with your modem's capabilities.

2. **Choose Connection and Terminal from the Settings menu, and set parameters to match the parameters that the service requires.** Be sure to enter the access number for the service in the Connection Settings dialog box. (As a starting point, you can use the communications document that you created in the section "Communication Essentials," earlier in this Topic.) You also may want to select a file transfer protocol at this time, or you can select it while on-line, prior to initiating the first transfer.

3. **Choose Open Connection from the Session menu (or press Shift-⌘-O).** The number that you entered in the Connection Settings dialog box is dialed.

4. **When the information service or BBS responds (you may see a message saying *CONNECT,* for example), enter any information that is requested.** It may ask you to present a user name or ID or to enter your full name, address, and so on. Many systems also expect users to provide a secret password that they have selected or that has been assigned to them. Entering this information is essential to the logon process.

5. **When you want to end the session, type or choose the command that the information service or BBS requires (Off, Bye, Quit, and Logoff are common examples). After the system responds, choose Close Connection (Shift-⌘-W) from the Session menu.** The modem disconnects and releases the phone line.

TIP

If the information service doesn't have a local access number in your city or town, don't choose one for the nearest city. Instead, pick one in a neighboring state. Out-of-state long-distance calls are usually much cheaper than long-distance in-state calls.

Down to business: Connecting with a Mac or a PC

From a communications standpoint, connecting with another PC or Mac differs little from connecting with a BBS or an information service. The main differences are

- *Speed.* Because you do not have to pay surcharges for high-speed connections, you can use the fastest baud rate that both modems can support.
- *Modem features used.* If both modems offer advanced error correction or data compression protocols in ROM, you can use those features to ensure error-free, speedy file transfers.

Step-by-Steps

To connect with a Mac or a PC:

1. **Agree on a set of communication parameters to use.** In particular, the parameters should include baud rate, parity, data bits, and stop bits. When you set the baud rate, select the highest speed that both modems support. (When one is a 9600-baud modem and the other is a 2400-baud modem, for example, set the baud rate at 2400 for both modems.)
2. **In ClarisWorks, choose Connection and Terminal from the Settings menu and set parameters to match the parameters that the other computer requires.** Be sure to enter the phone number for the other computer in the Connection Settings dialog box. You also may want to select a file transfer protocol at this time, or you can select it while you are on-line, prior to initiating the first transfer.

   The other computer user should open his or her communications program and set the initial communications parameters.
3. **If you are going to initiate the call, the other computer user should set the communications program to wait for your incoming call. In ClarisWorks, you then choose Open Connection from the Session menu (or press Shift-⌘-O).** The number that you entered in the Connection Settings dialog box is dialed.

— or —

3. **If you are going to receive the call, choose Wait for Connection from the Session menu (or press Shift-⌘-W).** The other computer user then instructs the communications program to dial your computer's phone number.

The receiving computer automatically answers the phone after the predetermined number of rings. During the first few seconds of the connection, the two modems negotiate about which special features, such as data compression and error correction, to use. They also may agree on an optimal baud rate for the session.

If the connection is successful, you should now be able to type in the terminal window and have your text appear on the other user's screen.

Transferring files while on-line

Transferring data and program files between two computers is a bit different from transferring them with an information service or BBS. No menus appear to help you through each step or help you choose a file transfer protocol. Setting matching protocols on the two systems is your responsibility, as is initiating the Send File and Receive File commands.

Step-by-Steps

To transmit a file:

1. **If you haven't already agreed on a file transfer protocol, select one now.** Both programs should be set to use the same protocol.
2. **Type a message to the receiving system to tell it that you are about to begin sending.** The other computer should choose the command to receive a file. (In ClarisWorks, choose Receive File from the Session menu.)
3. **In ClarisWorks, choose Send File from the Session menu, and choose the file to send.**

NOTE

You can set some protocols, such as Kermit, to receive files automatically without using the Receive File command.

Step-by-Steps

To receive a file:

1. **If you haven't already agreed on a file transfer protocol, select one now.** Both programs should be set to use the same protocol.
2. **Choose Receive File from the Session menu when the sending system is ready to begin transmitting the file and the other user instructs you to prepare for the transmission.**
3. **In the sending program, the other user should choose the command to send a file and choose the file to send.**

NOTE

You can set some protocols, such as Kermit, to automatically receive files without using a Receive File command.

Ending the session

When you are ready to end the session, type your intent to the other user and choose Close Connection from the Session menu (or press Shift-⌘-O).

The Direct Connection

You can transfer files between any two computers — including computers of different types, such as Macintoshes and PCs — by connecting their serial ports with a *null-modem cable.* (You don't need modems.) To connect a pair of Macs that are Mac Pluses or newer, use a mini DIN-8 to mini DIN-8 ImageWriter cable.

After you make the connection, all you need to do is launch a communications program on each machine, set matching communication parameters, and then use any communications protocol that they have in common — XMODEM, for example — to perform file transfers in either direction. Because you are using a cable and the Serial Tool, rather than communicating over a phone line with modems, file transfers can occur at much higher speeds.

Down to business: Transferring files between a pair of Macs

Here are some common examples of instances when you may want to transfer files between a pair of Macs that are connected by a cable:

- You have two Macs — a desktop Mac and one that you use outside the office, such as a PowerBook. You can use a direct hookup to transfer files that you've edited or created outside the office to your desktop system.
- You've prepared some important files for a presentation that you plan to give to a client. Use the direct connect method to transfer copies of the files to your PowerBook before you hit the road.
- You have purchased a new Mac and want to copy some important data files to it quickly.
- One or more of the files that you need to move between machines is too large to fit on a floppy disk.

Connecting the cable

You can use a standard ImageWriter II printer cable to connect any pair of Macs that are Mac Pluses or newer. Each end of the cable has a round 8-pin connector called a mini DIN-8. Attach the cable to the modem or printer port on the back of each Mac. Before you connect or disconnect the cable, turn off both machines.

Configuring the communications document

In this section, you will create a communications document that you can use to transfer data between a pair of Macs. After you create and save the document, you make a copy of it onto a floppy disk, install it on the second Mac, and perform a typical file transfer. The first step is to configure the communications document.

Step-by-Steps

To create a Mac-to-Mac communications document:

1. **Open a new communications document by choosing New from the File menu (or pressing ⌘-N).**
2. **When the document opens, choose Connection from the Settings menu.** The Connection Settings dialog box appears, as shown in Figure 8-9. Use the settings that are shown in Figure 8-9.

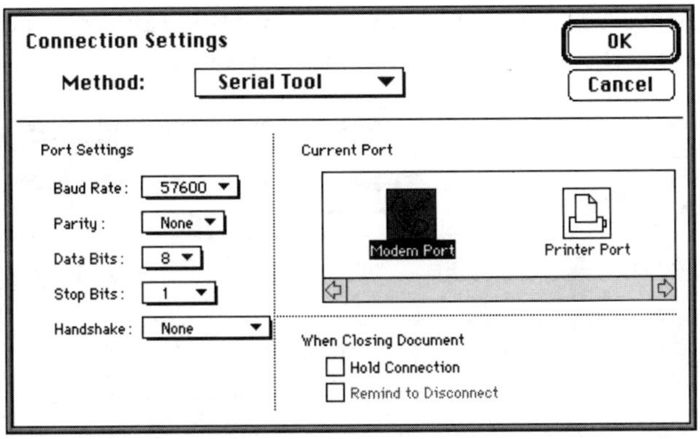

Figure 8-9: The Connection Settings dialog box.

3. **Choose the following settings from the pop-up menus:**

   Method: Serial Tool

   Baud Rate: 57600

   Parity: None

   Data Bits: 8

   Stop Bits: 1

   Handshake: None

   Be sure that the port to which the communications cable is connected is selected in the Current Port box. Click OK to accept the new settings.

   If another person is going to be involved in the file transfers, you can configure the Terminal settings so that you can type back and forth to each other between transfers (Steps 4 and 5). If not, skip to Step 6.

4. **Choose Terminal from the Settings menu.** The Terminal Settings dialog box appears. The Terminal Settings are divided into the following sections: General, Screen, Keyboard, and Character Set.

5. **Choose the VT102 Tool from the Emulation pop-up menu and set the following options (you can leave all other settings as they were initially):**

   General: On Line, Local Echo

   Screen: Auto Wrap to Next Line

   Keyboard: New Line on Return

   After making the changes, click OK to accept the new settings.

6. **Choose File Transfer from the Settings menu.** The File Transfer Settings dialog box appears, as shown in Figure 8-10.

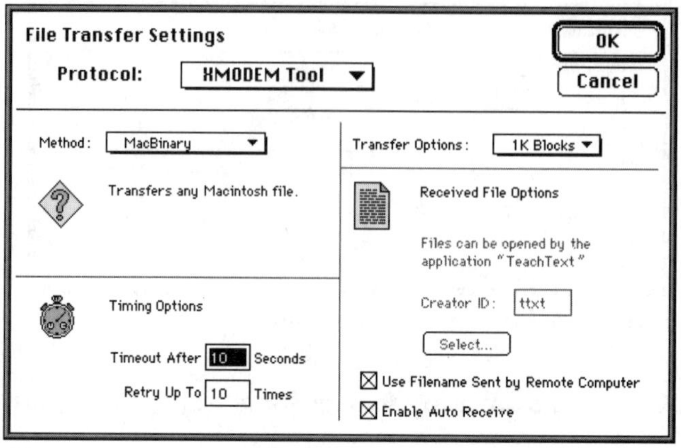

Figure 8-10: The File Transfer Settings dialog box.

7. **Choose the following settings from the pop-up menus:**

   Protocol: XMODEM Tool

   Method: MacBinary

   Transfer Options: 1K Blocks

   Check the boxes for Use Filename Sent by Remote Computer and Enable Auto Receive. Click OK to accept the new settings.

   Files will be received in the folder that you specified in the Communications section of the Preferences dialog box. For information on setting preferences, see Topic 12.

8. **Save the communications document (you might name it *Mac-to-Mac*, for example).**

9. **Make a copy of the communications document on a floppy disk and copy it to the other Mac.**

Next, test the file transfer process.

To transfer files:

1. **Launch ClarisWorks on both Macs and open the Mac-to-Mac communications document.**

2. **On both machines, choose Open Connection from the Session menu (or press Shift-⌘-O).**

3. **To test the connection, type some text on one of the Mac keyboards.** It should appear simultaneously in the terminal window on both Macs.

4. **Choose Send File from the Session menu on one of the Macs.** A standard file dialog box appears.

5. **Select a file to send and click the Send Button.** The file transfer occurs automatically.

Because you selected Enable Auto Receive, file transfers can occur without requiring the recipient to choose Receive File from the Session menu. You can use this configuration to send files in either direction. When you are through transferring files, choose Close Connection from the Session menu on both Macs (or press Shift-⌘-O).

For most users, the 1K XMODEM protocol is sufficiently speedy and error free for most file transfers. If you want to send a large number of files, however, you may prefer to use the Kermit protocol. Of the protocols that are provided with ClarisWorks, Kermit is the only one that permits unattended transfers of batches of files.

NOTE

If you check Overwrite Existing Files and you transfer a file with the same name as one that already exists in the destination folder on the receiving machine, the existing file will be replaced by the new one. (For details on using Kermit, see the box on the Kermit file transfer protocol later in this Topic.)

Down to business: Transferring files between a Mac and a PC

With Apple's continued penetration into the business market, finding both Macs and PCs in the same office is becoming more common. In the past, sharing files between the two platforms was difficult. Disks were formatted differently, and file formats varied widely between the systems.

The introduction of the Apple SuperDrive (the 1.4MB, 3.5-inch floppy disk drive) has helped minimize the differences between Mac and PC data. With Apple File Exchange, the newly released PC Exchange, and several other commercial programs from third-party software companies, Macs equipped with a SuperDrive can both read from and write to 3.5-inch PC floppies. Similar software is also available for the PC. Translation software that handles the differences in file formats is also widely available. Many programs, such as ClarisWorks, can import and export data by using file formats that are compatible with formats of other programs, so moving data between Macs and PCs is relatively easy.

This section explains how to use a direct connect cable to shuttle files between the two systems. This approach is particularly useful in the following circumstances:

- ◆ When some files are too large to fit on a single floppy disk
- ◆ When you need to move many files
- ◆ When you frequently need to move files between the systems

Although you also can use a pair of modems (one for each computer) that are connected over a telephone line to accomplish the same thing, a direct connect cable has one huge advantage — speed. You can move data easily and reliably across a serial cable at 57,600 baud. To accomplish the same throughput with modems requires a pair of 14,400 bps modems that are operating with quadruple data compression (v.32 bis) and a relatively static-free phone line.

The biggest problem with the direct connect approach to data transfer between Macs and PCs is the difficulty in locating an off-the-shelf cable that is designed to do the job. Unless you are up to the task of building your own cable (and I'm not), you will probably need to have one built for you. Figure 8-11 shows the appropriate cable pin-outs, depending on whether the PC has a 25-pin or 9-pin serial port.

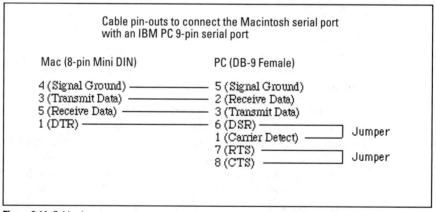

Cable pin-outs to connect the Macintosh serial port with an IBM PC 25-pin serial port

Mac (8-pin Mini DIN)	PC (DB-25 Female)	
4 (Signal Ground)	7 (Signal Ground)	
3 (Transmit Data)	3 (Receive Data)	
5 (Receive Data)	2 (Transmit Data)	
1 (DTR)	6 (DSR)	Jumper
	8 (Carrier Detect)	
	4 (RTS)	Jumper
	5 (CTS)	

Cable pin-outs to connect the Macintosh serial port with an IBM PC 9-pin serial port

Mac (8-pin Mini DIN)	PC (DB-9 Female)	
4 (Signal Ground)	5 (Signal Ground)	
3 (Transmit Data)	2 (Receive Data)	
5 (Receive Data)	3 (Transmit Data)	
1 (DTR)	6 (DSR)	Jumper
	1 (Carrier Detect)	
	7 (RTS)	Jumper
	8 (CTS)	

Figure 8-11: Cable pin-outs.

TIP

If you haven't dealt with a custom cable company before, contact Energy Electric Cable Inc. at 1-800-521-6520. They quoted me a price of $45 for an 8-foot Mac-to-PC null modem cable. Be sure to tell them whether you need the 9-pin or 25-pin connector for the PC end.

Connecting the cable

Attach the circular 8-pin end of the cable (the mini DIN-8 connector) to the modem or printer port on the back of the Mac. Connect the other end (either 9-pin or 25-pin) to any free serial port on the back of the PC. On some PCs, the ports will be labeled (Serial 1 and Serial 2, or COM1 and COM2). The number of serial ports varies from one manufacturer to another, but PCs usually have one to three such ports.

Configuring the communications programs

On the Mac side, use a ClarisWorks communications document as the communications software. For the PC, almost any communications program will do. The following instructions explain how to configure the two programs so that the machines can communicate with each other.

To configure ClarisWorks:

1. **Open a new communications document by choosing New from the File menu (or pressing ⌘-N).**
2. **Choose Connection from the Settings menu.** The Connection Settings dialog box that is shown in Figure 8-12 appears. Use the settings shown in Figure 8-12.

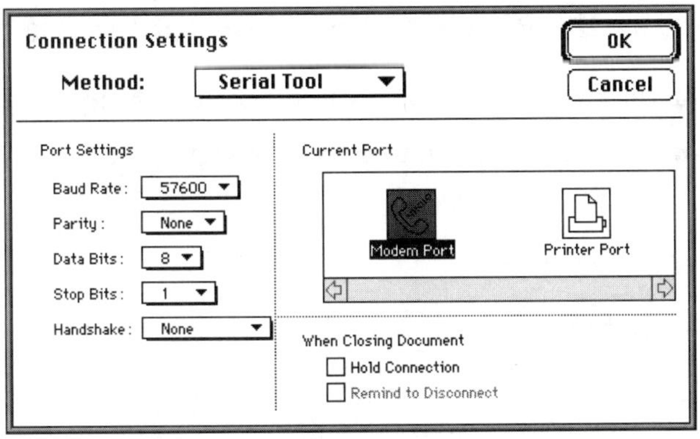

Figure 8-12: The Connection Settings dialog box.

3. **Choose the following settings from the pop-up menus:**

   Method: Serial Tool

   Baud Rate: 57600

   Parity: None

   Data Bits: 8

   Stop Bits: 1

   Handshake: None

Be sure that the port to which the communications cable is connected is selected in the Current Port box. Click OK to accept the new settings.

Because you are only transferring files from one computer to the other, the Terminal settings are irrelevant. They control what appears on the two screens when text is typed on either keyboard; therefore, they don't affect file transfers.

4. **Choose File Transfer from the Settings menu.** The File Transfer Settings dialog box appears.
5. **Choose the following settings from the pop-up menus:**

   Protocol: XMODEM Tool

   Method: Straight XMODEM

   Transfer Options: 1K Blocks

   You can ignore the other settings. Click OK to accept the new settings.
6. **Choose Terminal from the Settings menu.**
7. **With the General icon selected in the left window, click the On Line and Local Echo check boxes.**
8. **Choose Open Connection from the Session menu (or press Shift-⌘-O).**

Step-by-Steps

To configure the PC communications program:

1. **Run the DOS or Windows communications program.**
2. **Configure the program to match the settings in ClarisWorks:**

   Baud Rate: 57600

   Parity: None

   Data Bits: 8

   Stop Bits: 1

   Handshake: None

   Be sure that the port to which the communications cable is connected is selected in the program. In most cases, the port is COM1 or COM2.
3. **Set Local Echo (sometimes called Half Duplex) to On.**
4. **If the program allows you to set a default for the file transfer protocol, choose 1K XMODEM.**
5. **If the program does not automatically connect to the Mac, issue the command to put the program on-line.**

Testing the connection

When both programs are running, you can test the connection. Type a string of text on the Mac's keyboard. As you type, the characters should appear on the PC's screen.

Now perform the test again by typing something on the PC's keyboard. The characters should appear on the Mac's screen. In the tests, you don't need to be concerned if text overlaps on the same line or if you see extra blank lines between lines of text when you press Return. What's important is that the exact letters that you type on one machine appear on the screen of the other machine.

If nothing appears on the other machine's screen, you can probably trace the problem to one of the following causes:

- The wrong serial port is selected in either the Mac or the PC communications program.
- The cable is incorrectly wired.

If you see garbled characters on the other screen, the communication parameters between the two programs are probably mismatched. Check to make sure that you have set all of the parameters correctly. If they are correct, reduce the baud rate setting in the two programs and try again.

Transferring files

You can move document files of almost any type (word processing, spreadsheet, and graphics, for example) from one machine to the other. There is little point in moving programs, however. Mac programs cannot normally be run on a PC and vice versa.

Step-by-Steps

To transfer files from the Mac to the PC:

1. **If necessary, save or export the Macintosh documents to a format that the destination program on the PC can read.**

   If you use Microsoft Word for Windows, for example, you can save ClarisWorks word processing documents as Microsoft WinWord files. Be sure to check the import capabilities of the destination program on the PC. You may find that it can read some Macintosh files directly and does not require a conversion.

2. **In ClarisWorks, choose Send File from the Session menu.** A standard file dialog box appears.

3. **Select the file that you want to transmit and click Send.**

4. **On the PC, issue the communication program's command to receive a file.** If you are prompted for a file transfer protocol, select 1K XMODEM. You may also be asked what you want to name the file and in which directory the file should be saved. Respond appropriately, and the transfer begins.

During file transfers, ClarisWorks displays a window in which you can keep an eye on the progress (see Figure 8-13). Most PC communication programs display similar information.

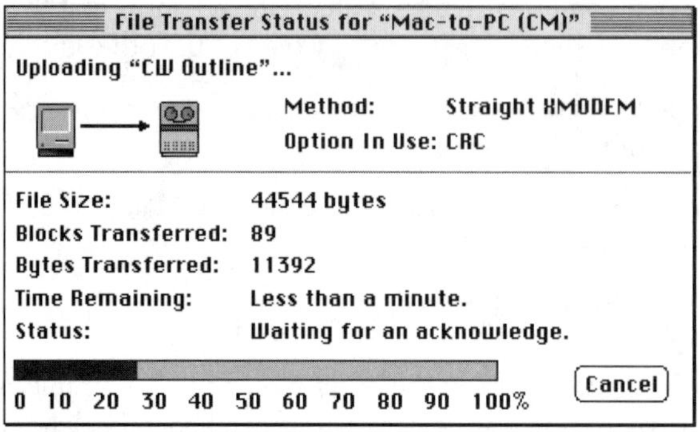

Figure 8-13: ClarisWorks displays this window during file transfers.

NOTE

Even though you have selected 1K XMODEM as the transfer protocol in both programs, don't be surprised if a different XMODEM protocol is used (as shown in Figure 8-13).

Step-by-Steps

To transfer files from the PC to the Mac:

1. **If necessary, save or export the PC documents to a format that the software on the Mac can read.**

   If you are running Microsoft Word for Windows, for example, no file conversion is necessary. The ClarisWorks word processor can read native Word documents in their original format (as Microsoft WinWord files). If you are transferring documents from a program for which ClarisWorks does not have translators, check the export capabilities of the PC program. It may offer an export or save option that ClarisWorks (or another destination program on the Mac) understands.

2. **On the PC, issue the communication program's command to send a file.** You are asked to type the name of the file or select it from a file list. Be sure to specify the correct drive and directory in which the file is located. If you are prompted for a file transfer protocol, select 1K XMODEM.

3. **In ClarisWorks, choose Receive File from the Session menu.** The transfer begins. After the file is received, a standard file dialog box appears, as shown in Figure 8-14.

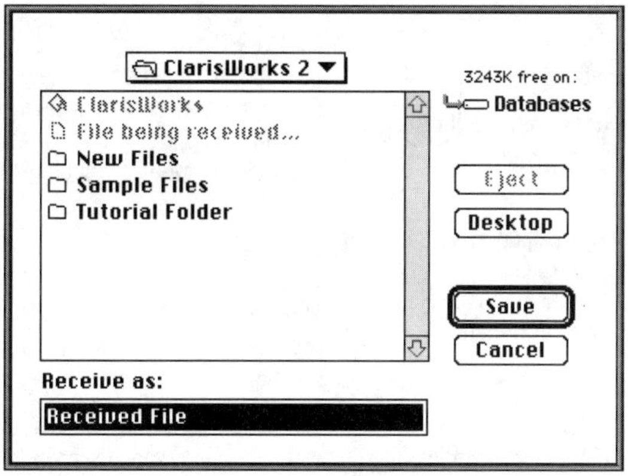

Figure 8-14: Because the original filename is not part of the information that is sent during the file transfer, you have to enter a filename here.

4. **Select the destination drive and folder, type a filename, and then click Save.**

ClarisWorks for Windows is now available. Unfortunately, it cannot read Macintosh ClarisWorks 2 documents unless you have ClarisWorks 3 for Windows. You'll have to save them in an intermediate format before transferring them to the PC. Files from ClarisWorks for Windows, on the other hand, can be read by the Macintosh version of ClarisWorks without translation.

Late in 1994, ClarisWorks 3.0 was released for both the Macintosh and Windows. Unlike in earlier versions of the program, the files from the two platforms are compatible. No translation is necessary when you move the files between the platforms. In addition, ClarisWorks 3.0 files are in the same format as those created by ClarisWorks 2.0 and 2.1. Thus, if you have ClarisWorks 3.0, you'll find that only ClarisWorks 1.0 files still require translation.

For occasional file transfers between two Macs or a Mac and a PC, the direct connect approach works fine. If you regularly make these types of transfers, however, you should check out some products that are dedicated to performing this task. Both MacLinkPlus/PC (DataViz) and LapLink Mac III (Traveling Software), for example, provide software that enables you to move files between computers effortlessly, as well as to translate them between a number of Mac and PC formats. Each product also includes an appropriate cable for connecting a Mac with another Mac or a PC.

The Kermit file transfer protocol

Although XMODEM will readily handle transfers of any file type from one machine to another, it has a couple of disadvantages:

- You can transfer only one file at a time.
- Because the filename is not transmitted with the file, you must name each file manually as it is received.

If you're willing to put up with Kermit's slower performance, you can use the Kermit protocol to transfer batches of files with a single command. When the files are received, they also can be named automatically.

To use Kermit:

1. **In ClarisWorks, choose File Transfer from the Settings menu.** The File Transfer Settings dialog box appears.
2. **Set options in the dialog box to match the settings shown in the figure.**

   Note: When you are connecting a Mac and a non-Mac (such as a PC), select Binary as the Method. The Binary option enables you to transfer ordinary text files or formatted documents. When you are connecting two Macs, use MacBinary as the Method. MacBinary can transfer any type of Mac document, including programs.

   Selecting a larger packet size (Extra Long Packets, in this example) can improve the speed of the transfer if both programs can use the larger packet size.
3. **On the PC, set Kermit as the new file transfer protocol.** Depending on the communications program, you may be able to set a file transfer protocol as a default, or you may have to select the protocol immediately prior to issuing the send or receive command.
4. **On the PC or Mac, choose the command to send a file or send a group of files.** (In ClarisWorks, choose Send File or Send Batch from the Session menu. If you choose Send Batch, you can specify several files to transmit together.)
5. **Set the other machine to receive a file.** (If the PC is the receiving machine, you may have to specify the Kermit protocol at this time.) The file transfer commences.

Note: When you are using the Kermit protocol to transfer PC files to the Mac, ClarisWorks may not recognize that the final transfer has been completed. If the transfer status window does not close by itself, click the Cancel Transfer button.

When you use Kermit, the transfer speed can be moderately or considerably slower than when you use XMODEM. But if you aren't in a rush, you can use Kermit to transfer a batch of files to either machine automatically while you occupy yourself with something more productive.

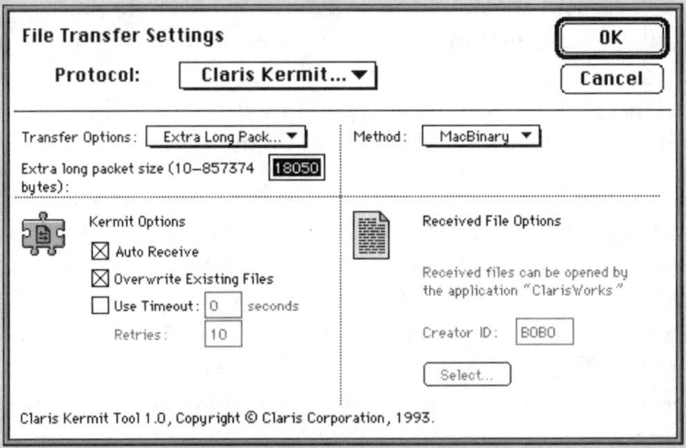

Quick Tips

The following Quick Tips tell you how to create an auto logon macro and macros to automate routine communications tasks, explain AT commands and tell you how to issue them manually.

Choosing the correct file transfer method

If you're hooked up to an on-line service or are simply downloading from another CPU, pay close attention to the file transfer method. MacBinary is the default and can only be used on Mac files. If you download from a service (GEnie or CompuServe, for example), chances are the files are not true Mac files — they are generic for multiple platforms. An "Out of Memory" error will occur, even if you have plenty of memory allocated. Switch to XModem if this problem occurs.

Creating an auto logon macro

Although ClarisWorks 2 and later versions include Phone Books for recording the numbers of the colleagues, friends, and information services with which you regularly connect, they do not enable you to save a logon sequence along with the phone number. For most of us, memorizing IDs and passwords is a pointless exercise. With a little bit of work, you can use the ClarisWorks macro feature to create auto logon sequences that respond to a series of prompts on your favorite BBS or information service and, optionally, take you to the first area of the service that you normally visit.

Step-by-Step

To record the macro:

1. **Open the communications document that you have created for the information service or BBS, and choose Open Connection from the Session menu (or press Shift-⌘-O).** ClarisWorks dials the number for the service.
2. **After the connection has been established, choose Record Macro from the Shortcuts submenu of the File menu.** The Record Macro dialog box appears.
3. **Name the macro, choose an Option-⌘-key combination with which you will execute the macro, and click the Document Specific check box.**
4. **Click Record to begin recording.**
5. **If required, press whatever keys are necessary to complete the connection.** (Some systems, for example, expect you to press Return immediately upon connection.)
6. **When the first system prompt appears (requesting a user ID, password, or both, for example), choose Macro Wait from the Shortcuts submenu of the File menu (or press Shift-⌘-J).** The Macro Wait dialog box that is shown in Figure 8-15 appears.

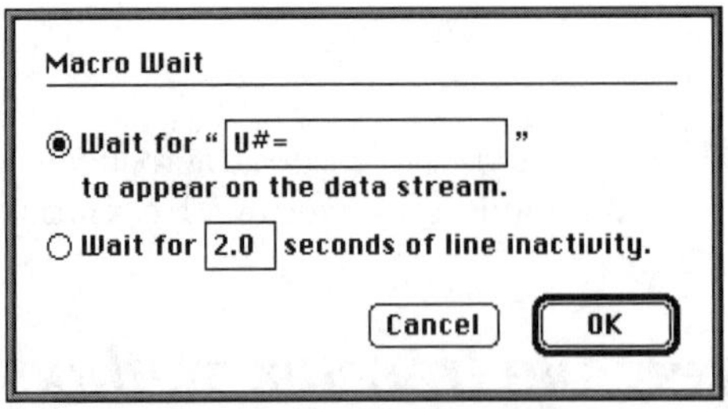

Figure 8-15: The Macro Wait dialog box offers two options: Wait for a text string, or wait for a specific number of seconds of line inactivity.

7. **Type the system prompt or enough of it to uniquely identify the text string for which you are waiting and click OK.** In the case of a GEnie logon (shown in Figure 8-15), U#= is the service's prompt for the user number and password.
8. **After the dialog box disappears, type your normal response to the system prompt — in this case, your user number and password — and then press Return.**
9. **If additional actions are required to complete the logon or to move to a particular part of the information service or BBS, record them now.**
10. **When the macro is completed, choose Stop Recording from the Shortcuts submenu of the File menu (or press Shift-⌘-J).**
11. **Continue with the on-line session or issue the command to log off the system.**

As an example, to move from the logon to the Macintosh software library in GEnie, you use a macro that is similar to the following steps:

1. Macro Wait for text string: *U#=*
2. In the terminal window, type your identification number, a comma, and your password, and then press Return.
3. Macro Wait for text string: *continue?*
4. Press Return in the terminal window.
5. Macro Wait for text string: *<H>elp?*
6. Type **Mac** in the terminal window and press Return.
7. Macro Wait for text string: *<H>elp?*
8. Type **3** in the terminal window and press Return.

To test or use the macro, choose Open Connection from the Session menu (or press Shift-⌘-O). As soon as the connection is established and before the first prompt from the service or BBS appears, execute the macro by pressing the Option-⌘-key combination that you defined for it. In the GEnie logon example, to avoid timing problems, you may want to eliminate Step 1 (Macro Wait for text string: *U#=*) and begin with Step 2. Then you can execute the macro after the ID prompt appears, instead of trying to sneak it in within the few seconds between the connection and the appearance of the ID prompt.

You have to observe a few precautions whenever you are working with communications macros. First, as the preceding example shows, macros are highly dependent on an unchanging information service or BBS structure and prompt sequences. If the service alters its logon sequence, reorganizes the names or locations of SIGs that you regularly visit, or changes the wording of its prompts, the macro may fail. Then you have to rerecord each macro that is affected because you cannot edit an existing macro.

Second, although auto logon macros are convenient, anyone can use them to log onto your account with the information service or BBS. If security is a problem in your office or home, you may want to purchase one of the many available security programs to make the communications document accessible only to individuals who know its password.

Third, you don't need to type the entire text string in the Macro Wait dialog box. However, you need to be careful to type a sufficient amount of text so that the string is unique. In the GEnie example, Steps 5 and 7 wait for the text string *<H>elp?.* If the macro had been instructed to simply wait for *elp,* the next step could have been mistakenly triggered by any sentence or text string that contained *elp,* such as *helpful.* If the macro responds too early, as in this example, it may fail.

Fourth, think twice before you check Play Pauses in a communications macro. Although recording the amount of time between each command that you issue (rather than using Macro Wait commands) may seem logical and easier, times vary significantly from one session to the next. The line conditions, the number of other users accessing the BBS or information service at the same time, and so on, affect the amount of time required. If your responses are sent before they are requested, the information service or BBS will often ignore them and kill the macro in the process.

If this approach doesn't work for you, you can try using Play Pauses in your logon macro.

If the macro doesn't work, you can halt its execution at any time by pressing ⌘-period.

Automating a communications session with macros

Just as you can create auto logon macros, you can create macros to perform other common actions, such as going to specific SIGs and the electronic mail section of the service, selecting a file transfer protocol for downloads, and logging off the system. For complex activities that require decision capabilities (such as checking for new mail and, if found, capturing the letters to a text file), you may want to investigate a more powerful commercial macro program, such as Tempo or QuicKeys.

Those ubiquitous AT commands

Your communications software — in this case, the ClarisWorks communications environment in combination with Apple's Communications Toolbox — controls the modem that is attached to your Mac. The software controls the modem by sending instructions that are called *AT commands* (*AT* stands for *Attention*) to the modem.

If you want to learn more about your modem's capabilities, you can send AT commands to it, too. Grab your modem manual, turn to the listing of its commands, and follow the steps for issuing AT commands. (Before you modify any of the modem's default commands, be sure that the modem has a command that you can use to reset it to its factory settings. Often, this command is AT&F. If you change a setting that shouldn't be changed, resetting the modem to its defaults will get you out of trouble.)

Step-by-Steps

To issue AT commands:

1. **Create or open a new communications document.**
2. **Choose Connection from the Settings menu.** The Connection Settings dialog box appears.
3. **Select Serial Tool as the Method and choose a Baud Rate from the pop-up menu that is supported by the modem. Leave the other settings alone. Click OK to accept the new settings.**
4. **Choose Terminal from the Settings menu.** The Terminal Settings dialog box appears.
5. **With the General icon selected (on the left side of the dialog box), enter check marks in the On Line and Local Echo check boxes. Leave the other settings alone. Click OK to accept the new settings.**
6. **Choose Open Connection from the Session menu (or press Shift-⌘-O).** The modem will now respond to commands that you type in the communications document.
7. **Because some commands will eventually scroll off the screen, choose Show Scrollback from the Settings menu (or press ⌘-L).**

As a test, type **AT** and press Return. (You have to end every instruction that you send to the modem by pressing Return.) The modem should respond by entering *OK* below your command.

One useful command that is supported by some modems is AT&H. On an Abaton InterFax 24/96, this command lists help information for controlling the modem, as shown in Figure 8-16. AT&H or AT&H0 lists an AT Command Set Summary; AT&H1 lists S Register Functions (user-modifiable information stored in the modem's ROM); AT&H2 lists a Dialing Command Code Summary; AT&H3 lists the MNP Command Set Summary; and AT&H4 lists the Evercom Proprietary Command Set Summary.

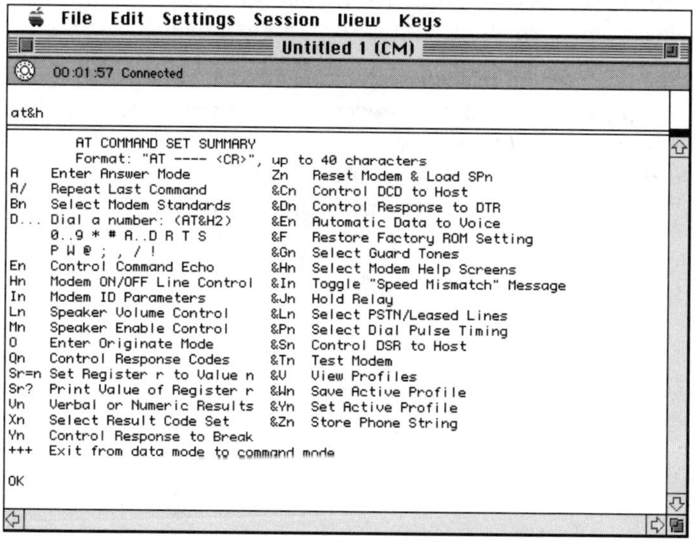

File Edit Settings Session View Keys
Untitled 1 (CM)
00:01:57 Connected
at&h
AT COMMAND SET SUMMARY
Format: "AT ---- <CR>", up to 40 characters
A Enter Answer Mode
A/ Repeat Last Command
Bn Select Modem Standards
D... Dial a number: (AT&H2)
0..9 * # A..D R T S
P W @ ; , / !
En Control Command Echo
Hn Modem ON/OFF Line Control
In Modem ID Parameters
Ln Speaker Volume Control
Mn Speaker Enable Control
O Enter Originate Mode
Qn Control Response Codes
Sr=n Set Register r to Value n
Sr? Print Value of Register r
Vn Verbal or Numeric Results
Xn Select Result Code Set
Yn Control Response to Break
+++ Exit from data mode to command mode
Zn Reset Modem & Load SPn
&Cn Control DCD to Host
&Dn Control Response to DTR
&En Automatic Data to Voice
&F Restore Factory ROM Setting
&Gn Select Guard Tones
&Hn Select Modem Help Screens
&In Toggle "Speed Mismatch" Message
&Jn Hold Relay
&Ln Select PSTN/Leased Lines
&Pn Select Dial Pulse Timing
&Sn Control DSR to Host
&Tn Test Modem
&V View Profiles
&Wn Save Active Profile
&Yn Set Active Profile
&Zn Store Phone String
OK

Figure 8-16: Some modems have built-in screens that can be displayed in the terminal window.

The normal format for an AT command is AT, the command, an optional parameter number, and Return. An ampersand (&) or backslash (\) symbol precedes some commands. You select an option in other commands by ending them with a number (ATM0 or ATM1, for example).

You can issue multiple AT commands on the same line, as in the following:

```
AT M1L0
```

If you like, you can add spaces between commands to improve readability. As usual, you have to end the command string by pressing Return.

You can do other useful things with AT commands:

- Change the volume of the modem's speaker or turn off the speaker entirely
- Dial a phone number through the modem, using a pulse or touch-tone phone line (ATDT[*phone number*], as in ATDT555-1212)

- Store frequently dialed numbers in the modem's memory (not all modems offer this feature)
- Store multiple communication setups, view them, and switch between them as needed (not all modems offer this feature)
- Switch between data and voice modes so that you can speak to the person on the other end of the line without having to hang up and call back (not all modems offer this feature)

NOTE

You can also use AT commands to modify the initialization string by selecting Custom from the Modem pop-up menu in the Modem Settings section of the Connection Settings dialog box. The default commands will be listed, which you can then change (turn off modem speaker, for example).

CAUTION!

If you want to learn more about the commands that your modem supports and how to issue them, refer to your modem manual. Remember, however, that unless you know what you're doing, you need to be sure to reset the modem to its factory defaults when you finish experimenting. Modern modems often include some special memory chips that retain your changes even after you turn off the modem.

Moving On Up

For basic communications, ClarisWorks serves most users very well. However, several major features have been omitted that you may eventually want to have. You may, for example, want the following features:

- *More-advanced file transfer protocols.* In particular, the YMODEM, YMODEM-G, and ZMODEM protocols provide faster data transfers and batch transfers. When the connection is broken during a file transfer, ZMODEM can pick up automatically where the transfer left off — instead of having to restart the download from the beginning. These protocols are often available in inexpensive shareware communications programs such as ZTerm.

- *A more powerful macro or scripting language.* The ClarisWorks macro facility is crude when compared to that of stand-alone macro programs or the advanced scripting options that are provided in a dedicated communications program such as MicroPhone II (Software Ventures Corporation). In particular, the inability to perform branching limits ClarisWorks macros.

  For example, you may want to create a macro or script that checks for new mail and, if it finds any, automatically downloads it or captures it to a text file for you. If new mail is not found, on the other hand, the macro or script could simply log off the system. You cannot use a ClarisWorks macro to perform this task.

Summary

- A communications document can connect your Mac to information services, BBSs, or other computers via a modem. With the proper ClarisWorks/Communication Toolbox settings, you also can link a pair of computers with a special direct-connect cable.
- To assure a trouble-free connection, you must set matching communication parameters in both communications programs.
- The Connection Settings dialog box enables you to specify whether you want to make a modem connection (Apple Modem Tool) or a direct link (Serial Tool), to select a communications port (modem or printer), and to specify the port settings.
- You use the Terminal Settings dialog box to specify a terminal emulation and set characteristics for how text will be displayed in the terminal pane, as well as how it will be transmitted to the other computer.
- In the File Transfer Settings dialog box, you select a protocol to use when sending or receiving files. The purpose of a file transfer protocol is to assure that data transfers are error-free. The protocol that you choose must be supported by both computer systems.
- You can store phone numbers for systems that you want to call in the Connection Settings dialog box or in the document's Phone Book. Every communications document can have its own Phone Book for dialing one or more information services, BBSs, or other computers.
- With the proper settings, you can either initiate a modem call or instruct ClarisWorks to wait for and answer an incoming modem call.
- Rather than storing old data in the terminal window, ClarisWorks provides a scrollback pane at the top of the window. As data is cleared from the terminal window, it is automatically transferred into the scrollback pane. You can scroll through the information in the scrollback pane, copy the information and paste it into the terminal window (or into other documents), force the current screen to be copied into the pane, and clear the contents of the pane.
- File transfers can occur between Macs and non-Macs, as well as between Macs.
- No modems are necessary if you want to connect a pair of computers over a direct-connect cable. You must, however, have the proper cable and a communications program running on both systems. Because direct-connect file transfers between systems are not limited by modem capabilities, they can occur at very high speeds.
- You can use the ClarisWorks macro recorder to create auto logon macros, as well as to automate many routine communications tasks.
- The communications program sends commands to the modem. You can issue the same commands manually by selecting the Serial Tool and typing the commands in the terminal window.

Part III

Integrating the ClarisWorks Environments

Topic 9

Generating a Mail Merge

Overview

A *merge* combines information from a database with a word processing document. In the most common use of a merge, a *mail merge,* you personalize form letters by inserting names from a database into a word processing document. For example, you use "Dear Mickey" or "Dear Mrs. Samuels," rather than "Dear Friend" or "Dear Customer."

Every merge has two components: a database and a merge form. The database contains the information that you want to insert into the merge form (names and addresses of friends, sales commission figures, or descriptions of catalog items, for example). The merge form is a text document, such as a form letter. You insert placeholders in the merge form, and each placeholder specifies the name of a database field («Last Name», for example). During the merge, data from the fields of each visible database record is inserted into the placeholders in the merge form. One copy of the merge document is printed for each visible database record.

NOTE

Although the merge form is usually a word processing document, you can create it within a text frame in any ClarisWorks environment. For example, you can design a party invitation in a draw document and personalize it with information that you place in a text frame.

The Elements of a Merge Form

As discussed previously, the merge form is a word processing document or frame that contains placeholders for information from database fields. Each placeholder contains the name of a database field, surrounded by special bracket symbols (as in «Company»). You create the left and right bracket symbols by pressing Option-\ and Shift-Option-\, respectively. (The \ is the backslash character.) However, because a misspelled field name will kill the merge, the preferable way to enter a field name and its surrounding brackets is to select the field from the Mail Merge dialog box, as explained in the step-by-step instructions for creating a merge form.

As with any other text in a word processing document or frame, you can apply different fonts, styles, colors, or other formatting options to the placeholders. You simply select the entire field name, including the brackets, and then apply formatting options.

You can use punctuation and spaces to separate merge fields from each other and from surrounding text. If the merge form contains two placeholders for the components of a name, as in «First»«Last», when the merge is performed, the result is TomJohnson. To separate the two fields in the merge, you add a space between the fields, as in «First» «Last».

You also can combine merge fields with normal text. For example, you can embed a merge field in a sentence:

- Just imagine your surprise when our prize van pulls up to the doorstep of the «Last Name» household.
- Because your sales were so extraordinary this quarter, «First Name», please find enclosed a commission check for «Commission» and a 15 percent bonus of «Bonus Amount».

Creating a Merge Form

To create a merge form, you simply type the basic text for the letter or document (that is, all the text that will be identical for each letter or document) and then, using the Mail Merge dialog box, insert field placeholders at the appropriate spots in the text.

Step-by-Steps

To use the Mail Merge dialog box to insert fields into a merge form:

1. **Open the database file with which you intend to merge.** (This file has to be open both when you select placeholders and when you perform the merge.)
2. **Open the merge document or create a new one.** (Remember that you can perform a merge with a word processing document or with a non-word processing document that contains a text frame.)
3. **Choose Mail Merge from the File menu (or press Shift-⌘-M).** The Select Data dialog box appears, as shown in Figure 9-1.
4. **Select the name of the database that you opened in Step 1 and then click OK.** The Mail Merge dialog box shown in Figure 9-2 appears.
5. **Switch back to the merge form by selecting it from the View menu.**
6. **Set the text insertion point where you want to insert the first field placeholder.**
7. **In the Field Name list box, select the field that you want to insert.**

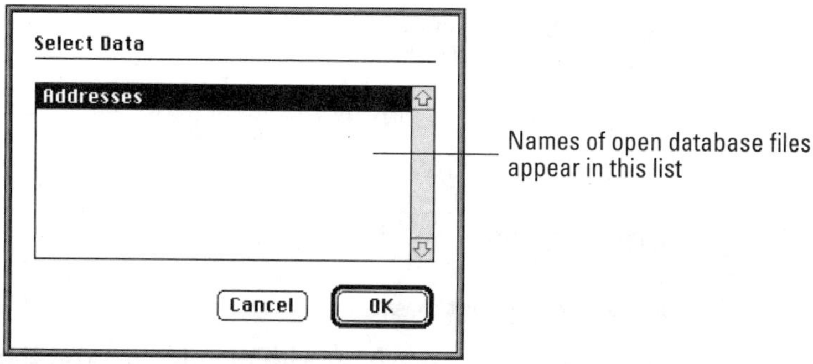

Figure 9-1: The Select Data dialog box.

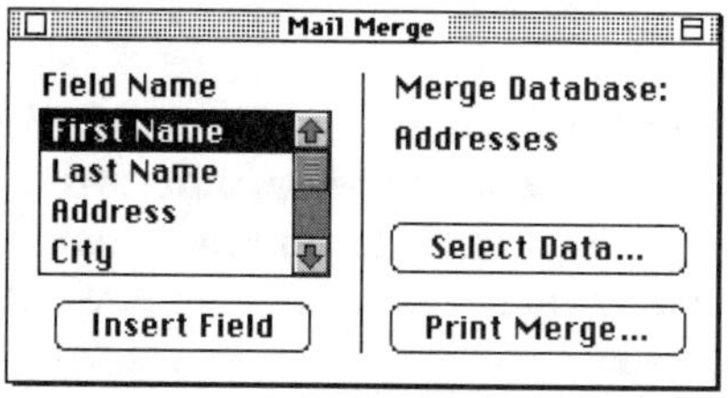

Figure 9-2: The Mail Merge dialog box.

8. **Click Insert Field to add the field name and its surrounding brackets at the present text insertion point.**
9. **Repeat Steps 6 through 8 for additional field placeholders that you want to add to the merge form.** Figure 9-3 shows a completed merge form.

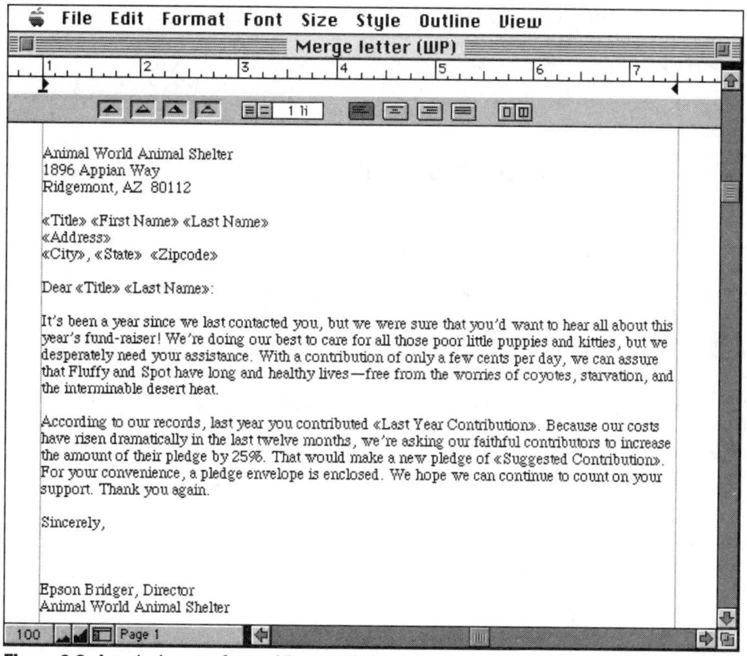

Figure 9-3: A typical merge form. All names in brackets are merge fields.

Performing a Merge

After the merge form is ready, the mechanics of performing the merge are straightforward.

Step-by-Steps

To perform a merge:

1. **Open the merge database.**
2. **To merge the entire database with the merge form, choose Show All Records from the Organize menu (or press Shift-⌘-A) and go to Step 3.**

— or —

2. **To merge selected records with the merge form, choose the Find command from the Layout menu (or press Shift-⌘-F). When the blank find request appears, specify criteria to find the record or records that you want to print. Click Visible to search only the visible records or All to search the entire database.**
3. ***Optional:* If you want the merge documents to print in a specific order (alphabetically by last name or in zip code order, for example), sort the records by choosing the Sort Records command from the Organize menu.**
4. **Open the merge document.**
5. **Choose Mail Merge from the File menu (or press Shift-⌘-M).**

   If the Select Data dialog box appears, choose the name of the database and click OK. The Mail Merge dialog box appears.

   If you have already chosen a database, the Mail Merge dialog box appears immediately.
6. **Click the Print Merge button.** The Print dialog box for the printer appears.
7. **Click Print, and the merge commences.** One copy of the merge document is produced for each visible database record.

TIP

Before committing yourself to a massive merge, hand-select a few records and try the merge on a smaller scale. You cannot preview the effects of a merge on-screen, so a trial run can save an enormous amount of paper if you have, for example, selected the wrong database field or incorrectly set the spacing between fields.

Down to Business: An Envelope Merge

After you understand the mechanics of a merge, the process becomes routine. Rather than step you through another typical mail merge, the following instructions tell you how to perform a type of merge that you may not have thought of: an envelope merge. With a little experimentation, you can not only format and print envelopes from ClarisWorks, but also use a merge to automate the process by grabbing the mailing addresses from a database.

NEW FEATURE 3.0

If you just want to print a single envelope now and then, you can use ClarisWorks 3.0's Envelope or Address Envelope Assistant. See Topic 4 for details.

Designing the merge form

This section explains how to create the envelope merge form as a document in the word processing environment. Figure 9-4 shows one such form that was designed for a center-feeding Apple LaserWriter IINT. The graphic rulers are displayed, rather than the normal word processing ruler, to show the approximate placement of the mailing address and return address sections.

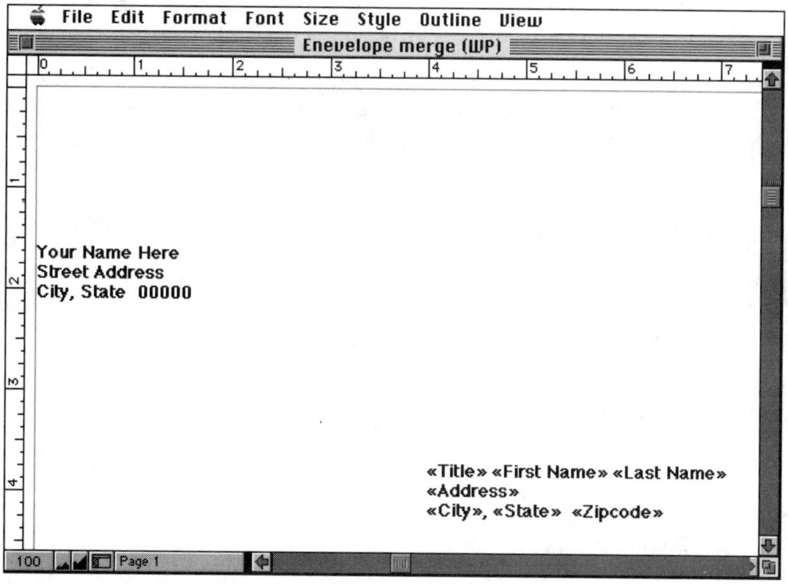

Figure 9-4: An envelope merge form.

To create the merge form:

1. **Create a new word processing document by choosing New from the File menu (or pressing ⌘-N). Click the Word Processing radio button and then click OK.**
2. **Choose Page Setup from the File menu.** The Page Setup dialog box appears.
3. **Click the icon for landscape mode printing (the sideways icon) and select the paper option that corresponds to a #10 business envelope. Then click OK.**
4. **Choose Rulers from the Format menu.** The Rulers dialog box appears.
5. **Click the Graphics and Inches radio buttons and then click OK.** The graphics rulers appear at the top and left sides of the blank word processing document, as shown in Figure 9-4. The outline of the document page should correspond to that of a #10 business envelope — 6.5 x 9 inches.
6. **Type the return address in the position shown in Figure 9-4.** (These instructions assume that you are using a center-feed printer. If the printer is a right- or left-feed printer, you enter the mailing address and return address at the top or nearer the bottom of the form, respectively.)
7. **For the mailing address section, press Return several times until you reach the 3½- to 4-inch mark on the vertical ruler. Set a left tab at about the 4-inch mark and then press Tab.** The text insertion point is now correct for the first field of the mailing address.
8. **Open the database that contains the mailing addresses.**

TIP

If you haven't created your own address database, you can use one of the ClarisWorks sample files — either the file in the Sample Files folder named Name & Address-Extended or the stationery file named Name & Address-Standard.

9. **Select the word processing document from the View menu again.**
10. **Choose Mail Merge from the File menu (or press Shift-⌘-M).** The Select Data dialog box appears.

NOTE

If you have already chosen the Mail Merge command during the current session and have selected a database, the Mail Merge dialog box appears instead. Go to Step 12.

11. **Select the name of the open address database and click OK.** The Mail Merge dialog box appears.
12. **In the Mail Merge dialog box, select the name of the first field that you want to insert and click Insert Field.** (For this example, insert a *Title* field — Mr., Ms., and so on.)

13. **Press the spacebar once to add a space after the field and insert the next field (in this case, First Name). To complete the first line of the mailing address, enter another space and insert the final field (Last Name).**

14. **Press Return to start a new line, followed by Tab to align the text with the line above it. Then insert the Address field.**

15. **Press Return to start another new line, followed by Tab to align the text with the line above it. Then insert the City field.**

16. **Type a comma and a space and then insert the State field.**

17. **Type one or two spaces and insert the Zip code field.**

18. **If you want to apply different fonts, sizes, or styles to the text, do so now.**

    If you format any of the placeholders, be sure to format the brackets that surround the field name, too.

NOTE

If the envelopes have a return address printed on them, leave the return address section of the template blank. If you routinely use both kinds of envelopes — blank envelopes and envelopes with a preprinted return address — you can create two envelope merge forms.

Testing the merge form

Now comes the fun part: making sure that the mailing and return addresses print correctly. Before even thinking of printing on an envelope, however, do a few test printouts on standard letter paper. You do test printouts for a more important reason than to avoid wasted envelopes. If you insert an envelope into the printer and it prints outside the area of the envelope, it is printing onto the printer drum rather than onto the envelope. You won't have that problem with letter paper.

Before printing, place a small pencil mark on the paper in the upper-right corner of the page. When you issue the Print command (don't do a merge at this point), you may see a message saying that some of the printing may be clipped. Ignore it. When the printout appears, the pencil mark tells you the following information:

- The side of the paper on which the printer prints (so that you know whether to insert the envelopes right side up or upside down)
- Which edge of the envelope to insert into the printer (left or right)

You can also tell from the test printout whether the printing is being clipped.

Now check the positions of the mailing and return addresses on the test printout. (You may want to lay the printout over an envelope to see how well they match up.) If necessary, adjust the positions of the mailing and return addresses and do another test. When you hold the printout sideways (so you can read it), the printing should be centered from top to bottom on a center-feed printer, near the top of the page on a right-feed printer, or near the bottom of the page on a left-feed printer. When the alignment looks correct, repeat the test with an envelope. After you print an envelope correctly, you can do the merge, as described in the next section.

Envelope feed methods and Page Setup dialog boxes

Unfortunately, no one method for printing envelopes is universal to all printers. Some printers, such as the original ImageWriter, weren't designed to handle envelopes. You can use the instructions in this Topic with such printers, but I don't recommend doing so.

In general, the laser and ink-jet printers (such as the StyleWriter and the HP DeskWriter) are best for printing envelopes. They have trays that assure that the envelopes are correctly aligned and that the envelopes' *paper path* (the route that paper takes after you feed it into the printer) is straight. The ImageWriters use a standard *platen* (roller bar) to feed paper. Although the platen is excellent for *tractor-feed paper* (paper with tiny holes on both sides) and reasonably good for letter paper, it's so-so for envelopes. Envelopes tend to slide around too much, and they frequently jam.

The method for feeding envelopes varies considerably among Apple-compatible and Macintosh-compatible ink-jet and laser printers. Some printers, such as the LaserWriter II series, expect you to center-feed envelopes (center them on the manual feed tray or in an envelope tray) and insert them facing up. Other printers require that you feed envelopes from the left or right side of the feed tray. Some printers are designed so that you have to feed paper upside down. The first figure shows how to position an envelope for an Apple LaserWriter IINT or NTX.

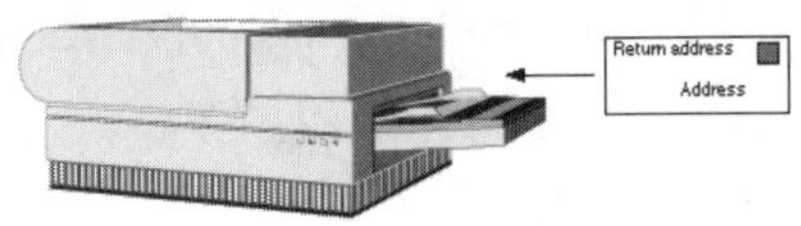

(LaserWriter image from EPS Business Art, courtesy of T/Maker Company)

For a LaserWriter II, center the envelope in the manual feed tray and insert it right side up (where the address will be printed), with the left edge of the envelope forward.

If you aren't sure of the printer's envelope feeding requirements, check its manual. The envelope template shown in this Topic was designed for a center-feed printer. You need to adjust the placement of the text to make it work properly with a right- or left-feed printer.

To make things more complicated, every printer also has its own version of the Page Setup dialog box. Luckily, the dialog boxes contain options that make formatting a standard #10 business envelope simple. The second figure shows the settings for the LaserWriter, Personal LaserWriter LS, and StyleWriter printers. Note the envelope choice in each dialog box, as well as the Landscape orientation option.

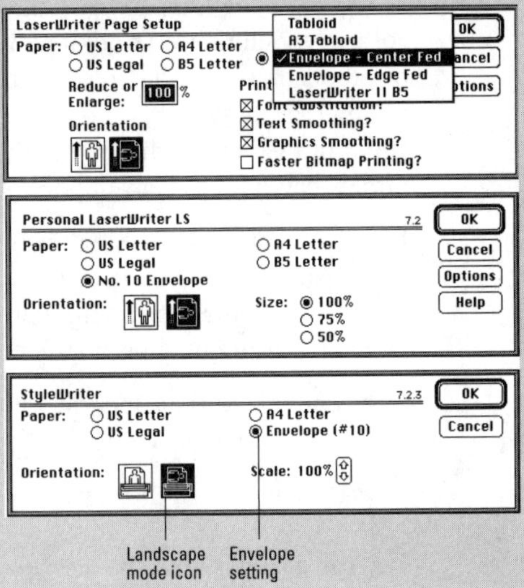

Performing the merge

Because different people have different merge needs, this section contains instructions for two types of envelope merges: printing a single envelope and printing a series of envelopes.

Step-by-Steps

To print a single envelope:

1. **Open the merge database.**
2. **Choose the Find command from the Layout menu (or press Shift-⌘-F).** A blank find request appears.
3. **Specify criteria to find the record that you want to print. Click Visible to search only the visible records or All to search the entire database.**

   If more than one record is found, use the mouse to select the specific record that you want to print. (To select a record, click anywhere in the record other than inside a field.) Then choose Hide Unselected from the Organize menu. All records other than the one that you selected are hidden.
4. **Open the word processing document.**
5. **Choose Mail Merge from the File menu (or press Shift-⌘-M).**

   If the Select Data dialog box appears, select the name of the address database and click OK. The Mail Merge dialog box appears.

   If you have already chosen a database, the Mail Merge dialog box appears immediately.
6. **Click the Print Merge button.** The Print dialog box for the printer appears.
7. **Insert an envelope into the manual feed tray of the printer and click Print to print the envelope.**

Occasionally, you may want to use the merge form to do a mass mailing, perhaps to send holiday greetings to all of your friends or a business message to your clients or coworkers.

Step-by-Steps

To print a set of envelopes:

1. **Open the merge database.**
2. ***Optional:* If you want to merge only a subset of records from the database, select the records that you want to use.** To select the records, use the Find command or the Match Records and Hide Unselected commands. (Remember, the merge prints an envelope for every visible database document, so you have to hide all the records that you do not want to print.) For instructions on using the Find and Match Records commands, refer to Topic 6.

3. ***Optional:* If you want the envelopes to print in a specific order (alphabetically by last name or in ZIP code order), sort the records by choosing the Sort Records command from the Organize menu.**

4. **Open the word processing document.**

5. **Choose Mail Merge from the File menu (or press Shift-⌘-M).**

   If the Select Data dialog box appears, choose the name of the address database and click OK. The Mail Merge dialog box appears.

   If you have already chosen the database, the Mail Merge dialog box appears immediately.

6. **Click the Print Merge button.** The Print dialog box for the printer appears.

7. **Insert an envelope into the manual feed tray or paper tray for the printer, turn on the printer, and click Print to print the envelopes. As each envelope feeds into the printer, insert the next one.** Continue until all of the envelopes have been printed.

TIP

If you have an envelope tray for your printer, you can print 15 to 20 envelopes at a time without having to stand and watch the process.

Quick Tips

The following Quick Tips explain how to use a calculation field to perform a conditional merge, how to use a merge to address a form letter when you don't know the names of all of the customers, and how to insert one of two different amounts in a merge.

Conditional merges

If you're searching for the conditional merge capabilities that many of the popular stand-alone word processing programs offer, you can stop looking. ClarisWorks doesn't have them. An example of a conditional merge is: If database field X contains information that matches these criteria, do this; otherwise, do something else.

Although ClarisWorks isn't equipped for sophisticated merges, you can jury-rig a conditional test by creating a calculation field that uses the IF database function. The following examples illustrate this application.

Problem 1

You have a customer database that contains a title, first name, last name, and address for each customer. Now you want to mail a form letter to all of them to tell them about your annual fall sale. Unfortunately, through sloppy record keeping, you didn't always record the customers' names. How do you address the letters?

To address a form letter when you don't know the names of all of the customers:

1. **In the address database, choose Define Fields from the Layout menu (or press Shift-⌘-D).** The Define Fields dialog box appears.
2. **Use the following formula to define a new calculation field that is called Name Present?**

   ```
   IF('Last Name'="","Customer",'Title'&" "&'Last Name')
   ```

   The result is formatted as text. The formula checks to see whether the Last Name field is blank. If it is, the word Customer is entered in the Name Present? field. If the Last Name field is not blank, the Title, a blank space, and the Last Name are combined and copied into the Name Present? field (Ms. Smith, for example).
3. **Use the following line as the salutation line of the form letter:**

   ```
   Dear «Title» «Name Present?»:
   ```

NOTE

You can use any properly defined field in the database as a placeholder in a merge form. The field does not need to be visible in the layout.

Problem 2

You've volunteered as a fund-raiser for a local nonprofit organization. The amount that each patron contributed last year is accurately recorded in a ClarisWorks database. You've decided that to increase contributions this year, you will ask patrons who gave $50 or more last year to consider increasing their donation by 25 percent. If they gave less than $50, you will ask them for the same amount. How can you accomplish this task?

To insert one of two different amounts in a merge:

1. **In the address database, choose Define Fields from the Layout menu (or press Shift-⌘-D).** The Define Fields dialog box appears.
2. **Define a new calculation field that is called Suggested Contribution.** Use the following formula for the field:

   ```
   IF('Last Year Contribution'>=50,'Last Year
   Contribution'*1.25,'Last Year Contribution')
   ```

   The result is formatted as a number. The formula checks the amount in the field named Last Year Contribution. If it is greater than $50, the amount is multiplied by 1.25 to increase the amount by 25 percent. Otherwise, the contents of the Last Year Contribution field are copied directly into the Suggested Contribution field.

3. In the form letter, insert the Suggested Contribution field in the line of text where you suggest a donation amount, as in the following line:

```
Based on your generous contribution last year, we suggest a
donation of «Suggested Contribution».
```

NOTE

You do not need to place the calculation field in the database layout. As long as you have properly defined a field, you can use it in the database as a placeholder in a merge form — whether or not it is visible in the layout.

Summary

- A merge requires two components: a database and a word processing document (or text frame). Information from the database fields is inserted into field placeholders in the merge document.
- You need to surround every merge field name with brackets («»). You can type them or insert them automatically by selecting the field names from the Mail Merge dialog box.
- Punctuation and spaces can separate merge fields from each other, as well as from surrounding text. You also can apply formatting, such as different fonts and styles, to the merge fields.
- In a merge, every visible database record produces its own merge document. You can restrict the number of records by using the Find or Match Records commands. You also can arrange the records in a particular order by using the Sort Records command.

Topic 10

Using the Spreadsheet to Create Charts and Tables for a Report

Overview

Only a few high-end word processing programs include a special feature for laying out tables. When you use a word processor without such a feature, your only recourse is to set a series of tabs and use them to format a table. Although you also can use tabs to create tables in the ClarisWorks word processor, a better way to make the table is to use a spreadsheet frame. This method enables you to reap the benefits of working in an environment that can not only format text but also understand and manipulate numbers.

This Topic discusses procedures essential to creating, sizing, and positioning tables. For other spreadsheet functions (to format the table or work with formulas, for example), refer to Topic 5.

TIP

This Topic explains how to add a spreadsheet table or chart to a word processing document. Because of the tight integration of ClarisWorks environments, however, you can apply the techniques that are described in this Topic in the other environments as well — in paint or draw documents, for example.

Spreadsheet Tables

Although you can design a spreadsheet table in the spreadsheet environment, creating a spreadsheet frame in the word processing document is simpler. This method also enables you to tell whether the table is the correct size for the document.

To create a spreadsheet table:

1. **Open an existing word processing document or create a new one by choosing the appropriate command from the File menu (Open or New).**
2. **If the Tool panel isn't visible, click the Show/Hide Tools control at the bottom of the document window.**
3. **Select the Spreadsheet tool (the large plus symbol near the top of the Tool panel).**
4. **To create the table, click where you want the upper-left corner to start and then drag down and to the right.** When you release the mouse button, a new spreadsheet frame appears, as shown in Figure 10-1.

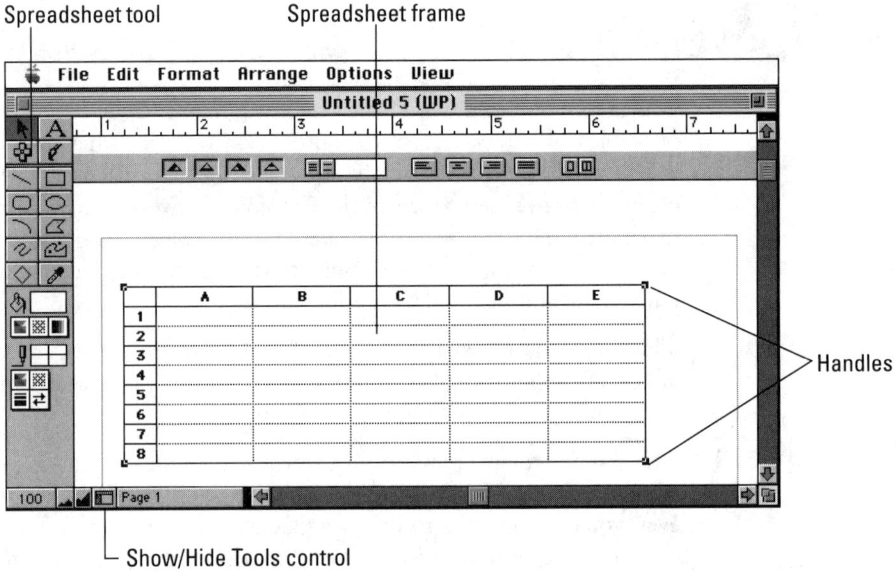

Figure 10-1: A new spreadsheet frame.

Don't be overly concerned about the initial appearance or dimensions of the table. You can change its size, the number of columns and rows, column widths, and row heights as needed.

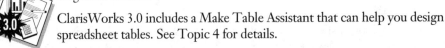

ClarisWorks 3.0 includes a Make Table Assistant that can help you design spreadsheet tables. See Topic 4 for details.

Entering data

To enter text and data into the spreadsheet table, click the table once to select it and then click any cell in the table. The cell that you selected has a dark border around it. You can now enter data in that cell or anywhere else in the spreadsheet.

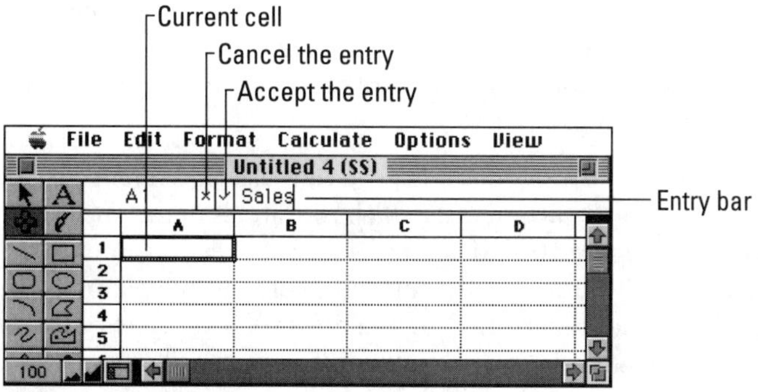

Figure 10-2: Entering data in a cell.

As you type an entry for a cell, text or numbers appear in the *entry bar*, which is shown in Figure 10-2. To accept the entry, click the check mark (which is the *accept* button), press Enter, press Return, press an arrow key, or press Tab or Shift-Tab.

In ClarisWorks 2.1, pressing an arrow key while editing a cell just changes the text insertion point. To accept an entry, press Option-arrow.

In ClarisWorks 3.0, the functions of the arrow and Option-arrow keys are defined in the spreadsheet preferences (see Topic 12).

Clicking the check mark or pressing Enter accepts the entry but leaves the cursor in the current cell. The other options (Return, arrow key, Tab, and Shift-Tab) accept the entry as well, but they move the cursor to a new cell, as described in Table 10-1.

Table 10-1
Cell Navigation

Key	***Movement***
Return	To the cell immediately below
Right arrow (Option-right arrow in 2.1) or Tab	To the cell immediately to the right
Left arrow (Option-left arrow in 2.1) or Shift-Tab	To the cell immediately to the left
Down arrow (Option-down arrow in 2.1)	To the cell immediately below
Up arrow (Option-up arrow in 2.1)	To the cell immediately above
Enter	No movement

You also can use the keys in Table 10-1 for pure cursor movements. If you are not entering data, pressing these keys simply moves the cursor in the direction stated.

You can move directly to any cell by clicking it with the mouse. In many cases, this method is the quickest way to get to any cell in the table that is not adjacent to the current cell.

NOTE: You also can choose the Go To Cell command from the Options menu (or press ⌘-G) and specify the coordinates of the desired cell (A7, for example) in the dialog box that appears. Because most tables are rather small, however, clicking a cell to select it is usually easier.

TIP: For fast data entry in contiguous cells, you can select a cell range by Shift-clicking (see Figure 10-3). The current cell (which is white) is in the upper-left corner of each selection in Figure 10-3. If you press *Return* after you enter the data for each cell, the current cell automatically shifts on a column-by-column basis, as shown in the table at the top of Figure 10-3. If you press *Enter* or *Tab* as you complete each cell entry, the current cell automatically shifts on a row-by-row basis, as shown in the table at the bottom of Figure 10-3.

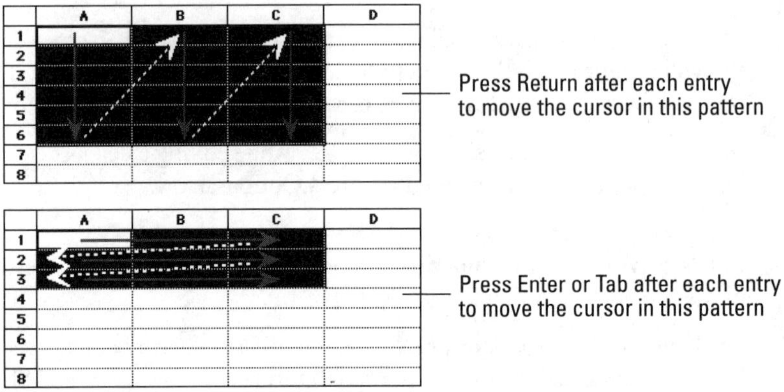

Press Return after each entry
to move the cursor in this pattern
Press Enter or Tab after each entry
to move the cursor in this pattern

Figure 10-3: Entering data into a selection of cells.

Changing the appearance of the table

By using the mouse and menu commands, you can make any of the following changes to the appearance of the table:

- Change individual row heights and column widths
- Change the number of columns or rows that are displayed
- Make text wrap within selected cells
- Display or hide the cell gridlines, column letters, and row numbers

Step-by-Steps

To change the number of columns or rows that are displayed:

1. **Click the spreadsheet table once to select it.** Handles appear at its four corners, and the cursor changes to a pointer.
2. **Click one of the table's handles and then drag.** When you release the mouse button, the table reforms and displays only the columns and rows that you have indicated.

NOTE Many finished tables look better if you hide the column and row headings (as described later in this Topic). If hiding the headings leaves an extra blank row at the bottom and a blank column at the right end of the table, you may need to resize the table again after you hide the row and column headings.

To change row heights and column widths:

1. **Click the spreadsheet table once to select it.** Handles appear at its four corners, and the cursor changes to a pointer.
2. **Select any cell in the column or row whose height or width you want to change.** You click the cell to select it.
3. **From the Format menu, choose Column Width or Row Height, as appropriate.** The Column width or Row height dialog box appears. Figure 10-4 shows the Column width dialog box.

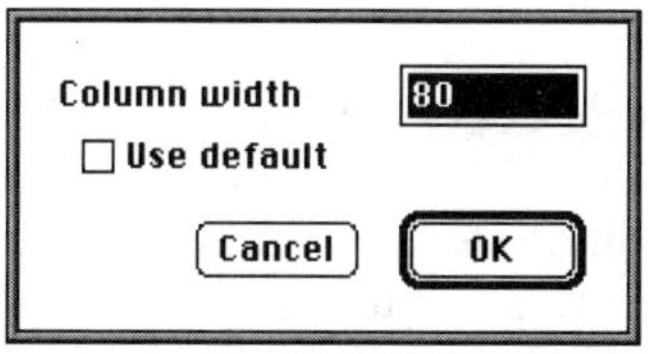

Figure 10-4: The Column width dialog box.

4. **Enter a new number for the width or height.** Numbers are shown in points rather than in characters. (Points are often used for measuring type. An inch contains 72 points.)
5. **Click OK.** The new column width or row height is put into effect.

Changing column widths or row heights manually by using the mouse may be easier.

To change row heights and column widths manually:

1. **Click the spreadsheet table once to select it.** Handles appear at the four corners, and the cursor changes to a pointer.
2. **Move the pointer into the heading area for the column or row whose height or width you want to change.** As the cursor moves over the right edge of the column or the bottom edge of the row, a special, two-headed pointer appears, as shown in Figure 10-5.
3. **While pressing the mouse button, drag to change the column width or row height.**
4. **When the width or height is correct, release the mouse button.**

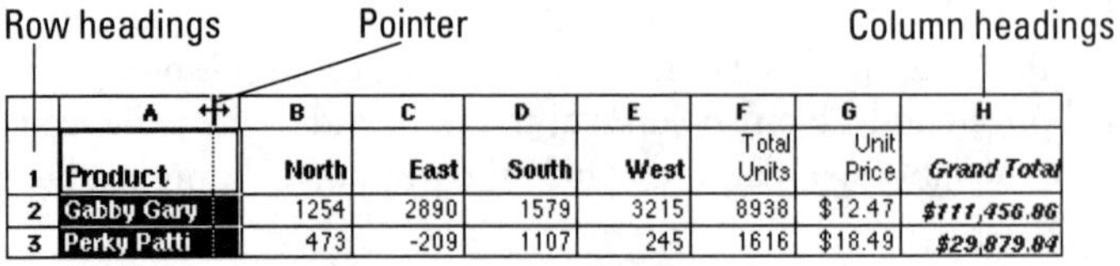

Row headings
Pointer
Column headings
A
B
C
D
E
F
G
H
1 Product
North
East
South
West
Total Units
Unit Price
Grand Total
2 Gabby Gary
1254
2890
1579
3215
8938
$12.47
$111,456.86
3 Perky Patti
473
-209
1107
245
1616
$18.49
$29,879.84

Figure 10-5: Changing the width of a column manually.

TIP

When a text string is too long to fit in a cell, it spills into adjacent empty cells. (The direction in which it spills depends on the original cell's Alignment setting.) To keep the entire string in its original cell, you can either widen the column (as described previously) or format the text to wrap within the cell.

You also can use either of these procedures to change the width or height of several columns or rows simultaneously. You simply Shift-click to select a series of contiguous columns or rows and then proceed as usual. When you're done, all of the selected rows or columns have identical widths or heights, respectively.

To make text wrap within selected cells:

1. **Click the spreadsheet table once to select it.** Handles appear at the four corners, and the cursor changes to a pointer.
2. **Select the cell or cells to which you want to apply the Wrap format.**
3. **Choose Wrap from the Alignment submenu in the Format menu.**

If the text no longer fits in the cell (some of it may be clipped at the bottom of the cell), you can change the row height by using either of the methods described previously.

To display or hide the cell gridlines, column letters, and row numbers:

1. **Click the spreadsheet table once to select it.** Handles appear at the four corners, and the cursor changes to a pointer.
2. **Click in any cell of the spreadsheet.** The spreadsheet menus appear in the menu bar.
3. **Choose Display from the Options menu.** The Display dialog box appears, as shown in Figure 10-6.

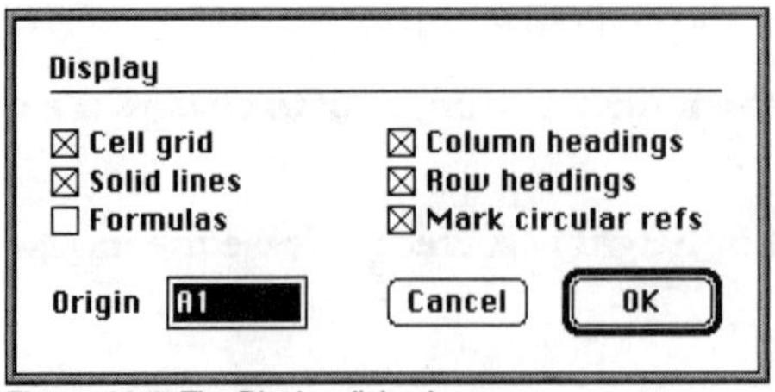

Figure 10-6: The Display dialog box.

4. **Select or deselect the display options by clicking the check boxes.** To change the table's appearance, consider these important options:

   - *Cell grid.* When this option is checked, the cell separators are dotted grid lines. When it is unchecked, lines do not appear.
   - *Solid lines.* When this option is checked, the cell separators are solid grid lines.
   - *Column headings and Row headings.* If these options are unchecked, you do not see the letters and numbers that the spreadsheet uses to label columns and rows.

5. **Click OK.** The changes in appearance are made.

TIP

You can shorten this procedure slightly by choosing Modify Frame from the Options menu immediately after you select the spreadsheet table in Step 1. In either case, the same Display dialog box appears.

Positioning the table

After you finish entering data and formatting the table, you may want to change the table's position on the page. Up to this point, the spreadsheet frame has been just another object that is floating on the document page. You can leave it that way and, optionally, specify a text wrap for it (remember, it's an object — just like a draw graphic), or you can move it into the text as an in-line graphic. Because ClarisWorks treats in-line graphics as text, you can apply paragraph formatting commands to center the table on the page and separate it from the surrounding paragraphs. Figures 10-7 and 10-8 show the two table treatments.

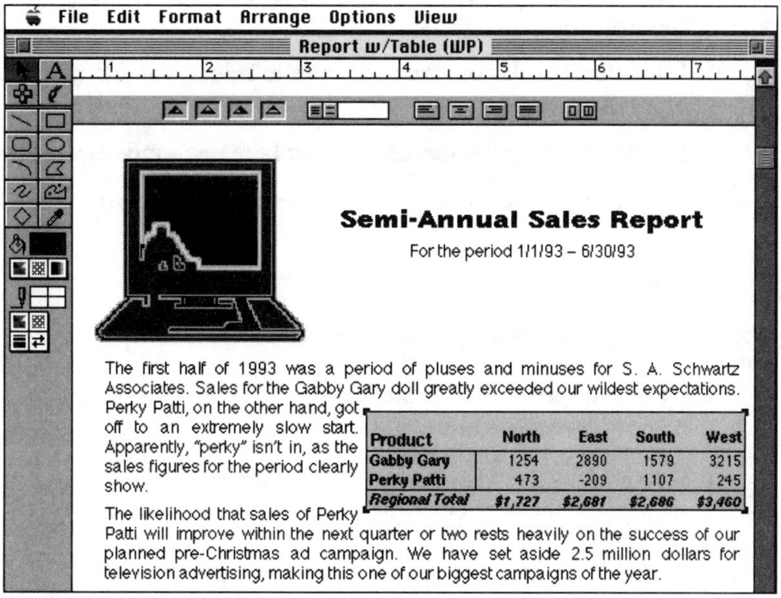

Figure 10-7: A spreadsheet table as an object.

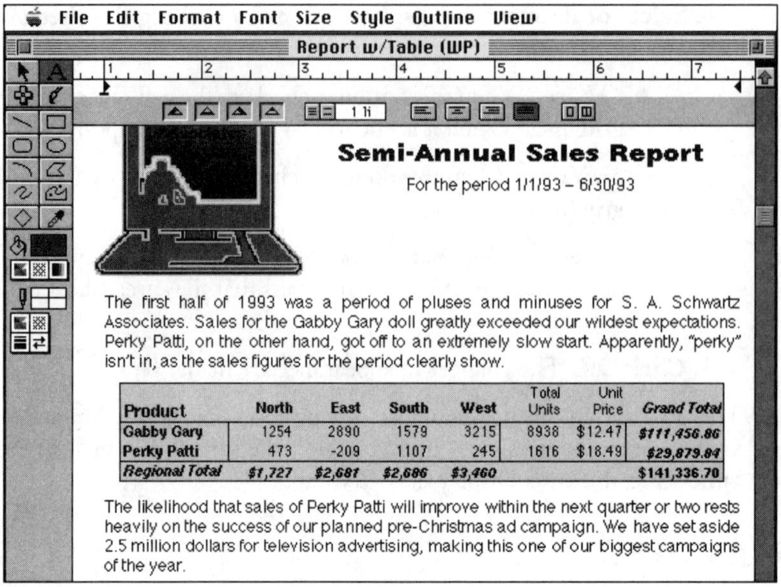

Figure 10-8: A spreadsheet table as an in-line graphic.

To treat a spreadsheet table as an object:

1. **Click the spreadsheet table once to select it.** Handles appear at the corners.
2. **Drag the table to its new position.**
3. **Choose Text wrap from the Options menu.** The Text Wrap dialog box appears.
4. **Click the Regular or Irregular icon to select it and then click OK.** Text near the table wraps around the table.
5. **Continue to drag the spreadsheet until the text wraps exactly as you want.**

NOTE: You can fine-tune the position of the table by pressing the arrow keys.

To treat a spreadsheet table as an in-line graphic:

1. **Click the spreadsheet table once to select it.** Handles appear at the corners.
2. **Choose Cut from the Edit menu (or press ⌘-X).** The spreadsheet is removed, and a copy of it is placed on the Mac's Clipboard.

3. **Click the Text tool (the capital A) and move the text insertion point to where you want to place the table.** (Because formatting is much simpler when the table is in a paragraph by itself, you may want to press Return to create a blank paragraph to receive the table.)

4. **Choose Paste from the Edit menu (or press ⌘-V).** The table is inserted at the text insertion point.

5. ***Optional:* If you want to center the table in its line, place the text insertion point at the end of the paragraph that contains the table and then click the Centered Alignment control in the ruler bar (see Figure 10-9).**

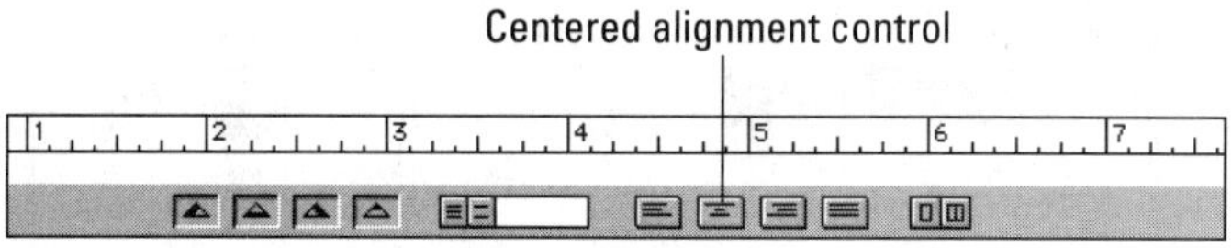

Figure 10-9: Use the Centered Alignment control to center the table.

6. ***Optional:* If you want to add some space between the table and the paragraphs that lie immediately above and below it, place the text insertion point at the end of the paragraph that contains the table. Then choose Paragraph from the Format menu. The Paragraph dialog box appears. Enter new figures for Space before and Space after (1 li, for example) and click OK.** The table is now separated from the surrounding paragraphs by the amount of space that you entered.

Deleting a table

At some point, you may decide that you don't need a table after all. To delete a table, click the table once to select it and then press Delete or Backspace. (If you want to use the table on a different page or in a different document, press ⌘-X or choose Cut from the Edit menu. You can then use the Paste Command to move the table to its new location.)

Spreadsheet Charts

You also can use spreadsheet charts in word processing reports. The major difference between adding a chart and adding a table is that creating the chart in the spreadsheet environment is easier than creating it within a spreadsheet frame in the word processing document.

To add a chart to a word processing document:

1. **Open an existing spreadsheet or create a new one by choosing Open or New from the File menu.**
2. **Select the cell range from which the chart will be created.**
3. **Choose Make Chart from the Options menu.** Figure 10-10 shows the Chart Options dialog box that appears. See Topic 5 for details on creating and modifying charts.

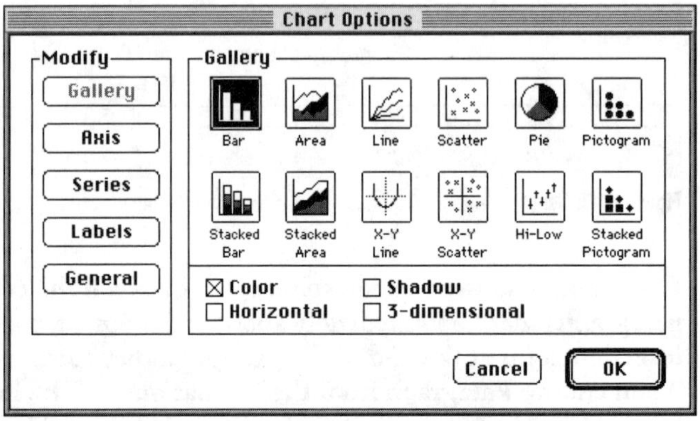

Figure 10-10: To design a chart, select options from the Chart Options dialog box.

4. **Click OK.** The chart appears on the current document page and is automatically selected (note the handles, as shown in Figure 10-11).
5. **Choose Copy from the Edit menu (or press ⌘-C).** A copy of the chart is placed on the Mac Clipboard.
6. **Switch to the word processing document by selecting its name from the list at the bottom of the View menu.** (If it isn't already open, choose Open from the File menu.)
7. **Choose Paste from the Edit menu (or press ⌘-V).** The chart appears in the word processing document.

You can change the chart's position and size, as well as treat it as an object or an in-line graphic, by following the directions given previously for spreadsheet tables.

Any chart pasted into a document in this manner is a static entity. If you later change the chart's spreadsheet, the pasted chart will not reflect the changes. If you want to maintain a link between the spreadsheet and the chart (and you are running System 7), use Publish & Subscribe as described in Topic 20.

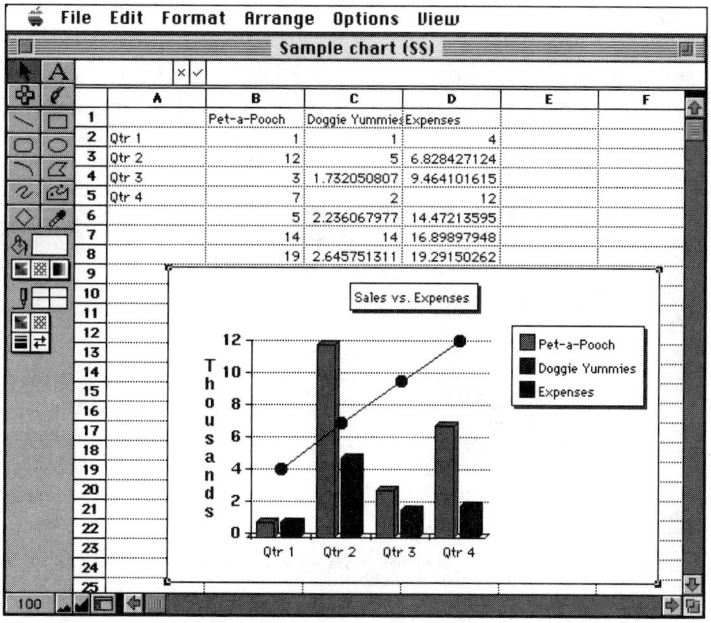

Figure 10-11: A new chart that is created in the spreadsheet environment simply floats on the page.

Quick Tips

The following Quick Tip points out ways that you can use spreadsheet formatting options to make the information in a table clearer and more attractive.

Other table formatting options

As you design the table, keep in mind that you are working in a spreadsheet that happens to be embedded within a word processing document. All the power of the spreadsheet environment can be brought to bear on the table. Not only can you enter calculations and formulas, but you also can choose from additional formatting options, such as the following:

- ◆ Choosing different fonts, styles, sizes, and colors for the text in selected cells
- ◆ Changing the alignment of text and numbers within cells
- ◆ Applying special formats for displaying numbers and dates
- ◆ Sorting cells
- ◆ Adding borders to cells
- ◆ Embellishing the table with background colors, patterns, and graphics

Refer to the instructions in Topic 5 for help in performing these tasks. As an example, Figure 10-12 shows a fully dressed spreadsheet table with multiple fonts, styles, sizes, and alignments; text wrap; background color; selective cell borders; and graphics embellishments (an oval around a number, an arrow, a callout that contains text, and a shadow).

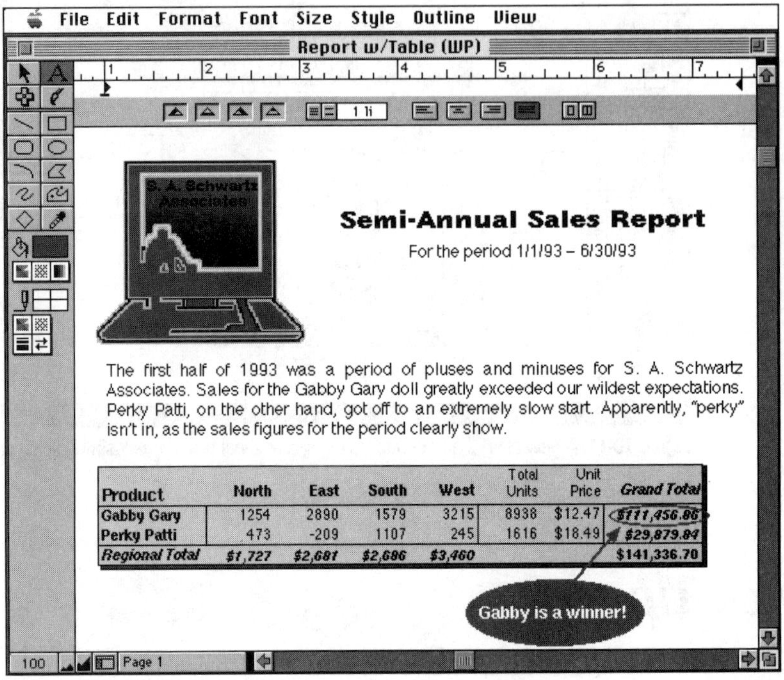

Figure 10-12: An example of a formatted spreadsheet table.

Summary

- Using a spreadsheet frame to make a table in a word processing environment enables you to reap the benefits of working in an environment that can not only format text but also understands and can manipulate numbers.
- Modifying row heights and column widths (to properly display text), changing the table's size, adding text wrap for some cells, and hiding row and column headings are some common changes that users make to spreadsheet tables.
- You can change column widths and row heights manually, or you can change them by entering numbers in a dialog box. Changing them manually is often more accurate and more direct than choosing menu commands.
- Like spreadsheet tables, charts can also be used to dress up a text-based report or memo.
- You can position tables and charts as floating objects (with text wrap) or as in-line graphics, which are subject to regular paragraph formatting commands. Both approaches work well.

Part IV

Advanced Topics

Topic 11

Using Stationery Documents and Assistants

Overview

When you have a document that you work with frequently but usually need to modify somewhat, the best way to save it is as a *stationery document* rather than as a normal ClarisWorks file. A stationery document is a template. It can include static text and graphics, as well as placeholders for other text elements that you intend to change each time you use the stationery document. An example of a document that would make a good stationery file is a letterhead template. In the template, you can include your return address, a date stamp (so you never have to enter the date manually), a standard salutation, and a closing. Then, whenever you want to write a new letter, you just open the stationery file, enter the addressee's name and address, and fill in the body of the text. Figure 11-1 shows a typical stationery document.

Figure 11-1: A fax template that was saved as a stationery document.

Assistants, intelligent helpers that make performing complex tasks in ClarisWorks a snap, are a new feature of ClarisWorks 3.0. Because you choose all stationery documents and many of the Assistants from the New Document dialog box, they are discussed together in this topic.

Stationery Documents versus Normal ClarisWorks Documents

Of course, you don't *have* to save a template as a stationery file. You can save it as a normal ClarisWorks document. However, if you accidentally issue the Save command while you are working with a template that is not a stationery file, you will replace the template with a filled-in copy of the letterhead, fax, or whatever type of document you are working on. Bye-bye, template. . . .

Saving the template as a stationery document protects you from this kind of mistake. When you open a ClarisWorks stationery file, you're opening a copy of the file, rather than the original. In fact, ClarisWorks treats the document that appears on-screen just as it treats a file that you create with the New command. It even names the file *Untitled* to remind you that it's not the original.

Creating Stationery Documents

You can easily create a stationery document from any ClarisWorks file.

To save a document as stationery:

1. **Choose Save As from the File menu.** The standard Save file dialog box appears.

2. **In ClarisWorks 2.0 or 2.1, choose Stationery from the Save As pop-up menu.**

— or —

2. **In ClarisWorks 3.0, click the Stationery radio button.**

3. **Enter a name for the document.**

4. **Save the stationery document to the desired folder.**

   If you want to be able to choose the stationery document from the Stationery pop-up menu in the New Document dialog box, save it in the ClarisWorks Stationery folder. (As Figure 11-2 shows, the ClarisWorks Stationery folder is located inside the Claris folder within the System Folder on the hard disk.) Any ClarisWorks stationery file that you save or move into this folder is automatically added to the Stationery pop-up menu, and you can choose it when you issue the New command. (In ClarisWorks 3.0, this folder is automatically chosen when you click the Stationery radio button.)

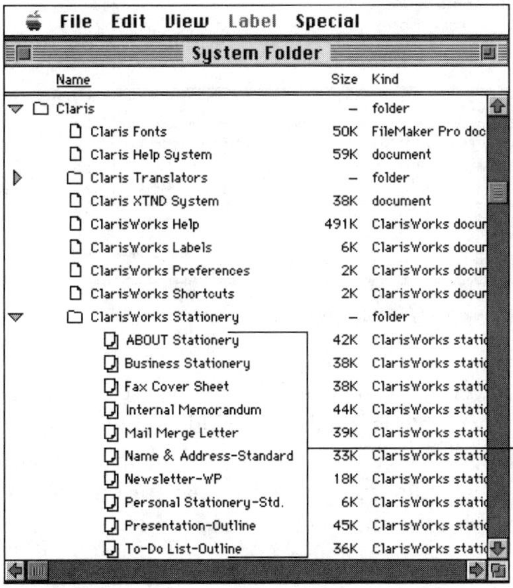

Documents in the ClarisWorks Stationery folder

Figure 11-2: The location of the ClarisWorks Stationery folder (as shown in System 7 with View By Name).

Of course, as with any other documents, you can save stationery files anywhere you choose. If you save them in a different location, they still function as stationery documents, but you have to load them by using the Open command from the File menu, rather than the New command.

NOTE

ClarisWorks enables you to set preferences (such as the date format to be used and palette options) that you can save with the current document. When you open the document, its preference settings override the normal ClarisWorks preferences. If you set preferences for a document and then save it as stationery, this rule still applies. Whenever you open a copy of the stationery document, any preferences settings that you have set for the document take precedence over the ClarisWorks preferences. For additional information on preferences, see Topic 12.

Special Considerations When Saving ClarisWorks 3.0 Stationery Documents

NEW FEATURE 3.0

When you save a ClarisWorks 3.0 document as a stationery file, it is presented in the New Document dialog box according to the information (or lack of it) that you have provided for the file in the Document Summary dialog box (see Figure 11-3). To ensure that you can easily find and promptly identify your stationery document, choose Document Summary Info from the File menu *prior to saving the file.* Be sure to fill in the following items:

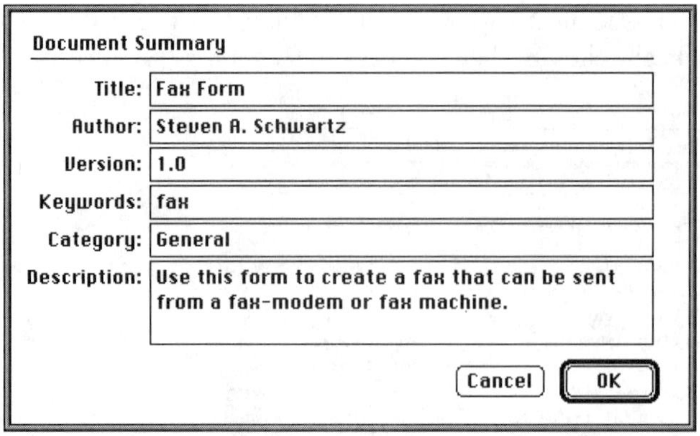

Figure 11-3: The Document Summary dialog box.

- *Category.* Whatever text you enter here will be used as the category in which the stationery document is listed. To include the file in an existing category (General, Home, or Small Business, for example), type that category name. You also can create a new category (Personal, for instance), or you can simply lump the file in with all other unclassified stationery documents (shown as None) by not listing any category.
- *Description.* This descriptive text appears whenever the stationery file is highlighted in the file list.

Other items in the Document Summary dialog box are optional. They do not affect the presentation of stationery files in the New Document dialog box. For additional information about the Document Summary dialog box, see "Saving New Files" in Topic 2.

Opening a Stationery Document

You open a stationery document in precisely the same way as you open any other document:

- Select it from the file list that ClarisWorks presents when you choose Open from the File menu (or press ⌘-O).
- Double-click the document icon on the desktop to launch ClarisWorks and open the document simultaneously.
- If the template is one that came with the program or one that you saved in the ClarisWorks Stationery folder, choose the template from the Stationery pop-up menu (shown in Figure 11-4) when you launch ClarisWorks or create a new file with the New command in ClarisWorks 2.0 or 2.1. In ClarisWorks 3.0, on the other hand, the New Document dialog box contains a Start with an Assistant or Stationery button that you can click to see several categories of stationery documents that you can open (see Figure 11-5).

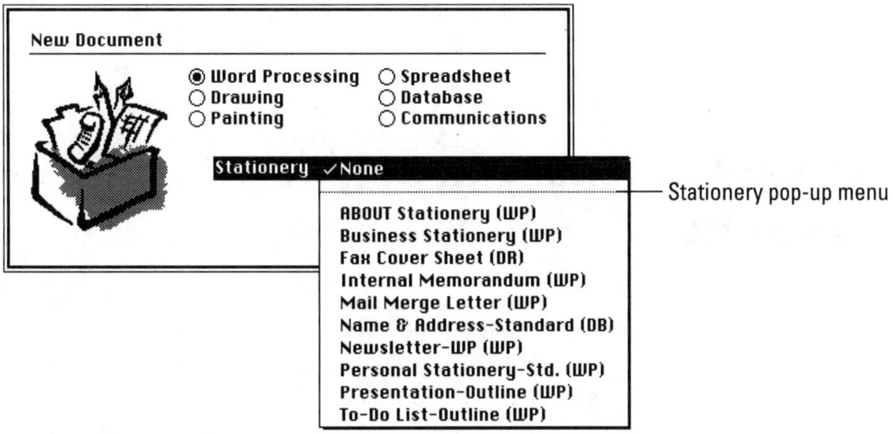

Figure 11-4: You can open many stationery documents from the Stationery pop-up menu in the New Document dialog box. The stationery documents shown here are included with ClarisWorks 2.

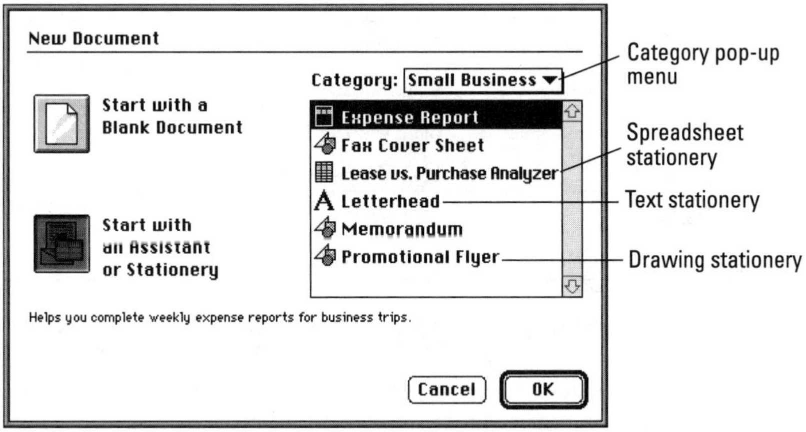

Figure 11-5: In ClarisWorks 3.0, you choose a document classification from the Category pop-up menu and then choose a stationery file to open.

Making a New Version of a Stationery Document

After you open a copy of a stationery document, you can edit the document and then save it under a new name, or you can simply close the file without saving it if you don't need a copy on disk. If, on the other hand, you've modified the stationery file with the intent of making a new, improved template, you can save the new file over the old one by typing the original stationery filename and choosing

Stationery again from the Save As pop-up menu (or by clicking the Stationery radio button in ClarisWorks 3.0). Click Replace when the program asks whether you want to replace the original file.

Using Stationary to Set New Environment Defaults

Although the Preferences command on the Edit menu enables you to set a handful of default options for several environments (see Topic 12), you can add many more settings as defaults so that they are automatically in effect whenever you create a new document. To add setting as defaults, simply create a document that contains the new default settings and then save it as a specially named stationery document in the Claris folder within the System Folder on the hard disk. Claris refers to these special documents as *ClarisWorks options stationery.* To save documents as options stationery, you need to name the files as follows:

Environment	***Name of Options Stationery Document***
Word Processing	ClarisWorks WP Options
Drawing	ClarisWorks DR Options
Painting	ClarisWorks PT Options
Spreadsheet	ClarisWorks SS Options
Database	ClarisWorks DB Options
Communications	ClarisWorks CM Options

For example, to make the word processing environment open new documents with my defaults, I created a blank stationery document, set the starting font to Times, defined four frequently used text styles, and added the styles to the Style menu. Now every new word processing document defaults to the Times font, and the four text styles are always available.

You can create your own options stationery documents with the defaults that you prefer. Note, however, that you can have only one options stationery document for each environment. If you want to change an existing options stationery document, the procedure is to save the new one over the old one — replacing it.

Step-by-Steps

To create an environment options stationery document:

1. **Choose New from the Edit menu.**
2. **Click the radio button for the environment of your choice and click OK.** A blank document appears.
3. **Set options for the document (and, if you want to, set preferences by using the Preferences command from the Edit menu).**

4. **Choose Save As from the File menu.** The normal file dialog box appears.
5. **Choose Stationery from the Save As pop-up menu (or, in ClarisWorks 3.0, click the Stationery radio button).**
6. **Use the Desktop button (System 7) or the Drive button (System 6) and then the folder pop-up menu to navigate to the Claris folder within the System Folder on the hard disk, which is shown in Figure 11-6.** (In ClarisWorks 3.0, you go to the Claris folder automatically.)

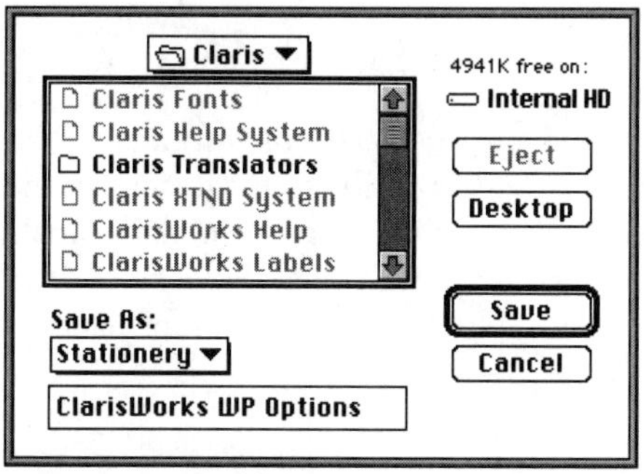

Figure 11-6: The ClarisWorks 2.0/2.1 file dialog box just before you click the Save button to create an options stationery document for the word processor.

7. **Name the file according to the conventions listed previously for saving options stationery.**
8. **Click Save.**

After you save an options stationery document, ClarisWorks adds it to the Stationery pop-up menu in the New Document dialog box (see Figure 11-7 for an example from ClarisWorks 2.0/2.1).

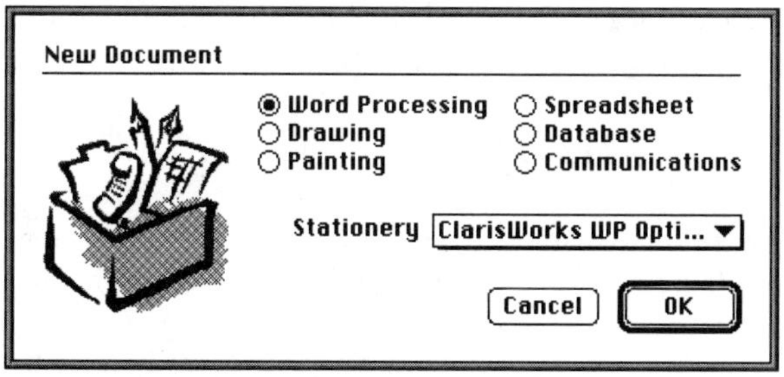

Figure 11-7: Any environment that contains an options stationery document presents that file as the new default in the Stationery pop-up menu (in place of the "None" choice).

If you have ClarisWorks 2.1 or a later version and are using PowerTalk messaging (refer to Topic 21), you can create a new type of options stationery document, called a *reply stationery document*, that ClarisWorks opens automatically whenever you choose the Reply command or choose the Reply shortcut (see Figure 11-8) to answer a message. (To learn more about shortcuts, refer to Topic 13).

Figure 11-8: The Reply shortcut.

Create your reply stationery in a word processing document, adding graphics and text elements as desired. Do not add a mailer to the document, however. Then save the document as a ClarisWorks Stationery file in the ClarisWorks Stationery folder (inside the Claris folder within the System Folder). In order to work, the stationery file must be named Reply. For additional information, see "Creating a reply stationery document" in Topic 21.

Using the ClarisWorks Assistants

ClarisWorks 3.0 includes eight Assistants, each designed to perform a specific task for you. You choose the majority of the Assistants in the New Document dialog box, and they create new documents. You need to invoke the other Assistants from within an existing document.

Each Assistant is self-explanatory. When you invoke an Assistant, you see a list on-screen of any preparatory steps that you need to perform, such as selecting a text insertion point or highlighting an address. Each Assistant is presented as a dialog box or a series of dialog boxes. You move forward (Next) and backward (Back) through the dialog boxes by clicking buttons. After you make selections from the pop-up menus, set necessary options, and type text entries, you click Create, Done, or Start (as appropriate) to make the Assistant execute.

New Document Assistants

You can choose five of the Assistants from the New Document dialog box. Each of these Assistants produces a new document that is created according to your specifications.

After you click the Start with an Assistant or Stationery button, you see the new document Assistants within the General category (see Figure 11-9). They include the following:

- *Name & Address List.* Creates a personal, business, or student name and address database.

- *Calendar.* Creates a single-month or multiple-month calendar. Each month is a separate ClarisWorks spreadsheet.

- *Envelope.* Creates a word processing document formatted as a business envelope (with an addressee and a return address).

- *Newsletter.* Designs a newsletter or informational booklet in a variety of styles with placeholders for copy.

- *Presentation.* Generates elaborate, multipage presentation templates that can be displayed on-screen, shown on an overhead projector, or printed.

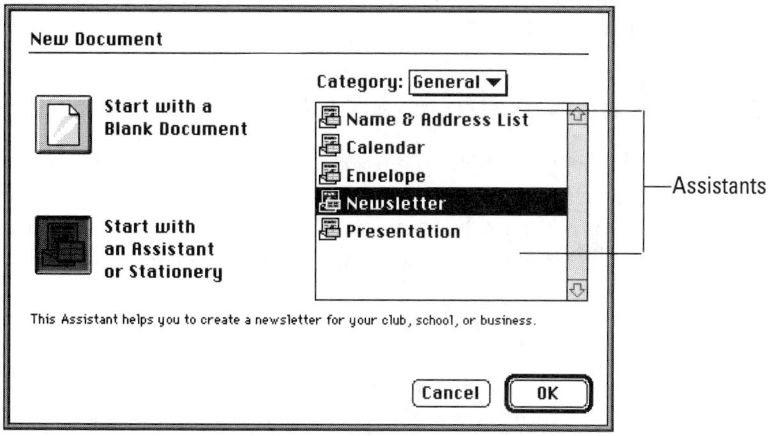

Figure 11-9: Selecting a New Document Assistant.

Other Assistants

You invoke three additional Assistants from within open ClarisWorks documents rather than from the New Document dialog box. To select one of these Assistants, choose ClarisWorks Assistants from the Help submenu of the Apple menu or from the Balloon Help menu (System 7 only):

- *Insert Footnote.* Adds a footnote to a word processing document, correctly formatted in the chosen style. See Topic 4, "Using the Word Processing Assistants," for instructions.

- *Make Table.* Adds a spreadsheet table to a word processing document, a draw document, or a database (in Layout mode only). See Topic 4, "Using the Word Processing Assistants," for instructions.

- *Address Envelope.* Copies the highlighted address from a word processing document and creates a new document that is formatted as a business envelope. You do not need to type the address information manually, as you do for the Envelope Assistant. Instead, the Address Envelope Assistant uses information that is already present in the document. See "Using the Word Processing Assistants," in Topic 4 for instructions.

The final Assistant, Find ClarisWorks Documents, helps you locate files to open. You can invoke it regardless of whether a document is on-screen. (Choose ClarisWorks Assistants from the Help submenu of the Apple menu or from the Balloon Help menu.) After you specify the criteria, this Assistant searches the current drive and lists all matching files. You can then open found files from within the Assistant. See Topic 2 for a more detailed discussion of this Assistant.

Quick Tips

The following Quick Tips suggest some practical applications for stationery documents.

More ideas for stationery documents

Any file that you intend to reuse can be a stationery document. Keep in mind, however, that if you never intend to alter the base document, saving it as a stationery file is pointless. For example, if you have a letter that you always send without changes, you can save it as a normal ClarisWorks file and simply reprint it as often as you like.

Here are a few more ideas for stationery documents:

- *Fax form or cover sheet.* Remove everything but the static information (the logo, return address, and phone number and the reserved areas for the date, subject, number of pages, recipient's name, and fax number) from your normal fax form or cover sheet (which is probably a word processing document). Then use the Insert Date command in the Edit menu to enter the date so that whenever you open a copy of the stationery document, the current date will be filled in automatically.
- *Letterhead.* If you have a laser or ink-jet printer, you can save money by printing your own letterhead.
- *Envelope templates.* Laser and ink-jet printers (such as the StyleWriter and HP DeskWriter) can easily handle envelope printing. Design templates that address different sizes of envelopes when you print in landscape mode (sideways).
- *Weekly, monthly, quarterly, or annual spreadsheets.* Many spreadsheets are reusable. (I keep my personal financial records in one, for example.) Open the spreadsheet and remove all the data, being sure to leave cells that contain labels or formulas intact. Then save the spreadsheet under a new name as a stationery document. Whenever the new week, month, quarter, or year begins, you open a copy of the template and plug in the new numbers. You can use the same tactic for record-keeping database templates.
- *Business forms.* Templates are perfect for standard business forms, such as invoices, statements, petty cash vouchers, and the like.

- *Contracts.* Most legal documents, whether they are wills, leases, or terms of work-for-hire, consist largely of standard language. By saving any of them as stationery, you can dramatically reduce writing time on subsequent contracts.
- *Common communication settings.* You can create a general-purpose communications stationery document that contains the options you most frequently use for the baud rate, transfer protocol, and so on. Most on-line sessions will require only slight modifications from the settings in the template.

Summary

- Save files as stationery documents when you want to use them as templates.
- When you open a stationery document, a copy of it is loaded into memory — protecting the original from unintentional modifications.
- When you launch ClarisWorks or create a new file, you can select any stationery document in the ClarisWorks Stationery folder from the Stationery pop-up menu (ClarisWorks 2.0/2.1), or you can select it by clicking the Start with an Assistant or Stationery button (ClarisWorks 3.0.).
- You can set defaults for any environment by designing a ClarisWorks options stationery document and following a special convention for naming the document when you save it in the Claris folder.

Topic 12

Setting Preferences

Overview

By setting preferences, you can customize ClarisWorks to fit the way you work. To view the current preferences settings or change them, choose Preferences from the Edit menu. The Preferences dialog box appears (see Figure 12-1). The left side of the Preferences dialog box contains icons that represent the different parts of ClarisWorks that you can customize. Each time you click an icon, a set of options for that particular program function appears in the right side of the dialog box. The four areas for which you can set preferences in ClarisWorks 2 are text, graphics, palettes, and communications.

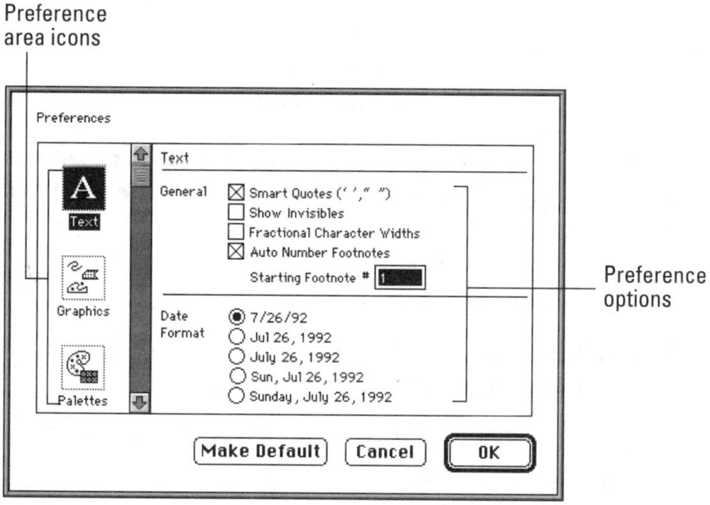

Figure 12-1: The Preferences dialog box, with options for text preferences.

VERSION 2.1

ClarisWorks 2.1 adds a fifth preference area: mail. (***Note:*** This area appears only if you are using System 7.5, System 7 Pro, or a later version of the system software.)

NEW FEATURE 3.0

ClarisWorks 3.0 adds two preference areas of its own: general and spreadsheet.

Default and Document-Specific Preferences

In ClarisWorks, you can set preferences in two ways. You can create a group of *default preferences* to be used automatically for all new documents in the current session and in future sessions. Or you can set *document-specific preferences* that apply to one document and are saved with that document.

Step-by-Steps

To set new default preferences:

1. **Choose Preferences from the Edit menu.**
2. **Click an icon on the left side of the Preferences dialog box to select the type of preferences settings that you want to modify.**
3. **Change the settings in the right side of the dialog box as desired.**
4. **Repeat Steps 2 and 3 for any other preferences that you want to change.**
5. **Click Make Default.**

The new preferences become the default settings for all new documents that you create in this session and in future sessions.

Step-by-Steps

To set document-specific preferences:

1. **Select the document whose preferences you want to set, making it the *active document* (bringing it to the front if you have two or more open documents).** You can use a document that you have just created or one that you have loaded from disk.
2. **Choose Preferences from the Edit menu.**
3. **Click an icon on the left side of the dialog box to select the type of preferences settings that you want to modify.**
4. **Change the settings in the right side of the dialog box as desired.**
5. **Click OK.**

The new settings apply only to the current document. Other new documents that you create in the session will still use the default settings, unless you also set preferences for them. Because preferences settings are saved with each document, the next time you run ClarisWorks 2 and open the document, the preferences will be intact.

NOTE

Preferences also are stored with files that you save as stationery documents.

General Preferences

You use general preferences to customize many of the basic options in ClarisWorks (see Figure 12-2), such as whether warnings are displayed and how graphics files are shown in Open dialog boxes and on the desktop. You also use general preferences to set the startup action for ClarisWorks.

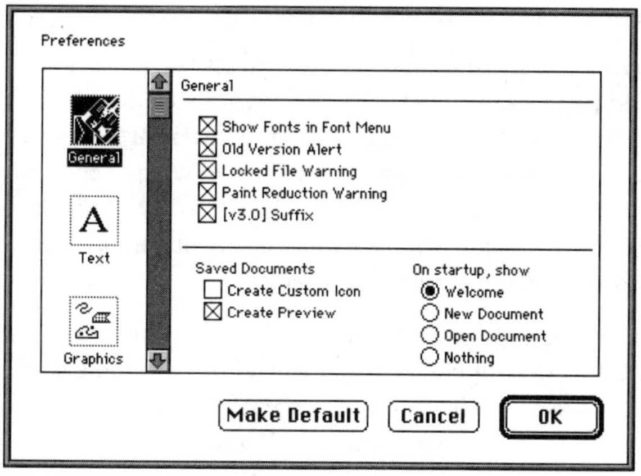

Figure 12-2: General preferences.

Although you normally use the Make Default and OK buttons to modify the ClarisWorks default and document-specific preferences settings, the OK button has a different function when you use it in conjunction with general preferences. Clicking OK puts the changed settings into effect for the entire session (until you quit the program), rather than just for the current document. For example, if you click the Create Custom Icon check box and then click OK, a custom icon will automatically be created for every draw or paint document that you save during the session. In the next ClarisWorks session, however, you'll find that the Create Custom Icon setting has been turned off again. To set new general preferences as *permanent* defaults, click the Make Default button.

General preferences settings include the following:

- *Show Fonts in Font Menu.* Shows font names in their respective typefaces in the Font submenu of the Format menu.
- *Old Version Alert.* Displays a warning message whenever a file created in an earlier version of the program is opened.
- *Locked File Warning.* Displays a warning whenever a locked file is opened. (Locked files can be read but not altered.) To unlock a file, quit ClarisWorks, select the file's icon on the desktop, press ⌘-I, remove the check mark from the Locked check box, and click the close box.

- *Paint Reduction Warning.* Warns when there is insufficient memory to create a full-page paint document. The document will be created at a reduced size. (See Quick Tips at the end of Topic 2 for instructions on avoiding this situation by increasing the memory allocation for ClarisWorks.)
- *[v3.0] Suffix.* Appends this suffix to the name of any file you open that was created with an earlier version of ClarisWorks. Because adding the suffix changes the filename, this option protects the original file from being overwritten by mistake.
- *Saved Documents.* This pair of check boxes affects the handling of graphics files (draw and paint) only. Click Create Custom Icon to instruct ClarisWorks to create file icons that are miniature representations of the images. This special icon is automatically created whenever a graphics file is saved. Click Create Preview to tell ClarisWorks to save a thumbnail preview of each image. The preview will be shown in the dialog box that appears when you choose Open from the File menu.
- *On startup, show.* Determines what you see first each time you launch ClarisWorks. The default choice is to display the Welcome screen — from which you can choose to view a guided tour of the program, create a new document, or open an existing document. If you normally begin each session by starting a new document or opening an existing one, you can click the New Document or Open Document radio button. If your initial action varies from one session to the next, you are better off clicking the Welcome or Nothing button; either choice enables you to select an appropriate startup action for each session.

NOTE

Clicking the “Don’t show this screen anymore” check box at the bottom of the Welcome screen has the same effect as choosing New Document in the general preferences. Instead of seeing the Welcome screen in future sessions, you go directly to the New Document dialog box.

Text Preferences

Text preferences apply to any text that you type in a ClarisWorks document, regardless of the environment you’re in. Figure 12-1 shows the options for text preferences.

Text preferences options include the following:

- *Smart Quotes.* With Smart Quotes enabled, ClarisWorks automatically translates your presses of the ' or " key into *curly quotes* (‘’ and “”), as shown in Figure 12-3. Smart Quotes are applied intelligently. In most cases, the program can correctly determine when a right-facing or left-facing quotation mark is appropriate.

NOTE

Curly quotes are preferred in modern correspondence and publications. Correct uses for straight quotes include displaying feet (') and inches (") in measurements.

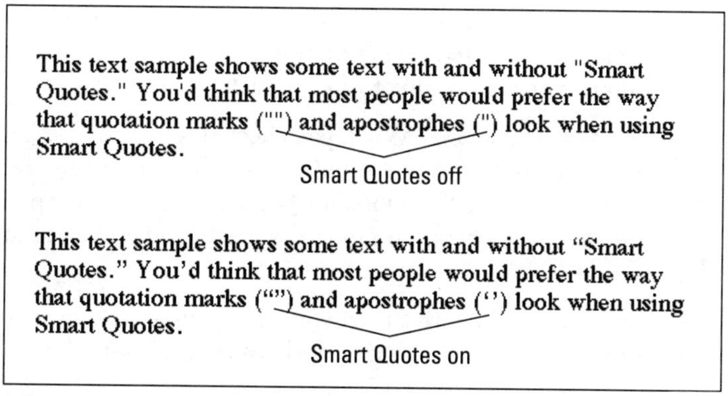

This text sample shows some text with and without "Smart Quotes." You'd think that most people would prefer the way that quotation marks ("") and apostrophes (') look when using Smart Quotes.
Smart Quotes off
This text sample shows some text with and without “Smart Quotes.” You’d think that most people would prefer the way that quotation marks (“”) and apostrophes (‘’) look when using Smart Quotes.
Smart Quotes on

Figure 12-3: Examples of the Smart Quotes settings.

TIP

To manually type curly quote characters (when Smart Quotes is off), use these keys:

Character	*Key*
“	Option-[
”	Shift-Option-[
‘	Option-]
’	Shift-Option-]

- *Show Invisibles.* When this option is checked, you can see characters that are normally invisible, such as tabs, spaces, and end-of-paragraph markers (see Figure 12-4). Turning this option on after you finish a report or letter makes clean-up editing simpler. For example, it enables you to find extra spaces between words. You also can toggle this option off and on in the shortcuts palette.

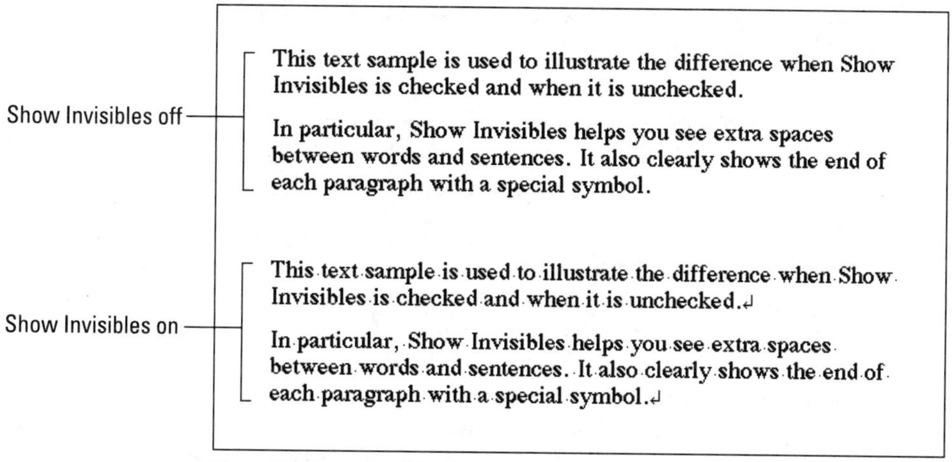

Show Invisibles off
This text sample is used to illustrate the difference when Show Invisibles is checked and when it is unchecked.
In particular, Show Invisibles helps you see extra spaces between words and sentences. It also clearly shows the end of each paragraph with a special symbol.
Show Invisibles on
This·text·sample·is·used·to·illustrate·the·difference·when·Show· Invisibles·is·checked·and·when·it·is·unchecked.↵
In·particular,·Show·Invisibles·helps·you·see·extra·spaces· between·words·and·sentences.·It·also·clearly·shows·the·end·of· each·paragraph·with·a·special·symbol.↵

Figure 12-4: Examples of the Show Invisibles settings.

- *Fractional Character Widths.* Choose this option to tighten spacing between characters (preferred when printing to a laser printer). Do not check this option if you are printing to an ImageWriter printer.
- *Auto Number Footnotes.* When you check this option, ClarisWorks automatically numbers footnotes, beginning with the number entered for Starting Footnote #. Leave the option unchecked if you want to specify footnote numbers manually or want to use characters other than numbers, such as asterisks (*).
- *Date Format.* The format that you select is used whenever you insert the current date into a document by choosing the Insert Date command from the Edit menu.

Graphics Preferences

The graphics preferences, shown in Figure 12-5, affect both draw and paint graphics, as the following explanations indicate:

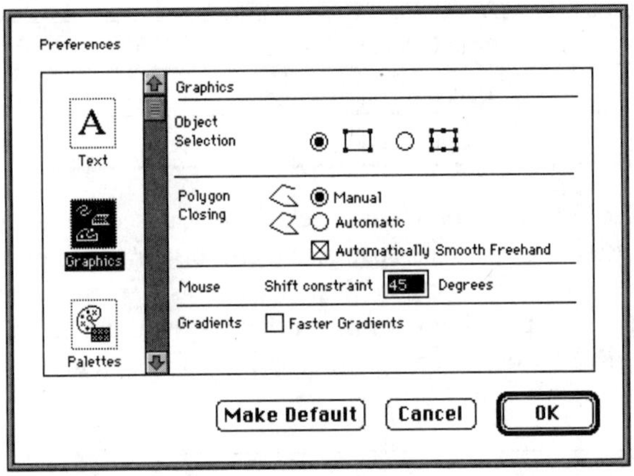

Figure 12-5: Graphics preferences options.

- *Object Selection (draw).* When you select draw objects with the pointer, they can be displayed with four or eight handles, as shown in Figure 12-6. Note that the extra handles do not provide additional object manipulation capabilities.
- *Polygon Closing (draw and paint).* Polygon closing can be Manual or Automatic. When you choose the Automatic setting, you don't have to complete the final side of a draw or paint figure. You simply click the handle on the end of the last line drawn, and the program completes the figure by connecting the handle to the beginning of the first line. In Manual mode, if you want a closed polygon, you have to finish the figure by clicking its starting point. (If most of your polygons will be closed, selecting Automatic can save considerable time when compared to manually attempting to click an object's starting point.)

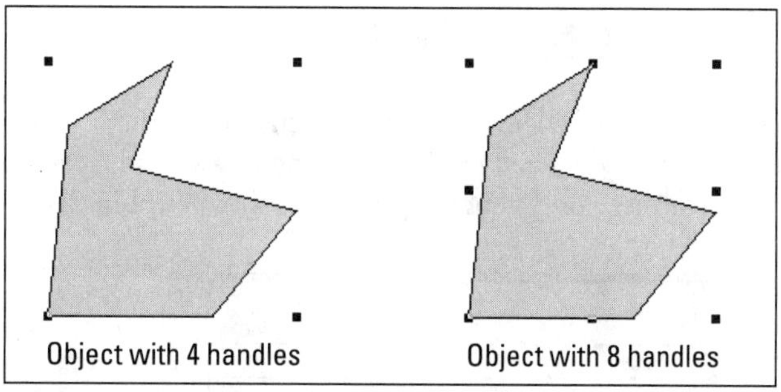

Figure 12-6: Object selection handles.

If you check Automatically Smooth Freehand (draw), the program transforms shapes that you draw freehand into relatively smooth curves.

- *Mouse Shift Constraint (draw).* You use this setting to specify an angular constraint for drawing with the mouse while the Shift key is pressed. The default setting enables you to draw in increments of 45 degrees, as shown in Figure 12-7. In paint mode, the Shift key always constrains lines to 90-degree angles (straight vertical or straight horizontal).

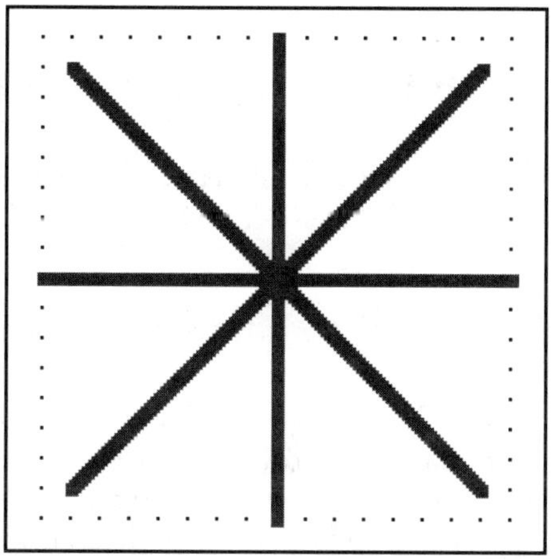

Figure 12-7: Lines drawn with a mouse Shift constraint of 45 degrees.

- *Gradients.* The Faster Gradients check box speeds up the display of gradients by temporarily showing them as rough approximations (frequently with banding lines), rather than as smooth transformations from one color to another.

Spreadsheet Preferences

The spreadsheet preferences enable you to customize the way that the arrow keys and Enter key are used when you are working in a spreadsheet document or frame. The new spreadsheet preferences options are shown in Figure 12-8.

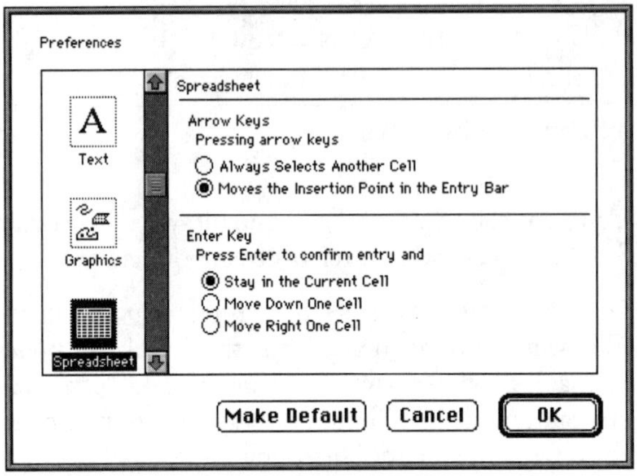

Figure 12-8: Spreadsheet preferences.

Depending on which Arrow Keys preference you choose, pressing an arrow key does one of the following:

- *Always Selects Another Cell.* Selects the cell to the immediate right, left, above, or below the current cell when you press the right, left, up, or down arrow key, respectively.
- *Moves the Insertion Point in the Entry Bar.* Used only for entering and editing data.

Regardless of which setting you choose, you can achieve the opposite function by pressing Option in combination with an arrow key. Thus, if you elect to use the arrow keys for cell selection, you can still move to the right or left when you enter or edit data by pressing Option-right arrow or Option-left arrow.

The Arrow Keys preference setting combines the two different ways that the arrow keys work in ClarisWorks 2.0 and 2.1 worksheets. In ClarisWorks 2.0, you use the arrow keys exclusively for cell-to-cell navigation. To move the cursor during editing, you press an Option-arrow combination. In ClarisWorks 2.1, these functions are reversed: arrow keys move the cursor in the entry bar, and you use Option-arrows for cell-to-cell movements. ClarisWorks 3.0 gives you a choice — *you* decide how you want the arrow keys to work.

The Enter Key preference setting enables you to set the action that occurs when you complete a cell entry by pressing the Enter key. If you've used other spreadsheet programs, you may prefer to use the default setting: Stay in the Current

Cell. Other options enable the Enter key to duplicate the function of the Return key (Move Down One Cell) or the Tab key (Move Right One Cell).

Remember that, as with other preferences, you can set spreadsheet preferences either for one document or globally. Most users prefer to choose one way of doing things and then click Make Default to set preferences for all future ClarisWorks worksheets.

Palettes Preferences

You use the palettes preferences options, shown in Figure 12-9, to customize the color palettes (Pen and Fill) and the Shortcuts palette.

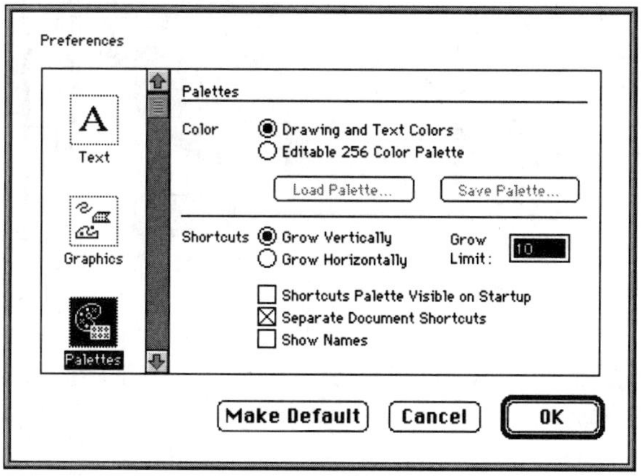

Figure 12-9: Palettes preferences options.

- *Color.* You can use the standard 81-color Drawing and Text Colors palette or load a color palette of your choice (Editable 256 Color Palette).

  ClarisWorks 2 includes a Colors and Gradients folder (stored in the Claris folder within the System Folder) that is installed when you install ClarisWorks. To see the sample palettes, click the Editable 256 Color Palette radio button, then the Load Palette button, and then select a palette from the Colors and Gradients folder. You also can load palettes that you've created in other graphics programs, such as MacDraw Pro.

  As with other preferences settings, loading a color palette affects only the active document. Thus, every document can have its own special color palette.

NOTE

ClarisWorks can save and load only color palettes. You cannot save Gradients as a palette.

To edit a color palette:

1. **Tear off the Fill or Pen color palette from its location in the Tool panel.**
2. **Double-click the color that you want to change.** A color wheel appears, as shown in Figure 12-10.

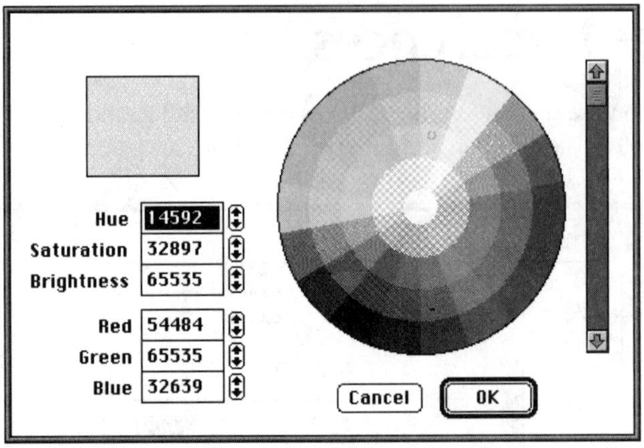

Figure 12-10: A Macintosh color wheel.

You can change directly to a different color by clicking the color in the wheel. Alternatively, you can enter different numerical settings in the boxes on the left or use the scroll bar to change the wheel's color scheme.

3. **Make the desired changes and then click OK.**

If you think that you may want to reuse a palette that you've customized, you can save it by clicking the Save Palette button in the Palettes Preferences dialog box.

- *Shortcuts.* The first group of options (Grow Vertically and Grow Horizontally) determines how the Shortcuts palette will be displayed (in long rows or tall columns, respectively), as well as how new buttons will be added (in rows from left to right or in columns from top to bottom). See Figure 12-11. The Grow Limit is the maximum number of buttons that will appear in each row or column.

  A check mark in the Shortcuts Palette Visible on Startup check box can save you some time at the beginning of each session. The Shortcuts palette appears automatically when you launch ClarisWorks. You don't have to choose Shortcuts from the File menu and then choose Show Shortcuts in order to see the Shortcuts palette.

The Separate Document Shortcuts check box enables you to save a specific set of shortcuts with a document. It also determines whether document-specific shortcuts that you've added to the palette appear with or without a dividing line to separate them from the application shortcuts.

When you check the Show Names setting, the program displays names for the shortcuts, rather than icons. Displaying the names is a great way to familiarize yourself with the shortcuts if you aren't up to deciphering the meanings of the tiny — and occasionally obscure — icons.

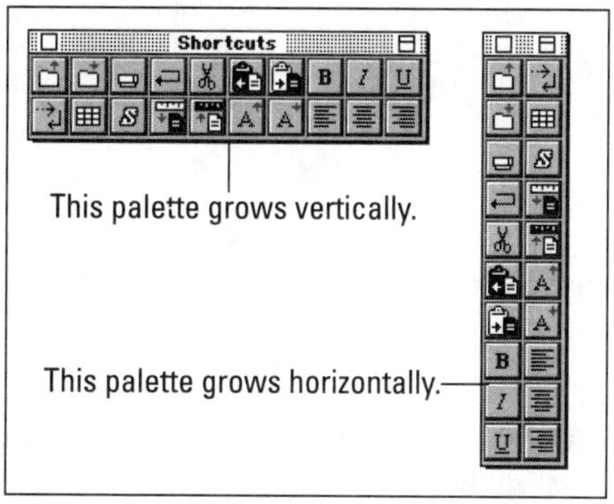
Shortcuts
This palette grows vertically.
This palette grows horizontally.

Figure 12-11: The left shortcuts palette expands vertically (by adding new rows) when new buttons are added. The palette on the right grows horizontally (by adding new columns).

NOTE

Note, however, that there is a limit to the number of names shown. Because of the nature of the *floating windoid*, no scroll bars are available. As a result, you could have more shortcuts loaded than you see displayed.

Communications Preferences

At a minimum, changing the default communications preferences is useful for setting a folder for receiving files and for other generic settings. You also may want to create several different communications documents, each with its own preferences settings.

For example, you can create a document for communicating with a friend that may start by automatically instructing the modem and software to wait for the friend's call. And for logging onto a communications service, you can create a document that attempts to connect the moment you open the document. Figure 12-12 shows the communications preferences options.

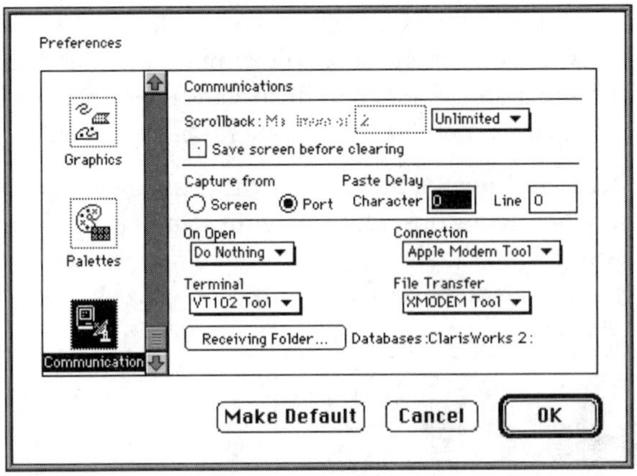

Figure 12-12: Communications preferences options.

The following descriptions tell you what various communications preferences do and how they affect activity during a session:

- *Scrollback.* Incoming text often arrives faster than you can read it, particularly if you are using a fast modem. The scrollback setting determines how many lines or screens of text will be available for you to scroll back through. You can choose a specific number of lines, kilobytes (sets of 1024 characters), or screens; or you can choose Unlimited. Unless you find yourself running out of memory, the best choice is Unlimited.

  If you choose anything other than Unlimited, ClarisWorks discards the oldest lines, kilobytes, or screens when the limit is reached. Similarly, some information services clear each screen before sending a new one. Check the Save screen before clearing check box if you want the program to store the old information in memory rather than discard it.

- *Capture from [Screen or Port].* This setting determines whether incoming text that is captured with the Capture to File command from the Session menu is formatted or unformatted. To save the formatting, choose Port. To ignore formatting, choose Screen. *Screen* ignores control characters, such as tabs, linefeeds, and formfeeds. The resulting file is straight text. *Port* includes these characters. In general, you should choose Port when you intend to use the information in a spreadsheet or database document. Choose Screen when you want to use the captured data in a word processing document.

- *Paste Delay.* This setting instructs ClarisWorks to pause between the characters or lines of text that it transmits. This feature enables a slower computer on the other end of the line to keep up. Numbers entered in either box are in $^1/_{60}$ of a second. (An entry of 5, for example, represents a $^5/_{60}$ of a second delay.) Normally, this option can be left as is (0, for no delays).

- *On Open.* This setting determines the action taken, if any, when you open a communications document. The choices are Do Nothing, Automatically Connect, and Wait for Connection. In general, you rarely need to change the default setting of Do Nothing.

  However, you may want to set an option for some communications documents. For example, the Automatically Connect setting is a good choice for a communications document that you use with bulletin boards (BBSs) or with an information service such as GEnie or CompuServe. Do Nothing is the best choice for documents when sometimes you initiate the connection and sometimes a friend or colleague initiates it.

- *Connection.* ClarisWorks ships with two connection tools: the Apple Modem Tool (for Apple and Hayes-compatible modems) and the Serial Tool (for direct communications between a pair of computers over a serial cable).

- *Terminal.* This option enables your Mac to work like a Teletype (TTY) or a DEC VT-102 terminal. A TTY is a very basic scrolling terminal. Text is sent as a continuous stream of characters and lines. The VT-102 terminal is more advanced and allows the other computer to send special commands, such as one that clears your screen. Most information services and BBSs support at least one of these terminal types.

- *File Transfer.* ClarisWorks supports three file transfer protocols: Text, Kermit, and XMODEM. XMODEM is the most widely used and supported protocol, and it is useful for transferring standard Mac files. For example, you can use XMODEM to transfer ClarisWorks word processing files between two Macs. The receiving Mac will be able to open the file in ClarisWorks.

  The Text option is useful for transferring text-only files between computers that don't have the same programs, as well as between different types of computers (Macs and PCs, for example).

- *Receiving Folder.* This setting identifies the folder that will be used to save captured text and protocol transfers (when you download files from an information service, for example). Click the button to select a different folder.

Mail Preferences

VERSION 2.1

If you have ClarisWorks 2.1 or a later version and System 7.5, System 7 Pro, or a later version of the system software, you can take advantage of PowerTalk, a new feature that makes exchanging electronic mail easy for Macintosh users. You can customize the way certain mail-handling tasks are performed. Mail preferences options (see Figure 12-13) include the following:

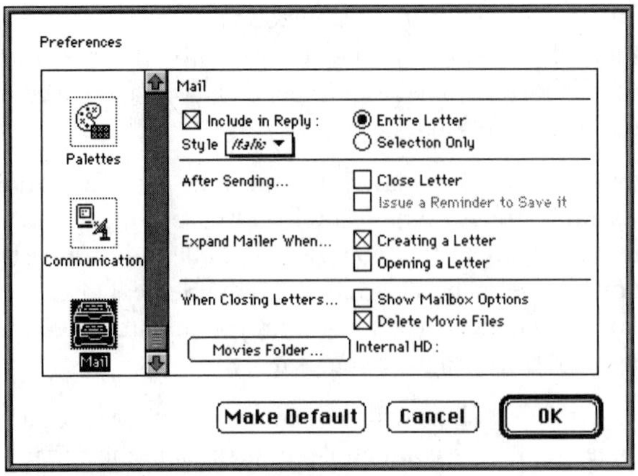

Figure 12-13: Mail preferences options.

- *Include in Reply.* When replying to a letter, you can determine how much text from the original letter is displayed beneath your reply. Choose Entire Letter if you want the entire text from the original message included in your reply. Choose Selection Only to include only the text that you have selected. Use the Style pop-up menu to select the font style (italics or bold, for example) in which you want the text of the original letter to be displayed. If you do not want to include any text from the original letter, click the Include in Reply check box to remove the check mark.

No matter which Include in Reply option you choose, you can edit any text that you include from the original letter. For example, you can choose the Entire Letter option and then edit it to show only the key points to which you are responding.

- *After Sending.* You can set in motion a couple of automatic actions to be performed after you send a letter. Click the Close Letter check box to automatically close a letter after you send it. And check the Issue a Reminder to Save It option (which is available only if you check Close Letter) to get ClarisWorks to automatically prompt you whenever you send a letter to ask whether you want to save the letter on disk. (***Note:*** Even if you do not save a copy of the letter to disk, you can still recall the letter from your Out Tray — as long as you haven't tossed the letter's icon into the Trash.)

- *Expand Mailer When.* By clicking the tiny triangle to the left of the From box in any mailer, you manually expand or collapse the mailer (see Figure 12-14). You can instruct ClarisWorks to automatically expand the mailer when Creating a Letter or Opening a Letter. Just click the appropriate check box(es).

Production Schedule (WP)

▷ **From** PowerBook 140 **Subject** Production Schedule

Production Schedule (WP)

▽ **From** **Subject**

 PowerBook 140 Production Schedule

 Recipients

 Ilci To ⬆ **Enclosures**

 ⬇ ⬆

 ⬇

 Sent Sat, Mar 26, 1994, 11:12 AM

—— Collapsed mailer Expanded mailer

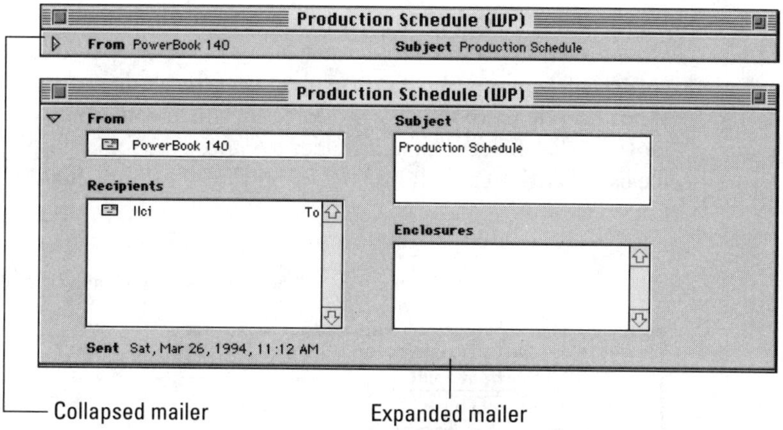

Figure 12-14: A collapsed mailer and an expanded mailer.

♦ *When Closing Letters.* You can set a couple of automatic actions to be performed when you close a letter.

If Show Mailbox Options is checked, the dialog box in Figure 12-15 appears when you close a letter. The Add Tag option helps you organize your mail by enabling you to add a key word or phrase to the letter. Every tag that you create is automatically added to the tag pop-up list; you then can assign it easily to other letters. Click Move to Trash if you want to delete the letter.

Click to display a pop-up list of tags
that have been used previously

Close letter and:

☐ **Add tag** [] ▼

☐ **Move to Trash**

[Cancel] [**Close**]

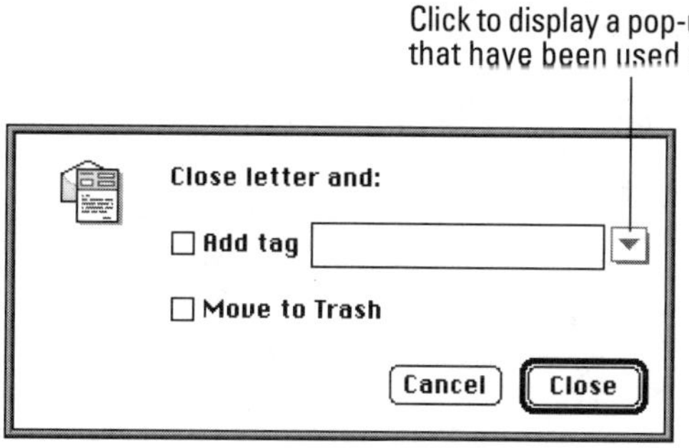

Figure 12-15: Set mailbox options in this dialog box.

You also can add or edit tags from the desktop by selecting a letter and then choosing Tag from the Mailbox menu. All tags, whether created in ClarisWorks or at the desktop, appear in all tag pop-up lists.

Delete Movie Files is checked by default, and with good reason. Movies that are attached to ClarisWorks letters are not in playable form; they must first be converted by ClarisWorks, which happens whenever you open a letter that contains a movie. As a result, leave this option checked to avoid creating duplicates of movies.

If you intend to replay movies that are enclosed in letters, click the Movies Folder button to select a folder in which to store the playable (that is, converted) versions of the movie files. After the file dialog box in Figure 12-16 appears, navigate to the disk and folder in which you want to store playable movies. Click Select Current Folder to choose the folder displayed above the file list; click Select to choose the folder that's currently highlighted in the file list.

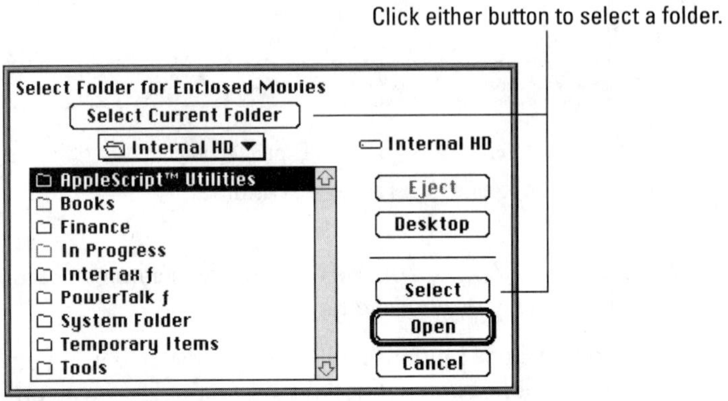

Figure 12-16: Select a folder in which to store any movie that you receive as part of a letter.

To learn more about the support in ClarisWorks for PowerTalk messaging, see Topic 21.

Summary

- ClarisWorks offers two kinds of preferences settings: default and document-specific. Changing a default preference affects all new documents. Setting a document-specific preference affects only that particular document.
- Program areas for which preferences can be set include text, graphics, palettes, communications, mail (in ClarisWorks 2.1 and later versions), and (in ClarisWorks 3.0) general and spreadsheet.
- Curly quotes, which are automatic with the Smart Quotes text preferences option, help create more professional-looking documents.
- The Show Invisibles text setting is useful when you perform a clean-up edit on documents.
- The Color option in the Palettes Preferences enables you to load and save custom color palettes that you can reuse with new documents.
- ClarisWorks can display buttons in the Shortcuts palette vertically or horizontally, and the buttons can show icons or names.
- The On Open preference item in the Communications Preferences can make a communications document automatically wait for an incoming call from another modem or connect with a particular information service, computer, or BBS.

Topic 13

The Shortcuts Palette

Overview

The Shortcuts palette (see Figure 13-1) is a floating *windoid* (a tiny window with close and collapse/expand boxes) that is covered with buttons (called *shortcuts*) that you click to execute common commands, such as printing the current document or changing the style of some text. (*Mac Trivia:* Palettes and windoids are said to *float* if you can freely change their on-screen location by dragging them to a more convenient position.) The shortcuts on the Shortcuts palette automatically change to match the environment in which you are currently working.

Figure 13-1: The Shortcuts palette for the Spreadsheet environment.

In addition to the standard shortcuts, ClarisWorks provides more than 70 predefined shortcuts that you can add to the palette. You also can add custom shortcuts for executing macros that you create. Other Shortcuts customization options include the following:

- Removing unwanted shortcuts from the palette
- Determining whether the Shortcuts palette appears automatically when ClarisWorks is launched or appears only when you choose Shortcuts from the File menu and then choose Show Shortcuts
- Setting the orientation of the palette (horizontal or vertical) to determine whether it will expand horizontally or vertically as new shortcuts are added

The Many Faces of the Shortcuts Palette

As mentioned previously, the contents of the Shortcuts palette automatically change to match the environment in which you're currently working. Tables 13-1 through 13-8 describe the functions of the standard ClarisWorks Shortcuts buttons in different ClarisWorks environments.

Table 13-1
The Shortcuts Palette with No Open Documents

Shortcut	***Description***
	Make a new word processing document.
	Make a new draw document.
	Make a new paint document.
	Make a new spreadsheet document.
	Make a new database document.
	Make a new communications document.
	Open a document on-disk.

Table 13-2
Shortcuts Available in All Palettes (Except Communications)

Shortcut	***Description***
	Open a document on disk.
	Save the current document.
	Print the current document.
	Undo the last operation.
	Cut selected text or object.
	Copy selected text or object to the Clipboard.

Shortcut	Description
	Paste the contents of the Clipboard at the current cursor location.
	Format selected text with boldface style.
	Format selected text with italic style.
	Format selected text with underline style.

Table 13-3
The Word Processing Shortcuts Palette

Shortcut	Description
	Show/hide invisibles.
	Add spreadsheet table to document. (***Note:*** If tab-delimited text is selected before the shortcut is executed, the text will be converted to a spreadsheet table. A tab-delimited paragraph contains a set of items separated by tab characters.)
	Create a custom style from the selected text.
	Copy the current paragraph settings from the ruler.
	Use the copied ruler settings to format the current paragraph.
	Increase size of selected text by one point.
	Decrease size of selected text by one point.
	Left-align the selected paragraphs.
	Center-align the selected paragraphs.
	Right-align the selected paragraphs.

Table 13-4
The Draw Shortcuts Palette

Shortcut	***Description***
	Align objects along their top edges.
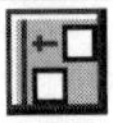	Align objects along their left edges.
	Align objects along their bottom edges.
	Align objects along their right edges.
	Align centers of selected objects.
	Arrange objects in a column so they are centered between the left edge of the left-most object and the right edge of the right-most object.
	Move selected objects forward (one layer closer to the front).
	Move selected objects back (one layer closer to the back).
	Set irregular text wrap for the current object.
	Rotate the selected object 90 degrees clockwise.

Table 13-5
The Paint Shortcuts Palette

Shortcut	***Description***
	Rotate the selected image 90 degrees clockwise.
	Switch to opaque mode.
	Switch to transparent mode.
	Switch to tint mode.
	Make the selected image lighter (whiter).
	Make the selected image darker (blacker).
	Tint the selected image with the current fill color.

Shortcut	Description
	Fill the selected object with the current color and pattern (or gradient).
	If the current selected image has more than one color, create a smooth blend of the colors.
	Invert (reverse) the colors in the selected image.

Table 13-6
The Spreadsheet Shortcuts Palette

Shortcut	Description
	Left-align the contents of the selected cells.
	Center-align the contents of the selected cells.
	Right-align the contents of the selected cells.
	Perform an ascending sort on the selected cell range.
	Perform a descending sort on the selected cell range.
	Sum the selected cell range, placing totals in the selected empty cells below and to the right.
	Apply the currency format to the selected cells.
	Apply the percentage format to the selected cells.
	Apply the comma numeric format to the selected cells.
	Draw an outline border for the selected cells.
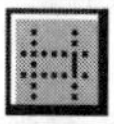	Draw a right border for the selected cells.
	Draw a bottom border for the selected cells.
	Toggle between showing formulas and showing values.
	Wrap text to fit the cell width.
	Insert selected rows or columns.

(continued)

Table 13-6 *(continued)*

Shortcut	***Description***
	Delete selected rows or columns.
	Create a bar chart based on the selected cells.
	Create a pie chart based on the selected cells.
	Create an area chart based on the selected cells.
	Create a line chart based on the selected cells.

Table 13-7
The Database Shortcuts Palette

Shortcut	***Description***
	Perform an ascending sort of the selected records, using the current database field as the key field.
	Perform a descending sort of the selected records, using the current database field as the key field.
	Re-sort the current set of selected/found records, using the current sort criteria.
	Select records that match (are equal to) the value in the current field.
	Select records that do not match (are not equal to) the value in the current field.
	Select records with values that are less than the value in the current field.
	Select records with values that are greater than the value in the current field.
	Add a new record.
	Select/show all records.
	Hide the currently selected records.

Table 13-8
The Communications Shortcuts Palette

Shortcut	*Description*
	Open a document on-disk.
	Save the current document.
	Print the current document.
	Copy selected text to the Clipboard.
	Paste the contents of the Clipboard at the current cursor location.
	Open the connection.
	Close the connection.
	Wait for call.
	Send a file.
	Prepare to receive a file.

Hiding and Showing the Shortcuts Palette

If the Shortcuts palette is not on-screen, you can make it appear by choosing the Shortcuts command from the File menu and then choosing Show Shortcuts (or by pressing Shift-⌘-X). To hide the Shortcuts palette from view, take any of the following actions:

- ◆ Choose the Shortcuts command from the File menu and then choose Hide Shortcuts.
- ◆ Press Shift-⌘-X.
- ◆ Click the close box in the upper-left corner of the Shortcuts palette.

Like other special ClarisWorks windoids, such as the tear-off Fill and Pattern palettes, the Shortcuts palette has another control box in its upper-right corner that is called the *collapse/expand box* (see Figure 13-2). If you click the collapse/expand box when the palette is completely displayed, the palette shrinks to show only its title bar and simultaneously moves out of the drawing area. If you click the box a second time, the palette expands to its normal size and instantly returns to its original location.

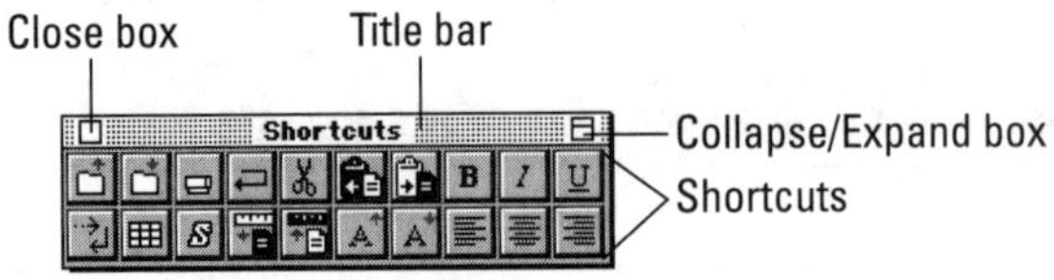

Figure 13-2: Control boxes appear in ClarisWorks windoids such as the Shortcuts palette.

As with other windoids, you can move the Shortcuts palette to a different position.

To move the Shortcuts palette:

1. **Click in the Shortcuts palette's title bar.**
2. **While pressing the mouse button, drag the palette to a new location.**
3. **When the palette is in the correct location, release the mouse button.**

Using a Shortcut

Shortcuts buttons work just like buttons in other Macintosh programs.

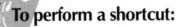

To perform a shortcut:

1. **If the Shortcuts palette is not visible, choose Shortcuts from the File menu and then choose Show Shortcuts.** You may have to position the cursor or select the text or object to be modified before you can perform some shortcuts.
2. **Click the button for the shortcut that you want to perform.**

Customizing the Shortcuts Palette

Although the standard Shortcuts palette offers a nice selection of common commands, the fact that you can customize the palette in so many ways adds appreciably to its power. You can customize the palette to suit your needs — even create special palettes for each of the environments you work in. If you don't like the commands that the palette includes, you can remove them and, optionally, replace them with commands that are more useful to you. You can even add shortcuts that execute macros you've created. And you can use the Preferences command to control how and when the Shortcuts palette is displayed.

Setting preferences for the Shortcuts palette

Choose Preferences from the Edit menu to see a dialog box where you can change the appearance and start-up actions of the Shortcuts palette. (For information on other ClarisWorks Preferences options, see Topic 12). As the options in Figure 13-3 show, you can set the direction in which the palette will expand as new buttons are added and determine whether the palette will automatically be displayed at start-up, whether document-specific shortcuts will be separated from application shortcuts, and whether icons or shortcut names will be shown.

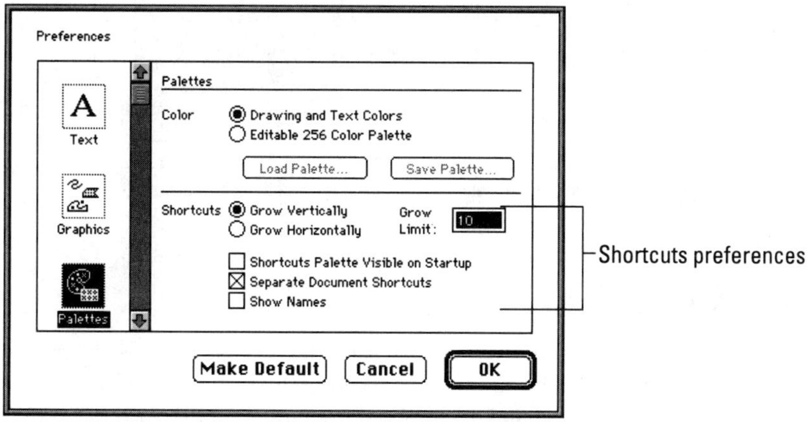

Figure 13-3: Click the Palettes icon in the Preferences dialog box to set options for the Shortcuts palette.

- Check Grow Vertically if you want to add new shortcuts in rows at the bottom of the palette. Check Grow Horizontally if you want to add new shortcuts in columns at the right side of the palette. The Grow Limit is the maximum number of shortcuts that will appear in each row or column. Grow Limit must be set to 30 or less.
- Check Shortcuts Palette Visible on Startup if you want the palette to appear automatically at the start of each session. If you normally use the Shortcuts palette, selecting this option saves you the trouble of manually choosing Shortcuts from the File menu and then choosing Show Shortcuts.
- Check Separate Document Shortcuts if you want to display document-specific shortcuts with a dividing line that separates them from the application shortcuts (see Figure 13-4). (Document-specific shortcuts are available only when the particular document in which they were saved is open.)
- Check Show Names to display shortcut names rather than icons (see Figure 13-4).

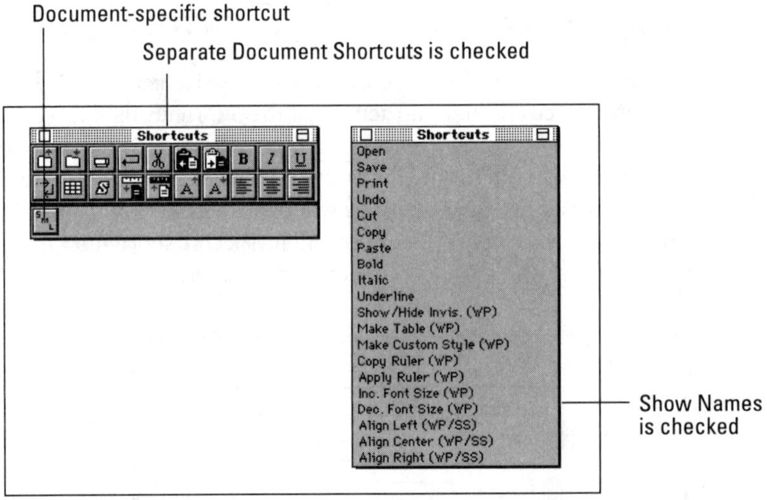

Figure 13-4: Preferences settings affect the display of the Shortcuts palette.

Adding buttons

The Shortcuts palette contains the set of buttons that Claris programmers think are most useful in the various ClarisWorks environments. However, you can choose from more than 70 additional predefined buttons to add to the palette. And, as described in Topic 14, you can create ClarisWorks *macros* (sequences of steps and commands), design icons to represent them, and then attach the macros to the shortcuts in the Shortcuts palette.

TIP

Whether or not you think the standard Shortcuts palette could stand some modification, you'll want to check out the other predefined shortcuts. Just choose Shortcuts from the File menu and then choose Edit Shortcuts. Each button in the Available Shortcuts list box is accompanied by a description in the box below the buttons. Click a few buttons to see what you're missing. You can also display the shortcut names rather than their icons. Choose Preferences from the Edit menu, click the Palettes icon, and then click in the Show Names check box. Note, however, that the Shortcuts palette can display only a limited number of names; luckily, most users will not exceed that limit.

Step-by-Steps

To add predefined buttons to the Shortcuts palette:

1. **Choose Shortcuts from the File menu and then choose Edit Shortcuts. The Edit Shortcuts dialog box appears, as shown in Figure 13-5.**
2. **Click any shortcut in the Available Shortcuts list box.** The button is shown as depressed. A brief description of the selected shortcut's function appears in the Description box below the list box. Note that the specific environment in which the shortcut is applicable (if any) is shown in parentheses at the end of the description line.

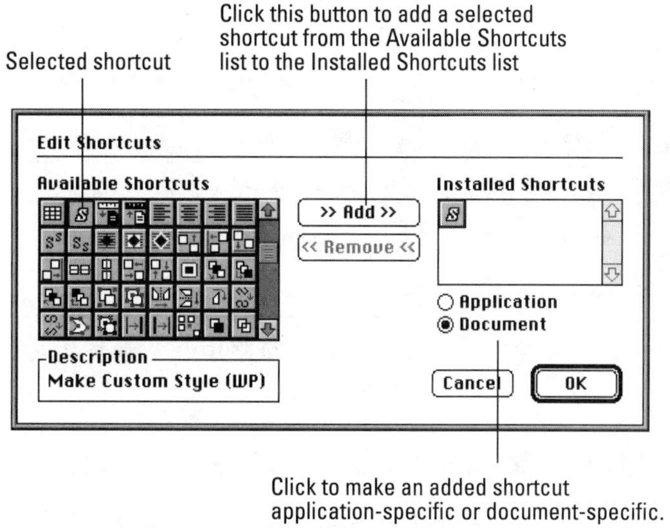

Figure 13-5: The ClarisWorks Edit Shortcuts dialog box.

3. **After you find a shortcut that you want to add to the Shortcuts palette, click the Application radio button if you want to add the shortcut to the palette for the environment that is shown in parentheses at the end of the description line.** This action makes the shortcut available in every document that uses that environment. (If no environment is shown in parentheses, the shortcut will automatically be available in *every* environment.)

— or —

3. **If you want to add a shortcut to the Shortcuts palette for the current document only, click Document.** Document-specific shortcuts appear in the palette only when the current document is open and active.
4. **Click Add.**
5. **Repeat Steps 2 through 4 for any additional shortcuts that you want to add to the Shortcuts palette.**
6. **Click OK to save your changes or Cancel to leave the Shortcuts palette unchanged.**

VERSION 2.1

If you recently upgraded to ClarisWorks 2.1, be sure to check the buttons in the Edit Shortcuts dialog box. At the bottom of the Available Shortcuts sit several new buttons that make it easier to handle PowerTalk electronic messages and to turn auto-hyphenation on and off (see Figure 13-6).

NEW FEATURE 3.0

ClarisWorks 3.0 adds nine more buttons that enable you to do a word count or invoke a ClarisWorks Assistant (see Figure 13-6).

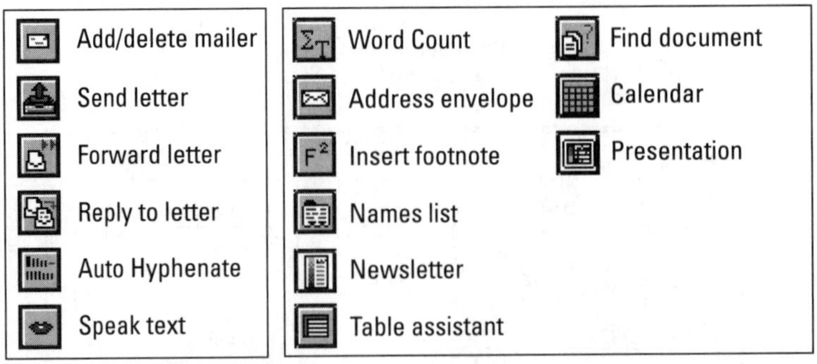

Figure 13-6: New Shortcuts buttons in ClarisWorks 2.1 (left) and ClarisWorks 3.0 (right).

To add user-defined buttons to the Shortcuts palette:

1. **Create a macro and design an icon for it (as described in the Step-By-Steps instructions in Topic 14 for recording a macro).**
2. **Choose Shortcuts from the File menu and then choose Edit Shortcuts.** The Edit Shortcuts dialog box shown in Figure 13-5 appears.
3. **Scroll to the bottom of the Available Shortcuts list box.** User-defined shortcuts are stored at the bottom of the list.
4. **Click the icon of the macro that you want to add to the Shortcuts palette.** A description of the selected shortcut's function appears below the Available Shortcuts list box.
5. **Click the Application radio button if you want to add the shortcut to the palettes for applicable environments.**

— or —

5. **If you want to add this shortcut to the Shortcuts palette for the current document only, click Document.**
6. **Click Add.**
7. **Repeat Steps 4 through 6 for any additional shortcuts that you want to add to the Shortcuts palette.**
8. **Click OK to save the changes or Cancel to leave the Shortcuts palette unchanged.**

Removing buttons

There's nothing sacred about the set of shortcuts that ClarisWorks initially provides in the Shortcuts palette. You can press ⌘-key equivalents to issue many of the shortcuts that are available in all environments (Cut, Copy, Paste, Open, Save, and Print, for example). By eliminating some of these shortcuts, you can keep the palette a manageable size. Similarly, shortcuts that you have added may no longer be necessary.

NOTE

Removing a shortcut from an application or document Shortcuts palette does not delete it. It merely removes the shortcut from the Shortcuts palette. To delete the shortcut and its associated macro, choose the Shortcuts command from the File menu and then choose Delete Macros (as explained in Topic 14).

Step-by-Steps

To remove buttons from the Shortcuts palette:

1. **Choose Shortcuts from the File menu and then choose Edit Shortcuts.** The Edit Shortcuts dialog box appears.

2. **To remove an application-specific shortcut, click the Application radio button.**

— or —

2. **To remove a shortcut that has been installed in this particular document (rather than in the environment), click the Document radio button.**

3. **In the Installed Shortcuts list box, click the shortcut that you want to remove.** The Remove button becomes active, as shown in Figure 13-7.

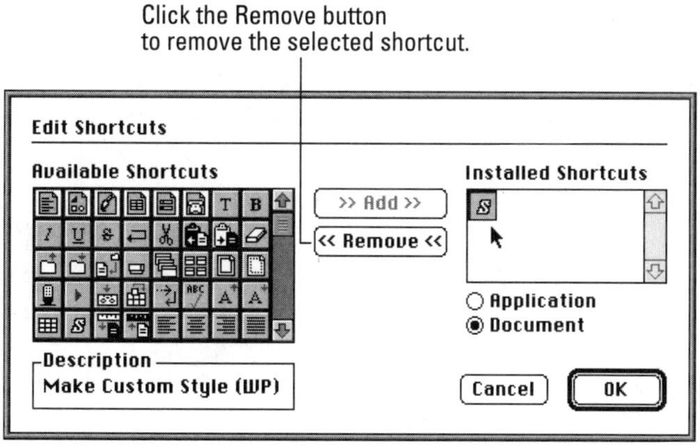

Figure 13-7: Removing a shortcut form the ClarisWorks 2.0 Shortcuts palette.

4. **Click the Remove button.**
5. **Repeat Steps 2 through 4 for any additional shortcuts that you want to remove.**
6. **Click OK to save the changes or Cancel to leave the Shortcuts palette unchanged.**

Application versus document shortcuts

Whether you are adding a predefined shortcut that is included with ClarisWorks or a custom shortcut that represents one of your macros, you can make any shortcut application-specific or document-specific by clicking the appropriate radio button in the Edit Shortcuts dialog box. Although the default is to make all new shortcuts application-specific, give some thought to your options. If you make all of the shortcuts application shortcuts, the palette will quickly grow so large that finding the shortcut you need may become difficult, and the purpose of using a palette will be defeated.

When selecting Application or Document, think about whether you can use the shortcut in all or many of the documents that you create in the particular environment. For example, a macro for a frequently used custom text style is highly appropriate as an application shortcut. On the other hand, a shortcut that automatically types a closing for letters is more appropriate as a document shortcut (unless all that you use the word processor for is writing letters). Carrying it a step further, you may want to save the document as a stationery file that you can use for all new letters; and you can create additional macros for several possible closings (Sincerely, Sincerely Yours, Yours Truly, Respectfully Yours, Your Obedient Servant, and so on).

NOTE

If you delete a macro that you also have assigned to a Shortcuts button (by choosing the Shortcuts command in the File menu and then choosing Delete Macros), the shortcut is simultaneously removed from the Shortcuts palette.

Quick Tips

The following tip explains how to share your shortcuts with other ClarisWorks users.

Sharing shortcuts

After you have modified the Shortcuts palette, a special document is created called ClarisWorks Shortcuts. You'll find it inside the Claris folder within the System Folder. This file contains details of the changes you have made to the Shortcuts palette, as well as a record of any global (not document-specific) macros that you've created. (Unless you've actually changed the default shortcuts or created a global macro, you won't find the ClarisWorks Shortcuts file.) Delete the file, and you're back to square one. That is, the Shortcuts palette returns to its original, unaltered state. This feature can be very useful if you've been experimenting with macros and the Shortcuts palette and simply want to put everything back the way it was when you first opened your copy of ClarisWorks.

If you want to share your shortcuts with others, all you have to do is give them a copy of your ClarisWorks Shortcuts file. After they copy it into their Claris folder, they'll have the same custom Shortcuts palette and global macros as you!

CAUTION!

If the ClarisWorks Shortcuts file is copied to another user's machine and that person already has global macros or shortcuts, they will be overwritten by the new ones.

For help with sharing your document-specific macros with other users, see Topic 14, "Using Macros."

Summary

- The shortcuts in the Shortcuts palette automatically change to reflect the environment in which you're working.
- You can hide, display, move, and collapse/expand the Shortcuts palette.
- You can use a variety of customization options to change the appearance of the Shortcuts palette. You can determine whether the palette will display vertically or horizontally, decide whether document-specific shortcuts will be separated from application-specific shortcuts, and add and remove shortcuts.
- In addition to using dozens of predefined shortcuts, you can create your own macros, design custom icons for them, and add them to the Shortcuts palette.
- Shortcuts can be application-specific or document-specific. Application-specific shortcuts appear in the Shortcuts palette in all appropriate environments; document-specific shortcuts appear only when a particular document is open and active.

Using Macros

Overview

Although the ClarisWorks macro recorder doesn't have many of the capabilities that stand-alone macro utilities have (such as repeating a macro; linking to other macros; and branching to different parts of a macro, based on certain conditions), it does provide an easier way to perform many repetitive, well-defined tasks in ClarisWorks.

The macro recorder works like a tape recorder. It simply watches the actions that you perform when you click the mouse (such as making choices in dialog boxes and choosing commands from menus) and keeps track of the characters that you type. It does not record mouse movements, however. You cannot, for example, use the recorder to capture figures that you create with the freehand drawing tool.

Recording a Macro

ClarisWorks makes recording a macro easy.

Step-by-Steps

To record a macro:

1. **To start the macro recorder, choose Shortcuts from the File menu and then choose Record Macro (or press Shift-⌘-J).** The Record Macro dialog box shown in Figure 14-1 appears.
2. **Name the macro and, optionally, specify a function key or Option-⌘-key combination that can be used to invoke the macro.**

   The Function Key radio button is *grayed out* (unselectable) if you do not have an extended keyboard.
3. **Set options for the macro.**
   - Choose Play Pauses if you want the macro to record the amount of time that it takes you to perform each step. Otherwise, the macro plays back at the fastest speed possible. This option is particularly useful when you're using ClarisWorks for step-by-step demonstrations or a slide show, for example.

◆ Choose Document Specific if you want the macro to be available only in this particular document, rather than in any ClarisWorks document of the appropriate type.

◆ If you want to add the macro to the Shortcuts palette, choose Has Shortcut to make the In Shortcuts Palette option available. Click that option to add the macro to the Shortcuts palette.

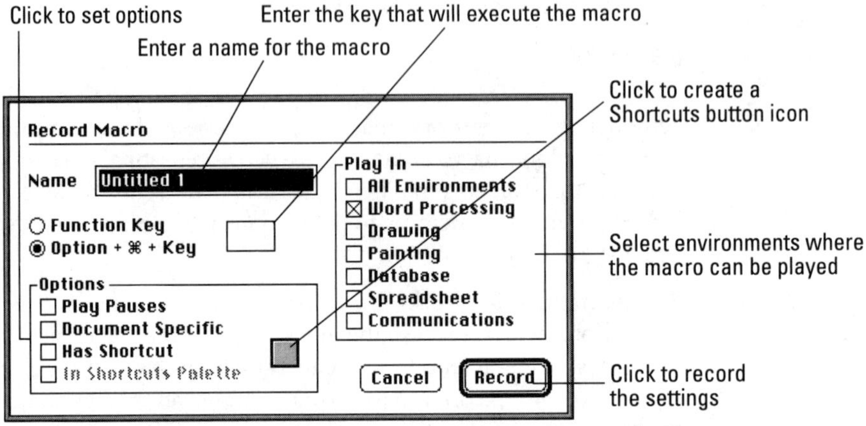

Figure 14-1: The Record Macro dialog box.

4. **Click the box to the right of the Has Shortcut option if you've assigned the macro to a Shortcuts button and want to create a button icon for it now.** The Edit Button Icon editor shown in Figure 14-2 appears. Design the button icon and then click OK to return to the Record Macro dialog box (or click Cancel if you change your mind about designing an icon at this time).

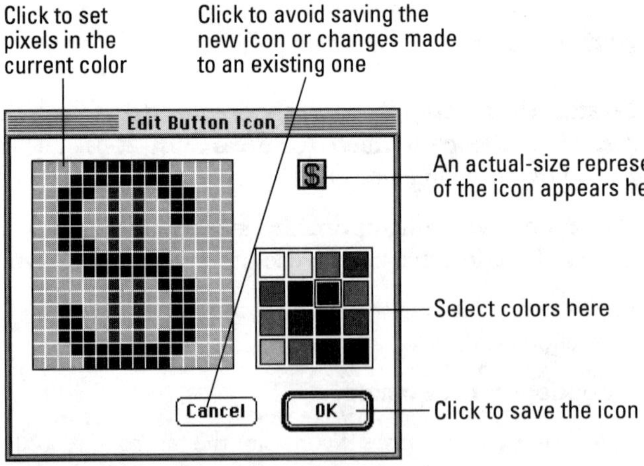

Figure 14-2: The Edit Button Icon dialog box.

5. **Choose the Play In environments on the right side of the Record Macro dialog box.** By default, ClarisWorks automatically chooses the environment that you are currently using. Check all of the environments in which you want to use the macro.

6. **To begin recording the macro, click Record. You return to the document.** To remind you that you are recording, a flashing microphone replaces the apple at the top of the Apple menu. If you decide not to record the macro, click Cancel in the dialog box.

7. **Perform the steps of the macro.**

8. **To end the macro, choose Shortcuts from the File menu and then choose Stop Recording (or press Shift-⌘-J).**

Playing a Macro

Depending on the options that you chose when you created the macro, you invoke the macro in different ways:

- Press the Option-⌘-key combination or the Function Key that you assigned to the macro.
- Click the Shortcuts button that you created for the macro.
- Choose Shortcuts from the File menu and then choose Play Macro. When the Play Macro dialog box appears (see Figure 14-3), choose the name of the macro and click Play.

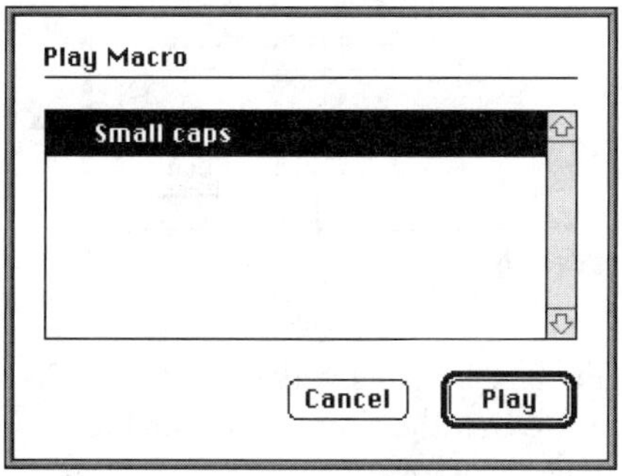

Figure 14-3: The Play Macro dialog box.

NOTE

Remember to set up the conditions that are needed for the macro before you execute it. For example, if you need to select some text before you can use a word processing macro, the macro will not work properly if you have not selected the text. If the macro does not execute when you press its hot key or if it is not on the list in the Play Macro dialog box, either you are in the wrong environment, or you clicked the Document Specific check box when you designed the macro and that particular document is not the active one.

Editing Macro Options

You cannot edit the steps of a macro. If you are dissatisfied with any step or need to make a change such as adding a step, you have to re-record the macro. (**Note**: you cannot use the same name or key combination for two macros. If you want to reuse either component, you have to delete the original macro first, as described in "Deleting a Macro," later in this Topic.)

On the other hand, if you want to change some of the options for a macro, you can alter as many of them as you like at any time. You can even create or edit a Shortcuts button icon whenever you like.

To edit macro options:

1. **Choose Shortcuts from the File menu and then choose Edit Macros.**
 The Edit Macros dialog box shown in Figure 14-4 appears.

Name of currently selected macro

Macro pop-up menu

```
Edit Macros

Macro  [Small caps ▼]          ┌Play In─────────────
                                │ ☐ All Environments
Name   [Small caps        ]     │ ☒ Word Processing
                                │ ☐ Drawing
○ Function Key                  │ ☐ Painting
● Option + ⌘ + Key    [c]       │ ☐ Database
                                │ ☐ Spreadsheet
┌Options─────────────┐          │ ☐ Communications
│ ☐ Play Pauses       │         └─────────────────
│ ☒ Document Specific │
│ ☐ Has Shortcut      │  [▓]    [ Cancel ] [ Done ]
│ ☐ In Shortcuts Palette│
└────────────────────┘
```

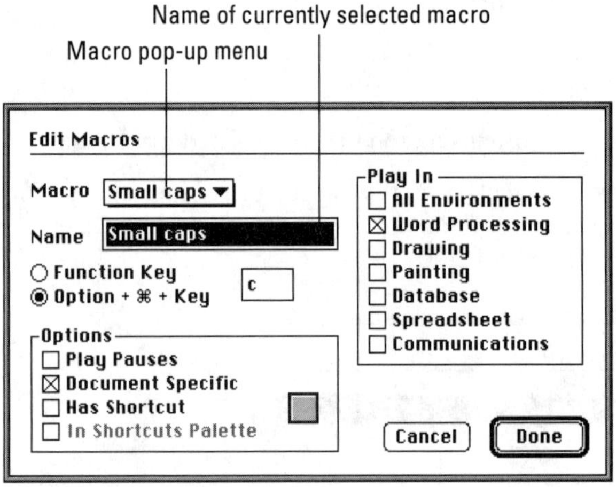

Figure 14-4: The Edit Macros dialog box.

The Edit Macros dialog box is virtually identical to the Record Macros dialog box. The sole difference is that the Edit Macros dialog box contains a pop-up menu that lists all installed macros.

2. **Choose the macro that you want to edit from the Macro pop-up menu.**
 The macro's name appears in the Name text-edit box below the Macro pop-up menu.

3. **Change whatever options you like.**

4. **Repeat Steps 2 and 3 for other macros that you want to change.**

5. **To record the changes and return to ClarisWorks, click Done. To ignore all changes (leaving your macros unaltered), click Cancel.**

Deleting a Macro

If you no longer want a particular macro, you can remove it from the document it was saved in or from ClarisWorks (depending on whether you chose the Document Specific option). You also should delete a macro if you made a mistake in it or if it doesn't play back correctly, because you can't reuse a macro name or key combination unless you first delete the old macro.

To delete a macro:

1. **Choose Shortcuts from the File menu and then choose Delete Macros.** The Delete Macros dialog box appears, as shown in Figure 14-5.

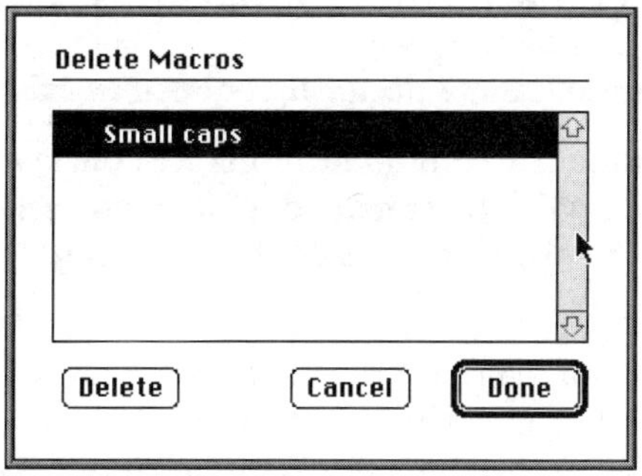

Figure 14-5: The Delete Macros dialog box.

2. **Choose a macro that you want to remove.**
3. **Click Delete.**
4. **Repeat Steps 2 and 3 for other macros that you want to remove at this time.**
5. **To record changes (deleting the macros), click Done.** If you change your mind and decide to leave the macro list unaltered, click Cancel.

Using the Macro Wait Command

In the communications environment, timing is everything. If you send your password to an information service before the service requests it, chances are excellent that the service won't receive it and you won't be able to *log on* (connect with the service) successfully.

Although you can record and play pauses in macros, often this capability isn't sufficient to ensure correct timing. Information services sometimes slow down (when they are handling large numbers of users, for example), so pauses between commands can vary dramatically from one session to the next. You can use a special command — Macro Wait — to remedy this situation in macros that you create for the communications environment. The Macro Wait command has two options:

- Wait for a specific text string to be received from the other computer.
- Wait for so many seconds of line inactivity.

When the condition is met, the macro continues to play. In a logon macro that automatically logs you onto an information service, you can use the Macro Wait command to wait for a specific prompt (*Password?,* for example) before transmitting your password.

Step-by-Steps

To create a communications macro that uses Macro Wait:

1. **Create a new communications document or open an existing document.**
2. **At the proper point in the communications session, start the macro recorder by choosing Shortcuts from the File menu and then choosing Record Macro (or by pressing Shift-⌘-J).** The Record Macro dialog box appears.

   Depending on what you want the macro to do, you may want to start the recorder (to record a logon sequence) just before you choose Open Connection from the Session menu, or you may want to start the recorder during the actual session.
3. **Name the macro and, optionally, specify a function key or Option-⌘-key combination to use to invoke the macro.**
4. **Choose options for the macro.**
5. **If you've assigned the macro to a Shortcuts button, you can create a button icon for it now. Click in the box to the right of the Has Shortcut option. The Edit Button Icon editor appears.**

   Design the button icon and then click OK to return to the Record Macro dialog box (or click Cancel if you change your mind about designing an icon at this time).

   Note: If you're on-line, you may want to create the icon *after* the communications session is over.
6. **Choose Communications as the Play In environment.** (Normally, this option is already selected.)
7. **To begin recording the macro, click Record.** You return to the communications document. To remind you that you are recording, a flashing microphone replaces the apple at the top of the Apple menu. If you decide not to record the macro, click Cancel.

8. **Perform the steps of the macro.** At the appropriate times, you can specify a wait period or a text string to wait for by choosing Shortcuts from the File menu and then choosing Macro Wait. The Macro Wait dialog box appears, as shown in Figure 14-6.

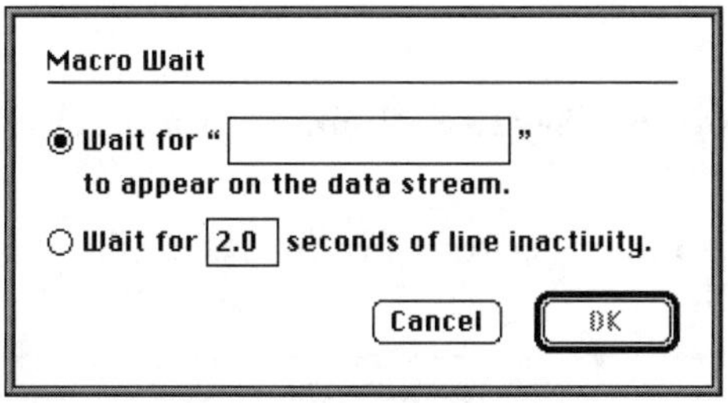

Figure 14-6: In the Macro Wait dialog box, type a text string or the number of seconds to wait.

9. **Choose a Macro Wait option by clicking the appropriate radio button.** If you choose the first option, enter the text string for which you want to wait. The text string has to be exact, with the correct spelling, capitalization, punctuation, and spaces. If you choose the second option (Wait for *x* seconds of line inactivity), enter the number of seconds.

10. **To end the macro, choose Shortcuts from the File menu and then choose Stop Recording (or press Shift-⌘-J).**

TIP

If you want to avoid the Macro Wait command or are having difficulty getting it to work reliably, you can create a normal macro and use it at the point in the session when you might otherwise use a Macro Wait command.

Designing Automatic Macros

NEW FEATURE 3.0

A special type of macro capability has been included in ClarisWorks 3.0: automatic macros. You can create automatic macros that play whenever

- ClarisWorks 3.0 is launched
- A new document is created in a particular environment (a new spreadsheet, for example)
- Any document from a selected environment is opened (a word processing file, for example)

To create an automatic macro:

1. **In the Record Macro dialog box (see Figure 14-1), enter one of the special names shown in Table 14-1 (spelling, capitalization, and hyphenation must be exact).**
2. **Set options.**
3. **Select the appropriate Play In environment (or deselect all environments).**
4. **Record the macro steps (as described in "Recording a Macro," earlier in this Topic).**

Table 14-1
Automatic Macro Names and Definitions

Macro Name	*Executes when . . .*
Auto-Startup	ClarisWorks is launched
Auto-Open WP	A word processing document is opened
Auto-Open DR	A draw document is opened
Auto-Open PT	A paint document is opened
Auto-Open SS	A spreadsheet document is opened
Auto-Open DB	A database document is opened
Auto-Open CM	A communications document is opened
Auto-New WP	A new word processing document is created
Auto-New DR	A new draw document is created
Auto-New PT	A new paint document is created
Auto-New SS	A new spreadsheet document is created
Auto-New DB	A new database document is created
Auto-New CM	A new communications document is created

As you can see, three classes of actions can cause an automatic macro to execute: ClarisWorks launches, a particular document type is opened, or a particular document type is created. You can have only one ClarisWorks macro for each of the names listed in Table 14-1.

You can easily create stationery documents or choose certain preference settings to accomplish many of the tasks that environment-specific automatic macros perform. For example, you can use a stationery or options stationery document (see Topic 11), rather than an Auto-New WP macro, to select a particular font, insert the current date, and type a Memo heading. To be truly useful, automatic macros should accomplish tasks that stationery and preferences cannot perform. For example, you can use an automatic macro to customize an environment by hiding or showing rulers, setting a zoom level, choosing a given tool in the Tool panel, or switching to a specific database layout.

Although the Auto-Open macros normally run whenever you open any document in the chosen environment, you can restrict an Auto-Open macro to a particular document by clicking the Document Specific check box when you define the macro. By linking the Auto-Open DB macro to one particular database file, for example, you can automatically sort that database and display the last record each time the file is opened. If any other database is opened, the macro will not play. If you use the Auto-Open DB macro in this manner, however, you cannot also create a similar macro for any other database; nor can you design a macro that will run when *any* database is opened. Remember . . . only one macro can be defined for each macro name.

If you want to delete on automatic macro, you must go to the Delete Macros dialog box (choose Delete Macros from the Shortcuts submenu of the File menu.)

Getting Down to Business: Creating a Small Caps Macro

Although ClarisWorks has many of the text formatting options that other word processing programs offer, it does not provide a *small caps* feature. (A phrase or text string that is formatted with small caps is completely capitalized, but the letters are slightly smaller than the surrounding text.)

By typing text in all caps and choosing a smaller point size, you can create small caps in ClarisWorks.

To create small caps:

1. **Type the text in all caps.**
2. **Select the part of the text that you normally would have typed in lowercase letters.** Ignore letters that you normally capitalize (the first letter in a proper noun or the first letter of the word at the beginning of a sentence, for example).
3. **In the Size menu, choose the next smaller point size.**

If you are using TrueType fonts, Adobe Type Manager (ATM) and PostScript fonts, or a PostScript laser printer, you aren't restricted to choosing just the next smaller point size from the Size menu. If the base text is 12 point, you can, for example, set the small cap text as 11 point rather than 10. To set type in a specific point size that isn't listed in the Size menu, choose Other from the Size menu and enter the new point size.

If you aren't sure whether your Mac and printer can handle the odd point sizes, format some text with the size (11 point, for example) and print it. By examining the output, you can quickly determine whether you can print odd text sizes. (If your setup doesn't qualify, the small cap text will look jagged and ugly. Before giving up, however, you may want to try some other fonts.)

Now that you know how to generate small caps, you can design a macro that will perform the small caps conversion for you.

Step-by-Steps

To create the small caps macro:

1. **In ClarisWorks, create a new word processing document or open an existing document.**
2. **Type a single word entirely in capital letters (MACROS, for example).**
3. **Position the cursor so that it's directly in front of the *M* in MACROS.**
4. **To start the macro recorder, choose Shortcuts from the File menu and then choose Record Macro (or press Shift-⌘-J).**
5. **Name the macro and set other options for it, such as the Option-⌘-key combination that you'll use to invoke the macro.**

   TIP

   Because you'll want to be able to use the macro in other word processing documents, be sure that you do not check the Document Specific check box.
6. **Click Record to begin recording the steps of the macro.**
7. **Press the right-arrow key once.** The cursor moves between the *M* and the *A*.
8. **Press Shift-Option-right arrow.** The remainder of the word (*ACRO*) is selected.
9. **From the Size menu, choose a slightly smaller point size than that of the base text.** If you are using a 12-point font, choose a 10-point font or choose Other from the Size menu and specify an 11-point font.
10. **To complete the process, choose Shortcuts from the File menu and then choose Stop Recording (or press Shift-⌘-J).** The macro is saved in the document or in ClarisWorks, depending on whether you checked Document Specific when you named the macro.

To play the macro, position the cursor immediately in front of the first letter of the word that you want to change to small caps. Then press the ⌘-Option keystroke that you assigned to the macro. If you didn't assign a special keystroke to the macro, you can invoke the macro by choosing Shortcuts from the File menu, choosing Play Macro, and then choosing the macro from the list that appears.

The macro automatically converts all but the first letter of the word to the smaller point size that you chose. Note, however, that the macro has two shortcomings:

- The text must already be in caps for the macro to work.
- It works correctly for only a single point size.

The first problem has no easy fix, because ClarisWorks has no command to change the case of text. If the size issue is of major importance, you can make the macro more general by skipping Step 9. When you execute the macro, you can then manually choose the desired point size from the Size menu.

Quick Tips

The following Quick Tips discuss one-time macros, ideas for macros, instructions for avoiding keystroke conflicts, and transferring macros to other users.

Sometimes once is enough

Most people normally think of using macros when they have a task that they will need to repeat, perhaps frequently. Sometimes, however, you have a task that may never come up again, but you need to perform it 25 times in the current document (changing every occurrence of "Ace Auto Parts" to Helvetica Italic, for example).

Just because you won't use a particular macro again after today is not a reason not to make a macro for it. Create the macro and make it specific to the document in which you use it, or just delete it when you're done.

Macro ideas

Having trouble coming up with reasons to create macros? Here are a few suggestions that may start those neurons firing.

- Create keyboard shortcuts for menu commands that don't have shortcuts.

  In the word processor, for example, you can create a macro that inserts the current date, one that pops up the Paragraph dialog box from the Format menu, and another that chooses a particular font and applies it to the currently selected text.

- Create complete paragraph styles for the word processor.

  Unlike the user-defined text styles that ClarisWorks supports, paragraph styles (which were popularized in Microsoft Word) enable you to maintain consistent formatting, both within a particular document and in other documents. Elements of a paragraph style can include paragraph formatting (ruler settings, line spacing, and so on), as well as font information (such as Times 12 point). For example, you can create a particular style for secondary heads that makes them flush left, Helvetica Bold 12 point, and followed by a single blank line. You also can define a style for hanging indents (to use in bulleted lists and sets of numbered steps). If you use the styles frequently, you can also create special buttons for each style and add them to the Shortcuts palette.

- Create a series of macros that perform on-line communications activities for you.

Examples include macros that take you directly to forums or special interest groups (SIGs), such as the Mac forum, a writers' forum, or a financial forum; a macro that automatically chooses the XMODEM file transfer protocol from an information service's menus; and a macro that performs a logoff for you (quitting from a communications session and closing the connection). You may also want to create separate Shortcuts buttons for the macros so you don't have to memorize any additional commands.

- Try to think in terms of *many steps.*

  You'll get the greatest gains in productivity by automating complex, multi-step procedures. You may create a macro that conducts an entire on-line communications session, for example. You can have ClarisWorks connect with GEnie or CompuServe, change to the Macintosh forum, capture a list of all new programs, and then log off. Why waste dollars browsing through this information on-line? After you have the list of files, read through it at your leisure and check off the ones you're interested in. Then log back onto the information service and download the files you want.

- Think about ClarisWorks activities that you routinely perform.

  Every macro doesn't need to have a grandiose purpose. You can, for example, assign an Option-⌘-key combination to any menu command that you frequently select. If you use a macro regularly for even small tasks such as this one, you will save a considerable amount of time.

Avoiding keystroke conflicts

You can assign ClarisWorks macros to function keys (if you have an extended keyboard) or to Option-⌘-key combinations. Because ClarisWorks uses neither of these approaches for invoking its menu commands and keyboard shortcuts, the particular key combinations that you choose should be of little consequence, right? Well, maybe. . . .

Many desk accessories and control panels have key combinations that you can use to pop them up or to make them perform particular functions. Watch out for conflicts. The usual symptom of a conflict is that the ClarisWorks macro will not function and is overridden by the desk accessory or control panel (or vice versa). The solution is either to choose another key combination for the ClarisWorks macro or to choose another key combination for the desk accessory or control panel, if you can.

Transferring macros to other users

Although the manual doesn't mention it, you can share macros with friends and colleagues. You simply save the macros in a document file, rather than in ClarisWorks itself. All that your friend has to do is open the file and change each macro from a document-specific macro to a ClarisWorks macro.

To transfer macros:

1. **Create a new document (choose New from the File menu) and record the macros.**
2. **When saving the macros, click the Document Specific check box.**
3. **Save the document and give a copy of it to your friend.**
4. **The other user launches ClarisWorks and opens the document in which you saved the macros.**
5. **The user chooses Shortcuts from the File menu and then chooses Edit Macros.** The Edit Macros dialog box appears.
6. **From the Macros pop-up menu, the user chooses a macro to add to ClarisWorks.**
7. **The user removes the check mark from the Document Specific check box by clicking once in the check box and then changes other options, such as the key combination used to invoke the macro, as desired.**

   To add other macros to ClarisWorks, the user repeats Steps 6 and 7.
8. **The user clicks Done to save the changes.**

Moving On Up

The ClarisWorks macros are fine for simple tasks, but you may want to investigate one of the more powerful commercial macro programs. In addition to working with ClarisWorks, these macro programs also work in other programs and with the Finder.

QuicKeys (CE Software) and Tempo (Affinity Microsystems) are general-purpose macro utilities that are intended for the typical Macintosh user. Both programs provide a recorder function that you can use to record most macros, as well as the ability to edit macros without re-recording them. If you're still using System 6, check out the MacroMaker utility that's included as part of the system software. It doesn't have the power of QuicKeys or Tempo, but it's free and simple to use.

Summary

- Macros enable you to automate simple and complex ClarisWorks tasks and perform them by clicking a button or pressing an Option-⌘-key combination.
- Every macro can be a general ClarisWorks macro (available in any new document of the correct type) or be document-specific (available only when a particular document is active).
- You can assign a macro to the Shortcuts palette and display a custom icon on the macro's button.
- Although you cannot edit the steps of a macro, you can edit the options for a macro.
- You can delete macros when you no longer need them.
- The communications environment has a special macro option called Macro Wait that causes the macro to wait a specific number of seconds or for a particular incoming text string before it continues.
- ClarisWorks 3.0 enables you to create automatic macros that automatically run when you launch ClarisWorks, open a particular document type, or create a new file in a specific environment.
- You can share macros with another user by creating several macros in the same document and making them document specific. The recipient then opens the file and changes the macros to general ClarisWorks macros.

Topic 15

Working with Frames

Overview

The concept of *frames* is what puts the integration into ClarisWorks. You can create a document in one environment and embed other environments in the document by adding frames. For example, in a word processing document, you can embed paint frames that have illustrations in them and embed spreadsheet frames to display tables and charts (see Figure 15-1).

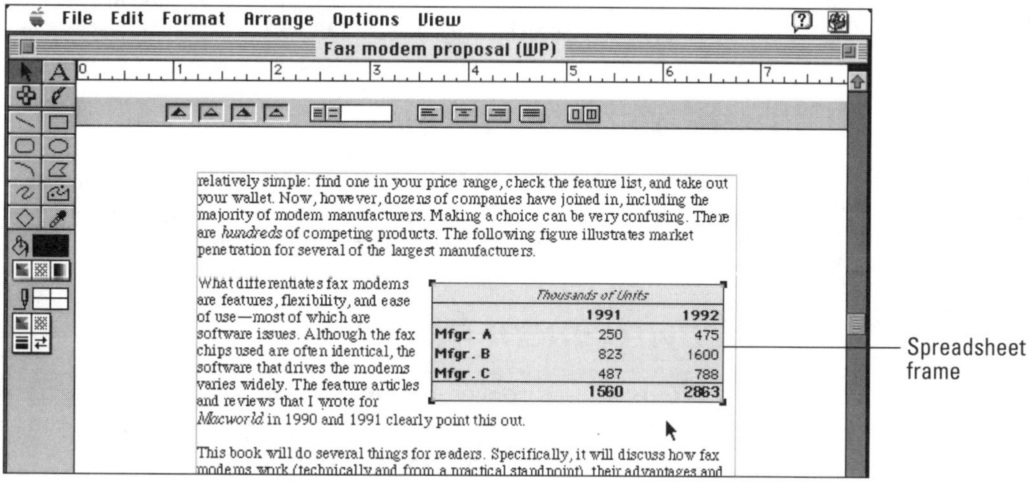

Figure 15-1: A spreadsheet frame within a word processing document.

Only the spreadsheet, word processing, and paint environments can be frames. When you work in a frame, it acts the same as a regular document that you create in that environment. The same menu commands and tools are available.

Unfortunately, the types of documents that enable you to use frames, the methods with which you create frames, the modes in which you can access the frames, and so on, are not consistent across environments. The next section lists the most important frame exceptions and "gotchas."

Frame Exceptions

You should be aware of the following list of rules and exceptions when you create and work with frames. Many of them are obvious and are based on common sense (no communications frames nor frames within communications documents, for example). Others are simply Claris design decisions — as in, that's the way it is.

Read the rules once and then go about your normal ClarisWorks business. If you don't remember whether a certain frame procedure works in a particular environment, just try it. Refer to this section only when you have problems. If you try to memorize any rules but the most critical ones, you'll needlessly confuse yourself.

No frames allowed

- Communications documents cannot contain frames, nor can you embed a communications document in any other type of document.
- Although you can embed frames within database documents (in Layout view only), you cannot create database frames in other kinds of documents.

Draw objects, not frames

- There are no draw frames. Draw objects are always drawn directly onto a document or within a frame. Environments in which draw objects can be added include the word processing, spreadsheet, database, and draw environments.

Same environment frames

- You can place word processing frames into word processing documents and spreadsheet frames into spreadsheet documents. To do so, you press the Option key while you draw the frame.

Adding frames to database documents

- Frames can be placed and edited in database documents, but only when you're in Layout view.

Behavior of frames added to paint documents

- The moment that you stop working in a frame that has been placed in a paint document, the contents of the frame become a regular paint image. You can no longer edit or manipulate the frame contents with its original environment tools. You can use only paint tools.
- You cannot add draw objects to paint documents, but draw documents can contain paint frames.

Text frame creation

- Unlike with spreadsheet and paint frames, you do not have to draw an outline to place a text frame in a document. You can simply click to position the cursor and begin typing.

Opening frames

- You can open spreadsheet or paint frames to display them separately in a full-sized window, but you cannot open text frames in this manner.
- You cannot open spreadsheet frames that are embedded in paint documents.

Linking frames

- You cannot link a pair of existing frames.
- You cannot link frames from different environments.
- You cannot link frames in a paint document.

See "Linking Frames," later in this Topic, for more information on linking.

Creating Frames

To create a spreadsheet, paint, or text frame within a document, select the appropriate tool from the Tool panel (see Figure 15-2), click to position one corner of the frame, and, while pressing the mouse button, drag to complete the frame. After you release the mouse button, the frame appears. Figure 15-3 shows the creation of a spreadsheet frame within a word processing document.

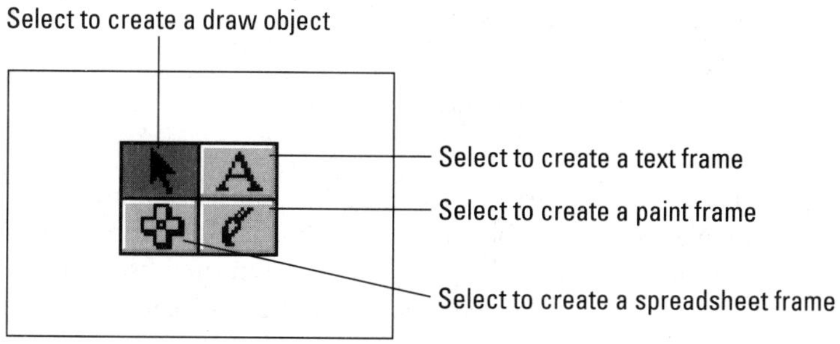
Select to create a draw object
Select to create a text frame
Select to create a paint frame
Select to create a spreadsheet frame

Figure 15-2: To create a frame, first select one of these tools from the Tool panel.

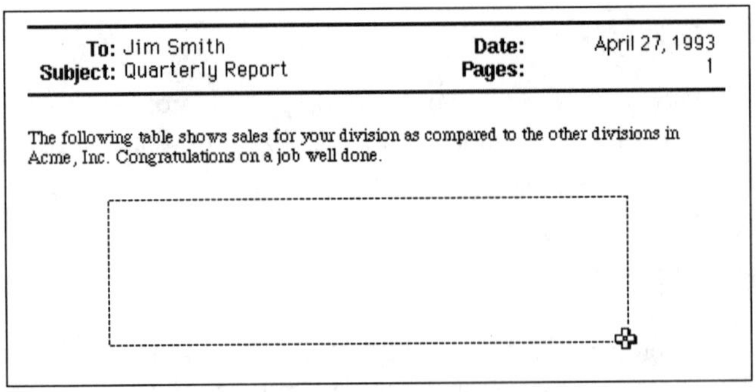

To: Jim Smith
Subject: Quarterly Report
Date: April 27, 1993
Pages: 1
The following table shows sales for your division as compared to the other divisions in Acme, Inc. Congratulations on a job well done.

Figure 15-3: Drag the mouse pointer to create a frame.

NOTE

If Autogrid — from the Options menu — is on, the frame aligns with the grid.

If frame links have not been set for the frame, a text frame will shrink to fit the text it contains. To retain a full WP frame (as you drew it), turn on frame links.

When you are creating frames, keep the following in mind:

NOTE

- Although there is no such thing as a draw frame, you can place a draw object into word processing, spreadsheet, draw, or database documents by choosing a draw tool and drawing.
- Spreadsheets and word processing documents can contain frames of their own type; that is, a spreadsheet can contain spreadsheet frames, and a word processing document can contain text frames. To create such a frame, start by selecting the text or spreadsheet tool, as appropriate. While pressing the Option key, click the mouse button and drag to make the frame. Figure 15-4 shows a text frame in a word processing document.

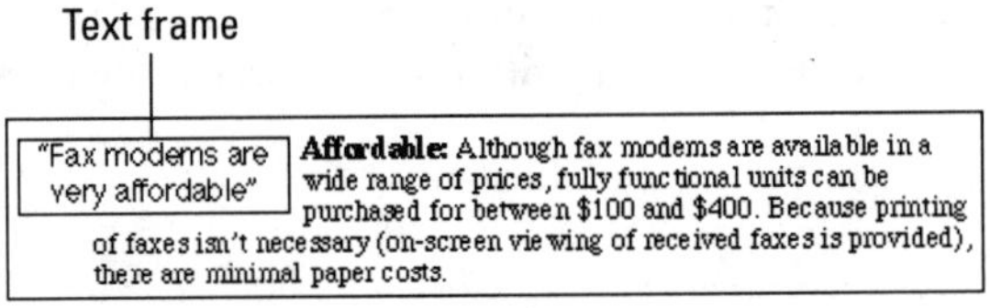

Figure 15-4: A text frame in a word processing document.

- You can select the text tool and drag to create a text frame, but you don't have to go to that trouble. Instead, you can click once to create a small text frame and immediately begin typing. You can later resize the frame as required (see "Resizing and Positioning Frames," later in this Topic).

Working in Frames

To work inside a frame, double-click it. The first click selects the frame; the second click moves you into the frame's environment and changes the pointer, tools, and menus to those of the new environment.

To stop working in a frame and return to the document's main environment, double-click anywhere outside the frame. If the click happens to hit another frame, rather than the main environment, the clicked frame is selected.

Resizing and Positioning Frames

After you place a frame in a document, you can treat its bounding rectangle just as you treat any other object. For example, to change the size of a frame, click it once to select the frame. Handles appear at the corners of the frame. Select any handle, press the mouse button, and drag to change the size of the frame. Release the mouse button to set the new size. Note that this procedure changes only the size of the frame, not the size of the image or data within the frame.

To change the location of a frame, click once to select it. Handles appear at its corners. Click anywhere inside the frame and, while pressing the mouse button, drag the frame to its new location. Release the mouse button to set the new position.

Keep in mind the following points about resizing and positioning frames:

- Although you can change the size of a text frame, the moment that you leave the frame, the frame is adjusted to the smallest height that still contains the text inside the frame. Only the new width is retained.
- You can drag spreadsheet frames to any size, but when you release the mouse button, the frame resizes itself to show only complete rows and columns.
- After you place a frame in a paint document, it ceases to be a frame. It becomes a paint image. To move the contents of a former frame, select its contents with the marquee tool and drag to a different location. To change the size of the contents of a former frame, select it with the marquee tool and choose the Resize command from the Transform menu.

Opening and Closing Frames

Because spreadsheet and paint frames are merely windows on what may be much larger documents, you can open frames to display them in separate document windows.

Being able to open these frames can make working with them easier. (Changes that you make while the frame is open are automatically carried to the frame in the document.) When you resize either type of frame by making it smaller, the rest of the image or cells don't disappear. They're simply outside the frame window — temporarily out of sight.

Step-by-Steps

To open a spreadsheet or paint frame:

1. **Click the spreadsheet or paint frame once to select it.** Handles appear at the edges.
2. **Choose Open Frame from the View menu.** If a spreadsheet frame was selected, a full-screen copy of the frame opens in a new document window. If a paint frame was selected, a same-size copy of the frame opens in a new document window.

— or —

1. **Press Option while double-clicking inside the frame.**

To close an opened frame, click the close box in the upper-left corner of the window. The frame disappears, and you return to your original document.

Changing the Display of Spreadsheet and Paint Frames

ClarisWorks has a Modify Frame command that you can use with either spreadsheet or paint frames. When you use it with a spreadsheet frame, you can decide whether the cell grid, row headings, and column headings should be visible or hidden and whether data or formulas are displayed; and you can set a different *origin* (the upper-left corner of the worksheet frame) to display. When you choose Modify Frame for a paint frame, you can set a different resolution and depth for the frame's contents, as well as specify a different origin.

Step-by-Steps

To modify a spreadsheet or paint frame:

1. **Select the frame.** Handles appear around the border of the frame.
2. **Choose Modify Frame from the Options menu (or press Shift-⌘-I).** One of two dialog boxes appears, depending on whether a spreadsheet or paint frame is currently selected (see Figure 15-5).

Display

☒ Cell grid ☒ Column headings
☐ Solid lines ☒ Row headings
☐ Formulas ☒ Mark circular refs

Origin `A1` [Cancel] [OK]

— Spreadsheet dialog box

Resolution and Depth

┌─**Resolution**─┐ ┌─**Depth**─────┐
◉ 72 DPI ○ Black & White
○ 144 DPI ○ 4
○ 288 DPI ○ 16
○ 300 DPI ◉ 256
○ 360 DPI ○ Thousands
 ○ Millions

Memory 14K

Origin
`0` `0` [Cancel] [OK]

— Paint dialog box

— Horizontal coordinate

— Vertical coordinate

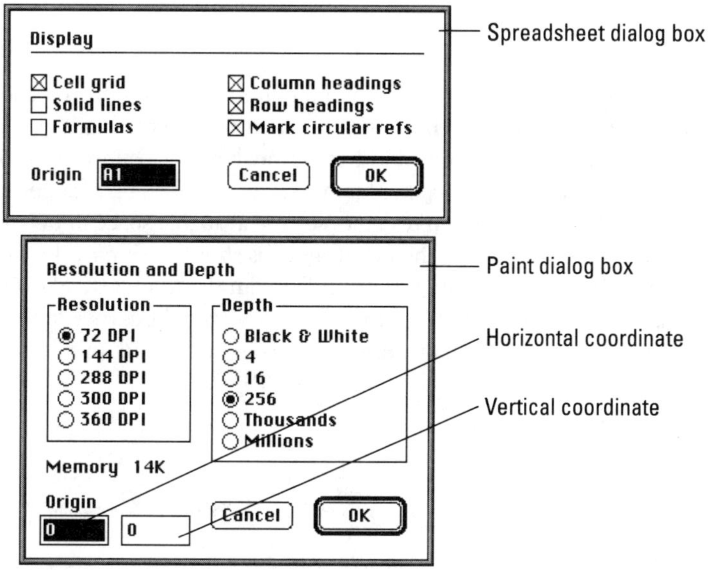

Figure 15-5: Dialog boxes for modifying spreadsheet and paint frames.

3. If a spreadsheet frame is selected, set options by clicking check boxes. To set a different cell origin (the cell that appears in the upper-left corner of the frame), type the new cell coordinates (B14, for example) in the Origin text-edit box.

— or —

3. If a paint frame is selected, you can set a different resolution (the number of dots per inch) and depth (number of colors/data bits) for the images in the frame. As you click different radio buttons, the amount of memory required is shown.

You also can specify a different origin used to display the image within its frame. The two Origin text-edit boxes are used to set the horizontal and vertical coordinates (in pixels). An inch contains 72 pixels. For example, to specify starting coordinates of 1 inch to the right and 1.5 inches down, you enter **72** and **108.**

4. Click OK to accept the changes.

When importing a PICT file into a paint frame or document, ClarisWorks 2.1 or higher automatically matches the resolution of the image and uses the document's original color table.

Linking Frames

Although you can easily create multicolumn text in the word processor, ClarisWorks provides a more flexible method for creating complex layouts. You can link text frames to one another — much as you can in desktop publishing programs. A document can contain a series of linked text frames that are placed wherever you like. When text exceeds the available space in one text frame, it automatically flows into the next frame (as shown in Figure 15-6). If the linked frames do not have enough room to contain the total text, an overflow indicator (a small box with an *X* in it) appears in the lower-right corner of the final frame. A document also can contain combinations of linked and unlinked frames.

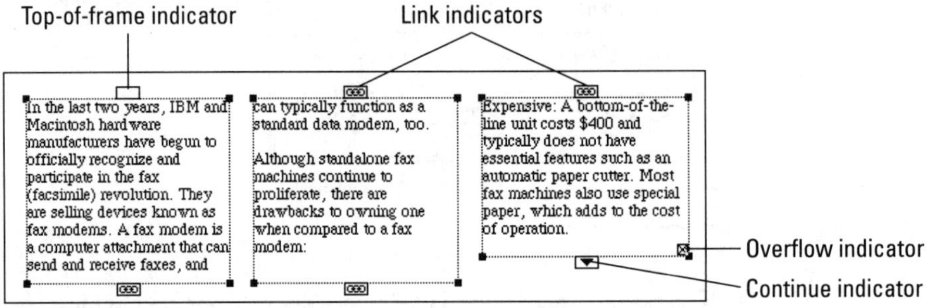

Figure 15-6: Linked text frames with indicator symbols.

You also can create linked spreadsheet frames and linked paint frames. Unlike linked text frames, any linked spreadsheet or paint frame is merely a window into the complete spreadsheet or paint document. The purpose of creating linked spreadsheet or paint frames is to provide multiple views into the same document. You can, for example, show some pertinent raw data from a worksheet in one frame and display summary figures from the same worksheet in another frame.

Step-by-Steps

To create linked text frames:

1. **Select the pointer tool in the Tool panel.**
2. **Choose Frame Links from the Options menu (or press ⌘-L).**
3. **Select the text tool from the Tool panel and draw a text frame.** (If the Tool panel isn't visible, choose Show Tools from the View menu or press Shift-⌘-T.)
4. **Click outside the text frame.** An empty text frame with top-of-frame and continue indicators appears, as shown in Figure 15-7.
5. **Click the continue indicator — the black triangle at the bottom of the frame — and draw a box for the next text frame.**

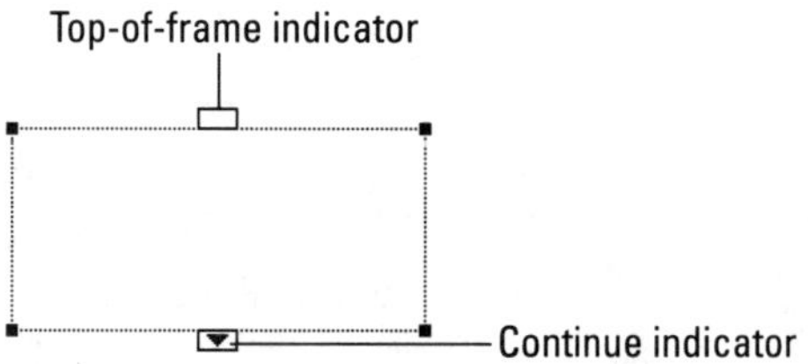

Figure 15-7: An empty linked text frame.

6. **Repeat Steps 4 and 5 for any additional continuation frames that you want to create.**
7. **Add text to the first frame by typing, pasting, or inserting.** When the frame fills, additional text automatically flows into the other frames that are linked to it.
8. **If additional frames are required, click the continue indicator of the last linked frame and draw another frame.** Repeat as necessary.

You also can start with a single frame that already contains text and then link new text frames to the first frame. Just use the pointer tool to select the first frame, choose Frame Links from the Options menu, and go to Step 5 in the preceding instructions.

TIP

You can insert a linked frame in the middle of several links — not just at the end. Simply use the pointer tool to click the link indicator on any linked frame and then draw the new frame.

NOTE

Draw documents can have multiple pages, and you can link frames across pages — linking an article that starts on page 1 to a continuation on page 5, for example. To add pages to a draw document, first choose Document from the Format menu. In the Size section of the dialog box that appears, indicate the number of pages that you want. To see the breaks between pages, choose Page View from the View menu (or press Shift-⌘-P).

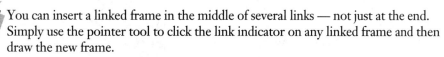

Step-by-Steps

To create linked spreadsheet or paint frames:

1. **Create a spreadsheet or paint frame and use the pointer tool to select the frame.**
2. **Choose Frame Links from the Options menu (or press ⌘-L).**
3. **Click the continue indicator at the bottom of the frame and draw a box for the continuation frame.** Repeat for any additional continuation frames that you want to create.

Why use linked frames?

In a word, *freedom.* Unlike in a word processing document — even a multicolumn one — you can place linked text frames anywhere you like. You also can have some text frames that are linked and other text frames that stand alone. By using linked text frames, you can create layouts that are as complex as layouts made with some desktop publishing programs. The following figure shows a simple newsletter layout in a draw document that incorporates linked text frames, standalone text frames, and draw objects.

To help align the different objects and frames, you can turn on the Autogrid. After you have placed objects in position, you can select the frames and then choose the Lock command from the Arrange menu (⌘-H) to lock the frames in position. Locking the frames keeps them from moving but lets you edit the text within.

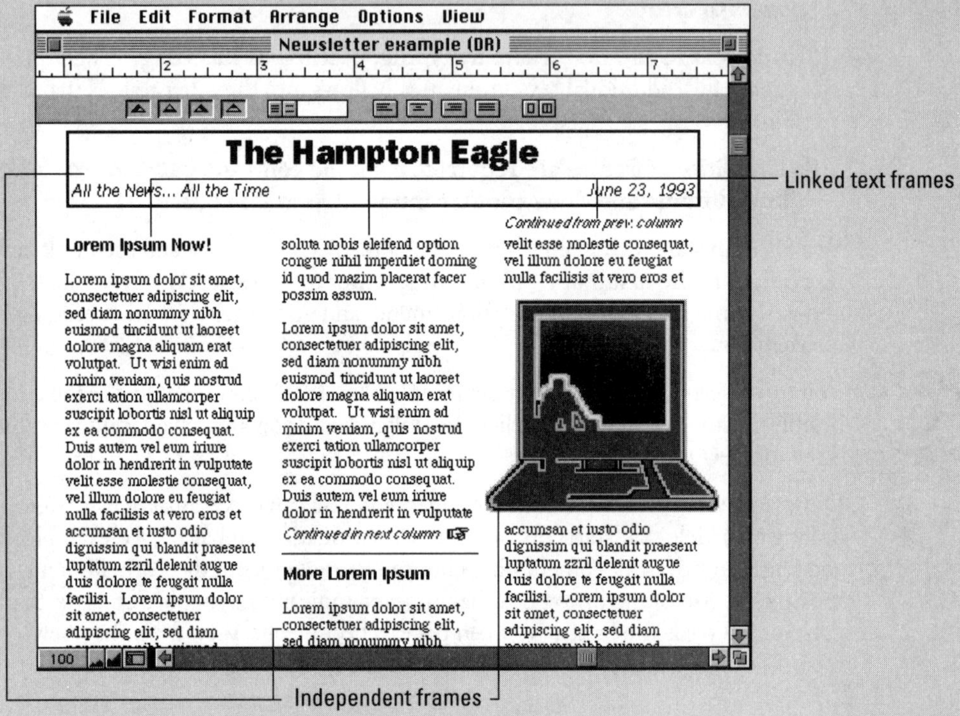

You can open a spreadsheet to full-screen size for editing or open a second view of a paint frame. You also can change the origin that is used to display any spreadsheet or paint frame. For details, refer to "Opening and Closing Frames" and "Changing the Display of Spreadsheet and Paint Frames," earlier in this Topic.

For additional information on working with spreadsheet charts in frames, see "Using Spreadsheet Charts in Frames," later in this Topic.

Quick Tips

The following Quick Tips give some examples of things that you can do to frames and provide instructions for using spreadsheet charts that are within a frame or are free floating.

Frames are objects

If it isn't apparent from the preceding discussion, I'll tell you now. Other than in the paint environment, *all frames are objects.* Anything that you can do to an object, you can do to a frame. Examples include the following:

- Changing the pen color, line width, and pattern for the border (or making the border transparent)
- Adding a background color
- Resizing the frame
- Placing one frame over another and sending frames forward or backward

Using spreadsheet charts in frames

You can embed spreadsheet charts in a spreadsheet frame or create them as free-floating objects.

To make a free-floating chart:

1. **Enter the spreadsheet frame by double-clicking a cell.**
2. **Select the data that you want to use for the chart.**
3. **Choose Make Chart from the Options menu (or press ⌘-M).** The Chart Options dialog box appears.
4. **Choose a chart type, choose options, and click OK.** The chart appears, separate from the worksheet.

To make a chart within a spreadsheet frame:

1. **Enter the spreadsheet frame by double-clicking a cell.**
2. **Choose Open Frame from the View menu.** The worksheet expands to a full-screen view.
3. **Select the data that you want to use for the chart.**
4. **Choose Make Chart from the Options menu (or press ⌘-M).** The Chart Options dialog box appears.

5. **Choose a chart type, choose options, and click OK.** The chart appears, embedded as an object in the worksheet.

6. **Click the close box on the spreadsheet window to return to the original document.**

To move or resize an embedded chart, either press Control while you click the chart or open the chart again with the Open Frame command.

Summary

- Any ClarisWorks document other than a communications document can contain frames from other environments.
- When you work in a frame, the menu commands and tools change to match the environment of the frame. When you leave the frame, they change back to match the base document's environment.
- Frames are objects, and, except for frames that you create in paint documents, you can resize or move them. You can apply any attribute to a frame that you can apply to an object.
- Spreadsheet frames are merely windows into larger documents, and you can expand them to full-screen size.
- You can link text, spreadsheet, and paint frames to like frames. When you link text frames, text can flow automatically from one frame to another. Linking spreadsheet or paint frames enables you to display multiple views of the same underlying spreadsheet or paint document.

Topic 16

Working with Outlines

Overview

Think back to your high school days. Remember making outlines — those numbered lists that you used to arrange your thoughts for a paper or speech into a coherent, meaningful order? Well, many of us still use outlines, and the ClarisWorks outline view for word processing documents makes using outlines easier than ever.

The main headings in an outline are called *topics*. Subordinate headings are called *subtopics*. Each subtopic is a point or an idea that is related to the topic above it, as shown in Figure 16-1. A ClarisWorks outline can have up to 16 levels of subtopics.

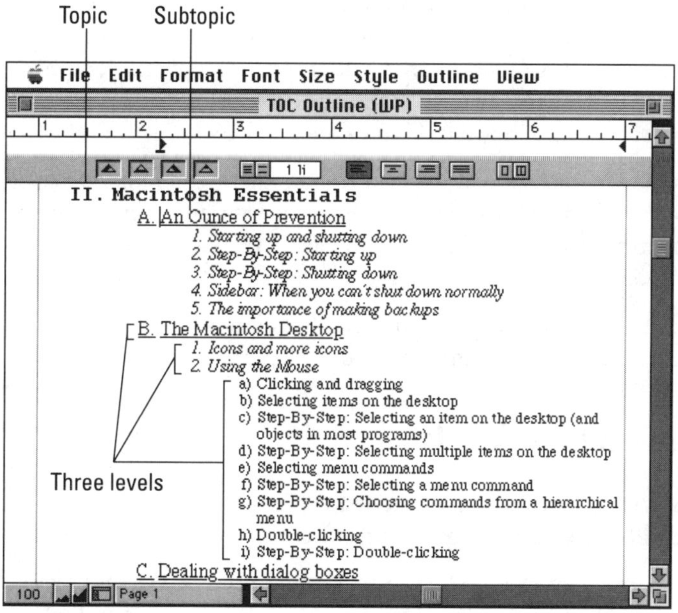

Figure 16-1: Topics and subtopics.

The Outline View command works as a toggle. Each time you choose the command, it toggles between the outline and the normal view of the current document.

NOTE

When you switch from outline view to a standard document (normal view), the formatting defined for topic labels is lost. You can easily reformat the text by using a macro or by defining and applying custom text styles. On the other hand, manual formatting applied to text in either outline or normal view *will* carry to the other view.

Step-by-Steps

To create a new outline:

1. **Choose New from the File menu (or press ⌘-N). The Word Processing radio button is already selected, so click OK or press Return to create a blank word processing document.**
2. **Choose Outline View from the Outline menu (or press Shift-⌘-I).**
3. **Select an outline format by choosing from the Outline Format submenu of the Outline menu.** You can now begin to create the outline.

Outline Formats and Topic Labels

Every outline has a general format that you choose from the Outline Format submenu of the Outline menu. Although you are still free to customize individual topics or subtopics (by changing their font or style, for example), an outline format specifies a default style for every new topic and subtopic that you create. Thus, you don't need to format individual topics and subtopics. The outline formats that you can choose from are shown in Figures 16-2 and 16-3.

As you can see, each format has its own method of assigning *topic labels* (the symbol, letter, or number that precedes each topic and subtopic in the outline), as well as the particular font and style for each level. ClarisWorks has 12 different types of topic labels, as shown in Figure 16-4.

Although the outline format automatically assigns a topic label to every topic and subtopic, you can change any topic label.

Step-by-Steps

To change a topic label:

1. **Select one or more contiguous topics or subtopics in the outline by clicking and dragging through them.**
2. **Choose a label style from the Topic Label submenu of the Outline menu.** The label style is applied to the selected topics and subtopics.

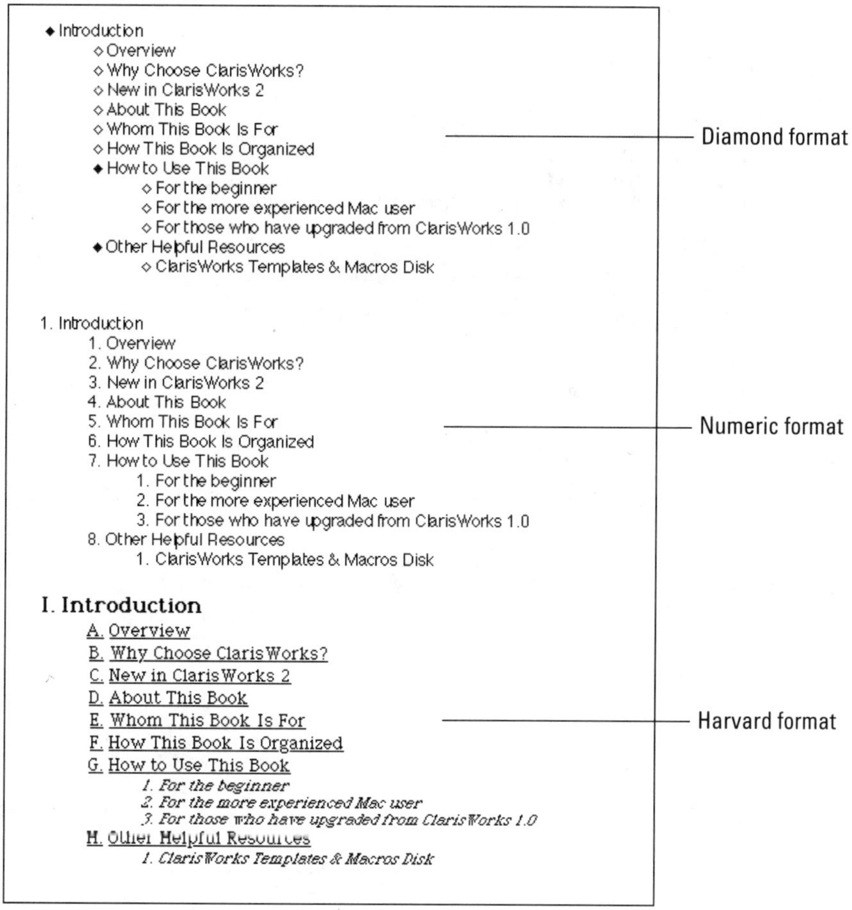

Figure 16-2: Diamond, Numeric, and Harvard outline formats.

Custom Formats

For a quick-and-dirty outline, stick with the level definitions that the program provides for the general format that you've selected. For presentations or formal papers, on the other hand, you may well want to design your own format for the outline so that you can select the topic labels, indents, fonts, styles, and sizes for each level.

Although you can alter the appearance of any topic or subtopic in the outline manually (by selecting the text and changing its font or size, for example), a better way to make the appearance of the levels in the outline consistent is to create a custom format.

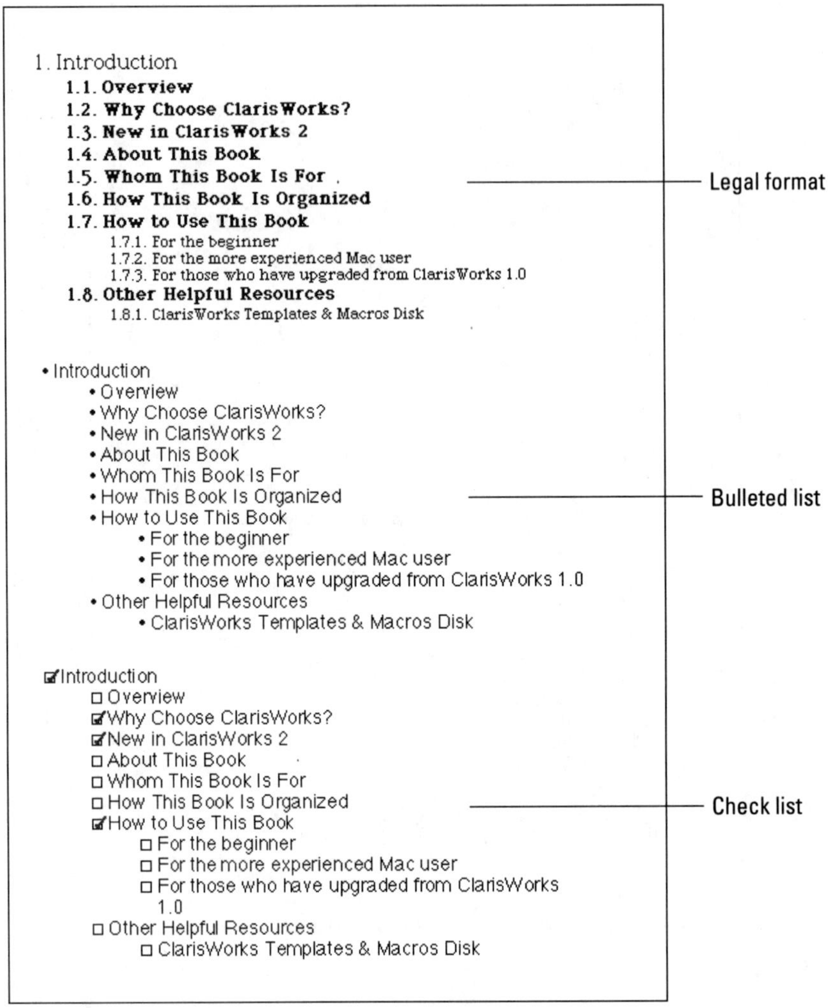

Figure 16-3: Legal format, Bulleted list, and Check list formats.

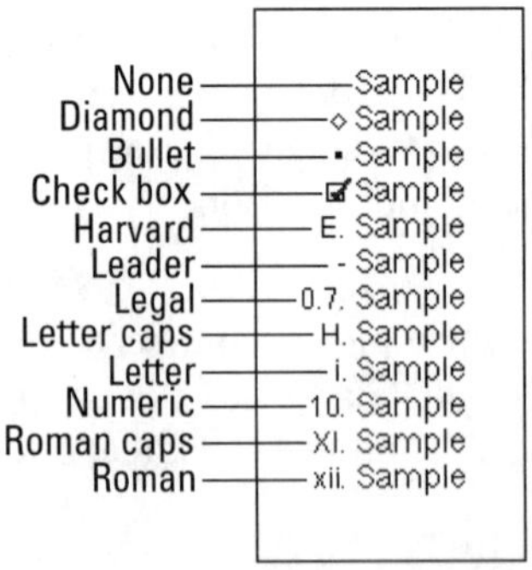

Figure 16-4: The different types of topic labels.

Regardless of which outline format you've chosen, you use the Edit Custom command to make changes to the format. When you choose the command, you see level specifications for the format that you've chosen.

To create a custom format:

1. **If you aren't already in outline view, choose Outline View from the Outline menu (or press Shift-⌘-I).**
2. **Choose Edit Custom from the Outline format submenu in the Outline menu.** The Level Format dialog box appears (Figure 16-5).

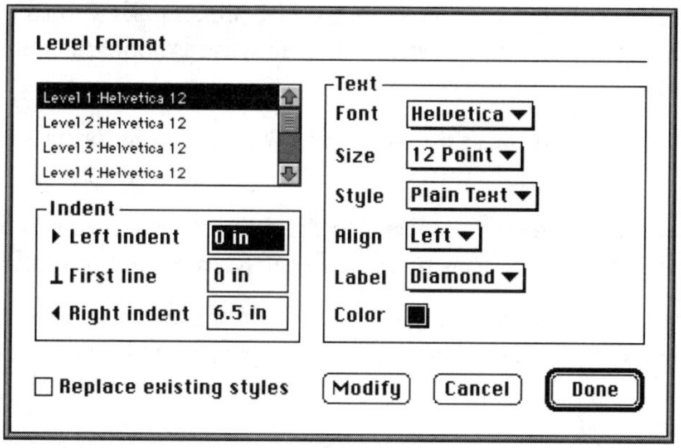

Figure 16-5: The Level Format dialog box.

3. **In the upper-left corner of the dialog box, choose the level that you want to change.**
4. **In the Indent section of the dialog box, change the left, right, or first line indent by typing new numbers if you want to change those settings.**
5. **Change any Text settings that you want to alter for the level by choosing options from the pop-up menus on the right side of the dialog box (Font, Size, Style, Align, Label, and Color).**
6. **When you finish making changes for the level, click Modify.**
7. **Repeat Steps 3 through 6 for other levels that you want to alter at this time.**
8. **Click Done.** Any new topics and subtopics that you create for levels that you've just modified will have the attributes that you specified.

   If you also want to change existing topics and subtopics in the outline to match the new formats, check the Replace existing styles check box before you click Done. Any formatting that you manually added to those levels, however, will be replaced by the new formatting definitions.

TIP

Using different text colors is an excellent way to differentiate levels. In a demonstration, for example, lecture items could all be one color, and points to be demonstrated could be formatted in another color.

Creating New Topics and Subtopics

Now that you know about the components of an outline and how to assign formats and labels to topics, you need to step back and examine the mechanics of entering outline topics and subtopics.

After you type a new topic, you can do the following:

- ◆ Create a new topic at the same level by pressing ⌘-Return or choosing New Topic from the Outline menu (these methods apply the default format for the level)
- ◆ Create a new topic at the same level with the same formatting as the previous topic by pressing Return
- ◆ Create a new topic below and to the right of the current topic (a subtopic) by pressing ⌘-R or choosing New Topic Right from the Outline menu
- ◆ Create a new topic below and to the left of the current one (at a higher level) by pressing ⌘-L or choosing New Topic Left from the Outline menu

Collapsing and Expanding

ClarisWorks enables you to expand and collapse the entire outline or just selected topics and subtopics. You may want to collapse the outline to show only one or two levels of topics so you can focus on the main points without the clutter of additional subtopics. Similarly, you may want to collapse only the levels below a particular topic or subtopic. When I am working with a book outline, I often use this approach to show that a chapter has been completed.

Step-by-Steps

To collapse or expand an entire outline:

1. **Choose the Expand to command from the Outline menu.** The Expand to dialog box appears, as shown in Figure 16-6.
2. **In the text-edit box, type the number of outline levels that you want to display and then click OK.** The outline changes to show only that number of levels.

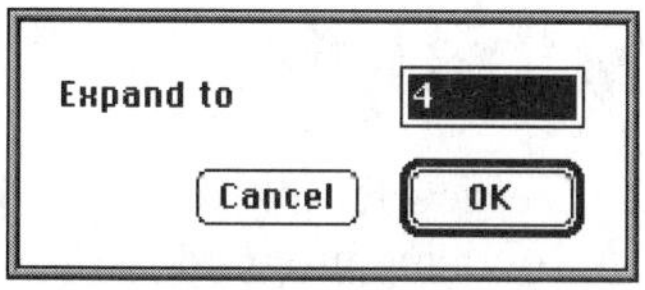

Figure 16-6: The Expand to dialog box.

Enter 1, for example, to display only the main topics for the outline. Type a larger number (the maximum is 16) to display all levels.

Step-by-Steps

To collapse or expand a single topic and associated subtopics:

1. **Choose the topic you want to collapse or expand.**
2. **Double-click the topic label, choose Collapse or Expand from the Outline menu, or press Control-spacebar.**

NOTE

If a topic cannot be collapsed or expanded, nothing happens. (For example, you cannot collapse the lowest level topic because it has no subtopics.)

TIP

You can collapse or expand multiple contiguous topics by choosing them before you choose the Collapse or Expand command. To choose several topics, click in the first topic to set the text insertion point and then drag to choose the additional topics.

Tips for expanding and collapsing

As you work with outlines, you'll find that the diamond outline format is easier to work with than the others, particularly when you are frequently expanding or collapsing individual topics. Only the diamond format shows whether hidden subtopics are below a topic. The normal diamond is empty; a gray diamond indicates that additional subtopics are hidden below.

Although check boxes are excellent for to-do lists, they pose a special problem when you expand or collapse levels. In a normal outline that uses diamond symbols, bullets, or numbers as topic labels, you can expand or collapse levels by double-clicking the label. (*Double-clicking* is much easier to remember than the keyboard shortcut — ⌘-spacebar — and handier than pulling down the Outline menu.) Unfortunately, double-clicking in a check box merely toggles the check mark on and off.

The trick to collapsing a check box level is to double-click *to the left* of the check box, rather than in it.

Rearranging Topics and Subtopics

One of the nice things about having a separate view for working with outlines (as opposed to creating one in a regular word processing program) is the ease with which you can rearrange topics and subtopics. ClarisWorks provides a variety of features for rearranging topics, including dragging them to different levels and using keyboard or menu commands.

Moving topics

By using the mouse, you can easily move a topic and its subtopics to a new position in the outline.

Step-by-Steps

To move a topic by using the mouse:

1. **Click the topic label to choose the topic and its associated subtopics.** (If the topic has a check box label, click to the left of the check box.)
2. **Click to the left of the selected topic and press the mouse button.** As you drag up or down, the cursor changes to a double-headed arrow, with a tiny horizontal line that separates the arrowheads. A thick horizontal line, called the insertion marker, appears, showing where the selected topic will move (see Figure 16-7).

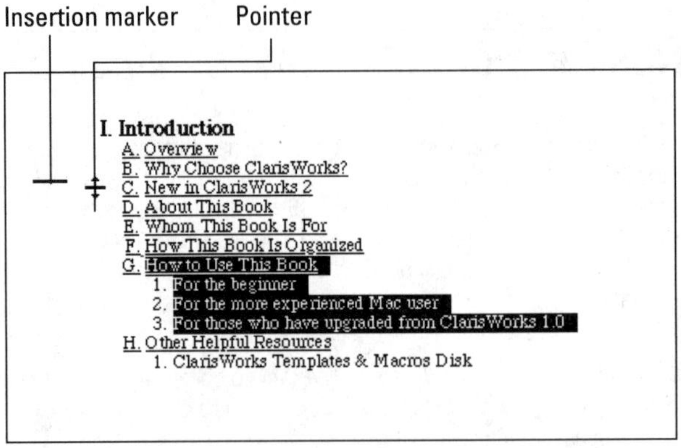

Figure 16-7: Moving a topic.

3. **When the insertion marker is in the spot where you want to move the topic, release the mouse button.** The topic and associated subtopics move to the new position, and the outline is relabeled as necessary.

You also can use menu commands to move a selected topic above or below adjacent topics.

To move a topic above or below an adjacent topic:

1. **Select the topic that you want to move by clicking anywhere within its text.**
2. **Choose Move Above (Shift-⌘-A or Control-up arrow) or Move Below (Shift-⌘-B or Control-down arrow) from the Outline menu.** The topic and its subtopics move to the new location while retaining the same level in the outline hierarchy.

— or —

2. **If you want to move a topic up or down without also moving its subtopics, press the Option key when you choose the Move Above or Move Below command from the Outline menu (or press Option-Control-up arrow or Option-Control-down arrow).**

Raising or lowering topic levels

Although you can use the mouse to move a topic anywhere in the outline, you cannot change a topic's level by moving it with the mouse. If a topic was at level 3 before the move, it will still be at level 3 after the move. To change a topic's level, you need to use the Move Left or Move Right command (or the keyboard equivalents).

To change a topic's level:

1. **Select the topic whose level you want to change by clicking anywhere within its text.**
2. **Choose Move Left (Shift-⌘-L or Control-left arrow) or Move Right (Shift-⌘-R or Control-right arrow) from the Outline menu.** The selected topic and all associated subtopics are promoted or demoted one level in the outline hierarchy.

— or —

2. **If you want to promote or demote a topic without affecting its subtopics, press Option when you choose the Move Left or Move Right command from the Outline menu (or press Option-Control-left arrow or Option-Control-right arrow).**
3. **Repeat Step 2 for each additional level that you want to promote or demote the selected items.**

Deleting Topics

As you work, you may decide to delete some topics or levels in the outline. The procedure differs, however, depending on whether you want to delete a topic and its subtopics or just delete a single level in the outline without eliminating its subtopics.

To delete a single level:

1. **Triple-click in the text of the level that you want to delete.** The entire line of text is selected (see Figure 16-8). If the topic contains more than one line, you have to quadruple-click to select it.

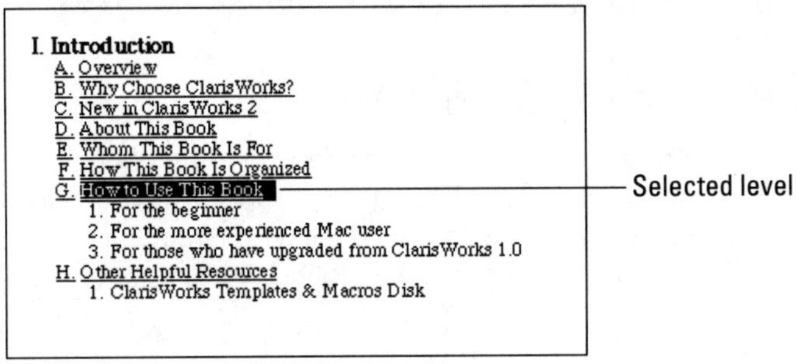

Figure 16-8: Selecting a single level in an outline.

— or —

1. **Drag to select all the text in the level.**
2. **Press Delete or Backspace.** The line is eliminated.

If the topic was one of several topics at the same level, the other topics below it move up and are renumbered. For example, if you delete point 2 of topic G in Figure 16-8, point 3 simply moves up and becomes point 2. If you delete a topic that has subtopics below it (as does topic G), the subtopics become subtopics of the level above it (in this case, topic F).

To delete a topic and associated subtopics:

1. **Click the topic label.** (If the topic has a check box label, click to the left of the check box.) The topic and all associated subtopics are selected (see Figure 16-9).
2. **Press Delete or Backspace.** The topic and its subtopics are eliminated.

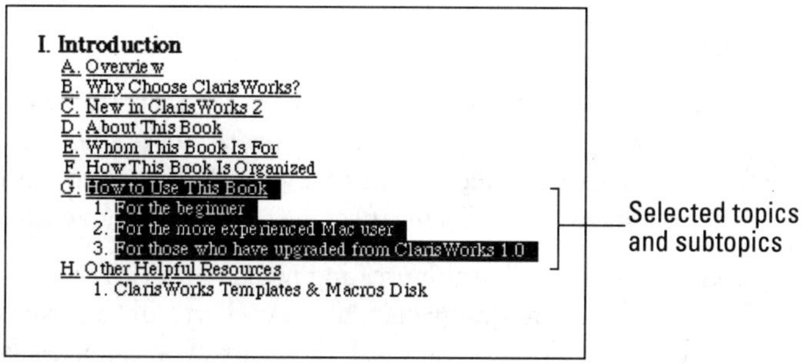

Figure 16-9: Selecting a topic and its subtopics.

Quick Tips

The following Quick Tips tell you how to make using the outline view feature more manageable if you don't use it regularly enough to learn all of the commands. They also suggest some applications for the outline view, including slide presentations.

Concentrate on the important commands

Because there are so many different commands for raising and lowering topics, moving topics, and creating new topics, you probably won't be able to remember them all unless you use the outliner on almost a daily basis. Instead, you are better off doing the following:

- ◆ For reorganizing topics and subtopics, try the visual approach. Select the topic and subtopics that you want to move and drag them to where they should go.
- ◆ Expand and collapse topics by double-clicking their labels.
- ◆ Concentrate on remembering only the most important commands, and use the Outline menu to choose the others. The following commands are the ones that you're likely to need the most.

Procedure	***Keystroke***
New topic at the same level	⌘-Return
New topic at the same level with the same formatting	Return
New topic to the left	⌘-L
New topic to the right	⌘-R
Shift topic to the left	Shift-⌘-L
Shift topic to the right	Shift-⌘-R

Outline ideas

Although the outlines that you created in high school or college were usually designed to organize points for a paper or speech, there's no reason that you can't write the entire paper or speech in outline view. Why use an outline just for notes? A topic doesn't have to be a point. It can just as easily be an entire paragraph.

Outline view is also excellent for creating presentations. You can use the Diamond or Bulleted list format to design standard text charts, or you can create a custom format, if you prefer. When you finish the charts, you can use a laser printer to print transparencies or handouts.

You also can use the ClarisWorks slide show feature to create an on-screen presentation. For an example of a slide show that is based on an outline, load one of the ClarisWorks sample files as follows:

1. Choose New from the File menu. The New Document dialog box appears.
2. Choose Presentation – Outline (WP) from the Stationery pop-up menu in the New Document dialog box.
3. Click OK. A copy of the template appears.
4. Choose Slide Show from the View menu. The Slide Show dialog box appears.
5. Click Start. The slide show begins.

You advance through the three slides by clicking the mouse button. When you're through, press Q. Click Done or Cancel to return to the Outline view. For more information about slide shows, see Topic 17.

Although a word processing document is normally used for outlines, you can also make an outline in a text frame. Insert a text frame into a slide show page, switch to outline view, and you can quickly make a bulleted list or text chart.

Summary

- You can switch freely back and forth between the outline and a normal view of your document.
- ClarisWorks outlines can have as many as 16 topic levels. (Levels are used to represent ideas that are subordinate to the preceding topic.)
- Six predefined formats are included in ClarisWorks. You can create custom formats, however, if the need arises.
- You can collapse or expand an entire outline or just selected topics and subtopics to change your perspective on the contents of the outline. You also can specify how many levels you want to view by using the Expand To command.
- You can move topics to a different location in the outline by dragging them with the mouse. You also can use keyboard and menu commands to shift topics to the left or right (promoting or demoting them), as well as to move them above or below adjacent topics.

Topic 17
Creating a Slide Show

Overview

You don't need fancy software to create and display most presentations. All you need is a program with a *slide show feature* — the capability to present a series of text charts, graphs, and other images on the Mac's screen. ClarisWorks has such a feature. You can use it from any environment except communications, and it is surprisingly flexible.

Slide Show Fundamentals

Every slide show is based on a single ClarisWorks document. Each page of the document is treated as a separate slide. You can rearrange pages to display them in a different order; make pages opaque, transparent, or hidden; specify special effects for the presentation, such as fading out between slides and looping (for continuous, self-running demonstrations); and place QuickTime movies on slides.

After you create a slide show document, you choose Slide Show from the View menu, set options, and then run the slide show. Creating an effective slide show tends to be an iterative process that consists of refining the slides, trying out different backgrounds, and experimenting with effects until you have the presentation you want.

Preparing for a Slide Show

Although you can take any document and instantly transform it into a serviceable slide show, a polished presentation requires that you spend some time examining different options and determining which options are best for the presentation. This Topic examines the slide show features and explains how each feature affects the presentation.

Setting the number of slides

In every environment except word processing, you have to set the number of slides that will appear in the slide show. Word processing is an exception because its documents are designed to accommodate multiple pages automatically. In most of the other environments, you have to add pages beyond the first one.

TIP

Regardless of the environment that you use, be sure that ClarisWorks is set for Page View in the View menu so that you can see where the page breaks occur.

The instructions that follow explain how to set the number of slides in different environments.

To set the number of slides for a draw document:

1. **Choose Document from the Format menu.** The Document dialog box appears, as shown in Figure 17-1.

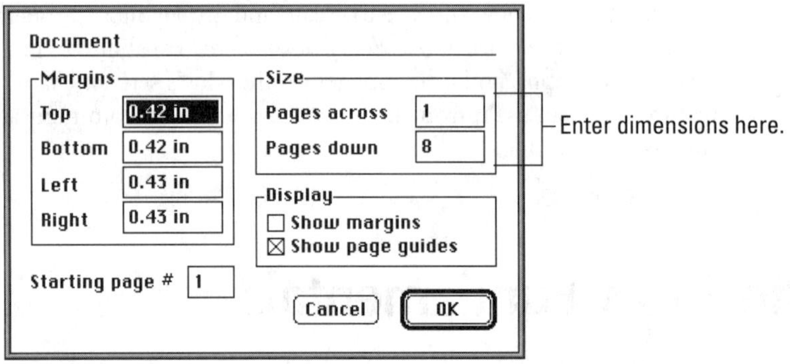

Figure 17-1: The Document dialog box for a draw document.

2. **In the Size section of the dialog box, enter the number of Pages across and Pages down.** When presented as a slide show, draw pages are shown across and then down.

NOTE

Draw documents also can have a *master page.* You use a master page to display a logo or other static objects on each slide. See Topic 18 for more information.

To set the number of slides for a paint document:

1. **Choose Document from the Format menu.** The Document dialog box appears, as shown in Figure 17-2.
2. **In the Size section of the dialog box, enter the number of Pixels across and Pixels down.** (An inch contains 72 pixels.)

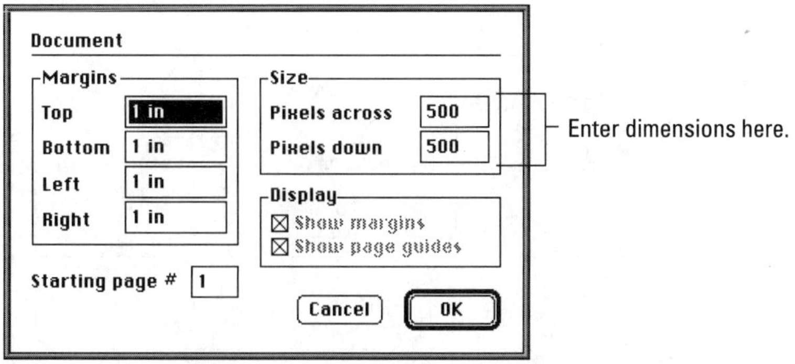

Figure 17-2: The Document dialog box for a paint document.

To set the number of slides for a spreadsheet document:

1. **Choose Document from the Format menu.** The Document dialog box appears, as shown in Figure 17-3.

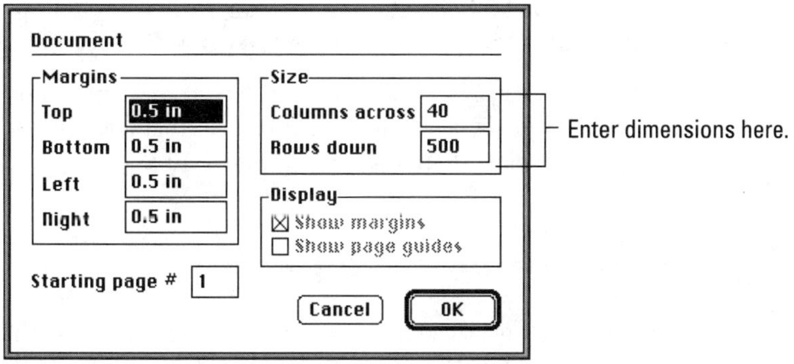

Figure 17-3: The Document dialog box for a spreadsheet document.

2. **In the Size section of the dialog box, enter the number of Columns across and Rows down.** Using the default column width and row height, a standard slide page is 7 columns wide and 50 rows high (or 9 columns wide and 37 rows high in landscape mode).

To set the number of slides for a database document:

1. **Create a layout that displays a single record per page.**
2. **Choose Browse (Shift-⌘-B) from the Layout menu.**
3. **Choose Slide Show from the View menu.** The Slide Show dialog box appears (see Figure 17-4).

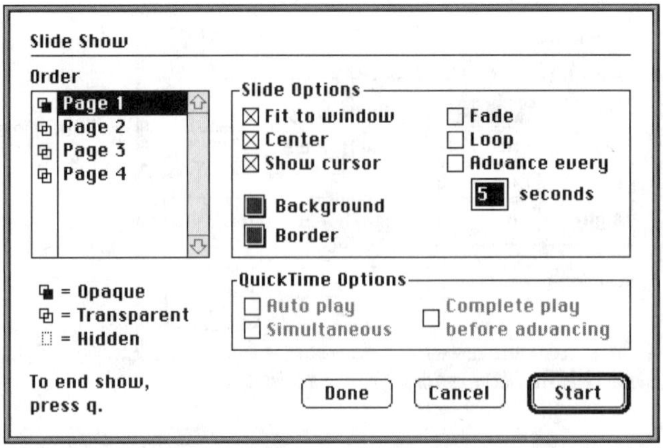

Figure 17-4: The Slide Show dialog box.

4. **Set options and click Start.**
5. **If more than one record appears on each slide or if the record isn't properly positioned on the slide screen, choose the Document command from the Format menu. Change the margins and then repeat Steps 3 and 4 until only a single record is displayed on each slide.**

When creating a database slide show, you can use the Find command in the Layout menu (Shift-⌘-F) to choose the records that you want to display as slides. If you want to display all records, choose Show All Records (Shift-⌘-A) from the Organize menu.

Changing the order of slides

The slide order is displayed in the left side of the Slide Show dialog box (see Figure 17-4). To alter the order, you simply select a page with the mouse and then drag it to a new position in the list.

Setting layering options

Each slide can be opaque, transparent, or omitted (hidden) from the presentation. An opaque slide is solid and completely obscures any slides that you have already shown. A transparent slide, on the other hand, lets the slide beneath it show. You can place several transparent slides on top of one another to create special effects. For an example of slides that are on top of one another, run the slide show for the ClarisWorks sample file named Presentation – Draw (which is located in the Sample Files folder).

To change a slide's layering in the Order list, click the icon to the left of the page number. As you click, the layering cycles through its three options: opaque, transparent, and hidden. Figure 17-5 shows examples of icons for pages that are opaque, transparent, and hidden.

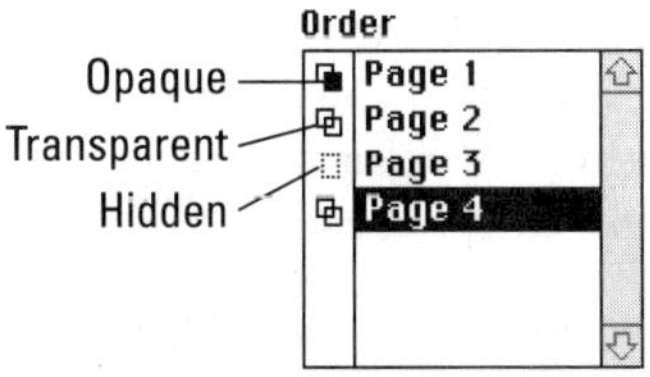

Figure 17-5: Slide layering options.

NOTE

If you are using a master page as a background, it will show through on all slides, regardless of whether they are opaque or transparent. Note that you can create master pages only for draw documents. (See Topic 18 for more information on master pages.)

Slide display options

You also set display options in the Slide Show dialog box.

Step-by-Steps

To set display options:

1. **Open the document that you want to use for the presentation.**
2. **Choose Slide Show from the View menu.** The Slide Show dialog box appears, as shown in Figure 17-4.
3. **Set the options that you want to use in the presentation (as described in the "Slide options" section later in this Topic).**
4. **Click Start to see the slide show.**
5. **Press Q to exit the slide show (⌘-period, Clear, and Esc also work).**
6. **Click Done to save the settings and return to the document or click Cancel to ignore the new settings and revert to the previous ones.**

You can repeat Steps 3 through 5 as many times as necessary. If you want to record the slide show settings permanently, save the document with the Save or Save As command from the File menu.

Options in the Order section of the Slide Show dialog box are discussed earlier in this Topic. The next two sections describe how the Slide Options and QuickTime Options affect a slide show.

Slide options

- *Fit to window.* This option resizes each slide to make it fit on the current screen, and it maintains the proportions of the original document pages.
- *Center.* Center causes slides to be centered on the screen.

- *Show cursor*. With Show cursor checked, the cursor remains on-screen as a pointer throughout the presentation. This feature is useful if you want to point at objects or text during the presentation. Leave Show cursor unchecked if the presentation is a self-running (looping) demonstration.
- *Fade*. When checked, Fade causes the screen to fade out and then fade back in between each pair of slides.
- *Loop*. Check Loop if you want the slide show to run continuously. After completing a cycle through the slides, the show starts over again from the beginning. Normally, you use Loop in conjunction with the auto-advance feature (advance every x seconds). You stop a looping presentation in the same manner as you stop a normal presentation — by pressing Q, ⌘-period, Clear, or Esc.
- *Advance every x seconds*. When this option is checked, slides automatically advance at the rate that is set in the text-edit box. When it is unchecked, you have to advance pages manually by clicking the mouse or by pressing special keys (see "Running a Slide Show," later in this Topic). Note that even when the auto-advance feature is set, you can still advance any slide manually.
- *Background*. Choose from this pop-up palette to add a color to the background of a slide. The background color is in effect for the entire slide show. The default background color is white.
- *Border*. Choose from this pop-up palette to add a color to the border of a slide (the area around the outside edges of the slide page). The border color is in effect for the entire slide show. The default border color is black.

TIP

If a slide fills the screen, the border may be very thin. In that case, you may want to set the background and border to the same color.

QuickTime options

You set the following QuickTime options in the Slide Show dialog box. Unless the QuickTime extension loaded when the Mac started up, the QuickTime options are dimmed and unselectable. (See Topic 19 for more information on working with QuickTime.)

- *Auto play*. When this option is checked, QuickTime movies automatically run when the slide in which they're embedded appears on-screen.
- *Simultaneous*. If you have more than one QuickTime movie on a slide, checking this option allows them to play at the same time. When it is unchecked, the movies play in sequence from back to front according to the draw layer in which they're embedded.
- *Complete play before advancing*. This option forces the slide show to wait until the QuickTime movie has finished before moving to the next slide — even if you have set Advance every *x* seconds.

TIP

In a slide show, QuickTime movies always play from the point at which they were last stopped. Be sure that the movie is set to its beginning before starting the presentation. You can halt a movie in a slide show prematurely by pressing the ⌘ or Option key while clicking the mouse.

Running a Slide Show

To run a slide show, you choose Slide Show from the View menu, set options, and click Start. You also can start the show without displaying the Slide Show dialog box by pressing the Option key while you choose Slide Show from the View menu.

While a slide show is running, you can use the following keyboard commands and mouse actions to control the presentation:

Command	***Key or Action***
Show next slide	Mouse click, right-arrow key, down-arrow key, Page Down, Return, Tab, or spacebar
Show previous slide	Left-arrow key, up-arrow key, Page Up, Shift-Return, Shift-Tab, or Shift-spacebar
Show final slide	End
Show first slide	Home
Play a QuickTime movie	Click in the movie frame
Pause or resume a movie	⌘-click or Option-click in the QuickTime movie frame
Halt a QuickTime movie	Click in the playing movie's frame
End the slide show	Q, ⌘-period, Esc, or Clear

Quick Tips

The following Quick Tips tell you how to use Page Setup to make slides fit on the screen, how to create overlays and animate objects, and how to create appealing bullet characters.

Using Page Setup for correct slide display

In most cases, monitors are considerably wider than they are tall. If you find that portions of the slides are falling off the right edge of the screen, choose Page Setup from the File menu and set the document for landscape mode (the sideways icon in the lower-left corner of the Page Setup dialog box (see Figure 17-6). ClarisWorks uses the Page Setup settings when displaying documents on screen, as well as when printing them.

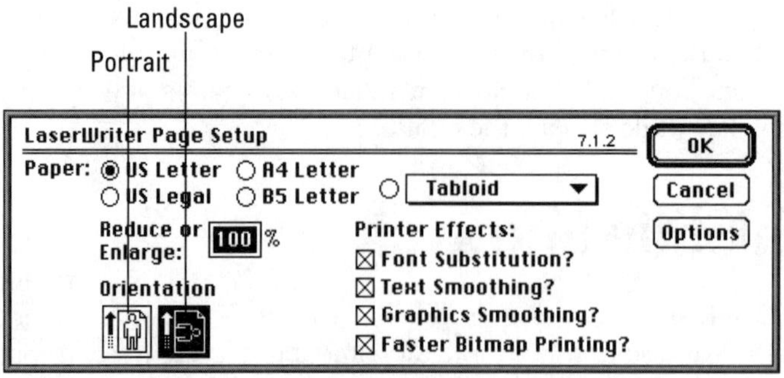

Figure 17-6: The Page Setup dialog box.

Movement in presentations

By making several consecutive transparent slides, you can create overlays and minor animation. One example is a bulleted list that adds a new bullet on each slide — enabling you to build on points as you move through the presentation.

Better bullets for text charts

Items in text charts are frequently preceded by a bullet character (•). Everyone recognizes the standard bullet (Option-8), and it's available for every font. Unfortunately, it's dull. If you have the Zapf Dingbats font, on the other hand, there are dozens of interesting characters to choose from. The following list contains some Zapf Dingbat characters that you may prefer to use as bullets to add visual appeal to your slides. (***Note:*** The Symbol font — available on every Mac — also has characters that you can use as bullets.)

Zapf Character	*Keystroke*
✓	3
✔	4
☛	Shift-8
✰	Shift-p
●	l
❍	m
■	n
❏	o
❐	p
❑	q
❒	r
▲	s
◆	u
➠	Shift-Option-7
➢	Shift-Option-0
➣	Shift-Option-W

Summary

- You can use documents from any environment (except communications) as the basis for a slide show.
- In every environment other than the word processor, you need to use a special procedure to create a multipage document if you want to include more than one slide in a presentation.
- You can change the order in which slides are presented without affecting the contents of the underlying document. You also can specify which slides are to be shown as opaque, transparent, or hidden.
- If you base a slide show on a draw document, you can create a master page and use it to display static information on every slide (a company logo, for example).
- You use the Slide Show dialog box to set most options for the presentation, including placement of the slide on-screen, background and border colors, special effects, and play settings for QuickTime movies.

Topic 18

Designing Master Pages

Overview

Although you can use headers and footers to add graphics and other items that should appear at the top and bottom of every page of a document, things get a bit sticky when you want an item to appear somewhere else on every page. To handle this situation, ClarisWorks provides a feature called the *master page.*

Think of a master page as an extra layer or special page that appears on-screen — and is printed — behind every page of the document. Objects that you may want to place on a master page include *rules* (solid lines that appear at the top of each page or that separate columns of text), page borders, a solid background or gradient, company logos, and presentation instructions ("Press Tab to advance to next slide; press Shift-Tab to view previous slide"). A master page lends consistency to the background elements in a document without forcing you to paste and realign the objects on every new page.

NOTE

You can create master pages only in draw documents. However, because you can place word processing, paint, and spreadsheet frames on draw documents, consider this limitation a minor one, rather than a major inconvenience.

Creating Master Pages for Your Documents

You can easily create master pages to add the same background elements to all of the pages in a document.

Step-by-Steps

To create a master page:

1. **Open an existing draw document (⌘-O) or create a new one (⌘-N).** You also can choose the Open or New command from the File menu.
2. **Choose Edit Master Page from the Options menu.** A check mark appears next to the Edit Master Page command in the menu, and a blank master page is displayed, as shown in Figure 18-1.
3. **Add the master page elements to the page.**

4. **Choose Edit Master Page from the Options menu.** The check mark next to the Edit Master Page command in the menu disappears, and the regular document is displayed.

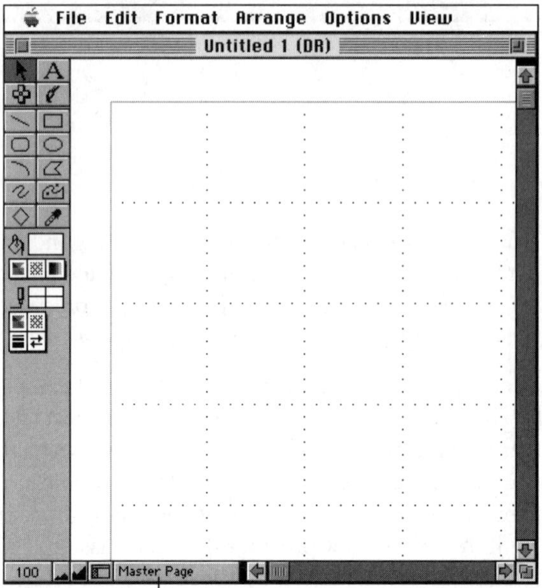

Master Page indicator

Figure 18-1: The Master Page indicator helps you distinguish a master page from other pages of the document.

You can edit master page elements, just as you can edit any other object, image, or text string that appears in a regular ClarisWorks document. Simply choose Edit Master Page from the Options menu and make whatever changes are necessary.

Quick Tips

The following Quick Tips tell you how to rotate text and how to hide a master page element.

Adding rotated text to a master page

The ClarisWorks manual teases you by showing an example of rotated text on a master page (an example of a *rubber stamp,* such as "Confidential," "Draft," or "Paid"), but the manual doesn't explain how to achieve this effect. You can rotate draw objects in 90-degree increments. Because text is treated by ClarisWorks as a draw object, you can rotate it in 90-degree increments too, but the example in the ClarisWorks manual is not for an angle that is a 90-degree increment.

The trick is to change the text into a paint image. Unlike with draw objects, you can rotate paint images at whatever angle you like (see Topic 7). The following instructions tell you how to design rotated text to use as a rubber stamp.

Step-by-Steps

To create rotated text:

1. **Launch ClarisWorks and create a new paint document.**
2. **Choose a font, size, and style from the Font, Size, and Style menus.**
3. **Choose Text Color from the Style menu and choose a color for the text.**

   Because you normally want to be able to read the text in the overlying document, a light color is best for rubber stamp text. A black rubber stamp would make the other text unreadable.
4. **Select the Text tool (the A) from the Tool panel. Click and drag to create a text frame that is large enough to hold the rubber stamp text.**
5. **Type the text string for the stamp.**
6. **Select the Selection Rectangle tool and draw a selection marquee around the text string.**
7. **Choose Rotate or Free Rotate from the Transform menu and rotate the text.**

   Rotate displays a dialog box in which you can enter a specific angle of rotation, such as 315.

   Free Rotate places hollow handles at the corners of the selection marquee that you drag to change the rotation.
8. **With the rotated text string still selected, choose Copy from the Edit menu (or press ⌘-C).**
9. **Choose New from the File menu and create a new draw document.**
10. **Choose Edit Master Page from the Options menu.** The master page is displayed.
11. **Choose Paste from the Edit menu (or press ⌘-V).** The rotated text string is pasted onto the master page. Drag to change its position, if necessary.
12. **Set the pen pattern to transparent (the two empty boxes) to hide the bounding box that surrounds the text.** Figure 18-2 shows the completed rubber stamp.

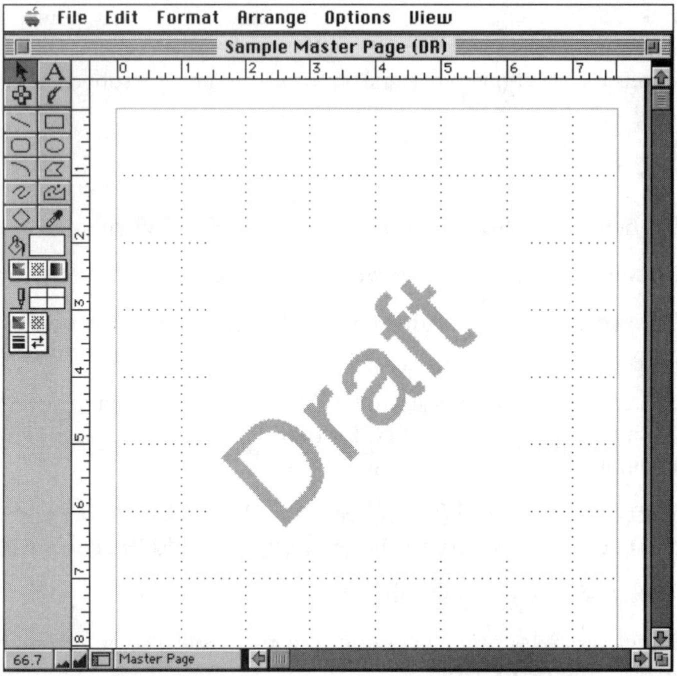

Figure 18-2: An example of rotated text that is pasted onto a master page.

Obscuring elements on the master page

Occasionally, you may want to obscure some of the elements on the master page. For example, you may want all elements to show through on every page except the first page of the document. (Perhaps you intend to use the first page as a title page.) A simple way to hide a master page element without altering the master page itself is to cover the element with an opaque white square that you place on the regular document page. The following instructions describe how to hide the "Draft" rubber stamp that is shown in Figure 18-3.

Step-by-Steps

To hide a master page element:

1. **Open the draw document that contains the master page.**
2. **Pull down the Options menu and make sure that Edit Master Page does not have a check mark beside it. If it does, choose it again.** (This action ensures that you are editing the regular document page, not the master page.)
3. **If you cannot see the master page elements, choose Page View from the View menu (or press Shift-⌘-P).**
4. **Select the Rectangle tool from the Tool panel.**

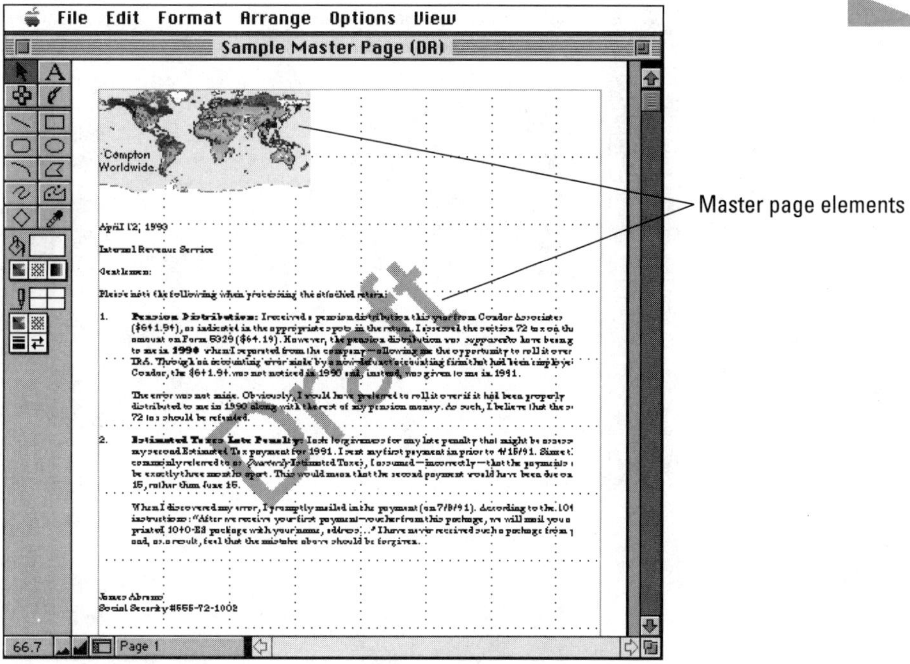

Figure 18-3: The original document with two master page elements: a logo and a "Draft" rubber stamp.

5. **Draw a rectangle that completely covers the master page element that you want to hide.**

6. **With the rectangle still selected, set the fill and pen color to white and the fill and pen pattern to opaque.** The document looks like the one shown in Figure 18-4.

   In addition to obscuring the master page "Draft" element, however, the white rectangle obscures much of the body text of the document. To correct this problem, you need to move the rectangle into the proper document layer.

7. **Choose Move Backward from the Arrange menu or press Shift-⌘-– (minus sign).** The rectangle moves into the layer between the master page and the body text, as shown in Figure 18-5.

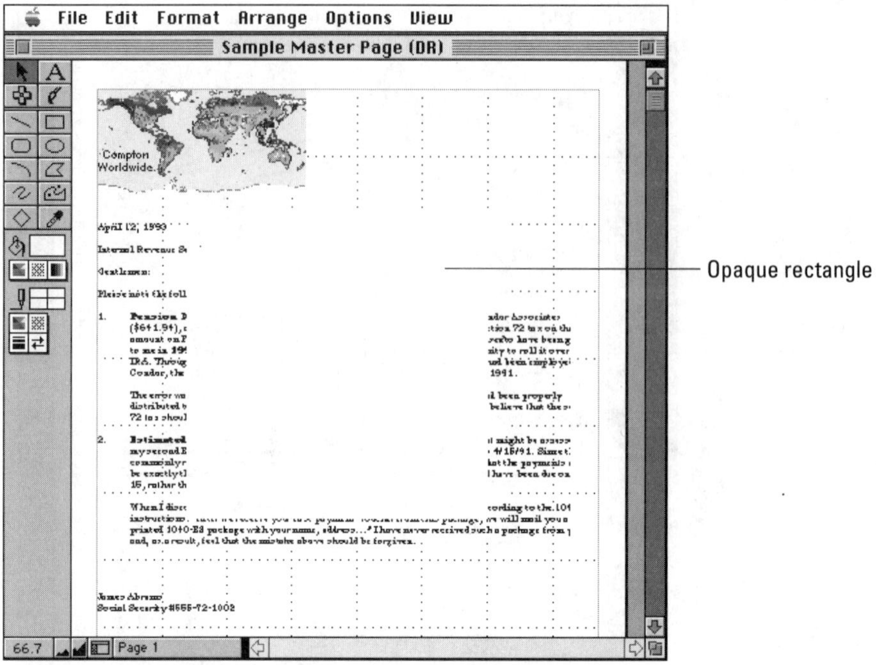

Figure 18-4: The opaque white rectangle obscures the master page "Draft" element.

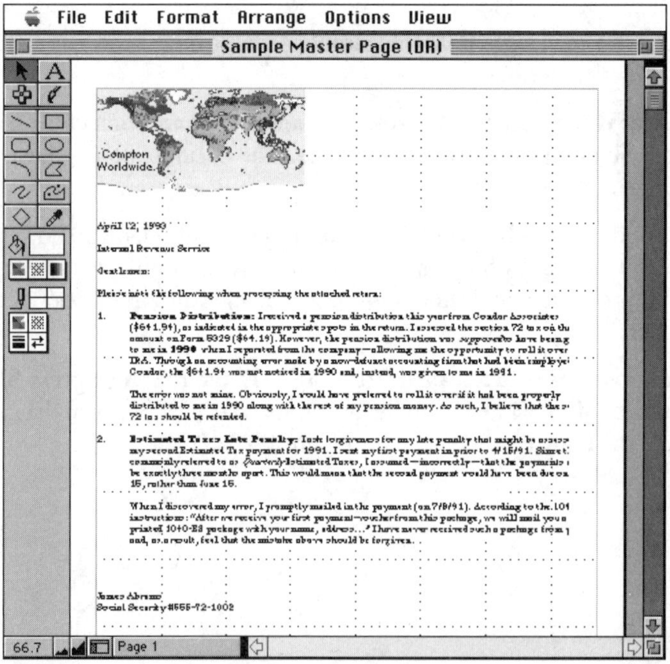

Figure 18-5: The master page element is hidden for this page only.

Summary

- Elements that you place on a master page automatically appear in the same position on every page of the document.

  Although you can create a master page only in a draw document, you can get around this limitation by placing word processing, paint, and spreadsheet frames on draw documents.

- You can edit master page elements as often as you like.

Topic 19

QuickTime Movies

Overview

QuickTime is an Apple-provided system extension that enables you to add movie clips to Macintosh documents. You can insert the clips into most ClarisWorks documents (and documents of other programs that support QuickTime), just as you add static images such as logos. Anyone else who has the QuickTime extension and the program in which you created the document can play the movie. To use QuickTime, you must be running system software Version 6.0.7 or later, have at least 2MB of memory, and have any Macintosh other than the Plus, SE, 512KE, 512K, or 128K.

NOTE

You can check which version of system software you're using by returning to the desktop (assuming that you're currently working in a program), pulling down the Apple menu, and choosing About This Macintosh (System 7) or About the Finder (System 6). The window that appears shows the system software version, along with the total memory installed in the Macintosh (see Figure 19-1).

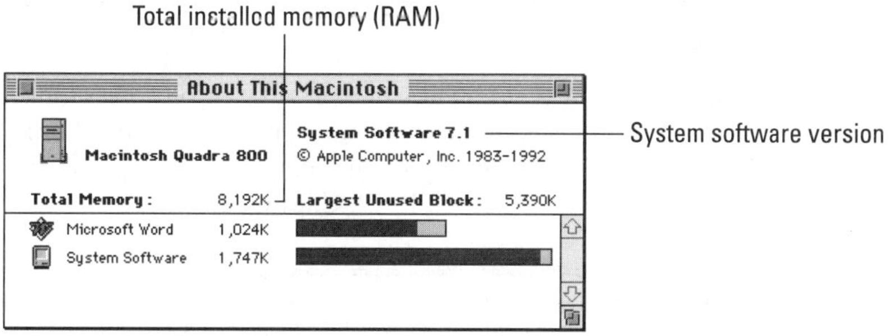

Figure 19-1: The system software version and the total installed memory are shown in the About This Macintosh or About the Finder window.

Installing QuickTime

You can obtain QuickTime in a number of ways. You can download it from most major information services (such as CompuServe, America Online, and GEnie) or purchase it as part of the QuickTime Starter Kit from Apple Computer. Or it may be included when you buy a new Macintosh. At this writing, the most current version of QuickTime is 2.0.

The heart of QuickTime — and the only essential component — is the QuickTime extension that you install in the System Folder on your start-up hard disk.

Depending on how you obtain QuickTime, it may or may not include an Installer program. (Installer works just like the Installer for ClarisWorks.) If an Installer is present, double-click its icon and follow the installation instructions that came with QuickTime.

If you do not have an Installer program, you have to install QuickTime manually.

Step-by-Steps

To install QuickTime manually:

1. **Insert the floppy disk that contains QuickTime in the floppy drive.**
2. **If the disk's window does not open automatically, double-click the disk icon.**
3. **Locate the System Folder on the start-up hard disk. Drag the QuickTime icon from the floppy disk onto the icon for the System Folder on the start-up hard disk.**

   If you are running System 6.0.7 or 6.0.8, this action copies QuickTime to the top level of the System Folder. If you are running System 7 or higher, you see a message that asks whether you want to copy QuickTime into the Extensions folder (see Figure 19-2). Click OK.

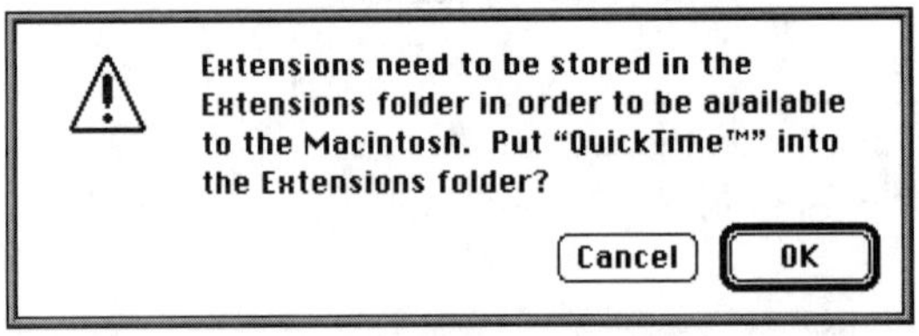

Extensions need to be stored in the Extensions folder in order to be available to the Macintosh. Put "QuickTime™" into the Extensions folder?
Cancel
OK

Figure 19-2: Click OK to copy QuickTime into the Extensions folder. (The message shown is from System 7.)

4. **Restart the Macintosh to load QuickTime.**

One QuickTime utility that also may be provided is a special version of the Scrapbook desk accessory that you can use for storing QuickTime movies. See the installation instructions that came with QuickTime for the proper installation procedure.

Inserting a QuickTime Movie into a Document

You can incorporate QuickTime movies in a ClarisWorks document in several ways:

- Open them by choosing Open (⌘-O) from the File menu and then choosing Drawing from the Document Type pop-up menu in the file dialog box.
- Insert them into a word processing, spreadsheet, draw, or database document by choosing Insert from the File menu.
- Copy and paste them into a word processing, spreadsheet, draw, or database document by selecting the movie in the Scrapbook or another program, and then choosing Copy (⌘-C) and Paste (⌘-V) from the Edit menu.

As with other ClarisWorks objects, you can add QuickTime movies either as in-line graphics or as objects (refer to Topic 4 for a discussion of in-line graphics and objects). In-line graphics become part of the paragraph into which you paste them, enabling you to format them with standard paragraph commands. To add a movie as an in-line graphic, set the text-insertion point within a word processing paragraph before choosing the Insert or Paste command.

Objects, on the other hand, are free floating, and you can move them anywhere on the page. You also can specify a text wrap style if you place the object in a word processing document or frame. To add a movie as a floating object, select the pointer tool from the Tool panel before choosing the Insert or Paste command.

NOTE

A QuickTime movie that you add to a paint document or frame appears as a static picture. You cannot play it. And although you can add a QuickTime movie to a database, you have to be in layout view to play the movie. Most ClarisWorks users spend almost all of their time in the database's browse mode, so this limitation makes working with QuickTime movies in databases extremely inconvenient — and almost pointless.

VERSION 2.1

For information on inserting movies into PowerTalk messages, see Topic 21.

Playing Movies

Figure 19-3 shows a word processing document with a QuickTime movie. The control badge (the film-strip icon) identifies the graphic as a QuickTime movie.

You can play a movie that is an object by double-clicking it or by using the special pop-up movie control bar. The only way to play movies that are in-line graphics is to double-click them. They have no control bar.

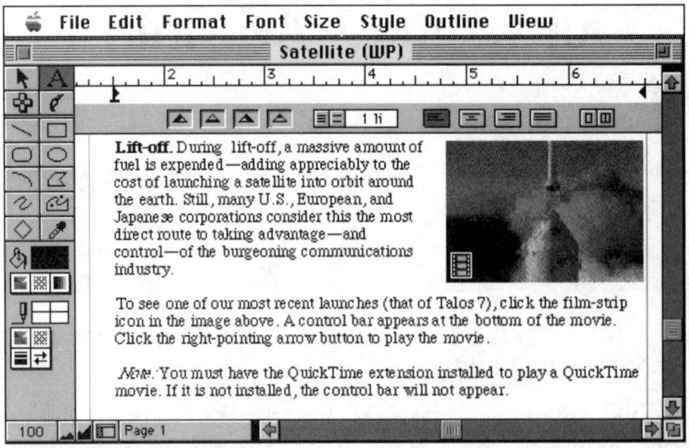

Figure 19-3: A document that includes the QuickTime movie *Liftoff* from the QuickTime Starter Kit (Apple Computer Inc.).

Using the double-click method

Double-clicking a movie automatically plays it with any options that are set for the movie. Normally, the movie plays from beginning to end with the default volume setting for audio that accompanies the clip. You can pause or stop the playback by clicking once anywhere on the screen. Double-click again to resume play from the point at which you halted the movie.

Using the movie control bar

For movies that are objects, clicking the film-strip icon exposes a movie control bar at the bottom of the movie, as shown in Figure 19-4.

The control bar contains the following buttons:

- *Volume control.* Click this button to expose a slider control for playback volume. Move the slider higher for louder volume and lower for less volume.

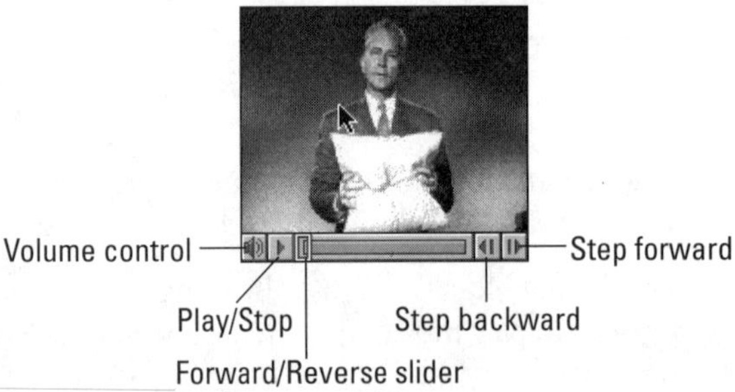

Figure 19-4: The movie control bar.

- *Play/Stop button.* When the movie is not playing, this button appears as a right-facing triangle. Click it once to begin playing the movie. When the movie begins to play, the button changes to a Stop button that has a pair of vertical lines on it. Click the Stop button to stop or pause the movie.
- *Forward/Reverse slider.* You can use the mouse to drag this slider forward or backward in the movie to any point that you want. As you drag the slider, the movie plays (without sound) either forward or backward until you release the mouse button.
- *Step backward and Step forward buttons.* The last two buttons enable you to step backward or forward through the movie one frame at a time — again, without audio.

Changing the Size of a Movie Frame

ClarisWorks enables you to change the size of any movie frame, regardless of whether the movie is an in-line graphic or an object.

Step-by-Steps

To resize a movie:

1. **Click once on the movie to select it.** If it is an in-line graphic, a single handle appears at the lower-right corner of the movie frame. If it is an object, handles appear at all corners of the movie frame.
2. **Select a handle with the mouse and then drag to resize the movie frame.** (To maintain the original proportions of the frame, press Shift as you drag diagonally.)
3. **Release the mouse button when the frame is the desired shape and size.**

Keyboard shortcuts for playback control

In addition to using the mouse, you also can control playback directly from the keyboard. Here are the keyboard shortcuts I've discovered:

Key	*Effect*
Return	Start/Stop playback
Spacebar	Start/Stop playback
Period (.)	Stop playback
Up-arrow key	Increase volume
Down-arrow key	Decrease volume
Right-arrow key	Step forward a frame at a time (hold the key down to step forward quickly)
Left-arrow key	Step backward a frame at a time (hold the key down to step backward quickly)

Setting Playback Options

You can set a variety of playback options for a movie that you have added to a ClarisWorks document as an object. (On the other hand, you can only play, pause, and restart in-line movies.) To see the different options, select the movie (the handles should appear) and then choose Movie Info from the Options menu (or press Shift-⌘-I). The Movie Info dialog box shown in Figure 19-5 appears.

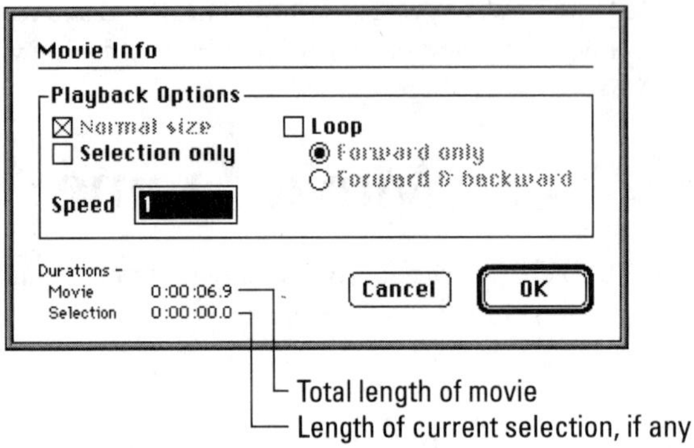

Figure 19-5: The Movie Info dialog box.

Playback options in the Movie Info dialog box include the following:

- *Normal size.* If you have changed the size of the movie window, clicking this check box restores the movie frame to its original size. If you have not resized the movie, this option is *grayed* (unselectable).
- *Selection only.* If you have selected only a portion of the movie, checking this option restricts playback to the selection, rather than to the entire movie (see "Working with Movie Selections," later in this Topic).
- *Speed.* By typing a number in the Speed text-edit box, you can change the playback speed, as well as make the movie play backward. The default or normal setting is 1. Table 19-1 shows how different settings affect playback.

Table 19-1
Effects of Different Speed Settings

	Slower Speed	*Normal*	*Faster Speed*
Play forward	Decimal between 0 and 1	1	Positive integer larger than 1
Play backward	Decimal between 0 and – 1	– 1	Negative integer smaller than – 1

You also can change the playback speed by pressing the Control key while you click either the Step forward or Step backward button on the control bar. A slider appears that you can use to select a new playback speed. The white area in the middle of the slider represents the normal speed setting. Moving the slider to the left of the white area sets backward playback speed, and moving it to the right of the white area sets forward playback speed.

- *Loop.* When this option is checked, the movie plays in a continuous loop. The radio button that you choose (Forward only or Forward & backward) determines the direction of playback. When Loop is set for a clip, you click once to halt the playback.

After setting options, click OK to put them into effect or click Cancel if you change your mind.

Working with Movie Selections

As the discussion on setting playback options states, you can also work with selections (or portions) of any movie that is an object. This capability enables you to do some rudimentary movie editing, such as cutting and pasting selections into the same or another QuickTime movie.

To make a selection within a movie:

1. **Use the Step backward and Step forward buttons or the Forward/Reverse slider in the movie control bar to find the starting frame of the selection.**
2. **Press Shift while you use the Step backward and Step forward buttons or the Forward/Reverse slider to move to the end of the intended selection.** The selected portion of the clip is shown as a dark area on the Play bar (see Figure 19-6).

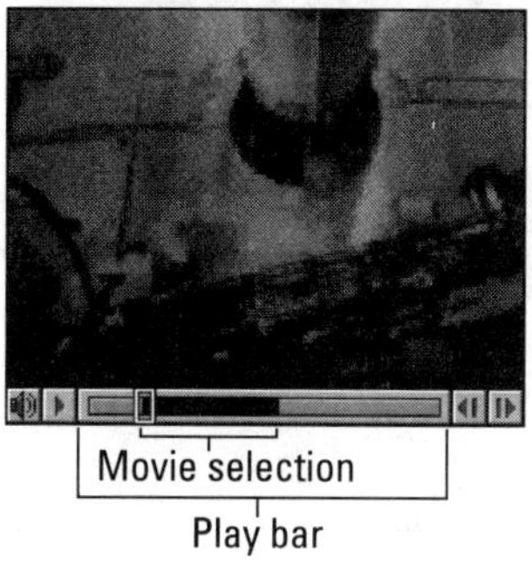

Figure 19-6: The Play bar shows what portion of the movie is selected.

3. **Release the Shift key and the mouse button when the selection is correct.**

TIP

You can extend a selection or reduce its size in the same way that you extend or reduce a text selection in a word processing document. Simply press Shift while dragging to the left or right. To clear a selection quickly, click the control bar once.

After you make a selection, you can perform either of the following tasks:

- ◆ Copy the selection by choosing Copy (⌘-C) from the Edit menu.
- ◆ Delete the selection by choosing Cut (⌘-X) or Clear from the Edit menu or by pressing the Delete Backspace, or Del key.

After you copy (⌘-C) or cut (⌘-X) a selection from a movie, the selection is transferred to the Macintosh Clipboard where it is available for pasting. You can paste the selection into a different spot in the same movie or into a different movie.

Step-by-Steps

To paste a movie selection:

1. **Click the control badge (the film-strip icon) on the destination movie to expose the control bar.**
2. **Use the Step backward and Step forward buttons or the Forward/ Reverse slider to move to the spot in the movie where you want to make the insertion.**
3. **Choose Paste from the Edit menu (or press ⌘-V).** The selection is pasted into the movie.

Quick Tips

The following Quick Tips tell you how to store QuickTime movies in the Scrapbook, how to find missing movies, how to share QuickTime movies with other users, and how to eliminate choppiness when you play movies.

Using the Scrapbook to store movies

If you install the new version of the Scrapbook desk accessory that comes with QuickTime, you can use it to store and play movies. Like movies pasted into documents, however, the movie does not actually reside in the Scrapbook. Instead, the Scrapbook merely maintains a pointer to the movie's real location on-disk.

To insert a movie into the Scrapbook:

1. **Open the movie in any application that can read it (you can insert it into a ClarisWorks document, for example).**
2. **Select the movie (its handles appear) and then choose Copy from the Edit menu (or press ⌘-C).**
3. **Choose the Scrapbook desk accessory from the Apple menu.** The Scrapbook opens.
4. **Using the scroll bar at the bottom of the Scrapbook window, move to the spot in the Scrapbook where you want to insert the movie.**
5. **Choose Paste from the Edit menu (or press ⌘-V).** The movie appears in the Scrapbook, as shown in Figure 19-7.

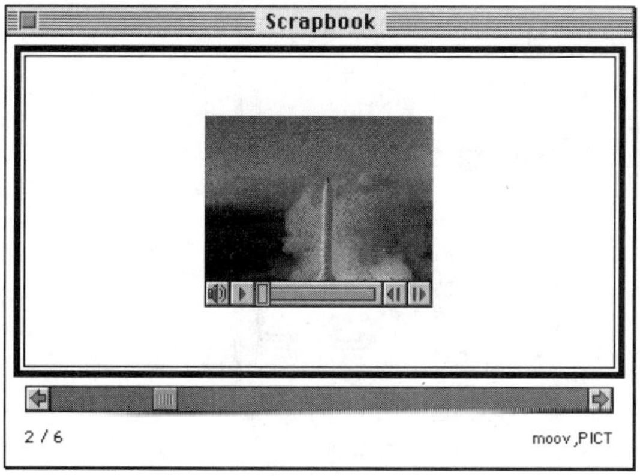

Figure 19-7: A movie in the Scrapbook.

Locating missing movies

When you attempt to display a movie file — either one that is embedded in a document or one that is on a page in the Scrapbook — QuickTime immediately searches for the disk on which the movie file is stored. If the original disk is not mounted on the desktop, the program asks you to insert it.

Insert the requested disk. If the disk isn't available, click Cancel.

If you click Cancel, QuickTime automatically searches all mounted disks for a copy of the missing movie file. If it finds the movie file, it makes a record of the file's location and uses that file for all future requests. If it doesn't find the file, you get one last chance to help locate it, as Figure 19-8 shows.

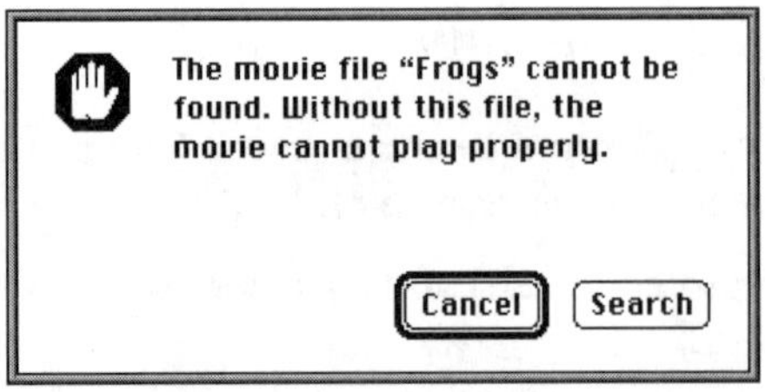

Figure 19-8: Last chance to find the movie file.

If you click Cancel in the new dialog box and the movie is *not* found, the movie is automatically changed to a static picture. If you think that you can still find it (you have it on a different disk that is not currently mounted, for example), click Search. The file dialog box in Figure 19-9 appears.

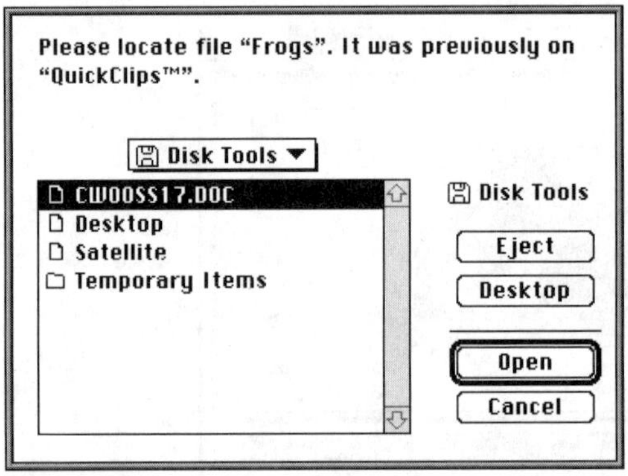

Figure 19-9: Insert the disk that contains the movie file or use this dialog box to search for it manually.

Sharing QuickTime movies with other users

Again, because QuickTime movies aren't actually stored in the documents in which they're embedded, if you give someone a ClarisWorks document or another type of document that contains a QuickTime movie, you need to give them a copy of the movie, too.

The first time that the other person attempts to view the movie, a dialog box appears, explaining that the original disk cannot be found and that it should be inserted. Clicking Cancel forces QuickTime to search for the file, and it will locate the file if your friend or colleague has copied the movie to a hard disk or has the document distribution disk inserted in a drive.

Improving QuickTime playback

If you want to play a movie with minimal choppiness, you can improve playback by storing the movie on the fastest disk drive that you own. CD-ROM and floppy drives, for example, are extremely slow. SyQuest, Bernoulli, and optical disk cartridges are somewhat faster. A hard disk is better still.

If you intend to use QuickTime movies in a presentation, are running System 7, and have the memory to spare, consider copying the movie to a RAM disk. A RAM disk is a temporary disk that is created from the Mac's memory. Because files and programs that are run from a RAM disk are accessed almost instantly (unlike a hard disk, a RAM disk has no moving parts), movie playback from a RAM disk is exceptional.

NOTE

Depending on the amount of RAM that is installed in the Mac and the size of the movie file(s), using a RAM disk may not be a workable solution. (If you don't have at least 8MB of RAM, for example, a RAM disk for use with QuickTime isn't practical.) Any memory that is allocated for a RAM disk is not available for you to use to run programs or desk accessories.

Step-by-Steps

To create and use a RAM disk:

1. **Choose Control Panels from the Apple menu.** The Control Panels folder opens.
2. **Double-click the Memory control panel.** If your model of Mac supports it, the bottom section of the Memory control panel contains a RAM disk section (see Figure 19-10).

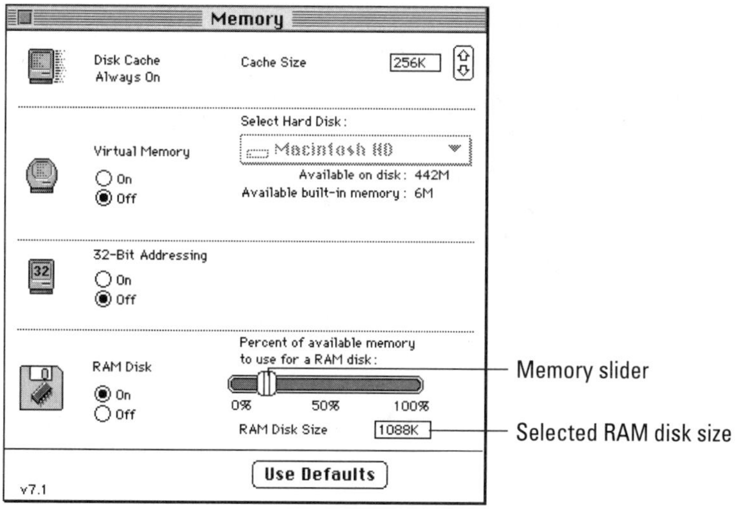

Figure 19-10: The System 7 Memory control panel.

3. **Click the On radio button in the RAM disk section and move the slider to set the size of the RAM disk.** (Try setting it to the total size of the ClarisWorks document plus the movie file.)
4. **Click the Memory control panel's close box to save the changes.**
5. **Restart the Macintosh.** A RAM disk appears on the right side of the desktop.
6. **Copy the ClarisWorks document and movie files to the RAM disk.**
7. **Make a backup copy of the movie file on a floppy disk or removable hard disk and then delete the original.**
8. **Double-click the ClarisWorks document that is on the RAM disk to launch ClarisWorks and load the document.**
9. **Because the QuickTime movie is no longer in its original location, a dialog box may appear to inform you of that fact. If so, click Cancel.** QuickTime will locate the file on the RAM disk and use that copy to play the movie.

Later, to regain the memory that has been allocated to the RAM disk, open the Memory control panel again, click the Off button in the RAM disk section, close the control panel, and restart the Mac.

Moving On Up

ClarisWorks wasn't really designed for heavy-duty QuickTime editing. Also, you can use it only to play movies that have been provided to you (in the QuickTime Starter Kit, for example). If you want more control over the content of movies, want to add your own sound track, or want to make your own movies, you need to invest in some additional hardware and software.

If you want to capture video from an external source, such as a TV, videotape, or video camera, you need a way to change the video signals into a form that's compatible with the Macintosh. In most cases, you can use a video capture board, such as the Video Spigot (SuperMac Technologies), to accomplish this. Even if you only want improved editing capabilities, you may want to invest in a video editing program such as Premiere (Adobe Systems).

Summary

- You can add QuickTime movies to most ClarisWorks documents. However, the word processing, spreadsheet, and draw environments are preferable for movie clips.
- As with static graphic images, you can paste or insert movies into documents as objects or as in-line graphics. If you want access to the movie control bar, however, you have to add the movies as objects.
- Movies that you add as objects contain a pop-up movie control bar with which you can vary the playback direction and speed and do minor editing of the movie. You can only play, pause, and restart movies that are in-line graphics.
- You can change the size of any movie that is embedded in a ClarisWorks document by dragging a handle on the movie frame.
- In the Movie Info dialog box, you can change playback settings for movies that are objects.
- In addition to working with the entire movie, you can select a portion of the movie (for selective playback or editing).

Topic 20 Publish & Subscribe

Overview

Publish & Subscribe is a major advance that was introduced in System 7. It provides a simple way to integrate and share data among multiple programs, documents, and users without having to resort to the normal Macintosh copy-and-paste procedure. Publish & Subscribe maintains an active link between elements from two or more documents. If the published material (text or an object such as a spreadsheet chart, for example) is changed in the original document, the revised text or object can be automatically or manually updated in any document that is subscribing to the material. This feature makes Publish & Subscribe an ideal tool for coordinating the work of several individuals, as well as for linking frequently changing data and objects from different programs.

Some of the ways to use Publish & Subscribe include the following:

- To incorporate the work of several individuals on a network in a single master document (a departmental report that requires budget data from every department head, for example)
- To combine data from several different programs (adding ClarisWorks charts and Adobe Illustrator drawings to a shareholders' report created in Aldus PageMaker, for example)
- To maintain live links between elements created in different ClarisWorks environments

Every Publish & Subscribe transaction has three components: a publisher, an edition, and a subscriber. Figure 20-1 shows the relationship among the components.

- The *publisher* is the portion of the document that is the source data — the text or object that you want to make available for use by others or in other documents.
- The *subscriber* is the area in a second document in which you see the published information or object.
- The *edition* is a special file that serves as the link between the publisher and the subscriber. It contains a copy of the publisher's contents. This intermediate file transparently notifies the subscriber whenever the publisher's data has changed and then executes whatever updates are required.

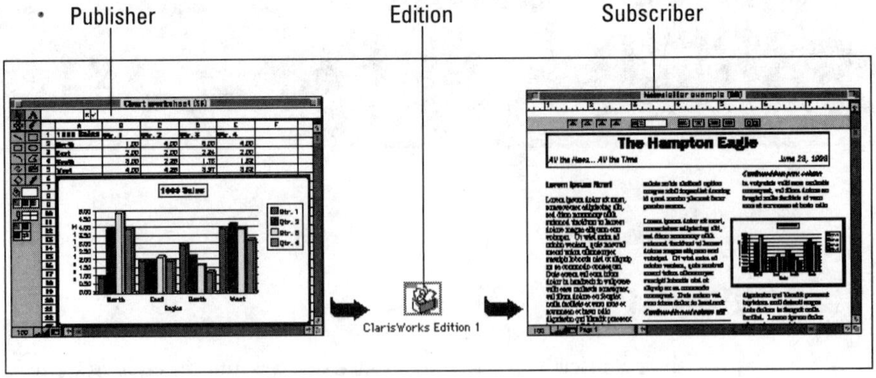

Figure 20-1: An example of Publish & Subscribe.

You can publish database elements only from Layout mode, and you cannot publish or subscribe to information from the ClarisWorks communications or paint environments. Otherwise, documents from all other environments and elements, such as word processing text, worksheet sections, charts, and draw objects, are eligible for Publish & Subscribe.

At a minimum, every Publish & Subscribe transaction has a single publisher and a single subscriber. Note, however, that you can have multiple publishers and subscribers in any document. You can also have multiple subscribers — in different documents — to any published material.

Using Publish & Subscribe

Two steps create the link between the publisher and the subscriber: publishing the item and subscribing to the item's edition.

To publish an item:

1. **Open the document that contains the item you want to publish (make available to other users or use in other documents).**
2. **Select the item to be published, such as a text segment, a spreadsheet chart, a range of cells, or a draw object.**
3. **Choose Create Publisher from the Publishing submenu of the Edit menu. The dialog box in Figure 20-2 appears.**
4. **Navigate to the drive and folder where you want to store the edition file, type a name for the new edition, and click Publish.** The edition file is created, and the selected text or object is surrounded by a border (to show you and remind you that it is now a publisher).

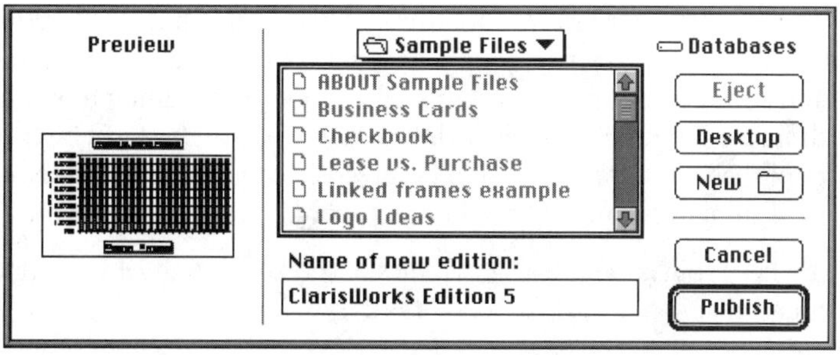

Figure 20-2: The publishing file dialog box shows a preview of the object or data that will be published.

Step-by-Steps

To subscribe to an edition:

1. **Open the document in which the published item will be placed.**
2. **Select the spot in the document where you want the edition to be placed (a text insertion point in a word processing document or frame, a location in a draw document, or a range of spreadsheet cells, for example).**

   NOTE

   If the edition contains an object that you intend to place in a word processing document, you can make it a free-floating object by choosing the pointer tool. Otherwise, the object will be placed as an in-line graphic at the text insertion point.

   If the edition is to be placed in a spreadsheet, be sure to choose a range that is large enough to hold the data. If the range is too small, the new data will spill over into additional cells — overwriting any data that they contain.
3. **Choose Subscribe To from the Publishing submenu of the Edit menu.** A dialog box similar to the one in Figure 20-2 appears.
4. **Navigate to the drive and folder where the edition file is stored, select the edition's filename from the list, and click Subscribe.** A copy of the edition is placed in the document.

Publish & Subscribe: An Example

The easiest way to learn more about Publish & Subscribe is to work through a simple example — one that you can do by yourself entirely within ClarisWorks. Using Publish & Subscribe, you'll create a ClarisWorks worksheet with a chart in it, publish the chart, and then subscribe to it in a report created in the ClarisWorks word processor. When a chart is simply pasted into another document, it loses all connection with the worksheet in which it was created. By using Publish & Subscribe, however, you maintain the link between the chart and the worksheet in which it was created. If you later modify the chart or the data on which it is based, the chart in the word processing report can be updated automatically.

As you read and work through this example, keep in mind that the following steps can also be done by two people on a network — one person publishing the chart and another person (the author of the report) subscribing to it. Similarly, two different programs can be used. For example, the chart can be created in and published from the ClarisWorks spreadsheet and subscribed to by a desktop publishing program or by a different word processing program.

To keep things simple, use two files (a spreadsheet and a word processing document) that come with ClarisWorks 2 or 3.

- ◆ If you have ClarisWorks 2.0 or 2.1, use Mortgage Analyzer and ABOUT Sample files (both files are in the Sample Files folder). Make a copy of ABOUT sample files and use it to avoid changing the original.
- ◆ If you have ClarisWorks 3.0, use Mortgage Analyzer and Résumé A (both files are in the ClarisWorks Stationery folder inside the Claris folder within the System Folder on your start-up hard disk). Because these files are stationery documents, you do not need to make a copy of them to use in this example.

Follow these steps to see how Publish & Subscribe works:

1. If you have ClarisWorks 2.0 or 2.1, choose Open from the File menu (or press ⌘-O). Choose the Mortgage Analyzer file and click the Open button.

— or —

1. If you have ClarisWorks 3.0, choose New from the File menu (or press ⌘-N). In the New Document dialog box that appears, click Start with an Assistant or Stationery, choose Home from the Category pop-up menu, choose Mortgage Analyzer, and then click OK.
2. Using the mouse, click to select the chart that begins at cell K21. Handles appear at the corners of the chart to show that it is selected.
3. Select Create Publisher from the Publishing submenu of the Edit menu. A file dialog box appears, as shown in Figure 20-2.
4. Type a filename for the new edition or accept the one that is presented. ClarisWorks uses the convention shown in Figure 20-2 to name all edition files (*ClarisWorks Edition x*). Click Publish to create the edition.
5. If you have ClarisWorks 2.0 or 2.1, use the Open command to load the word processing file named ABOUT Sample files. The document opens in a new window.

— or —

5. If you have ClarisWorks 3.0, choose New from the File menu (or press ⌘-N). In the New Document dialog box that appears, click Start with an Assistant or Stationery, choose Home from the Category pop-up menu, choose the Résumé A word processing stationery document, and then click OK. The document opens in a new window.

6. Click the Show/Hide Tools control at the lower-left corner of the word processing document window to make the Tool panel appear. Select the pointer tool. (This ensures that the chart is placed as a free-floating graphic that you can drag to any spot in the document.)

7. Select Subscribe To from the Publishing submenu of the Edit menu. A file dialog box appears, similar to the one in Figure 20-2. Select the name of the edition file created in Step 4 and click Subscribe. A copy of the chart appears in the word processing document.

The chart is surrounded by a gray border to show that it is a subscriber object. If you like, you can turn the border off by choosing Hide Borders from the Publishing submenu of the Edit menu.

8. With the chart selected, drag one of the chart's handles to reduce the size of the chart (make it approximately 2 inches wide and 1.5 inches high).

9. With the chart still selected, choose Text Wrap from the Options menu, click the Regular icon, and then click OK. Drag the chart anywhere you like. The surrounding text wraps around the chart. Figure 20-3 shows what the finished document may look like in ClarisWorks 2.

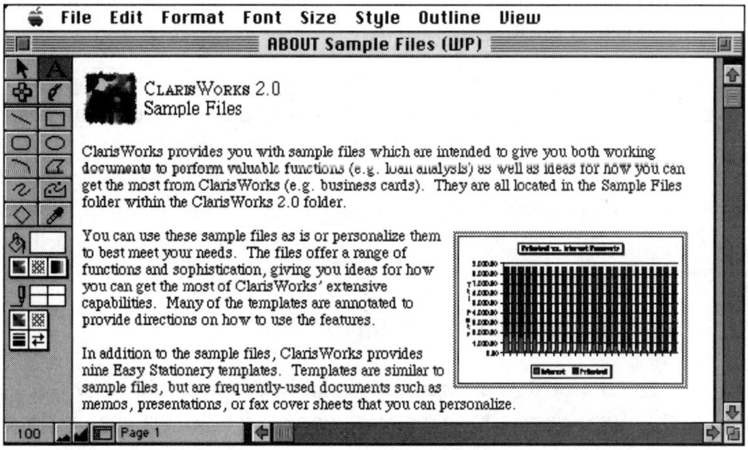

Figure 20-3: The word processing document now includes a chart to which it subscribes.

10. To see how updating works, make a change to the chart. In the worksheet, select the chart and choose Modify Chart from the Options menu. In the Modify Chart dialog box, click a new chart type, such as Stacked Area, and then click OK to close the dialog box.

11. Because the published chart is updated in the edition only when its document is saved, choose the Save command from the File menu. (If you like, you can use the Save As command to save the document under a new name.)

12. Return to the word processing document and you'll see that the chart has been replaced with the revised chart. When you are done experimenting with Publish & Subscribe, close both documents.

This example demonstrates two important points. First, when you save a file that contains published material, the edition can track the file even if it has been renamed. The edition also knows when the file has been moved to a new location, and, of course, it tracks normal Saves too. Second, the updated chart is the same size as the original rather than the size to which you previously reduced it in the word processing document. The text wrap that you set remains intact, but you have to resize the chart.

Updating an Edition

Until their edition is updated, subscribed to elements remain unchanged (unless, of course, you edit them in the subscribing program). Although you can continue to edit the text or object in the original document from which they were published, the subscriber will reflect changes only when one of the following conditions is met:

- The original document is saved again.
- The edition is manually or automatically updated.

After the edition has been updated, changes in published material are sent to all subscribing documents.

By default, editions are automatically updated whenever a published document is saved. (It doesn't matter whether the subscribing document is open at the time the update occurs. The next time you open the subscribing document, you'll see the updated material.) However, automatic updating may not always be what you want. To control when updates occur, either the person publishing the material or the one subscribing to it can set updates to occur manually or force an update.

Step-by-Steps

To update an edition manually:

1. **Select the published material in the publishing or the subscribing document.** (If the material is an object, be sure that its outer border is selected).
2. **If you're working in the publishing document, choose Publisher Options from the Publishing submenu of the Edit menu.** The Publisher to dialog box appears, as shown in Figure 20-4.
3. **Click the Send Edition Now button.** The most recently saved copy of the published material is sent from the edition to the subscribing document.

— or —

2. **If you're working in the subscribing document, choose Subscriber Options from the Publishing submenu of the Edit menu.** The Subscriber to dialog box appears, as shown in Figure 20-5.

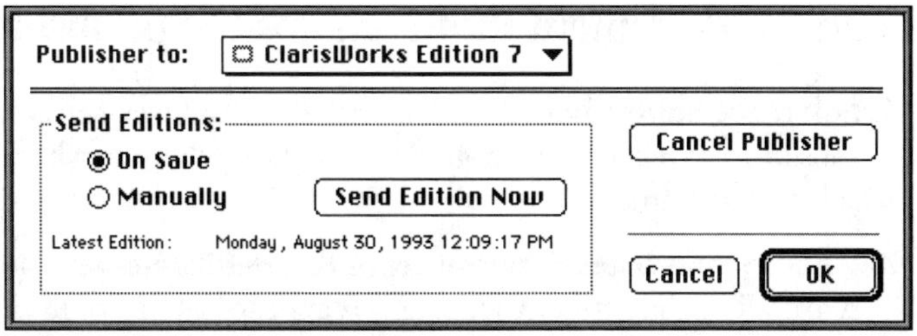

Figure 20-4: The Publisher to dialog box.

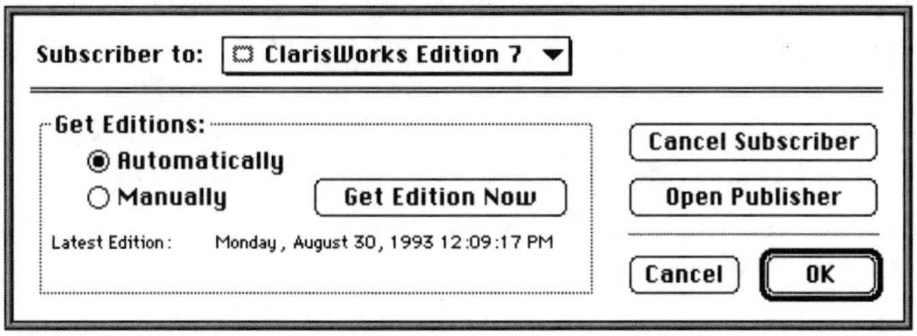

Figure 20-5: The Subscriber to dialog box.

3. **Click the Get Edition Now button.** The most recently saved copy of the published material is sent from the edition to the subscribing document.

NOTE

When you are performing a manual update, it doesn't matter whether the Get Editions or Send Editions setting in the dialog boxes in Figures 20-4 and 20-5 is set to be done automatically or manually. Clicking the Send Edition Now or Get Edition Now buttons forces an update to occur based on the most recently saved copy of the published material.

CAUTION!

To ensure that *only* manual updates can occur (if you want to exercise total control over the update process), select the Manually option in either dialog box. When you select Automatically or On Save, an update occurs every time the document that contains the published material is saved.

Setting Subscriber Options

In addition to specifying an edition update method (automatic or manual), you can use the Subscriber Options command to find and open the publisher file, break the Publish & Subscribe link for any subscribed-to edition, and allow modification of the subscriber.

Opening a publisher

When you are using Publish & Subscribe, you don't need to have the documents that contain the publisher and the subscriber open at the same time. If, on the other hand, the subscriber document is open and you need to view or work with the publisher, ClarisWorks provides a command to quickly locate and open the file.

To open the document that contains the publisher:

1. **Select the subscriber.** If the subscriber is an object, select its border. If the subscriber is text or a portion of a worksheet, click anywhere inside the subscribed material.
2. **Choose Subscriber Options from the Publishing submenu of the Edit menu.** The Subscriber to dialog box appears, as shown in Figure 20-5.
3. **Click the Open Publisher button.** ClarisWorks locates and opens the document that contains the publisher in a new window.

TIP

Open Publisher is a very powerful feature. You can use it not only to open ClarisWorks documents, but also to open published documents from *other* programs! For example, you can design and publish an illustration in a high-end graphics program and then subscribe to it in a ClarisWorks document. If you later find that you need to edit the graphic (to set a different background color, for example), clicking Open Publisher launches the graphics program instantly and loads the document for editing.

Canceling a subscriber

To break the link to a subscriber (so you can prevent further updates), you cancel the subscriber.

To cancel a subscriber:

1. **Select the subscriber.** If the subscriber is an object, select its border. If the subscriber is text or a portion of a worksheet, click anywhere inside the subscribed material.
2. **Choose Subscriber Options from the Publishing submenu of the Edit menu.** The Subscriber to dialog box appears, as shown in Figure 20-5.
3. **Click Cancel Subscriber.**

Modifying a subscriber

Rather than just maintain a link to the publisher, sometimes you want to make your own alterations to a subscriber. However, if the subscriber is an object (such as a draw image), changes to the object are limited to changing its size, placement, and text wrap. To make other modifications, return to the document from which the object was published, make the changes, and then update the edition to transfer the changes to the subscriber.

Modifying a subscriber that is placed as text is a simple procedure.

To modify a text subscriber:

1. **Select the subscriber text by clicking anywhere within it.**
2. **Choose Subscriber Options from the Publishing submenu of the Edit menu.** The Subscriber to dialog box appears.
3. **Click the Allow Modification check box**. (If the box is not present, the text has probably been placed as an object rather than as text.)
4. **Click OK.** You can now edit the text subscriber and add formatting to it. However, if the published text is later updated, it will replace any edits that you have made to the subscriber.)

Setting Publisher Options

Other than specifying whether a publisher will be automatically or manually updated, there is only one publisher option: canceling the publisher. Canceling a publisher has no effect on the edition or its subscribers. It merely cuts the link between publisher and subscribers. Any additional changes that are made to the published material will not be sent as updates to the subscribers.

To cancel a publisher:

1. **Select the publisher.** If the publisher is an object, select its border. If the publisher is text or a portion of a worksheet, click anywhere inside the published material.
2. **Choose Publisher Options from the Publishing submenu of the Edit menu.** The Publisher to dialog box appears, as shown in Figure 20-4.
3. **Click Cancel Publisher.**

NOTE: Canceling a publisher does not eliminate its edition file (*ClarisWorks Edition 3* or whatever else you happened to name it). After you cancel a publisher, you should drag its edition to the Trash.

Quick Tips

The following tips explain how to deal with subscribed-to objects that are larger than the document page in which they are placed and give suggestions for using Publish & Subscribe with other programs.

Handling large subscribers

Finding that a subscriber in a ClarisWorks document is too wide to display completely is not unusual. And because many subscribers are objects, the resize handle (the black dot in the lower-right corner) may be off-screen. Here are two ways that you can deal with this situation:

- If the object is free floating, click anywhere inside the object and drag to the left until the resize handle appears. You can then resize the object as needed.
- If the object has been placed as an in-line graphic (embedded in a sentence or paragraph as a "graphic character" of sorts), you can't drag it. Instead, select the object and use the Scale Selection command from the Format menu to shrink the object to the proper size. (***Note:*** You can also apply the Scale Selection command to free-floating objects.)

Program differences in the implementation of Publish & Subscribe

If you examine different programs that support Publish & Subscribe, you'll find that implementations of this feature can vary considerably. To determine the differences in Publish & Subscribe capabilities, options, and procedures, you need to carefully check the manuals of the programs involved. And don't be afraid to experiment. Sometimes it's the quickest way to find out how a feature works.

Summary

- Publish & Subscribe allows data to be shared by multiple users (over a network) and among multiple programs. For example, a non-Claris desktop publishing program can subscribe to a chart that was created in a ClarisWorks spreadsheet.
- The three components in every Publish & Subscribe transaction are a publisher, an edition, and a subscriber. If necessary, you can have multiple publishers and/or subscribers.
- Editions can be updated automatically (whenever the published material is saved) or manually (on request by either the individual who published the material or by the one who subscribed to it).
- Additional Publish & Subscribe options enable you to break the link between the publisher and the subscriber (so that future changes in the published material will not be reflected in the subscribed to material), find and open the document that contains the published material, and modify a subscriber.
- Publish & Subscribe standards are still a little loose. Different programs may handle the process differently — offering and supporting different options, for example.

Topic 21

Electronic Mail

Overview

System 7.5, System 7 Pro (also called System 7.1.1), and later versions of the system software include PowerTalk system software, an interesting new feature for creating, sending, and receiving electronic mail. If you buy the optional Direct Dialup Mail Accessory Kit from Apple Computer, you also can use a modem to exchange messages with other PowerTalk users.

To send PowerTalk messages from ClarisWorks, you must have ClarisWorks 2.1 or a later version *and* System 7.5, System 7 Pro, or a later version of the system software.

At its simplest, PowerTalk enables you to easily exchange files of any type with individuals on a network. If you have a program that provides direct PowerTalk support (ClarisWorks 2.1 or later, for instance), you can do the following:

- Create messages and then route them to people on the network
- Reply to messages
- Forward messages to others

Messages can be accompanied by whole documents, called *enclosures*.

ClarisWorks 2.1 and later versions have a new Mail submenu (which holds the new message-handling functions) and special PowerTalk-specific buttons for the Shortcuts palette. (For help with installing the new buttons, see the "Customizing the Shortcuts Palette" section in Topic 13.) ClarisWorks also supports PowerTalk *mailers* (message headers that list a letter's sender, recipient, subject, and enclosures). And ClarisWorks enables you to create a special stationery file that you can use to reply to messages.

This Topic provides the information you need to use PowerTalk to create, send, and respond to messages in ClarisWorks. (***Note:*** The Topic is not designed as a complete reference on PowerTalk, but rather to show you how you can use this system with ClarisWorks. Familiarity with key PowerTalk terms and concepts will help you understand and use the information in this Topic.) For additional details on installing and using PowerTalk, refer your system software's documentation.

If you are just beginning a computing session or have locked your PowerTalk Key Chain (see page 7 of your user's guide for information), PowerTalk prompts you to enter your access code when you attempt to perform any mail-related task.

Sending Letters from ClarisWorks

No matter which ClarisWork environment you're working in (except Communications), you can send any document created in ClarisWorks 2.1 or later versions as a *letter* — an e-mail document. A letter can be accompanied by enclosures.

Attaching a *mailer* (a message header that lists the letter's sender, recipient, subject, and enclosures) to a document changes it to a letter. You can attach mailers to new or existing documents. If you later decide to return the letter to its original form (a word processing or draw document, for example), remove the mailer.

Step-by-Steps

To create and send a letter from ClarisWorks:

1. **Open or create a ClarisWorks document that you want to use as the basis of your letter.** The document can exist in any environment except communications.

   TIP

   If you want to send a previously created letter, you can locate the file quickly by choosing Letter from the File Type pop-up menu in the Open dialog box.

2. **Enter or edit the message as necessary.**

3. **Choose Add Mailer from the Mail submenu of the File menu.** A mailer appears at the top of the document, as shown in Figure 21-1.

   Alternatively, you can click the Add/Delete Mailer button in the Shortcuts palette (see Figure 21-2).

   NOTE

   Unlike other Shortcuts buttons, the PowerTalk-specific buttons are dynamic — they come and go as appropriate. To read how to add buttons to the Shortcuts palette, see the "Customizing the Shortcuts Palette" section in Topic 13.

4. **To change the sender, click the button next to From and provide the information requested.** By default, the From box initially contains the name of the owner of the machine — your name, in most cases.

5. **Type subject information in the Subject box.** (You *must* fill in this box.)

6. **Click the button next to Recipients to select the recipient(s) for the letter.** The window in Figure 21-3 appears. (A shortcut is to *drag* the addresses of individuals or groups from catalogs, the desktop, or any disk into the Recipients box.)

7. **When you find a recipient, select the name in the dialog box and click the To button.**

   To send a copy of the letter to individuals or groups, choose the appropriate names and click CC (carbon copy). To send a blind carbon copy to someone, hold down the Option key — which changes the CC button to BCC (blind carbon copy) — and click BCC. (When you send a blind carbon copy, the recipient's name does not appear in the distribution list seen by the other recipients.)

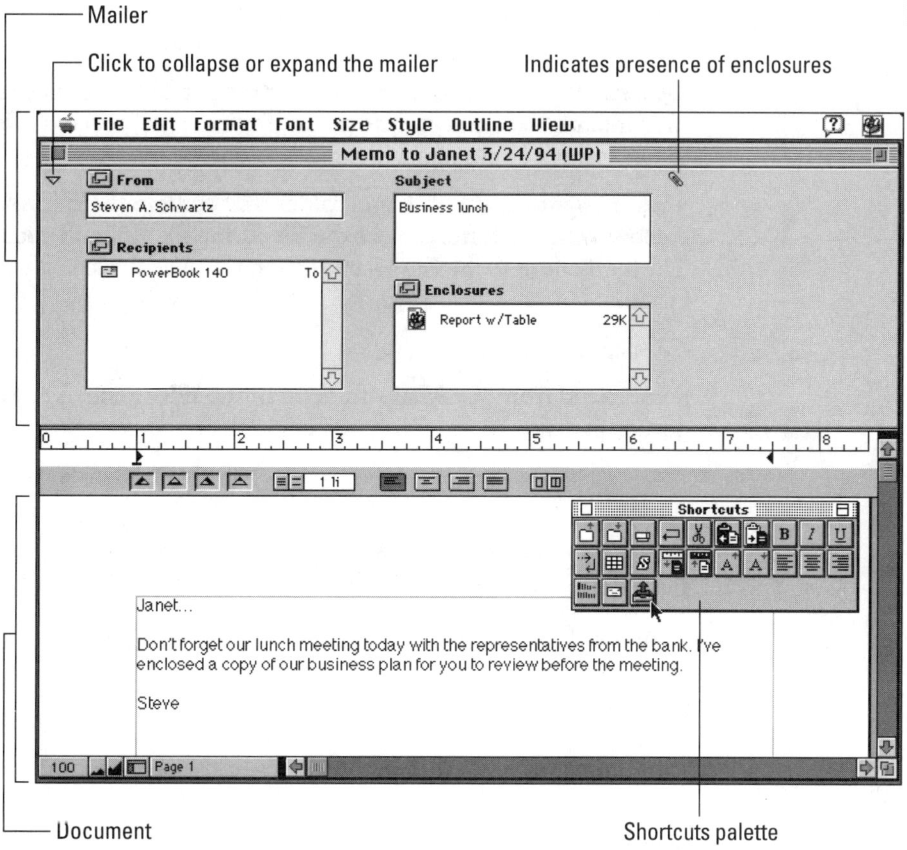

Figure 21-1: A ClarisWorks document with a mailer.

Figure 21-2: The Add/Delete Mailer button.

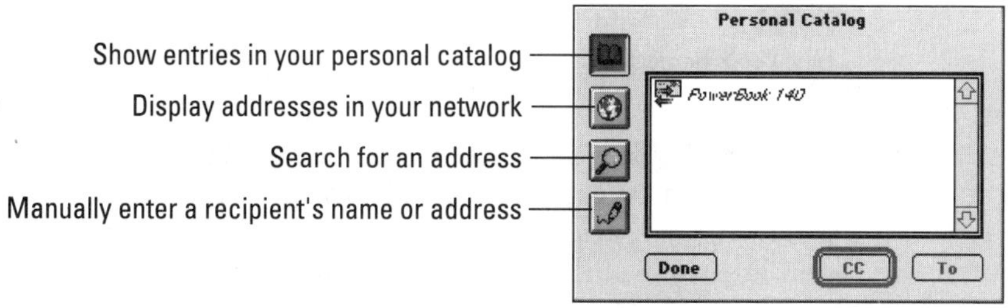

Figure 21-3: From this dialog box, you specify who should receive your letter.

You can add as many normal recipients, carbon copies, and blind carbon copies as you like. When you are through specifying the distribution list, click Done.

8. ***Optional:* If you want to attach one or more additional files to the letter (documents, data files, or programs, for example), click the button next to Enclosures. A standard file dialog box appears.**

   Then navigate to the disk and folder that contain the file you want to enclose with the letter, select the file in the file list, and click Enclose. The file is added to the Enclosures list, and a paper clip icon is added to the mailer.

   To enclose additional files, repeat Step 8.

9. **Select Send from the Mail submenu of the File menu.** The Send document dialog box appears (see Figure 21-4).

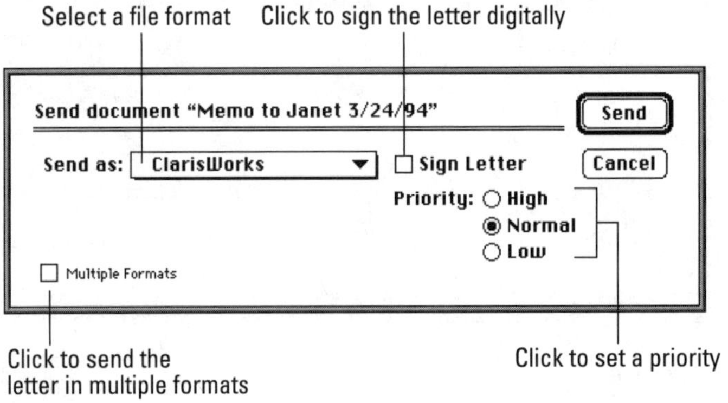

Figure 21-4: The Send document dialog box.

Alternatively, you can click the Send button in the Shortcuts palette, as shown in Figure 21-5.

Figure 21-5: The Send button.

10. **Set a priority for your letter by clicking the High, Normal, or Low radio button.** The default setting is Normal. The priority that you set is indicated in the recipient's In Tray. (All mail that a user receives is automatically listed in the In Tray on the desktop.)

    The priority does not affect delivery time or the method used to notify the recipient of the message's arrival.

11. ***Optional:* If you want your digital signature affixed to the letter, click Sign Letter.** (If you do not already have an approved digital signature, refer to your system software's documentation for details.)

12. **Select a file format for the letter.**

    Because your letter is a ClarisWorks document, the default format is ClarisWorks. If the recipient(s) cannot read a ClarisWorks file, select a different file format from the Send as pop-up menu.

    If you don't know which formats the recipient can read, click the Multiple Formats check box. The dialog box changes its appearance, as shown in Figure 21-6. You can choose up to three formats (AppleMail, SnapShot, plus one other) for the document:

    - *AppleMail* — The document can be read and edited in any AppleMail-compatible program.
    - *Snapshot* — The letter is sent as a graphic rather than as text. This is a less-than-perfect choice if the recipient needs to edit or reuse portions of the letter. However, Snapshot works well when you want to send the document through a fax gateway or when the recipient does not have ClarisWorks.
    - *A program-specific format* — You can select any format listed in the Send As pop-up menu (Microsoft Word, for example). You can choose only one program-specific format, however.

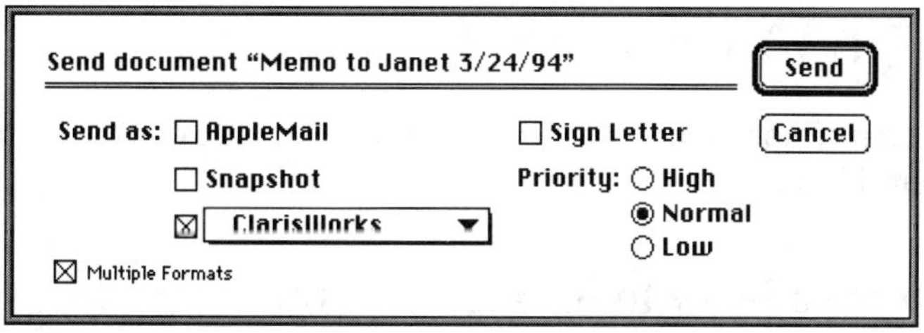

Figure 21-6: The Send document dialog box after you select the Multiple Formats option.

NOTE

The Send As formatting affects only the letter. Enclosures retain their native formats.

13. **Click the Send button.** The letter and any enclosures are sent.

14. **(Optional) To save the file to disk, choose the Save As command from the File menu and select Letter or Letter Stationery as the file format.** If you'd prefer to save the file as an ordinary document rather than as a letter, first choose Delete Mailer from the Mail submenu of the File menu and then choose Save As.

NOTE

If you need additional help with filling in a mailer, refer to your system software's documentation.

Saving Letters

You can save any letter to disk in either of two formats: letter or letter stationery. The stationery format is useful if you want to use the letter as a template for creating other letters — suppose that you want to design a basic letter layout that contains a graphic or logo, has blanks for standard memo information, and uses a particular font. (For more information about creating stationery documents, see Topic 11.)

To save a letter:

1. **Choose Save As from the File menu.** The Save As dialog box appears.
2. **Choose Letter or Letter Stationery from the Save As pop-up menu.**
3. **Enter a filename in the text-edit box.**
4. **Navigate to the disk and folder where you want to save the file.**
5. **Click Save.**

Deleting Mailers

You can remove a mailer at any time; the underlying document reverts to its original form.

To return a letter to its original form:

1. **Open the letter in ClarisWorks.**
2. **Choose Delete Mailer from the Mail submenu of the File menu.**

   Alternatively, click the Add/Delete Mailer button in the Shortcuts palette (see Figure 21-2).

Handling Incoming Mail

When mail arrives, you can open, reply to, and forward the message.

Opening a letter

After you're notified that a letter has arrived, choose Open Next Letter from the Mail submenu of the File menu. The letter is converted (if necessary) and opens as a ClarisWorks document.

You can set the manner in which you are notified of incoming mail by returning to the desktop and choosing Preferences from the Mailbox menu. You can choose from displaying an alert dialog box, blinking an icon in the menu bar, and playing a particular sound.

Letters that are sent to you as Snapshots open as draw documents.

To open an enclosure, double-click its icon (found in the Enclosures box in the mailer) or drag its icon onto the desktop and then open it through an appropriate application.

If you receive a letter that was sent by someone who used the drag-and-drop procedure described in this Topic's Quick Tips, you cannot open the letter by using the Open Next Letter command; although the letter sits in your In Tray, it is invisible to ClarisWorks. To open the letter, you have to return to the desktop, open the In Tray, and double-click the letter's icon. If the letter is a ClarisWorks document, ClarisWorks launches and opens the letter. If the letter is in another format, a different program may open it.

You can force ClarisWorks to attempt to open almost any letter: Just return to the desktop and drag the letter icon onto the ClarisWorks program icon. If ClarisWorks contains an appropriate file translator, ClarisWorks launches (if it's not already running) and automatically translates the letter into a ClarisWorks format.

Replying to a letter

Many letters require a reply.

To reply to a letter:

1. **Open the letter in ClarisWorks (see the preceding section, "Opening a letter").**
2. **Choose Reply from the Mail submenu of the File menu or click the Reply button in the Shortcuts palette (see Figure 21-7).** A new untitled word processing document appears (see Figure 21-8). Type your reply. (The text insertion point is already placed for you.) If the received letter was also created in the word processing environment, it appears at the bottom of the reply document.

Figure 21-7: The Reply button.

3. ***Optional:* Add enclosures or other recipients as desired.**
4. **Choose Send from the Mail submenu of the File menu or click the Send button in the Shortcuts palette (see Figure 21-5).** The Send document dialog box appears, as shown in Figure 21-4.

5. **Select your send options, as described earlier in this Topic.**

6. **Click the Send button.**

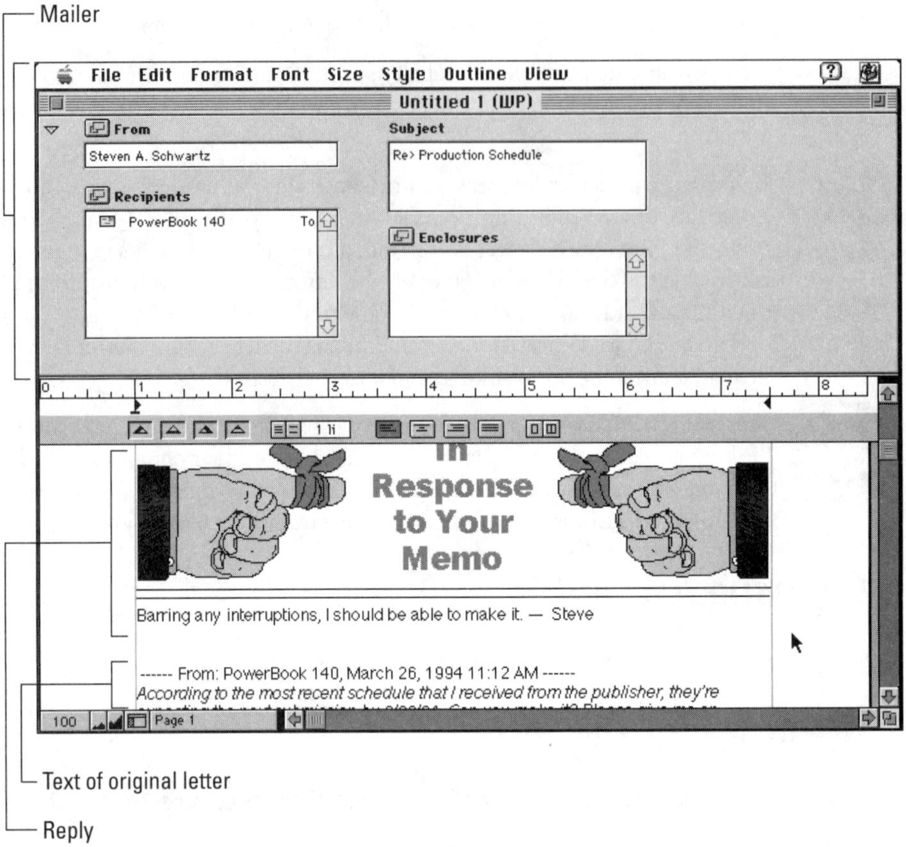

Figure 21-8: The reply document already contains the appropriate mailer information and a copy of the original letter. (Clip art courtesy of T/Maker Co., ClickArt Business Cartoons.)

Creating a reply stationery document

Normally, when you select the Reply command from the Mail submenu of the File menu, an ordinary blank document appears. ClarisWorks 2.1 and later versions, however, support a new PowerTalk reply stationery document (much like the options stationery documents described in Topic 11) in which you can dress up e-mail, giving your replies a more personal touch.

To create a reply stationery document:

1. **Open a new, blank document in the environment where you intend to write your replies.**
2. **Add any elements you want to appear in every reply, such as a base font and graphics (see Figure 21-9).**

   Make sure that you have a line of text in the correct font, size, and style for your actual message text embedded in your reply stationery. In fact, create a Return before that line and assign to it the font, size, and attributes you want, or the following text may not turn out as you expect it.

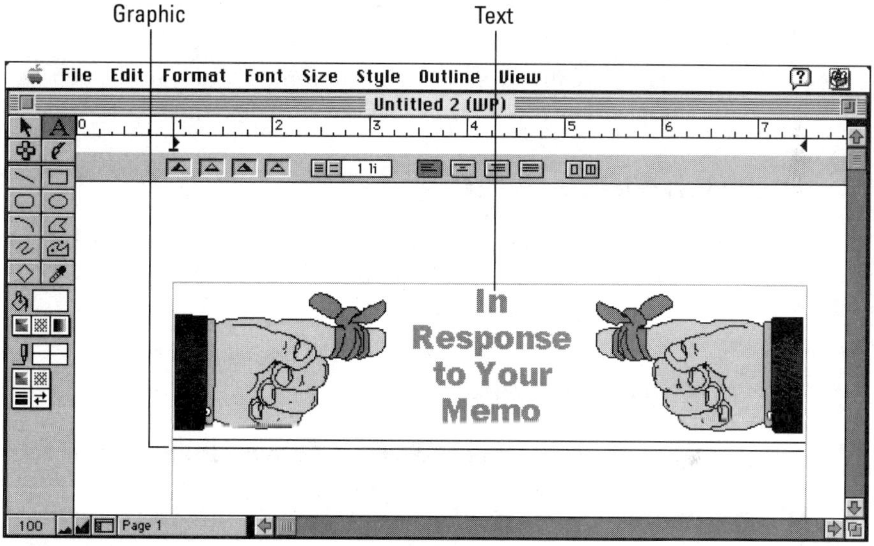

Figure 21-9: Creating a reply stationery document.

3. **Choose Save or Save As from the File menu.** The Save dialog box appears.
4. **Navigate to the ClarisWorks Stationery folder (located in the Claris folder within the System Folder of the start-up hard disk), name the file Reply, select ClarisWorks Stationery as the file type, and then click Save (see Figure 21-10).**

   In ClarisWorks 3.0, clicking the Stationery radio button automatically navigates to the ClarisWorks Stationery folder.

   Now whenever you select the Reply command, the Reply stationery document is used.

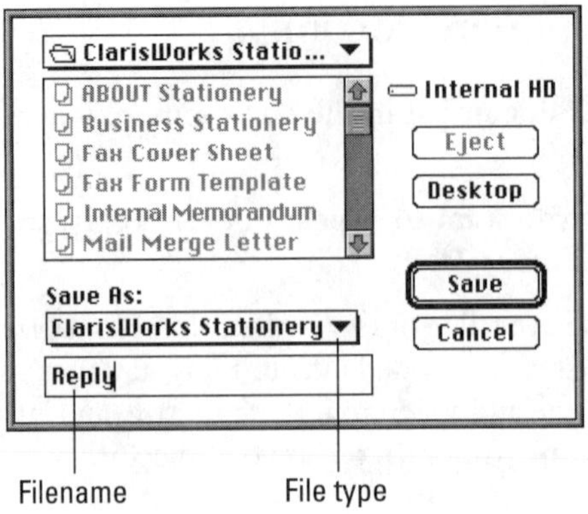

Figure 21-10: Saving the Reply stationery document.

NOTE

Do not save the Reply stationary document with a mailer attached. ClarisWorks automatically adds the mailer when you choose the Reply command.

Forwarding a letter

Occasionally, you may want to forward a received letter to someone else. For example, if you receive a letter that you think your supervisor also should read, you can forward a copy of the letter.

Step-by-Steps

To forward a letter:

1. **Open the letter and choose Forward from the Mail submenu of the File menu.**

   Or you can click the Forward button in the Shortcuts palette (see Figure 21-11). A new mailer is added *over* the old one, as shown in Figure 21-12.

   Figure 21-11: The Forward button.

2. **If the mailer is collapsed, expand it.**
3. **Select recipients for the forwarded letter.**
4. **Choose Send from the Mail submenu of the File menu.** The Send document dialog box appears.
5. **Select send options,** as described earlier in this Topic (see the "Sending Letters from ClarisWorks" section).
6. **Click the Send button.** The letter is forwarded to the selected recipients.

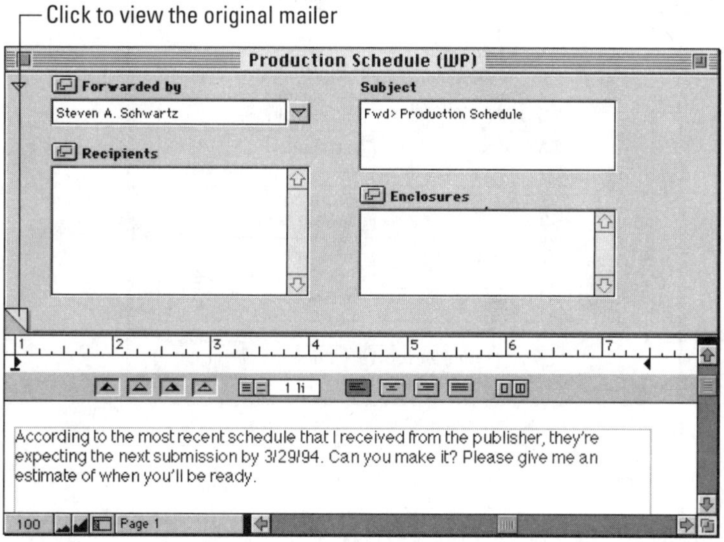
Click to view the original mailer
Production Schedule (WP)
Forwarded by
Steven A. Schwartz
Subject
Fwd> Production Schedule
Recipients
Enclosures
According to the most recent schedule that I received from the publisher, they're expecting the next submission by 3/29/94. Can you make it? Please give me an estimate of when you'll be ready.
100
Page 1

Figure 21-12: The new mailer.

Quick Tips

The following Quick Tips mention the new Preferences options introduced in ClarisWorks 2.1 for handling mail, discuss the importance of font selection when writing letters, show how to send mail immediately, explain how to delete old mail, and show how to send documents from the desktop.

Setting mail preferences

As with any other major ClarisWorks component, you can set the preferred way for handling many mail-related tasks. (***Note:*** The Mail icon, however, appears only if System 7.5, System 7 Pro, or a later version of the system software is installed.) For details, refer to Topic 12, "Setting Preferences." The Mail Preferences are shown in Figure 21-13.

Select your fonts carefully

Be cautious about using esoteric fonts in your letters. If the recipients do not have the same fonts installed, a message to that effect appears on their screens, and every instance of a missing font is converted to a generic font — spoiling your document's look.

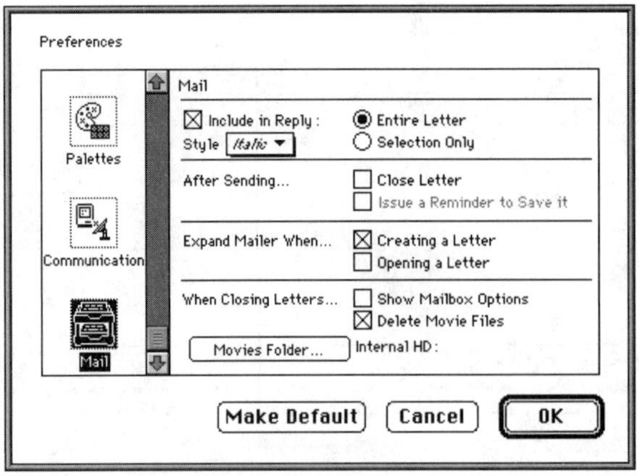

Figure 21-13: Mail Preferences.

Handling reluctant mail

When checking your Out Tray on the desktop, you may see mail whose status is "Waiting." You can force PowerTalk to send the message immediately by selecting the letter in the Out Tray and then choosing Send Now from the Mailbox menu.

Discarding mail

Old mail — sent or received — cannot be deleted from within ClarisWorks. To delete old mail, return to the desktop, open your In or Out Tray, and drag the icons of unwanted letters into the Trash.

Sending files from the desktop

If you want to transfer some files to another user but don't need or want to attach a message, you can use the *drag-and-drop* method.

To send a document via drag-and-drop:

1. **From the desktop, open the PowerShare, AppleTalk, or personal catalog that contains the address of the file's intended recipient.**

   Alternatively, you can find the recipient's information card. See Figure 21-14 for examples of these two PowerTalk elements.

   If you need help locating a particular individual or group, select the Find in Catalog desk accessory from the Apple menu. (See your system software's documentation for details.)

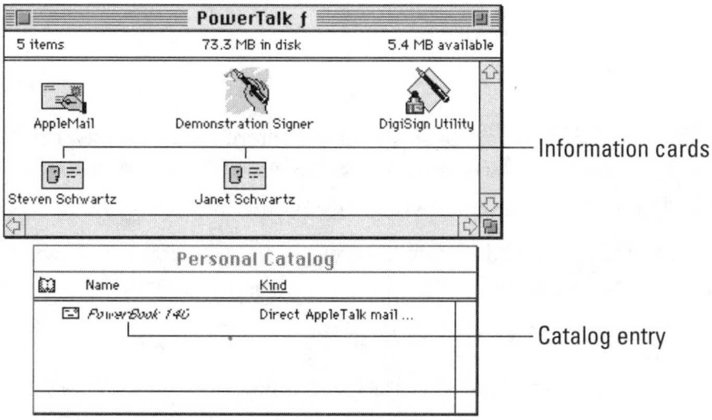

Figure 21-14: Choosing recipients via their information cards or catalog entries.

2. **Click the file you want to transfer and then drag it onto the recipient's icon in the personal catalog or onto the recipient's information card.** When you release the mouse button, a dialog box like the one in Figure 21-15 appears.

3. **Click OK.** A copy of the file is sent and the normal notification procedure is executed.

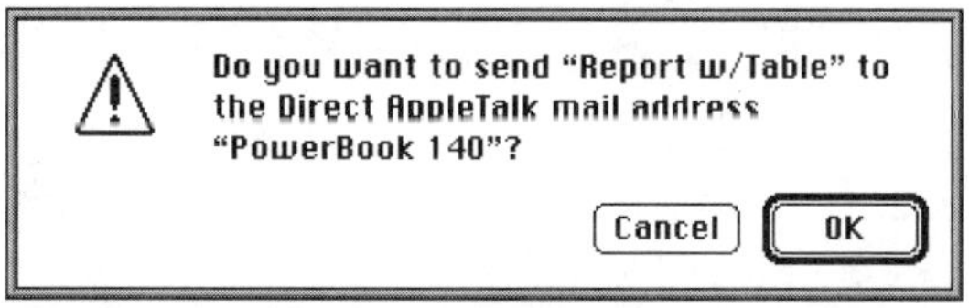

Figure 21-15: This dialog box changes to reflect the actual filename, the recipient's name, and the mail address (Direct AppleTalk mail or AppleShare file server, for example).

Summary

- With ClarisWorks 2.1 or higher and System 7.5, System 7 Pro, or a later version of the system software, you can use the new PowerTalk system software to send electronic mail and documents from within ClarisWorks.
- ClarisWorks 2.1 and higher versions include several new PowerTalk-specific buttons for the Shortcuts palette, as well as a Mail submenu for the File menu.
- Adding a mailer to a ClarisWorks document changes it to a PowerTalk letter.
- A letter created in ClarisWorks can contain non-ClarisWorks files as enclosures.
- To ensure that a recipient can read your letter, send the letter in any format supported by the XTND translators. (See "Opening non-ClarisWork documents" in Topic 2.) You also can send a letter in AppleMail or Snapshot format. To be sure that a recipient can read the letter, you can send it in multiple formats.
- Mail can be saved to disk as a letter (a document with a mailer attached) or as a normal ClarisWorks document (with the mailer removed). Letters that you want to reuse as templates can be saved as Letter Stationery documents.
- Letters created and sent from ClarisWorks can be opened directly from within ClarisWorks. Mail sent via drag-and-drop must be opened from the desktop.
- When you receive a letter, you can send a reply or forward the letter to others.

Part V
Appendixes

Appendix A

Installing ClarisWorks 2 or 3

Regardless of whether you have ClarisWorks 2.0, 2.1, or 3.0, the procedure that you use to install the program is very similar. You run the ClarisWorks installation program, select options, and watch as the appropriate files are copied to the hard disk. When the process concludes, ClarisWorks is ready to run.

Although this appendix steps you through the installation of ClarisWorks 2.0, the installation procedure also applies to ClarisWorks 2.1. (If, on the other hand, you're *upgrading* a copy of ClarisWorks 2.0 to 2.1, refer to Appendix B for instructions.) If you're installing ClarisWorks 3.0, check the end of this appendix for information concerning the small differences in the general installation procedure.

Installing ClarisWorks 2

To install ClarisWorks 2, you need the following:

- A Macintosh Plus or later machine (ClarisWorks 2 does not run on a Mac 128K or Mac 512K.)
- Macintosh system software Version 6.0.5 or later. (You can determine the version by choosing About This Macintosh or About the Finder from the Apple menu.)
- At least 1MB of memory for System 6 and 2MB for System 7
- An internal or external hard disk with at least 3.1MB of free space

To install ClarisWorks 2, you need to run a special Installer program. (If you have installed any version of the system software in the past few years, you will recognize the Installer.) Using the Installer — rather than installing by hand — ensures that ClarisWorks and its support files are correctly installed, uncompressed, and ready to run.

Begin by locking each of the ClarisWorks master disks to protect them from inadvertent changes. (To lock a floppy disk, slide the tab in the upper-right corner of the disk so that the tiny window is open.)

Now insert Disk 1 and double-click its icon (if the disk window is not open). If it contains a TeachText READ ME file, double-click the file's icon to view late-breaking news about the program and the installation process. After reading and, optionally, printing the READ ME document, choose Quit from the File menu. You return to the desktop.

CAUTION!

Before starting the installation, turn off any active antivirus program, extensions (INITs), and control panels. Antivirus software can interfere with the installation process. If you aren't sure how to turn off an antivirus utility, check its instruction manual. You also should quit other programs that you are running and close any open desk accessories and control panels.

If you have a PowerBook with an internal modem, some of the communication tools may already be installed and active. ClarisWorks cannot overwrite or update these files while they are active. Restart with the Shift key held down to turn off your extensions.

Performing an Easy Install

To run the Installer, you need to do two things:

- Decide whether to perform an easy or custom installation.
- Select the hard disk on which to install the software.

The Easy Install option copies the program and all support files to the hard disk of your choice. The Customize option copies only the program components that you select.

Most users should choose Easy Install and install ClarisWorks to their start-up hard disk — the one that contains the System Folder. The following steps explain how to use Easy Install. If you think that you want to perform a Customized Install or install ClarisWorks on a disk other than the start-up hard disk, read "Performing a Customized Install" and "Selecting a different hard disk," later in this appendix, before proceeding with the installation.

Step-by-Steps

To install ClarisWorks with Easy Install:

1. **Double-click the Installer icon, as shown in Figure A-1.** Figure A-2 shows the opening screen that appears.
2. **To continue, click OK (or press Return or Enter).**
3. **The default procedure for the Installer is to perform an Easy Install on the start-up hard disk. Be sure that the correct hard disk is selected and then click Install, as shown in Figure A-3.**

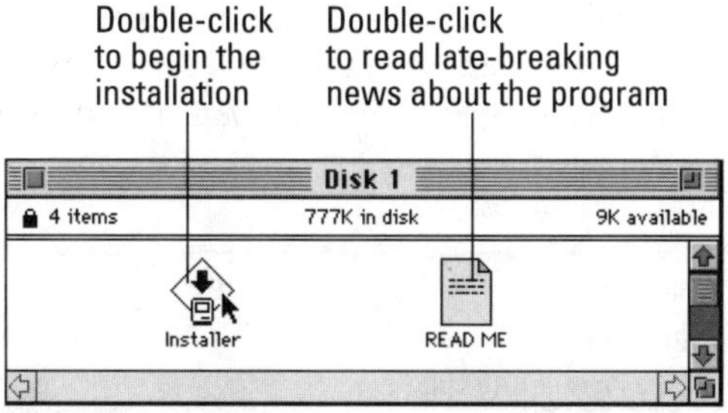

Figure A-1: The Installer program icon and READ ME document icon.

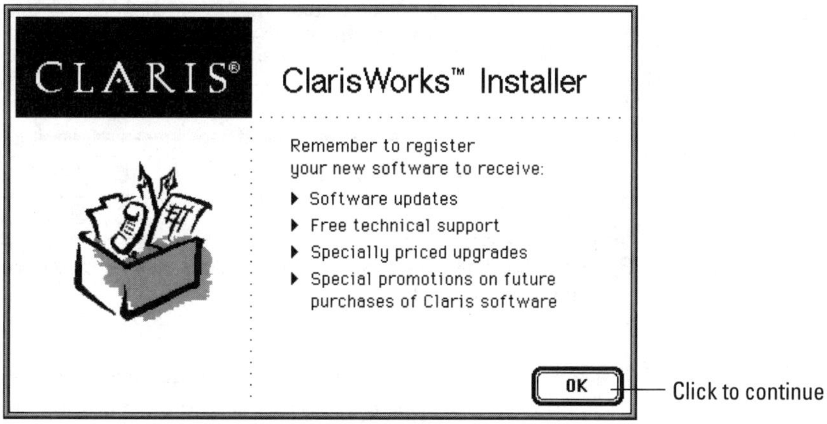

Figure A-2: The ClarisWorks Installer opening screen.

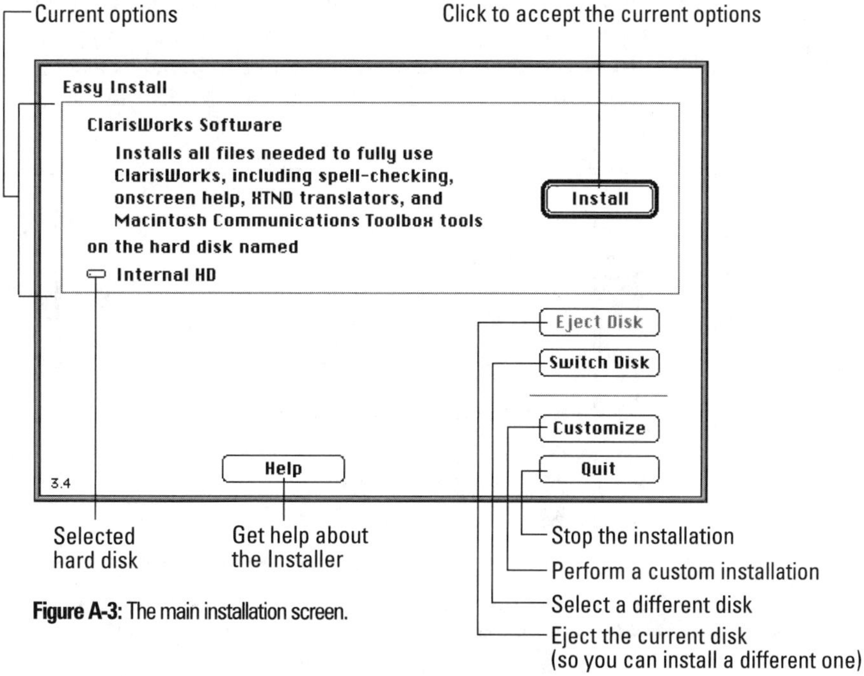

Figure A-3: The main installation screen.

Because you are installing ClarisWorks 2 on the start-up hard disk, the Installer requires that any open programs, desk accessories, and control panels be shut down. If any of these items is detected, the screen shown in Figure A-4 appears.

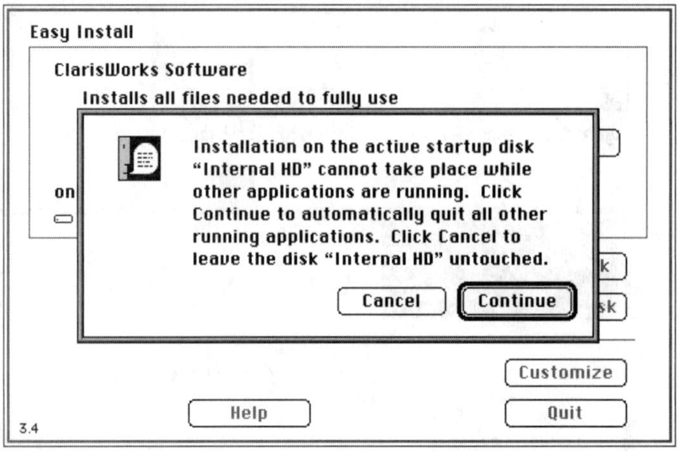

Figure A-4: This warning box is displayed if any programs, desk accessories, or control panels are open during installation.

If you want the Installer to quit any programs that are currently running, click Continue. If you have files that you want to save before continuing with the installation, click Cancel. The Installer quits, and you can save files as needed. After quitting the programs, begin again at Step 1.

4. **The Installer continues the installation, requesting different disks as they are needed, as shown in Figure A-5. After copying all files to the hard disk and uncompressing them, the Installer asks you to restart the Macintosh.** After the Mac restarts, ClarisWorks 2 is ready to run.

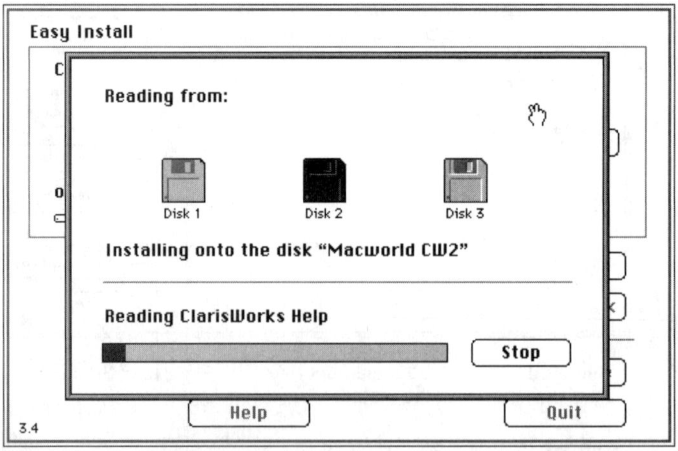

Figure A-5: The installation process.

Performing a Customized Install

Why would you want to do a customized install? The most common reason is that you want to install only some of the ClarisWorks files because you have limited hard disk space. (This can be a problem on some PowerBooks, for example.)

To install ClarisWorks with Customized Install:

1. **Double-click the Installer icon.** The opening screen appears.
2. **To continue, click OK (or press Return or Enter).**
3. **Click Customize.** A screen similar to the one in Figure A-6 appears.

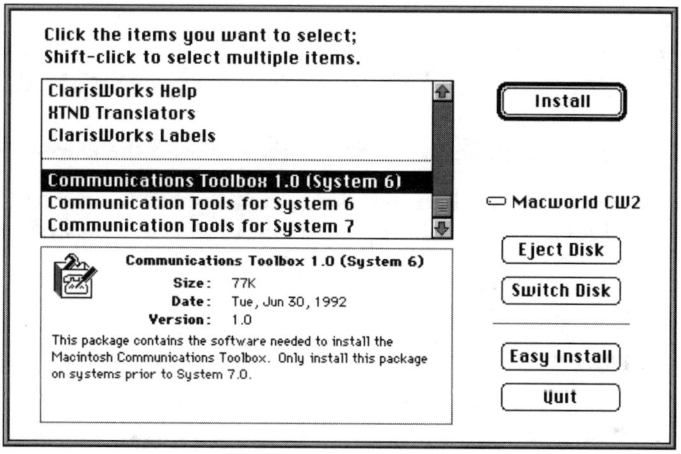

Figure A-6: Selecting custom options.

4. **Choose the parts of ClarisWorks that you want to install.** Click to select an individual item. Shift-click to select more than one item.

   Before selecting the set of items to install, click each one individually. A help message like the one in Figure A-6 appears, explaining a little about each item.

5. **Click Install.**

   As described for Easy Install, the Installer completes the installation, requesting new disks as they are needed.

Selecting a different hard disk

Regardless of whether you perform an Easy or Customized Install, you can install ClarisWorks on any hard disk that has sufficient space. To install on a different hard disk, click Switch Disk. Each time that you click the button, the Installer cycles through the mounted disk drives, displaying the name of the next one in line. Stop when you see the name of the correct destination drive.

CAUTION!

Selecting any disk other than the start-up disk does not result in a proper install.

This problem occurs because critical Claris files are copied into the System Folder on the start-up disk during a normal installation. The Installer also makes sure that only the newest versions of files are copied. For example, it prevents an older copy of the Claris Help System or User Dictionary from replacing a more recent one. When you choose a different hard disk, on the other hand, the Installer copies all files to that disk — completely ignoring the start-up disk and System Folder. You need to make sure that only the most recent files make their way into the Claris folder.

You can solve this problem the easy way or the hard way. The easy way is to install ClarisWorks on the start-up hard disk and then move the ClarisWorks 2 folder to a different hard disk. The hard way is to install directly on the destination hard disk and then move the essential files back into the System Folder on the start-up hard disk.

Step-by-Steps

To install ClarisWorks on a different hard disk the easy way:

1. **Use the Installer to install ClarisWorks on the start-up hard disk.**
2. **When the installation is done, drag the newly created ClarisWorks 2 folder from the start-up hard disk to the hard disk of your choice.**

   The program places a copy of the folder and its contents on the destination drive.
3. **Drag the ClarisWorks 2 folder that's on the start-up hard disk into the Trash.**
4. **Choose Empty Trash from the Special menu.**

   The ClarisWorks 2 folder that was on the start-up hard disk is deleted.

Step-by-Steps

To install ClarisWorks on a different hard disk the hard way:

1. **Double-click the Installer icon. The opening screen appears.**
2. **To continue, click OK (or press Return or Enter).**
3. **Click Switch Disk until the destination hard disk appears.**
4. **Perform an Easy or Customized Install, as described previously.** Following the installation, a new folder named ClarisWorks 2 appears on the hard disk that you selected in Step 3. The contents of the folder should look similar to what you see in Figure A-7.
5. **Double-click the System Folder on the start-up hard disk.** The folder opens.

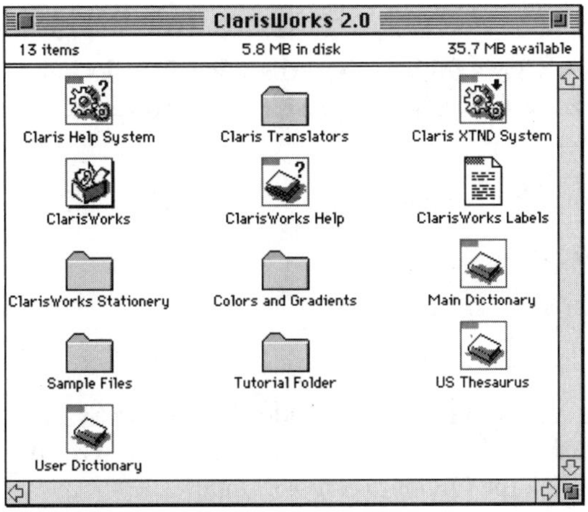

Figure A-7: The ClarisWorks 2 folder.

6. **Choose by Name from the View menu.**
7. **Look for a folder named Claris.** If you have installed any Claris program, including a previous version of ClarisWorks, you should see the Claris folder.

   The remaining steps depend on whether the Claris folder already exists.
8. **If you do not have a Claris folder, choose New Folder from the File menu.**

   A folder named untitled folder (System 7) or Empty Folder (System 6) is created for you. (If you already have a Claris folder, skip to Step 8.)
9. **Rename the folder *Claris*.**
10. **Open the ClarisWorks 2 folder (where ClarisWorks was installed).**
11. **Within the ClarisWorks 2 folder, Shift-click to select all files and folders *except* the following ones:**
    - ClarisWorks
    - Sample Files
    - Tutorial Folder
12. **Drag the selected files onto the Claris folder icon.**

    The program copies the files into the Claris folder.
13. **Go back to the ClarisWorks 2 folder and Shift-click to select the same items again.**
14. **Drag the items to the Trash and choose Empty Trash from the Special menu.**

— or —

8. **If you have a Claris folder, open the ClarisWorks 2 folder (where ClarisWorks was installed) and Shift-click to select the following files and folders:**
   - ClarisWorks Help
   - ClarisWorks Labels
   - ClarisWorks Stationery
   - Colors and Gradients
9. **Drag these items to the Claris folder inside the System Folder on the start-up hard disk.** You may see a message that you're about to replace some files. Click the OK button to continue.
10. **Set the View for both the ClarisWorks 2 and Claris folders to by Name.** (Click anywhere inside each folder and choose by Name from the View menu.)
11. **Expand the two folder windows so that you can see the Last Modified date for each file. Arrange the windows one above the other so you can see them both at the same time.**
12. **Visually compare the Last Modified dates for the following files in the two folders:**
    - Claris Help System
    - Claris XTND System
    - Main Dictionary
    - US Thesaurus

    If the date for any of these files in the ClarisWorks 2 folder is more recent than the date for the same file in the Claris folder, drag the new file into the Claris folder (replacing the old file). Similarly, if any of these files is not already in the Claris folder, drag it there.
13. **If the Claris folder does not have a User Dictionary file, drag the file there from the ClarisWorks 2 folder.**
14. **Open the Claris Translators folders on both disks and compare the file dates as you did in Step 12. If any translator in the ClarisWorks 2 folder is more recent than the same file in the Claris folder, drag the new file into the Claris folder (replacing the old file). Similarly, if any of the new translator files is not found on the start-up disk, drag it there.**

NOTE

If a Claris Translators folder is not found within the Claris Folder, drag the entire folder there.

15. **Return to the ClarisWorks 2 folder and drag all files and folders — except ClarisWorks, Sample Files, and Tutorial Folder — into the Trash. Choose Empty Trash from the Special menu.**

16. **System 7 users only: If you replaced any old translators with new ones in Step 14, open the Preferences folder (which is found inside the System Folder) and drag the file named XTND Translator List into the Trash. Choose Empty Trash from the Special menu.** The next time you launch ClarisWorks (or any other Claris program), the XTND Translator List will be rebuilt, based on the new translators.

As you can see, the easy method is the preferred approach, and you should definitely use it if you have sufficient free space on the start-up disk (3 to 4MB). You should use the hard installation method only when you don't have the necessary disk space on the start-up hard disk.

Installing ClarisWorks 3.0

To install ClarisWorks 3.0, you need the following:

- A Macintosh Plus or later machine (ClarisWorks 3.0 does not run on a Mac 128K or Mac 512K.)
- Macintosh system software Version 6.0.5 or later (You can determine the version by choosing About This Macintosh or About the Finder from the Apple menu.)
- At least 1MB of memory for System 6, 2MB of memory for System 7 and communications, or 4MB for a Power Macintosh
- An internal or external hard disk (requires approximately 12MB of free space for a full installation, including the clip art)

As mentioned previously, when you install ClarisWorks 3.0, you can follow the instructions provided for installing ClarisWorks 2.0. Here are the few important differences that you should note:

- The installation program is named Install ClarisWorks.
- If you choose to perform a Custom Install, you click check boxes to select components to install and click tiny *I* buttons to get information about the components (see Figure A-8).

As in the ClarisWorks 2 installation procedure, you are prompted for additional floppy disks as they are needed.

TIP

If you intend to install ClarisWorks 3.0 on a hard disk other than the startup hard disk, save yourself some grief . . . Follow the Step-by-Steps labeled "To install ClarisWorks on a different hard disk the easy way."

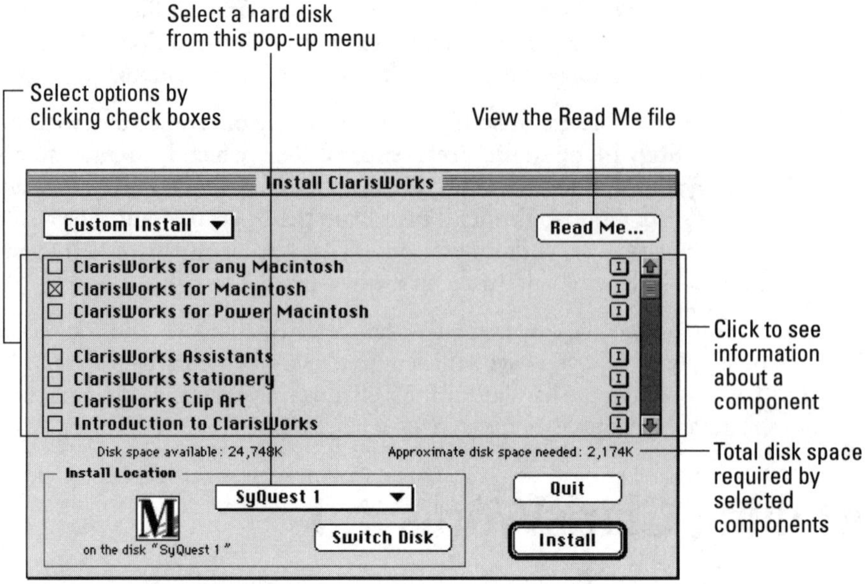

Figure A-8: Performing a Custom Install.

Registering ClarisWorks

The first time that you run a newly installed copy of ClarisWorks, a registration screen appears, as shown in Figure A-9. Enter your name, the company name, and the serial number for the program. (The serial number is on the product registration card.) Click OK to begin the program or click Cancel to halt the registration and return to the desktop.

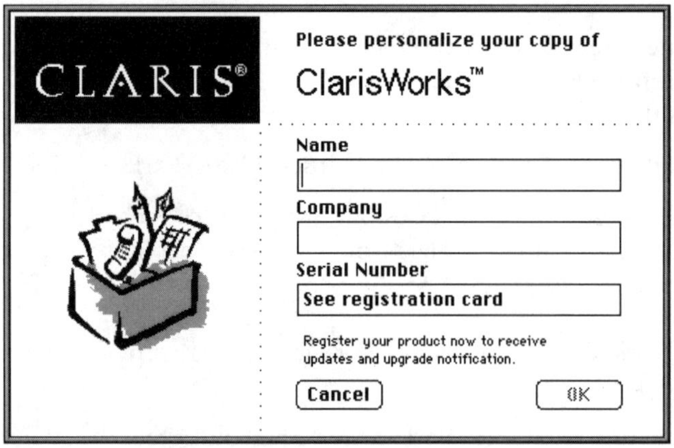

Figure A-9: The registration screen.

Appendix **B**

Installing the ClarisWorks 2.1 Updater

Obtaining the ClarisWorks 2.1 Updater

If you still have ClarisWorks 2.0, you can inexpensively upgrade to Version 2.1 by getting the Claris utility program called ClarisWorks 2.1v2 Updater. The Updater modifies your copy of ClarisWorks 2, converting it to Version 2.1. You can obtain the Updater by doing either of the following:

- ◆ Calling Claris Customer Relations (800-544-8554 or 408-727-8227). If you obtain the Updater through Claris, it costs $13, which you can charge by using MasterCard or VISA.
- ◆ Using a modem to download the Updater — at no cost! — from one of the popular on-line information services, such as America Online.

NOTE

Before you rush to acquire the Updater, first check your copy of ClarisWorks; you may already have version 2.1 or a later version. To determine the version number of your copy of ClarisWorks do one of the following:

- ◆ *If ClarisWorks is running*, choose About ClarisWorks from the Apple menu. A dialog box appears, listing the version number. Click OK to close the dialog box.
- ◆ *If ClarisWorks is not running*, go to the desktop and click the ClarisWorks program icon. Then choose Get Info from the File menu or press ⌘-I. An Info window appears, listing the version number. Click the Info window's close box.

Running the Updater Program

NOTE

Please note that you must have ClarisWorks 2 to run the Updater program. You cannot update earlier versions of ClarisWorks to Version 2.1.

The Updater consists of a single file, named CW2.1v2 Installer. When you run the Installer, new XTND filters, the hyphenation dictionary, and other new and changed files are copied into the Claris Folder (within the System Folder on your start-up hard disk). At the same time, a new folder named ClarisWorks 2.1v2 Update is added to the start-up hard disk.

The newly created ClarisWorks 2.1v2 Update folder holds several files that explain the changes in ClarisWorks 2.1, as well as a program called ClarisWorks 2.1v2 Updater. Running the Updater updates your copy of ClarisWorks 2 to 2.1.

To update a copy of ClarisWorks 2:

1. Double-click the CW2.1v2 Installer icon.

The program launches, and the screen shown in Figure B-1 appears. Click Continue to go to the next screen (see Figure B-2), which explains what happens during the update procedure and presents the terms of the software license.

Figure B-1: The ClarisWorks 2.1v2 Updater opening screen.

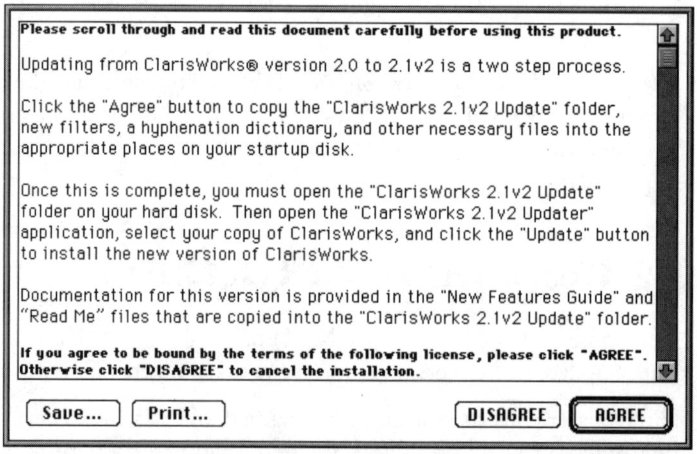

Figure B-2: An explanation of the update process, followed by the software license agreement.

2. **Click Agree to proceed with the update; click Disagree to cancel the update.** (You can save or print a copy of the agreement by clicking the Save or Print buttons, respectively.)

3. **ClarisWorks copies the necessary files to your start-up hard disk. If the installation is successful, the dialog box in Figure B-3 appears. Click OK to conclude the installation.**

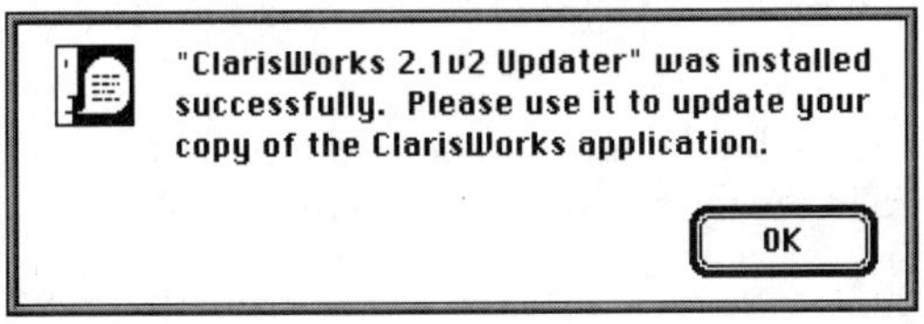

Figure B-3: You are informed that Updater was successfully installed.

4. **During the installation, a new folder named ClarisWorks 2.1v2 Update is created on your start-up hard disk. To finish the installation, open the ClarisWorks 2.1v2 Update folder and double-click the ClarisWorks 2.1v2 Updater icon.** (Updater is the program that changes ClarisWorks 2 into ClarisWorks 2.1.)

   The UpdateMaker 2.2 file dialog box (shown in Figure B-4) appears.

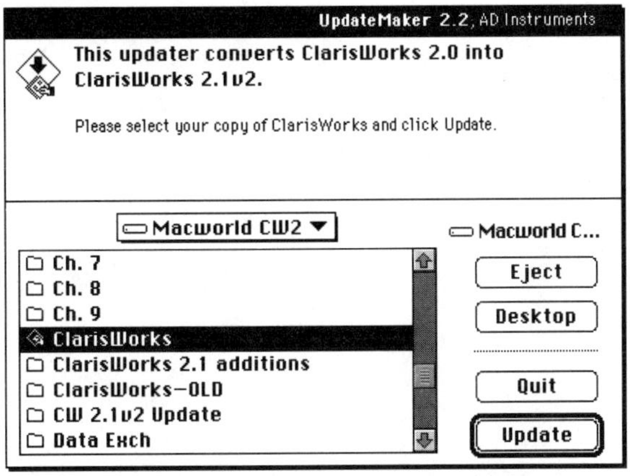

Figure B-4: Locate your copy of ClarisWorks 2 in this dialog box.

5. **Navigate to the disk and folder that contain your copy of ClarisWorks 2, select the program in the file list, and then click Update.**

   If the update is successful, you see the dialog box shown in Figure B-5. Click OK.

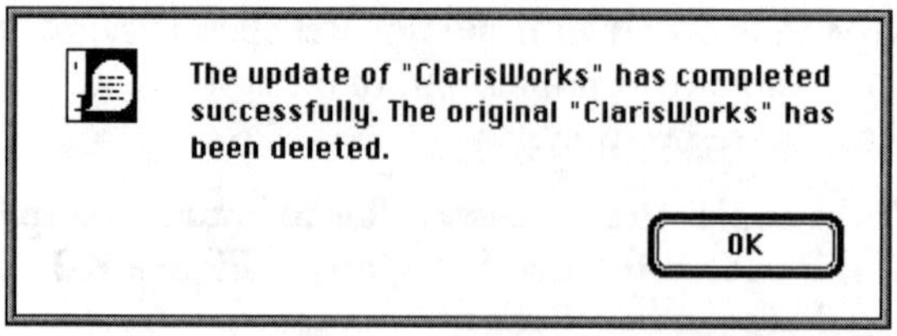

Figure B-5: You are informed that your copy of ClarisWorks 2 has been successfully converted to ClarisWorks 2.1.

For a quick rundown on the changes and new features in ClarisWorks 2.1, read the text files that are in the ClarisWorks 2.1v2 Update folder.

TIP

After the conversion to version 2.1, you no longer need the files in the ClarisWorks 2.1v2 Update folder. Rather than simply delete the files, however, copy them to a floppy disk and then store the disk in a safe place. That way, if your copy of ClarisWorks 2.1 is ever damaged, you can reinstall ClarisWorks 2.0 and then run Updater again.

Appendix C

Keyboard Shortcuts

The following table is a listing of ClarisWorks keyboard shortcuts that will increase your productivity and make you feel at ease if you're not used to using a mouse or don't like to take your hands off the keyboard.

General Menu Commands (Available in Most Environments)

Command	***Key Sequence***	***Menu***
Bold	⌘-B	Style (Format)
Center	⌘-\	Alignment (Format)
Check Document	⌘-=	Spelling or Writing Tools in 2.1/3.0 (Edit)
Check Selection	Shift-⌘-Y	Spelling or Writing Tools in 2.1/3.0 (Edit)
Clear	Clear (Extended keyboard)	Edit
Close	⌘-W	File
Copy	⌘-C, F3 (Extended keyboard)	Edit
Cut	⌘-X, F2 (Extended keyboard)	Edit
Find Again	⌘-E	Find/Change (Edit)
Find Selection	Shift-⌘-E	Find/Change (Edit)
Find/Change	⌘-F	Find/Change (Edit)
Frame Links	⌘-L	Options
Help	⌘-?, Help (Extended keyboard)	Apple
Italic	⌘-I	Style (Format)
Justify	Shift-⌘-\	Alignment (Format)
Left	⌘-[	Alignment (Format)
Mail Merge	Shift-⌘-M	File
New	⌘-N	File
Open	⌘-O	File
Other	Shift-⌘-O	Size (Format)
Page View	Shift-⌘-P	View
Paste	⌘-V, F4 (Extended keyboard)	Edit
Plain Text	⌘-T	Style (Format)
Print	⌘-P	File

(continued)

General Menu Commands *(continued)*

Command	*Key Sequence*	*Menu*
Quit	⌘-Q	File
Record Macro/ Stop Recording	Shift-⌘-J	Shortcuts (File)
Right	⌘-]	Alignment (Format)
Save As	Shift-⌘-S	File
Save	⌘-S	File
Select All	⌘-A	Edit
Show/Hide Rulers	Shift-⌘-U	View
Show/Hide Shortcuts	Shift-⌘-X	Shortcuts (File)
Show/Hide Tools	Shift-⌘-T	View
Thesaurus	Shift-⌘-Z	Spelling or Writing Tools in 2.1/3.0 (Edit)
Underline	⌘-U	Style (Format)
Undo	⌘-Z, F1 (Extended keyboard)	Edit

General Navigation Commands

Command	*Key Sequence*
Go to beginning of document	Home (Extended keyboard)
Go to end of document	End (Extended keyboard)
Scroll down one screen	Page Down (Extended keyboard)
Scroll up one screen	Page Up (Extended keyboard)

Other General Commands

Command	*Key Sequence*
Cancel printing and most dialog boxes	⌘-.
Delete character to left of cursor	Delete/Backspace
Delete character to right of cursor	Del (Extended keyboard)
Discretionary hyphen (ClarisWorks 2.1 only)	⌘-hyphen
First slide	Home (Extended keyboard)
Last slide	End (Extended keyboard)

Communications Menu Commands

Command	*Key Sequence*	*Menu*
Info	⌘-I	Settings
Open/Close Connection	Shift-⌘-O	Session
Phone Book	⌘-B	Settings
Save Lines Off Top	⌘-T	Session
Show/Hide Scrollback	⌘-L	Settings
Wait for Connection	Shift-⌘-W	Session

Database Menu Commands

Command	*Key Sequence*	*Menu*
Browse	Shift-⌘-B	Layout
Define Fields	Shift-⌘-D	Layout
Duplicate Record	⌘-D	Edit
Field Format	Shift-⌘-I	Options
Find	Shift-⌘-F	Layout
Go To Record	⌘-G	Organize
Hide Selected	⌘-(	Organize
Hide Unselected	⌘-)	Organize
Layout	Shift-⌘-L	Layout
Match Records	⌘-M	Organize
New Record	⌘-R	Edit
Show All Records	Shift-⌘-A	Organize
Sort Records	⌘-J	Organize

Database Navigation Commands

Command	*Key Sequence*
Move to beginning of field	⌘-up arrow
Move to end of field	⌘-down arrow
Move to next field	Tab
Move to previous field	Shift-Tab
Move to next record (same field)	⌘-Return
Move to previous record (same field)	Shift-⌘-Return

Other Database Commands

Command	*Key Sequence*
Deselect records	Enter
Insert a tab in a text field	⌘-Tab
Paste current date, time, or record number	⌘- -(hyphen)[1]

Draw Commands

Command	*Key Sequence*	*Menu*
Align Objects	Shift-⌘-K	Arrange
Align to Grid	⌘-K	Arrange
Duplicate	⌘-D	Edit
Group	⌘-G	Arrange
Lock	⌘-H	Arrange
Move Backward	Shift-⌘--(hyphen)	Arrange
Move Forward	Shift-⌘-+	Arrange
Reshape	⌘-R	Edit
Rotate	Shift-⌘-R	Arrange
Round Corners	Shift-⌘-I	Options[2]
Smooth	⌘-(	Edit
Turn Autogrid On/Off	⌘-Y	Options
Ungroup	Shift-⌘-G	Arrange
Unlock	Shift-⌘-H	Arrange
Unsmooth	⌘-)	Edit

Other Draw Commands

Command	*Key Sequence*
Complete open or closed polygon or bezigon	Enter
Move selected image one pixel or gridpoint	Any arrow key
Select Eyedropper tool	Tab

[1] You must be in correct field type (for example, must be in date field for date insert).
[2] You must have rectangle selected.

Paint Menu Commands

Command	*Key Sequence*	*Menu*
Duplicate	⌘-D	Edit
Turn Autogrid On/Off	⌘-Y	Options

Other Paint Commands

Command	*Key Sequence*
Complete open or closed polygon or bezigon	Enter
Move selected image one pixel or gridpoint	Any arrow key
Select Eyedropper tool	Tab

Spreadsheet Menu Commands

Command	*Key Sequence*	*Menu*
Calculate Now	Shift-⌘-=	Calculate
Copy Format	Shift-⌘-C	Edit
Delete Cells	Shift-⌘-K	Calculate
Fill Down	⌘-D	Calculate
Fill Right	⌘-R	Calculate
Go to Cell	⌘-G	Options
Insert Cells	Shift-⌘-I	Calculate
Make Chart	⌘-M	Options
Modify Chart	Shift-⌘-I	Options
Number	Shift-⌘-N	Format
Paste Format	Shift-⌘-V	Edit
Protect Cells	⌘-H	Options
Sort	⌘-J	Calculate
Unprotect Cells	Shift-⌘-H	Options

Spreadsheet Navigation Commands

Command	Key Sequence
Move one cell down	Return, down arrow (Option-down arrow in 2.1)
Move one cell up	Shift-Return, up arrow (Option-up arrow in 2.1)
Move one cell right	Tab, right arrow (Option-right arrow in 2.1)
Move one cell left	Shift-Tab, left arrow (Option-left arrow in 2.1)
Move one character right (in entry bar)	Option-right arrow (2.0); right arrow (2.1)
Move one character left (in entry bar)	Option-left arrow (2.0); left arrow (2.1)
Stay in current cell	Enter

Note: You also can use each of these commands to complete a cell entry. The functions of these keys in ClarisWorks 3.0 are determined by the settings in spreadsheet preferences.

Other Spreadsheet Commands

Command	Key Sequence
Cancel entry	Esc
Clear cell contents and format	Clear (Extended keyboard)
Delete cell contents	Delete, Backspace, Del (Extended keyboard)

Word Processing Menu Commands

Command	Key Sequence	Menu
Apply Ruler	Shift-⌘-V	Format
Copy Ruler	Shift-⌘-C	Format
Insert Footnote	Shift-⌘-F	Format
Move Above	Shift-⌘-A/Control-up arrow	Outline
Move Below	Shift-⌘-B/Control-down arrow	Outline
Move Left	Shift-⌘-L/Control-left arrow	Outline
Move Right	Shift-⌘-R/Control-right arrow	Outline
New Topic Left	⌘-L	Outline
New Topic Right	⌘-R	Outline
Outline View	Shift-⌘-I	Outline
Subscript	Shift-⌘-- (hyphen)	Style (Format)
Superscript	Shift-⌘-+	Style (Format)

Word Processing Navigation Commands

Command	*Key Sequence*
Move up one line	up arrow
Move down one line	down arrow
Move left one character	left arrow
Move right one character	right arrow
Move to beginning of document	⌘-up arrow
Move to beginning of line	⌘-left arrow
Move to beginning of paragraph	Option-up arrow
Move to beginning of word	Option-left arrow
Move to end of document	⌘-down arrow
Move to end of line	⌘-right arrow
Move to end of paragraph	Option-down arrow
Move to end of word	Option-right arrow

Other Word Processing Commands

Command	*Key Sequence*
Accept footnote entry and return to main body of document	Enter
New outline topic at same level	⌘-Return
New outline topic with same format as previous topic	Return
Select outline topic and its subtopics	Shift-Control-spacebar
Select text from insertion point to beginning of document	Shift-⌘-up arrow
Select text from insertion point to end of document	Shift-⌘-down arrow
Select text from insertion point to beginning of paragraph	Shift-Option-up arrow
Select text from insertion point to end of paragraph	Shift-Option-down arrow
Show/Hide invisible characters	⌘-;

TIP

Shortcuts for Dialog Box Buttons

With the exception of the *default button* in dialog boxes (a button surrounded by a double line that you can select by pressing Enter or Return), you normally have to use the mouse to click buttons. But some people are lazy. Dragging the mouse to the correct position just so you can click a button sometimes seems like more work than it's worth. Recognizing this fact, Claris built several keyboard shortcuts into ClarisWorks so that you can click buttons from the keyboard.

To click a button, do the following: while pressing ⌘, press the first letter in the button's name. For example, you can press ⌘-C to select Cancel, ⌘-A to select Apply, and ⌘-D to select Desktop.

Appendix D

Task Index

Topic 1: Macintosh Essentials

Topic 2: ClarisWorks Essentials

Topic 4: The Word Processing Environment

Topic 5: The Spreadsheet Environment

Topic 6: The Database Environment

Topic 7: Graphics: The Draw and Paint Environments

Topic 8: The Communications Environment

Topic 9: Generating a Mail Merge

Topic 10: Using the Spreadsheet to Create Charts and Tables for a Report

Topic 11: Using Stationery Documents and Assistants

Topic 12: Setting Preferences

Topic 13: The Shortcuts Palette

Topic 14: Using Macros

Topic 15: Working with Frames

Topic 16: Working with Outlines

Topic 17: Creating a Slide Show

Topic 18: Designing Master Pages

Topic 19: QuickTime Movies

Topic 20: Publish & Subscribe

Topic 21: Electronic Mail

Appendix A: Installing ClarisWorks 2 or 3

Appendix B: Installing the ClarisWorks 2.1 Updater

Index

Symbol

A

Index

D

E

F

G

H

I

J

K

L

M

N

O

Index

P

Index

S

T

X

Y

Z

IDG BOOKS WORLDWIDE REGISTRATION CARD

RETURN THIS REGISTRATION CARD FOR FREE CATALOG

Title of this book: ClarisWorks 3.0 Companion

My overall rating of this book: ❑ Very good [1] ❑ Good [2] ❑ Satisfactory [3] ❑ Fair [4] ❑ Poor [5]

How I first heard about this book:

❑ Found in bookstore; name: [6] ❑ Book review: [7]

❑ Advertisement: [8] ❑ Catalog: [9]

❑ Word of mouth; heard about book from friend, co-worker, etc.: [10] ❑ Other: [11]

What I liked most about this book:

What I would change, add, delete, etc., in future editions of this book:

Other comments:

Number of computer books I purchase in a year: ❑ 1 [12] ❑ 2-5 [13] ❑ 6-10 [14] ❑ More than 10 [15]

I would characterize my computer skills as: ❑ Beginner [16] ❑ Intermediate [17] ❑ Advanced [18] ❑ Professional [19]

I use ❑ DOS [20] ❑ Windows [21] ❑ OS/2 [22] ❑ Unix [23] ❑ Macintosh [24] ❑ Other: [25] ________ (please specify)

I would be interested in new books on the following subjects:
(please check all that apply, and use the spaces provided to identify specific software)

❑ Word processing: [26] ❑ Spreadsheets: [27]

❑ Data bases: [28] ❑ Desktop publishing: [29]

❑ File Utilities: [30] ❑ Money management: [31]

❑ Networking: [32] ❑ Programming languages: [33]

❑ Other: [34]

I use a PC at (please check all that apply): ❑ home [35] ❑ work [36] ❑ school [37] ❑ other: [38] ________

The disks I prefer to use are ❑ 5.25 [39] ❑ 3.5 [40] ❑ other: [41] ________

I have a CD ROM: ❑ yes [42] ❑ no [43]

I plan to buy or upgrade computer hardware this year: ❑ yes [44] ❑ no [45]

I plan to buy or upgrade computer software this year: ❑ yes [46] ❑ no [47]

Name: Business title: [48] Type of Business: [49]

Address (❑ home [50] ❑ work [51]/Company name:)

Street/Suite#

City [52]/State [53]/Zipcode [54]: Country [55]

❑ **I liked this book!** You may quote me by name in future IDG Books Worldwide promotional materials.

My daytime phone number is ________

IDG BOOKS®
THE WORLD OF COMPUTER KNOWLEDGE

❑ **YES!**

Please keep me informed about IDG's World of Computer Knowledge. Send me the latest IDG Books catalog.

SECRETS™

...FOR DUMMIES™ COMPUTER BOOK SERIES FROM IDG

MACWORLD MW AUTHORIZED EDITION

AUTHORIZED PC WORLD EDITION

NO POSTAGE NECESSARY IF MAILED IN THE UNITED STATES

BUSINESS REPLY MAIL

FIRST CLASS MAIL PERMIT NO. 2605 FOSTER CITY, CALIFORNIA

IDG Books Worldwide
919 E Hillsdale Blvd, STE 400
Foster City, CA 94404-9691